PELHAM CRICKET YEAR

THIRD EDITION

September 1980 to September 1981

A chronological record of
first-class cricket
throughout the world

Edited by David Lemmon

Pelham Books
London

First published in Great Britain by
Pelham Books Ltd
44 Bedford Square
London WC1B 3DU
1981

British Library Cataloguing in Publication Data
Pelham cricket year. – 3rd ed.
1. Cricket – Periodicals
I. Lemmon, David
796.35′8′05   GV911

ISBN 0 7207 1363 3

Filmset by
Northumberland Press Ltd, Gateshead, Tyne and Wear
Printed and bound in Great Britain by
Richard Clay (The Chaucer Press) Ltd, Bungay, Suffolk

Contents

Editor's Note

The aim of *Pelham Cricket Year* is that the cricket enthusiast shall be able to read through the happenings in world cricket, from each October until the following September (the end of the English Season). Form charts are printed and a player's every appearance will be given on these charts, and date and place allow those appearances to be readily found in the text.

The symbol * indicates 'not out' or 'wicket-keeper' according to context.

Photo Credit

The editor and publishers are grateful to Patrick Eagar for permission to use his photographs in this book.

A

Padding Up

Cricket Year 1981 commences

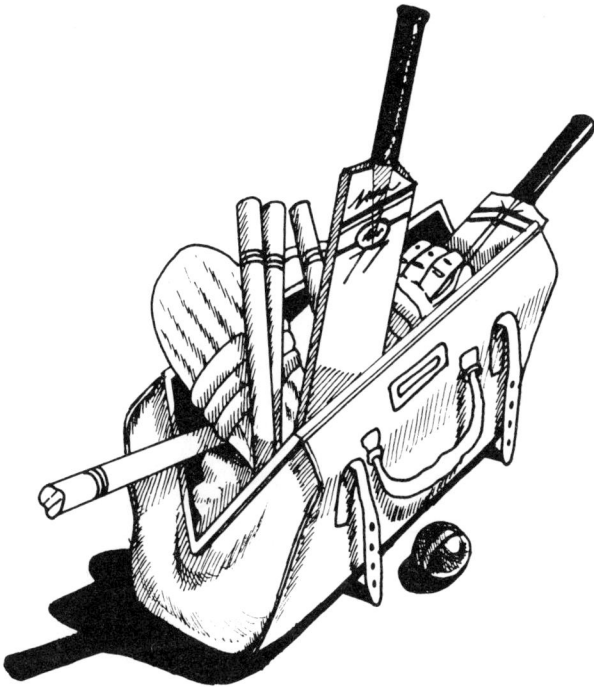

The debates on Cricket Year 1980 were still at their fiercest when Cricket Year 1981 began.

Wounds are slow to heal and the M.C.C. announced that after full investigation into incidents at The Centenary Test some members had been reprimanded for their behaviour. So be it, but perhaps the saddest aspect of the confrontations on the pavilion steps at Lord's was that they had been magnified so as to eclipse the fact that a great occasion had been reduced to farce and that a game which should have been remembered for its dignity and grandeur had ended in cat-calls and boos for the English batsmen. It all seemed symbolic of the greatest danger facing cricket in the 1980s, the danger of becoming detached from its roots.

Cricket is the most cherished of games because those who watch it still feel an affinity with those who play it. At county matches throughout England it is still possible for the people of the county to chat with those who represent them. The players are honoured, but they are not distanced. When this closeness is threatened, cricket is threatened.

The greatest threat comes from the proliferation of Test matches, an argument that we have forwarded in these pages in previous issues. We are nearing the stage, already reached in Australia, where a cricketer of Test standard may find himself playing no games for his county or state or province. Such a state of affairs begins to detach the man and the game from the very roots which give them substance.

The decision to shorten the Australian tour of England in 1981 and yet to play six Test matches did nothing to allay our fears as to the direction in which the game was moving. Only ten of the seventeen counties would be able to play three-day games against the tourists, and Leicester was to lose the one-day international previously scheduled for Grace Road. There was to be monetary compensation, but this could hardly balance the disappointment to those who had worked so hard to bring a representative match to Leicester.

Economy, it seems, must dictate every action these days, but the economy will prove to be false if the goose which lays the golden egg is killed by being asked to produce without respite.

Short-sightedness afflicted counties. In spite of the T.C.C.B.'s request that English players should be appointed to lead county sides, three counties chose overseas players to succeed English players as county captains. Alan Ealham was deposed as Kent captain and Asif Iqbal whose career one had thought to be nearing its close was appointed in his stead. Frank Hayes was replaced as captain of Lancashire by Clive Lloyd. Once more Lloyd, never very impressive as a captain and plagued by injury, was believed to be at the end of his career. Glenn Turner succeeded Norman Gifford as leader of Worcestershire.

Elsewhere, Geoff Cook became captain of Northants, Chris Old succeeded John Hampshire who resigned after two uneasy years as captain of Yorkshire, and John Barclay became captain of Sussex in succession to Arnold Long who retired after doing much good for Surrey, Sussex and cricket. Barclay's vice-captain was to be Paul Parker, an enterprising choice by Sussex, and a youthful combination which could have exciting results.

John Spencer left Sussex and Richard Hills left Kent. Bob Ratcliffe was released by Lancashire and Curzon, the Nottinghamshire keeper, moved to Hampshire who had managed to persuade Southern to change his mind and to continue with his cricket career.

On the umpires list it was cheering to see David Shepherd's name; a genial man of cheery disposition, Shepherd would brighten any ground. Barry Leadbeater and Peter Eele joined Shepherd as newcomers and replaced John Langridge, Derek Dennis and Tom Spencer.

Whilst Middlesex and Worcestershire announced new venues, Derbyshire broke the news that all their home matches would be played at Derby which meant the end of Chesterfield as a county ground. There was hostile reaction among many members, but the Derbyshire Committee carried the day. Norman Graham, the Chesterfield groundsman and one of most respected in the country, became head groundsman for Essex.

Having seen his place at Middlesex go to Paul Downton, Ian Gould joined Sussex which was a little hard on Head who had performed splendidly as Long's understudy.

The greatest upheavals came at Edgbaston. Sadly, John Claughton retired from the game after the recurrence of a knee injury had determined him to concentrate on his business career and, surprisingly, John Whitehouse also announced his retirement in order to follow his profession as an accountant. With Sam and Clifford not re-engaged, Warwickshire faced some rebuilding after their John Player League triumph of 1980.

We lost old friends who had given much pleasure when Jim Parks senior, Arthur Wellard, Walter Keeton and Bruce Dooland passed from us, and the world was diminished by their leaving.

Graham Dilley and Bill Athey were named Commercial Union Cricketers of the Year though Athey would probably have rather been selected for the West Indian tour. Dilley passed his fitness test for the tour as did Willis, Old, Miller and Willey. There continued to be rumours as to Botham's fitness, and discussion as to his suitability for the position of England captain. It was announced that the English players could be fined for misdemeanours on and off the field in the West Indies.

The three young men to be awarded Whitbread scholarships enabling them to play grade cricket in Australia were Hogg of Lancashire, Cook of Leicestershire and David Smith of Surrey. A former winner, Jonathan Agnew, was flown home from Australia where he was playing grade cricket with glandular fever so continuing his run of misfortune.

The witty and urbane Christopher Martin-Jenkins was named as next editor of *The Cricketer* in succession to Reg Hayter though a sporting scene without Reg around was unthinkable.

David Evans joined the Test panel of umpires and Kepler Wessels became eligible to play for Australia, leaving many even more hazy as to what constituted qualification to play for a country.

The commercial jamboree continued with news that there was to be a floodlit cricket tournament at the end of the 1981 season in England. On Thursday 17 September there would be four regional tournaments and the next evening the final would be played in London. The teams were to be eight-a-side and would play ten over games. Football grounds would be used. As one county player said at a dinner at which the editor was a speaker, 'We should not dignify this enterprise with the name of cricket.'

More happily, John Arlott was named as one of the thirty new life members of the M.C.C., an honour richly deserved.

The most important pronouncements came from the T.C.C.B. The one hundred over first innings limit in County Championship was abolished and a new ball granted after eighty-five overs. County wickets were to be covered and sixteen points given for a win instead of twelve.

Fielding circles were to be introduced in the Benson and Hedges Cup competition, and here, one felt, the Board erred, for it was the John Player League competition which seemed most in need of an injection of some sort to revivify it. The BBC seemed to recognise this by announcing that they were reducing their coverage of the League on television.

Sunday play was to be allowed in three of the Test matches if rain caused abandonment of any of the first three days. Nothing, it seems, could be done to prevent us once more witnessing a Test series as miserable as that of 1980 when England and West Indies had bowled 14·5 and 13·5 overs an hour, respectively.

The remedy for that sickness lay in the hands of the cricketers themselves, as, indeed, did the remedy for much else. An attitude of mind which recognises the game is greater than any individual, or group of individuals, is cricket's only real legislation. As Cricket Year 1981 began, we turned to the players in hope and anticipation.

B

Another World Conquered

The West Indies in Pakistan

In their restless search for further triumphs the West Indies followed their con-
quest of England in 1980 with a sixty-eight day tour of Pakistan, the only
country in which they had not won a Test series. The West Indian selectors,
anxious to avoid staleness and to ensure that their victorious side did not all
grow old together, decided to rest Andy Roberts, who was replaced by Sylvester
Clarke, and to drop Deryck Murray in favour of David Murray. Milton
Pydanna of Guyana was brought into the side as second wicket-keeper. Larry
Gomes and Ranjie Nanan, an off-break bowler, were others who had not toured
England, but were included in the side for Pakistan.

5, 6 and 7 November 1980   **at Rawalpindi**
West Indies 247 (C. H. Lloyd 53, Iqbal Sikander 5 for 110) and 186 for 3 dec
    (C. G. Greenidge 81)
Pakistan Board President's XI 120 (C. E. H. Croft 5 for 41) and 314 for
    5 (Javed Miandad 130)
Pakistan Board President's XI won by 5 wickets

The tour began with a surprise defeat at the hands of the President's XI in
Rawalpindi. The first day saw the West Indies struggle after Javed Miandad,
the Pakistan captain elect, had won the toss and asked them to bat. Only an
aggressive knock by Lloyd gave them any substance, but then their quick
bowlers were too fierce for the home side and when Gordon Greenidge got
in full flow in the second innings a West Indian victory seemed a formality.
The President's XI lost 2 for 28, but Javed batted at his best to give them
a thrilling victory.

9, 10 and 11 November 1980   **at Peshawar**
North West Frontier Province Governor's XI 91 (S. T. Clarke 5 for 29) and
    215 (Ejaz Faqih 61 retired hurt, S. T. Clarke 4 for 58)
West Indies 267 (D. L. Haynes 86, H. A. Gomes 85, Sarfraz Nawaz 4 for 54)
    and 40 for 0
West Indies won by 10 wickets

On a wicket which was severely criticised by Clive Lloyd, the home side had
a fearful time against the West Indian pace attack of Clarke, Garner and
Marshall. The West Indians themselves struggled against Sarfraz and Sikhander
Bakht and were 26 for 3 before Haynes, whose technical application in all
conditions makes him among the most accomplished of West Indian batsmen,
and Gomes added 114. The Governor's XI fared better at the second attempt
and were unlucky to lose all-rounder Ejaz Faqih who was batting well when
struck on the hand by a rising ball from Marshall and forced to retire. Left
with forty to win, Haynes and Bacchus hit off the runs in an hour.

14, 15 and 16 November 1980   **at Sukkur**
West Indies 213 and 149 (Wasim Raja 5 for 44)
Sind Governor's XI 228 (Mansur Akhtar 75, M. D. Marshall 4 for 30) and
    70 (M. D. Marshall 5 for 9)
West Indies won by 64 runs

After looking to be struggling for much of the game, the West Indians snatched a remarkable victory on the last day thanks to Malcolm Marshall who took 5 for 9 in 5·3 overs. The West Indians had an uneasy time on the first day against a varied attack on a newly laid pitch. Three men were out for 48, but then Bacchus batted with good sense and the last three wickets added 66. The Governor's XI gained a lead of 15 on the first innings and Mansur, pressing for a Test place, batted impressively. When the visitors batted again Greenidge went at ten, but Haynes and Richards saw the total to 73. Nine wickets then fell for the addition of 76 runs, mainly to the leg-spin of Wasim Raja. The Governor's XI were left 40 minutes plus 20 overs in which to make 135 for victory, but Marshall and Croft bowled the West Indians to an unexpected win with five overs remaining. All ten batsmen were either bowled or lbw, Mudassar fell lbw to Holding on the first ball of the innings.

First One-Day International

The West Indians, well equipped for limited over cricket and with two victories behind them, entered the first of the internationals in high spirits. They were not disappointed. Holding and Croft cramped the early batsmen and scoring was so slow that the later batsmen were forced to sacrifice themselves in an effort to improve the rate. Such was the scramble that Richards and Kallicharran were able to pick up two wickets each with their combined spin. 127 from 40 overs was a miserable effort and after Haynes had fallen early to Iqbal Qasim, Richards and Bacchus seemed to be strolling to victory, but the West Indians became bogged down and the end was dramatic. The final over saw Kallicharran and Greenidge confronted by Imran. Kallicharran became fifth out at 124, leaving the West Indies to score four runs off the last four balls. Marshall was immediately run out and then Garner survived an appeal for a catch at the wicket from which a bye was run. Three runs were needed for victory from the last ball and, incredibly, Greenidge drove majestically and three were run.

First One-Day International: Pakistan *v.* West Indies

21 November 1980

Pakistan   **at Karachi**

*Taslim Arif	c Marshall, b Croft	4
Sadiq Mohammad	c Holding, b Richards	40
Mansur Akhtar	b Garner	24
Javed Miandad (capt)	c Pydanna, b Croft	8
Wasim Raja	c Holding, b Richards	2
Majid Khan	c Lloyd, b Kallicharran	16
Mudassar Nazar	c and b Holding	4
Imran Khan	c Bacchus, b Kallicharran	2
Sarfraz Nawaz	run out	8
Iqbal Qasim	not out	6
Nazir Junior	not out	2
Extras	b 1, lb 5, w 4, nb 1	11
	(for 9 wkts)	127

	O	M	R	W
Holding	6	3	5	1
Croft	7	1	17	2
Marshall	8	—	34	—
Garner	8	—	26	1
Richards	8	—	24	2
Kallicharran	3	—	10	2

Fall of Wickets
1–5, 2–59, 3–74, 4–81, 5–83, 6–97, 7–102, 8–114, 9–119.

West Indies

D. L. Haynes	b Iqbal	4
S. F. A. Bacchus	hit wkt, b Mudassar	36
I. V. A. Richards	st Taslim, b Majid	36
C. H. Lloyd (capt)	c Sadiq, b Mudassar	9
A. I. Kallicharran	lbw, b Imran	14
C. G. Greenidge	not out	21
M. D. Marshall	run out	0
J. Garner	not out	0
Extras	b 2, lb 4, w 1, nb 1	8
	(for 6 wkts)	128

*M. R. Pydanna, C. E. H. Croft and M. A. Holding did not bat.

	O	M	R	W
Imran Khan	7	3	14	1
Sarfraz Nawaz	6	—	25	—
Iqbal Qasim	8	2	21	1
Nazir Junior	8	1	25	—
Mudassar Nazar	4	—	13	2
Majid Khan	7	1	22	1

Fall of Wickets
1–18, 2–69, 3–85, 4–93, 5–124, 6–124.

West Indies won by 4 wickets

First Test Match

West Indies left out Holding and Greenidge, neither of whom was completely fit, which gave opportunities to Clarke and Gomes. Javed won the toss and Pakistan took first innings on a lifeless pitch. Shafiq Ahmed and Sikhander Bakht were the players omitted and this meant a return to Test cricket after an absence of Nazir Junior, the off-break bowler, who toured England in 1971 (as a late replacement) and 1974 without playing in a Test. At that time he was known as Mohammad Nazir. He had had a successful series against New Zealand in 1969–70 and was now beginning a new Test career at the age of thirty-four. The first day was a tedious affair. By mid-afternoon Pakistan were 95 for 5. A stand of 93 by Wasim Raja and Imran Khan gave some respectability to the score. Raja batted with uncharacteristic restraint against the unrelenting accuracy of the speed attack. As in England, it was Garner who produced consistently accurate and economic length. As in England, the over-rate was parsimonious with only seventy-three overs bowled during the day. This included six overs from Richards whose spin brought about the dismissal of Wasim Raja. He lost patience and miss-hit to Kallicharran in the covers. Pakistan finished the day at 218 for 6, but the next day they moved into a good position through a fine innings by Imran Khan who, on his twenty-eighth birthday, hit his maiden hundred in Test cricket. He was seventh out with the score at 356, Abdul Qadir having retired after being struck on the shoulder by a ball from Croft. Sarfraz reached his highest score in Test cricket and the Pakistani innings had changed complexion from the mid-afternoon of the first day. During the course of his innings Imran became only the second Pakistani Test cricketer to complete a thousand runs and take a hundred wickets in Test cricket, Intikhab Alam was the first. There was no play on the third day which, inevitably, doomed the match to be drawn. Haynes completed a thousand runs in Test cricket in his fourteenth Test, and Richards, Gomes and David Murray all batted well. The Pakistani spinners Abdul Qadir and Nazir Junior performed creditably, but their main batsmen gave an inept display in the second innings and the match was abandoned as a miserable draw with half an hour of scheduled playing time still left. Pakistan suffered a bad set-back when Taslim broke a finger batting against Clarke.

First Test Match   Pakistan *v.* West Indies
24, 25, 27, 28 and 29 November 1980   at Lahore

Pakistan

	First Innings		*Second Innings*	
Sadiq Mohammad	c Murray, b Marshall	19	(2) lbw, b Clarke	28
*Taslim Arif	c Murray, b Garner	32	(1) retired hurt	8
Mansur Akhtar	c Murray, b Croft	13	b Clarke	0
Javed Miandad (capt)	c Richards, b Croft	6	run out	30
Majid Khan	c Bacchus, b Garner	4	not out	62
Wasim Raja	c Kallicharran, b Richards	76	lbw, b Clarke	3
Imran Khan	lbw, b Marshall	123	c Marshall, b Richards	9
Abdul Qadir	retired hurt	18	c Haynes, b Richards	1
Sarfraz Nawaz	c Richards, b Croft	55	c Garner, b Haynes	4
Iqbal Qasim	b Marshall	3		
Nazir Junior	not out	1		
Extras	b 1, lb 5, w 1, nb 12	19	b 2, lb 3, nb 6	11
		369	(for 7 wkts)	156

	O	M	R	W		O	M	R	W
Clarke	22	3	68	—		12	2	26	3
Croft	28	4	89	3		20	7	38	—
Marshall	22.4	4	91	3		15	4	30	—
Garner	27	6	71	2		9	3	17	—
Richards	7	—	31	1		11	4	19	2
Gomes						4	1	9	—
Kallicharran						1	—	4	—
Haynes						1	—	2	1

Fall of Wickets
1–31, 2–65, 3–67, 4–71, 5–95, 6–188, 7–356, 8–368, 9–369,
1–15, 2–57, 3–101, 4–112, 5–125, 6–133, 7–156.

West Indies

	First Innings	
D. L. Haynes	c Qasim, b Nazir	40
S. F. A. Bacchus	lbw, b Imran	0
I. V. A. Richards	b Nazir	75
A. I. Kallicharran	c Sadiq, b Qadir	11
C. H. Lloyd (capt)	c Javed, b Qasim	22
H. A. Gomes	b Raja	43
*D. A. Murray	c Majid, b Qadir	50
M. D. Marshall	b Sarfraz	9
J. Garner	c Taslim, b Qadir	15
C. E. H. Croft	not out	7
S. T. Clarke	st Taslim, b Qadir	15
Extras	b 3, lb 6, nb 1	10
		297

	O	M	R	W
Imran Khan	16	2	39	1
Sarfraz Nawaz	13	3	40	1
Abdul Qasim	40.4	4	131	4
Iqbal Qasim	12	4	18	1
Wasim Raja	10	3	21	1
Nazir Junior	17	4	38	2

Fall of Wickets
1–1, 2–118, 3–119, 4–143, 5–158, 6–225, 7–255, 8–275, 9–276.

Match drawn

1, 2 and 3 December 1980   **at Sahiwal**
West Indies 304 for 9 dec (S. F. A. Bacchus 80, M. R. Pydanna 56 not out,
   Mian Fayyaz 4 for 86) and 171 for 1 dec (S. F. A. Bacchus 70 not out,
   D. L. Haynes 63)
Punjab Governor's XI 170 (R. Nanan 6 for 48, D. R. Parry 4 for 84) and
   143 for 5
Match drawn

An uninspiring first day was brightened only by a second wicket stand of 122
between Gomes and Bacchus. There was some brisker scoring by the late order
batsmen on the second morning after which the spinners Nanan and Parry
bemused the Punjabi batsmen. Ranjee Nanan was particularly impressive,
taking 6 for 48 in 24 overs. Haynes and Bacchus opened with a stand of 134,
but Lloyd delayed his declaration until after lunch, leaving the Governor's XI
306 to make in 190 minutes. Azmat Rana hit seven fours in his 34 before being
hit on the head by a ball from Sylvester Clarke and being forced to retire,
and after that the game faded to a limp draw.

Second One-Day International

Playing his first match after a long absence through illness and injury, Zaheer Abbas rekindled hopes of a Pakistan victory after they had three wickets for 80 in 24 overs. He evoked memories of his former glories with an innings of power and charm, but it was nullified by some superb batting by Bacchus and Richards who not only hit with sustained aggression, but also stole every conceivable run with their briskness between the wickets. They added 176 and were both out at the same score, but by that time West Indies needed only three to win, a feat they accomplished with 27 balls to spare.

Second One-Day International: Pakistan *v.* West Indies

5 December 1980   at Sialkot

Pakistan

Mudassar Nazar	c Marshall, b Croft	3
Sadiq Mohammad	c Lloyd, b Garner	13
Zaheer Abbas	not out	95
Javed Miandad (capt)	st Pydanna, b Richards	16
Majid Khan	c Clarke, b Richards	34
Wasim Raja	not out	22
Extras		17
	(for 4 wkts)	200

Imran Khan, *Ashraf Ali, Sikhander Bakht, Sarfraz Nawaz and Iqbal Qasim did not bat.

	O	M	R	W
Clarke	8	1	28	—
Croft	8	2	28	1
Garner	8	2	36	1
Marshall	8	2	38	—
Richards	8	—	53	2

Fall of Wickets
1–5, 2–35, 3–80, 4–134.

West Indies

D. L. Haynes	c Qasim, b Imran	16
S. F. A. Bacchus	lbw, b Sarfraz	79
I. V. A. Richards	lbw, b Sikhander	83
*M. R. Pydanna	not out	2
C. H. Lloyd (capt)	not out	1
Extras		20
	(for 3 wkts)	201

A. I. Kallicharran, H. A. Gomes, S. T. Clarke, M. D. Marshall, J. Garner and C. E. H. Croft did not bat.

	O	M	R	W
Imran Khan	8	1	30	1
Sarfraz Nawaz	7.3	—	29	1

Sikhander Bakht	4	—	22	1
Iqbal Qasim	8	—	37	—
Majid Khan	2	—	20	—
Wasim Raja	4	—	27	—
Mudassar Nazar	2	—	16	—

Fall of Wickets
1–22, 2–198, 3–198.

West Indies won by 7 wickets

Second Test Match

Nanan replaced the injured Garner in the West Indian side, with Parry as twelfth man. As neither Holding, nor Greenidge was available, this was the only change in the West Indian side. Nanan's Test debut marked the first time for eight Test matches that the West Indies had played a recognised spinner in their side. Taslim played for Pakistan in spite of his injured finger, but the decision was not altogether a wise one. Lloyd won the toss and the West Indies were dismissed on the opening day by the spin trio of Nazir Junior, off-break, Abdul Qadir, leg-spin, and Iqbal Qasim, slow left arm. Nazir Junior's 5 for 44 in his sixth Test match represented his best figures in Test cricket. West Indies would not have passed two hundred but for a second wicket stand of 60 by Bacchus and Richards, and a defiant innings by David Murray at number seven. Pakistan would have prospered more had Imran been able to hold a chance given by Richards off Iqbal Qasim when he had only scored five. Richards was in his customary sparkling form after this escape and was surprisingly bowled by Nazir when he seemed certain to reach another Test hundred. The good that the Pakistani bowlers had done on the first day was eroded by some ineffective batting on the second. Taslim was lbw to Clarke on the third ball of the day and Zaheer was bowled in Clarke's next over. In spite of a brave innings by their skipper, Pakistan never recovered from these set-backs. By the end of the day West Indies led by 88 runs and had nine second innings wickets standing.

The West Indian second innings followed an almost identical pattern to the first. Once more it was the spinners who dominated and once more it was Viv Richards who responded to their challenge. The spinners reduced West Indies from 150 for 3 to 242 all out, but this still left Pakistan needing 302 for victory when no innings in the match had produced 250. This time it was the slow left arm of Iqbal Qasim that earned most of the honours with 6 for 89. The West Indies owed much to a last wicket stand of 44 between Nanan and the hard-hitting Sylvester Clarke. Before the close of the third day Pakistan lost Mansur, caught at square leg at 14, and Taslim, dismissed by a diving slip catch at 43. Zaheer stood firm, but the task before him and the rest of the side looked an enormous one. The enormity grew rapidly on the fourth morning. Sikhander, the night-watchman, was out to the first ball of the day and within forty minutes 60 for 2 had become 77 for 5. Javed and Wasim Raja, surely too low at number seven, briefly halted the slide, but there was little backbone in the Pakistani side and they lost their first Test match at home for eleven years shortly after lunch. It was a limp performance by their batsmen though West Indies bowled well and caught splendidly.

Second Test Match   Pakistan *v.* West Indies
8, 9, 11 and 12 December 1980   **at Faisalabad**

West Indies

	First Innings		*Second Innings*	
D. L. Haynes	lbw, b Qasim	15	lbw, b Qadir	12
S. F. A. Bacchus	c Sikhander, b Qadir	45	b Qasim	17
I. V. A. Richards	b Nazir	72	(5) c sub, b Qasim	67
A. I. Kallicharran	lbw, b Qadir	8	(6) lbw, b Nazir	27
C. H. Lloyd (capt)	c Mansur, b Nazir	20	(4) lbw, b Qasim	37
H. A. Gomes	c Qasim, b Nazir	8	(7) c Mansur, b Qasim	1
*D. A. Murray	c Majid, b Qadir	31	(8) b Nazir	19
M. D. Marshall	b Nazir	0	(9) c Javed, b Nazir	1
R. Nanan	lbw, b Nazir	8	(10) c Raja, b Qasim	8
C. E. H. Croft	c Taslim, b Qasim	2	(3) lbw, b Qasim	1
S. T. Clarke	not out	8	not out	35
Extras	b 12, lb 5, nb 1	18	b 9, lb 7, nb 1	17
		235		242

	O	M	R	W		O	M	R	W
Imran Khan	10	—	36	—		3	—	6	—
Sikhander Bakht	7	2	22	—		4	—	9	—
Iqbal Qasim	19	3	54	5		32.2	5	89	6
Abdul Qadir	15.3	1	48	3		17	4	45	1
Nazir Junior	22	7	44	5		33	13	76	3
Wasim Raja	4	—	13	—					

Fall of Wickets
1–39, 2–99, 3–127, 4–150, 5–176, 6–187, 7–187, 8–207, 9–223.
1–22, 2–47, 3–129, 4–150, 5–153, 6–171, 7–186, 8–189, 9–198.

Pakistan

	First Innings		*Second Innings*	
*Taslim Arif	lbw, b Clarke	0	c Richards, b Croft	18
Mansur Akhtar	c Lloyd, b Marshall	16	c Nanan, b Marshall	
Zaheer Abbas	b Clarke	2	lbw, b Marshall	3
Javed Miandad (capt)	c and b Clarke	50	(5) c Lloyd, b Croft	2
Majid Khan	c Murray, b Marshall	26	(6) b Clarke	
Wasim Raja	st Murray, b Nanan	21	(7) not out	3
Imran Khan	c Richards, b Croft	29	(9) c Richards, b Nanan	
Abdul Qadir	b Nanan	4	b Croft	
Iqbal Qasim	b Croft	0	(10) c Richards, b Nanan	
Sikhander Bakht	c Lloyd, b Richards	6	(4) c Lloyd, b Marshall	
Nazir Junior	not out	2	c Nanan, b Marshall	
Extras	b 4, lb 7, nb 9	20	b 4, lb 4, nb 10	1
		176		14

	O	M	R	W		O	M	R	W
Clarke	13	2	28	3		12	2	36	1
Croft	16	4	35	2		13	—	29	3
Marshall	9	1	39	2		9.4	—	25	4
Nanan	20	1	54	2		16	6	37	2
Richards	0.2	—	0	1					

Fall of Wickets
1–0, 2–2, 3–32, 4–73, 5–122, 6–132, 7–149, 8–150, 9–167.
1–14, 2–43, 3–60, 4–71, 5–77, 6–122, 7–122, 8–124, 9–132.

West Indies won by 156 runs

15, 16 and 17 December 1980 **at Bahawalpur**
West Indies 380 for 5 dec (D. L. Haynes 98, C. H. Lloyd 97, H. A. Gomes
   86, C. G. Greenidge 82) and 144 for 3 (A. I. Kallicharran 55 not out)
Pakistan Combined XI 232 (Ejaz Faqih 78, Rizwanus Zaman 58, D. R. Parry
   5 for 48)
Match drawn

While Haynes and Lloyd came close to recording the first centuries of the tour
it was events off field that caused most comment. Sarfraz Nawaz flew to England
for treatment for a groin injury and Wasim Bari was recalled to the Test squad
so being given an opportunity to become the most capped player in Pakistan
Test history. At Bahawalpur Greenidge, having missed four matches with a
back injury, hit three sixes and nine fours in his 82. He and Haynes put on
171 for the first wicket. Sadly, Greenidge's injury was aggravated by his innings
and it was decided that he should return home for treatment. Ejaz steered the
Combined XI to safety when they had looked at one time to be in danger
of being forced to follow-on. The game was abandoned as a draw when both
captains agreed that there was no hope of a result. Kallicharran took the
opportunity of batting practice to register his first fifty of the tour.

Third One-Day International

In the unusual spot as opener, Alvin Kallicharran played his best innings in
international cricket for over a year. Though they were without both Imran
and Sarfraz, Pakistan had initial success when Haynes and Richards were dismissed with only ten runs scored. Kallicharran batted with much of his old
charm, however, and with Gomes again showing good form and Clarke hitting
three sixes, West Indies climbed to 170 in their forty overs. It seemed an
inadequate score when Salim and Taslim opened steadily for Pakistan. They
reached 44 in 13 overs and a first victory for Pakistan over West Indies in
limited over cricket looked likely. Salim then fell to Garner and Taslim, still
nursing his broken finger, was brilliantly run out by Murray after he had played
and missed at Marshall. Zaheer gave Pakistan new hope, but Clarke bowled
him and Javed and, in spite of Wasim Raja's effort, there was just not enough
power left in the Pakistani batting to give them victory, so West Indies took
the one-day series by three matches to nil.

Third One-Day International: Pakistan *v.* West Indies
19 December 1980   at Lahore

West Indies

A. I. Kallicharran	lbw, b Raja	50
D. L. Haynes	b Rashid	2
I. V. A. Richards	c Taslim, b Rashid	0
C. H. Lloyd (capt)	c Bari, b Raja	13
H. A. Gomes	c and b Majid	32
D. R. Parry	run out	32
S. T. Clarke	b Majid	20
M. D. Marshall	run out	12
J. Garner	not out	3
Extras	lb 3, w 3	6
	(for 8 wkts)	170

*D. A. Murray and C. E. H. Croft did not bat.

	O	M	R	W
Sikhander Bakht	1	—	3	—
Rashid Khan	8	2	31	2
Tahir Naqqash	8	1	37	—
Ejaz Faqih	8	1	30	—
Wasim Raja	8	—	28	2
Majid Khan	7	—	35	2

Fall of Wickets
1–10, 2–10, 3–36, 4–92, 5–110, 6–134, 7–164, 8–170.

Pakistan

Salim Pervez	c Murray, b Garner	18
Taslim Arif	run out	24
Zaheer Abbas	b Clarke	42
Javed Miandad (capt)	b Clarke	23
Wasim Raja	not out	22
Majid Khan	run out	16
Ejaz Faqih	run out	0
Rashid Khan	not out	4
Extras	b 1, lb 8, nb 5	14
	(for 6 wkts)	163

*Wasim Bari, Sikhander Bakht and Tahir Naqqash did not bat.

	O	M	R	W
Clarke	8	—	25	2
Croft	7	—	28	—
Garner	8	2	18	1
Marshall	6	—	27	—
Parry	8	1	33	—
Richards	3	—	18	—

Fall of Wickets
1–44, 2–65, 3–116, 4–123, 5–155, 6–157.

West Indies won by 7 runs

Third Test Match

There was no play possible on the first day because of rain and, in fact, no play was possible until mid-way through the second day, Javed won the toss, as he did in the one-day international when he asked West Indies to bat. This time, however, he decided to bat on a drying wicket and must have quickly regretted his decision when four wickets went down for fourteen runs and Zaheer retired hurt after being hit on the forehead by a short delivery from Croft. Croft it was who caused most of the early damage and though Javed batted courageously, Pakistan finished the day at 68 for 6. They reached 128 the following day, but six men had failed to score and so created a new Test record. West Indies fared little better against a combination of pace and spin and were struggling with their five leading batsmen out for 44 runs. David Murray and Larry Gomes once more showed their emergence as Test players with a stand of 99 for the sixth wicket, and once more one could reflect on the way in which Gomes had matured from the shy, uncertain and likeable young man who had played with no great success for Middlesex. At the beginning of the last day it still seemed that West Indies might force a win, but Wasim Raja again batted with great assurance and the match was saved so keeping Pakistan's hopes of saving the series alive.

Third Test Match   Pakistan *v*. West Indies
22, 23, 24, 26 and 27 December 1980   at Karachi
Pakistan

	First Innings		*Second Innings*	
Shafiq Ahmed	lbw, b Clarke	0	lbw, b Garner	17
Sadiq Mohammad	lbw, b Croft	0	c Bacchus, b Clarke	36
Zaheer Abbas	not out	13	(4) b Croft	1
Javed Miandad (capt)	c Lloyd, b Clarke	60	(5) c Haynes, b Clarke	5
Majid Khan	c Bacchus, b Croft	0	(3) c Murray, b Croft	18
Wasim Raja	c Bacchus, b Croft	2	not out	77
Imran Khan	lbw, b Garner	21	c Murray, b Marshall	12
Ejaz Faqih	b Marshall	0	c Murray, b Marshall	8
*Wasim Bari	c Murray, b Clarke	23	b Garner	3
Iqbal Qasim	c Richards, b Clarke	0	b Croft	2
Nazir Junior	b Garner	0	not out	2
Extras	lb 1, w 1, nb 7	9	b 4, lb 3, nb 16	23
		128	(for 9 wkts)	204

	O	M	R	W		O	M	R	W
Clarke	15	7	27	4		11	3	14	2
Croft	14	5	27	3		23	6	50	3
Garner	18.1	8	27	2		19	4	39	2
Marshall	14	—	38	1		17	1	54	2
Richards						8	2	10	—
Gomes						6	—	14	—

Fall of Wickets
1–0, 2–0, 3–5, 4–14, 5–53, 6–57, 7–111, 8–112, 9–112.
1–30, 2–76, 3–78. 4–82, 5–85, 6–122, 7–146, 8–150, 9–178.

West Indies

	First Innings	
D. L. Haynes	lbw, b Iqbal	1
S. F. A. Bacchus	b Imran	16
I. V. A. Richards	c Zaheer, b Iqbal	18
A. I. Kallicharran	b Imran	4
C. H. Lloyd (capt)	c Javed, b Imran	1
*D. A. Murray	c Javed, b Iqbal	42
H. A. Gomes	c Javed, b Nazir	61
M. D. Marshall	b Nazir	0
S. T. Clarke	b Iqbal	17
J. Garner	lbw, b Imran	1
C. E. H. Croft	not out	3
Extras	lb 1, w 4	5
		169

	O	M	R	W
Imran Khan	29	5	66	4
Iqbal Qasim	34.1	11	48	4
Nazir Junior	9	2	21	2
Ejaz Faqih	4	1	9	—
Wasim Raja	1	—	8	—
Majid Khan	8	3	12	—

Fall of Wickets
1–19, 2–21, 3–43, 4–43, 5–44, 6–143, 7–143, 8–160, 9–161.

Match drawn

Fourth Test Match

West Indies took first knock on a pitch which was showing signs of breaking up at the end of the first day. They started badly, but Viv Richards, limping with leg strain, played his best innings of the series to hold the innings together and on the second day completed the only century of the tour by a West Indian. It was his eleventh in Test cricket. He was 95 when Croft joined him, but 41 were added for the last wicket. Clive Lloyd, who was leading West Indies for the forty-second time, a new Test record (Peter May had led England forty-one times), had been run out for nine, but must have been satisfied with the final score of 249. He became even more satisfied when Clarke dismissed both openers for 4. Javed and Majid took the score past a hundred, but were both out at the same score. Unhappily, all these events were overshadowed by an incident concerning Sylvester Clarke. Evidently, he was upset by the throwing of oranges by a section of the crowd when he was fielding in the deep, and, seizing a brick at the side of the field, he threw it into the crowd where it struck and injured a young student who was taken to hospital. The game was held up for twenty minutes as the crowd showed their anger at Clarke's action. It was left to Kallicharran to calm the situation so that play could be restarted. Manager Jackie Hendricks later visited the hospital to tender an apology. Clarke was later disciplined by the West Indian authorities and suspended for three Tests. Play resumed on the third day in an atmosphere of unreality under damp conditions. West Indies took a first innings lead of 83, but were shattered in the closing overs of the day when, after a stop for drizzle, they lost three wickets while one run was scored. They closed at 85 for 5, having been 84 for one just before tea. There was only forty minutes play possible on the fourth day and none at all on the last day. As we had learned that Croft and Richards had been warned by the umpires for allegedly using foul language against them, it was perhaps an occasion when rain was welcome. So West Indies took the series 1–0, their first win in Pakistan. Sadly, as in New Zealand the previous year, these wonderful cricketers had lost a few friends, and we mourned for cricket.

Fourth Test Match   Pakistan *v.* West Indies
30 and 31 December 1980, 2, 3 and 4 January 1981   **at Multan**

West Indies

	First Innings		*Second Innings*	
D. L. Haynes	b Imran	5	st Bari, b Qasim	31
S. F. A. Bacchus	lbw, b Imran	2	c Zaheer, b Qasim	39
I. V. A. Richards	not out	120	c Sadiq, b Nazir	12
A. I. Kallicharran	lbw, b Imran	18	not out	12
H. A. Gomes	lbw, b Qasim	32		
C. H. Lloyd (capt)	run out	9	(7) not out	17
*D. A. Murray	c Bari, b Qasim	0	(6) lbw, b Nazir	0
S. T. Clarke	c Javed, b Imran	28		
M. D. Marshall	c Javed, b Nazir	3		
J. Garner	c Nazir, b Imran	2		
C. E. H. Croft	lbw, b Sarfraz	3	(5) lbw, b Nazir	1
Extras	b 15, lb 6, w 3, nb 3	27	lb 3, w 1	4
		249	(for 5 wkts)	116

	O	M	R	W		O	M	R	W
Imran Khan	22	6	62	5		11	—	27	—
Sarfraz Nawaz	15.2	6	24	1		5	1	15	—
Iqbal Qasim	28	9	61	2		12	2	35	2
Nazir Junior	26	8	69	1		15	3	35	3
Wasim Raja	2	—	6	—					

Fall of Wickets
1–9, 2–22, 3–58, 4–134, 5–146, 6–153, 7–198, 8–201, 9–208.
1–57, 2–84, 3–84, 4–85, 5–85.

Pakistan

	First Innings	
Shafiq Ahmed	c Garner, b Clarke	0
Sadiq Mohammad	b Clarke	3
Majid Khan	c Richards, b Garner	41
Javed Miandad (capt)	c Haynes, b Croft	57
*Wasim Bari	run out	8
Zaheer Abbas	c Murray, b Marshall	8
Wasim Raja	not out	29
Imran Khan	c Haynes, b Croft	10

Sarfraz Nawaz	b Garner	1
Iqbal Qasim	c Richards, b Garner	1
Nazir Junior	lbw, b Garner	0
Extras	nb 8	8
		166

	O	M	R	W
Clarke	12	1	43	2
Croft	16	3	33	2
Marshall	12	1	44	1
Garner	17.2	4	38	4

Fall of Wickets
1–2, 2–4, 3–104, 4–104, 5–120, 6–137, 7–163, 8–164, 9–166.

Match drawn

Pakistan v. West Indies – Test Match Averages

Pakistan Batting

	M	Inns	NOs	Runs	HS	Average	100s	50s
Wasim Raja	4	7	3	246	77*	61.50		2
Javed Miandad	4	7		230	60	32.85		3
Sarfraz Nawaz	2	3	1	60	55	30.00		1
Imran Khan	4	7		204	123	29.24	1	
Majid Khan	4	7	1	154	62*	25.66		1
Taslim Arif	2	4	1	58	32	19.33		
Sadiq Mohammad	3	5		86	36	17.20		
Zaheer Abbas	3	5	1	57	33	14.25		
Wasim Bari	2	3		34	23	11.33		
Mansur Akhtar	2	4		36	16	9.00		
Abdul Qadir	2	4	1	23	18*	7.66		
Shafiq Ahmed	2	3		17	17	5.66		
Iqbal Qasim	4	6		11	5	1.83		
Nazir Junior	4	6	3	5	2*	1.66		

Played in one Test: Ejaz Faqih 0 and 8; Sikhander Bakht 6 and 1.

Pakistan Bowling

	Overs	Mdns	Runs	Wkts	Average	Best	5/inn
Iqbal Qasim	137.3	34	305	21	14.52	6–89	2
Nazir Junior	122	37	283	16	17.68	5–44	1
Imran Khan	91	13	236	10	23.60	5–62	1
Abdul Qadir	73.1	9	224	8	28.00	4–131	
Sarfraz Nawaz	33.2	10	79	2	39.50	1–24	
Wasim Raja	17	3	48	1	48.00	1–21	

Bowled in one Test: Ejaz Faqih 4–1–9–0; Majid Khan 8–3–12–0; Sikhander Bakht 11–2–31–0.

Pakistan Catches
7 – Javed Miandad; 3 – Taslim Arif (ct 2 st 1); 2 – Zaheer Abbas, Mansur Akhtar, Iqbal Qasim, Majid Khan, Sadiq Mohammad and Wasim Bari (ct 1, st 1); 1 – Sikhander Bakht, Wasim Raja, Nazir Junior and sub (Iqbal Sikander).

West Indies Batting

	M	Inns	NOs	Runs	HS	Average	100s	50s
I. V. A. Richards	4	6	1	364	120*	72.80	1	3
S. T. Clarke	4	5	2	103	35*	34.33		
H. A. Gomes	4	5		145	61	29.00		1
D. A. Murray	4	6		142	50	23.66		1
C. H. Lloyd	4	6	1	106	37	21.20		
S. F. A. Bacchus	4	6		119	45	19.83		
D. L. Haynes	4	6		104	40	17.33		
A. I. Kallicharran	4	6	1	80	27	16.00		
J. Garner	3	3		18	15	6.00		
C. E. H. Croft	4	6	2	17	7*	4.25		
M. D. Marshall	4	5		13	9	2.60		

Played in one Test: R. Nanan 8 and 8.

West Indies Bowling

	Overs	Mdns	Runs	Wkts	Average	Best	5/inn
I. V. A. Richards	26.2	6	60	4	15.00	2–19	
S. T. Clarke	97	20	242	15	16.13	4–27	
C. E. H. Croft	130	29	301	16	18.81	3–27	
J. Garner	90.3	25	192	10	19.20	4–38	
M. D. Marshall	99.2	11	321	13	25.69	4–25	

Bowled in two Tests: H. A. Gomes 10–1–23–0.
Bowled in one Test: R. Nanan 36–7–91–4; A. I. Kallicharran 1–0–4–0;
D. L. Haynes 1–0–2–1

West Indies Catches

10 – D. A. Murray (ct 9, st 1); 9 – I. V. A. Richards; 5 – C. H. Lloyd; 4 – D. L. Haynes
and S. F. A. Bacchus; 2 – R. Nanan and H. A. Gomes; 1 – S. T. Clarke, A. I. Kallicharran and M. D. Marshall.

West Indies in Pakistan, 1980–81
First-Class Matches – Batting

	v. Pakistan Board President's XI (Rawalpindi) 5–7 November		v. N.W.F.P. Governor's XI (Peshawar) 9–11 November		v. Sind Governor's XI (Sukkur) 14–16 November		First Test Match (Lahore) 24–29 November		v. Punjab Governor's XI (Sahiwal) 1–3 December		Second Test Match (Faisalabad)
C. G. Greenidge	16	81			10	5			16	63	15
D. L. Haynes	26	34	86	9*	10	39	40	—	16	63	15
I. V. A. Richards	18	—	8	—	21	32	75	—			72
S. F. A. Bacchus	37	20	0	26*	49	3	0	—	80	70*	45
A. I. Kallicharran	37	37*	1	—	25	4	11	—	22	—	8
C. H. Lloyd	53	—	0	—			22	—	19	—	20
D. A. Murray	11	—			5	3	50	—	12	—	31
D. R. Parry	10	7*			9	16			18	—	
M. A. Holding	19	—	3	—	2	3	15	—	5*	—	8*
S. T. Clarke	0	—	3	—			15	—	5*	—	8*
C. E. H. Croft	1*	—			1*	1*	7*	—			2
H. A. Gomes			85	—			43	—	49	20*	8
M. R. Pydanna			5	—					56*	—	
M. D. Marshall			13	—	20	24	9	—			0
R. Nanan			17	—	32	1			5	—	8
J. Garner			8*	—			15	—	1	—	
Byes	15	6	21	2	16	8	3		13	9	12
Leg byes	1		9	1	5	4	6		4	6	5
Wides					2	1			1		
No balls	3	1	11	2	6	5	1		3	3	1
Total	247	186	267	40	213	149	297		304	171	235
Wickets	10	3	10	0	10	10	10		9	1	10
Result	L		W		W		D		D		W

Catches
15 – D. A. Murray (ct 14, st 1)
13 – I. V. A. Richards
12 – C. H. Lloyd
 9 – S. F. A. Bacchus
 7 – D. L. Haynes
 4 – H. A. Gomes
 3 – A. I. Kallicharran, R. Nanan and D. R. Parry
 2 – M. D. Marshall, J. Garner, and M. R. Pydanna
 1 – S. T. Clarke

(Bahawalpur) 15–17 December	Third Test Match (Karachi) 22–27 December		Fourth Test Match (Multan)	30 December– 4 January		Inns	NOs	Runs	HS	Av
—						5	—	194	82	38.80
—	1	—	5	31		15	1	485	98	34.64
0	18	—	120	12		11	—	443	120	40.27
	16	—	2	39		14	2	404	80	33.66
55*	4	—	18	12*		14	3	263	55*	23.90
—	1	—	9	17*		10	1	275	97	30.55
	42	—	0	0		10	—	173	50	17.30
42						6	1	102	42	20.40
—						3	—	24	19	8.00
	17	—	28	—		8	3	111	35*	22.20
	3*	—	3	1		9	5	20	7*	5.00
—	61	—	32	—		9	1	385	86	48.12
39						4	2	104	56*	52.00
—	0	—	3	—		8	—	70	24	8.75
						6	—	71	32	11.83
—	1	—	2	—		5	1	27	15	6.75

(Bahawalpur) 15–17 December	Third Test Match (Karachi) 22–27 December		Fourth Test Match (Multan)	30 December– 4 January
			15	
3	1		6	3
1	4		3	1
4			3	
144	169		249	116
3	10		10	5
D	D		D	

West Indies in Pakistan, 1980–81
First-Class Matches – Bowling

	M. A. Holding	S. T. Clarke	C. E. H. Croft	D. R. Parry	M. D. Marshall	J. Garner
v. Pakistan Board President's XI (Rawalpindi) 5–7 Nov.	10–2–32–1	13.4–6–26–3	13–2–41–5	4–1–13–0		
	17–0–64–1	16–2–56–1	16–2–65–3	15–0–120–0		
v. N.W.F.P. Governor's XI (Peshawar) 9–11 Nov.		14–4–29–5			6.2–1–14–1	10–2–27–3
		14–2–58–4			8–0–44–0	15–1–55–3
v. Sind Governor's XI (Sukkur) 14–16 Nov.	11–4–15–2		9–1–34–0	17.4–3–54–2	18–4–30–4	
	5–3–11–1		9–2–27–3	1–0–6–0	5.3–1–9–5	
First Test Match (Lahore) 24–29 Nov.		22–3–68–0	28–4–89–3		22.4–4–91–3	27–6–71–2
		12–2–26–3	20–7–38–0		15–4–30–0	9–3–17–0
v. Punjab Governor's XI (Sahiwal) 1–3 Dec.		10–0–25–0		34–6–84–4		5–2–8–0
		11–2–31–1		19–6–42–1		6–1–19–0
Second Test Match (Faisalabad) 8–12 Dec.		13–2–28–3	16–4–35–2		9–1–39–2	
		12–2–36–1	13–0–29–3		9.4–0–25–4	
v. Pakistan Combined XI (Bahawalpur) 15–17 Dec.	14–2–47–1			21–5–48–5	15–2–49–2	16.4–5–50–2
Third Test Match (Karachi) 22–27 Dec.		15–7–27–4	14–5–27–3		14–0–38–1	18.1–8–27–2
		11–3–14–2	26–3–50–3		17–1–54–2	19–4–39–2
Fourth Test Match (Multan) 30 Dec.–4 Jan.		12–1–43–2	16–3–33–2		12–1–44–1	17.2–4–38–4
	57–11–	175.4–36–	180–33–	111.4–21–	152.1–19–	143.1–36–
	169–6	467–29	468–12	367–12	467–25	351–18
	av. 28.16	av. 16.10	av. 17.33	av. 30.58	av. 18.68	av. 19.50

† Azmat Rana, absent hurt.
* Ejaz Faquih, retired hurt.
‡ Abdul Qadir, retired hurt.

R. Nanan	I. V. A. Richards	H. A. Gomes	A. I. Kallicharran	D. L. Haynes	B	Lb	W	Nb	Total	Wkts
						1	2	5	120	9†
					3	3		3	314	5
					(12)				91	10
0–9–1					5	1		2	215	9*
0–50–2					25	5	1	9	228	10
–4–55–2					5	2	4	6	70	10
					1	5	1	12	369	9‡
	7–0–31–1				2	3		6	156	7
	11–4–19–2	4–1–9–0	1–0–4–0	1–0–2–1	(5)				170	10
–10–48–6					5	1		7	143	5
–4–38–3					4	7		9	176	10
–1–54–2	0.2–0–0–1				4	4		10	145	10
–6–37–2					10	5		9	232	10
		3–0–14–0								
						1	1	7	128	10
	8–2–10–0	6–0–14–0			4	3		16	204	9
								8	166	10
–25–	26.2–6–	13–1–	1–0–	1–0–						
–18	60–4	37–0	4–0	2–1						
6.16	av. 15.00	—	—	av. 2.00						

C

Eternal Triangle

New Zealand and India in Australia
Test series and Benson and Hedges
World Series Cup Competition

Once more the Australian public was presented with an almost indigestible diet of international cricket. Though there was to be a concession in that the Test series against New Zealand was to be completed before the one against India began, the number of one-day internationals in the qualifying section of the Benson and Hedges tournament was to be increased to fifteen. Surely such familiarity must breed contempt.

The programme for both touring teams once more emphasised how the increase in international matches meant that so little time was available for adequate preparation in the form of first-class games for those matches. Instant form would be demanded of both the New Zealanders and the Indians.

The decision by Glenn Turner not to join the New Zealand party was, of course, a disappointment, but the man has served his country so ill over the past few years that his withdrawal hardly constituted a surprise, nor could it be said to weaken the New Zealand side as he had not been part of it when they beat the West Indies.

With this triumph fresh in their minds, the New Zealanders began the tour in good heart, and, indeed, in good form.

31 October, 1, 2 and 3 November 1980   **at Melbourne**
Victoria 195 for 5 dec (G. N. Yallop 59) and 167 for 6 dec (J. M. Wiener
   61, G. N. Yallop 51)
New Zealanders 167 for 4 dec (G. P. Howarth 73 not out) and 196 for 2
   (G. P. Howarth 78 not out, J. G. Wright 69)
New Zealanders won by 8 wickets

The opening match of the New Zealand tour provided a dull start and an exciting finish. Robinson elected to bat when he won the toss, but, on a placid wicket, Victoria managed only 152 for 3 on the first day. The tourists' attack was accurate rather than penetrative and both Wiener and Matthews were run out. Howarth played a fine knock, refreshing after his miserable summer in England, and he and Burgess added 89 in 116 minutes before Burgess fell to Higgs. Howarth declared 28 behind – at one time New Zealand had been 20 for 3, all three to Max Walker – and Victoria batted with more enterprise in their second innings. Eventually, the visitors had to make 196 at a run a minute. Howarth and Wright scored 88 in 80 minutes and, in a tense finish, New Zealand won with four balls to spare.

5 November 1980   **at Traralgon**
New Zealanders 221 (J. M. Parker 55, J. V. Coney 51, G. Challis 4 for 47,
   C. Hogan 5 for 65)
Victorian Country XI 124
New Zealanders won by 97 runs

The New Zealanders gained their second win of the tour when they proved far too strong for a Victorian Country XI in a fifty over game. The home side's opening bowlers did well, but Coney and Parker put on 59 for the third wicket and both reached half centuries.

7, 8 and 9 November 1980 at Canberra
New Zealanders 262 for 8 dec (B. A. Edgar 85)
Australian Capital Territory 38 for 1
Match drawn

Rain which had curtailed play in the game at Melbourne returned to thwart the New Zealanders at Canberra where only six hours' play was possible in the three days. Bruce Edgar batted well on the opening day.

12 November 1980 at Armidale
New Zealanders 209 for 9 (J. G. Bracewell 70, N. Johnson 4 for 42)
Northern New South Wales XI 125 (B. Whatham 51, M. C. Snedden 4 for 11)
New Zealanders won by 84 runs

Johnson caused the tourists early discomfort, but John Bracewell hit fiercely to bring his side to some respectability in their fifty overs. The country side stumbled badly against a varied and accurate attack and were out in 47.2 overs.

14, 15, 16 and 17 November 1980 at Brisbane
New Zealanders 193 (G. S. Chappell 4 for 28) and 461 for 8 dec (R. J. Hadlee
103, J. V. Coney 96, J. G. Wright 78, P. E. McEwan 73, B. A. Edgar 51,
T. V. Hohns 4 for 131)
Queensland 203 (A. R. Border 69, R. J. Hadlee 5 for 61) and 323 for 6
(A. R. Border 80 not out, K. C. Wessels 64)
Match drawn

With skipper Howarth unable to play with a groin injury, the New Zealanders began the game with some trepidation and their worries increased as both McEwan and Troup suffered injuries during the match, Troup being unable to bowl in the Queensland second innings. Chappell and Thomson dismissed the visitors for a disappointing score on the first day, but Richard Hadlee brought his side back into contention with a magnificent all-round display. Queensland slipped from 102 for 3 to 102 for 7 as Hadlee produced a marvellous spurt which saw Chappell, among others, out for a duck. At the second attempt, the New Zealanders batted with consistency and Coney and Hadlee added 159 for the seventh wicket in 99 minutes, Hadlee hit three sixes and fourteen fours in his third century in first-class cricket. Queensland faced their huge target with determination and panache, but a draw always seemed the most likely result.

19, 20 and 21 November 1980 at Newcastle
Newcastle 215 (G. J. Gilmour 59, J. G. Bracewell 4 for 64) and 176 (R. Neal
58, J. G. Bracewell 7 for 76)
New Zealanders 360 (P. E. McEwan 63, J. G. Wright 98, B. L. Cairns 59,
M. Hill 4 for 66) and 34 for 0
New Zealanders won by 10 wickets

In their last match before the first of the international matches, the New Zealanders again overwhelmed minor opposition. Ex-Test all-rounder Gary Gilmour was top scorer for Newcastle side who also included state leg-spinner

Holland. The most successful of the New Zealanders was young off-spinner John Bracewell who took eleven wickets in the match and enhanced his chances of being chosen for the representative side.

With the New Zealanders having started their tour well, the Indians arrived with Gavaskar breathing confidence in his team. The Indian party included three who had had no Test experience: Srinivasan, an opening batsman, Yograj Singh, an opening bowler, and Azad, a batsman.

22, 23, 24 and 25 November 1980   **at Perth**
Western Australia 296 for 5 dec (M. O'Neill 100, B. M. Laird 68, C. S. Serjeant 56 not out) and 262 for 5 dec (B. M. Laird 110, R. S. Langer 84, K. D. Ghavri 4 for 65)
Indians 312 for 4 dec (S. M. Gavaskar 157, G. R. Viswanath 75) and 116 for 1 (D. B. Vengsarkar 59 not out)
Match drawn

On a beautiful wicket in Perth batsmen enjoyed themselves and three centuries were recorded in a game which moved inevitably to a draw. On the opening day Mark O'Neill recorded his first century in first-class cricket and on the second day Sunil Gavaskar reached his fifty-eighth. The third century of the match was recorded by Bruce Laird who, ironically, had been omitted from the Australian Test side on the previous day. It was hard on Laird who had batted well in the first innings, sharing in a stand of 108 with O'Neill after Shipperd and Langer had gone for fourteen. Gavaskar and Chauhan began the Indian innings with a stand of 111. The Indian captain was missed three times on his way to his hundred. He was finally caught behind by Tim Zoehrer, a nineteen-year-old, who was keeping wicket in the state side for the first time.

First One-Day International – Australia *v.* New Zealand

The Australian side showed two surprising choices, Shaun Graf, who had had an inept season with Hampshire in England, but had performed creditably for Victoria, and Trevor Chappell, the youngest of the three brothers. Howarth declared himself fit and, with New Zealand in good heart after their fine start to the tour, asked Australia to bat when he won the toss. There were no early upsets. Dyson and Wood began steadily before Wood was caught by substitute John Bracewell, the first of four catches taken by the twelfth man. They reached 142 with only two wickets down and then, in the space of nine overs, lost six wickets while 29 runs were scored. Hadlee had bowled an immaculate length, but it was Chatfield who reaped the harvest, taking three of the wickets in the middle order collapse and finishing with 5 for 34 to win the Man of the Match award. That Australia reached 217 was due to a ferocious assault in the last over of their innings by Rodney Marsh. He hit Lance Cairns for three sixes and two fours before being caught by John Bracewell off the final delivery. New Zealand had bowled tidily and fielded splendidly and now they batted with consistent application. Edgar and Wright began with caution and put on 61 in 19 overs. McEwan was run out, but Howarth, in his best form, and Wright added 73 in 14 overs. When New Zealand seemed to be slipping behind the clock Richard Hadlee hit 39 runs off 29 deliveries, profiting from a dropped catch by Border at mid-wicket. Three wickets went for 13 runs, but Coney and Cairns kept calm to see the visitors home with five balls to spare.

First One-Day International: Australia v. New Zealand
23 November 1980   **at Adelaide**

Australia

J. Dyson	c sub (J. G. Bracewell), b Chatfield	69
G. M. Wood	c sub (J. G. Bracewell), b Chatfield	19
G. S. Chappell (capt)	c Lees, b Chatfield	25
K. J. Hughes	c Wright, b McEwan	20
A. R. Border	c Lees, b Chatfield	5
*R. W. Marsh	c sub (J. G. Bracewell), b Cairns	44
S. F. Graf	c sub (J. G. Bracewell), b Chatfield	0
T. M. Chappell	c Hadlee, b Cairns	12
D. K. Lillee	c Wright, b Cairns	3
G. F. Lawson	not out	4
Extras	lb 1, nb 15	16
	(for 9 wkts)	217

L. S. Pascoe did not bat

	O	M	R	W
Hadlee	10	1	25	—
Snedden	10	1	34	—
Coney	4	—	14	—
Cairns	10	—	58	3
Chatfield	10	1	34	5
McEwan	6	—	36	1

Fall of Wickets
1–37, 2–92, 3–142, 4–147, 5–150, 6–150, 7–167, 8–171, 9–217.

New Zealand

J. G. Wright	c Dyson, b G. Chappell	60
B. A. Edgar	c. T. Chappell, b Graf	25
P. E. McEwan	run out	3
G. P. Howarth (capt)	run out	37
R. J. Hadlee	lbw, b Lillee	39
J. M. Parker	c and b Lillee	16
J. V. Coney	not out	10
*W. K. Lees	c Lawson, b Lillee	2
B. L. Cairns	not out	4
Extras	lb 15, nb 8	23
	(for 7 wkts)	219

E. J. Chatfield and M. C. Snedden did not bat.

	O	M	R	W
Lillee	10	2	40	3
Pascoe	10	3	30	—
Lawson	9.1	1	42	—
T. Chappell	5	—	21	—
Graf	10	1	40	1
G. Chappell	5	—	23	1

Fall of Wickets
1–61, 2–67, 3–140, 4–151, 5–198, 6–203, 7–211.

New Zealand won by 3 wickets

Second One-Day International – Australia v. New Zealand

The elation which New Zealand felt at winning the first of the one-day internationals was tempered by concern over injuries. Troup was still incapacitated with cartilage trouble, and Brendon Bracewell, playing grade cricket in Perth, was asked to join the party as a stand-by. Wright had injured his ankle in Adelaide and he and Coney were replaced by Burgess and Smith. On a beautiful wicket at Sydney, the game belonged entirely to Australia and Greg Chappell. The Australians included Doug Walters in their side and Kim Hughes was sent in first with Dyson. They added 29 and then came Chappell. With Dyson, a resolute player, Chappell added 151 in 28 overs. Dyson was bowled by Hadlee for 79, at which time Chappell was on 66. In the last ten overs of the innings he went on the rampage. Walters came in to a standing ovation, for services rendered and enthusiasm maintained, and he and Chappell scored at ten an over. To their credit, New Zealand started at the required rate, but they were unable to match the slaughter that Chappell had inflicted upon them in the closing overs and Australia were easy winners, having taken full advantage of batting first on a splendid wicket, and possessing, in Greg Chappell, one of the world's great batsmen of power and dignity.

Second One-Day International: Australia v. New Zealand
25 November 1980   **at Sydney**

Australia

K. J. Hughes	c Smith, b McEwan	19
J. Dyson	b Hadlee	79
G. S. Chappell (capt)	not out	138
A. R. Border	c Snedden, b Chatfield	9
K. D. Walters	not out	26
Extras	b 6, lb 12	18
	(for 3 wkts)	289

T. M. Chappell, *R. W. Marsh, D. K. Lillee, L. S. Pascoe, G. F. Lawson and S. F. Graf did not bat.

	O	M	R	W
Hadlee	10	1	66	1
Snedden	10	1	58	—
Cairns	10	—	41	—
Chatfield	10	—	55	1
McEwan	10	—	51	1

Fall of Wickets
1–29, 2–180, 3–207.

New Zealand

B. A. Edgar	lbw, b G. Chappell	34
J. M. Parker	c Dyson, b Pascoe	6
P. E. McEwan	c G. Chappell,	23
	b Lawson	
G. P. Howarth (capt)	c Marsh, b Pascoe	46
M. G. Burgess	b Lillee	29
R. J. Hadlee	c Dyson, b Graf	10
B. L. Cairns	c Border, b Pascoe	16
I. D. S. Smith	c Marsh, b Graf	1
*W. K. Lees	c Dyson, b Pascoe	8
M. C. Snedden	b Pascoe	3
E. J. Chatfield	not out	4
Extras	lb 11, w 1, nb 3	15
		195

	O	M	R	W
Lillee	7	—	26	1
Pascoe	7.5	1	30	5
Lawson	10	—	43	1
G. Chappell	10	1	41	1
Graf	8	—	40	2

Fall of Wickets
1–14, 2–63, 3–73, 4–138, 5–155, 6–173, 7–176, 8–181, 9–190.

Australia won by 94 runs

25 November 1980   **at Perth**
Indians 250 for 6 (Kirti Azad 56, Kapil Dev 55 not out, T. E. Srinivasan 53)
Western Australia 154 for 8 (D. R. Doshi 5 for 24)
Indians won on faster scoring rate

The Indians gained a comfortable win in their one-day game with Western
Australia whose innings was restricted to 45 overs by the weather. The tourists
batted consistently, but it was the Doshi's spin and nagging accuracy which
provided the dominant feature of the day.

27 November 1980   **at Geraldton**
Indians 180 (T. E. Srinivasan 59)
Western Australian Country XI 182 for 4 (I. Herbert 70 not out)
Western Australian Country XI won by 6 wickets

The Indians were surprisingly beaten by a country side after Srinivasan and Chauhan had given them a good start with a stand of 83. Their last six wickets fell for only 22, however, and one of them was Gavaskar, batting at number ten and bowled first ball by Ross Ditchburn who had 3 for 40. The Country XI's success was founded on a fourth wicket partnership of 96 in 77 minutes between Ian Herbert and skipper Terry Waldron. The home side won with two overs and a ball remaining.

First Test Match – Australia *v.* New Zealand

The buoyancy that had seen New Zealand make such an impressive start to the tour evaporated on the opening day of the First Test match. Chappell won the toss and asked New Zealand to bat. The visitors included Smith as wicket-keeper for Lees, and Brendon Bracewell was thrust straight into the Test side as replacement for Troup as Coney and Chatfield were both unfit. The host of injuries that plagued New Zealand could not excuse some dreadful batting, however. All began well with Wright and Edgar taking the score to 64 before Wright flashed wildly at Pascoe who had just gone round the wicket. Wright edged the ball to Marsh and a few minutes later Edgar fell to Lawson in exactly the same manner. McEwan was caught at slip off Lillee shortly after lunch and three wickets had gone for 12 runs. Howarth and Parker repaired the damage though neither of them looked at ease; both, however, looked magnificent in comparison to what followed. The leg-spin of Higgs, contrasting with the pace of Lillee and Pascoe, bemused the visitors and the last seven wickets went down for 32 runs. It was a good wicket and a terrible batting display. Australia finished the day at 14 without loss. On the following morning Wood and Dyson took their stand to 80. Chappell looked in fine form, hitting with cleanliness and power, but after a brisk 35, he lofted Cairns to McEwan. The out of form Hughes failed again, but Wood and Border ended any thoughts of a collapse. Wood batted with customary grit and when he was fourth out he had scored 111 out of 225. Some good bowling at the close of the day by Hadlee and Cairns gave New Zealand hope as Australia finished only 53 ahead with seven men out. The lead was extended to 80 the following morning, but New Zealand lost seven wickets before clearing off this deficit. It was batting that lacked both technique and application and bowling by Lillee that was both intelligent and fiery. The courage of Edgar and Hadlee salvaged some pride, but New Zealand's score was their lowest in Australia and they had lost in three days.

First Test Match   Australia *v.* New Zealand
28, 29 and 30 November 1980   **at Brisbane**

New Zealand

	First Innings		*Second Innings*	
J. G. Wright	c Marsh, b Pascoe	29	c Walters, b Lillee	1
B. A. Edgar	c Marsh, b Lawson	20	c Hughes, b Lillee	51
P. E. McEwan	c Border, b Lillee	6	c Hughes, b Lillee	0
G. P. Howarth (capt)	c and b Higgs	65	c Wood, b Lillee	4

J. M. Parker	b Pascoe	52	c Dyson, b Lawson	4
M. G. Burgess	c Chappell, b Pascoe	0	c Wood, b Lillee	2
*I. D. S. Smith	c Hughes, b Lillee	7	c Hughes, b Pascoe	7
R. J. Hadlee	c Marsh, b Higgs	10	(9) not out	51
B. L. Cairns	c Border, b Higgs	0	(10) c Border, b Lillee	0
J. G. Bracewell	not out	6	(8) c Border, b Lawson	0
B. P. Bracewell	b Higgs	0	b Pascoe	8
Extras	lb 18, w 5, nb 7	30	b 4, lb 4, w 1, nb 5	14
		225		142

	O	M	R	W		O	M	R	W
Lillee	18	7	36	2		15	1	53	6
Pascoe	19	4	41	3		13.1	2	30	2
Lawson	12	2	39	1		8	—	26	2
Chappell	4	1	18	—					
Higgs	16.1	3	59	4		5	1	19	—
Walters	1	—	2	—					

Fall of Wickets
1–64, 2–71, 3–76, 4–193, 5–193, 6–209, 7–209, 8–209, 9–221.
1–6, 2–9, 3–14, 4–30, 5–34, 6–58, 7–61, 8–114, 9–114.

Australia

	First Innings		*Second Innings*	
G. M. Wood	c Parker, b J. Bracewell	111	not out	32
J. Dyson	lbw, b Cairns	30	not out	24
G. S. Chappell (capt)	c McEwan, b Cairns	35		
K. J. Hughes	c Wright, b Hadlee	9		
A. R. Border	run out	36		
K. D. Walters	b Cairns	17		
*R. W. Marsh	b Hadlee	8		
D. K. Lillee	c Parker, b Cairns	24		
G. F. Lawson	c sub (Boock), b Hadlee	16		
L. S. Pascoe	b Cairns	5		
J. D. Higgs	not out	1		
Extras	b 1, lb 7, nb 5	13	b 2, lb 2, nb 3	7
		305	(for no wkt)	63

	O	M	R	W		O	M	R	W
Hadlee	37	8	83	3		6	—	28	—
B. Bracewell	22	8	71	—		3	3	0	—
Cairns	38.5	11	87	5		7.3	3	16	—
J. Bracewell	18	5	51	1		5	—	12	—

Fall of Wickets
1–80, 2–145, 3–160, 4–225, 5–235, 6–250, 7–258, 8–299, 9–299.

Australia won by 10 wickets

29 and 30 November, 1 and 2 December 1980   **at Adelaide**
South Australia 302 (P. R. Sleep 90 not out, R. J. Zadow 61) and 275 (D. C.
    Lovell 74, W. M. Darling 61, J. J. Crowe 50, D. R. Doshi 4 for 60)

Indians 456 for 9 dec (D. B. Vengsarkar 153, S. M. Patil 116, K. Azad 59)
    and 78 (R. M. McLellan 4 for 18, G. R. Attenborough 4 for 20)
South Australia won by 43 runs

In remarkable fashion, and one which may be considered uniquely their own,
the Indians contrived to lose the game against South Australia which, for three
days, they looked to be winning with ease. South Australia struggled at 139
for 5 on the opening day until Peter Sleep batted with sense and aggression
to lead them past the three hundred. This seemed a completely inadequate total
in the face of some elegant batting by Vengsarkar and Patil who added 212
for the fifth wicket. The Indians led by 153 on the first innings and seemed
to be heading for an innings victory when Kapil Dev dismissed Goodman and
Hookes with successive balls and then had Zadow caught behind to have the
home side at 29 for 3. They were rallied by Darling and Crowe, but finished
the third day only 27 ahead with but four wickets left. Lovell and the tail wagged
well, but India's task of 122 in three hours did not seem too burdensome. They
produced a strange batting order, and some stranger shots, and crumbled
inexplicably before the medium pace of Geoff Attenborough and Ross
McLellan who gave their side victory by 43 runs with twenty minutes remaining.

4 December 1980   **at Whyalla**
South Australian Country XI 119
Indians 188 for 4 (Kapil Dev 105 not out, C. P. S. Chauhan 53 not out)
Indians won by 6 wickets

Slumping from 75 for 2 to 119 all out, Dev taking three wickets, the Country
XI fought back to have India in trouble at 39 for 4. Gavaskar was bowled
for nought and Viswanath went for seven, but Kapil Dev hit fiercely and saw
India to victory with Chauhan. They batted on and Dev reached his hundred
and the stand realised 149.

5 December 1980   **at Wagga**
New Zealanders 174 for 9
Southern New South Wales 108 (S. L. Boock 5 for 27)
New Zealanders won by 66 runs

The New Zealanders did not bat well, but gained a comfortable win over the
Southern side. Most reassuring for the tourists was the reappearance of their
walking wounded. Troup, in particular, bowled well, taking 1 for 9 in ten overs.
It was also pleasing to see Boock meet with success, but the New Zealand
joy was ended when Howarth damaged a finger, an injury which needed seven
stitches and was likely to deprive the team of his services for at least two
matches.

Third One-Day International – Australia v. India

India's preparation for the representative matches had inspired little confidence
and, as they were the country least at ease in the limited over situation and
Australia were fielding the side that trounced New Zealand in Sydney, an
Australian victory seemed inevitable. When India were floundering at 111 for

6, their main batting gone, the predictions of an overwhelming Australian victory were being realised. At this point Patil and Kirmani batted quite splendidly, both going for their shots and showing no fear of the Australian attack as they added 92. It proved a match-winning stand and Patil's contribution was to be a deciding factor in gaining him the Man of the Match award. The wicket was slow and the ball tended to keep low so that the Indian score of 208 was a creditable one. The Indians were helped by some poor Australian catching, Lillee, in particular, offered Patil three lives. A sparkling start by Hughes and Dyson was ended when Patil who, in an economic spell of medium pace, bowled Hughes. Dyson was the first of three batsmen to be run out and Doshi then took three wickets as Australia slumped to defeat in an inept batting display.

Third One-Day International: Australia v. India
6 December 1980   **at Melbourne**

India

S. M. Gavaskar (capt)	c Lawson, b Lillee	4
D. B. Vengsarkar	b G. Chappell	22
T. E. Srinivasan	c G. Chappell, b Lillee	6
G. R. Viswanath	b T. Chappell	22
Kirti Azad	c Lawson, b Pascoe	4
S. M. Patil	b G. Chappell	64
Kapil Dev	b Lawson	6
*S. M. H. Kirmani	not out	48
R. Binny	run out	0
K. D. Ghavri	run out	0
D. R. Doshi		
Extras	b 11, lb 15, nb 6	32
	(for 9 wkts)	208

	O	M	R	W
Lillee	7	1	22	2
Pascoe	10	2	32	1
Graf	10	—	30	—
Lawson	9	—	46	1
T. Chappell	5	—	14	1
G. Chappell	8	1	32	2

Fall of Wickets
1–12, 2–22, 3–58, 4–65, 5–73, 6–111, 7–203, 8–208, 9–208.

Australia

K. J. Hughes	b Patil	35
J. Dyson	run out	23
G. S. Chappell (capt)	c Gavaskar, b Doshi	11
A. R. Border	c Azad, b Doshi	6
K. D. Walters	st Kirmani, b Doshi	27
T. M. Chappell	run out	14
*R. W. Marsh	b Ghavri	7
S. F. Graf	b Binny	5

D. K. Lillee	run out	5
G. F. Lawson	c Doshi, b Binny	0
L. S. Pascoe	not out	0
Extras	lb 2, nb 7	9
		142

	O	M	R	W
Ghavri	9.1	1	32	1
Binny	6	—	23	2
Kapil Dev	7	2	15	—
Doshi	10	1	32	3
Patil	10	1	31	1

Fall of Wickets
1–60, 2–62, 3–73, 4–80, 5–118, 6–129, 7–137, 8–139, 9–139.

India won by 66 runs

Fourth One-Day International – Australia *v.* New Zealand

With each side having won one match, but Australia having played three, it was imperative that the home country should beat New Zealand in Melbourne if they were to retain interest in the Benson and Hedges competition. Chappell complained to the Australian Board that he felt that the Melbourne wicket was unsuitable for first-class cricket, and he was not alone in his view that the pitch was not conducive to good batting with its slowness and low bounce. New Zealand made a mockery of the pitch with a fine opening stand, but then the New Zealand batsmen, with Howarth absent, made another terrible mess of things. Edgar and Wright reached 74 in 25 overs and the score was barely doubled by the remaining batsmen. It was another miserable display. Border who, like Hughes, had not been in the best of form, went in first with Dyson so as to give him a chance to play an innings. He responded for, after Dyson had gone at 15, he and Chappell put on 92 in a manner which suggested that they would steer Australia to victory with ease. There was a collapse, however, and in the end it was Marsh and Wood who edged Australia home. It was a rather uninspiring match for which the wicket was largely to blame.

Fourth One-Day International: Australia *v.* New Zealand
7 December 1980   **at Melbourne**

New Zealand

B. A. Edgar	run out	33
J. G. Wright	b Pascoe	57
J. V. Coney	run out	9
P. E. McEwan	b Lillee	17
R. J. Hadlee	c T. Chappell, b Pascoe	1
M. G. Burgess (capt)	c Border, b Pascoe	14
J. M. Parker	lbw, b G. Chappell	3
*W. K. Lees	c G. Chappell, b Lillee	0
G. B. Troup	not out	7

S. L. Boock	lbw, b Lillee	2
E. J. Chatfield	lbw, b Pascoe	0
Extras	b 2, lb 10, w 1	13

| | | 156 |

	O	M	R	W
Lillee	10	3	19	3
Pascoe	9.5	3	37	4
Graf	4	—	15	—
G. Chappell	10	1	23	1
T. Chappell	10	2	27	—
Walters	6	—	22	—

Fall of Wickets
1–74, 2–95, 3–112, 4–116, 5–138, 6–141, 7–142, 8–147, 9–153.

Australia

J. Dyson	lbw, b Hadlee	3
A. R. Border	c Edgar, b Chatfield	55
G. S. Chappell (capt)	st Lees, b Boock	48
K. J. Hughes	run out	19
K. D. Walters	lbw, b Boock	7
T. M. Chappell	b Hadlee	6
G. M. Wood	not out	1
*R. W. Marsh	not out	10
Extras	b 2, lb 8	10

| | (for 6 wkts) | 159 |

D. K. Lillee, S. F. Graf and L. S. Pascoe did not bat.

	O	M	R	W
Troup	9	3	15	—
Hadlee	10	—	34	2
Chatfield	9.2	1	34	1
McEwan	5	—	18	—
Boock	10	1	30	2
Coney	4	—	18	—

Fall of Wickets
1–15, 2–107, 3–116, 4–124, 5–143, 6–145.

Australia won by 4 wickets

Fifth One-Day International – New Zealand *v.* India

The unhappiness of New Zealand continued in Perth, and so, too, did the surprising success of India. It was an exciting game of fluctuating fortune and some very bad batting on a good wicket. Once more Gavaskar failed, being caught behind off Hadlee's first ball of the match. Hadlee's bowling and courageous batting rightly earned him the Man of the Match award. He appeared to have won the game for New Zealand when, aided by Cairns, he had India at 119 for 8. That India had reached so many was due to the effort and application of Sharma and Patil who added 70 for the fifth wicket and then saw four wickets fall for three runs. Kirti Azad and Ghavri produced surprising resistance for India who reached 162, far better than they could have expected at one time and far more than New Zealand should have allowed them to reach. Hadlee took five wickets in all and took a wicket with the first delivery of each of his four spells. Once again without Howarth, the New Zealand batting was most inept and they disintegrated to 80 for 6 with only Paul McEwan showing any resolution. Hadlee and Cairns then put bat to ball to add 50 before Hadlee was caught behind and Cairns died as he had lived, bravely, skying the ball to Vengsarkar. When the last pair, Lees and Chatfield, came together 27 runs were needed from four overs. Chatfield was struck on the head by a bouncer from Dev, but, helmeted, he was saved from the near tragedy of 1974. When Binny began the last over New Zealand needed nine runs to win. Three came from the first three balls, but Lees failed to score from the fourth and attempting to hit a winning six off the fifth ball, he skied to mid-wicket where Vengsarkar took another most able catch.

Fifth One-Day International: New Zealand *v.* India
9 December 1980   **at Perth**

India

S. M. Gavaskar (capt)	c Lees, b Hadlee	0
R. Binny	c Parker, b Chatfield	14
D. B. Vengsarkar	c Coney, b Troup	12
G. R. Viswanath	c Coney, b Hadlee	10
Yashpal Sharma	b Cairns	23
S. M. Patil	c Parker, b Hadlee	39
Kapil Dev	c Lees, b Hadlee	0
*S. M. H. Kirmani	c Parker, b Cairns	1
Kirti Azad	c and b Chatfield	29
K. D. Ghavri	b Hadlee	14
D. R. Doshi	not out	2
Extras	b 9, lb 6, w 2, nb 1	18
		162

	O	M	R	W
Hadlee	9	1	32	5
Chatfield	8.4	—	33	2
Troup	10	2	36	1
Coney	10	1	25	—
Cairns	10	2	18	2

Fall of Wickets
1–0, 2–27, 3–35, 4–46, 5–116, 6–116, 7–116, 8–119, 9–157.

New Zealand

J. G. Wright	c Vengsarkar, b Dev	4
B. A. Edgar	b Binny	16
P. E. McEwan	c Sharma, b Doshi	41
J. M. Parker	c Dev, b Binny	1
J. V. Coney	c Kirmani, b Patil	5

M. G. Burgess (capt)	c sub (Yadav), b Doshi	10
R. J. Hadlee	c Kirmani, b Binny	20
B. L. Cairns	c Vengsarkar, b Ghavri	26
*W. K. Lees	c Vengsarkar, b Binny	16
G. B. Troup	run out	5
E. J. Chatfield	not out	6
Extras	lb 4, w 1, nb 2	7
		157

	O	M	R	W
Kapil Dev	10	2	33	1
Ghavri	10	—	30	1
Binny	9.5	1	41	4
Patil	10	3	24	1
Doshi	10	4	22	2

Fall of Wickets
1–13, 2–22, 3–28, 4–50, 5–80, 6–80, 7–130, 8–130, 9–136.

India won by 5 runs

11, 12 and 13 December 1980   **at Hobart**
Indians 275 (R. Binny 51, K. D. Ghavri 51, M. B. Scholes 4 for 63) and 220
    for 3 dec (S. M. Gavaskar 85, C. P. S. Chauhan 66)
Tasmania 233 for 5 dec (B. F. Davison 76 not out, D. C. Boon 63) and 62
    for 1
Match drawn

Some good bowling from Yadav, who took 3 for 67 in bowling 32 overs, and
a return to form innings from Gavaskar were the Indian highlights in a game
which ended in a draw in spite of the efforts of the two captains to effect a
result. The tourists were handicapped by an injury to Ghavri who could not
bowl on the second day after hurting his neck while batting.

Second Test Match – Australia v. New Zealand

Once more the New Zealanders crumpled miserably before the Australia pace
attack. Lillee, Hogg, reappearing in the Test side, and Pascoe reduced New
Zealand to 28 for 4 on the opening morning, and but for a spirited stand by
Coney and acting captain Burgess, and some lusty blows from Hadlee, the
visitors' position at the end of the first day would have been much worse. Coney
was one of three changes in the New Zealand side from the First Test. He
replaced the injured Howarth while Lees and Troup, both fit again, came in
for Brendon Bracewell and Smith. There was still no place for Chatfield who
had had success in the one-day games. Burgess and Coney added 88 for the
fifth wicket, but Burgess fell to Lillee shortly before tea, and though the last
five wickets showed some resilience, it was in all a poor display by the New
Zealand batsmen, Coney excepted. Once more Dennis Lillee took the honours
with sustained hostility and accuracy in a performance which fully justified
his captain's decision to ask New Zealand to bat first. The Australians one

set back on the first day came off the second ball of their innings when Wood was caught at short leg in attempting to glance a ball from Richard Hadlee. Early on the second day, however, it seemed as though New Zealand would emulate Australia's performance in the field. Chappell fell to Troup at twenty-two and Hughes was out three runs later. Dyson and Border saw the score to fifty, but both went in quick succession and the home side were tottering at 68 for 5. The veterans, Walters and Marsh, produced some fine shots and some less authentic smites to hit Australia out of trouble. Walters, whose return to Test cricket was both surprising and romantic, played a most useful innings, but when he fell to Hadlee Australia were still forty runs behind. Lillee and Hogg did not stay long and with Australia 187 for 8, the first innings looked likely to end in stalemate. Then came a fierce and unorthodox partnership between Marsh and Pascoe which gave Australia a vital lead and disheartened the New Zealanders. Marsh was caught nine short of his century off the bowling of Hadlee who took five wickets and bowled quite splendidly. In the debris that often appeared around him, Hadlee never looked anything but one of the world's very greatest cricketers and certainly no better bowler has ever played for New Zealand. The second New Zealand innings was even more dismal than the first though the visitors were unfortunate in that they lost three wickets to controversial decisions by umpire Wester. A stand of 42 for the seventh wicket between Lees and Burgess was the only stand of any substance, but this time it was mainly the leg spin of Jim Higgs that destroyed New Zealand. Needing only 53 to win, Australia lost Wood caught behind without a run scored and then Chappell had a most torrid time, being dropped and surviving a confident appeal for lbw before he, too, was caught at the wicket off the unquenchable Hadlee. Hughes and Dyson gave Australia victory without further mishap and with victory in this match came victory in the series. It was another humiliation for New Zealand who had again lost in three days and had once more failed to give a true indication of their batting ability. It was rather sad, but Hadlee's performance and endeavour were things of which his countrymen could feel justly proud. Australia had twice overwhelmed New Zealand and yet they had not played particularly well on either occasion and their batting, in particular, looked rather brittle with Hughes and Border out of touch.

Second Test Match   Australia *v.* New Zealand

12, 13 and 14 December 1980   at Perth

New Zealand

	First Innings		*Second Innings*	
J. G. Wright	b Pascoe	10	c Marsh, b Hogg	3
B. A. Edgar	c Border, b Lillee	0	c Hughes, b Pascoe	0
J. M. Parker	c Chappell, b Hogg	3	(6) c Hughes, b Hogg	18
P. E. McEwan	c Marsh, b Lillee	8	c Marsh, b Lillee	16
J. V. Coney	b Hogg	71	c Marsh, b Higgs	0
M. G. Burgess (capt)	c Hughes, b Lillee	43	(7) lbw, b Higgs	18
*W. K. Lees	c Marsh, b Pascoe	5	(8) not out	25
R. J. Hadlee	c Hughes, b Pascoe	23	(9) c Chappell, b Higgs	0

J. G. Bracewell	lbw, b Lillee	6	(3) run out	16
B. L. Cairns	c Pascoe, b Lillee	13	c Border, b Higgs	6
G. B. Troup	not out	0	c Marsh, b Lillee	0
Extras	lb 3, w 2, nb 9	14	lb 12, w 2, nb 5	19
		196		121

	O	M	R	W		O	M	R	W
Lillee	23.5	5	63	5		15.1	7	14	2
Hogg	16	5	29	2		10	2	25	2
Pascoe	20	3	61	3		10	1	30	1
Chappell	7	3	5	—		3	1	7	—
Higgs	5	1	13	—		8	2	25	4
Walters	2	—	11	—		2	1	1	—

Fall of Wickets
1–6, 2–13, 3–24, 4–28, 5–116, 6–133, 7–171, 8–177, 9–196.
1–0, 2–27, 3–38, 4–63, 5–64, 6–73, 7–115, 8–115, 9–121.

Australia

	First Innings		*Second Innings*	
G. M. Wood	c Bracewell, b Hadlee	0	c Lees, b Hadlee	0
J. Dyson	c Bracewell, b Cairns	28	not out	25
G. S. Chappell (capt)	c Cairns, b Troup	12	c Lees, b Hadlee	13
K. J. Hughes	c Lees, b Hadlee	3	not out	16
A. R. Border	b Cairns	10		
K. D. Walters	c Coney, b Hadlee	55		
*R. W. Marsh	c Coney, b Hadlee	91		
D. K. Lillee	c and b Hadlee	8		
R. M. Hogg	b Cairns	3		
L. S. Pascoe	not out	30		
J. D. Higgs	c Coney, b Cairns	7		
Extras	b 3, lb 4, w 1, nb 10	18	lb 1	1
		265	(for 2 wkts)	55

	O	M	R	W		O	M	R	W
Hadlee	27	8	87	5		11.1	4	20	2
Troup	22	5	57	1		1	—	1	—
Cairns	28.1	7	88	4		5	2	17	—
Bracewell	4	1	15	—		5	—	16	—

Fall of Wickets
1–0, 2–22, 3–25, 4–50, 5–68, 6–156, 7–176, 8–187, 9–244.
1–3, 2–31.

Australia won by 8 wickets

14 December 1980   **at Launceston**
Indians 141 for 9 (R. J. McCurdy 5 for 15)
Tasmania 143 for 7 (B. F. Davison 76)
Tasmania won by 3 wickets

The one-day game at Launceston was reduced to thirty-five overs by the weather ınd it did not seem as if this many overs would be necessary when the tourists were 12 for 4, all four wickets to the pace of Rod McCurdy. Kirti Azad and Kapil Dev gave the Indian innings some substance and some valuable runs from Kirmani meant that Tasmania were chasing 142. They, in their turn, were n disarray at 12 for 3, but Davison and Jeffery added 111 and though the ınnings faltered again, Tasmania won with three overs and three wickets remaining. Davison hit four sixes and six fours in his match-winning 76.

Sixth One-Day International – Australia v. India

The success of India came to an abrupt end when Australia overwhelmed them ıt Sydney. Chappell won the toss and asked India to bat. They made a brisk start with Gavaskar suggesting that his show of form in Hobart had indeed been a sign of his restoration to his normal level of excellence. He was bowled between bat and pad by Pascoe's first ball, but then Viswanath and Sharma batted soundly and scored quickly to take the score to 129 in 19 overs. The return of Lillee heralded a collapse in which four wickets went down in three overs. Kirmani and Ghavri hit 29 in the last five overs, but 180 was a miserably disappointing score. Allan Border opened with Dyson and was soon in commanding form, lashing the ball through the covers to reach 50 out of 77. Dyson had left at 56 and Greg Chappell, in need of a long innings, batted with elegant restraint and made sure that Border would reach a splendid hundred. It was a crushing defeat for India and the form of Border and Chappell, which had caused some concern of late, was an added bonus for Australia who now seemed to be capable of winning both the Test series and the Benson and Hedges World Series Cup. A crowd of nearly twenty-eight thousand reflected the Australian confidence.

Sixth One-Day International: Australia v. India
8 December 1980   at Sydney

India

S. M. Gavaskar (capt)	b Pascoe	22
R. Binny	c Marsh, b Graf	31
D. B. Vengsarkar	c Marsh, b Pascoe	4
G. R. Viswanath	b Graf	43
Yashpal Sharma	b Lillee	34
S. M. Patil	b T. Chappell	0
Kirti Azad	lbw, b Lillee	1
Kapil Dev	c Dyson, b Hogg	4
S. M. H. Kirmani	run out	24
K. D. Ghavri	not out	11
D. R. Doshi		
Extras	b 1, lb 3, nb 2	6
	(for 9 wkts)	180

	O	M	R	W
Lillee	10	1	29	2
Hogg	10	1	48	1

Pascoe	9	2	34	2
Graf	10	1	23	2
T. Chappell	10	—	40	1

Fall of Wickets
1–31, 2–42, 3–64, 4–129, 5–130, 6–133, 7–139, 8–151, 9–180.

Australia

J. Dyson	c Kirmani, b Dev	20
A. R. Border	not out	105
G. S. Chappell (capt)	not out	52
Extras	lb 4, nb 2	6
	(for 1 wkt)	183

K. J. Hughes, T. M. Chappell, K. D. Walters, *R. W. Marsh, S. F. Graf, D. K. Lillee,
L. S. Pascoe and R. M. Hogg did not bat.

	O	M	R	W
Ghavri	8	—	25	—
Binny	7	—	29	—
Kapil Dev	8	1	27	1
Patil	8	—	49	—
Doshi	10	—	40	—
Gavaskar	1.2	—	7	—

Fall of Wickets
1–56.

Australia won by 9 wickets

19 December 1980   **at Currambin**
New Zealanders 252 for 6 (G. P. Howarth 66, J. M. Parker 63, J. V. Coney
    53 not out)
Queensland Country XI 141
New Zealanders won by 111 runs

With morale low after two Test defeats and a series of injuries, New Zealand
treated the country game at Currambin with a seriousness not usually associated
with such fixtures. They fielded a strong side as this game gave the only
opportunity for match practice in between the Second Test match and the
one-day international with India in Brisbane, one of the distressing factors in
an itinerary crowded with limited over matches and international fixtures. The
tourists gained an easy victory, but far the most encouraging aspect of their
win was the innings of Geoff Howarth who played with caution in an effort
to re-establish himself after injury. Parker, too, showed good form as did all
rounder Coney. Once more Richard Hadlee bowled finely, finishing with
for 10 and being far too lively for the country batsmen.

Seventh One-Day International – India *v.* New Zealand

A splendid game of cricket ended with New Zealand winning by three wickets
with only two balls remaining though with twenty minutes to go, New Zealand

had looked beaten. Gavaskar won the toss and decided to bat, but once more the Indian captain failed, falling in Troup's second over. None of the Indian batsmen, apart from the dependable Chauhan, showed any durability and with India at 84 for 5 after 32 overs, New Zealand had victory in their grasp. At this point Kapil Dev came in and though at first unable to find any sort of timing, he suddenly hit Cairns for two fours to leg and then savaged the bowling in spectacular style. Three overs from Coney produced 43 runs and Kapil Dev hit him for sixes off successive balls, having previously hit for six through the off-side. It was the return of Hadlee and Troup to the attack that brought an end to Kapil Dev's fireworks. He hit 75 off 51 deliveries, including nine fours as well as his three sixes. Many felt that Howarth should have confronted him with Troup and Hadlee earlier for, as it was, India scored 120 runs off the last 18 overs. Wright and Edgar gave New Zealand a sound start with 67 in 19 overs though, like the later New Zealand batsmen, they were aided by dropped catches. Wright skied Kapil Dev to cover and then Doshi turned the game India's way with some immaculate bowling that reduced New Zealand to 166 for 7 with only five and a half overs left. Coney and Cairns were the heroes who won the game for New Zealand so revenging the mauling that they had received from Kapil Dev earlier in the day, but once more it was India's lapses in the field which gave the advantage to their opponents. A vital miss was when Doshi dropped Coney off Ghavri. The forty-seventh over was important for New Zealand for it was then that Cairns took 15 runs off Yograj Singh. Cairns and Coney made the last 49 runs off 31 deliveries and Coney's 47 came from 52 balls.

Seventh One-Day International: India *v.* New Zealand
21 December 1980   at Brisbane

India

S. M. Gavaskar (capt)	c Coney, b Troup	1
C. P. S. Chauhan	c Hadlee, b Snedden	46
D. B. Vengsarkar	c Lees, b Cairns	13
G. R. Viswanath	b Snedden	2
Yashpal Sharma	c Wright, b Snedden	16
S. M. Patil	c Wright, b Cairns	16
Kapil Dev	c Cairns, b Troup	75
*S. M. H. Kirmani	c Edgar, b Troup	18
K. D. Ghavri	not out	9
Yograj Singh	c Burgess, b Troup	0
D. R. Doshi	run out	0
Extras	b 2, lb 6	8
		204

	O	M	R	W
Hadlee	9.5	1	21	—
Troup	9	2	19	4
Snedden	10	—	33	3
Cairns	10	1	53	2
Coney	10	—	70	—

Fall of Wickets
1–3, 2–45, 3–52, 4–79, 5–84, 6–136, 7–190, 8–203, 9–204.

New Zealand

J. G. Wright	c sub, b Kapil Dev	42
B. A. Edgar	b Doshi	28
*W. K. Lees	c Yograj, b Doshi	20
G. P. Howarth (capt)	c Kapil Dev, b Doshi	0
J. M. Parker	c Kirmani, b Doshi	11
J. V. Coney	not out	47
M. G. Burgess	b Yograj	13
R. J. Hadlee	c Vengsarkar, b Yograj	0
B. L. Cairns	not out	27
Extras	b 6, nb 9, w 1, nb 1	17
	(for 7 wkts)	205

M. C. Snedden and G. B. Troup did not bat.

	O	M	R	W
Yograj Singh	8.4	—	44	2
Ghavri	10	1	38	—
Kapil Dev	10	—	37	1
Patil	10	1	39	—
Doshi	10	—	30	4

Fall of Wickets
1–67, 2–93, 3–97, 4–103, 5–130, 6–158, 7–166.

New Zealand won by 3 wickets

Eighth One-Day International – India *v.* New Zealand

For the third time India and New Zealand contrived a most exciting finish, but this time the victory went to India who thereby drew level on points with Australia, with New Zealand two points behind. Once more Gavaskar failed to impress and with Vengsarkar falling to the ever-improving Snedden, India were struggling at 30 for 2. Chauhan and Yashpal Sharma gave the Indian score some respectability without ever threatening to dominate the bowling. Chauhan left at 95 and Patil went seven runs later, but then Kapil Dev changed the tempo of the innings with some fine driving. Howarth confronted Kapil Dev with Hadlee, but the all-rounder was not to be subdued and his 27 was a most significant contribution. His innings appeared to have a liberating effect upon Sharma who cut loose in spectacular fashion, pulling four sixes and reaching 72 with a variety of aggressive shots that brought him the Man of the Match award. Kirmani, though handicapped by injury, gave good support and Ghavri's final gesture was to hit the last ball of the innings for six. India's 230 was their biggest score in the Benson and Hedges competition. New Zealand's start was similar to India's, but Howarth and Coney were progressing at a good rate until the captain was lured forward and beaten by Doshi. Some panic then set in and New Zealand slumped to 134 for 6 and looked well beaten. It was then that Burgess, recovering much of his old form and poise, and Cairns brought renewed hope to New Zealand. Cairns attacked the medium pacers as soon as Doshi's quota was complete and suddenly only eighteen were needed with more than three overs left. Then came disaster. Cairns tried to force Ghavri to leg and was bowled and at the same score, 213, Burgess, now batting with a runner, was run out. Snedden, Troup and Chatfield were a little too agitated and though Doshi dropped Troup in the penultimate over when only nine were needed, India won with three balls and six runs to spare.

Eighth One-Day International: India v. New Zealand

23 December 1980   **at Adelaide**

India

S. M. Gavaskar (capt)	c Lees, b Troup	17
C. P. S. Chauhan	c Coney, b Snedden	43
D. B. Vengsarkar	b Snedden	3
Yashpal Sharma	c Cairns, b Troup	72
S. M. Patil	c Coney, b Chatfield	6
Kapil Dev	c Lees, b Snedden	27
*S. M. H. Kirmani	not out	39
R. Binny	c Wright, b Troup	4
K. D. Ghavri	not out	10
Extras	lb 8, nb 1	9
	(for 7 wkts)	230

Yograj Singh and D. R. Doshi did not bat.

	O	M	R	W
Hadlee	10	2	42	—
Troup	10	—	65	3
Snedden	10	2	30	3
Cairns	10	3	30	—
Chatfield	10	—	54	1

Fall of Wickets
1–23, 2–30, 3–95, 4–102, 5–153, 6–192, 7–209.

New Zealand

J. G. Wright	b Patil	18
J. M. Parker	c Chauhan, b Yograj	13
G. P. Howarth (capt)	st Kirmani, b Doshi	26
J. V. Coney	run out	49
*W. K. Lees	lbw, b Ghavri	6
M. G. Burgess	run out	42
R. J. Hadlee	c Gavaskar, b Doshi	4
B. L. Cairns	b Ghavri	39
M. C. Snedden	c Ghavri, b Dev	4
G. B. Troup	not out	5
E. J. Chatfield	b Dev	0
Extras	b 12, lb 2, nb 4	18
		224

	O	M	R	W
Yograj Singh	9	1	39	1
Binny	10	—	47	—

Ghavri	10	1	49	2
Patil	1	—	3	1
Kapil Dev	9.3	1	34	2
Doshi	10	1	34	2

Fall of Wickets
1–36, 2–36, 3–105, 4–123, 5–125, 6–134, 7–213, 8–213, 9–224.

India won by 6 runs

26, 27, 28 and 29 December 1980   **at Brisbane**
Indians 308 (S. M. Gavaskar 79, D. B. Vengsarkar 75, S. M. Patil 60,
   G. Dymock 5 for 101) and 344 for 8 dec (S. M. Gavaskar 108, S. M. Patil
   97)
Queensland 259 for 9 dec (G. M. Ritchie 75, W. R. Board 61, Yograj Singh
   4 for 72) and 85 for 2
Match drawn

In search of some sort of batting form, Gavaskar handed over the captaincy
for the game against Queensland, originally scheduled as a one-day contest,
to Viswanath. The effect on Gavaskar was remarkable. Playing better than
at any other time since his arrival in Australia, he hit 79 and 108. Viswanath
was less successful in his search for form, but Patil assured himself of a place
in the Test side with two fine innings and Vengsarkar also showed a glimpse
of his true ability. The worry from the Indian point of view was that, on the
eve of the First Test, they were left with fitness doubts concerning Binny, Ghavri
and Chauhan, and Kirmani had had no opportunity to play a first-class innings
on the tour.

Third Test Match – Australia v. New Zealand

Winning the toss, Howarth asked Australia to bat and was rewarded with
immediate success when Wood was out to the second ball of the day, unable
to remove his bat in time from a ball of Hadlee's which lifted. It was Wood's
third consecutive Test duck, following centuries in the two previous Tests.
Suspicious of the pitch, which the New Zealand bowlers did not exploit to
their best advantage early on, the Australians batted doggedly, but late in the
day Doug Walters showed some good form and much depended on him when
Australia restarted at 222 for 6. He did not disappoint and reached a fine century
on the second morning to complete a remarkable return to Test cricket and,
probably, to assure himself of a fifth tour to England. The match was still
in favour of New Zealand, however, when three wickets went down in one
over with the score on 261. It was then that Higgs joined Walters. Higgs not
only stayed while Walters completed his century, but batted for nearly an hour
and three quarters while 60 runs were added. He was aided by a somewhat
bizarre incident. Before the score had reached three hundred, Higgs was caught
behind off Cairns, only for umpire Ballihache to call no-ball on the grounds
of intimidatory bowling, Cairns having bowled a bouncer at a number eleven
batsman. There was a lengthy and heated discussion between Howarth and

the umpire, Howarth's argument being, presumably, that Cairns is of only medium pace and the batsman was in no danger. Higgs had a further reprieve when he should have been run out a few minutes later, but Bracewell and Lees bungled the chance. It all made Walters' eloquent and story-book hundred possible. New Zealand replied well with some good batting by Howarth and Parker after early lapses. Howarth was unsettled by some barracking after an appeal for a catch by Wood had been turned down and Howarth had stood his ground and was out shortly after and Pascoe was troubling the New Zealand batsmen when a thunderstorm brought play to an abrupt end on the third day. Coney saw New Zealand to within sight of the Australian total, but by now the pitch had grown slow and the bounce was so low as to make strokes impossible. The Australians ended the day at 121 for 3 and a draw seemed inevitable. Hadlee, named Man of the Series, bowled with great heart to give New Zealand some hope and their final target was 193 in 205 minutes. Glory seemed to be within their grasp when they reached 95 for the loss of Edgar, but Hogg and Chappell took four wickets in five overs and a draw was all that was left for either side in a match which did credit to the players when one considers the difficulties of the pitch.

Third Test Match   Australia *v.* New Zealand

26, 27, 28, 29 and 30 December 1980   **at Melbourne**

Australia

	First Innings		*Second Innings*	
G. M. Wood	c Lees, b Hadlee	0	c Lees, b Hadlee	21
J. Dyson	b Troup	13	lbw, b Cairns	16
G. S. Chappell (capt)	c Coney, b Hadlee	42	b Hadlee	78
K. J. Hughes	c Parker, b Hadlee	51	b Hadlee	30
A. R. Border	c Cairns, b Coney	45	c Lees, b Hadlee	9
K. D. Walters	b Coney	107	run out	2
*R. W. Marsh	c Parker, b Coney	1	lbw, b Cairns	0
D. K. Lillee	b Cairns	27	c Coney, b Bracewell	8
R. M. Hogg	run out	0	b Hadlee	12
L. S. Pascoe	b Cairns	0	not out	0
J. D. Higgs	not out	6	b Hadlee	0
Extras	b 7, lb 13, w 3, nb 6	29	b 6, lb 4, nb 2	12
		321		188

	O	M	R	W		O	M	R	W
Hadlee	39	8	89	3		27.2	7	57	6
Troup	26	5	54	1		11	1	31	—
Cairns	35	6	83	2		33	13	65	2
Bracewell	9	—	38	—		15	5	22	1
Coney	12.3	6	28	3		1	—	1	—

Fall of Wickets
1–0, 2–32, 3–75, 4–159, 5–190, 6–192, 7–261, 8–261, 9–261.
1–25, 2–64, 3–111, 4–128, 5–131, 6–131, 7–149, 8–185, 9–188.

New Zealand

	First Innings		*Second Innings*	
J. G. Wright	c Chappell, b Higgs	4	c Wood, b Hogg	44
B. A. Edgar	lbw, b Higgs	21	run out	25
G. P. Howarth (capt)	b Hogg	65	lbw, b Chappell	20
J. M. Parker	c Marsh, b Pascoe	56	lbw, b Chappell	1
M. G. Burgess	lbw, b Pascoe	49	(6) not out	10
J. V. Coney	not out	55	(5) lbw, b Hogg	3
J. G. Bracewell	c Chappell, b Pascoe	0		
*W. K. Lees	lbw, b Hogg	4	(7) b Lillee	7
R. J. Hadlee	c Border, b Hogg	9	(8) not out	5
B. L. Cairns	lbw, b Higgs	18		
G. B. Troup	c Hughes, b Hogg	1		
Extras	b 13, lb 12, nb 10	35	b 2, lb 8, w 1, nb 2	13
		317	(for 6 wkts)	128

	O	M	R	W		O	M	R	W
Lillee	21	4	49	—		13	3	30	1
Hogg	26.2	9	60	4		8	1	14	2
Higgs	19	6	87	3		12	4	24	—
Pascoe	26	6	75	3		11	1	35	—
Border	4	1	6	—		2	1	5	—
Chappell	2	—	5	—		7	4	7	2
Hughes						1	1	0	—

Fall of Wickets
1–27, 2–32, 3–157, 4–163, 5–247, 6–247, 7–264, 8–280, 9–316.
1–50, 2–95, 3–97, 4–101, 5–101, 6–121.

Match drawn

Australia *v.* New Zealand – Test Match Averages

Australia Batting

	M	*Inns*	*NOs*	*Runs*	*HS*	*Average*	*100s*	*50s*
K. D. Walters	3	4	—	181	107	45.25	1	1
G. S. Chappell	3	5	—	180	78	36.00		1
J. Dyson	3	6	2	136	30	34.00		
G. M. Wood	3	6	1	164	111	32.80	1	
K. J. Hughes	3	5	1	109	51	27.25		1
A. R. Border	3	4	—	100	45	25.00		
R. W. Marsh	3	4	—	100	91	25.00		1
L. S. Pascoe	3	4	2	35	30*	17.50		
D. K. Lillee	3	4	—	67	27	16.75		
J. D. Higgs	3	4	2	14	7	7.00		
R. M. Hogg	2	3	—	15	12	5.00		

Also batted: G. F. Lawson 16 (one match).

Australia Bowling

	Overs	*Mdns*	*Runs*	*Wkts*	*Average*	*Best*	*5/inn*
R. M. Hogg	60.2	17	128	10	12.80	4–60	
D. K. Lillee	106	27	245	16	15.31	6–53	2
J. D. Higgs	75.1	17	227	11	20.63	4–25	

| G. S. Chappell | 23 | 9 | 42 | 2 | 21.00 | 2–7 |
| L. S. Pascoe | 99.1 | 17 | 272 | 12 | 22.66 | 3–41 |

Also bowled: G. F. Lawson 20–2–65–3; K. D. Walters 5–1–14–0; A. R. Border 6–2–11–0; K. J. Hughes 1–1–0–0.

Australia Catches

10 – R. W. Marsh; 9 – K. J. Hughes; 7 – A. R. Border; 5 – G. S. Chappell; 3 – G. M. Wood; 1 – J. D. Higgs, K. D. Walters, J. Dyson and L. S. Pascoe.

New Zealand Batting

	M	*Inns*	*NOs*	*Runs*	*HS*	*Average*	*100s*	*50s*
J. V. Coney	2	4	1	129	71	43.00		2
G. P. Howarth	2	4	—	154	65	38.50		2
R. J. Hadlee	3	6	2	98	51*	24.50		1
M. G. Burgess	3	6	1	122	49	24.40		
J. M. Parker	3	6	—	134	56	22.33		2
B. A. Edgar	3	6	—	117	51	19.50		1
J. G. Wright	3	6	—	91	44	15.16		
W. K. Lees	2	4	1	41	25*	13.66		
P. E. McEwan	2	4	—	30	16	7.50		
B. L. Cairns	3	5	—	37	18	7.40		
J. G. Bracewell	3	5	1	28	16	7.00		
G. B. Troup	2	3	1	1	1	0.50		

Also batted: B. P. Bracewell 0 and 8 (one match) I. D. S. Smith 7 and 7 (one match).

New Zealand Bowling

	Overs	*Mdns*	*Runs*	*Wkts*	*Average*	*Best*	*5/inn*
R. J. Hadlee	147.3	35	364	19	19.15	6–57	2
B. L. Cairns	147.3	42	356	13	27.38	5–87	1
G. B. Troup	60	11	143	2	71.50	1–54	
J. G. Bracewell	56	11	154	2	77.00	1–22	

Also bowled: J. V. Coney 13.3–6–29–3; B. P. Bracewell 25–11–71–0.

New Zealand Catches

6 – W. K. Lees; 5 – J. V. Coney; 4 – J. M. Parker; 2 – B. L. Cairns and J. G. Bracewell; 1 – J. G. Wright, R. J. Hadlee, P. E. McEwan and sub (S. L. Boock).

1, 2, 3 and 4 January 1981   **at Launceston**

New Zealanders 494 (M. G. Burgess 134, J. G. Wright 106, G. P. Howarth 53, J. V. Coney 51, R. J. McCurdy 7 for 91)

Tasmania 188 (R. F. Jeffery 61, J. G. Bracewell 5 for 67) and 286 for 6 (R. F. Jeffery 145 not out, L. Allen 55, M. C. Snedden 4 for 74)

Match drawn

The New Zealand batting form returned too late to influence the course of the Test matches, but, nevertheless, the first day run spree was encouraging for the visitors in the quest for the Benson and Hedges World Series Cup. Burgess and Wright, who batted at number six, were in particularly aggressive form and Jeremy Coney once more emphasised his consistency and immense value to the side. Rod McCurdy, whose first-class debut had been for Derbyshire in 1979, returned a remarkable career best with his medium pace bowling. That Tasmania were able to save the game after following on 306 behind was due to some fine batting from opener Jeffery and the loss of play on the third day when unsupervised repairs to the wicket at one end made it unsafe for play. The match tended to highlight the inadequacy of preparation for the Tests that had been inflicted upon the tourists with the very limited number of first-class fixtures. Snedden played his first first-class game of the tour, Smith his second, his first having been as a late replacement in the First Test. Boock again found himself without a game. McKechnie, the most durable of cricketers, came into the side as replacement for Troup who had returned to New Zealand because of injury.

First Test Match – Australia v. India

The Indians were expected to provide stronger opposition to the might of Australia than the New Zealanders, but their form in the matches leading up to the First Test provided no evidence for this optimism. In effect, they were completely outplayed and their batting, in the main, was a miserable affair. India won the toss and batted first on a wicket which held some dampness likely to give aid to the quick bowlers, but certainly not expected to be viciously unplayable. Graf and Yadav were named as twelfth men and Gavaskar and Chauhan opened the Indian innings. Once more the Indian captain failed, hanging out his bat to Lillee in the first over to provide Marsh with the first of his five dismissals in the innings, a record for an Australian wicket-keeper against India. Worse was to follow as Pascoe, Lillee and Hogg, encouraged by both the pitch and the frailty of the batting, reduced India to a rabble who were struggling at 78 for 5 at lunch. Some courageous and forceful batting by Patil and Kapil Dev brought 67 runs in 49 minutes before Patil, who had already been struck by a bouncer from Hogg, was knocked unconscious by a ball from Pascoe and taken to hospital. Kirmani batted with his usual determination, but Binny once more failed to establish his claim to be an all-rounder at the top level and India were out for a meagre 201. Kapil Dev lifted Indian hopes when he dismissed both openers in his first two overs, but before the close Chappell and Hughes had shown ominous contempt for the visitors' bowling by adding 58 in the last hour and a quarter.

The second day belonged entirely to Greg Chappell. He was reported to have been unwell overnight with an upset stomach, but it is impossible to conceive how any player who was one hundred per cent fit could have batted better. He was 41 not out at the close of the first day and by the time he was seventh out, with the score at 363, he had scored 204 from 196 balls that he received. He hit 27 fours and his innings was the highest ever recorded for Australia against India, beating by three Don Bradman's score at Adelaide in 1948. Chappell was given magnificent support by Walters who once more displayed that his riper years have only added to his lustre as a batsman. He and Chappell added 172 for the fifth wicket. Ghavri claimed three wickets in five overs with second new ball and both he and Kapil Dev, who took the first four wickets to fall, finished with five wickets. Batting for the second time 205 runs in arrears, India gave a most inept display. The Australian pace attack made the early inroads and the leg-spin of Jim Higgs destroyed the later batsmen, and India, like New Zealand before them, had been beaten inside three days.

First Test Match　　**Australia *v.* India**
2, 3 and 4 January 1981　　　　　　　　　　　　　　**at Brisbane**

India

	First Innings		*Second Innings*	
S. M. Gavaskar (capt)	c Marsh, b Lillee	0	c Marsh, b Hogg	10
C. P. S. Chauhan	c Border, b Pascoe	20	c Walters, b Pascoe	36
D. B. Vengsarkar	c Marsh, b Lillee	22	c Marsh, b Pascoe	34
G. R. Viswanath	b Hogg	26	st Marsh, b Higgs	24
Yashpal Sharma	c Marsh, b Pascoe	6	c Walters, b Lillee	4
S. M. Patil	retired hurt	65	(8) c Wood, b Lillee	4
Kapil Dev	c Marsh, b Pascoe	22	(6) c sub (Graf), b Higgs	19
*S. M. H. Kirmani	c Walters, b Lillee	27	(7) not out	43
R. Binny	c Marsh, b Pascoe	3	lbw, b Lillee	0
K. D. Ghavri	c Wood, b Lillee	7	c Hogg, b Higgs	21
D. R. Doshi	not out	0	c Lillee, b Higgs	0
Extras	lb 1, nb 2	3	b 2, lb 3, w 1	6
		201		201

	O	M	R	W	O	M	R	W
Lillee	20.2	3	86	4	18	2	79	3
Hogg	14	1	51	1	9	1	24	1
Pascoe	19	6	61	4	11	2	35	2
Higgs					18	8	45	4
Walters					6	3	12	—

Fall of Wickets
1–0, 2–36, 3–62, 4–70, 5–78, 6–145, 7–183, 8–186, 9–201.
1–21, 2–74, 3–92, 4–110, 5–120, 6–140, 7–144, 8–144, 9–201.

Australia

	First Innings	
G. M. Wood	c Kirmani, b Dev	9
J. Dyson	c Gavaskar, b Dev	0
G. S. Chappell (capt)	c Dev, b Ghavri	204
K. J. Hughes	c Kirmani, b Dev	24
A. R. Border	c Kirmani, b Dev	31
K. D. Walters	c Viswanath, b Ghavri	67
*R. W. Marsh	c Binny, b Ghavri	12
D. K. Lillee	c Doshi, b Ghavri	5
R. M. Hogg	not out	26
L. S. Pascoe	c Doshi, b Ghavri	7
J. D. Higgs	b Dev	2
Extras	b 4, lb 3, w 3, nb 9	19
		406

	O	M	R	W
Kapil Dev	36.1	7	97	5
Ghavri	30	7	107	5
Binny	15	1	70	—
Doshi	27	—	103	—
Chauhan	1	—	10	—

Fall of Wickets
1–3, 2–14, 3–95, 4–169, 5–341, 6–355, 7–363, 8–365, 9–376.

Australia won by an innings and 4 runs

6, 7 and 8 January 1981   **at Geelong**
Geelong and Districts 306 for 5 dec (P. Oxlade 95 retired hurt, G. Ward 51
  not out) and 85 (B. L. Cairns 4 for 17)
New Zealanders 319 for 7 dec (J. M. Parker 135, F. Meek 4 for 95) and 73
  for 1
New Zealanders won by 9 wickets

After a bad first day when sloppy fielding and a good innings by Peter Oxlade
took Geelong to a good score, New Zealand recovered to win easily. Oxlade's
fine innings was brought to an end when he was struck by Hadlee for the third
time and taken to hospital. Parker batted well and with consistent support
was able to see the tourists to a first innings lead. Then Cairns destroyed the
Geelong batting so that New Zealand won early on the third day.

Ninth One-Day International – Australia *v.* India

Put in to bat on a wicket which, affected by rain on the previous day, gave
the bowlers some assistance, India gave a miserable showing. Viswanath alone
showed any idea of how to bat in the conditions and the Indians succumbed
within twenty-six overs. Gavaskar, batting at number five, once more demonstrated a lack of form and confidence, swinging hopefully at the sixth ball he
received to be bowled by Greg Chappell who swung the ball mightily to take
five wickets. A rather dour opening stand by Dyson and Wood was followed
by Greg Chappell's demonstration of the art of batsmanship for the second
time in four days.

Ninth One-Day International: Australia *v.* India
8 January 1981   **at Sydney**

India
C. P. S. Chauhan	b Lillee	2
R. Binny	c Marsh, b G. Chappell	16
D. B. Vengsarkar	c Marsh, b Pascoe	3
G. R. Viswanath	c Marsh, b Hogg	23
S. M. Gavaskar (capt)	b G. Chappell	1
Yashpal Sharma	lbw, b G. Chappell	6
Kapil Dev	lbw, b Hogg	0
*S. M. H. Kirmani	run out	4
K. D. Ghavri	c Marsh, b G. Chappell	1
Yograj Singh	not out	0
D. R. Doshi	b G. Chappell	2
Extras	lb 3, w 1, nb 1	5

	O	M	R	W
Lillee	5	2	3	1
Hogg	7	2	14	2
G. Chappell	9.5	5	15	5
Pascoe	4	—	26	1

Fall of Wickets
1–2, 2–24, 3–26, 4–32, 5–50, 6–54, 7–55, 8–60, 9–61.

Australia

J. Dyson	not out	13
G. M. Wood	c Binny, b Dev	11
G. S. Chappell (capt)	not out	33
Extras	lb 3, w 1, nb 3	7
	(for 1 wkt)	64

K. J. Hughes, A. R. Border, K. D. Walters, T. M. Chappell, *R. W. Marsh,
D. K. Lillee, L. S. Pascoe and R. M. Hogg did not bat.

	O	M	R	W
Kapil Dev	9	5	15	1
Ghavri	4	—	14	—
Yograj Singh	4	1	9	—
Doshi	1	—	6	—
Binny	3	1	13	—

Fall of Wicket
1–18.

Australia won by 9 wickets

Tenth One-Day International – India *v.* New Zealand

Melbourne proved to be no kinder to India than Brisbane or Sydney had been and they suffered their third annihilation in a week. The match was reduced to 34 overs because of rain, a fact which caused adverse comment from Wing Commander Durani, the Indian manager. The Wing Commander's complaint was as inappropriate as some of the shots by which the Indian batsmen surrendered their wickets. Gavaskar reverted to opening, but with no more success and, at one time, India were 13 for 3. Edgar was in sparkling form for New Zealand and he and Wright reached the winning target with five overs still remaining.

Tenth One-Day International: India *v.* New Zealand
10 January 1981   **at Melbourne**

India

S. M. Gavaskar (capt)	lbw, b Chatfield	8
T. E. Srinivasan	b Coney	4
D. B. Vengsarkar	c Parker, b Coney	0
G. R. Viswanath	run out	33
S. M. Patil	c Coney, b Snedden	8

Yashpal Sharma	c Coney, b Cairns	5
Kapil Dev	run out	21
*S. M. H. Kirmani	run out	7
K. D. Ghavri	c Howarth, b Snedden	6
R. Binny	not out	5
D. R. Doshi	not out	5
Extras	lb 10	10
	(for 9 wkts)	112

	O	M	R	W
Hadlee	8	3	15	—
Chatfield	8	2	14	1
Coney	6	3	18	2
Cairns	7	—	39	1
Snedden	5	—	16	2

Fall of Wickets
1–13, 2–13, 3–13, 4–46, 5–60, 6–66, 7–82, 8–98, 9–100.

New Zealand

J. G. Wright	not out	39
B. A. Edgar	not out	65
Extras	lb 8, nb 1	9
	(for no wkt)	113

J. M. Parker, G. P. Howarth (capt), J. V. Coney, *W. K. Lees, M. G. Burgess, R. J. Hadlee, B. L. Cairns, E. J. Chatfield and M. C. Snedden did not bat.

	O	M	R	W
Kapil Dev	8	—	29	—
Ghavri	7	2	15	—
Binny	4	—	23	—
Patil	2	—	10	—
Doshi	8	—	27	—

New Zealand won by 10 wickets

Eleventh One-Day International – Australia *v.* India

A return to form by Gavaskar who shared an elegant second wicket partnership of 101 with Vengsarkar helped India to reach a score of 192 in their fifty overs, a huge total by their recent standards, but still insufficient to give them victory. The two left-handers, Wood and Border, gave Australia a sound start, but at 69, Border was bowled when slashing across the line at Patil. Chappell did not settle and was caught at mid-wicket off Doshi and then Hughes was run out for nought when going for a second run after Wood had square cut Doshi. Momentarily India had hopes of victory, but Wood and Walters dispelled these hopes with some firm strokes and good running between the wickets and saw Australia home with just under four overs remaining. The game was watched by 31,882 people, the largest crowd for any game in the season. Australia's win virtually assured them of a place in the World Series Final for, with three matches to play, they had ten points. Both New Zealand and India were on six points with three and two games to play respectively.

Eleventh One-Day International: Australia v. India
11 January 1981   **at Melbourne**

India

S. M. Gavaskar (capt)	b T. Chappell	80
R. Binny	c G. Chappell,	21
	b T. Chappell	
D. B. Vengsarkar	c Hughes, b Lillee	46
Kapil Dev	c T. Chappell,	4
	b G. Chappell	
S. M. Patil	c Hughes, b G. Chappell	3
Yashpal Sharma	not out	21
*S. M. H. Kirmani	not out	3
Extras	b 2, lb 11, nb 1	14
		—
	(for 5 wkts)	192

G. R. Viswanath, Yograj Singh, K. D. Ghavri and D. R. Doshi did not bat.

	O	M	R	W
Lillee	10	1	29	1
Pascoe	9	1	33	—
Graf	6	—	31	—
G. Chappell	10	4	23	2
T. Chappell	9	—	41	2
Border	6	—	21	—

Fall of Wickets
1–57, 2–158, 3–165, 4–165, 5–169.

Australia

A. R. Border	b Patil	39
G. M. Wood	not out	98
G. S. Chappell (capt)	c Viswanath, b Doshi	7
K. J. Hughes	run out	0
K. D. Walters	not out	43
Extras	b 1, lb 5	6
		—
	(for 3 wkts)	193

J. Dyson, T. M. Chappell, *R. W. Marsh, D. K. Lillee, L. S. Pascoe and S. F. Graf did not bat.

	O	M	R	W
Binny	9.2	1	42	—
Ghavri	9	1	37	—
Kapil Dev	9	1	27	—
Patil	10	—	43	1
Doshi	10	—	38	1

Fall of Wickets
1–69, 2–96, 3–97.

Australia won by 7 wickets

12 and 13 January 1981   **at Canberra**
Indians 302 for 6 dec (Yashpal Sharma 74, Kapil Dev 68, Kirti Azad 56)
Australian Capital Territory 304 for 6 (T. Khan 69, N. Bulger 57, P. Rogers 53,
    S. Yadav 4 for 94)
Match drawn

Though officially recorded as a draw, the match was greeted by the local crowd
as a triumphant victory for the Capital Territory. The hero was the Aboriginal
all-rounder Bulger who, after bowling well, hit 57 in 76 minutes to bring his
side victory. The Indians batted well, but after Kapil Dev was forced to withdraw from the attack, the Indian bowling came in for some punishment.

Twelfth One-Day International – Australia *v.* New Zealand

With Australia needing only one point to ensure that they would reach the
Benson and Hedges World Series Final and New Zealand needing to win to
keep their hopes alive, the scene was set for a classic one-day encounter at
Sydney, and for once there was to be no anti-climax as the two teams produced
a memorable match in which fortunes fluctuated almost over by over. New
Zealand elected to bat and suffered an early set-back when Edgar went without
scoring. Howarth seemed in good form, but left with the score at 30. Runs and
wickets came with a pattern of regularity, but it was Wright who provided the
foundation to the New Zealand innings, scoring a sensible 78 out of 176 in
43 overs. Three overs later New Zealand were 191 for 8 and struggling. It was
then that Ian Smith, who had come into the side as a replacement for Lees
injured by a lift at the hotel, played a most resourceful innings in scoring 23
off 19 balls and, with Snedden, raised the total to 220. Australia's task had
now become more difficult than had seemed likely with only four overs of
the New Zealand innings remaining and their chances were not improved when
Chatfield bowled Border. Wood and Greg Chappell put on 56 in 15 overs to
give Australia the impetus needed to force victory, but Wood went at 74 and
Chappell fell to a poor shot at 90 to tilt the game back in New Zealand's favour.
Hughes and Walters played some flourishing shots and all seemed well with
the Australians again until Hughes and Trevor Chappell fell within one run
of each other. Walters and Marsh silenced any New Zealand rejoicing with
a blistering attack on the bowling. In 15 overs 78 runs were added. Marsh
hit 49 off 48 balls and Australia had victory within her grasp. Marsh mishooked
Hadlee and was caught behind, but Australia needed only 20 off 21 balls.
Eighteen were needed off three overs, 13 from the last two. When Snedden
began the last over 8 runs were needed for an Australian victory. Graf was
facing the bowling and though he failed to connect with the first delivery, five
runs were scrambled from the next four balls. Walters faced the last ball with
three needed to win. He pulled the ball viciously, but Hadlee sprawled full
length to make the stop and, while still on the ground, flicked the ball to the
bowler's end to run out Graf and give New Zealand victory by one run. The
visitors owed much to the cool and astute captaincy of Geoff Howarth and
to a fine team spirit.

Twelfth One-Day International: Australia *v.* New Zealand
13 January 1981   at Sydney

New Zealand

J. G. Wright	c T. Chappell,	78
	b G. Chappell	
B. A. Edgar	b Hogg	0
G. P. Howarth (capt)	lbw, b Pascoe	20
J. M. Parker	c Pascoe, b T. Chappell	23
M. G. Burgess	c Walters, b Graf	14
J. V. Coney	c Marsh, b Pascoe	18
R. J. Hadlee	c Hogg, b Graf	9
B. L. Cairns	b Pascoe	7
*I. D. S. Smith	not out	23
M. C. Snedden	not out	8
Extras	lb 16, w 1, nb 3	20

	(for 8 wkts)	220

E. J. Chatfield did not bat.

	O	M	R	W
Lillee	10	2	27	—
Hogg	8	—	40	1
Pascoe	10	—	37	3
G. Chappell	9	2	35	1
Graf	10	—	40	2
T. Chappell	3	—	21	1

Fall of Wickets
1–2, 2–30, 3–75, 4–105, 5–134, 6–176, 7–181, 8–191.

Australia

A. R. Border	b Chatfield	8
G. M. Wood	c Smith, b Coney	37
G. S. Chappell (capt)	c Coney, b Cairns	30
K. J. Hughes	c Smith, b Snedden	21
K. D. Walters	not out	50
T. M. Chappell	run out	0
*R. W. Marsh	c Smith, b Hadlee	49
S. F. Graf	run out	7
Extras	b 3, lb 12, w 1, nb 1	17

	(for 7 wkts)	219

D. K. Lillee, R. M. Hogg and L. S. Pascoe did not bat.

	O	M	R	W
Hadlee	10	1	46	1
Chatfield	10	2	26	1
Coney	10	—	41	1
Cairns	10	1	48	1
Snedden	10	—	41	1

Fall of Wickets
1–18, 2–74, 3–90, 4–122, 5–123, 6–201, 7–219.

New Zealand won by 1 run

Thirteenth One-Day International – Australia *v.* India

The Indians died bravely against Australia at Sydney, failing by twenty-seven runs to reach the home side's total of 242 for 8, the highest in the series. The Australian score was most creditable in view of the fact that Greg Chappell was dismissed for 2. Allan Border played a faultless innings for Australia which provided them with a sound basis in both runs and tempo and the middle order all made some contribution. The Indians faced a stiff task and it was made harder when Gavaskar was given out lbw with only two on the board. It seemed a harsh decision. As with the Australian innings consistency was the main quality of the Indians though 58 in 11 overs from Binny and Vengsarkar was a magnificent early flourish, mainly at the expense of Pascoe, which could not quite be maintained. The Australian victory meant that they had qualified for the final and the Indian defeat meant that New Zealand now seemed to be the side that Australia would meet in the final.

Thirteenth One-Day International: Australia *v.* India
15 January 1971   **at Sydney**

Australia

G. M. Wood	c Binny, b Patil	26
A. R. Border	c Azad, b Doshi	85
G. S. Chappell (capt)	c Sharma, b Patil	2
K. J. Hughes	c Dev, b Binny	39
K. D. Walters	b Ghavri	38
T. M. Chappell	c Vengsarkar, b Dev	14
*R. W. Marsh	c Reddy, b Ghavri	12
S. F. Graf	c Azad, b Dev	2
D. K. Lillee	not out	4
R. M. Hogg	not out	1
Extras	b 1, lb 16, nb 2	19

	(for 8 wkts)	242

L. S. Pascoe did not bat.

	O	M	R	W
Kapil Dev	10	1	46	2
Ghavri	10	—	39	2
Binny	10	—	45	1
Patil	10	2	34	2
Doshi	10	—	59	1

Fall of Wickets
1–48, 2–55, 3–135, 4–181, 5–216, 6–230, 7–233, 8–240.

India

S. M. Gavaskar (capt)	lbw, b Lillee	1
R. Binny	lbw, b Graf	34
D. B. Vengsarkar	c Marsh, b Hogg	52
G. R. Viswanath	c and b G. Chappell	7
Yashpal Sharma	c and b G. Chappell	25

S. M. Patil	b Lillee	27
Kapil Dev	c Marsh, b Lillee	20
Kirti Azad	b Lillee	19
K. D. Ghavri	not out	11
*B. Reddy	not out	8
Extras	lb 10, nb 1	11
	(for 8 wkts)	215

D. R. Doshi did not bat.

	O	M	R	W
Lillee	10	1	32	4
Hogg	10	1	34	1
Pascoe	10	—	64	—
Graf	10	2	36	1
G. Chappell	10	—	38	2

Fall of Wickets
1–2, 2–59, 3–78, 4–112, 5–135, 6–161, 7–196, 8–197.

Australia won by 27 runs

15 and 16 January 1981   **at Bundaberg**
New Zealanders 281 for 4 dec (B. A. Edgar 96, P. E. McEwan 81) and 103
   for 3 dec (B. McKechnie 61 not out)
Queensland Country XI 82 and 207
New Zealanders won by 95 runs

After the incident at Geelong when Peter Oxlade was knocked out by a ball
from Hadlee, Geoff Howarth urged the local batsmen at Bundaberg to wear
protective helmets in view of the wicket and the pace of bowlers like Hadlee.
The bitter irony was that it was McEwan, opening the New Zealanders second
innings, who was injured when his nose was broken by a rising ball from
Glover. McEwan had recaptured form in the match in which Edgar and
McKechnie, promoted to open in the second innings, had also batted well.
The Country Eleven twice failed against a consistently accurate attack.

Fourteenth One-Day International – India *v.* New Zealand

Needing not only to beat New Zealand, but also to score a very fast rate,
India elected to field when they won the toss. New Zealand gave a thoroughly
workmanlike batting display against some rather moderate bowling and
reached 242 for 9. This meant that India had to make 243 in 15 overs if they
were to overtake New Zealand on the faster over-all run rate, an impossible
task. With Vengsarkar again batting well, they did make a fine show of trying
to win the game, however, though they were not helped by some indecisive
running between the wickets. In the field New Zealand were certainly the
superior side and deserved to reach the final.

Fourteenth One-Day International: India *v.* New Zealand
18 January 1981   **at Brisbane**

New Zealand

J. G. Wright	b Ghavri	14
B. A. Edgar	b Doshi	34
G. P. Howarth (capt)	c Patil, b Doshi	45
J. M. Parker	c Reddy, b Dev	6
M. G. Burgess	c Viswanath, b Azad	26
J. V. Coney	run out	49
*I. D. S. Smith	c sub, b Dev	12
R. J. Hadlee	b Ghavri	32
B. L. Cairns	b Dev	0
M. C. Snedden	not out	6
E. J. Chatfield	not out	0
Extras	b 1, lb 13, w 1, nb 3	18
	(for 9 wkts)	242

	O	M	R	W
Kapil Dev	10	3	37	3
Ghavri	10	—	61	2
Binny	4	—	25	—
Patil	10	—	38	—
Doshi	10	—	25	2
Kirti Azad	3	1	26	1
Yashpal Sharma	3	—	12	—

Fall of Wickets
1–28, 2–95, 3–108, 4–108, 5–166, 6–199, 7–207, 8–207, 9–241.

India

R. Binny	c Cairns, b Coney	35
S. M. Gavaskar (capt)	run out	9
D. B. Vengsarkar	run out	66
G. R. Viswanath	b Coney	9
Kapil Dev	b Coney	0
S. M. Patil	run out	48
Yashpal Sharma	c Smith, b Snedden	13
Kirti Azad	c Parker, b Snedden	19
K. D. Ghavri	b Snedden	2
*B. Reddy	not out	3
D. R. Doshi	lbw, b Hadlee	0
Extras	b 4, lb 11, nb 1	16
		220

	O	M	R	W
Hadlee	9.2	1	15	1
Chatfield	10	1	42	—
Coney	10	1	28	3
Cairns	10	—	54	—
Snedden	8	—	57	3
Burgess	1	—	8	—

Fall of Wickets
1–32, 2–73, 3–86, 4–86, 5–178, 6–179, 7–197, 8–213, 9–220.

New Zealand won by 22 runs

20 January 1981   **at Portland**
Indians 232 for 7 (S. M. Patil 62, T. E. Srinivasan 61, S. M. Gavaskar 58)
Victorian Country XI 168 (D. R. Doshi 4 for 41)

Indians won by 64 runs

The Indians showed an agreeable return to batting form which was an
encouragement with the Second Test close at hand. Yograj Singh made the
early inroads into the local side's batting before Doshi, who had lost form
after a fine start to the tour, and Yadav completed the job.

Fifteenth One-Day International – Australia v. New Zealand

The last of the preliminary matches, the result of which would have no bearing
on the competition for the Benson and Hedges World Series Trophy, was
rained off just as the night session was beginning. Greg Chappell played another
majestic innings for Australia, his 74 coming off 78 balls. He shared a second
wicket partnership of 88 in 17 overs with Allan Border. Max Walker returned
to the Australian side in place of Pascoe, but had little opportunity to show
his bowling talents.

Benson and Hedges World Series – Preliminary Competition

Final Table	P	W	L	D	Pts
Australia	10	6	3	1	13
New Zealand	10	5	4	1	9
India	10	3	7	—	6

Australia and New Zealand qualified for final.

Fifteenth One-Day International: Australia v. New Zealand
21 January 1981   **at Sydney**

Australia

A. R. Border	c Hadlee, b McKechnie	40
G. M. Wood	c Smith, b Chatfield	5
G. S. Chappell (capt)	c Burgess, b McEwan	74
K. J. Hughes	c Coney, b McEwan	14
K. D. Walters	run out	16
T. M. Chappell	lbw, b Cairns	14
*R. W. Marsh	c Hadlee, b McKechnie	0
S. F. Graf	lbw, b Hadlee	2
D. K. Lillee	c Coney, b Cairns	0
R. M. Hogg	run out	1

M. H. N. Walker	not out	0
Extras	lb 12, w 2	14
		180

	O	M	R	W
Hadlee	8	4	13	1
Chatfield	8.1	2	15	1
Coney	4	—	19	—
Cairns	8	2	37	2
McKechnie	10	—	53	2
McEwan	5	—	29	2

Fall of Wickets
1–10, 2–98, 3–125, 4–149, 5–173, 6–175, 7–179, 8–179, 9–179.

New Zealand

B. A. Edgar	not out	2
J. G. Wright	c Marsh, b G. Chappell	8
G. P. Howarth (capt)	not out	0
Extras	b 8, lb 4, nb 1	13
	(for 1 wkt)	23

M. G. Burgess, P. E. McEwan, J. V. Coney, *I. D. S. Smith, B. McKechnie, R. J. Hadlee, B. L. Cairns and E. J. Chatfield did not bat.

	O	M	R	W
Lillee	3	1	6	—
Walker	4	3	3	—
G. Chappell	1	—	1	1

Fall of Wicket
1–22.

Match abandoned as a draw

Second Test Match – Australia *v.* India

For remote reasons probably more akin to defence than attack Gavaskar asked Australia to bat when he won the toss. It could have been an inspired decision if a chance that Wood offered in Kapil Dev's first over had been taken, but Kirmani dived in front of slip and the edge went to ground. From that point Wood and Dyson prospered in their best opening stand for Australia. Wood hit one six off Ghavri, who laboured somewhat, and ten fours in his return to form century, and though, by his high standards, Greg Chappell failed, Kim Hughes sparkled brighter than at any time since the Centenary Test at Lord's. Eighty-five not out at the end of the first day, he dominated the second with a series of fierce and elegant shots that brought him past the records of Bradman and Greg Chappell to reach the highest score for an Australian in a Test against India. India faced a formidable total, but Gavaskar and Chauhan gave them a sound start. Gavaskar was out shortly before the close, but Yadav, who, considering the lack of encouragement he had been given, bowled well in the Australian innings, batted doggedly as night-watchman. India looked

in trouble when Yadav, Viswanath and Vengsarkar were dismissed in quick
succession to reduce the visitors to 130 for 4, but Patil, first with the under-
praised and courageous Chauhan, and then with Yashpal Sharma, batted them
to safety. Though the Indians added only another 48 runs on the fourth
morning, Sandeep Patil took his score to 174 before falling to Hogg. It was
a splendidly aggressive innings and the all-rounder reached the highest score
by an Indian in a Test against Australia. He won high praise from Greg
Chappell on the power of his hitting. Doshi opened the bowling with Kapil
Dev and Yadav, too, was quickly brought on when the Australians began the
second innings with a lead of 109. Both spinners posed problems, but not as
great as those that confronted India when Chappell declared, belatedly, and
left them four and a half hours to survive. It was Pascoe, not fully fit, who
caused the Indian breakdown and within an hour they were 57 for 4. Vengsarkar
batted for over two hours before falling to Border's left-arm spin and Sharma
batted for ten minutes short of three hours, an innings which did much to
save India. Kirmani was victim of Chappell's leg-spin, and, when the eighth
wicket fell there were still more than ten overs to be bowled, but Ghavri and
Yadav held out with grim determination to earn India a draw.

Second Test Match   Australia *v.* India
23, 24, 25, 26 and 27 January 1981   at Adelaide

Australia

	First Innings		*Second Innings*	
J. Dyson	c Gavaskar, b Dev	30	lbw, b Ghavri	28
G. M. Wood	c Doshi, b Yadav	125	c Patil, b Doshi	3
G. S. Chappell (capt)	c Chauhan, b Doshi	36	st Kirmani, b Doshi	52
K. J. Hughes	c Sharma, b Yadav	213	b Dev	53
A. R. Border	c Gavaskar, b Dev	57	b Doshi	7
K. D. Walters	c Viswanath, b Yadav	20	not out	33
*R. W. Marsh	run out	0	c Kirmani, b Yadav	23
B. Yardley	c Viswanath, b Doshi	12	c Vengsarkar, b Yadav	2
D. K. Lillee	c Dev, b Doshi	2	not out	10
R. M. Hogg	c and b Yadav	11		
L. S. Pascoe	not out	1		
Extras	lb 13, w 1, nb 7	21	b 2, lb 5, nb 3	10
		528	(for 7 wkts dec)	221

	O	M	R	W		O	M	R	W
Kapil Dev	32	5	112	2		17	3	55	1
Ghavri	27	3	106	—		11	2	37	1
Doshi	48	6	146	3		33	11	49	3
Yadav	42.4	6	143	4		29	6	70	2

Fall of Wickets
1–84, 2–152, 3–234, 4–363, 5–393, 6–399, 7–435, 8–461, 9–505.
1–5, 2–74, 3–118, 4–138, 5–165, 6–204, 7–208.

India

	First Innings		*Second Innings*	
S. M. Gavaskar (capt)	b Pascoe	23	c Chappell, b Pascoe	5
C. P. S. Chauhan	c Marsh, b Lillee	97	c Marsh, b Pascoe	11
S. Yadav	c Chappell, b Yardley	16	(10) not out	0
G. R. Viswanath	lbw, b Hogg	3	b Pascoe	16
D. B. Vengsarkar	lbw, b Lillee	2	(3) c Chappell, b Border	37
S. M. Patil	lbw, b Hogg	174	(5) lbw, b Lillee	9
Yashpal Sharma	c Marsh, b Lillee	47	(6) lbw, b Yardley	13
Kapil Dev	c Border, b Lillee	2	(7) c Marsh, b Lillee	7
*S. M. H. Kirmani	b Pascoe	6	(8) c Marsh, b Chappell	14
K. D. Ghavri	c Wood, b Yardley	3	(9) not out	7
D. R. Doshi	not out	6		
Extras	b 11, lb 10, w 2, nb 17	40	b 7, lb 1, nb 8	16
		419	(for 8 wkts)	135

	O	M	R	W		O	M	R	W
Lillee	34	10	80	4		19	7	38	2
Hogg	28	6	100	2		3	—	11	—
Pascoe	17	2	62	2		11	2	32	3
Yardley	44.4	16	90	2		24	13	25	1
Chappell	6	2	14	—		9	6	4	1
Walters	3	—	21	—					
Border	4	1	11	—		9	5	9	1
Hughes	1	—	1	—					

Fall of Wickets
1–77, 2–112, 3–115, 4–130, 5–238, 6–385, 7–393, 8–399, 9–409.
1–13, 2–16, 3–44, 4–57, 5–90, 6–103, 7–126, 8–128.

Match drawn

24, 25 and 26 January 1981   **at Sydney**
New Zealanders 202 (B. L. Cairns 68, G. R. Beard 5 for 58) and 166
   (P. E. McEwan 87, G. R. Beard 5 for 37)
New South Wales 228 for 3 dec (R. B. McCosker 109, T. M. Chappell 100)
   and 130 for 8

Match drawn

The New Zealanders had an unhappy time in their three-day game against
New South Wales. Their batting disintegrated against the medium pace of
Graeme Beard and only a characteristically hurricane innings by Lance Cairns
saved them from complete humiliation. Then the New South Wales opening
pair flayed the weakened New Zealand attack before Beard again destroyed
their batting. It was only a brave innings by McEwan that gave New South
Wales any sort of target, but still victory seemd a formality for the home side.
That New South Wales did not win was due entirely to their inability to
overcome the New Zealanders' defensive tactics when they adopted a limited
over approach.

Benson and Hedges World Series – First Final

The Australian team showed changes from that which, in the main part, had taken them to the final of the competition. Kent was brought in to open the innings with Wood, and Walker held his place at the expense of Trevor Chappell. Beard, whose performance against the New Zealanders in the three-day game at Sydney had earned him a recall to the Australian squad, was kept in reserve. The New Zealanders were not impressed by the Australian changes. Their innings began steadily and then flourished excitingly. They owed much to Wright who provided both solidity and flair and who shared a commanding second wicket partnership of 103 with Geoff Howarth. The innings stumbled a little after this, but Richard Hadlee and Lance Cairns produced a violent burst at the close of the innings which ensured New Zealand their highest total in the competition. With rain threatening, Australia needed to score quickly and twenty-two came in the first five overs, but then Hadlee destroyed the batting and won the match when he dismissed Wood, Kent and Hughes. Chatfield sent back Marsh and Australia were 28 for 4. There was some resurgence, mainly from Border and Walters, but Hadlee returned to end the innings and complete a fine victory for New Zealand. Hadlee's five wickets at meagre cost, his three wicket spell in nine balls, and his aggressive innings made him the unchallenged Man of the Match.

Benson and Hedges World Series – First Final
Australia v. New Zealand
29 January 1981   **at Sydney**

New Zealand

J. G. Wright	b Chappell	81
B. A. Edgar	c Walker, b Lillee	21
G. P. Howarth (capt)	c Border, b Walker	47
J. V. Coney	c and b Pascoe	0
M. G. Burgess	lbw, b Lillee	15
R. J. Hadlee	not out	23
B. L. Cairns	c Walker, b Pascoe	18
B. McKechnie	not out	1
Extras	b 18, w 7, nb 2	27
	(for 6 wkts)	233

*I. D. S. Smith, M. C. Snedden and E. J. Chatfield did not bat.

	O	M	R	W
Hogg	10	1	37	—
Walker	10	1	31	1
Lillee	10	—	47	2
Pascoe	10	—	48	2
Chappell	10	—	43	1

Fall of Wickets
1–43, 2–148, 3–152, 4–172, 5–198, 6–231.

Australia

G. M. Wood	c Burgess, b Hadlee	13
M. F. Kent	c Howarth, b Hadlee	12
*R. W. Marsh	c Coney, b Chatfield	0
G. S. Chappell (capt)	c Wright, b Chatfield	31
K. J. Hughes	lbw, b Hadlee	0
A. R. Border	c Coney, b McKechnie	55
K. D. Walters	b McKechnie	20
D. K. Lillee	c Cairns, b McKechnie	7
M. H. N. Walker	c Smith, b Hadlee	4
R. M. Hogg	c Smith, b Hadlee	1
L. S. Pascoe	not out	3
Extras	b 2, lb 6, w 1	9
		155

	O	M	R	W
Chatfield	10	3	38	2
Hadlee	8.3	4	26	5
McKechnie	9	1	23	3
Snedden	6	1	25	—
Cairns	6	—	34	—

Fall of Wickets
1–28, 2–28, 3–28, 4–28, 5–93, 6–135, 7–145, 8–147, 9–148.

New Zealand won by 78 runs

30 and 31 January, 1 and 2 February 1981   **at Geelong**
Victoria 267 for 7 dec (J. K. Moss 125) and 231 (G. N. Yallop 64)
Indians 398 for 9 dec (Yashpal Sharma 201 not out, C. P. S. Chauhan 68)
    and 102 for 0 (T. E. Srinivasan 69 not out)
Indians won by 10 wickets

The morale of the Indian side was boosted considerably by their fine win over Victoria. The state had batted well on the opening day with Jeff Moss giving yet another indication that he was perhaps cruelly unlucky to have won only one Test cap. Srinivasan was dismissed before the close, but the rest of the game belonged to India. Yashpal Sharma hit the first double century of his career, an innings which lasted 465 minutes and included three sixes and eleven fours. He shared a solid stand with Chauhan which produced 119 for the third wicket and a sparkling stand of 63 in 70 minutes with Gavaskar for the fourth wicket. He was helped to his double century by Doshi who stayed while 42 runs were added for the last wicket. Though Kapil Dev and Doshi were unable to bowl, India dismissed Victoria for 231 with some good efforts from Yograj Singh, Binny and Kirti Azad, and, in particular, from the less regular bowlers, Chauhan and Sharma. Srinivasan and Gavaskar had little problem in hitting off the runs though Robinson tried nine bowlers, including himself.

Benson and Hedges World Series – Second Final

Following their success in the first final, the New Zealanders gave a disappointing display in the second match. Beard and Trevor Chappell came into the Australian side instead of Hogg and Kent, and the New Zealanders replaced Snedden by McEwan. This last change seemed a little hard on Snedden who, though he had not taken a wicket in the first final, had been a great success in the one-day matches. Greg Chappell won the toss and put the visitors in. They scored only 126 in 47 overs. The Australian bowling was accurate, but once more the Melbourne wicket was largely responsible for the tedium. The Australians won with more than ten overs to spare and were much indebted to a grafting innings by Greg Chappell. It was among the least memorable of matches.

Benson and Hedges World Series – Second Final
Australia v. New Zealand
31 January 1981   at Melbourne

New Zealand

J. G. Wright	c Marsh, b Lillee	11
B. A. Edgar	c Border, b T. Chappell	28
G. P. Howarth (capt)	b Walker	7
J. V. Coney	lbw, b Lillee	4
M. G. Burgess	run out	13
P. E. McEwan	run out	12
B. McKechnie	lbw, b T. Chappell	0
*I. D. S. Smith	b G. Chappell	13
R. J. Hadlee	c G. Chappell, b Beard	16
B. L. Cairns	c T. Chappell, b Beard	14
E. J. Chatfield	not out	2
Extras	lb 4, w 1, nb 1	6
		126

	O	M	R	W
Lillee	8	—	25	2
Walker	10	—	25	1
Beard	8.4	3	20	2
G. Chappell	10	2	22	1
T. Chappell	10	1	28	2

Fall of Wickets
1–14, 2–21, 3–30, 4–62, 5–70, 6–71, 7–92, 8–95, 9–113.

Australia

G. M. Wood	c Smith, b Chatfield	32
A. R. Border	c Burgess, b Howarth	19
G. S. Chappell (capt)	not out	58
K. J. Hughes	st Smith, b Cairns	12
K. D. Walters	not out	4
Extras	b 2, lb 2, w 1	5
	(for 3 wkts)	130

G. R. Beard, T. M. Chappell, *R. W. Marsh, L. S. Pascoe, D. K. Lillee and M. H. N. Walker did not bat.

	O	M	R	W
Hadlee	10	2	29	—
Chatfield	6	1	21	1
McEwan	4	—	18	—
Howarth	4	—	13	1
Cairns	10	1	23	1
McKechnie	5.3	1	21	—

Fall of Wickets
1–30, 2–85, 3–118.

Australia won by 7 wickets

Benson and Hedges World Series – Third Final

A crowd of just under 53,000 gathered to see the third match in the final series of the Benson and Hedges competition. The Melbourne wicket, so excessively watered on the Saturday, had dried out to provide a surface on which more entertaining stroke play had become possible. Snedden for Chatfield, Parker for Coney, Kent for Pascoe were the changes. Australia batted first and New Zealand had an early success when Hadlee had Border taken by Parker. Greg Chappell and Wood now engaged in a stand of 145 which was rich in strokes. The quality of Chappell's innings was diminished, however, by an incident that occurred when he had scored 58. He skied a ball from Cairns to mid-wicket where young Snedden ran thirty yards and dived to hold a brilliant catch. The fieldsman immediately signalled that he had made the catch, but Chappell stood his ground, refusing to accept the catcher's claim. The New Zealanders appealed to the umpires who held a conference after which Chappell was given not out. When Howarth enquired as to the reason he was told that the umpires had been looking at the popping creases, neither had watched the ball and so neither had seen the catch. Chappell went on to make 90 and the Australians reached 235 in their fifty overs, but an ethic of cricket had been violated and all the New Zealanders could do was ponder on the television action replay which showed clearly that Snedden had taken a good and clean catch. Wright and Edgar gave New Zealand a splendid start with 85 in 24 overs, but there was no one robust enough in the middle order to sustain the necessary tempo. Edgar, who had taken a fine catch to get rid of Greg Chappell, stayed to give New Zealand hope and became the first New Zealander to hit a hundred in the competition. With three overs remaining New Zealand needed 32 runs to win and the odds were heavily against them. Eleven runs came from Trevor Chappell's over and in the penultimate over, bowled by Lillee, six were scored and Parker was dismissed. This left Trevor Chappell to bowl the last over with 15 needed. Hadlee drove the first ball for four and was lbw to the second. Smith swung twos off successive deliveries and then was bowled. McKechnie came in to face one ball which he needed to hit for six to give New Zealand a tie. Greg Chappell consulted with his brother and the last ball of the innings was bowled underarm and along the ground. McKechnie threw his bat down in disgust as he left the field and he was not the only one who felt that emotion. Later there were angry words from prime-ministers, eminent cricketers and chairmen of boards of control, and the tactic which the Chappells had adopted was made illegal. Yet their action seemed to many to be simply the logical conclusion to the moves of the past few years which have made monetary considerations paramount to many of those who play and rule the game at the top level. Perhaps the beast which some have created has now got out of control.

Benson and Hedges World Series – Third Final
Australia v. New Zealand
1 February 1981   **at Melbourne**

Australia

A. R. Border	c Parker, b Hadlee	5
G. M. Wood	b McEwan	72
G. S. Chappell (capt)	c Edgar, b Snedden	90
M. F. Kent	c Edgar, b Snedden	33
*R. W. Marsh	not out	18
K. D. Walters	not out	6
Extras	b 8, lb 3	11
	(for 4 wkts)	235

K. J. Hughes, G. R. Beard, T. M. Chappell, D. K. Lillee and M. H. N. Walker did not bat.

	O	M	R	W
Hadlee	10	—	41	1
Snedden	10	—	52	2
Cairns	10	—	34	—
McKechnie	10	—	54	—
McEwan	7	1	31	1
Howarth	3	—	12	—

Fall of Wickets
1–8, 2–153, 3–199, 4–215.

New Zealand

J. G. Wright	c Kent, b G. Chappell	42
B. A. Edgar	not out	102
G. P. Howarth (capt)	c Marsh, b G. Chappell	18
B. L. Cairns	b Beard	12
M. G. Burgess	c T. Chappell, b G. Chappell	2
P. E. McEwan	c Wood, b Beard	11
J. M. Parker	c T. Chappell, b Lillee	24
R. J. Hadlee	lbw, b T. Chappell	4
*I. D. S. Smith	b T. Chappell	4
B. McKechnie	not out	0
Extras	lb 10	10
	(for 8 wkts)	229

M. C. Snedden did not bat.

	O	M	R	W
Lillee	10	1	34	1
Walker	10	—	35	—
Beard	10	—	50	2
G. Chappell	10	—	43	3
T. Chappell	10	—	57	2

Fall of Wickets
1–85, 2–117, 3–136, 4–139, 5–172, 6–221, 7–225, 8–229.

Australia won by 6 runs

Benson and Hedges World Series – Fourth Final

With Coney still injured and Cairns far from fit, New Zealand had to rely upon a good performance by their batsmen to give them any chance of beating Australia in the fourth match in the final series. Howarth won the toss and with Sydney giving more encouragement to the batsmen than Melbourne, he had no hesitation in batting first. Once more Wright and Edgar gave New Zealand a fine start and Howarth, too, batted well for his 46, but the final total fell short of expectations. Wood and Border began the Australian chase with a stand of 37. Border was bowled by Snedden and Greg Chappell came in to a cacophony of boos from the crowd of 29,117. He replied by playing with the elegant assurance which makes him the most noble of batsmen. He scored 87 and shared a stand of 99 in 18 overs with Kim Hughes. Still Australia were a little behind the asking rate and it was Marsh who helped to lift the scoring to the required tempo. The anger that the crowd had first shown to Chappell melted to pleasure and applause as he reached his fifty. Their anger was now centred on Hadlee who had roughly handled a young spectator who had fielded a ball before it reached the boundary. Australia won with more than two overs left, but New Zealand had put up a brave effort as they had had to attack without Cairns who strained a groin muscle when batting. The nineteenth match had seen Australia win the cup and the money. Unfortunately, cricket had lost a few friends along the way.

Benson and Hedges World Series – Fourth Final
Australia v. New Zealand
3 February 1981   at Sydney

New Zealand

J. G. Wright	c Border, b T. Chappell	57
B. A. Edgar	run out	38
G. P. Howarth (capt)	c Kent, b Hogg	46
M. G. Burgess	b G. Chappell	20
R. J. Hadlee	c Border, b Lillee	15
J. M. Parker	c Marsh, b Lillee	12
P. E. McEwan	c Hogg, b Lillee	4
B. L. Cairns	b Pascoe	7
*I. D. S. Smith	not out	2

Extras   lb 9, nb 5   14
                                                          ——
                          (for 8 wkts)   215
M. C. Snedden and E. J. Chatfield did not bat.

	O	M	R	W
Lillee	10	2	27	3
Hogg	10	—	46	1
Pascoe	10	—	51	1
G. Chappell	10	1	36	1
T. Chappell	10	—	41	1

Fall of Wickets
1–90, 2–119, 3–171, 4–177, 5–200, 6–201, 7–210, 8–215.

Australia

G. M. Wood	run out	34
A. R. Border	b Snedden	19
G. S. Chappell (capt)	b Snedden	87
K. J. Hughes	b Snedden	47
*R. W. Marsh	not out	18
M. F. Kent	not out	4
Extras	lb 8, w 1	9
		——
	(for 4 wkts)	218

K. D. Walters, T. M. Chappell, D. K. Lillee, R. M. Hogg and L. S. Pascoe did not bat.

	O	M	R	W
Chatfield	10	1	30	—
Hadlee	8.4	1	43	—
Snedden	9	—	27	3
McEwan	10	1	58	—
Burgess	10	—	51	—

Fall of Wickets
1–37, 2–89, 3–188, 4–219.

Australia won by 6 wickets
Australia won the Final by 3 matches to 1

3 and 4 February 1981   **at Ballarat**
Indians 363 for 5 dec (Kirti Azad 103 not out, S. M. Patil 63, Kapil Dev 60,
    T. E. Srinivasan 59)
Victorian Country XI 193 for 4
Match abandoned

The Indians gained comfort from their batting in this rain-restricted match.
Kirti Azad reached a hundred in under three hours. He reached the target
with a six.

Third Test Match – Australia v. India

On a pitch in which there was enough moisture to give some uncharacteristic
life, both sides included their two spinners, but, of the bowlers, it was Dennis

Lillee who was the centre of attention as he began the match needing only five wickets to equal Richie Benaud's record of 248 Test wickets for Australia. Chappell asked India to bat and they lost Chauhan before a run was scored. Gavaskar batted with grim determination, but he fell to a fine ball from Pascoe which lifted and left him late and Vengsarkar fell to an equally good delivery from Lillee. Viswanath had had a miserable tour, but he now played with great certainty to reach a majestically impressive century. Patil, Kirmani and Yadav all batted bravely, but the Australian bowling was on top form and, but for Viswanath's innings of quality, India would have been in a sorry state. As it was their 237 faded insignificantly on the second day when Australia passed the score with only four wickets down. They had begun the day at 12 for 0 and though they lost both openers early on – Dyson once more failing to reproduce his state form – and Kim Hughes at 81, they battled back to take the initiative. Inevitably, it was Greg Chappell who led the counter attack though, on the Melbourne wicket, he could not indulge in his usual repertoire of majestic shots. He drove early at Ghavri and gave a simple return catch and his 76 had occupied three and three-quarter hours. Border and Walters consolidated the position and Australia ended the day 35 ahead with six wickets in hand. Border reached his century the next day and Walters with whom he added 131 for the fifth wicket again batted with confidence, soundness and aggression. Marsh swotted merrily and Australia led by 182 on the first innings. India replied courageously and Gavaskar and Chauhan were undefeated with 108 before the close. The stand was increased to 165 the following morning when Gavaskar was given out lbw to Lillee by umpire Rex Whitehead. Gavaskar stood his ground for some seconds, protesting that he had hit the ball, and when he left the wicket he beckoned Chauhan to come with him, seemingly withdrawing India from the match as a protest against the umpiring. The Indian team manager Shahid Durani came on to the pitch and ordered Chauhan back to the wicket as Vengsarkar came out. The game continued. Chauhan's concentration had obviously been disturbed and this plucky batsman was denied his first Test century when, having added eight more runs to the score, he went to square cut Lillee and mishit the ball to cover. This was Lillee's 249th Test wicket, a new Australian record. India now stumbled as the ball kept low. There were some brave flourishes, particularly from Patil, but in the end they were bowled out for 324 and Australia needed only 143 to win. With Yadav out of the match with a fractured toe and Kapil Dev unable to take the field on the fourth evening because of a pulled muscle, Australia seemed to have an easy task. It became appreciably more difficult when Ghavri had Dyson caught behind and bowled Greg Chappell with successive balls. Then Wood was stumped off Doshi and Australia closed at 24 for 3. The last day was one of the greatest in the history of Indian cricket. Just over a quarter of an hour after lunch Jim Higgs was lbw to Kapil Dev and India had won a remarkable match by 59 runs, one of the great reversals in Test history. Scorning his injury, Kapil Dev returned to the attack to inspire the victory as Australia batted limply on a wicket of uneven bounce. Doshi, handicapped by a foot injury, also bowled splendidly and took the vital wicket of Kim Hughes. These two bowled unchanged throughout the last morning and the combination of accurate pace and subtle spin was devastating. Against all probabilities India had drawn the series and their jubilation could only have been tempered by the fact that they came very close to forfeiting the game on the fourth morning.

Third Test Match   Australia *v.* India
7, 8, 9, 10 and 11 February 1981   **at Melbourne**
India

	First Innings		Second Innings	
S. M. Gavaskar (capt)	c Hughes, b Pascoe	10	lbw, b Lillee	70
C. P. S. Chauhan	c Yardley, b Pascoe	0	c Yardley, b Lillee	85
D. B. Vengsarkar	c Border, b Lillee	12	c Marsh, b Pascoe	41
G. R. Viswanath	c Chappell, b Yardley	114	b Lillee	30
S. M. Patil	c Hughes, b Lillee	23	c Chappell, b Yardley	36
Yashpal Sharma	c Marsh, b Lillee	4	b Pascoe	9
Kapil Dev	c Hughes, b Pascoe	5	(8) b Yardley	0
*S. M. H. Kirmani	c Marsh, b Lillee	25	(7) run out	9
K. D. Ghavri	run out	0	not out	11
S. Yadav	not out	20	absent hurt	0
D. R. Doshi	c Walters, b Yardley	0	(10) b Lillee	7
Extras	b 1, lb 8, w 6, nb 9	24	b 11, lb 8, nb 7	26
		237		324

	O	M	R	W		O	M	R	W
Lillee	25	6	65	4		32.1	5	104	4
Pascoe	22	11	29	3		29	4	80	2
Chappell	5	2	9	—					
Yardley	13	3	45	2		31	11	65	2
Higgs	19	2	65	—		15	3	41	—
Border						2	—	8	—

Fall of Wickets
1–0, 2–22, 3–43, 4–91, 5–99, 6–115, 7–164, 8–190, 9–230.
1–165, 2–176, 3–243, 4–245, 5–260, 6–296, 7–296, 8–308, 9–324.

Australia

	First Innings		Second Innings	
J. Dyson	c Kirmani, b Dev	16	c Kirmani, b Ghavri	3
G. M. Wood	c Doshi, b Ghavri	10	st Kirmani, b Doshi	10
G. S. Chappell (capt)	c and b Ghavri	76	b Ghavri	0
K. J. Hughes	c Chauhan, b Yadav	24	b Doshi	16
A. R. Border	b Yadav	124	(6) c Kirmani, b Dev	9
K. D. Walters	st Kirmani, b Doshi	78	(7) not out	18
*R. W. Marsh	c sub, b Doshi	45	(8) b Dev	3
B. Yardley	lbw, b Doshi	0	(5) b Dev	7
D. K. Lillee	c and b Patil	19	b Dev	4
L. S. Pascoe	lbw, b Patil	3	run out	6
J. D. Higgs	not out	1	lbw, b Dev	0
Extras	b 12, lb 6, nb 5	23	lb 5, nb 2	7
		419		83

	O	M	R	W		O	M	R	W
Kapil Dev	19	7	41	1		16.4	4	28	5
Doshi	52	14	109	3		22	9	33	2

Ghavri	39	4	110	2		8	4	10	2
Yadav	32	6	100	2					
Chauhan	2	—	8	—					
Patil	12.3	4	28	2		2	—	5	—

Fall of Wickets
1–30, 2–32, 3–81, 4–189, 5–320, 6–356, 7–356, 8–413, 9–413.
1–11, 2–11, 3–18, 4–40, 5–50, 6–55, 7–61, 8–69, 9–79.

India won by 59 runs

Australia v. India – Test Match Averages

Australia Batting

	M	Inns	NOs	Runs	HS	Average	100s	50s
G. S. Chappell	3	5		368	204	73.60	1	2
K. D. Walters	3	5	2	216	78	72.00		2
K. J. Hughes	3	5		330	213	66.00	1	1
A. R. Border	3	5		228	124	45.60	1	1
G. M. Wood	3	5		157	125	31.40	1	
R. W. Marsh	3	3		83	45	16.60		
J. Dyson	3	5		77	30	15.40		
D. K. Lillee	3	5	1	40	19	10.00		
L. S. Pascoe	3	4	1	17	7	5.66		
B. Yardley	2	4		21	12	5.25		
J. D. Higgs	2	3	1	3	2	1.50		

Also batted: R. M. Hogg 26* and 11 (two matches).

Australia Bowling

	Overs	Mdns	Runs	Wkts	Average	Best	5/inn
L. S. Pascoe	109	27	299	16	18.68	4–61	
D. K. Lillee	148.3	33	452	21	21.52	4–65	
G. S. Chappell	20	10	27	1	27.00	1–4	
A. R. Border	15	6	28	1	28.00	1–9	
B. Yardley	112.4	43	225	7	32.14	2–45	
J. D. Higgs	52	13	151	4	37.75	4–45	
R. M. Hogg	54	8	186	4	46.50	2–100	

Also bowled: K. D. Walters 9–3–33–0; K. J. Hughes 1–0–1–0.

Australia Catches
16 – R. W. Marsh (ct 15, st 1); 5 – G. S. Chappell; 4 – G. M. Wood; 3 – A. R. Border,
K. J. Hughes and K. D. Walters; 2 – B. Yardley; 1 – R. M. Hogg, D. K. Lillee and sub.

India Batting

	M	Inns	NOs	Runs	HS	Average	100s	50s
S. M. Patil	3	6	1	311	174	62.20	1	1
C.P.S. Chauhan	3	6		249	97	41.50		2
S. Yadav	2	3	2	36	20*	36.00		
G. R. Viswanath	3	6		213	114	35.50	1	
S. M. H. Kirmani	3	6	1	124	43*	24.80		
D. B. Vengsarkar	3	6		148	41	24.66		
S. M. Gavaskar	3	6		118	70	19.66		1
Yashpal Sharma	3	6		83	47	13.83		
K. D. Ghavri	3	6	2	49	21	12.25		
Kapil Dev	3	6		55	22	9.16		

D. R. Doshi   3   5   2   13   7   4.33
Also batted: R. Binny 3 and 0 (one match).

India Bowling

	Overs	Mdns	Runs	Wkts	Average	Best	5/inn
S. M. Patil	14.3	4	33	2	16.50	2–28	
Kapil Dev	120.5	26	333	14	23.78	5–28	2
K. D. Ghavri	115	20	370	10	37.00	5–100	1
S. Yadav	103.4	18	313	8	39.12	4–143	
D. R. Doshi	182	40	440	11	40.00	3–49	

Also bowled: C. P. S. Chauhan 3–0–18–0; R. Binny 15–1–70–0.

India Catches

10 – S. M. H. Kirmani (ct 7, st 3); 4 – D. R. Doshi; 3 – S. M. Gavaskar and G. R. Viswanath; 2 – Kapil Dev, C. P. S. Chauhan and S. M. Patil; 1 – Yashpal Sharma, S. Yadav, D. B. Vengsarkar, R. Binny, K. D. Ghavri and sub.

Benson and Hedges World Series Averages

Australia Batting

	M	Inns	NOs	Runs	HS	Average	100s	50s
G. S. Chappell	14	14	4	686	138*	68.60	1	5
K. D. Walters	13	10	5	237	50*	47.40		1
J. Dyson	7	6	1	207	79	41.40		2
G. M. Wood	11	11	2	348	98*	38.66		2
A. R. Border	14	13	1	450	105*	37.50	1	3
R. W. Marsh	14	9	3	158	49	26.33		
M. F. Kent	3	3	1	49	33	24.50		
K. J. Hughes	14	11		226	47	20.54		
T. M. Chappell	13	6		60	14	10.00		
D. K. Lillee	14	5	1	19	7	4.75		
S. F. Graf	9	5		16	7	3.20		
R. M. Hogg	7	3	1	3	1*	1.50		

Also batted: G. F. Lawson 0 and 4* (three matches); L. S. Pascoe 0 and 3* (twelve matches); M. H. N. Walker 4 and 0* (four matches); G. R. Beard played in two matches, but did not bat.

Australia Bowling

	Overs	Mdns	Runs	Wkts	Average	Best	5/inn
D. K. Lillee	120	17	366	25	14.64	4–32	
G. S. Chappell	112.5	17	375	22	17.04	5–15	1
G. R. Beard	18.4	3	70	4	17.50	2–20	
L. S. Pascoe	99.4	12	422	19	22.21	5–30	1
T. M. Chappell	72	3	290	10	29.00	2–28	
S. F. Graf	68	4	255	8	31.87	2–23	
R. M. Hogg	55	5	219	6	36.50	2–14	
M. H. N. Walker	34	4	94	2	47.00	1–25	
G. F. Lawson	28.1	1	131	2	65.50	1–43	

Also bowled in one match: A. R. Border 6–0–21–0; K. D. Walters 6–0–22–0.

Australia Catches

15 – R. W. Marsh; 7 – T. M. Chappell and G. S. Chappell; 6 – A. R. Border; 5 – J. Dyson;

3 – G. F. Lawson; 2 – K. J. Hughes, L. S. Pascoe, R. M. Hogg, M. H. N. Walker and M. F. Kent; 1 – D. K. Lillee, K. D. Walters and G. M. Wood.

New Zealand Batting

	M	Inns	NOs	Runs	HS	Average	100s	50s
B. A. Edgar	13	13	3	426	102*	42.60	1	1
J. G. Wright	13	13	1	511	81	42.58		5
G. P. Howarth	12	11	1	292	47	29.20		
J. V. Coney	11	9	2	191	49	27.28		
B. L. Cairns	13	11	2	170	39	18.88		
M. G. Burgess	13	11		198	42	18.00		
G. B. Troup	4	3	2	17	7*	17.00		
P. E. McEwan	8	7		111	41	15.85		
R. J. Hadlee	14	12	1	173	39	15.72		
I. D. S. Smith	8	6	2	55	23*	13.75		
J. M. Parker	11	10		115	24	11.50		
M. C. Snedden	10	4	2	21	8*	10.50		
W. K. Lees	7	6		52	20	8.66		
E. J. Chatfield	12	6	4	12	6*	6.00		
B. McKechnie	4	3	2	1	1*	1.00		

Also batted: S. L. Boock 2 (one match).

New Zealand Bowling

	Overs	Mdns	Runs	Wkts	Average	Best	5/inn
G. B. Troup	38	7	135	8	16.87	4–19	
M. C. Snedden	88	5	373	17	21.94	3–27	
E. J. Chatfield	110.1	14	396	16	24.75	5–34	1
R. J. Hadlee	131.2	22	448	17	26.35	5–26	2
B. McKechnie	34.3	2	151	5	30.20	3–23	
J. V. Coney	58	5	233	6	38.83	3–28	
B. L. Cairns	111	10	469	12	39.08	3–58	
P. E. McEwan	47	2	241	5	48.20	2–29	

Also bowled: G. P. Howarth 7–0–25–1 (two matches); M. G. Burgess 11–0–59–0 (two matches); S. L. Boock 10–1–30–2 (one match).

New Zealand Catches

12 – J. V. Coney; 10 – I. D. S. Smith (ct 9, st 1); 8 – W. K. Lees (ct 7, st 1); 6 – J. G. Wright and J. M. Parker; 4 – R. J. Hadlee, B. A. Edgar, B. L. Cairns and sub (J. G. Bracewell); 3 – M. G. Burgess; 2 – G. P. Howarth; 1 – E. J. Chatfield and M. C. Snedden.

India Batting

	M	Inns	NOs	Runs	HS	Average	100s	50s
C. P. S. Chauhan	3	3		91	46	30.33		
S. M. H. Kirmani	8	8	3	144	48*	28.80		
Yashpal Sharma	9	9	1	215	72	26.87		1
S. M. Patil	9	9		211	64	23.44		1
D. B. Vengsarkar	10	10		221	66	22.10		2
R. Binny	9	9	1	160	35	20.00		
G. R. Viswanath	9	8		149	43	18.62		
Kapil Dev	10	10		157	75	15.70		1
Kirti Azad	5	5		72	29	14.40		
S. M. Gavaskar	10	10		143	80	14.30		1
K. D. Ghavri	10	9	4	64	14	12.80		

D. R. Doshi   10   5   2   9   5*   3.00

Also batted: T. E. Srinivasan 6 and 4 (two matches); B. S. Reddy 8* and 3* (two matches); Yograj Singh 0 and 0* 9 (four matches).

India Bowling

	Overs	Mdns	Runs	Wkts	Average	Best	5/inn
D. R. Doshi	89	6	313	15	20.86	4–30	
Kapil Dev	90.3	16	300	11	27.27	3–37	
Yograj Singh	21.4	2	92	3	30.66	2–44	
R. Binny	63.1	3	288	7	41.14	4–41	
K. D. Ghavri	97.1	6	340	8	42.50	2–39	
S. M. Patil	71	7	271	6	45.16	2–34	

Also bowled in one match: Kirti Azad 3–1–26–1; Yashpal Sharma 3–0–12–0; S. M. Gavaskar 1.2–0–7–0.

India Catches

6 – S. M. H. Kirmani (ct 4, st 2); 5 – D. B. Vengsarkar; 3 – Kirti Azad, Kapil Dev and subs; 2 – S. M. Gavaskar, Yashpal Sharma, R. Binny, G. R. Viswanath and B. S. Reddy; 1 – D. R. Doshi, Yograj Singh, C. P. S. Chauhan, K. D. Ghavri and S. M. Patil.

India in Australia, 1980–81
First-Class Matches – Batting

	v. Western Australia (Perth) 22–25 November		v. South Australia (Adelaide) 29 November–2 December		v. Tasmania (Hobart) 11–13 December		v. Queensland (Brisbane) 26–29 December		First Test Match (Brisbane) 2–4 January		Second Test Match (Adelaide) 23–27 January	
S. M. Gavaskar	157	—			19	85	79	108	0	10	23	5
C. P. S. Chauhan	48	19	30	8	35	66			20	36	97	11
D. B. Vengsarkar	0	59*	153	5			75	4	22	34	2	37
G. R. Viswanath	75	—	8	13	4	—	3	47	26	24	3	16
Yashpal Sharma	23*	31*			9	31			6	4	47	13
Kapil Dev	—	—	39	0					22	19	2	7
K. D. Ghavri	—	—			51	—	11	0	7	21	3	7*
Yograj Singh	—	—			17	—	7	2*				
S. Yadav	—	—	0*	10	3	—	17*	—			16	0*
D. R. Doshi	—	—	2*	1*					0*	0	6*	—
S. M. H. Kirmani	—	—							27	43*	6	14
T. E. Srinivasan			33	10	25	29*	2	31				
K. Azad			59	3	33	—	8	40				
S. M. Patil			116	2			60	97	65*	4	174	9
R. Binny			1	10	51	—	17	1	3	0		
B. Reddy			1	8	4*	—	16	—				
Byes	1	.			1	4		1		2	11	7
Leg byes	4	4	14	8	9	1	3	5	1	3	10	1
Wides					1		1			1	2	
No balls	4	3			13	4	9	8	2		17	8
Total	312	116	456	78	275	220	308	344	201	201	419	135
Wickets	4	1	9	10		3	10	8	9†	10	10	8
Result	D		L		D		D		L		D	

† S. M. Patil, retired hurt.
‡ S. Yadav, absent hurt.

Catches
13 – B. Reddy (ct 11, st 2)
11 – S. M. H. Kirmani (ct 8, st 3)
 8 – S. M. Gavaskar
 6 – D. B. Vengsarkar
 5 – Kapil Dev and G. R. Viswanath
 4 – Yashpal Sharma, S. Yadav, C. P. S. Chauhan and D. R. Doshi
 3 – S. M. Patil
 2 – Yograj Singh, Kirti Azad, T. E. Srinivasan and subs
 1 – R. Binny and K. D. Ghavri

v. Victoria (Geelong) 30 January–2 February		Third Test Match (Melbourne) 7–11 February		Inns	NOs	Runs	HS	Av
31	28*	16	70	13	1	625	157	52.08
68	—	0	85	13	—	523	97	40.23
6	—	12	41	13	1	450	153	37.50
		114	30	12	—	363	114	30.25
201*	—	4	9	11	3	378	201*	47.25
18	—	5	0	9	—	112	39	12.44
		0	11*	9	2	111	51	15.85
12	—			4	1	38	17	12.66
		20*	—	7	4	66	20*	22.00
13*	—	0	7	8	5	29	13*	9.66
		25	9	6	1	124	43*	24.80
4	69*			8	2	203	69*	33.83
14	—			6	—	157	59	26.16
		23	36	10	—	586	174	58.60
8	—			8	—	91	51	11.37
3	—			5	1	32	16	8.00
3		1	11					
4		8	8					
1	2	6						
12	3	9	7					
398	102	237	324					
9	0	10	9‡					
W		W						

India in Australia, 1980–81 First-Class Matches – Bowling	Kapil Dev	K. D. Ghavri	Yograj Singh	Yashpal Sharma	S. Yadav	D. R. Doshi
v. Western Australia (Perth) 22–25 Nov.	13–3–33–2 13–2–39–0	13–1–52–1 19.4–4–65–4	13–4–49–0 15–3–56–1		15–2–62–1 5–0–15–0	30–3–84–1 17–1–68–0
v.South Australia (Adelaide) 29 Nov.–2 Dec.	25.2–4–87–3 20–3–64–3				22–6–36–2 38–8–71–3	35–11–69–2 42.2–14–60–
v. Tasmania (Hobart) 11–13 Dec.			18–6–42–1 8.5–2–26–1		32–7–67–3 5–1–16–0	
v. Queensland (Brisbane) 26–29 Dec.		14–7–35–3	26–8–72–4 8–4–20–0		24–3–86–0 13–5–23–1	
First Test Match (Brisbane) 2–4 Jan.	36.1–7–97–5	30–7–107–5				27–0–103–0
Second Test Match (Adelaide) 23–27 Jan.	32–5–112–2 17–3–55–1	27–3–106–0 11–2–37–1			42.4–6–143–4 29–6–70–2	48–6–146–3 33–11–49–3
v. Victoria (Geelong) 30 Jan.–2 Feb.	5–0–15–0		14–2–46–0 16–3–44–1	3–0–6–0 8–3–15–1		26–2–81–2
Third Test Match (Melbourne) 7–11 Feb.	19–7–41–1 16.4–4–28–5	39–4–110–2 8–4–10–2			32–6–100–2	52–14–109– 22–9–33–2
	197.1–38– 571–22 av. 25.95	161.4–32– 522–18 av. 29.00	118.5–32– 355–8 av. 44.37	11–3– 21–1 av. 21.00	257.4–50– 689–18 av. 38.27	332.2–71– 802–20 av. 40.10

R. Binny	S. M. Patil	Kirti Azad	C. P. S. Chauhan	B	Lb	W	Nb	Total	Wkts
					12	2	2	296	5
				11			8	262	5
-6-56-1	10-6-25-0	5-0-16-1			10		3	302	10
-1-39-0	3-0-14-0	2-0-11-0		4	11		1	275	10
-3-66-1		16-2-49-0		4	2	3		233	5
)-13-0		1-0-1-0			2		4	62	1
-2-33-2		3-0-18-0		4	9		2	259	9
-18-1	12-3-22-0	2-1-1-0			1			85	2
-1-70-0			1-0-10-0	4	3	3	9	406	10
					13	1	7	528	10
				2	5		3	221	7
-2-46-2		23-9-53-3		4	10		6	267	7
-3-50-3		38-10-60-2	29-4-51-3	1	4	1	5	231	10
	12.3-4-28-2		2-0-8-0	12	6		5	419	10
	2-0-5-0				5		2	83	10
2-19-	39.3-13-	90-22-	32-4-						
-10	94-2	209-6	69-3						
39.10	av. 47.00	av. 34.83	av. 23.00						

New Zealand in Australia, 1980–81
First-Class Matches – Batting

	v.Victoria (Melbourne) 31 October–3 November		v. Queensland (Brisbane) 14–17 November		First Test Match (Brisbane) 28–30 November		Second Test Match (Perth) 12–14 December		Third Test Match (Melbourne) 26–30 December		v. Tasmania (Launceston) 1–4 January	
J. G. Wright	1	69	21	78	29	1	10	3	4	44	106	—
B. A. Edgar	5	15	18	51	20	51	0	0	21	25	10	—
P. E. McEwan			23	73	6	0	8	16				
J. M. Parker	10	24*	13	3	52	4	3	18	56	1	26	—
M. G. Burgess	49	—	18	14	0	2	43	18	49	10*	134	—
J. V. Coney	23*	—	7	96			71	0	55*	3	51	—
W. K. Lees	—	—	16	16			5	25*	4	7		
R. J. Hadlee	—	—	48	103	10	51*	23	0	9	5*		
E. J. Chatfield	—	—	0	—							4*	—
G. B. Troup	—	—	6*	4*			0*	0	1	—		
S. L. Boock	—	—	9	—								
G. P. Howarth	73*	78*			65	4			65	20	53	—
I. D. S. Smith					7	7					30	—
B. L. Cairns					0	0	13	6	18	—		
J. G. Bracewell					6*	0	6	16	0	—	24	—
B. P. Bracewell					0	8						
B. McKechnie											30	—
M. C. Snedden											3	—
Byes		7				4			13	2	5	
Leg byes	5	3	7	3	18	4	3	12	12	8	10	
Wides				1	5	1	2	2		1	3	
No balls	1		6	20	7	5	9	5	10	2	5	
Total	167	196	193	461	225	142	196	121	317	128	494	
Wickets	4	2	10	8	10	10	10	10	10	6	10	
Result	W		D		L		L		D		D	

Catches

9 – J. V. Coney and W. K. Lees

8 – J. M. Parker

4 – G. P. Howarth

3 – J. G. Wright, B. L. Cairns and J. G. Bracewell

2 – R. J. Hadlee, I. D. S. Smith, M. G. Burgess and B. A. Edgar

1 – P. E. McEwan, M. C. Snedden, B. McKechnie and S. L. Boock (as sub)

		Inns	NOs	Runs	HS	Av
4	40	13	—	410	106	31.53
29	6	13	—	251	51	19.30
11	87	8	—	224	87	28.00
26	4	13	1	240	56	20.00
13	21	12	1	371	134	33.72
20	2	10	2	328	96	41.00
		6	1	73	25*	14.60
		8	1	249	103	35.57
		2	1	4	4*	4.00
		5	3	11	6*	5.50
		1	—	9	9	9.00
11	0	9	2	369	78*	52.71
10	5	5	—	59	30	11.80
68	0	7	—	105	68	15.00
		6	1	52	24	10.40
		2	—	8	8	4.00
3	0	3	—	33	30	11.00
1*	0*	3	2	4	3	4.00
2						
1	1					
1						
2						
202	166					
10	10					
	D					

v New South Wales (Sydney) 24–26 January

New Zealand in Australia, 1980–81
First-Class Matches – Bowling

	R. J. Hadlee	G. B. Troup	E. J. Chatfield	J. V. Coney	S. L. Boock	J. M. Parker
v. Victoria (Melbourne) 31 Oct.–3 Nov.	26–7–52–1 10–3–14–1	24–6–61–1 14–3–35–0	24–13–25–1 16–2–39–1	14–6–25–0 8–0–34–1	12–6–18–0 11–3–38–1	
v. Queensland (Brisbane) 14–17 Nov.	26–6–61–5 20–1–76–1	11–4–31–1	24.2–10–61–1 41–10–93–3	13–6–37–1 6–1–22–0	8–3–10–1 40–14–95–2	1–0–9–0
First Test Match (Brisbane) 28–30 Nov.	37–8–83–3 6–0–28–0					
Second Test Match (Hobart) 12–14 Dec.	27–8–87–5 11.1–4–20–2	22–5–57–1 1–0–1–0				
Third Test Match (Melbourne) 26–30 Dec.	39–8–89–3 27.2–7–57–6	26–5–54–1 11–1–31–0		12.3–6–28–3 1–0–1–0		
v. Tasmania (Launceston) 1–4 Jan.			21.1–4–46–3 23–3–62–0	17–7–37–0		2–0–7–0
v. New South Wales (Sydney) 24–26 Jan.				8–1–27–0 7–3–16–0		7–0–37–1
	229.3–52– 567–27 av. 21.00	109–24– 270–4 av. 67.50	149.3–42– 326–9 av. 36.22	86.3–30– 227–5 av. 45.40	71–26– 161–4 av. 40.25	10–0– 53–1 av. 53.00

A. J. G. Wright 2–0–15–0.
B. P. E. McEwan 13–1–40–1: G. P. Howarth 1–0–1–0.

M. G. Burgess	B. P. Bracewell	B. L. Cairns	J. G. Bracewell	M. C. Snedden	B. McKechnie	B	Lb	W	Nb	Total	Wkts
							11		3	195	5
						2	5			167	6
–20–0							3			203	10
						4	4			323	6
	22–8–71–0	38.5–11–87–5	18–5–51–1			1	7		5	305	10
	3–3–0–0	7.3–3–16–0	5–0–12–0			2	2		3	63	0
		28.1–7–88–4	4–1–15–0			3	4	1	10	265	10
		5–2–17–0	5–0–16–0				1			55	2
		35–6–83–2	9–0–38–0			7	13	3	6	321	10
		33–13–65–2	15–5–22–1			6	4		2	188	10
			22–5–67–5	15–1–50–2	8–1–16–0	4	3		2	188	10
2–7–0			26–4–62–2	24–6–74–4		10	9		3	286	6A
		18–3–42–0		20–9–50–0	9–1–26–0		4		1	228	2
–26–1		14–5–22–2		11–0–36–2	15–7–26–1		3		1	130	8B
–4–	25–11–	179.3–50–	104–20–	70–16–	32–9–						
–1	71–0	420–15	283–9	210–8	68–1						
53.00	—	av. 28.00	av. 31.44	av. 26.25	av. 68.00						

D

Western Shield

The Australian Domestic Season

The Sheffield Shield Competition had been swamped by international cricket in 1979–80 to the extent that several of the leading cricketers had played only a handful of matches in their state sides. A more intelligent fixture list gave promise that this would not happen in 1980–81. The challenge to Victoria, champions for the past two seasons, was likely to be strong. Queensland, seeking their first title, had added Allan Border from New South Wales to their array of talent and, even after Border's departure, the strong New South Wales side could find no place for Andrew Hilditch, vice-captain of Australia in 1979 and only twenty-four years old. The might of Western Australia had smouldered for two seasons and, with their strength in depth, they would be main contenders for the championship, particularly as Kim Hughes would be able to play state, as well as Test, cricket. Western Australia had their problems. Rodney Marsh and Dennis Lillee had both declined the post of vice-captain, presumably unwilling to serve under Hughes, and Bruce Laird had accepted the position. Victoria, to the bewilderment of all, had dispensed with Yallop and Whatmore as captains, though these two had led them successfully to their two titles, and appointed wicket-keeper Robinson, captain before he joined W.S.C.

17, 18, 19 and 20 October 1980 **at Perth**
Victoria 183 (D. K. Lillee 5 for 57) and 268 (S. F. Graf 64, B. Yardley 5 for 112)
Western Australia 303 (G. M. Wood 78, K. S. McEwan 67, R. W. Marsh 61, M. H. N. Walker 4 for 82) and 149 for 3 (R. S. Langer 75 not out, K. S. McEwan 57 not out)
Western Australia won by 7 wickets
Western Australia 19 pts, Victoria 5 pts

at Brisbane
Queensland 189 (G. S. Chappell 94, L. S. Pascoe 4 for 38) and 295 (G. S. Chappell 113, A. R. Border 106)
New South Wales 304 for 5 dec (I. C. Davis 91 not out, J. Dyson 88) and 37 for 0
Match drawn
New South Wales 11 pts, Queensland 4 pts

The opening matches of the competition showed that Victoria would face the strongest possible challenges for the title. In Perth they were bowled out by the home state's pace attack on the opening day. At one time Victoria were 99 for 7 and only some brave batting by Bright and Graf gave any respectability. Western Australia batted steadily to a big lead and then Lillee and the off-spin of Bruce Yardley accounted for Victoria a second time. Needing 149 to win, Western Australia lost 3 for 26, but Rob Langer and Ken McEwan, who had batted finely in the first innings, saw them to victory. Rain reduced play to under half an hour on the second day in Brisbane and almost certainly robbed New South Wales of victory. Wessels and Chappell had stood alone on the first day and in Queensland's second innings a stand of 201 in 215 minutes for the fourth wicket between Chappell and state debutant Allan Border, both of whom hit centuries, was nullified by the fact that seven men failed to reach double figures. New South Wales also had their debutant in new ball bowler Michael Whitney. The visitors batted consistently and impressively and for the first time in thirty matches Jeff Thomson failed to take a wicket for Queensland. After the match Queensland created a major surprise when they omitted Phil Carlson, an all-rounder of Test standard, from their side.

23, 24, 25 and 26 October 1980   **at Adelaide**
Tasmania 395 (B. F. Davison 126, R. D. Woolley 90, W. Prior 4 for 92) and 137
South Australia 465 for 9 dec (P. R. Sleep 102 not out, B. L. Causby 102, J. J. Crowe 82, W. M. Darling 81, S. Saunders 4 for 154) and 68 for 4
South Australia won by 6 wickets
South Australia 20 pts, Tasmania 9 pts

                                                                    at Sydney
New South Wales 340 for 3 dec (R. B. McCosker 168, J. Dyson 152)
Western Australia 176 (G. F. Lawson 4 for 34, L. S. Pascoe 4 for 47) and 103 (R. G. Holland 4 for 30)
New South Wales won by an innings and 61 runs
New South Wales 22 pts, Western Australia 3 pts

A record sixth wicket stand of 213 between Brian Davison and Roger Woolley helped Tasmania to a formidable total, but South Australia, for whom wicket-keeper Kevin Wright, formerly of Western Australia, was making his debut, passed the Tasmanian total with only five wickets down. Darling and Causby put on 124 for the second wicket and Causby went on to reach his hundred. That fine all-rounder Peter Sleep also hit a century to give the home state a lead of 70 on the first innings. Stuart Saunders bowled his leg-spin bravely to take 4 for 154 in just under 38 overs. The Tasmanian second innings disintegrated and South Australia won with an hour to spare. Hogg bowled well after his absence through back injury. South Australia were captained in this match by Ashley Mallett who temporarily filled the void left by the retirement of Ian Chappell. There was no play on the second day in Sydney, but this did not prevent New South Wales from recording their first victory of the season and moving to the top of the embryo Shield table. A record New South Wales opening stand of 319 by McCosker and Dyson was the platform of the home side's victory, but the visitors were very disappointing. They batted limply against the pace of Pascoe and Lawson, and then succumbed to the leg-spin of Rob Holland.

24, 25, 26 and 27 October 1980   **at Brisbane**
Victoria 250 for 7 dec (R. G. Matthews 62, J. M. Wiener 52)
Queensland 358 for 5 dec (K. C. Wessels 134, G. S. Chappell 102 not out, M. F. Kent 77)
Match drawn
Queensland 10 pts, Victoria 7 pts

No play on the second day and very little on the third made the contest for bonus points the only interest in this match. Wiener and Matthews had an opening stand of 90 and Whatmore and Laughlin batted well, but Wessels and Kent replied with 179 for the first wicket for Queensland. Wessels reached 134 before he was out with the score at 276. Greg Chappell then took over and reached the fourteenth century he had hit for Queensland.

30 and 31 October, 1 November 1980   **at Adelaide**
New South Wales 338 (I. C. Davis 64, J. Dyson 62, K. D. Walters 54,
   T. M. Chappell 50, P. M. Toohey 50, R. M. Hogg 4 for 50)
South Australia 89 (L. S. Pascoe 5 for 27) and 152 (R. G. Holland 4 for 50)
New South Wales won by an innings and 97 runs
New South Wales 20 pts, South Australia 2 pts

New South Wales overwhelmed South Australia and consolidated their position at the top of the table. Five New South Wales players hit half centuries in a solidly consistent batting performance and then Lawson and Pascoe destroyed the home side on the second day. Pascoe finished the South Australian innings by having Hogg caught by Holland, dismissing Attenborough lbw, and bowling Mallett first ball to record the hat-trick. South Australia fared little better in their second innings when Steve Rixon took five catches behind the stumps and the leg-spin of Holland supplemented the place of Lawson and Pascoe. The match was decided on the third day.

31 October, 1, 2 and 3 November 1980   **at Brisbane**
Western Australia 261 (B. Yardley 78) and 420 (K. J. Hughes 149, R. W. Marsh
   67)
Queensland 439 (G. S. Chappell 194, K. C. Wessels 76, T. V. Hohns 74,
   D. K. Lillee 6 for 97) and 82 for 0
Match drawn
Queensland 11 pts, Western Australia 6 pts

Western Australia recovered from 58 for 5 to reach 261 due to the efforts of Marsh, Yardley and Lillee, but Queensland quickly passed this total and built up a commanding lead. Lillee bowled admirably and passed the six hundred wicket mark in first-class cricket, but it was the batting of Greg Chappell that dominated. He reached his highest score in Sheffield Shield cricket and hit his third century in four innings for Queensland, bringing his aggregate to 503 in four innings, average 167.66. The two left-handers, Hohns and Wessels, batted well in support and Queensland led by 178. Carl Rackemann had the visitors struggling at 83 for 3, but he retired from the attack injured and with debutant off-spinner Kelly also injured, Queensland could not force home their advantage. Kim Hughes hit a career best and the game was saved. Hughes had fine support from Marsh and Shipperd, but the Western Australian catching deserved to lose the game – Chappell was missed five times.

McDonald Cup – First Round of Matches

8 November 1980   **at Melbourne**
Victoria 121 for 5 (J. M. Wiener 73 not out)
Queensland 70 for 6 (M. H. N. Walker 4 for 37)
Victoria won by 51 runs

9 November 1980   **at Melbourne**
Victoria 138
New South Wales 139 for 2 (J. Dyson 55 not out, P. M. Toohey 55 not out)
New South Wales won by 8 wickets

                                                       at Perth
South Australia 176 for 7 (P. R. Sleep 50 not out, G. W. Goodman 50)
Western Australia 178 for 3 (G. Shipperd 65 not out, K. S. McEwan 52 not
    out)
Western Australia won by 7 wickets

The weather was unkind to the opening of the competition and only a twenty
over game before 836 people could be played on the first day. Wiener and
Walker took all the honours. Wiener hit seven fours and a huge six, off Jeff
Thomson. Chappell conceded 29 runs in 3 overs. Queensland could not match
the Victoria run rate. The following day Victoria were less successful. Wiener
again batted well, but Dyson and Toohey stroked New South Wales to victory
with five overs to spare. There was a closer finish in Perth where the home
side, thanks to a 96 run stand in 81 minutes by McEwan and Shipperd, won
with 28 deliveries remaining. Shipperd won the man-of-match award and
McEwan hit Mallett for one of the biggest sixes ever seen on the W.A.C.A.
ground. Former Tasmanian, Goodman, batted solidly, but too slowly for the
visitors and it was Peter Sleep who gave the innings impetus.

13, 14, 15 and 16 November 1980   **at Sydney**
South Australia 302 (J. J. Crowe 131, G. F. Lawson 4 for 61, L. S. Pascoe
    4 for 62) and 206 (J. J. Crowe 67, R. G. Holland 5 for 82, L. S. Pascoe
    4 for 39)
New South Wales 349 (K. D. Walters 186, G. R. Beard 51, G. R. Atten-
    borough 5 for 94) and 160 for 4 (J. Dyson 85 not out)
New South Wales won by 6 wickets
New South Wales 19 pts, South Australia 8 pts

Opening the innings for the first time, New Zealander Jeff Crowe batted
faultlessly. He was well supported by Zadow in a stand of 104 for the sixth
wicket, but the last five wickets fell for 47 runs. New South Wales were
struggling at 61 for 4 when Doug Walters arrived to play one of the finest
innings of his splendid career. His 186 was scored in $5\frac{1}{4}$ hours and included
26 boundaries. He was dropped by Hookes on 43. Surprisingly, New South
Wales had grabbed the lead and Pascoe, who had another fine match, and
Holland consolidated their advantage. Crowe again batted well, but the last
nine wickets fell for only 105 runs and the consistent Dyson saw New South
Wales to another triumph.

14, 15, 16 and 17 November 1980   **at Melbourne**
Western Australia 187 and 234 (G. Shipperd 62, J. D. Higgs 4 for 67)
Victoria 401 for 8 dec (J. K. Moss 131, S. F. Graf 100 not out, R. J. Bright
    53, W. M. Clark 4 for 100) and 24 for 3
Victoria won by 7 wickets
Victoria 17 pts, Western Australia 4 pts

Victoria hauled themselves off the bottom of the table with a comfortable win
over Western Australia. Ian Callen returned to first-class cricket for the first
time in a year and, with Graf, was instrumental in dismissing the visitors on
the opening day. Callen had 3 for 36, Graf 3 for 25. Victoria lost both openers
for a duck, but Whatmore and Bright repaired the damage, and then Moss
and Graf put on 103 for the seventh wicket in 108 minutes. Moss was as
aggressive as ever, but it was Graf who won the plaudits for his maiden century
in first-class cricket. The spin of Higgs and Bright accounted for Western
Australia in the second innings and Victoria needed only 21 to win. They lost
three wickets in getting the runs for the ball was keeping very low and the
win was accomplished with four leg-byes.

McDonald Cup – Second Round of Matches

20 November 1980   **at Sydney**
New South Wales 214 for 6 (I. C. Davis 84)
Queensland 215 for 5 (M. F. Kent 68, G. S. Chappell 58)
Queensland won by 5 wickets

On an easy wicket New South Wales never forced the pace sufficiently, Trevor
Chappell and Dyson were particular offenders. Kent and Chappell set the
platform for Queensland's victory with a second wicket partnership of 98, and
Carlson and Ritchie made victory certain after New South Wales had taken
3 quick wickets.

                                                    at Hobart
Western Australia 203 for 9 (C. S. Sergeant 65, A. L. Mann 59 not out)
Tasmania 144 (M. F. Malone 4 for 30)
Western Australia won by 59 runs

Tasmania were reduced to 55 for 6 and only Allen and Faulkner gave them
a hint of respectability with a stand of 84.

4, 5 and 6 December 1980   **at Adelaide**
South Australia 114 (M. H. N. Walker 5 for 29, I. W. Callen 4 for 30) and
    162 (I. W. Callen 5 for 47)
Victoria 223 (R. T. Robinson 120, R. M. Hogg 6 for 75) and 54 for 1
Victoria won by 9 wickets
Victoria 17 pts, South Australia 5 pts

The pace men dominated the match and Victoria, at 50 for 6, were struggling
as much as the home state had done. Robinson then saved them with his highest
score of the season, but Victoria's ultimate victory hinged on the fact that he

was recalled after having been caught off Hogg. Umpire Wilson ruled that Hogg had bowled in an intimidatory manner. It was this performance, however, that won Hogg his Test place back. Bright bowled well in the second innings and Goodman, formerly of Tasmania, made his debut for South Australia, scoring 43. Dav Whatmore, former captain and Test player scored 33 not out in the second innings, but was dropped for the rest of the season.

11, 12, 13 and 14 December 1980   **at Melbourne**
New South Wales 347 for 9 dec (P. M. Toohey 145, D. M. Welham 100, M. H. N. Walker 6 for 120)
Victoria 188 (G. F. Lawson 5 for 50, G. R. Beard 4 for 34) and 111 for 5
Match drawn
New South Wales 9 pts, Victoria 2 pts

12, 13, 14 and 15 December 1980   **at Brisbane**
South Australia 283 (P. R. Sleep 71, J. R. Thomson 5 for 61) and 160 for 4 (R. J. Inverarity 52)
Queensland 393 for 9 dec (K. C. Wessels 76, G. M. Ritchie 74, T. V. Hohns 63, R. B. Phillips 51, P. R. Sleep 5 for 90)
Match drawn
Queensland 10 pts, South Australia 9 pts

Rain saved Victoria from defeat in Melbourne after Peter Toohey and Dirk Welham, in his first game of the season, had both hit hundreds and shared a fifth wicket stand of 221. Toohey was missed three times. Victoria batted with painful slowness, but could not avoid the follow-on. Rain was also the winner in Brisbane where Jeff Thomson recovered from a spate of no-balls to give Queensland the edge. Peter Sleep had a fine all-round performance for the visitors and John Inverarity batted dourly in the second innings. Queensland gave an impressively even batting display, but, in the field, were handicapped by an injury to Carl Rackemann.

20, 21, 22 and 23 December 1980   **at Perth**
Western Australia 350 for 9 dec (G. M. Wood 126, R. M. Hogg 4 for 87) and 192 (K. J. Hughes 97)
South Australia 221 (K. J. Wright 105, T. M. Alderman 4 for 74) and 233 (R. J. Inverarity 59, W. M. Darling 55, B. Yardley 5 for 85)
Western Australia won by 88 runs
Western Australia 23 pts, South Australia 7 pts

                                              at Sydney
New South Wales 269 (T. M. Chappell 111, G. R. Beard 50, J. R. Thomson 4 for 42, T. V. Hohns 4 for 78) and 320 (J. Dyson 106, G. R. Beard 58, A. R. Border 4 for 61)
Queensland 422 for 6 dec (K. C. Wessels 160, G. S. Chappell 86 not out) and 36 for 1
Match drawn
Queensland 10 pts, New South Wales 6 pts

at Hobart

Tasmania 425 (B. F. Davison 173, D. C. Boon 114, D. Robinson 60) and
211 (D. C. Boon 67, R. J. Bright 4 for 59)
Victoria 543 for 9 dec (J. W. Scholes 156, G. N. Yallop 121, R. J. Bright
108) and 94 for 4
Victoria won by 6 wickets
Victoria 17 pts, Tasmania 10 pts

Although being forced to retire hurt after he had been struck by a ball from
Hogg, Graeme Wood returned to hit a fine century and lift the home state
from 197 for 7. South Australia were in disarray against Alderman and Malone
and were 111 for 7. Then Kevin Wright hit a maiden first-class hundred
against his former state. Kim Hughes saved his side with a sparkling 97. They
had been 78 for 6 in their second innings, but in the end they were able to
set South Australia 322 to win, a task they found impossible against the spin
of Yardley on the last day. Batsmen thrived at Sydney where a draw always
seemed most likely. Two important innings by Graeme Beard saved the home
side when it looked as if Queensland would gain the advantage. When Tasmania
closed the first day at 335 for 4, they seemed immune from defeat. Nineteen-
year-old David Boon hit 114 in 4 hours and shared a fourth wicket stand of
174 in 160 minutes with Brian Davison who hit his third Sheffield Shield
century in successive matches. Victoria savaged the Tasmanian bowling to reach
their highest total for sixteen years. There was a highest score from John
Scholes and a maiden hundred from Ray Bright. Yallop hit a hundred in $3\frac{1}{2}$
hours and Tasmania wilted at the second attempt. Left to score 94 in 83 minutes,
Victoria won with eleven balls to spare.

8, 9, 10 and 11 January 1981   **at Adelaide**

South Australia 171 (T. M. Alderman 4 for 45, M. F. Malone 4 for 68) and
243 (D. W. Hookes 67, W. M. Darling 65 not out)
Western Australia 359 (C. S. Serjeant 144 not out, K. S. McEwan 68, A. A.
Mallett 5 for 88) and 58 for 4 (W. Prior 4 for 23)
Western Australia won by 6 wickets
Western Australia 19 pts, South Australia 4 pts

9, 10, 11 and 12 January 1981   **at Brisbane**

Tasmania 211 (B. F. Davison 51, G. Dymock 4 for 61) and 347 (B. F. Davison
118, D. C. Boon 73, D. J. Lillee 4 for 48)
Queensland 458 for 8 dec (M. F. Kent 171, W. R. Broad 75, W. Morgan 61,
R. B. Phillips 52 not out) and 101 for 1 (M. F. Kent 68 not out)
Queensland won by 9 wickets
Queensland 26 pts, Tasmania 5 pts

Wins for Western Australia and Queensland made New South Wales' grip on
the Sheffield Shield look very much weaker. Queensland amassed a record 26
points against Tasmania. Kent and Morgan hit career best scores and hit
furiously as did the late order batsmen. Eleven batting points were won. Davison
and Boon again performed nobly for Tasmania, but Denis Lillee's leg-spin
turned the game back to Queensland. Kent's 171 included 26 fours and 3 sixes.

In spite of Wayne Prior's late burst, Western Australia always looked in charge at Adelaide after Craig Serjeant and Ken McEwan had rescued them from 58 for 4 with a stand of 120. There were some brave rearguard actions from Darling and Hookes, but South Australia never really threatened the visitors' supremacy.

17, 18 and 19 January, 1981   **at Sydney**

Victoria 300 for 9 dec (J. W. Scholes 65, G. N. Yallop 52, L. S. Pascoe 4 for 62, M. R. Whitney 4 for 62) and 245 for 7 (G. N. Yallop 70, R. D. Robinson 70)

New South Wales 398 (J. Dyson 95, D. M. Welham 66, S. J. Rixon 63 not out, K. D. Walters 56)

Match drawn

New South Wales 11 pts, Victoria 9 pts

at Adelaide

Queensland 366 for 8 dec (G. S. Chappell 172, M. F. Kent 78, A. A. Mallett 5 for 110) and 230 for 1 dec (M. F. Kent 101 not out, A. R. Border 85 not out)

South Australia 236 (G. Dymock 5 for 59) and 304 (P. R. Sleep 122, R. J. Inverarity 70, D. W. Hookes 53)

Queensland won by 56 runs

Queensland 23 pts, South Australia 7 pts

at Devonport

Tasmania 246 (B. F. Davison 114, B. Yardley 7 for 62) and 123 (B. Yardley 4 for 36)

Western Australia 252 for 8 dec (G. M. Wood 103) and 121 for 3

Western Australia won by 7 wickets

Western Australia 19 pts, Tasmania 7 pts

Queensland had another masterly victory which brought them a further abundance of points. Excellent batting from Greg Chappell and Martin Kent and good bowling from Thomson, Dymock and Rackemann, with fine spin support from Lillee, Hohns and Border, which both restricted and fretted the South Australian batsmen, clinched the northerners victory. Peter Sleep played a valiant innings in an attempt to stave off defeat. Poor 'Rick' Darling was again injured. He was concussed by a ball from Thomson and taken to hospital. Western Australia maintained their challenge with a resounding win over Tasmania. After Lillee had made early inroads it was Yardley's spin that defeated the islanders. Graeme Wood was again in fine form and there was yet another hundred from Brian Davison, 114 in 169 minutes off 130 deliveries. He was certainly leading by example. The game at Sydney was quite dreadful. There was a lack of urgency in the batting, Dirk Welham excepted, and the game drew barracking from the crowd as New South Wales batted on tediously and a draw became inevitable. Although they failed to beat Victoria, New South Wales led the Shield table with 98 points, four more than Queensland and five more than Western Australia. The last two matches for each side would be decisive.

McDonald Cup – Final Stages

at Hobart

South Australia 218 for 8 (D. W. Hookes 84, R. J. McCurdy 4 for 37)
Tasmania 181 (T. Docking 59)
South Australia won by 37 runs

Semi-Finals
14 February 1981   **at Perth**
Western Australia 214 for 8 (C. S. Serjeant 59 not out, M. D. O'Neill 52)
Victoria 187 (R. J. Bright 70)
Western Australia won by 27 runs

15 February 1981   **at Adelaide**
South Australia 217 for 9 (W. M. Darling 51)
Queensland 219 for 5 (A. R. Border 97)
Queensland won by 5 wickets

Only a brave flourish from the late batsmen gave Victoria any respectability in
Perth after Lillee and Malone, aided by Marsh behind the stumps, had reduced
them to 13 for 5. The home state had recovered from 22 for 3 with a stand
of 78 between O'Neill and Serjeant. There was some fine late order hitting
from Yardley and Smith and after the opening burst from Lillee and Malone
the match was decided. The hottest day in Adelaide for thirty-two years did
little for the South Australian bowlers. Their batsmen had accumulated runs
steadily, but, Hogg and Prior apart, their bowling was poor and Allan Border
showed them no mercy.

Consolation Final
21 February 1981   **at Adelaide**
South Australia 209 (W. M. Darling 53)
Victoria 176
South Australia won by 33 runs

Final
22 February 1981   **at Brisbane**
Queensland 188 for 9 (K. C. Wessels 53)
Western Australia 116
Queensland won by 72 runs

Before a record crowd of 20,237 people, Wessels and Kent gave Queensland
a fine start with 68 in the first 16 overs. It proved to be decisive for, with
a slow outfield, Queensland's 188 was a good score. Western Australia began
badly and never recovered. They were 19 for 4 and 55 for 7 and were all out
in 32.5 overs of suicidal batting. Carl Rackemann's accuracy gave him 2 for
11 in 6.5 overs.

26, 27, 28 February and 1 March 1981   **at Geelong**
Queensland 330 for 4 dec (G. M. Ritchie 140 not out, G. S. Chappell 83) and
    258 (A. R. Border 86, M. F. Kent 52)
Victoria 301 for 3 dec (G. M. Watts 99, J. W. Scholes 80 not out) and 268

(R. D. Robinson 69 not out, S. F. Graf 51)
Queensland won by 19 runs
Queensland 19 pts, Victoria 7 pts

27, 28 February, 1 and 2 March 1981   **at Perth**
Western Australia 328 for 6 dec (K. J. Hughes 94, G. Shipperd 80) and 319
  for 7 dec (R. W. Marsh 76 not out, K. J. Hughes 73, G. Shipperd 65)
New South Wales 262 for 8 dec (T. M. Chappell 71) and 270 (J. Dyson 134,
  S. J. Rixon 66)
Western Australia won by 115 runs
Western Australia 22 pts, New South Wales 7 pts

Western Australia's victory over New South Wales moved them to the top
of the table and with one game to play put them in a commanding position
though their main challenge now would come in the deciding match with
Queensland, victors in an exciting game in Geelong. A fine hard hitting innings
from Greg Ritchie who shared an unbeaten stand of 103 for the fifth wicket
with Trevor Hohns gave Queensland an advantage on the opening day, but
this was nullified by some sound Victorian batting led by Garry Watts. The
twenty-two year old left-hander, given only his third game in three years by
the state selectors, cut a ball onto his stumps when one short of his century.
In their second innings Queensland collapsed from 196 for 2 to 258 all out,
mainly through some superb fielding, especially by Moss, which ran out three
batsmen. Victoria needed 288 to win, but, in spite of some hard hits from Moss,
they were 156 for 6. In a dust-storm, Graf and Robinson added 82 in 85
minutes, but Dymock and Chappell decided the issue in favour of Queensland.
In Perth, Western Australia were always leading New South Wales. Their
bowling was relentless and there was some sparkling batting from Hughes and
Marsh. Sadly, Dyson and Marsh were fined for bad behaviour, but this could
not detract from Dyson's rousing second innings century when he and Rixon
put on 159 in 128 minutes for the seventh wicket in a brave attempt to save
the game.

6, 7 and 8 March 1981   **at Sydney**
New South Wales 222 (R. B. McCosker 88, T. M. Chappell 59) and 297 for
  5 dec (D. M. Welham 128 not out, S. J. Rixon 92, K. D. Walters 55)
Tasmania 226 (B. F. Davison 82) and 133 (D. W. Hourn 6 for 33, R. G.
  Holland 4 for 40)
New South Wales won by 160 runs
New South Wales 17 pts, Tasmania 8 pts

7, 8, 9 and 10 March 1981   **at Geelong**
South Australia 312 for 6 dec (W. B. Phillips 111, W. M. Darling 50) and
  309 for 5 (W. B. Phillips 91, R. McLean 89, D. W. Hookes 73 not out)
Victoria 328 for 2 dec (P. A. Hibbert 153 not out, G. N. Yallop 122) and
  164 for 5 (G. N. Yallop 66)
Match drawn
Victoria 10 pts, South Australia 7 pts

at Perth

Western Australia 305 for 8 dec (G. Shipperd 140, G. S. Chappell 4 for 66)
and 289 (C. S. Serjeant 72)

Queensland 186 (M. F. Kent 67, T. M. Alderman 4 for 33) and 232 for 9
(A. R. Border 83 not out)

Match drawn

Western Australia 11 pts, Queensland 5 pts

Rain on the last day prevented a result at Geelong where batsmen thrived.
Yallop and Hibbert added 263 for the second wicket for Victoria, and Wayne
Phillips played two fine innings for the visitors. In Sydney, New South Wales
did not bat well enough in the first innings to secure more than two batting
points and though another impressive century by Dirk Welham and an excellent
knock from Rixon revived them in the second innings, their chance had gone.
Leg-spinners Holland and Hourn routed Tasmania on the last day, but, by
then, the Sheffield Shield had escaped New South Wales again. The Shield,
in fact, went to Western Australia who once more denied Queensland their
ambition. Greg Shipperd hit his first century of the season to put Western
Australia in a commanding position on the first day. Queensland then collapsed
before Lillee, Alderman and Yardley. Queensland were left needing 409 to win
on the last afternoon and with Chappell failing again, a draw was all that they
could hope for, and this was only narrowly achieved with Border standing
firm.

Sheffield Shield
Final Table

	P	W	D	L	Pts
Western Australia	9	5	2	2	125
New South Wales	9	4	4	1	122
Queensland	9	3	6	—	118
Victoria	9	3	4	2	91
Tasmania	5	—	—	5	70.2
South Australia	9	1	2	6	69

First Class Averages

Batting

	M	*Inns*	*NOs*	*Runs*	*HS*	*Average*	*100s*	*50s*
P. A. Hibbert	2	4	2	204	153*	102.00	1	
G. S. Chappell	14	22	2	1502	204	75.10	5	6
B. F. Davison	7	13	1	824	173	68.66	4	3
D. M. Welham	5	8	2	408	128*	68.00	2	1
M. F. Kent	11	20	4	941	171	58.81	2	5
J. Dyson	13	22	4	1028	152	57.11	3	4
K. C. Wessels	10	17	1	814	160	50.87	2	3
A. R. Border	14	22	3	914	124	49.68	2	6

K. D. Walters	14	20	2	781	186	48.81	2	5
G. N. Yallop	11	20	2	796	122	44.22	2	6
J. W. Scholes	7	13	3	430	156	43.00	1	2
R. D. Robinson	11	18	5	553	120	42.53	1	2
J. K. Moss	11	19	3	666	131	41.62	2	1
K. J. Hughes	14	26	1	1036	213	41.44	2	5
P. R. Sleep	10	20	4	663	122	41.43	2	2
S. F. Graf	8	11	4	286	100*	40.85	1	2
R. B. McCosker	10	16	2	571	168	40.78	2	1
D. C. Boon	7	13		518	114	39.84	1	3
T. M. Chappell	10	15	1	550	111	39.28	2	3
W. G. Morgan	4	6	1	196	61	39.20		1
G. Shipperd	9	18	1	646	140	38.00	1	3
R. F. Jeffery	7	14	2	443	145*	36.91	1	1
G. M. Ritchie	10	15	3	432	140*	36.00	1	2
W. R. Broad	4	6		215	75	35.83		2
G. M. Wood	14	27	2	863	126*	34.52	4	1
W. M. Darling	10	20	3	573	81	33.70		5
G. M. Watts	3	6		202	99	33.66		1
P. M. Toohey	9	12	1	357	145	32.45	1	1
R. J. Bright	11	14	4	308	108	30.80	1	1
R. W. Marsh	14	23	2	625	91	29.76		4
D. W. Hookes	7	14	1	387	73*	29.76		3
S. J. Rixon	10	12	1	315	92	28.63		3
K. J. Wright	10	17	3	399	105	28.50	1	
G. R. Beard	10	11	1	285	58	28.50		4
J. J. Crowe	10	20		565	131	28.25	1	3
K. S. McEwan	8	16	2	390	68	27.85		3
B. M. Laird	7	14		387	110	27.64	1	2
B. L. Causby	3	6		161	102	26.83	1	
R. J. Inverarity	7	14	2	321	70	26.75		3
I. C. Davis	8	12	2	267	91*	26.70		2
R. B. Phillips	11	13	3	267	55*	26.70		3
T. V. Hohns	11	16	4	315	74	26.25		2
T. J. Laughlin	4	7	1	146	41	24.33		
M. D. O'Neill	7	13		302	100	23.23	1	
R. S. Langer	5	10	1	206	84	22.88		2
M. B. Scholes	4	6	1	114	34	22.80		
R. L. Knight	6	12	1	234	47	21.27		
D. B. Robinson	6	12		252	60	21.00		1
J. M. Wiener	9	12	1	334	61	20.87		2
B. Yardley	11	19	3	333	78	20.81		1
D. C. Lovell	3	6		124	74	20.66		1
R. J. Zadow	6	12	1	220	61	20.00		1
R. G. Matthews	7	13		234	62	18.00		1
D. F. Whatmore	5	9	1	143	47	17.87		
D. K. Lillee	13	20	5	251	31*	16.73		
M. H. N. Walker	10	9	2	116	44	16.57		
G. W. Goodman	4	8		109	43	13.62		
L. G. Allen	5	10	1	119	55	13.22		1
J. R. Thomson	11	11	1	126	34	12.60		
G. R. Attenborough	8	14	3	134	42	12.18		
S. L. Saunders	6	11	1	100	31*	10.00		

(Qualification 100 runs; average 10.00)
R. D. Woolley 90 & 41 *; I. R. McLean 89 & 23; W. B. Phillips 11.1 & 91 scored over
100 runs but played in only one match.

Bowling

	Overs	Mds	Runs	Wkts	Average	Best	5/inn	10/m
L. S. Pascoe	451	102	1230	63	19.52	5–27	1	
D. K. Lillee	545	138	1462	69	21.18	6–53	4	
R. M. Hogg	353.4	78	960	42	22.85	6–75	1	
G. F. Lawson	364	88	947	41	23.09	5–50	1	
G. S. Chappell	228.3	69	549	23	23.86	4–28		
J. R. Thomson	378.1	73	1149	46	24.97	5–61	1	
G. R. Beard	385	167	732	29	25.24	5–37	2	1
B. Yardley	489.3	154	1193	47	25.38	7–62	3	1
T. M. Alderman	277.5	55	835	32	26.09	4–33		
I. W. Callen	236.4	47	751	28	26.82	4–30		
S. F. Graf	223.5	40	606	20	30.30	3–25		
R. J. McCurdy	224.5	41	773	25	30.92	7–91	1	
R. G. Holland	339.4	87	931	30	31.03	5–82	1	
M. R. Whitney	111	22	347	11	31.54	4–62		
M. H. N. Walker	389.1	105	999	31	32.22	6–120	2	
M. F. Malone	174	45	463	14	33.07	4–68		
D. J. Lillee	129.4	26	399	12	33.25	5–48	1	
W. Prior	207.5	40	713	21	33.95	4–23		
P. R. Sleep	189.4	28	749	22	34.04	5–90	1	
A. A. Mallett	386.2	104	923	27	34.18	5–88	2	
J. D. Higgs	454.3	89	1395	38	36.71	4–25		
G. R. Attenborough	279.2	58	865	22	39.31	5–94	1	
T. V. Hohns	355.2	82	974	24	40.58	4–78		
C. L. Broadby	131.2	30	407	10	40.70	2–35		
R. J. Bright	392.5	131	898	22	40.81	4–59		
C. G. Rackemann	313.2	86	863	21	41.09	3–9		
W. M. Clark	203.4	48	513	12	42.75	4–100		
P. M. Clough	237	40	712	14	50.85	3–62		
S. L. Saunders	150.1	27	546	10	54.60	4–154		

(Qualification 10 wickets)

Wicket-keeping
61 – R. W. Marsh (ct 59/st 2)
39 – S. J. Rixon (ct 35/st 4)
35 – R. B. Phillips (ct 30/st 5)
28 – R. D. Robinson (ct 26/st 2)
27 – K. J. Wright (ct 22/st 5)
13 – L. G. Allen (ct 12/st 1)

Leading catchers
24 – G. S. Chappell
18 – K. J. Hughes and A. R. Border
16 – M. F. Kent
12 – G. M. Wood
11 – K. D. Walters

10 – G. N. Yallop and R. B. McCosker
9 – J. J. Crowe, T. M. Alderman and T. V. Hohns
8 – J. K. Moss, J. M. Wiener, K. C. Wessels and J. Dyson

FRANK TYSON, *distinguished player, commentator and coach, reviews the season in Australia –*

The Australian Cricket Board's innovation of asking two Test teams to bask in the sun of one Australian summer brought in its wake neither great rewards nor dire punishment, but merely foreseeable consequences. The prospect of witnessing the talents of a greater number of international stars in the space of one season, certainly stimulated public interest in the highest level of the game; but it also seriously depleted the following of Australia's domestic competition: the Sheffield Shield. The watching public it seems, on the evidence of 1979–80, would far sooner spend its valuable leisure time revering the awesome talents of Viv Richards or the obduracy of Geoff Boycott than tasting the more pedestrian wares of the local first-class tradesmen.

Alarmed by the continuing sad Sheffield Shield story of escalating travel and accommodation costs and diminishing gates and revenue, the A.C.B. in 1980–81 sought to inject the sick man of Australian cricket with a life-saving serum. One stimulant was to programme state games to avoid clashes with international fixtures, thus affording spectators the opportunity of seeing Test stars in action in Shield clashes. So successful was this ploy that most of the country's leading cricketers missed only two of their state's games. In January 1981 an experiment in curtailing costs was tried by playing three Shield games over extended hours in three rather than the normal four days. Significantly two of those three trial matches produced outright decisions. Spice was added to the competition by the introduction of a more efficient incentive bonus points scheme, more akin to the English system.

At such close quarters it is difficult to ascertain the efficacity of the treatment of the Shield's ills. It would not, however, be too premature a judgement to state that the physical demands of the past season on the players involved at Test, one-day international and Shield levels were excessive. In certain instances, individuals who appeared in a Benson and Hedges/World Series Cup match, ending amidst great tension at 10.30 pm, were compelled to rise at six on the following morning, fly 500 miles and begin a Shield match at 11 am. It was small wonder that, against this background of unremitting physical challenge, the strain began to tell on players towards the end of the season. It was certainly no great source of surprise to me that players such as Greg Chappell and Len Pascoe chose to withdraw from the 1981 tour of England and that Marsh and Lillee sought medical permission to bypass the Sri Lankan segment of that tour.

One conclusion emerged quite clearly from the experiments to revitalise the Sheffield Shield: the competition was considerably more representative of the comparative strengths of the participants than it had been in the previous year. Illustrative of this point was the fact that Victoria and South Australia, the two teams who fought out the grand final of the competition in the previous season, when they had been relatively unaffected by international demands, found themselves, in 1980–81, occupying the number 4 and last positions. By contrast, Western Australia, restored to its full glory by the regular availability of Hughes, Lillee, Marsh and Wood, carried off the trophy for the seventh time in fourteen years in 1980–81 and came within a whisker of emulating Victoria's achievement of the previous season of winning the coveted double of the Sheffield Shield and the McDonald's Cup.

For Kim Hughes, captain of Western Australia, 1980–81 was an *annus mirabilis*. Elected to guide the destiny of his state, not without radical dissent from some of the senior members of his team, he performed an arduous task well. He had to fill the oversized shoes of that astute and experienced skipper, John Inverarity, who migrated to South Australia to assume the educational post of vice-principal of Pembroke College. The twenty-seven year old Hughes wrested the Shield from Victoria, its holder for two years, at his first attempt and, in so doing, was instrumental in earning for himself and his team mates a reputed $81,000 in sponsorship money. Nor was that the conclusion of the Hughes saga of success. There was, of course, his remarkable and record-breaking 213 in the Adelaide Test against India, a fortnight after the birth of twin sons to his wife Jenny. As if that were not enough to cause celebration in the Hughes household, there was the head of the house's third position in the season's Test averages; and to cap the year for a man, whose grooming for leadership was begun at an early age by his election to the position of head boy at school and president of the students' union at college, came his nomination as captain of the Australian touring team to England.

Western Australia's margin of victory in the Sheffield Shield was a mere three point supremacy over the season's early front runner, New South Wales. It was not an ascendancy great enough to permit the Perth side unbounded complacency about its season's performance; but it sufficed, and importantly the win was well deserved. The summer was not all a bed of roses for Hughes' men; their early season form away from their native heath was nothing short of disastrous. In the space of four games they went down to New South Wales by an innings and 61 runs, were defeated by Victoria by seven wickets and had the worst of a drawn game against Queensland. Injury further blighted their aspirations of success when it robbed them of the services of key opening batsman Bruce Laird, who ruptured an Achilles tendon in November and did not play again until his side's penultimate game against New South Wales in Perth. In spite of McCosker's team opening up a commanding points lead early in the competition, Western Australia showed admirable staying power and sprinted home to the winning post in a withering burst which saw it account for Tasmania by seven wickets, South Australia twice by six wickets and 88 runs, New South Wales by 115 runs and only fail to defeat Queensland by one wicket. It was a performance reminiscent of the pre-December 1978 days; a period which saw the western state play thirty-one games without defeat.

The final match of the season drew to a close on the W.A.C.A. ground in Perth with Border and Rackemann, Queensland's last men, defending desperately against the Western Australian bowlers and 177 runs still needed for victory. It was a bitter situation for Greg Chappell's men to savour, for it meant that after fifty-four years in the Sheffield Shield competition, its first

premiership still eluded the northern side. Only seven points separated Queensland from its crowning ambition; but they might have well as been 700.

One does not have to look far for the reasons for Western Australia's
triumph in 1980–81. The consistency of its success was founded upon the
evenness of the ability found in the eighteen players used by the Perth side
in its quest for the Shield. Such was the strength of its reserves that its selectors could afford to ignore the undoubted talents of Springbok, Ken McEwan,
and his 350 runs for the final two deciding games of the competition; other
occasions saw them embarrassed by a surfeit of international ability personi-
fied in the names of Serjeant, Clark, Porter and Mann. Such was the striking
power of Hughes' team that three of his bowlers, Lillee, Alderman and Yardley
figured in the top half dozen bowlers in the national averages and captured
a joint 104 wickets. In a season of impressive batting statistics, the Western
Australian batsmen were less prominent. The diminutive Shipperd led the van
with 607 runs at a mean figure of 40.47; even so, he could do no better than
earn himself the eleventh position in the national averages. The saving grace
about the Perth side's batting performances was undoubtedly its reliability;
when one man failed there was usually a competent substitute to step into
the breach and this self-complementary co-operation produced an evenness of
batting performances which no other state could match. Hughes and Wood
each surpassed the 500 run mark, whilst Marsh fell only eight runs short of
the 450 milestone. A revitalised Craig Serjeant donned glasses and immediately
found the touch which gained him an Australian cap in 1977; he, like McEwan,
scored more than 350 runs during the summer.

It was the bowlers Lillee and Yardley, however, who engineered the first
Western Australian victory of the season over Victoria, the Shield holders, in
Perth. Each captured five wickets in an innings in a game which saw the visitors'
early batting fail twice, reducing them to the early successive losing absurdities
of 7 for 99 and 5 for 80. Had it not been for some staunch resistance from
the bat of the Australian all-rounder of the approaching season, Shaun Graf,
Victoria's losing margin of seven wickets would have been much greater.

Western Australia's jubilation at its impressive beginning to the season
proved to be short-lived. In a match reduced to three days by rain in Sydney,
the full-strength Perth combination were crushed by an innings and 61 runs by the
New South Wales juggernaut. In the early days of the season McCosker's men
had an impressive air of invincibility about them. McCosker, himself, contributed largely to his team's triumph over Hughes' men with a massive 168.
He and Dyson opened the New South Wales account with a record stand of
319 against an attack which included Lillee, Alderman, Clark and Yardley.
Facing a total of 3 for 340 declared, the Western Australian batting capitulated
twice against the ferocity of Pascoe and Lawson and the guile of leg-spinner
Holland and were dismissed for unworthy totals of 176 and 103.

A first innings batting fragility again asserted itself when Western Australia
moved northwards to Brisbane for the Queensland clash; at one stage the
Perth side were 6 for 151, and only reached the respectability of 261 thanks
to a spirited 78 from Yardley, who figured large in a seventh wicket stand of
107. Greg Chappell thereupon capitalised on being missed six times to amass
a Shield best score of 194 and gave his team an advantage of 178 on the

first innings. Chappell's understudy for the Australian captaincy, Hughes, responded in kind, however, with a career highest score of 149, to enable his side to scramble to the safety of a draw.

There was no escape when the western team migrated south to Melbourne and found themselves totally unable to come to grips with the low-bouncing, sluggish M.C.G. pitch. The former Test paceman Callen made his comeback in this game, after being sidelined for twelve months with a serious back injury, and, in collaboration with Hampshire's medium-pacer, Graf, twice discomfitted Western Australian for 187 and 234. The Victorian batsmen, more accustomed to the vagaries of their home wicket, proved more durable than their opponents, compiling 401 for 8 declared. The left-handed Moss grafted his way to his seventh first class hundred and Graf notched his first, thus enabling their side to gain revenge for its initial defeat of the season by seven wickets.

The debacle against Victoria proved to be the final sad chapter in Western Australia's story of the season. Just before the Christmas festivities, Hughes' men dispatched South Australia, the team led by their former captain, John Inverarity, by 88 runs, with Wood contributing 126 in the first innings and Hughes 97 in the second, to the victory. After digesting their turkey and plum duff, the two teams met once more in the New Year and once again the westerners proved superior, this time by six wickets. The game was characterised by two mediocre batting performances from South Australia who could manage no more than successive totals of 171 and 243; it was also lifted from mediocrity by a brilliant 144 not out from the bat of Craig Serjeant, who rescued Western Australia from yet another incipient first innings collapse and the danger of being 4 for 58. Set 56 to win, Hughes' early batsmen again experienced another rude shock when South Australian paceman Prior sent Shipperd, O'Neill and Langer back to the pavilion in his first over to hoist the score of 15 for 4 on the scoreboard. Serjeant steadied the ship once again and was fittingly unbeaten on 23 when victory was won.

A match-winning bowling performance of 11 for 98 from off-spinner, Bruce Yardley, sealed Tasmania's fate in Devonport. Western Australia won with six and a half overs to spare and with seven wickets in hand: most of its opposition flowed from the bat of Rhodesian, Brian Davison, whose 114 in Tasmania's first innings was his fourth century of the season and contained an over against Dennis Lillee which yielded 14 runs including a six over the head of extra-cover.

Tempers were honed to a fine razor's edge when the potential Sheffield Shield champions, New South Wales, encountered the challengers, Western Australia, in late February in Perth. The match was virtually decided by the home side reaching 328 for 6 in a first day which saw 144 runs scored in the last two hours of play. A Western Australian aggregate of 647 met a New South Wales response of only 532 and the home side won by 115 runs, thereby gaining 21 points from the match. New South Wales' plight might have been much worse had it not been for a second innings seventh wicket partnership of 159 in 128 minutes between Dyson and wicket-keeper Rixon. Dyson scored 134 at his second attempt and was one of the two players reported to the A.C.B.'s disciplinary committee for kicking over his stumps when given out;

Marsh, too, was reported for abusing umpire Peter McConnell in this game and both players incurred token fines from their peers.

The grand finale of the Shield season took place in Perth in early March. An outright victory to Queensland would have given the Brisbane side its maiden premiership; but after Shipperd had scored his first century of the season and steered Western Australia to a first innings total of 305, the destination of the Shield was decided by one over from Dennis Lillee who snatched the wickets of Wessels and Chappell in the space of four deliveries. In the final analysis, Queensland required 409 runs for victory but, having lost the wickets of Wessels, Kent and Chappell for a handful of runs, it was hard pressed to salvage a face-saving, but Shield-losing, draw from the encounter.

Two remarkable riches-to-rags stories to emerge from the season were those of New South Wales and Victoria. From the outset, New South Wales was the pace-setter for the competition. Its initial annihilation of Western Australia, prefaced by a draw against Queensland, was succeeded by an innings and 97 runs win over South Australia: a match which saw Pascoe take 5 for 27 in South Australia's first innings, including the hat-trick. The return fixture in Sydney also went the way of New South Wales by the handsome margin of six wickets. Former New Zealand schoolboy representative Crowe notched 131 in South Australia's first innings total of 302; but this was more than matched by a vintage Walters' innings of 186 in 315 minutes in a first innings New South Wales tally of 349. South Australia's second innings disintegrated against Holland's accurate brand of leg-spinners, the last nine wickets falling for only 105 runs, and it was left to Dyson to steer his team home to victory with an unbeaten 85.

In Melbourne a stand of 221 for the fifth wicket between the effervescent Toohey and the twenty-one year old Dirk Wellham laid the foundations for a New South Wales first innings total of 347 for 9 declared. For the remainder of the game, Victoria were in the toils of the accurate off-spin of Beard, who, on a creeping wicket, was virtually impossible to score off; he sent down a thrifty 61 overs in the match and conceded only 47 runs in taking six wickets. The home side, dismissed at its first attempt for 188, was compelled to follow-on and, when the merciful umpires finally called time, was 111 for 5 in its second innings.

At this stage of the season, after five games, New South Wales had established a lead of 31 points over its nearest rival in the Shield table, Victoria. The only question remaining about the destination of the trophy seemed to be; who was to be runner-up? Then, inexplicably, just as the second last team, Western Australia, received the fillip of its first innings defeat of South Australia, New South Wales faltered. A fine innings of 160 from the bat of South African import, Wessels, gave Queensland a first innings advantage of 153 over the league leaders, and only centuries from Trevor Chappell and Dyson enabled New South Wales to escape with a draw from a game in which they looked far from potential champions.

The ship from Sydney really lost way, however, in the return fixture against Victoria. After Victoria declared its first innings at the expiration of the bonus points period of 100 overs with 300 for 9 on the board, McCosker declined to make a comparable closure, and batted on for a further two and a half hours, during which time his batsmen gained him a meagre and costly 98 runs. The New South Wales captain's excuse for his negative tactic was that the opposition would not have given his team an opportunity to get back into the game if he had closed. Ten points for the outright victory went begging as Victoria met negation with negation and batted out the rest of a game, which one of the Victorian players described as the worst in which he had ever played. His comment was occasioned by the many instances of verbal abuse of players which occurred in this game.

Briefly the New South Wales flame of hope flickered more brightly as wrist-spinners Holland and Hourn took all ten wickets to fall in Tasmania's second innings in Sydney to dismiss the Apple Isle batsmen for 133 and win by 160 runs; the flame was an *ignus fatuus*, however, for by its dying light even the most myopic statistician could see that in allowing themselves to be dismissed for 222 in the first innings, the New South Wales batsmen had thrown away the chance of scoring the vital batting bonus points which might have brought home both the bacon and the Shield.

So it was on to Perth, the final exercise in acrimony, the ultimate loss to Western Australia by 115 runs, and the crushing realisation on the part of the New South Wales players that they had squandered the fortune which they must have surely thought would be theirs half-way through the season.

Victoria's masochistic inclinations in 1980–81 were the equal of those of New South Wales. Even before the season began, the southern selectors embarked upon a policy of self-flagellation by dismissing Graham Yallop from the captaincy which he had held during Victoria's two previous Shield-winning seasons. Former W.S.C. wicket-keeper, Richie Robinson, was appointed in Yallop's place, but found the leadership an unrewarding task, as the voluntary blood-letting continued in Melbourne. The previous vice-captain of the successful Victorian combination, Dav Whatmore, was not only moved sideways out of the captaincy, to which he could confidently have expected to succeed after Yallop, he was also moved downwards and right out of the team. Wiener, the golden-haired opener of the Australian team of the previous year, after playing well in the McDonald Cup matches of the early season, also experienced a slump in form which carried him right out of the bottom of the team of which he had so recently been a key player.

To make matters worse, Test bowler, Alan Hurst, disheartened by the recurrence of a back injury, announced his retirement from first-class cricket and the once proud holders of the Sheffield Shield were no more than a shadow of their former selves by the time that the half-way point in the season was reached. By the end of the season there were only five Victorian survivors of the combination who, two years previously, had swept so confidently through the indian summer of February and March 1979 to victory in the Shield. Not surprisingly, the inconsistent Victorian performances reflected the instability in certain departments of the team. The southern state ended the season in fourth position in the premiership ladder, 34 points behind Western Australia. Indicative of the Victorian batting fragility was the fact that skipper, Robinson, was the leading batsman in the side with an average of 44.18; his eighth position in the national averages placed him two notches above his predecessor, Yallop, who was the only other Victorian to figure in the first fifteen places.

Ian Callen led the Melbourne side's bowling averages with 26 wickets at 24.67; he captured two wickets less than the redoubtable Max Walker, whose nip off the wicket seemed to have deserted him, with a consequent loss of penetration: a fact which was reflected by the reduction of his wicket tally by 15 from the previous season.

The exigencies of the wet southern spring usually demand that Victoria play its first two fixtures in the more clement climate and firmer wickets of Western Australia and Queensland. Lack of outdoor and match practice produced its perennial consequences for the Melbourne team: a defeat by seven wickets in Perth and a lucky draw in Brisbane where Greg Chappell reeled off his habitual three-figure score against Robinson's men. Wessels also contributed 134 to Queensland's first innings supremacy of 108 in a game which was restricted by weather to just one innings per side.

Returning to its native heath for the first time, Victoria fired on all cylinders against Western Australia and followed its initial seven wickets victory with another against South Australia in Adelaide, this time by an even more convincing nine wickets. The South Australian clash was a low scoring game, with the home team gleaning only 276 runs in two innings against the effective pace bowling of Callen and Walker. Skipper Robinson's 120 in Victoria's first innings of 223 proved the decisive innings of the game; but it has to be admitted that the wicket-keeper-batsman was fortunate. When he was two, he was caught at short leg off a Hogg bouncer, but was reprieved by umpire Wilson's call of no-ball against the bowler for intimidatory tactics under the new interpretation of Law 42. In spite of this setback, Hogg bowled in true Test match style to capture 6 for 75 in Victoria's only major innings.

Victoria's hopes of retaining the Shield for an unprecedented three consecutive seasons plummeted when, in spite of a solo Max Walker bowling performance of 6 for 120 in an innings, it gathered only two points from a dreary draw with New South Wales at the Melbourne Cricket Ground. In stark contrast with this dismal contest against their traditional rivals was the display put on by the Victorian batsmen against Tasmania in Hobart, where Yallop, Scholes and Bright each reached the century mark. Hundreds from the bats of Taswegians Davison and Boon, however, enabled the home team to answer Victoria's first innings total of 543 with an equally formidable 425; it was only because of the unexpected batting collapse of Tasmania in its second innings that the mainland side managed to edge its way to a six wicket victory in the dying moments of the game. In Sydney the war of attrition between Victoria and New South Wales resumed with the game in which McCosker's refusal to declare extinguished all hope of a result. In a team of disgruntled Victorians, only Yallop with a sound double of 52 and 70 had any cause for personal satisfaction.

In February the Victorian side became the homeless orphans of the storm centred around the poor conditions of the Melbourne Cricket Ground; summarily it was evicted from its traditional home and compelled to play its last two first class games in the provincial centre of Geelong, some fifty miles from Melbourne. The batting perfection of the Kardinia Park pitch was much to the liking of the visiting Queensland batsmen, who quickly ran up a first innings total of 330 for 4 declared with Chappell and Ritchie contributing a joint 144 in 159 minutes. The twenty-one year old Ritchie was particularly impressive in an upright, hard-driving innings of 140 not out. Not to be outdone Victoria riposted with 301 for 3, with the diminutive left-handed opener Gary Watts cutting the ball on to his stumps when he was one run short of his maiden century. Set 288 runs to win in their last knock, the home batsmen fell disappointingly 20 runs short of their target as the last wickets tumbled in a blinding dust storm.

Only 18 wickets fell in the drawn Victorian finale against South Australia at an average cost of 61 runs. The tall, elegant and bespectacled left-handed opener, Phillips, fulfilled the promise which had earlier gained him a place in the Australian Under 19 side by achieving the convincing double of 111 and 91 in South Australia's totals of 312 for 6 declared and 309 for 5 declared.

It was a 'molly dukers'' game; Hookes notched 73 not out in his side's second innings and, for Victoria, former Test opener, Hibbert scored 153 not out and Yallop 122 and 66 in the host team's totals of 328 for 2 declared and 164 for 5. The sad 1980–81 season ended on a frustrating and drably symbolic note for the former Shield holders; with a Victorian win still a remote possibility, rain prevented all but 32 minutes play before lunch on the final day.

Queensland have probably never had a better chance of winning its maiden Sheffield Shield than its golden but wasted opportunity of 1980–81. The Sunshine State was capably led by the Australian captain, Greg Chappell, whose batting average of 113.25 not only placed him head and shoulders above any other player in the country but was also representative of the immense power embodied in the Queensland batting machine. No fewer than four Queenslanders finished the season in the top six positions in the national averages. Lured from the south of the New South Wales state line by offers of an attractive business career Allan Border quickly made himself at home on the Woolloongabba wickets and aggregated 459 runs at 51 per innings. One place higher than the former New South Welshman in the pecking order of achievement was the former South African, Wessels, who totted up 718 runs at 51.29. Just above the new Australian citizen was Kent, the only native in the quartet, with 834 runs to his name at a mean figure of 69.5. The significant statistic in the Queensland averages however, was that, whilst its batsmen figured prominently in the ranks of the country's leading exponents of the art, only Jeff Thomson made his presence felt amongst the leading dozen bowlers in the Shield competition. The truism that bowlers win matches and premierships was completely vindicated by the Queensland performance in 1980–81; for in spite of the fact that the northern state scored more batting bonus points than any of its rivals and went through the season unbeaten, its lack of consistent bowling penetration and rain interruptions to three of its home games, prevented it forcing an issue in six of its nine matches.

Chappell's men all but lost their first home game against a rampant New South Wales, who accumulated an impressive 304 for 5 declared, thanks to an 88 from Dyson and 91 not out from Davis. Queensland's southern neighbours had previously dismissed their opponents for 189 in a first innings which owed most of its substance to a 94 from Greg Chappell. Chappell carried on in the second innings where he had left off in the first and reached 113; together with Border, who recorded 106, the Queensland skipper helped to stave off a defeat which at one stage seemed a foregone conclusion. As Queensland began, so it continued; four more draws ensued and it was twelve days into the New Year before the northerners registered their first win.

Most of Queensland's inconclusive games were drawn in its favour. Such was certainly the case in the match against the visiting Victorians who only scored 250 for 7 in reply to their opponents 358 for 5 in the only two innings possible. Thanks to the butter-fingered propensities of the Western Australian fieldmen, the home side also scored heavily when Hughes' men played in Brisbane. Wessels added 76 and Hohns 74 to yet another Chappell hundred and helped hoist 439 Queensland first innings runs on the 'Gabba scoreboard. Western Australia however, refused to emulate its weak first batting attempt and also scored more than 400 in its second innings to save its face. Favoured by the home draw for the third time in the season, a Chappell-less Queensland were still unable to defeat the lowly South Australia, in spite of a 5 for 61 performance from Jeff Thomson and half-centuries from Wessels, Ritchie, Hohns and Phillips in the only Queensland innings of 393 for 9. Rain deprived Queensland of 190 minutes play on the third day and this curtailment, together with a recurrence of fast bowler Rackemann's shoulder injury, allowed South Australia to survive, in spite of moderate totals of 283 and 160 for 4. Ten points from this game would surely have earned Queensland the Shield.

The return game against New South Wales in Sydney saw the bat dominate the ball for most of the game, Queensland replying to New South Wales' innings of 269 and 320 with 422 and 1 for 36. Two crucial knocks played in this game were those of Graeme Beard, the home team's all-rounder, whose scores of 50 and 58 prevented Queensland pressing on to victory, just when it appeared to have the game in its grasp. Importantly, for the first time in the season, Queensland made New South Wales look less than invincible.

Heartened by its performance against the team which many critics were already hailing as the champions, Queensland steamrollered its way to victory by nine wickets when Tasmania visited Brisbane. Kent enjoyed a magnificent match, thrashing a personal best of 171 in the habitual 400 plus Queensland first innings and following this score with 68 not out in a total of 101 for 1, reached in a mere 78 minutes in the second innings sprint for the finishing line. The most effective home state bowler was Denis Lillee, who captured 5 for 48 in Tasmania's second innings of 347. It was not *the* Dennis Lillee, but a contrasting slow leg-spinner who was in his thirty-fifth year, and who had made previous appearances for his state.

Kent's purple patch continued when Queensland journeyed to Adelaide where it defeated South Australia by 56 runs. The tall right-hander with the bent-kneed stance scored 78 and 101 not out in his side's totals of 366 for 8 declared and 230 for 1 declared. Chappell dominated Queensland's first knock with an innings of 172, which many observers believed should have ended when he was one and dropped by Hookes, or alternatively, when he was 29 and ostensibly caught off his glove by keeper Wright. When his side batted again it was all Kent, and he and Border added 176 in 140 minutes in an unfinished second wicket stand. The Queensland triumph was not as comfortable as its batting supremacy suggested; set 361 runs to win in 418 minutes South Australia paced its innings admirably and when the last wicket fell, it was only 57 runs short of its target with 58 balls remaining to be bowled. Had not opening batsman Darling been compelled to retire hurt after being struck by a Thomson bouncer, the Adelaide team might have reached its goal.

The margin of Queensland's win at Geelong against Victoria was even more slender than that against South Australia: a mere 19 runs. It was deserved, however, if only for the classical innings of Greg Ritchie. Nonetheless Chappell must have experienced many moments of anxiety as Robinson and Graf added 82 in 85 minutes of Victoria's second innings and brought their team to within 50 runs of their target score of 288.

After being borne to heights of great expectation by three successive victories, Queensland was dashed to the depths of disappointment by its final flop in Perth. To my eyes the match proved the folly of misguided over-reliance on one player; for there was no doubt that Queensland's lowly first innings total of 186 was directly attributable to the psychological advantage established by the West Australian bowlers over their Queensland batting opponents, when Lillee dismissed both Wessels and Chappell in four balls when the visitors' total was eight. The visible weariness of Chappell at the end of an onerous international and domestic programme was immense; and the thought of having to go out to the middle yet again to score a Sheffield-Shield-winning hundred must have been crushing and overwhelming. Not surprisingly, Chappell could not toe the mark for this last challenge and his team only just salvaged a draw from the clash by a finger-nail grip on its last wicket. Chappell, in mitigation of the final outcome of the Shield competition, could always point with justification, to the ill-luck experienced by Queensland in its home games at the hands of the weather.

South Australia sadly missed the inspirational leadership and dynamic batting of Ian Chappell in 1980–81 and slumped from being the previous season's runner-up in the championship to the 'Tail-End Charlie' position. Even Tasmania, the only side whom the Adelaide side defeated all summer, finished above it in the table. Inverarity took over the reins from the retired Ian Chappell, but found the team under his command a vastly different proposition to the one he had led from success to success in Perth. The unreliability of the South Australian batting resulted in only 28 batting bonus points from nine games – the least number of incentive points gained by any team in the competition. Only Sleep and Darling earned a mention in the first 20 places in the national averages. Hookes in particular was a grave disappointment.

In the bowling department, it was a slightly different story; for here Hogg performed with all of the sterling qualities expected of a Test bowler and finished the season third in the averages with 24 wickets at a cost of 23.54. Prior, too, bowled well to gain tenth spot in the averages with 21 wickets and the spinners, Sleep and Mallett, were not disgraced with returns of 17 and 23 wickets respectively.

The first game of the season augured well for the fortunes of Inverarity's side. Tasmania were dispatched by six wickets, with Sleep and Causby scoring centuries in South Australia's major innings of 465 for 9 declared. That result must have fostered false confidence in South Australian breasts, for the next game produced a batting debacle against New South Wales. Before the eyes of their own mortified spectators, the South Australian batsmen were twice dismissed for 89 and 152 to go down to defeat by an innings. Nor was the return match a much better experience for supporters of the southern side; the only consolations they could draw from their six wicket loss were that the margin of defeat was less, that Crowe scored an aggregate of 198 in the game and the left-handed paceman Attenborough captured 5 for 94 in New South Wales' first innings.

The pattern of batting fragility continued against Victoria in Adelaide. Totals of 114 and 162 were insufficient to avoid a nine wickets loss. It must have made Hogg extremely frustrated to witness the tame capitulation of his team's batting after he had bowled magnificently to take 6 for 75 and restrict the Victorian first innings total to 223. Rain in Brisbane gave South Australia a draw and relief from the gloomy monotony of defeat; but the respite was only temporary and two defeats against Western Australia followed in quick succession. The first loss by 88 runs reflected a good bowling performance against the eventual Shield champions; Wright, however, unearthed very little support for his maiden first-class century in South Australia's first innings and Inverarity and Darling failed to expand their half-centuries in the second into match-winning scores. In Adelaide, Hookes, who had been regularly used throughout the summer as a medium-paced left-handed bowler, eventually succeeded with the bat; but neither his 67 nor Darling's undefeated 65 could prevent a Western Australian victory by six wickets.

In mid-January South Australia surprised the pundits by coming within 57 runs of vanquishing the much fancied Queensland combination. The result was perhaps misleading, since Chappell's team declared twice and did not use 11 of its available wickets in the match; nonetheless the game provided an encouraging improvement in South Australian batting form with Sleep scoring 122 and Hookes 53 in totals of 236 and 304.

The South Australian selectors placed their trust in youth for the final game of the season against Victoria. Their young openers, Ian McLean and Wayne Phillips did not betray that trust, adding 112 for the first wicket in the first innings and 187 in the second. Phillips notched over 200 runs for the game. McLean had the satisfaction of aggregating 112, but also experienced the disappointment of falling just 11 runs short of a century in his first game for his state. The youngsters' form in the drawn game at Geelong was perhaps one of the brightest aspects of an otherwise dismal South Australian season.

Tasmania, the Cinderella state of the Sheffield Shield, usually embark upon each year in the competition more in hope than expectation. In 1980–81, however, its first-class campaign was endowed with more fixity of purpose. As in the previous season, the island side called in overseas professional stiffening in the person of Rhodesian Brian Davison and, in the absence of its previous fast bowling star, Richard Hadlee, seconded to the touring New Zealand team, recruited the pace duet of Rod McCurdy and Brian Clough and opening batsman David Robinson from the mainland states of Victoria and New South Wales. On the deficit side, opening bat Goodman departed for South Australian pastures.

Tasmania failed to record a single victory in its Shield matches; nor did it enjoy its previous successes in the one-day arena. Its team, however, was far from disgraced and not only finished one place above South Australia in the premiership table, but also recorded outstanding collective and individual performances against its more senior brethren in the two competitions. Its imported captain Davison had an outstanding season with the bat, scoring four centuries, aggregating 699 runs at an average of 69.9 and coming third in the Australian averages. Not far behind his skipper in the batting rankings was the locally produced nineteen-year-old David Boon who averaged 42.80, scored a century against Victoria, finished ninth in the averages and must have been desperately unlucky to have missed a place in the Australian touring party to England.

In its limited season of five games, Tasmania put together some impressive first innings scores against the mainland teams, but appeared to lack the mental and physical stamina to bat well twice in succession. Its 395 total against the South Australian bowling of Hogg, Prior and Mallett in Adelaide accrued from a fine innings of 126 from Davison and a sound supportive knock of 90 from Woolley; together they added a record 213 runs for their side's sixth wicket. Davison featured in another large stand with Boon against Victoria; the pair scored 174 in 160 minutes for the fourth wicket on a flawless Hobart pitch which produced 1273 runs in four days – 636 of those runs coming from Tasmanian bats. Davison's 173 was his highest tally of the season and was compiled against an attack containing four international bowlers.

He followed this three figure score with equally impressive innings of 118 and 114 against Queensland and Western Australian bowlers of the calibre of Thomson, Dymock, Lillee, Malone, Alderman and Yardley. The Rhodesian missed the grand slam of a hundred in each of Tasmania's five Shield games by only 18 runs; he scored 82 in Sydney in a first innings total of 226 which gave the small island state gain a lead of four runs over the strong New South Wales side. No doubt Davison derived some vicarious pleasure from the fact that, whilst he had been denied his fifth hundred, his bowlers gained his revenge by restricting the New South Wales batting bonus points to two and thus effectively ending the Sydney team's designs on the Shield.

In the late 1970s Tasmania's two professional English Jacks, Simmons and Hampshire, established for the Apple Isle the reputation of being a giant killer in the one-day competition of the time, the Gillette Cup. The zenith of its limited-over accomplishment was marked by the winning of the trophy in 1979. No similar success has since attended the efforts of the Taswegians in the McDonalds' Cup: the replacement for the razor blade sponsor's competition. Tasmania's performances in the 1980–81 knock-out contest was barren of victory, with Western and South Australia both defeating Davison's men in the preliminary rounds in Hobart. The Perth team won by 59 runs with Tasmania failing to utilise 13 of its alloted 50 overs. Serjeant's 65 and Mann's unbeaten 59 were the backbone of the visitors' first innings total of 203 for 9; for their part, the Tasmanian batsmen showed very little backbone being at one stage 55 for 6. The captain of the Tasmanian colts team, Faulker, then added 84 for the seventh wicket in conjunction with wicket-keeper Allen; but the illusion of a possible victory disappeared when the last four wickets realised a mere five runs.

South Australia's win by 37 runs with two overs of Tasmania's batting allowance remaining, was based on a third wicket partnership of 96 between Hookes and Sleep, after their side had lost its first two wickets for six runs. Tasmania never looked likely to match South Australia's total of 218 for 8 and at one stage were 76 for 7 before managing 181, thanks to a lusty 42 from fast bowler, McCurdy.

South Australia and Western Australia's opponents in the semi-finals of the competition eventuated as Victoria and Queensland. The second half of the draw proved to be an evenly balanced affair with New South Wales, Queensland and Victoria each winning one game and the semi-finalists being decided by the run-rate and a gross miscalculation on the part of McCosker, the New South Wales skipper.

In the first Cup match of the season, on a sluggish Melbourne pitch, Victoria defeated Queensland by 51 runs with the eventual Man-of-the-Match, Wiener, scoring 73 and Walker taking 4 for 37, in a game reduced to 20 overs by the fickle southern weather. On the following day, New South Wales evened matters up by accounting for Robinson's men with 28 balls to spare. Dyson and Toohey each contributed unbeaten 55s in the visitors' total of 139 for 2.

It was back to square one when New South Wales were in turn beaten by Queensland in Sydney with Kent and Chappell adding 98 for the northerners' second wicket and steering their side to 215 for 5 and victory with 29 balls in hand. New South Wales could have qualified for the semi-finals had its batsmen made an effort to lift its scoring rate above that of its nearest rival Victoria; but because of an extremely unfunny comedy of errors, Dyson and Chappell dawdled at the batting crease and forfeited the right of their team to a place in the semi-finals.

The penultimate act in the McDonalds' Cup drama unfolded on the weekend of 14 and 15 February. Western Australia demolished Victoria in Perth by 27 runs in a game which saw the eastern state's batsmen fail yet again to be all out for 187, after having been 13 for 5 when Dennis Lillee finished his first spell. On a day of broiling Adelaide heat, Queensland defeated the host state with two deliveries of an exciting match remaining. The trauma of losing Wessels and Chappell in the same Prior over did not disconcert Border, whose 97 decided the match.

After the excitement of the Adelaide encounter, the final, played in Brisbane, proved an anticlimax, although the record partisan crowd of 20,237 were more than delighted with the ease of their local team's 72 runs triumph. Queensland began with panache, Kent and Wessels adding 68 in handsome style for the first wicket. It was only desperate Western Australian fielding which prevented Queensland translating a 110 for 1 total into a score much larger than the eventual 188 for 9. A required scoring rate of just over $3\frac{1}{2}$ runs per over should have been well within the batting capabilities of Wood, Hughes, McEwan, Serjeant, Marsh, O'Neill and Yardley – if they were permitted to get into their stride. They were not allowed, however, to settle down to their task; three disturbingly fast overs from Thomson, a dubious lbw decision against O'Neill and a suicidal Hughes run-out completely disconcerted and demoralised a West

Australian team who capitulated for 116. Queensland, frustrated in its bid for the Sheffield Shield by its opponents, had achieved a modicum of revenge.

The enormity of the crowd which witnessed the McDonalds' Cup final was symptomatic of the trends which characterised Australian cricket in the summer of 1980–81. There is no doubt that one-day matches, in both the international and state arenas, increased tremendously in popularity. Perhaps it was the fact that there were so many games which were close encounters of the most attractive kind which drew the customers in such large numbers through the gates; but draw them they did.

It is debatable whether the new breed of spectators were the *cognoscenti* of the game; it is more probable that they were sensation seekers lured through the turnstiles by the promise of cricket action, 'aggro' on the field and a result at the end of six hours play. One sensed as the season progressed that a dichotomy was occurring within cricket, partitioning the game into an entertainment, television-oriented, quick-moving, spectacle and a more traditional, thoughtful, deliberate contest between long-time rivals. Each product appeared to have its own supporters. Neither, it seems, can survive without either the financial or staffing support of the other. In this fact there is great consolation. For it appears to me that, if one-day cricket continues to be able to subsidise the nurseries of the game, there is little need for the administrators to worry about the continuing welfare of Sheffield Shield cricket. My only concern would be for qualitative control over the limited-over format of the game to ensure a continuance of the true skills of cricket.

New South Wales First-Class Matches – Batting 1980–81

	v. Queensland (Brisbane) 17–20 October		v. Western Australia (Sydney) 23–26 October		v. South Australia (Adelaide) 30 October–2 November		v. South Australia (Sydney) 13–16 November		v. Victoria (Melbourne) 11–14 December		v. Queensland (Sydney) 20–23 December	
R. B. McCosker	18	18*	168	—	13	—	2	26	26	—	0	4
J. Dyson	88	18*	152	—	62	—	25	85*			25	100
S. J. Rixon	13	—	—	—	7	—	10	—	4	—	13	
T. M. Chappell	39	—	2*	—	50	—	19	16	7	—	111	2
I. C. Davis	91*	—	3	—	64	—	0	4	36	—	34	
P. M. Toohey	27	—	8*	—	50	—	23	9	145	—	6	1
K. D. Walters	8*	—	—	—	54	—	186	15*			1	4
G. R. Beard	—	—	—	—	16	—	51	—	3	—	50	5
G. F. Lawson	—	—	—	—	9	—	8	—	4*	—	5	
M. R. Whitney	—	—										
L. S. Pascoe	—	—	—	—	3*	—	14	—			10	
R. G. Holland			—	—	0	—	2*	—	2*	—	3*	
D. Welham									100	—		
S. Small												
A. M. Hilditch									4	—		
R. P. Done									1	—		
D. W. Hourn												
Byes	1				3		6		6			
Leg byes	5		5		6		3		1		4	
Wides	3	1							3		3	
No balls	11		2		1			5	5		4	
Total	304	37	340		338		349	160	347		269	32
Wickets	5	0	3		10		10	4	9		10	1
Result	D		W		W		W		D		D	
Points	11		22		20		19		9		6	

Catches
39 – S. J. Rixon (ct 35, st 4)
10 – R. B. McCosker
 7 – P. M. Toohey, and T. M. Chappell
 6 – M. R. Whitney, J. Dyson and K. D. Walters
 5 – I. C. Davis and D. M. Welham
 4 – G. F. Lawson
 3 – G. R. Beard and L. S. Pascoe
 2 – S. Small

v. Victoria (Sydney) 17–19 January		v. New Zealanders (Sydney) 24–26 January		v. Western Australia (Perth) 27 Feb–2 March		v. Tasmania (Sydney) 6–8 March		Inns	NOs	Runs	HS	Av
33	—	109	15*	3	0	88	6	16	2	571	168	40.78
95	—			25	134			11	2	815	152	90.55
63*	—		4	24	66	18	92	12	1	315	92	28.63
89	—	100	14	71	1	59	0	15	1	550	111	39.28
		8*	8			11	7	12	2	267	91*	26.70
21	—		15	36	0			12	1	357	145	32.45
8	—			0	13	4	55	11	—	384	186	34.90
66	—		2	44	4	1	0*	11	1	285	58	28.50
1	—		1	4*	21*	8	—	10	3	66	21*	9.42
3	—				2	1	—	2	—	4	3	2.00
0	—				2			6	2	30	14	7.50
			5*		4	0*	—	8	5	22	6	7.33
66	—	6*	38	35	14	21	128*	8	2	408	128*	68.00
			24					1	—	24	24	24.00
								1	—	4	4	4.00
								1	—	1	1	1.00
						0	—	1	—	0	0	—

v. Victoria		v. New Zealanders		v. Western Australia		v. Tasmania	
2						2	6
9		4	3		5	3	3
				(20)	6	1	
2		1	1			5	
8		228	130	262	270	222	297
0		2	8	8	10	10	5
D		D		L		W	
11		—		7		17	

New South Wales
First-Class Matches – Bowling, 1980–81

	L. S. Pascoe	G. F. Lawson	M. R. Whitney	G. R. Beard	T. M. Chappell	R. B. McCosker
v. Queensland (Brisbane) 17–20 October	15.5-6-38-4 / 17-3-55-2	15-1-41-0 / 20.3-3-76-3	15-2-52-2 / 13-3-39-1	9-3-28-1 / 23-7-61-3	12-5-22-3 / 8-1-37-0	3-1-13-0
v. Western Australia (Sydney) 23–26 October	19-5-47-4 / 14-6-15-3	19.2-9-34-4 / 10.5-2-31-1		15-7-27-0		
v. South Australia (Adelaide) 30 Oct–2 Nov	11.5-3-27-5 / 13-2-40-2	12-2-34-3 / 14-4-35-2		23.1-12-20-2		
v. South Australia (Sydney) 13–16 November	24.1-4-62-4 / 17-7-39-4	21-3-61-4 / 15-2-41-0		35-14-82-1 / 17-10-23-1	10-4-21-1 / 5-2-10-0	
v. Victoria (Melbourne) 11–14 December		30.4-11-50-5 / 11-2-28-0		53-37-34-4 / 8-3-13-2	3-1-9-0 / 1-0-1-0	
v. Queensland (Sydney) 20–23 December	32-8-106-0 / 9-1-27-1	25.4-8-79-3 / 4-3-4-0		40-14-66-2	12-4-40-1 / 2-2-0-0	
v. Victoria (Sydney) 17–19 January	20.2-2-62-4 / 17-3-43-2	20-4-69-0 / 16-5-42-2	22-5-62-4 / 17-6-44-0	31-9-85-1 / 35-18-53-0	10-3-14-2	4-0-18-0
v. New Zealanders (Sydney) 24–26 January		11-6-11-2 / 13-3-26-1	13-1-48-1 / 6-0-26-0	27.1-11-58-5 / 21.4-8-37-5	3-1-3-0	
v. Western Australia (Perth) 27 Feb–2 Mar	19.4-4-65-0 / 13-4-33-0	25-5-81-2 / 28-5-77-3		25-7-79-1 / 15-3-61-1	5-2-21-0	
v. Tasmania (Sydney) 6–8 March		22-6-41-3 / 10-2-21-0	19-5-50-3 / 6-0-26-0	7-4-5-0	6-2-8-1	
	242.5-58-659-35 av. 18.82	344-86-882-38 av. 23.20	111-22-347-11 av. 31.54	385-167-732-29 av. 25.24	79-27-196-8 av. 24.50	7-0-31-0 –

K. D. Walters	R. G. Holland	R. P. Done	I. C. Davis	D. M. Welham	D. W. Hourn	B	Lb	W	Nb	Total	Wkts
							2		6	189	10
						1	3		10	295	10
2–5–0	17–2–49–1					3	8		3	176	10
4–25–1	14–7–30–4								2	103	10
4–1–0	12–3–23–2						3		1	89	10
	28–9–50–4								7	152	10
0–12–0	13–5–48–0						8	1	7	302	10
	28.4–5–82–5					3	4		4	206	10
	29–11–54–1	16–2–29–0				4	5	2	1	188	10
	17–3–40–2	5–1–20–1	1–0–7–0				1		1	111	5
0–16–0	33–7–110–0						3	2		422	6
2–1–0	3–2–4–0					1				36	1
3–13–1				1–1–0–0		2	8		1	300	9
							8	1	9	245	7
	14–2–79–1					2	1	1	2	202	10
2–15–1	33–11–73–2						1			166	10
2–9–0	22–4–78–1						3	4	3	328	6
	24–3–101–2					1	9	2	5	319	7
0–2–0	31–8–70–1				14.2–3–44–2		(11)			226	10
1–3–0	21–5–40–4				14.2–4–33–6		2		3	133	10
5–20–	339.4–87–	21–33–	1–0–	1–1–	28.4–7–						
02–3	931–30	49–1	7–0	0–0	77–8						
v. 34.00	av. 31.03	av. 49.00	–	–	av. 9.62						

Queensland First-Class Matches – Batting 1980–81

	v. New South Wales (Brisbane) 17–20 October		v. Victoria (Brisbane) 24–27 October		v. Western Australia (Brisbane) 31 October–3 November		v. New Zealanders (Brisbane) 14–17 November		v. South Australia (Brisbane) 12–15 December		v. New South Wales (Sydney) 20–23 December	
K. C. Wessels	38	28	134	—	76	39*	32	64	76	—	160	—
M. F. Kent	5	22	77	—	16	36*	37	20	26	—	48	29*
W. G. Morgan							2	29	33	—		
R. B. Phillips	0	0	—	—	11	—	14	5*	51	—	55*	—
A. R. Border	13	106	0	—	25	—	69	88*			34	—
G. M. Ritchie			7	—	1	—	0	47	74	—	12	4*
T. V. Hohns	13	0	27*	—	74	—	0	14	63	—	22	—
G. S. Chappell	94	113	102*	—	194	—	0	48			86*	—
G. Dymock	6*	0	—	—	1	—	11	—	27*	—	—	—
J. R. Thomson	0	0	—	—	17*	—	34	—	16	—	—	—
W. R. Broad	4	4										
P. H. Carlson	6	8*							0	—	0	2
C. G. Rackemann	2	0			1	—			4*	—		
A. D. Parker			2	—								
I. D. C. Kelly					3	—						
D. Rathie												
D. J. Lillee									2	—		
M. S. Mainhardt							1*	—				
Byes		1	1		4	4			16			1
Leg byes	2	3	4		13	2	3	4	5		3	
Wides				1	1						2	
No balls	6	10		3	2	1						
Total	189	295	358		439	82	203	323	393		422	36
Wickets	10	10	5		10	10	10	6	9		6	1
Result	D		D		D		D		D		D	
Points	4		10		11		—		10		10	

Catches

35 – R. B. Phillips (ct 30, st 5)
16 – M. F. Kent
14 – G. S. Chappell
 9 – T. V. Hohns
 8 – A. R. Border and K. C. Wessels
 7 – G. M. Ritchie
 4 – C. G. Rackemann
 3 – J. R. Thomson and D. J. Lillee (one as sub)
 1 – G. Dymock, W. R. Broad, D. Rathie and W. G. Morgan

v. Indians (Brisbane) 26–29 December		v. Tasmania (Brisbane) 9–12 January		v. South Australia (Adelaide) 17–19 January		v. Victoria (Geelong) 26 February–1 March		v. Western Australia (Perth) 7–10 March		Inns	NOs	Runs	HS	Av
		0	28	3	39	30	27	2	38	17	1	814	160	50.87
9	41	171	68*	78	101*	25	52	67	13	20	4	941	171	58.81
48	23*	61								6	1	196	61	39.20
4	—	52*		28	—	—	11	12	24	13	3	267	55*	26.70
				0	85*	17	86	10	83*	13	3	616	106	61.60
75	—	32	4*	0	—	140*	11	23	2	15	3	432	140*	36.00
6	3*	16	—	49*	—	24*	3	1	0	16	4	315	74	26.25
				172	—	83	27	0	35	12	2	954	172	95.40
31*	—	0	—	1	—	—	2	7	0	11	3	86	31*	10.75
0	—	31	—	15	—	—	9	4	0	11	1	126	34	12.60
61	—	75	—					46	25	6	—	215	75	35.83
										5	1	16	8*	4.00
0	—	—	—	—	—	—	3*	1*	0*	8	4	11	4*	2.75
										1	—	2	2	2.00
										1	—	3	3	3.00
9	17									2	—	26	17	13.00
1*	—	1*	—	8*	—	—	5			5	3	17	8*	8.50
										1	1	1	1*	—
4		9		3		1	8		5					
9	1	8	1	2	4	5	9	10	7					
		1					2							
2		1		7	1	5	3	3						
259	85	458	101	366	230	330	258	186	232					
9	2	8	1	8	1	4	10	10	9					
D		W		W		W		D						
—		26		23		19		5						

Queensland First-Class Matches – Bowling 1980–81

	J. R. Thomson	G. Dymock	G. S. Chappell	T. V. Hohns	A. R. Border	C. G. Rackemann
v. New South Wales	17–2–44–0	21–4–62–0	1–0–9–0	25–3–93–1	8–1–24–1	23–11–43–
(Brisbane) 17–20 October	5–0–20–0	1–0–3–0				4–0–13–0
v. Victoria	20–5–46–3	32–7–85–0		18.3–10–29–3	3–1–16–0	26–11–63–
(Brisbane) 24–27 October						
v. Western Australia	20–5–75–3	22–6–52–2	7–1–24–1	6–1–24–3		15–2–42–
(Brisbane) 31 Oct–3 Nov	26.1–4–91–2	27–7–57–2	10–1–43–1	38–7–123–1	15–4–36–0	14–9–9–3
v. New Zealanders	20–2–71–3	20–6–40–2	18.5–7–28–4	38–7–131–4	6–0–40–0	
(Brisbane) 14–17 November	18–6–62–1	33.3–4–109–2	4–0–20–0			
v. South Australia	22.3–6–61–5	26–8–50–2		10–1–31–0		11–1–34–
(Brisbane) 12–15 December	10–2–21–1	5–1–7–0		26–9–46–2		14.2–9–10
v. New South Wales	19–4–42–4	15–9–13–0	5–1–13–0	27.5–3–78–4	4–2–7–0	20–2–78–
(Sydney) 20–23 December	21–4–45–2	17–11–23–1	26–3–85–2	23.3–9–50–1	25–8–61–4	8–2–26–0
v. Indians	13.2–2–44–3	28–8–101–5		8–2–23–0		15–1–71–
(Brisbane) 26–29 December	18–3–58–3	17.2–3–56–2		12–3–49–0		27–4–109–
v. Tasmania	16–4–43–3	31–10–61–4		6–3–5–0		22–4–59–
(Brisbane) 9–12 January	22–2–76–2	20–6–69–0		32–6–77–3		16–4–53–
v. South Australia	19–5–58–1	19.3–4–59–5	2–1–2–0	6–1–12–0		18–5–48–
(Adelaide) 17–19 January	19–6–48–3	11.2–0–41–1	15.4–4–46–0	14–4–32–0	12–4–26–0	14–1–31–
v. Victoria (Geelong)	12–1–35–0	19–3–40–0	20–5–41–1	32–10–81–1		16–3–51–
26 Feb–1 Mar	16–2–52–1	31–9–59–3	22–6–39–3	21–3–54–2		9–1–29–0
v. Western Australia	25–3–94–2	18–12–44–1	19.3–4–66–4	9–3–32–0		9–3–31–0
(Perth) 7–10 March	19.1–5–63–4	33–9–78–1	16–7–35–1	21–7–33–2		32–13–63–
	378.1–73–	447.4–127–	185.3–50–	355.2–82–	73–20–	313.2–86–
	1149–46	1109–33	480–20	974–24	210–5	863–21
	av. 24.97	av. 33.60	av. 24.00	av. 40.58	av. 42.00	av. 41.09

† W. M. Darling retired hurt.

P. H. Carlson	W. R. Broad	I. D. C. Kelly	D. J. Lillee	M. S. Mainhardt	B	Lb	W	Nb	Total	Wkts
4-2-8-0	1-0-1-0				1	5	3	11	304	5
						1			37	0
						6		5	250	7
		12-5-27-0			5	4		8	261	10
		5-1-26-0			17	7	5	6	420	10
				11-4-40-1		7	1	6	193	10
				17-3-76-0		3		20	461	8
16-4-29-2			17-3-50-1		4	7	1	16	283	10
12-6-9-0			17-2-47-1		5	2		13	160	4
8-2-27-1						4	3	4	269	10
7-0-13-0					6	5	2	4	320	10
	1-0-18-0		15-2-38-1			3	1	9	308	10
	1-1-0-0		16-4-58-0		1	5		8	344	8
	2-0-11-0		5-0-14-0			2	1	15	211	10
			19.4-4-48-5		9	8	2	5	347	10
			11-5-36-2		4	5	4	8	236	10
			19-6-68-2		1	1		10	304	9†
			6-0-29-0		9	8	2	5	301	3
			4-0-11-0		3	15		6	268	10
	5-2-17-0					9	1	11	305	8
						9	2	6	289	10
47-14- 36-3 av. 28.66	10-3- 47-0 –	17-5- 53-0 –	129.4-26- 399-12 av. 33.25							

South Australia First-Class Matches – Batting 1980–81

	v. Tasmania (Adelaide) 23–26 October		v. New South Wales (Adelaide) 30 October–2 November		v. New South Wales (Sydney) 13–16 November		v. Indians (Adelaide) 29 November–2 December		v. Victoria (Adelaide) 4–6 December		v. Queensland (Brisbane) 12–15 December	
J. J. Crowe	82	24	16	0	131	67	32	50	32	7	17	9
G. W. Goodman							27	2	3	43	10	15
D. W. Hookes	21	6	17	0	35	17	4	0				
R. J. Zadow					45	6	61	4	0	10	41	7*
W. M. Darling	81	0*	6	46	16	27	26	61	19	15	21	40
D. C. Lovell							1	74	7	14		
P. R. Sleep	102*	4*	3	7	16	25	90*	13	0	16	71	17*
K. J. Wright	42	—	14*	22	29	16*	14	13	18	3	8	—
G. R. Attenborough	0	—	0	5*	0*	5	17	42	14	10	21	—
R. M. Hogg	1	—	0	3	5	0	15	0*	0	14		
R. M. McLellan							2	0				
J. E. Nash	5	10										
B. L. Causby	102	17	10	23	9	0						
A. A. Mallett	8	—	0	1	0	6			0*	0	6	—
W. Prior	11*	—							0	14*	1*	—
R. J. Inverarity			10	5	0	26					41	52
J. R. Hammond			9	33								
R. G. Vincent											18	—
D. J. Rolfe												
R. McLean												
W. B. Phillips												
Byes		6				3		4	1	1	4	5
Leg byes	5	1	3		8	4	10	11	5	4	7	2
Wides					1		3				1	
No balls	5		1	7	7	4		1	15	11	16	13
Total	465	68	89	152	302	206	302	275	114	162	283	160
Wickets	9	4	10	10	10	10	10	10	10	10	10	4
Result	W		L		L		W		L		D	
Points	20		2		8		—		5		9	

† W. M. Darling, retired hurt

Catches
27 – K. J. Wright (ct 22, st 5)
9 – J. J. Crowe
6 – W. Prior, A. A. Mallett, R. J. Inverarity and R. J. Zadow
5 – W. M. Darling and G. W. Goodman
3 – R. M. Hogg and G. R. Attenborough
2 – P. R. Sleep, J. E. Nash, D. C. Lovell and D. J. Rolfe
1 – B. L. Causby, R. G. Vincent and W. B. Phillips

v. Western Australia (Perth) 20-23 December		v. Western Australia (Adelaide) 8-11 January		v. Queensland (Adelaide) 17-19 January		v. Victoria (Geelong) 7-10 March		Inns	NOs	Runs	HS	Av
11	8	34	14	17	2	8	4	20	—	565	131	28.25
4	5							8	—	109	43	13.62
		33	67	26	53	35	73*	14	1	387	73*	29.76
3	37	4	2					12	1	220	61	20.00
23	55	1	65*	1	6*	50	14	20	3	573	81	33.70
				28	0			6	—	124	74	20.66
21	16	46	25	24	122	23	22	20	4	663	122	41.43
105	25	2	16	28	17	27*	—	17	3	399	105	28.50
2	0	18*	0					14	3	134	42	12.18
21	10			27	1	—	—	13	4	97	27	8.08
								2	—	2	2	1.00
								2	—	15	10	7.50
								6	—	161	102	26.83
13	5	4	0	23	12	—	—	14	1	78	23	6.00
4*	0*	2	0	18*	0*	—	—	10	7	50	18*	16.66
11	59	10	12	6	70	15*	4*	14	2	321	70	26.75
								2	—	42	33	21.00
								1	—	18	18	18.00
		7	29	17	9			4	—	62	29	15.50
						23	89	2	—	112	89	56.00
						111	91	2	—	202	111	101.00
	4	2	5	4	1							
1	7	7	4	5	1	11	9					
	1			4		2	1					
2	1	1	4	8	10	7	2					
221	233	171	243	236	304	312	309					
10	10	10	10	10	9†	6	5					
	L		L		L		D					
	7		4		7		7					

South Australia First-Class Matches – Bowling 1980–81	G. R. Attenborough	R. M. Hogg	R. M. McLellan	P. R. Sleep	D. W. Hookes	G. W. Goodman
v. Tasmania (Adelaide) 23–26 October	32–6–97–2 11.3–4–32–3	22–4–74–2 9–3–21–1		11–0–32–0 10–3–32–1	3–1–15–0	
v. New South Wales (Adelaide) 30 Oct–2 Nov	36.2–6–109–3	28–8–50–4		6–1–22–0		
v. New South Wales (Sydney) 13–16 November	34.3–11–94–5 10–2–23–0	24–5–46–2 13–3–33–2		14–3–50–3 20–5–61–2	6–2–13–0	
v. Indians (Adelaide) 29 Nov–2 Dec	20–2–105–1 11–4–20–4	19–3–67–3 8–2–14–1	18–2–92–1 7–1–18–4	24–1–125–3 3.5–1–18–1	5–0–42–0	2–0–10–0
v. Victoria (Adelaide) 4–6 December	16–2–44–1	25.2–4–75–6		3–1–12–0 8–0–33–1		
v. Queensland (Brisbane) 12–15 December	26–4–94–0			26–5–90–5		
v. Western Australia (Perth) 20–23 December	21–4–86–0 29–6–85–2	25–4–87–4 12–3–29–3		8–0–45–0 2–0–8–1		
v. Western Australia (Adelaide) 8–11 January	26–5–65–1 6–2–11–0			16.2–1–69–2 0.3–0–7–0	5–0–23–0	
v. Queensland (Adelaide) 17–19 January		13–4–40–0 10–0–39–0		20–7–58–2 4–0–30–0	10–2–22–0 3–0–16–0	
v. Victoria (Geelong) 7–10 March		24–7–53–0 7–2–18–0		9–0–46–0 4–0–11–1	5–1–12–0 2–0–9–0	
	279.2–58– 865–22 av. 39.31	239.2–52– 646–28 av. 23.07	25–3– 110–5 av. 22.00	189.4–28– 749–22 av. 34.04	39–6– 152–0 –	2–0– 10–0 –

A. J. J. Crowe 1–0–6–0; R. J. Zadow 0.2–0–1–0

W. Prior	A. A. Mallett	J. R. Hammond	R. J. Inverarity	W. M. Darling	R. G. Vincent	B	Lb	W	Nb	Total	Wkts
21–3–92–4	35.1–14–65–2					3	7		10	395	10
7–3–9–2	27–14–25–3					1	15		2	137	10
	33–9–95–2	21–4–52–0	1–1–0–0			3	6		1	338	10
	32–8–96–0		14–4–41–0			6	3			349	10
	14–7–30–0		4–1–7–0	0.2–0–1–0					5	160	4
							(15)			456	10
									8	78	10
17–6–56–2	17–7–26–1					1	6		3	223	10
	9–4–11–0			1–0–2–0					1	54	1A.
25–4–79–0	36–8–78–2				8.3–3–31–2	16	5			393	9
25–5–82–3	19.4–5–41–2					5			4	350	9
18–5–45–3	3.3–0–14–1					1	9		1	192	10
29–7–85–1	45–12–88–5		6–0–24–1					4	1	359	10
8–2–23–4	5–0–17–0									58	4
12–0–53–1	37–5–110–5		12–2–71–0			3	2		7	366	8
15.5–2–66–1	20–3–74–0						4		1	230	1
17–3–67–0	35–5–105–2		10–1–30–0			1	1		13	328	2
13–0–56–0	18–3–48–2		6–1–15–2				2		5	164	5
207.5–40– 713–21 av. 33.95	386.2–104– 923–27 av. 34.18	21–4– 52–0 –	53–10– 188–3 av. 62.66	1.2–0– 3–0 –	8.3–3– 31–2 av. 15.50						

Tasmania
First-Class Matches – Batting
1980–81

	v. South Australia (Adelaide) 23–26 October		v. Indians (Hobart) 11–13 December		v. Victoria (Hobart) 20–23 December		v. New Zealand (Launceston) 1–4 January		v. Queensland (Brisbane) 9–12 January		v. Western Australia (Devonport) 17–19 January	
D. B. Robinson			18	8	60	40	0	15	28	43	2	3
R. F. Jeffery	17	2	1	43*	14	9	61	145*	26	16	31	9
R. L. Knight	47	26	43	5*	12	26	3	18	4	41	9	0
D. C. Boon	28	23	63	—	114	67	27	0	17	73	40	18
B. F. Davison	126	17	76*	—	173	2	45	4	51	118	114	3
S. L. Saunders	2	0	16	—	0	1	5	11			23	31*
C. G. Hargrave	4	3	7*	—								
R. J. McCurdy	8	3	—	—	5	0	7	—	6	0	11	5
P. M. Clough	0*	0	—	—	5*	0*	0*	—	29	21	1*	22
C. L. Broadby			—	—	4	0	0	—	14*	1*		
M. B. Scholes	34	1	—	—	12	34	17	16*				
N. J. Allanby	19	3										
R. D. Woolley	90	41*										
L. G. Allen					13	13	14	55	0	5	0	0
D. A. Smith									5	0		
P. A. Blizzard									13	5	7	0
I. Beven											6	20
D. O'Halloran												
Byes	3	1	4		3	6	4	10		9	1	4
Leg byes	7	15	2	2	3	9	3	9	2	8	1	5
Wides			3						1	2		
No balls	10	2		4	7	4	2	3	15	5		3
Total	395	137	233	62	425	211	188	286	211	347	246	123
Wickets	10	10	5	1	10	10	10	6	10	10	10	10
Result	L		D		L		D		L		L	
Points	9		—		10		—		5		7	

Catches

13 – L. G. Allen (ct 12, st 1)
7 – M. B. Scholes
6 – D. C. Boon
4 – R. F. Jeffery, R. D. Woolley (ct 2, st 2), P. M. Clough and R. L. Knight
3 – B. F. Davison, S. L. Saunders, C. L. Broadby, C. G. Hargrave (ct 2, st 1) and R. J. McCurdy
2 – D. B. Robinson, I. Beven and D. O'Halloran
1 – D. A. Smith

v. New South Wales (Sydney) 6–8 March

		Inns	NOs	Runs	HS	Av
1	34	12	—	252	60	21.00
22	47	14	2	443	145*	36.91
		12	1	234	47	21.27
41	7	13	—	518	114	39.84
82	13	13	1	824	173	68.66
11	0	11	1	100	31*	10.00
		3	1	14	7	7.00
0	7	11	—	52	11	4.72
0	2	11	5	80	29	13.33
		5	2	19	14*	6.33
		6	1	114	34	22.80
		2	—	22	19	11.00
		2	1	131	90	131.00
18*	1	10	1	119	55	13.22
		2	—	5	5	2.50
17	6*	6	1	48	17	9.60
0	4	4	—	30	20	7.50
23	7	2	—	30	23	15.00

(11)	2
	3

226	133
10	10
	L
	8

Tasmania
First-Class Matches – Bowling
1980–81

	R. J. McCurdy	P. M. Clough	S. L. Saunders	C. L. Broadby	M. B. Scholes	R. F. Jeffery
v. South Australia (Adelaide) 23–26 October	26–6–78–1 5–1–12–1	21–7–59–0 3–0–8–0	37.5–5–154–4 10–3–27–1		18–2–63–1	16–2–54–2 5–3–9–1
v. Indians (Hobart) 11–13 December	17–7–41–1 14–0–49–0	17–3–43–2 19–3–59–0	6.2–1–30–2 12–3–43–0	21–6–48–1 17–2–39–2	18–2–63–4 7.4–3–21–1	10–3–26–0
v. Victoria (Hobart) 20–23 December	28–5–103–2 7–0–32–0	30–4–109–2 7–1–22–1	23–2–90–0 1–1–0–0	37–10–99–2 8.1–1–35–2	29–2–87–2	12–3–28–1
v. New Zealanders (Launceston) 1–4 January	27.2–5–91–7	25–1–96–0	14–1–67–0	21–5–84–1	20–1–90–0	10–1–43–2
v. Queensland (Brisbane) 9–12 January	26–3–140–3 4–0–29–0	30–7–88–2 7–0–31–0		25–5–93–1 2.1–1–9–1		11–4–43–1 1–0–8–0
v. Western Australia (Devonport) 17–19 January	23–1–90–3 10–4–19–0	28–3–62–3 9–3–20–1	8–4–23–1 15–3–42–2			6–1–12–0
v. New South Wales (Sydney) 6–8 March	16.3–7–37–3 21–3–52–4	15–5–34–2 26–3–81–1	4–1–15–0 19–3–55–0			12–4–34–2 8–2–15–0
	224.5–41– 773–25 av. 30.92	237–40– 712–14 av. 50.85	150.1–27– 546–10 av. 54.60	131.2–30– 407–10 av. 40.70	92.4–10– 324–8 av. 40.50	91–23– 272–9 av. 30.22

N. J. Allanby	C. G. Hargrave	B. F. Davison	P. A. Blizzard	I. Beven	D. O'Halloran	B	Lb	W	Nb	Total	Wkts
12–0–47–1							5		5	465	9
	1.2–0–5–0					6	1			68	4
						1	9	1	13	275	10
						4	1		4	220	3
		1–1–0–0				2	6		19	543	9
							5			94	4
						5	10	3	5	494	10
			18–1–75–1			9	8	1	1	458	8
			5–0–23–0						1	101	1
			26–5–54–1			2	3	3	3	252	8
			6–3–9–0	11.1–5–26–0			4		1	121	3
			13–1–40–1	14–4–31–2	8–1–20–0	2	3	1	5	222	10
				13–2–36–0	15–1–49–0	6	3			297	5
12–0–	1.2–0–	1–1–	68–10–	38.1–11–	23–2–						
47–1	5–0	0–0	201–3	93–2	69–0						
av. 47.00	–	–	av. 67.00	av. 46.50	–						

Victoria
First-Class Matches – Batting
1980–81

	v. Western Australia (Perth) 17–20 October		v. Queensland (Brisbane) 24–27 October		v. New Zealanders (Melbourne) 31 October–3 November		v. Western Australia (Melbourne) 14–17 November		v. South Australia (Adelaide) 4–6 December		v. New South Wales (Melbourne) 11–14 December	
J. M. Wiener	29	0	52	—	4	61	0	4	0	4	42	11
R. G. Matthews	15	25	62	—	48	14	0	6			27	5
D. F. Whatmore	1	5	47	—	14	0	43	0	0	33*		
G. N. Yallop	33	40	7	—	59	51*	7	5*	13	—	10	25
J. K. Moss	5	35	4	—	37	4	131	2*	5	—	25	19
T. J. Laughlin	5	0	41	—							24	37*
R. D. Robinson	8	29	18	—	12*	14	30	—	120	—	18	—
R. J. Bright	36	11	7*	—	7*	6	53	—	27	—	0	—
S. F. Graf	34	64	1*	—	—	10*	100*	—				
M. H. N. Walker	8	44	—	—	—	—	4	—	13	—	0	—
J. D. Higgs	0*	0*	—	—	—	—	—	—	2*	—		
A. G. Hurst					—	—						
I. W. Callen							1*	—	3	—	3*	—
J. W. Scholes									29	16*	0	0
G. M. Watts												
G. J. Cosier									1	—	27	12*
J. F. Leehane												
P. A. Hibbert												
Byes	5	8				2	9	1	1		4	
Leg byes	1	6	6		11	5	17	6	6		5	1
Wides							3				2	
No balls	3	1	5		3		3		3	1	1	1
Total	183	268	250		195	167	401	24	223	54	188	111
Wickets	10	10	7		5	6	8	3	10	1	10	5
Result	L		D		L		W		W		D	
Points	5		7		—		17		17		2	

Catches
28 – R. D. Robinson (ct 26, st 2)
10 – G. N. Yallop
 8 – J. K. Moss and J. M. Wiener
 5 – J. W. Scholes
 3 – D. F. Whatmore, R. J. Bright, S. F. Graf and I. W. Callen
 2 – R. G. Matthews and M. H. N. Walker
 1 – J. D. Higgs, A. G. Hurst, G. J. Cosier, G. M. Watts and P. A. Hibbert

v. Tasmania (Hobart) 20–23 December		v. New South Wales (Sydney) 17–19 January		v. Indians (Geelong) 30 January–2 February		v. Queensland (Geelong) 26 February–1 March		v. South Australia (Geelong) 7–10 March		Inns	NOs	Runs	HS	Av
36	38*	5	16	29	3					17	1	334	61	20.87
2	16	14	0							13		234	62	18.00
										9	1	143	47	17.87
121	2	52	70	0	64	28	21	122	66	20	2	796	122	44.22
62	12	45	34	125*	44	1	48	—	28*	19	3	666	131	41.62
				36	3					7	1	146	41	24.33
4	11	37	70	15	26	47*	69*	21*	4*	18	5	553	120	42.53
108	—	28	6*	3*	12	—	4	—	—	14	4	308	108	30.80
		3*	0	0	13	—	51	—	10	11	4	286	100*	40.85
6	—	38*	0*			—	3	—	—	9	2	116	44	16.57
12*	—	2	—	—	5*	—	7	—	—	7	5	28	12*	14.00
										—				
2	—	0	—	—	21	—	0	—	—	7	2	30	21	6.00
156	10*	65	31	23	17	80*	3	—	0	13	3	430	156	43.00
				16	12	99	18	17	40	6	—	202	99	33.66
										3	1	40	27	20.00
7*	—									1	1	7	7*	—
						22*	20	153*	9	4	2	204	153*	102.00

v. Tasmania		v. New South Wales		v. Indians		v. Queensland		v. South Australia	
2		2		4	1	9	3	1	
6	5	8	8	10	4	8	15	1	2
			1		1	1	2		
19		1	9	6	5	5	6	13	5

v. Tasmania		v. New South Wales		v. Indians		v. Queensland		v. South Australia	
543	94	300	245	267	231	301	268	328	174
9	4	9	7	7	10	3	10	2	5
W		D		L		L		D	
17		9		—		7		10	

Victoria First-Class Matches – Bowling 1980–81	S. F. Graf	M. H. N. Walker	T. J. Laughlin	R. J. Bright	J. D. Higgs	J. M. Wiener
v. Western Australia (Perth) 17–20 October	27–6–73–3 9–2–27–1	43.2–16–82–4 11–3–44–2	8–2–21–0 2.3–0–14–0	26–7–80–3 6–0–29–0	6–0–32–0 5–1–24–0	1–0–7–0
v. Queensland (Brisbane) 24–27 October	25–5–73–1	26–10–67–0	16–1–45–0	23.2–2–80–3	29–7–84–1	
v. New Zealanders (Melbourne) 31 Oct–3 Nov	10–2–22–0 4–0–14–0	12–3–33–3 14–7–26–0		15–1–46–0 16–3–50–0	11–0–42–1 24–4–85–2	0.2–0–1–0
v. Western Australia (Melbourne) 14–17 Nov	15–3–25–3 8–3–21–0	20–9–37–1 28–7–51–2		16–9–10–1 33–17–46–3	26–7–65–2 30–8–67–4	3–0–8–0
v. South Australia (Adelaide) 4–6 December		15.5–7–29–5 11–2–41–0		11–4–21–0 14.3–10–12–3	1–1–0–0 11–1–34–1	
v. New South Wales (Melbourne) 11–14 Dec		44–8–120–6	3–1–12–0	28–11–67–0		
v. Tasmania (Hobart) 20–23 December		29–7–75–3 18–5–36–3		27–4–79–0 29–12–59–4	24–5–76–2 16.2–2–42–2	1–1–0–0
v. New South Wales (Sydney) 17–19 January	24.3–3–62–2	28–6–77–0		26–6–67–2	24–1–81–2	
v. Indians (Geelong) 30 Jan–2 Feb	29–4–82–3 4–0–11–0		14–6–21–1 2–0–16–0	25–11–51–1 12–7–13–0	23–3–94–2 7–0–16–0	5–0–17–0 1–0–1–0
v. Queensland (Geelong) 26 Feb–1 Mar	20–3–57–3 17.2–1–50–3	22–3–79–0 16–3–48–1		29–11–71–0 18–4–36–0	14–4–49–0 16–5–55–1	
v. South Australia (Geelong) 7–10 March	11–1–44–0 20–7–45–1	26–7–71–1 25–2–83–0		22–5–50–1 16–7–31–1	28–6–83–2 32–4–88–1	
	223.5–40– 606–20 av. 30.30	389.1–105– 999–31 av. 32.22	45.3–10– 129–1 av. 129.00	392.5–131– 898–22 av. 40.81	327.2–59– 1017–23 av. 44.21	12.2–1– 34–0 –

A. A. G. Hurst 12–5–18–0; 4–1–10–0

B. R. D. Robinson 5–2–6–0; G. M. Watts 1–1–0–0

C. P. A. Hibbert 1–0–4–0

G. N. Yallop	I. W. Callen	J. K. Moss	J. W. Scholes	G. J. Cosier	J. F. Leehane	B	Lb	W	Nb	Total	Wkts
						2	2	2	9	303	10
							1		3	149	3
-1-0-0						1	4	1	3	358	5
							5		1	167	4 A
						7	3			196	2
	9.5-2-36-3					3	3	2	6	187	10
	12-4-17-1					14	7		3	234	10
	12-5-30-4			5-1-13-1		1	5		15	114	10
	18-4-47-4			8-4-12-1		1	4		11	162	10
	30-8-69-3		2-0-9-0	16-1-55-0		6	1	3	5	347	9
-0-7-0	22-1-111-1				20.3-4-64-2	3	3		7	425	10
	13-4-41-1				4-1-14-0	6	9		4	211	10
	29-5-98-3					2	9		2	398	10
	30-6-95-2	3-1-12-0	4-1-6-0			3	4	1	12	398	9
	4-0-14-0		3.3-0-20-0					2	3	102	0 B
	14-0-59-1					1	5		5	330	4 C
	17-2-47-2					8	9	2	3	258	10
	14-4-44-2						11	2	7	312	6
-0-2-0	11.5-2-43-1	1-0-5-0					9	1	2	309	5
-1- -0 -	236.4-47- 751-28 av. 26.82	4-1- 17-0 –	9.3-1- 35-0 –	29-6- 80-2 av. 40.00	24.3-5- 78-2 av. 39.00						

Western Australia First-Class Matches – Batting 1980–81	v. Victoria (Perth) 17–20 October		v. New South Wales (Sydney) 23–26 October		v. Queensland (Brisbane) 31 October–3 November		v. Victoria (Melbourne) 14–17 November		v. Indians (Perth) 22–25 November		v. South Australia (Perth) 20–23 December	
G. Shipperd			26	7	35	47	2	62	5	34	37	3
B. M. Laird	10	0	2	24	2	23	8	39	68	110		
R. S. Langer	9	75*	10	13	4	4			1	84		
M. D. O'Neill	1	—					9	5	100	1	40	22
K. S. McEwan	67	57*	41	9	4	26	35	5	8	8	12	4
C. S. Serjeant									56*	6*	0	9
C. E. Penter							14	16	42*	—		
G. D. Porter									—	—		
T. M. Alderman	3	—	0	1	0	10*					5*	19
W. M. Clark	2*	—	12	19	1	14	1	1	—	—	24	13*
T. Zoehrer									—	—		
G. M. Wood	78	5	23	14	29	29	17	17			126*	7
K. J. Hughes	16	8	16	2	12	149	12	9			17	97
R. W. Marsh	61	—	31*	8	48	67	37	32			40	0
B. Yardley	11	—	1	1	78	6	37*	9			6	7
D. K. Lillee	30	—	0	3*	31*	10	1	15*				
M. F. Malone											34	0
A. L. Mann												
Byes	2		3		5	17	3	14		11	5	1
Leg byes	2	1	8		4	7	3	7	12			9
Wides	2					5	2		2			
No balls	9	3	3	2	8	6	6	3	2	8	4	1
Total	303	149	176	103	261	420	187	234	296	262	350	192
Wickets	10	3	10	10	10	10	10	10	5	5	9	10
Result	W		L		D		L		D		W	
Points	19		3		6		4		—		23	

Catches

35 – R. W. Marsh (ct 34, st 1)
 9 – T. M. Alderman
 7 – G. Shipperd and C. S. Serjeant
 6 – K. J. Hughes, G. M. Wood and B. M. Laird
 5 – K. S. McEwan and B. Yardley
 3 – W. M. Clark and T. Zoehrer
 2 – G. D. Porter, A. L. Mann, M. F. Malone and D. K. Lillee
 1 – R. S. Langer and M. D. O'Neill

v. South Australia (Adelaide) 8-11 January		v. Tasmania (Devonport) 17-19 January		v. New South Wales (Perth) 27 February-2 March		v. Queensland (Perth) 7-10 March		Inns	NOs	Runs	HS	Av
18	0	42	39*	80	65	140	4	18	1	646	140	38.00
				21	21	0	59	14	—	387	110	27.64
6	0			31	6	42	29	10	1	206	84	22.88
16	0							13	—	302	100	23.23
68	29*	5	12					16	2	390	68	27.85
44*	23*	6	17*	6*	6	8	72	12	6	353	144*	58.83
								3	1	72	42*	36.00
14	6							2	—	20	14	10.00
0	—	—	—	—	—	—	7*	9	3	45	19	7.50
								9	2	87	24	12.42
25	—							1	—	25	25	25.00
		103	16	38	3	36	1	16	1	542	126*	36.13
		13	32	94	73	20	27	16	—	597	149	37.31
		8	—	22	76*	7	5	14	2	442	76*	36.83
32	—	19	—	26*	42	20*	17	15	3	312	78	26.00
		5	—	—	10*	11	28	11	4	144	31*	20.57
21	—	13*	—	—	—	—	23	5	1	91	34	22.75
10	—	27*	—					2	1	37	27*	32.00
		2			1							
4		3	4	3	9	9	9					
1		3	3	4	2	1	2					
		3	1	3	5	11	6					
59	58	252	121	328	319	305	289					
10	4	8	3	6	7	8	10					
W		W		W		D						
19		19		21		11						

Western Australia First-Class Matches – Bowling 1980–81	T. M. Alderman	W. M. Clark	C. E. Penter	G. D. Porter	M. D. O'Neill	R. S. Langer
v. Victoria (Perth)	15–3–50–1	19–5–40–2			2–0–5–0	
17–20 October	8–2–29–1	15–6–20–0				
v. New South Wales	26–3–95–1	24–3–96–1				
(Sydney) 23–26 October						
v. Queensland	29–3–117–2	37.5–5–110–2				
(Brisbane) 31 Oct–3 Nov	4–1–11–0	3–0–14–0				3–2–5–0
v. Victoria (Melbourne)		54–15–100–4	24–7–78–0		13.1–4–47–1	
14–17 November		5–0–15–1				
v. Indians (Perth)	26–7–74–0	18.5–5–38–1	27–3–76–0	11–0–38–2	11–2–55–0	6–1–22–1
22–25 November	7–3–14–0	6–2–10–0	10–2–43–0	6–3–12–1	7–2–13–0	5–0–15–0
v. South Australia (Perth)	24–4–74–4	8–1–40–1				
20–23 December	26–8–64–3	13–6–30–0				
v. South Australia (Adelaide)	20.5–7–45–4				6–1–26–0	
8–11 January	14–4–31–2			6.2–2–17–2		
v. Tasmania (Devonport)	6–0–40–0					
17–19 January	8.2–3–11–2					
v. New South Wales	22–4–56–2					
(Perth) 27 Feb–2 Mar	12–0–50–3				2–0–14–0	
v. Queensland	11.4–2–33–4					
(Perth) 7–10 March	18–1–41–3					
	277.5–55–	203.4–48–	61–12–	23.2–5–	41.1–9–	14–3–
	835–32	513–12	197–0	67–5	160–0	42–1
	av. 26.09	av. 42.75	–	av. 13.40	–	av. 42.00

G. Shipperd	D. K. Lillee	B. Yardley	G. M. Wood	M. F. Malone	A. L. Mann	B	Lb	W	Nb	Total	Wkts
	25.5–8–57–5	6–1–22–1				5	1		3	183	10
	32–7–92–3	37.4–9–112–5				8	6		1	268	10
	26–6–68–0	24–6–74–0					5		2	340	3
	46–13–97–6	22–4–79–0	2–0–16–0			4	13	1	2	439	10
-0–2–0	5–0–16–0	9–2–27–0				4	2		1	82	0
	29–7–73–2	36–13–71–1				9	17	3	3	401	8
	5.2–3–2–2					1	6			24	3
-0–2–0						1	4		4	312	4
		16–5–29–1		24–4–75–3			1		2	221	10
		41–15–85–5		25–10–41–1		4	7	1	1	233	10
		7–1–22–2		26–6–68–4		2	7		1	171	10
		44–13–87–3		6–2–13–0	33–6–82–3	5	4		4	243	10
	18–3–79–3	23.4–4–62–7		14–1–46–0	14–5–17–0	1	1			246	10
	21–6–49–3	23–12–36–4		8–2–14–1	3–2–1–0	4	5		3	123	10
	24–7–66–1	26.3–8–69–2		25–9–51–2			(20)			262	8
	15.2–5–41–2	26–5–119–3		11–3–35–2			5	6		270	10
	22–10–59–3	16–6–40–3		17–5–41–0			10		3	186	10
-1–0–0	21–3–66–2	19–7–34–3		18–3–79–1		5	7			232	9
-1–	290.3–78–	376.5–111–	2–0–	174–45–	50–13						
-0	765–32	968–40	16–0	463–14	100–3						
	av. 23.90	av. 24.20	–	av. 33.07	av. 33.33						

E

Growing in Stature

The Domestic Season in New Zealand
including the Test series *v.* India
Review of the year by Don Cameron

The New Zealand section should start with an apology to an Englishman. In reviewing the 1980 season in New Zealand we omitted to pay tribute to Bernard Simmonds, assistant secretary of Kent County Cricket Club, who managed D. H. Robins' Young England side on their tour of the country. A man of passionate love for the game and concern for his fellow human beings, Bernard Simmonds stamped his name indelibly on New Zealand cricket history and his return to the Dominion is eagerly awaited. The matches against Derek Robins' side which followed the Test victory over the West Indies had raised interest in cricket in New Zealand to a high level, and, as DON CAMERON, editor of *The New Zealand Cricket Player*, relates, this interest was fostered and broadened by the events of the New Zealand season which started with the Test side in Australia.

The sight and sound of the Prime Minister fulminating on some mischief visited upon the New Zealand team in Australia was one, perhaps the strongest, indication of the grip which cricket took upon New Zealanders in the last southern summer.

There is an inherent interest in cricket among New Zealanders even if this is seldom shown in the numbers going to watch games. The previous summer the New Zealand team had re-awakened much of this latent interest, although the West Indians and their erratic behaviour did much to move cricket from the sports pages onto the street-front billboards.

But this was a minor epidemic compared with the cricket fever which gripped New Zealand in mid-summer, which infected even the leader of the land, Robert Muldoon. A year or so before the fever would have been known as Packeritis for it was the New Zealanders' stumbling progress through an ill-planned tour of Australia, and then into the final against Australia in the one-day international series which raised everyone's temperatures. It was New Zealand's first-hand encounter with what the Australians call the modern game which sometimes produced cricket of the highest quality, and at other times produced a pastime that might have been devised by the Marx Brothers.

Whatever the standard, and whatever the worries that the classical strain of the game had also been infected, New Zealanders were caught up in the colours and sights and sounds – and arguments – of the side-show game in Australia.

Before I elaborate on this, and Mr Muldoon's astonishing interjection, might I be permitted to sketch in a little background. The New Zealanders had been invited, for the first time, to take part in the three-team series (it might not be kind to talk of three-ring circuses at this stage) with India and Australia, in Australia. Each visitor was to play three Tests against Australia, and to play the ten-match one-day series leading up to the five-match finals.

New Zealanders were fascinated at the prospect. They had a useful conceit for their players, the novelty of the tour appealed, and the promise of riches beyond the New Zealand Cricket Council's means did not go unnoticed.

Unfortunately the planning was not accurate. New Zealand were offered an itinerary which offered only one major game, against Queensland, before the First Test and after some horse-trading (which involved New Zealand agreeing to forgo rest days in two Tests) Australia included a four-day match against Victoria to stiffen the build-up to the Test. At about the same time the New Zealand selectors, holding close to the side which had defeated West Indies, tried to fashion a side which would be strong enough in the Tests, and adaptable enough to handle the differing demands of the one-day game.

They took two risks, picking two fulltime spinners, Stephen Boock, the slow left-armer whose recent Test results had been modest, and John Bracewell, the budding young off-spinner, and also decided on the luxury of two wicket-keepers, Warren Lees, the senior man, and Ian Smith.

Even before the tour it was obvious that Boock would have a very quiet tour. By the end of the Test series – and Boock should have played in the Third Test on the Melbourne Cricket Ground – Boock took the astonishing step of asking to leave the tour. Just as remarkably the New Zealand Cricket Council agreed, and Boock went home to take another harvest of wickets for Otago in the remaining Shell Trophy matches. At about the same time Gary Troup, the left-arm new-ball bowler, broke down and was replaced by Brian McKechnie – that remarkable man-about-sport whose career with New Zealand cricket and rugby teams so often causes a sensation.

Had not Lees damaged a hamstring before the First Test Smith would have spent the first seven weeks twiddling his thumbs, while another injury to Lees let Smith into the later one-day matches where he performed well enough to hold his place on merit.

The great need was a 'charger', a tearaway batsman in the middle of the list who could turn the course of a one-day game in an over or two. Graham or 'Jock' Edwards, the rumbustious Central Districts batsman, was the obvious man, but apparently he was still suffering from the backwash of his unfortunate first tour to England in 1978. New Zealand selectors tend to have long memories.

However, in the early days in Australia the personnel of the team was of secondary interest. Rain made the Victoria game rather a waste of time, and a three-day game against Australian Capital Territory was also severely restricted by bad weather. So the New Zealanders approached the start of the one-day internationals and the First Test against Australia with a quite ridiculously inadequate build-up for players coming out of their home winter. It did not help, either, that the Indians, after starting in Perth, had a much more sensible series of major matches before the one-dayers and the Tests.

The New Zealanders caused a flutter – and had the World Series Cricket organisers over-joyed – by winning their first one-day game against Australia. It turned out to be the last piece of comfort the New Zealanders had for several weary weeks.

They lost the second one-day match to Australia and obviously needed all the luck in the world to be competitive in the First Test at Brisbane. So much for luck. Lees and Troup and Jeremy Coney could not play because of injury and Dennis Lillee scythed through the rusty batting to finish the Test in three days. One-day losses to Australia and to India were followed by the second three-day Test loss at Perth, New Zealand this time without their foremost batsman Geoff Howarth who had a hand injury. A win over India at Brisbane was followed by a loss to Australia in a one-dayer at Melbourne.

By now the morale of the team was low, only the faithful home supporters were interested and my temporary masters of the New Zealand Press Association were wondering whether my own journey was especially necessary.

However, the New Zealanders had always fancied their chances on the slow, low-bouncing MCG pitch, for two reasons. The Australians, especially Greg Chappell, were becoming paranoic about the MCG pitch, while New Zealanders, without wishing to be cynical, regarded the pitch as being rather similar to too many of their home pitches.

On the last day, with the pitch abysmal, New Zealand needed 193 to win in 145 minutes and 20 overs, perhaps four runs an over, but lost wickets (some to rather exotic umpiring) and settled for a draw.

Only then did the full impact of an umpiring decision of the second day become exasperatingly evident. With Australia 279 for nine in their first innings Lance Cairns, of medium-pace, bowled a bumper at Jim Higgs, Australia and everyone's No 11, who squatted underneath it but left his bat up and the edge went to Lees. Robin Bailhache ruled it a no-ball for intimidatory bowling, and Higgs was to hold on in a 60-run stand while Doug Walters finished his century.

Richie Benaud, as a television commentator, had a lovely time with this incident, which he criticised fiercely. At his age, said Benaud, he could bowl a nastier bouncer than Cairns.

But the ruling could not be changed, the Test was drawn, the New Zealanders had only a slim prospect of qualifying for the one-day finals, and a great wave of sympathy washed across the Tasman from the home folk who said unkind things about Australian administrators who devised such a tour, and unkinder remarks about Australian umpires.

But Howarth said after the Third Test that by then he felt his New Zealanders were ready to play cricket in keeping with their ability – and he proceeded to prove it. There were victories in Tasmania and Geelong, a wet win over India at Melbourne and then a dramatic last-over win over Australia in a day–night game at Sydney; a staggering result which set the whole of New Zealand alight again. A win over India put New Zealand into the finals and the first raging signs of Packeritis swept through New Zealand.

A sweeping victory in the first final at Sydney had millions (or so it felt) of New Zealanders hovered over transistors and television sets. Then to Melbourne for a double-header, with Australia taking the first and New Zealand entering the second minus Coney who had a back strain.

The New Zealanders always felt that Greg Chappell was the key to the one-day matches and he was 59, and Australia 130 for one from 30 overs, when he hoisted a ball high and deep to midwicket. Martin Snedden raced in, dived and held what 52,000 spectators hailed as an unbelievable catch. But the two people at the ground who really mattered, Peter Cronin and Don Weiser, the umpires, ruled that Chappell was not out. On the field Cronin told a very irate Howarth that he had not seen the catch, or non-catch, as he was watching to see if the batsman grounded his bat before turning for the second run.

It was the most staggering, if not the first, piece of erratic umpiring during the New Zealanders' campaign. As an instance Graeme Wood, the Australian opener, was given out caught for nought in three consecutive Tests. The New Zealanders, in the modern fashion, appealed mightily, but later allowed that the catches had come from thigh-pad, bat and back pad, in that order.

Chappell went on to score 90, Australia 235, and Bruce Edgar led the New Zealand effort so nobly, amid fierce excitement, that 15 runs were needed from the last over, and five of these brought eight and the remarkable McKechnie to the crease for the last ball, which he had to hit for six to tie the match.

The grisly details of Greg Chappell's organisation that his brother Trevor should bowl the last ball underarm do not need repeating, and the hooting and the booing went on for about 36 hours.

The New Zealanders themselves took some wicked humour out of the event for the next day every time Howarth appeared before a television camera he rather pointedly had a copy of the New Zealand Lawn Bowler magazine prominently in his hand.

But at home New Zealanders were in an uproar and during a nationally-telecast press conference Mr Muldoon took himself away from affairs of state to belabour Australia about the under-arm ball, with pointed reference that the Australians were playing in yellow uniforms. The telecast was repeated in Australia the next day, amid the furious criticism of Greg Chappell who, so the Australian critics maintained, had destroyed the great Australian tradition of sportsmanship ... a remark that caused a certain wry amusement among New Zealanders who have sometimes in the past had other views of Australian sportsmen.

If nothing else, the under-arm incident projected Howarth's team into the minds, and many of the hearts, of New Zealanders and the fact that New Zealand lost the next match and the final went virtually unnoticed.

The New Zealand Cricket Council, with the Indian tour following so closely, also found itself with a highly-saleable asset, which they happily emphasised by having the Indians and New Zealand wear their coloured clothing ('disco gear' according to the New Zealanders) for the opening two one-day internationals in New Zealand, both of which the New Zealanders won easily, and to the great comfort of their television army.

Playing the Indians over five-day Tests would obviously be a more difficult assignment. For years New Zealand batsmen had suffered at the hands of the Indian spinners. The precautionary word had gone about that grass should be encouraged, or at least not discouraged, to grow on the Test pitches at Wellington, Christchurch and Auckland, although it was questionable whether Dilip Doshi and Shivlal Yadav, the Indian spinners, would be more menacing than the Indian seamers, Kapil Dev and Karsan Ghavri. And there was the doubly uncomfortable feeling that Sunil Gavaskar was due to regain his throne as a prince among Test batsmen, and that by defeating Australia at Melbourne (and squaring the series) India had performed better in a tight situation than had New Zealand.

For once good fortune smiled upon New Zealand in the First Test at Wellington, although it was difficult to assess whether Howarth's majestic century in the first innings could displace the new-look Basin Reserve as the show-piece of the match.

The Basin in the bad old days was no-one's favourite ground, a vast open space usually buffeted by strong and cold winds, a tatty old grandstand containing very few of the creature comforts, a cheerless, characterless place which could be bearable on a sunny day, but as utterly miserable as a Siberian steppe in unkinder weather. Bishen Bedi, after losing a Test there amid Antarctic conditions, described it as the worst Test ground in the world, and there would be many, including New Zealanders, who would chatter agreement.

As the pitch was of sometimes indifferent standard the Basin was also not on the regular Test roster, another fact which bit deep into the soul of Mr Bob Vance, for so many years an outstanding player and administrator in Wellington, and more recently chairman of the board of the New Zealand Cricket Council.

Vance has persuasive ways and, against many odds, won support both from the Wellington City Council, and cricketers, to revamp the ground. Grass terraces were built on the flat eastern side, and a circular field enclosed by a white picket fence. The pitch block was changed 45 degrees so that bowlers would not need to plough into whichever wind was blowing straight down the pitch, and various other improvements were made, including a very effective scoreboard which has room for the attendants to post such messages as 'Nice one, Geoff' to mark Howarth's hundred.

Best of all a new pavilion, complete with facilities luxurious by New Zealand standards, was built in the north-west corner of the ground and containing, among other comforts, a press box running high across the front of the stand which is not the place for those who suffer from vertigo.

I hope I shall be pardoned for digressing from the tread of the India tour to interpolate such a description, but the re-birth of the Basin Reserve was one of the great events of the New Zealand season. Unlike the bigger grounds such as Lancaster Park and Eden Park, designed with rugby utilitarianism, the Basin is the first New Zealand ground planned specifically for cricket. The stately shape of the new pavilion (grandstand is not the right word) has given the Basin a distinctive character. It is also an intimate ground, ideal for spectators. It was bursting at the seams on the first two days of the Indian Test, making its capacity about 12,000. But even when there were only about 5000 or 6000 people on the following workaday days they spread round the ground and still provided atmosphere.

As I mentioned earlier the early luck was with the New Zealanders. Both Doshi and Yadav came with injuries, could not be considered for the First Test and a youngster Ravi Shastri was hurriedly summoned to do the spinning.

Ghavri was also injured and unable to play, but the mottled pitch, with its grassy patches, persuaded Gavaskar to send New Zealand in. It was a sensible move for no-one could predict how the pitch would play. It promised life and lift, and Gavaskar obviously preferred to bowl Kapil Dev on it rather than have his batsmen face Richard Hadlee, Gary Troup and Martin Snedden, who had frequently embarassed them in Australia.

Unfortunately for Gavasker the bowling was more notable for eagerness than accuracy. The pitch did have some life, but the fast and rather bare outfield encouraged strokes. So New Zealand prospered, Bruce Edgar, John Wright and John Reid, recalled after his solitary Test against Pakistan two years before, all making useful scores and early on the second day Howarth finished his century, his sixth in 13 tests since he became a fully-fledged Test player in 1978. Before than Howarth's Test batting was speculative. But there was a poise and certainty about this hundred which was quite captivating. The better Kapil Dev bowled, and he did improve in mid-innings, the better Howarth batted.

So New Zealand worked to 375 in their first innings and the medium-fast attack, nicely honed in Australia, swung quickly into action. Cairns struck two critical blows by bowling, with the full inswinger which had returned to his armoury, Gavaskar and Gundappa Viswanath in one over. After that, and despite some breezy boundary hitting by Sandip Patil, the New Zealand bowlers kept chipping away at the wickets. It said much for the new-found command of Troup, Snedden and Cairns, who finished with five wickets, that they removed India for 223 without Hadlee having to take a wicket.

With the luxury of a lead of 152 and some eight sessions to play New Zealand were in a powerful position, and proceeded to squander this command by foolish batting against a much better directed Indian attack. By the time three batsmen John Wright, Coney and Jock Edwards, restored at last, had committed suicide on the hook shot the New Zealand innings was on the slide to ruin, and young Shastri finished off the innings with one astonishing over in which he took wickets with the third, fifth and sixth balls.

New Zealand were out for an even 100 and India were left with two days to score 253, with conditions still in favour of the batsmen.

From this unpromising position Howarth drew a remarkable response from his bowlers. In their modest number of Test wins New Zealand have sometimes bowled with spectacular success on the last day, but generally when the pitch favoured the bowlers. This time the New Zealanders produced a quite remarkable and sustained assault on the Indians, each bowler pinning the batsmen down, the fielding accurate and aggressive. Again Patil batted briskly, but the rest were removed, almost remorselessly, this time Hadlee getting four wickets and Troup, Snedden and Cairns two each. It must rank among the finest, most consistent pieces of attacking out-cricket which New Zealand have managed, and by 5.25 p.m. the victory was complete with 62 runs and a day to spare.

With public interest again so keen it was the greatest shame that the Second Test at Christchurch should be reduced by rain to an academic exercise. Some 94 minutes were lost to bad light on the first day, only 49 minutes possible on the second, none at all on the third and fourth days. The Indians, amid all this confusion, reached 200 for two wickets, but Hadlee struck them down and they reached only 255.

So the only dramatic events of the Test were that Walter Hadlee, the former chairman of the NZCC, should hover about the rain guage and watch with glee the level rise sufficiently for the council to win $16,000 in rain insurance, and that on the last day as New Zealand batted out the match Reid should put together a patient 123 not out, his first century in only his Third Test.

Already the alarm bells were ringing that the Eden Park pitch, affected by some soil complaint, would be like home away from home for the Indian spinners. In fact they played all three, Doshi, Yadav and Shastri (while New Zealand brought in John Bracewell as their only front-line spinner) and Gavaskar won a very important toss. But again Gavaskar failed with the bat, the middle of the innings evaporated and it took a 105-run stand by Syed Kirmani and Yadav, lifting India from 124 for eight to 229 for nine, to give any substance to an innings of 238. The New Zealand innings was notable for Wright at last reaching a Test century in a seven-hour struggle, more runs to Reid, and useful efforts from Coney, Edwards and Cairns.

As the pitch became worn and torn, with the ball turning awkwardly, Bracewell (who had four for 61 from 42 overs in the first innings) and Cairns worked steadily through the Indian second innings and a second New Zealand win seemed a formality. Bracewell took another five, for 75 runs from 41 overs, and from lunch onward on the last day New Zealand needed 157 to win.

Edgar went quickly, Edwards and Hadlee were promoted to hit the spinners while Wright blocked up one end. Edwards blazed away for 47 before he was second out at 83. Hadlee went at 87, with the ball by now turning fiendishly. The crowd waited for Cairns to come out for a last explosive blast at the bowling. They waited in vain. Howarth decided the risk was too great, came out himself and decided that New Zealand would not lose.

This decision, which caused hoots of dismay from the crowd, was the result of long and earnest dressing-room discussions. The feeling seemed to be that the New Zealanders had travelled a long and rocky road since late October, they were tired, they had a Test series 1–0 in the bag (New Zealand's third series win) and they were not of a mind to offer the Indian spinners the chance of squaring the series. Howarth was heavily criticised for his decision but his point did have some validity. The New Zealanders had had a long and tiring campaign. They had been beset with injuries, not very much good luck, and some highly questionable umpiring. Various prizes had been within reach, and snatched away. This series win was one prize they would make sure of, regardless of the manner of achievement.

So the long season left the New Zealanders again in the headlines, although not so complimentary this time. It was a pity, for through all the trials and travail the New Zealanders had done much to strengthen the fabric of the country's cricket. They had shaken the Australians, and beaten the Indians. They had done much to strengthen cricket's hold on a sometimes fickle home crowd, they had spurred even more the youngsters who were flocking in larger numbers than before to the game. These things, I am sure, far outweighed the disappointment of them failing to try that last winning jump at Eden Park.

They came back from Australia, too, to find the sub-structure of New Zealand cricket in a very healthy state. After flirting for years with a one-day knockout series before Christmas the NZCC last summer decided to run the three-day Shell Trophy and one-day Shell Cup matches in conjunction, with the one-day game usually preceding the three-day match. It became a very successful experiment, particularly as the one-day matches were designed to bring together the two leading teams in a national final. The round-robin series, and final, had much more impact than the old knockout system.

With the New Zealand side away for almost all the domestic matches it was obvious that the batsmen especially would prosper with the leading bowlers absent.

Auckland, with most of their batting intact (whereas Northern Districts who won everything the previous summer had lost Howarth, Wright and Parker) were first to realise that this would be a batsman's season and laid their plans accordingly. They started with a sweeping victory over an under-prepared Canterbury side, had the better of a draw with Wellington, and then defeated Otago. Central Districts started even more quickly, with wins over Northern, Otago and Canterbury.

The fourth series produced the key match, Auckland versus Central at Napier, one of the sunniest cities in New Zealand until a major match is placed there. Again the rains came, Auckland took four points from a draw, Central only three. The Central challenge faded after that, Canterbury came with a rush, but Auckland finished off with two wins, over Wellington and Otago, and finished four points clear of Canterbury.

Auckland also beat Canterbury in the one-day cup final to complete a quite staggering season of improvement. They were without Troup and Snedden, in Australia, but still developed a very strong and consistent team effort. The batting figures tell much of the story ... John Reid 567 runs at 56.7, John Wiltshire 368 at 40.89, Peter Webb 431 at 39.18, Martin Crowe 303 at 33.67, Austin Parsons, 393 at 32.75. The bowling was equally impressive and consistent – John McIntyre 31 wickets at 15.61, John Cushen 23 at 19.30, Warren Stott 26 at 20.92.

The Auckland bowlers may not concern the national selectors, but the improvement of Reid, Webb and Crowe, a youngster in only his second season will be most significant. Reid was into the Test side against Pakistan in 1978–79 for one Test, and then discarded. He had progressed steadily through the grades as a batsman-wicketkeeper, but his form seemed to fall below international class at either art.

His keeping became too variable in quality, and his batting lost its thrust – he could occupy the crease, but laboured for his runs. Also he seemed to lack the fitness or agility which the modern game, especially the one-day variety, demands. Before the start of last season Reid made three important decisions. He would forsake wicket-keeping, he would hit the ball and play strokes, and he would work on his fitness and fielding. The improvement in a man who already had technique and concentration was quite remarkable, and two centuries for Auckland, and a brilliant 97 not out in the Shell Cup final, were followed by Test scores of 46, 7, 123 not out, 74 and 0 against India. These scores suggest quite accurately that against the best bowling Reid may be an uncertain starter, and he still needs to work hard on his fielding. But there is also the promise of a rich Test career, and perhaps next summer will put him on that path.

Webb, tried and then dropped after the West Indies series in 1979–80, made almost as much progress for he also had two hundreds for Auckland, and like Reid was more eager to play his strokes. Sometimes Webb tried too eagerly to hit for the fence, but he is now a much stronger and better-balanced player than the young man who struggled, without any luck at all, against the West Indians.

Other home batsmen made significant progress, although in the case of John Morrison (Wellington) topping the trophy aggregates with 599 runs this was more an instance of a fine batsman maintaining his form. Vaughan Brown, the batsman and off-spinner from Canterbury had 513 runs, one century, and his early promise is very close to fulfilment. Gary Robertson, a rather angular young fast bowler from Central Districts, took 37 wickets even though occasionally troubled by a neck injury, and he was promoted on merit to the one-day squad against the Indians. A young batsman and leg-spinner from Canterbury, Richard Leggat, made his debut. He scored only 182 runs, and took 17 wickets, but will bear watching. Barry Cooper of Northern Districts, Richard Hoskin and Geoff Blakely of Otago emerged as distinctly promising batsmen.

So as the long, intriguing and sometimes sensational season came to an end New Zealand could look with some pleasure at much profit. Especially the New Zealand Cricket Council who might expect a profit close to $200,000 from the Indian tour, with $100,000 of this coming from the gate for the third Indian Test.

And there should be a final word of tribute to Gavaskar's Indians. Like the New Zealanders they had had a hard, and often difficult, tour of Australia. Yet in New Zealand they played with charm and good humour. It seems par for the Test tour course these days that every series should be marked by argument, controversy and bitterness. Gavaskar and his men, and the New Zealanders too, played a Test series with nary a sour note.

The Indians accepted their defeat with old-fashioned courtesy, and Howarth's men their win with pleasant dignity. The two teams seemed firm friends off the field, and played their Tests with touches of chivalry. After all the side-show atmosphere of what the Australians call the modern game, the sight of two teams playing Test matches as if they were games to be enjoyed became the most pleasant part of the whole summer.

Shell Trophy

27, 28 and 29 December 1980   **at Eden Park, Auckland**
Auckland 300 for 5 (J. F. Reid 113 not out, P. N. Webb 58)
Canterbury 77 (L. W. Stott 5 for 41) and 124
Auckland won by an innings and 99 runs
Auckland 20 pts, Canterbury 2 pts

                                     at Molyneux Park, Alexandra
Wellington 215 (R. H. Vance 52, E. J. Gray 55, G. B. Thomson 4 for 39)
    and 199 (J. F. M. Morrison 52, R. H. Vance 51, G. B. Thomson 6 for 41)
Otago 266 for 9 (B. Milburn 103, W. L. Blair 50, E. J. Gray 4 for 50) and 149
    for 9 (P. J. Petherick 4 for 46)
Otago won by 1 wicket
Otago 17 pts, Wellington 4 pts

                                     at Trafalgar Park, Nelson
Northern Districts 242 for 9 (C. W. Dickeson 58) and 186 (D. R. O'Sullivan
    4 for 64)
Central Districts 264 for 9 (G. N. Edwards 79, C. W. Dickeson 7 for 79) and
    168 for 7 (A. H. Jones 61, G. J. Langridge 50)
Central Districts won by 3 wickets
Central Districts 19 pts, Northern Districts 6 pts

The first round of matches saw a result in each match. Auckland, bottom of the table in 1980, overwhelmed Canterbury and John Reid began his climb back to the Test side with an impressive hundred with won him the Man of the Match award. There was also an award for Barry Milburn who was rewarded for his epic century at the expense of Graeme Thomson who took 10 for 80 and joined in the last wicket stand of 29 with Richard Webb which brought Otago victory by one wicket. There was defeat too for reigning Trophy holders Northern Districts whose one consolation was the fine all-round performance of Cliff Dickeson.

Shell Cup

30 December 1980   **at Eden Park, Auckland**
Canterbury 158 (L. W. Stott 4 for 23)
Auckland 128 for 5 (T. Franklin 54)
Auckland won on faster scoring rate

                                        at Molyneux Park, Alexandra
Wellington 206 for 6
Otago 126
Wellington won by 80 runs

                                        at Trafalgar Park, Nelson
Central Districts 199 for 8 (S. J. Scott 4 for 54)
Northern Districts 204 for 2 (B. G. Cooper 77 not out, J. G. Gibson 75)
Northern Districts won by 8 wickets

In the limited over matches the result of the first-class game was reversed at Nelson and Alexandra, but Auckland completed the double over Canterbury in a rain restricted match. The most impressive performance came from Barry Cooper, who had spent the previous months with Derbyshire second eleven, though mostly as twelfth man and scorer. He had obviously benefited from his months in the nets in England.

Shell Trophy

1, 2 and 3 January 1981   **at Seddon Park, Hamilton**
Canterbury 307 for 6 (V. R. Brown 78, B. R. Hadlee 76) and 264 (V. R. Brown
   79, B. D. Ritchie 75 not out)
Northern Districts 353 for 8 (J. G. Gibson 119, C. M. Kuggeleijn 116, S. R.
   McNally 4 for 73) and 186 (B. G. Cooper 62, D. W. Stead 4 for 72)
Canterbury won by 32 runs
Canterbury 19 pts, Northern Districts 7 pts

                                        at Basin Reserve, Wellington
Auckland 318 for 7 (P. N. Webb 119, J. F. Reid 56, E. J. Gray 4 for 84) and
   177 for 6 (S. B. Cater 5 for 71)

Wellington 194 (E. J. Gray 77, L. W. Stott 4 for 61) and 251 for 7 (E. J. Gray 88 not out)
Match drawn
Auckland 8 pts, Wellington 4 pts

at Carisbrook, Dunedin
Otago 112 (G. K. Robertson 6 for 47) and 162 (B. R. Blair 57, D. C. Aberhart 4 for 35)
Central Districts 228 (G. N. Edwards 96) and 47 for 4 (R. Webb 4 for 23)
Central Districts won by 6 wickets
Central Districts 18 pts, Otago 4 pts

The Shell Trophy slipped further from the grasp of Northern Districts when they suffered their second defeat of the season. They led on the first innings and Barry Cooper again batted impressively, but the bowling of David Stead was decisive. Vaughan Brown gave further indication of his batting form, but Northern could take heart from a maiden century from Chris Kuggeleijn who shared a second wicket stand of 237 with Grant Gibson. Evan Gray gave a fine all-round display which saved Wellington from defeat against Auckland for whom Peter Webb hit a career best. The pace bowling of Gary Robertson and the forceful batting of 'Jock' Edwards gave Central an easy win in Dunedin though they did lose four wickets to Richard Webb in the rush for runs.

Shell Cup

4 January 1981   **at Seddon Park, Hamilton**
Canterbury 231 for 9 (D. A. Dempsey 104)
Northern Districts 191
Canterbury won by 40 runs

at Basin Reserve, Wellington
Wellington 204
Auckland 208 for 6 (A. E. W. Parsons 91, R. Aitken 54)
Auckland won by 4 wickets

at Carisbrook, Dunedin
Otago 173 (M. F. Gill 4 for 27)
Central Districts 176 for 7 (W. G. Hodgson 71)
Central Districts won by 3 wickets

6 January 1981   **at Rangiora**
Canterbury 228 (R. T. Latham 83, M. F. Gill 4 for 42)
Central Districts 218 (G. J. Langridge 78)
Canterbury won by 10 runs

at Eden Park, Auckland
Auckland 188 for 9 (M. D. Crowe 59, B. R. Blair 4 for 47)
Otago 178 for 5 (I. A. Rutherford 100)
Auckland won by 10 runs

at Basin Reserve, Wellington
Wellington 195 for 9 (R. H. Vance 68, R. B. Reid 57)
Northern Districts 196 for 7 (A. D. G. Roberts 80, M. J. E. Wright 54)
Northern Districts won by 3 wickets

Three wins out of three made it virtually certain that Auckland, rapidly
emerging as the team of the season, would qualify for the final of the Shell
Cup. They had a remarkable victory over Otago where accurate bowling, particularly by Cushen, stifled Otago's batting and gave Auckland a narrow victory
in spite of a splendid hundred from Rutherford. Canterbury, for whom
Dempsey had a rumbustious knock against Northern, also had a narrow win
over Central which allowed them to challenge Auckland's supremacy. Chasing
229, Central reached 210 with only five men out, but in the panic for quick
runs lost their last five wickets for 8 runs. Against Otago Wayne Hodgson had
given Central a sensational win. Facing a total of 173, they were 83 for 5 when
he came to the wicket. He hit 71 of the 81 runs scored while he was batting
and snatched a win for Central

Shell Trophy

7, 8 and 9 January 1981   **at Lancaster Park, Christchurch**
Central Districts 326 for 9 (R. A. Pierce 84, M. H. Toynbee 58) and 232 for
   8 dec (R. A. Pierce 65, E. B. McSweeney 50 not out)
Canterbury 266 (B. R. Hadlee 130, G. K. Robertson 5 for 79) and 168 (D. W.
   Stead 66 not out, D. R. O'Sullivan 4 for 33, G. K. Robertson 4 for 48)
Central Districts won by 124 runs
Central Districts 20 pts, Canterbury 7 pts

at Eden Park, Auckland
Auckland 312 for 8 (A. E. W. Parsons 132) and 185 for 4 dec (J. R. Wiltshire
   72 not out)
Otago 203 for 8 (G. Blakely 74, L. W. Stott 5 for 53) and 185 (R. Hoskin 50,
   J. Ackland 5 for 44)
Auckland won by 109 runs
Auckland 19 pts, Otago 5 pts

at Basin Reserve, Wellington
Wellington 315 for 8 (E. J. Gray 63, R. H. Vance 61) and 210 for 4 dec
   (J. F. M. Morrison 138 not out)
Northern Districts 174 (B. W. Cederwall 6 for 42, S. B. Cater 4 for 73) and
   277 (B. G. Cooper 105, A. D. G. Roberts 81, P. J. Petherick 4 for 63)
Wellington won by 74 runs
Wellington 20 pts, Northern Districts 4 pts

Central Districts won their third successive match in the Shell Trophy when
they outplayed Canterbury. It was a splendid team performance, but once more
it was the pace bowling of Gary Robertson that took the eye. Central's win
gave them a ten point lead over Auckland who also had a comfortable win
over Otago. Austin Parsons was the foundation of their victory with a fine

hundred, but the all-round contribution of John McIntyre was also a big factor in their win. Wellington notched their first win of the season with a good performance against Northern Districts for whom nothing was going right. Evan Gray and the consistent mature play of John Morrison gave solidity to the batting and Brian Cederwall returned career best bowling figures. He and Stewart Cater shot out Northern in the first innings. The visitors' morale was lifted by a maiden century from the excitingly promising Barry Cooper. Roberts also played well, but Peter Petherick spun them to defeat.

Shell Cup

11 January 1981   **at Whangerei**
Northern Districts *v*. Otago
Match abandoned. Rain

at Nelson Park, Napier

Central Districts 207 (W. G. Hodgson 59)
Auckland 147 (M. D. Jamieson 4 for 12)
Central Districts won by 60 runs

at Timaru

Canterbury 265 for 9 (D. A. Dempsey 61, V. R. Brown 56)
Wellington 152 (R. H. Vance 64)
Canterbury won by 113 runs

Canterbury's big victory over Wellington, which was founded on some more fine hitting from the ever improving Dave Dempsey and Vaughan Brown, brought them level with Auckland who went down to Central Districts for whom Wayne Hodgson was once again dominant. As Northern Districts' game was abandoned they moved to within a point of Canterbury and Auckland. The last round of matches would be decisive.

Shell Trophy

12, 13 and 14 January 1981   **at Cobham Oval, Whangerei**
Northern Districts 200 (S. L. Boock 7 for 84) and 225 for 8 dec (A. D. G.
   Roberts 68, S. L. Boock 6 for 62)
Otago 193 (R. Hoskin 57, G. Dawson 50) and 196 for 8 (R. Hoskin 117)
Match drawn
Northern Districts 6 pts, Otago 5 pts

at McLean Park, Napier

Auckland 204 for 8 dec (J. R. Wiltshire 77 not out) and 38 for 2
Central Districts 89 for 6 dec (J. A. J. Cushen 4 for 33)
Match drawn
Auckland 4 pts, Central Districts 3 pts

at Lancaster Park, Christchurch
Wellington 262 (J. F. M. Morrison 80) and 263 for 6 dec (B. W. Cederwall 94,
R. H. Vance 50)
Canterbury 253 (V. R. Brown 104, E. J. Gray 5 for 65) and 276 for 2
(D. A. Dempsey 121, R. T. Latham 63 not out, D. W. Stead 55)
Canterbury won by 8 wickets
Canterbury 19 pts, Wellington 7 pts

The vital contest between Auckland and Central Districts was ruined by rain,
and Canterbury snatched the opportunity to close the gap on the leaders with a
marvellous victory over Wellington. Brian Cederwall hit a career best for
Wellington which was overshadowed by Vaughan Brown's maiden hundred
and then a spectacular career best from Dave Dempsey. After a lean time in
the Shell Trophy matches at the start of the competition he came back to form
in the most aggressive style. Canterbury were set 273 to win and reached the
target at over five runs an over. Dempsey and Stead put on 175 for the first
wicket and Latham continued the onslaught for a memorable victory. It was
a credit to skipper Cran Bull's positive approach to the game that he had
instilled in his Canterbury side. There was great cheer, too, at Whangerei where
Stephen Boock announced his return with a haul of 13 for 146, and Richard
Hoskin hit a maiden hundred. This was in his first season of first-class cricket
and showed once more that talent is emerging in New Zealand cricket.

Shell Cup

17 January 1981   **at Pukekohe**
Auckland 229 for 7 (J. F. Reid 86, P. N. Webb 52, S. J. Scott 4 for 49)
Northern Districts 201 (C. W. Dickeson 62)
Auckland won by 28 runs

at Lancaster Park, Christchurch
Otago 140 for 8
Canterbury 134 (R. Webb 4 for 17)
Otago won by 6 runs

at Masterton
Wellington 215 for 9 (J. F. M. Morrison 56, M. D. Jamieson 5 for 35)
Central Districts 150 (W. G. Hodgson 59, S. B. Cater 5 for 26)
Wellington won by 65 runs

A consistently aggressive batting display by Auckland was too much for
Northern Districts who were wilting at 93 for 7 before a valiant innings by
Cliff Dickeson raised them to some respectability. Central Districts lost their
chance of joining Auckland in the final when they were routed by Wellington.
Wellington batted consistently in spite of another good spell from Jamieson,
but it was Tim Vogel, who reduced Central to 22 for 3 when he dismissed
Anderson, Jones and Toynbee in his opening spell, who took the Man of the
Match award. Canterbury lost a thrilling game to Otago but still reached the
final. Geoff Blakely batted well for Otago and Canterbury never really

recovered from being 9 for 3. They moved to 88 for 7 before McNally and Leggat added 43, but Webb dismissed them both to give Otago their first win in the competition.

Shell Cup Qualifying Tournament Final Positions

	P	W	L	D	Pts
Auckland	5	4	1	—	8
Canterbury	5	3	2	—	6
Northern Districts	5	2	2	1	5
Central Districts	5	2	3	—	4
Wellington	5	2	3	—	4
Otago	5	1	3	1	3

18, 19 and 20 January 1981   **at Seddon Park, Hamilton**
Auckland 360 for 7 (J. F. Reid 173, M. D. Drowe 75) and 81 for 3
Northern Districts 292 for 7 (A. D. G. Roberts 100, B. G. Cooper 86, M. J. E. Wright 55)
Match drawn
Auckland 8 pts, Northern Districts 6 pts

at Lancaster Park, Christchurch
Canterbury 409 for 5 (B. R. Hadlee 163 not out, D. A. Dempsey 131) and 83 for 1
Otago 224 (W. L. Blair 88, D. W. Stead 4 for 49) and 266 (W. L. Blair 140)
Canterbury won by 9 wickets
Canterbury 22 pts, Otago 4 pts

at Palmerston North
Central Districts 445 for 6 (G. N. Edwards 177 not out, A. H. Jones 64, M. H. Toynbee 61) and 18 for 1
Wellington 250 for 8 (B. W. Cederwall 50, G. K. Robertson 5 for 59) and 360 (R. Ormiston 85, B. W. Cederwall 81, E. J. Gray 50)
Match drawn
Central Districts 9 pts, Wellington 5 pts

Canterbury's win over Otago brought them level at the top of the table with Central Districts. An opening stand of 218 between Dave Dempsey, establishing himself as one of the most exciting batsmen in the country, and 39-year-old Barry Hadlee was the foundation of Canterbury's victory. Both batsmen hit career bests. Otago faced an enormous task to save the game, but there were some brave performances, notably from Wayne Blair with a maiden century in the second innings. Auckland remained only ten points behind the two leaders after drawing with Northern Districts. John Reid hit the highest score of his career. He was well supported by Martin Crowe, but Roberts and Cooper thwarted Auckland after Cushen had taken the first two wickets for 9 runs. There was mighty scoring at Palmerston North too where 'Jock' Edwards hit the highest score of his career in his customary ebullient manner. Gary Robertson's bowling gave Central hope of victory, but some solid second innings application saved the game for Wellington.

24, 25 and 26 January 1981 **at Rotorua**
Central Districts 157 and 349 for 8 dec (A. H. Jones 77, G. J. Langridge
  62, E. B. McSweeney 56 not out, W. G. Hodgson 51)
Northern Districts 235 (D. J. White 64, D. R. O'Sullivan 6 for 71) and 174
  for 7
Match drawn
Northern Districts 6 pts, Central Districts 4 pts

at Eden Park, Auckland
Auckland 304 (P. N. Webb 136, A. E. W. Parsons 69) and 196 for 5 dec
  (M. D. Crowe 51 not out)
Wellington 156 (P. Holland 55, J. M. McIntyre 4 for 30) and 174 (R. H. Vance
  65, J. M. McIntyre 5 for 39)
Auckland won by 170 runs
Auckland 20 pts, Wellington 5 pts

Central Districts recovered from a weak first innings batting display with some
solid hitting in their second innings which enabled them to set Northern Districts
272 to win. O'Sullivan and Toynbee bowled them to the brink of victory, but
Roberts offered the straight bat of defence and thwarted them. Central's failure
to beat Northern meant that they surrendered the leadership of the trophy to
Auckland who devastated Wellington at Eden Park. Peter Webb became the
latest batsman of the season to record a career best and Wellington surrendered
limply twice to McIntyre's slow left-arm and Cushen's reliable speed.

30, 31 January and 1 February 1981 **at Pukekura Park, New Plymouth**
Canterbury 146 (M. F. Gill 6 for 53) and 376 for 8 dec (D. W. Stead 193
  not out, G. K. Robertson 4 for 104)
Central Districts 296 (R. A. Pierce 80, G. K. Robertson 65, G. J. Langridge
  52, D. W. Stead 6 for 76) and 227 for 7 (G. N. Edwards 75, G. C. Bateman
  4 for 41)
Central Districts won by 3 wickets
Central Districts 19 pts, Canterbury 4 pts

at Carisbrook, Dunedin
Otago 98 (G. B. Troup 4 for 21, J. A. J. Cushen 4 for 48) and 189 (B. R.
  Blair 57, J. M. McIntyre 5 for 59)
Auckland 219 (M. D. Crowe 81, J. F. Reid 56, S. L. Boock 6 for 65) and
  69 for 7 (S. L. Boock 6 for 22)
Auckland won by 3 wickets
Auckland 18 pts, Otago 4 pts

In thrilling matches of contrasting styles both Auckland and Central Districts
won and Auckland's win gave them the Shell Trophy, a remarkable achievement
considering that they had finished last in 1980. In both matches it was the
losers who provided the hero of the contest. David Stead, left handed bat and
right arm leg-break bowler, hit the highest score of his career and produced
the best bowling he has ever accomplished, but Central answered Cran Bull's
challenge to score at more than five an over with resounding hitting from 'Jock'

Edwards and the rest. Gary Troup returned to the Auckland side and, with John Cushen, routed Otago on the opening day. Auckland moved solidly to a substantial lead with a career best from Martin Crowe. Auckland were left needing only 69 to win the Shell Trophy. Stephen Boock, neglected at international level, gave them a terrible attack of the jitters with some splendid left-arm bowling. They scraped home by 3 wickets and Boock had match figures of 12 for 87.

6, 7 and 8 February 1981   **at Basin Reserve, Wellington**
Otago 271 (W. L. Blair 83, G. Dawson 61) and 185 (D. Walker 58, P. J. Petherick 5 for 48)
Wellington 219 (S. L. Boock 4 for 48) and 231 for 9 (J. F. M. Morrison 84 not out, P. Holland 52, D. Walker 4 for 53)
Match drawn
Otago 6 pts, Wellington 6 pts

7, 8 and 9 February 1981   **at Lancaster Park, Christchurch**
Canterbury 311 for 8 (B. D. Ritchie 61 not out) and 257 for 5 dec (R. T. Latham 67, D. W. Stead 52 not out, B. G. Cooper 4 for 82)
Northern Districts 270 (A. D. G. Roberts 95, R. Broughton 70, D. W. Stead 5 for 86) and 203 (R. I. Leggat 5 for 37)
Canterbury won by 95 runs
Canterbury 20 pts, Northern Districts 6 pts

The season of Shell cricket competitions ended in a flourish. John Morrison failed by 7 runs and Man of the Match Derek Walker failed by one wicket to give their respective sides victory in a wonderful match at Basin Reserve. Canterbury's fine win over Northern Districts, who finished the season without a win and went from top to bottom, moved them into second place, a just reward for some enterprising cricket under Cran Bull's leadership.

Shell Trophy Final Table

	P	W	L	D	Pts
Auckland (6)	7	4	—	3	97
Canterbury (3)	7	4	3	—	93
Central Districts (5)	7	4	—	3	92
Wellington (2)	7	1	3	3	51
Otago (4)	7	1	4	2	45
Northern Districts (1)	7	—	4	3	41

(1980 Position in Brackets)

Shell Cup Final

6 February 1981   **at Eden Park, Auckland**
Canterbury 186 (V. R. Brown 65, B. R. Hadlee 45, J. M. McIntyre 3 for 43)
Auckland 188 for 7 (J. F. Reid 96 not out, M. D. Crowe 34, C. H. Thiele 3 for 15)
Auckland won by 3 wickets
Man of the Match – John Reid
Fielding prize – Peter Webb

The positions in the Shell Cup were a duplicate of those in the Shell Trophy with Auckland beating Canterbury by 3 wickets with 5 balls to spare. Canterbury began very well. Dempsey hit 22 out of 26 before falling to Troup and then Hadlee and Brown added 109 for the second wicket. After that the innings fell apart, but Auckland began badly, Parsons being bowled by Thiele in the first over. Franklin also went quickly, but the majestic and confident Reid, first with Crowe and then with Webb, steered Auckland to victory in spite of some alarms.

First One-Day International

Once more the Indians displayed their lack of appetite for the one-day game and were outplayed from start to finish by the zestful and ever-improving New Zealand side. A second wicket stand of 88 between Edwards and Edgar was the foundation of the New Zealand innings of 218 scored at just under five an over, and Hadlee and Cairns made useful late hard-hit contributions. Edgar was unlucky to be denied a well-deserved century. Chauhan and Vengsarkar were out with only ten on the board for India and when Gavaskar, Viswanath and Patil followed before the score reached fifty, the contest was over. Kapil Dev made a characteristic brave flourish, but the task was beyond even him.

First One-Day International **New Zealand v. India**
14 February 1981 at Eden Park, Auckland

New Zealand

J. G. Wright	c Binny, b Ghavri	10
B. A. Edgar	not out	99
G. N. Edwards	c Chauhan, b Ghavri	36
G. P. Howarth (capt)	c Yograj Singh, b Patil	11
J. V. Coney	c and b Kapil Dev	2
* I. D. S. Smith	lbw, b Patil	10
R. J. Hadlee	c Vengsarkar, b Ghavri	22
B. L. Cairns	not out	12
Extras	lb 11, w 1, nb 4	16
	(for 6 wkts)	218

M. C. Snedden, G. B. Troup and E. J. Chatfield did not bat.

	O	M	R	W
Kapil Dev	10	1	40	1
Ghavri	10	1	40	3
Binny	6	2	26	—
Yograj Singh	9	—	57	—
Patil	10	1	39	2

Fall of Wickets
1–24, 2–112, 3–127, 4–132, 5–156, 6–196.

India

| C. P. S. Chauhan | b Hadlee | 6 |
| S. M. Gavaskar (capt) | c Smith, b Snedden | 14 |

D. B. Vengsarkar	run out	0
G. R. Viswanath	b Chatfield	14
S. M. Patil	b Chatfield	4
Yashpal Sharma	c Edwards, b Cairns	17
Kapil Dev	run out	50
R. Binny	c Edwards, b Cairns	12
K. D. Ghavri	not out	6
Yograj Singh	c Hadlee, b Troup	1
*S. M. H. Kirmani	not out	10
Extras	lb 5, nb 1	6
		140

	O	M	R	W
Hadlee	6	3	6	1
Troup	10	3	21	1
Chatfield	10	2	36	2
Snedden	8	2	26	1
Coney	3	—	7	—
Cairns	7	2	33	2
Howarth	1	—	5	—

Fall of Wickets
1–9, 2–10, 3–31, 4–40, 5–41, 6–86, 7–122, 8–122, 9–124.

New Zealand won by 78 runs

Second One-Day International

Without Gavaskar the Indians fared only marginally better in the second match. Robertson replaced Cairns in the New Zealand side so winning international recognition for the first time. The New Zealanders started less comfortably this time, but a solid batting display saw them past two hundred. They had been put into bat on a green wicket, but the Indian bowlers, Kapil Dev apart, had failed to exploit the conditions to advantage. India, in fact, began well and their second wicket, that of Chauhan, did not fall until the score had reached 82, but by then more than half of their fifty overs had been used and the later batsmen succumbed in the mad rush for runs.

Second One-Day International   **New Zealand v. India**
15 February 1981   at Seddon Park, Hamilton

New Zealand

J. G. Wright	c Kirmani, b Binny	38
B. A. Edgar	b Kapil Dev	1
G. N. Edwards	c Vengsarkar, b Yograj Singh	17
G. P. Howarth (capt)	c Chauhan, b Patil	17
J. V. Coney	c Vengsarkar, b Ghavri	46
*I. D. S. Smith	c Vengsarkar, b Patil	0
R. J. Hadlee	c Kirti Azad, b Ghavri	23

G. K. Robertson	c Patil, b Kapil Dev	17
M. C. Snedden	not out	11
G. B. Troup	not out	14
Extras	b 1, lb 10, w 1, nb 5	26
	(for 8 wkts)	210

E. J. Chatfield did not bat.

	O	M	R	W
Kapil Dev	10	1	34	2
Yograj Singh	10	2	37	1
Ghavri	10	1	47	2
Binny	10	2	38	1
Patil	10	1	28	2

Fall of Wickets
1–15, 2–43, 3–89, 4–91, 5–92, 6–165, 7–166, 8–183.

India

G. P. S. Chauhan	b Snedden	31
R. Binny	c Howarth, b Chatfield	18
D. B. Vengsarkar	b Hadlee	41
Kirti Azad	b Robertson	10
G. R. Viswanath (capt)	b Snedden	5
S. M. Patil	b Robertson	20
Yashpal Sharma	lbw, b Hadlee	9
Kapil Dev	lbw, b Troup	1
* S. M. H. Kirmani	c Smith, b Troup	2
K. D. Ghavri	c Wright, b Troup	3
Yograj Singh	not out	0
Extras	b 6, lb 4, w 2, nb 1	13
		153

	O	M	R	W
Hadlee	8	1	27	2
Troup	9.2	2	18	3
Chatfield	10	1	31	1
Robertson	10	1	29	2
Snedden	8	1	35	2

Fall of Wickets
1–34, 2–82, 3–104, 4–111, 5–127, 6–140, 7–141, 8–149, 9–153.

New Zealand won by 57 runs

17, 18 and 19 February 1981   **at McLean Park, Napier**
Indians 312 for 7 dec (Kirti Azad 127 not out and 195 for 3 dec (T. E. Srinavasan 90, C. P. S. Chauhan 79)
Central Districts 277 for 7 dec (G. N. Edwards 103, R. W. Anderson 101) and 29 for 0
Match drawn

Central Districts gave a fine account of themselves in the match which preceded the First Test and a stand of 176 between Anderson and Edwards was the highlight of the match. They came together when Central had lost both openers for 36. Chauhan and Srinivasan countered with an opening partnership of 144 in the second innings. Kirti Azad dominated the first day with an attractive and aggressive hundred.

First Test Match

John Reid and 'Jock' Edwards were brought into the New Zealand side to join nine who had toured Australia and both of them performed well. Reid and Howarth put on 99 for the third wicket and the New Zealand captain continued in his most elegant vein to give his side a grip on the match which they did not relinquish until an unaccountable second innings collapse which saw the young spinner Shastri take the last three wickets in one over. With two days in which to make 253, the Indians were destroyed by some inspired pace bowling and enthusiastic, unflagging fielding. The wave of optimism surging through New Zealand cricket had proved well founded.

First Test Match   New Zealand v. India
21, 22, 23 and 25 February 1981   **at Basin Reserve, Wellington**

New Zealand	*First Innings*		*Second Innings*	
J. G. Wright	c Binny, b Yograj	32	c Viswanath, b Dev	8
B. A. Edgar	c Kirmani, b Patil	39	c Patil, b Binny	28
J. F. Reid	c Kirmani, b Patil	46	lbw, b Dev	7
G. P. Howarth (capt)	not out	137	c Kirmani, b Patil	7
J. V. Coney	c and b Shastri	4	c sub, b Dev	8
G. N. Edwards	c Kirmani, b Dev	23	c sub, b Dev	6
*I. D. S. Smith	c Vengsarkar, b Dev	20	not out	15
R. J. Hadlee	c Kirmani, b Binny	20	c Kirmani, b Binny	7
B. L. Cairns	c Gavaskar, b Dev	13	c Vengsarkar, b Shastri	0
M. C. Snedden	b Shastri	2	c Vengsarkar, b Shastri	0
G. B. Troup	c Gavaskar, b Shastri	0	c Vengsarkar, b Shastri	0
Extras	b 4, lb 18, w 1, nb 16	39	lb 9, w 2, nb 3	14
		375		100

	O	M	R	W		O	M	R	W
Kapil Dev	38	9	112	3		16	4	34	4
Yograj Singh	15	3	63	1					
Binny	22	4	67	1		12	4	26	2
Shastri	28	9	54	3		3	—	9	3
Patil	16	4	40	2		17	10	12	1
Kirti Azad						1	—	5	—

Fall of Wickets
1–60, 2–101, 3–200, 4–215, 5–245, 6–292, 7–331, 8–364, 9–375.
1–17, 2–35, 3–57, 4–58, 5–73, 6–78, 7–99, 8–100, 9–100.

India	*First Innings*		*Second Innings*	
S. M. Gavaskar (capt)	b Cairns	23	b Snedden	12
C. P. S. Chauhan	c Coney, b Troup	17	b Hadlee	1
D. B. Vengsarkar	lbw, b Cairns	39	c Smith, b Hadlee	26
G. R. Viswanath	b Cairns	0	b Troup	9

S. Patil	c Smith, b Troup	64	c Smith, b Cairns		42
Kirti Azad	b Cairns	20	b Hadlee		16
Kapil Dev	c Smith, b Troup	0	c Hadlee, b Troup		9
*S. M. H. Kirmani	run out	13	b Cairns		11
R. M. Binny	b Snedden	11	not out		26
R. Shastri	not out	3	c Smith, b Snedden		19
Yograj Singh	c Smith, b Cairns	4	c Smith, b Hadlee		6
Extras	b 10, lb 13, nb 6	29	b 2, lb 5, nb 6		13
		223			190

	O	M	R	W		O	M	R	W
Hadlee	16	4	62	—		22.3	7	65	4
Troup	17	5	43	3		13	4	34	2
Cairns	19.4	8	33	5		19	9	30	2
Snedden	20	7	56	1		17	4	39	2
Coney						4	1	9	—

Fall of Wickets
1–32, 2–70, 4–116, 5–183, 6–183, 7–198, 8–213, 9–218.
1–10, 2–30, 3–50, 4–75, 5–111, 6–117, 7–136, 8–136, 9–170.

The substitute catches for India were taken by T. E. Srinivasan

New Zealand won by 62 runs

28 February, 1 and 2 March   **at Carisbrook, Dunedin**
Otago 187 (B. R. Blair 65, Kirti Azad 6 for 50) and 117 (R. Shastri 5 for 22)
Indians 318 (Yashpal Sharma 89, C. P. S. Chauhan 83, J. G. Bracewell 7 for 155)
Indians won by an innings and 14 runs

The Indians were encouraged by an innings victory over Otago and a return to form and fitness by Yashpal Sharma. It was a match in which the spinners took all the bowling prizes, Boock and Bracewell dismissing three and seven of the Indians respectively.

Second and Third Test Matches

These matches are covered by Don Cameron in his review of the season. The rain ruined Second Test was notable for John Reid's maiden Test hundred. The Third Test disappointed home supporters when Geoff Howarth gave up the chase for victory. India were all out just before lunch on the last day and New Zealand needed 157 to win. Edgar went quickly, but Wright and Edwards gave hope of victory until Edwards was brilliantly caught and bowled. At 4.20 New Zealand needed 70 to win with 7 wickets in hand, but Howarth decided to play out time.

Second Test Match   New Zealand v. India
6, 7, 8, 10 and 11 March 1981   **at Lancaster Park, Christchurch**

India   *First Innings*
S. M. Gavaskar (capt)   c Smith, b Hadlee   53

C. P. S. Chauhan	c Smith, b Hadlee	78
D. B. Vengsarkar	b Snedden	61
G. R. Viswanath	b Hadlee	7
S. M. Patil	c Reid, b Hadlee	4
Yashpal Sharma	c Howarth, b Hadlee	0
*S. M. H. Kirmani	retired hurt	9
Kapil Dev	c and b Snedden	0
K. D. Ghavri	c Reid, b Coney	17
R. Shastri	not out	12
D. R. Doshi	b Coney	0
Extras	b 4, lb 5, nb 5	14
		255

	O	M	R	W
Hadlee	33	12	47	5
Troup	26	6	60	—
Cairns	33	16	57	—
Snedden	23	8	63	2
Coney	9	4	12	2
Howarth	3	2	2	—

Fall of Wickets
1–114, 2–168, 3–200, 4–210, 5–210, 6–224, 7–224, 8–255, 9–255.

New Zealand	*First Innings*	
J. G. Wright	c Vengsarkar, b Ghavri	18
B. A. Edgar	lbw, b Shastri	49
J. F. Reid	not out	123
G. P. Howarth (capt)	c sub (Srinivasan), b Doshi	26
J. V. Coney	c Chauhan, b Patil	15
G. N. Edwards	b Shastri	23
*I. D. S. Smith	not out	11
Extras	b 6, lb 8, nb 7	21
	(for 5 wkts)	286

R. J. Hadlee, G. B. Troup, B. L. Cairns and M. C. Snedden did not bat.

	O	M	R	W
Kapil Dev	22	2	60	—
Ghavri	10	4	33	1
Patil	12	4	14	1
Doshi	49	23	67	1
Shastri	42	21	65	2
Chauhan	5	1	12	—
Gavaskar	3	1	11	—
Vengsarkar	2	1	3	—

Fall of Wickets
1–27, 2–152, 3–201, 4–235, 5–265.

Match drawn

Third Test Match   New Zealand *v.* India
13, 14, 15, 17 and 18 March 1981   **at Eden Park, Auckland**

India	*First Innings*		*Second Innings*	
S. M. Gavaskar (capt)	c Smith, b Snedden	5	c Wright, b Bracewell	33
C. P. S. Chauhan	c Cairns, b Bracewell	36	c Cairns, b Bracewell	7
D. B. Vengsarkar	c Smith, b Snedden	0	not out	52
S. M. Patil	b Cairns	19	b Bracewell	57
G. R. Viswanath	lbw, b Hadlee	2	run out	46
T. E. Srinivasan	c Smith, b Bracewell	29	c Wright, b Cairns	19
R. Shastri	c and b Cairns	5	run out	9
*S. M. H. Kirmani	b Bracewell	78	b Bracewell	1
Kapil Dev	b Cairns	4	c Edgar, b Cairns	14
S. Yadav	c Hadlee, b Bracewell	43	c Smith, b Bracewell	1
D. R. Doshi	not out	3	b Cairns	2
Extras	b 5, lb 3, nb 6	14	b 23, lb 7, nb 13	43
		238		**284**

	O	M	R	W		O	M	R	W
Hadlee	27	11	49	1		21	3	65	—
Snedden	22	7	52	2		13	4	40	—
Cairns	27	13	37	3		35.5	16	47	3
Coney	9	1	14	—		4	1	3	—
Bracewell	42.3	17	61	4		41	19	75	5
Howarth	3	—	11	—		6	3	11	—

Fall of Wickets
1–9, 2–10, 3–43, 4–50, 5–97, 6–100, 7–114, 8–124, 9–229.
1–43, 2–50, 3–93, 4–143, 5–236, 6–260, 7–261, 8–271, 9–279.

New Zealand	*First Innings*		*Second Innings*	
J. G. Wright	c Kirmani, b Chauhan	110	not out	33
B. A. Edgar	c Shastri, b Patil	0	c Kirmani, b Dev	1
J. F. Reid	c Viswanath, b Shastri	74	(5) lbw, b Doshi	0
G. P. Howarth (capt)	c sub (Binny), b Shastri	0	(6) c Chauhan, b Doshi	2
J. V. Coney	c and b Doshi	65	(7) not out	0
G. N. Edwards	c and b Doshi	34	(3) c and b Shastri	47
R. J. Hadlee	c Chauhan, b Yadav	0	(4) b Shastri	2
B. L. Cairns	c Gavaskar, b Shastri	41		
*I. D. S. Smith	b Shastri	10		
J. G. Bracewell	lbw, b Shastri	1		
M. C. Snedden	not out	0		
Extras	b 14, lb 10, nb 7	31	b 3, lb 4, nb 3	10
		366	(for 5 wkts)	**95**

	O	M	R	W		O	M	R	W
Kapil Dev	20	6	34	—		10	5	15	1
Patil	6	4	2	1		4	—	8	—
Yadav	33	8	91	1		9.1	4	20	—
Doshi	69	34	79	2		19	9	18	2
Shastri	56	13	125	5		18	8	24	2
Chauhan	2	—	4	1					

Fall of Wickets
1–0, 2–148, 3–152, 4–251, 5–301, 6–302, 7–332, 8–354, 9–365.
1–1, 2–83, 3–87, 4–94, 5–95.

Match drawn

New Zealand *v.* India – Test Match Averages

New Zealand Batting

	M	Inns	NOs	Runs	HS	Average	100s	50s
J. F. Reid	3	5	1	250	123*	62.50	1	1
J. G. Wright	3	5	1	201	110	50.25	1	
G. P. Howarth	3	5	1	172	137*	43.00	1	
I. D. S. Smith	3	4	2	56	20	28.00		
G. N. Edwards	3	5		133	47	26.60		
B. A. Edgar	3	5		117	49	23.40		
J. V. Coney	3	5	1	92	65	23.00		1
B. L. Cairns	3	3		54	41	18.00		
R. J. Hadlee	3	4		29	20	7.25		
M. C. Snedden	3	3	1	2	2	1.00		
G. B. Troup	2	2		0	0	0.00		

Also batted: J. G. Bracewell 1 (one Test).

New Zealand Bowling

	Overs	Mdns	Runs	Wkts	Average	Best	5/inn
J. G. Bracewell	83.3	36	136	9	15.11	5–75	1
B. L. Cairns	134.3	62	204	13	15.69	5–33	1
J. V. Coney	26	7	38	2	19.00	2–12	
G. B. Troup	56	15	137	5	27.40	3–43	
R. J. Hadlee	119.3	37	288	10	28.80	5–47	1
M. C. Snedden	95	30	250	7	35.71	2–39	
G. P. Howarth	12	5	24	0	—	0–2	

New Zealand Catches
13 – I. D. S. Smith; 3 – B. L. Cairns; 2 – R. J. Hadlee, J. G. Wright and J. F. Reid;
1 – B. A. Edgar, G. P. Howarth, J. V. Coney and M. C. Snedden.

India Batting

	M	Inns	NOs	Runs	HS	Average	100s	50s
D. B. Vengsarkar	3	5	1	178	61	44.50		2
S. M. Patil	3	5		186	64	37.20		2
S. M. H. Kirmani	3	5	1	112	78	28.00		1
C. P. S. Chauhan	3	5		139	78	27.80		1
S. M. Gavaskar	3	5		126	53	25.20		1
R. Shastri	3	5	2	48	19	16.00		
G. R. Viswanath	3	5		64	46	12.80		
Kapil Dev	3	5		27	14	5.40		
D. R. Doshi	2	3	1	5	3*	2.50		

Also batted in one Test: R. M. Binny 11, 7 and 26*; T. E. Srinivasan 29 and 19;
S. Yadav 43 and 1; Kirti Azad 20 and 16; K. D. Ghavri 17; Yograj Singh 4 and 6;
Yashpal Sharma 0.

India Bowling

	Overs	Mdns	Runs	Wkts	Average	Best	5/inn
S. M. Patil	55	22	76	5	15.20	2–40	
C. P. S. Chauhan	7	1	16	1	16.00	1–4	
R. Shastri	147	51	277	15	18.46	5–125	1
R. M. Binny	34	8	93	3	31.00	2–26	
Kapil Dev	106	26	255	8	31.87	4–34	
D. R. Doshi	137	66	164	5	32.80	2–18	
S. Yadav	42.1	12	111	1	111.00	1–91	

Also bowled: S. M. Gavaskar 3–1–11–0; K. D. Ghavri 10–4–33–1; D. B. Vengsarkar 2–1–3–0; Yograj Singh 15–3–63–1; Kirti Azad 1–0–5–0.

India Catches

8 – S. M. H. Kirmani; 5 – D. B. Vengsarkar; 3 – C. P. S. Chauhan, R. Shastri, S. M. Gavaskar and T. E. Srinivasan (all as sub); 2 – G. R. Viswanath, D. R. Doshi and R. M. Binny (one as sub); 1 – S. M. Patil.

First-Class Averages

Batting

	M	Inns	NOs	Runs	HS	Average	100s	50s
J. F. Reid	10	18	4	817	173	58.35	3	3
J. F. M. Morrison	7	14	3	599	138*	54.45	1	3
V. R. Brown	7	12	2	513	104	51.30	1	2
J. G. Wright	3	5	1	201	110	50.25	1	
A. D. G. Roberts	7	13	2	541	100	49.18	1	3
G. N. Edwards	11	19	2	812	177	47.76	2	3
D. W. Stead	7	13	3	477	193*	47.70	1	3
B. R. Hadlee	6	12	1	477	163*	43.36	2	1
G. P. Howarth	3	5	1	172	137	43.00	1	
B. D. Ritchie	7	11	4	287	75*	41.00		2
J. R. Wiltshire	7	11	2	368	77*	40.88		2
B. G. Cooper	7	13		520	105	40.00	1	2
E. J. Gray	7	14	2	473	88*	39.41		5
P. N. Webb	7	13	2	431	136	39.18	2	1
D. A. Dempsey	7	14	1	471	131	36.23	2	
W. L. Blair	8	16		556	140	34.75	1	3
R. A. Pierce	5	10	1	312	84	34.66		3
G. K. Robertson	8	10	3	240	65	34.28		2
M. D. Crowe	7	12	3	303	81	33.66		2
A. E. W. Parsons	7	13	1	393	132	32.75	1	1
R. T. Latham	7	13	1	381	67	31.75		2
R. W. Anderson	5	8	1	222	101	31.71	1	
A. H. Jones	7	12	1	343	77	31.18		3
R. Broughton	3	5		149	70	29.80		1
B. W. Cederwall	7	13	2	320	94	29.09		3
R. H. Vance	7	14		389	65	27.78		5
E. B. McSweeney	7	11	3	221	56*	27.62		2
J. G. Gibson	7	13		349	119	26.84	1	
P. J. Holland	6	11		290	55	26.36		2
M. J. E. Wright	7	13		341	55	26.23		1
G. Dawson	6	12	2	262	61	26.20		2
R. I. Leggat	5	8	1	182	44	26.00		
G. J. Langridge	8	13	2	284	62	25.81		3

	M	I	NO	Runs	HS	Avge	100	50
D. Henry	6	9	3	153	40*	25.50		
R. Ormiston	7	10		242	85	24.20		1
W. G. Hodgson	7	12	1	265	51	24.09		1
R. Hoskin	8	16		380	117	23.75	1	2
B. A. Edgar	3	5		117	49	23.40		
B. R. Blair	7	14		312	65	22.28		3
C. M. Kuggeleijn	7	13		272	116	20.92	1	
M. H. Toynbee	7	12		247	61	20.58		2
T. Franklin	7	13		256	42	20.38		
J. M. McIntyre	7	9	4	100	31	20.00		
G. Blakely	8	16		291	74	18.18		1
G. A. Newdick	7	14		253	42	18.07		
C. W. Dickeson	7	13	3	174	58	17.40		1
I. A. Rutherford	8	16		270	45	16.87		
C. L. Bull	7	12	1	175	31	15.90		
S. R. Gillespie	6	10	2	120	32	15.00		
B. Milburn	7	14		207	103	14.78	1	
S. B. Cater	7	12		147	36	12.25		
D. Walker	5	10		119	58	11.90		1

(Qualification 100 runs, average 10.00.)

Bowling

	Overs	Mdns	Runs	Wkts	Average	Best	5/inn	10/m
J. M. McIntyre	279.3	120	484	31	15.61	5–39	2	
B. L. Cairns	134.3	62	204	13	15.69	5–33	1	
J. G. Bracewell	123.5	45	291	16	18.18	7–155	2	
S. L. Boock	329.4	123	757	41	18.46	7–84	4	2
G. B. Troup	124.5	37	244	13	18.76	4–21		
J. A. J. Cushen	181.3	41	444	23	19.30	4–33		
G. K. Robertson	272	68	736	38	19.36	6–47	4	
L. W. Stott	250	72	544	26	20.92	5–41	2	
D. C. Aberhart	188.1	73	342	16	21.37	4–35		
D. R. O'Sullivan	443.3	164	880	40	22.00	6–71	1	
P. J. Petherick	207	54	536	24	22.33	5–48	1	
R. I. Leggat	111.2	20	398	17	23.41	5–37	1	
G. B. Thomson	166.3	50	382	16	23.87	6–41	1	1
C. W. Dickeson	379.5	134	857	34	25.20	7–79	1	1
G. C. Bateman	167	47	455	17	26.76	4–41		
D. W. Stead	286	53	877	32	27.40	6–76	2	
E. J. Gray	271.5	84	741	27	27.44	5–65	1	
M. F. Gill	201.1	51	552	20	27.60	6–53	1	
K. Treiber	102.3	27	276	10	27.60	3–21		
S. B. Cater	197.2	43	601	21	28.61	5–71	1	
R. J. Hadlee	119.3	37	288	10	28.80	5–47	1	
S. R. Gillespie	203.1	33	534	18	29.66	3–57		
M. H. Toynbee	147	49	327	11	29.72	3–60		
C. H. Thiele	166	37	507	17	29.82	3–45		
B. R. Blair	149.4	37	424	12	35.33	3–36		
B. W. Cederwall	177.1	66	438	12	36.50	6–42	1	
S. R. McNally	151	35	453	12	37.75	4–73		
R. Webb	177.2	41	546	13	42.00	4–23		

(Qualification 10 wickets.)

Wicket-keeping

26 – E. B. McSweeney (ct 21/st 5) and B. Milburn (ct 21/st 5)
20 – J. Mackie (ct 16/st 4)
16 – I. D. S. Smith (ct 16)
14 – R. H. Vance (ct 11/st 3) and N. Scott (ct 10/st 4)
13 – M. J. E. Wright (ct 11/st 2)
12 – B. D. Ritchie (ct 11/st 1) (not all catches while keeping wicket)

Leading catchers

13 – J. F. M. Morrison
11 – G. N. Edwards
10 – C. M. Kuggeleijn
 9 – W. G. Hodgson and W. L. Blair
 8 – C. W. Dickeson
 7 – R. Ormiston, M. D. Crowe, J. R. Wiltshire, M. H. Toynbee and A. H. Jones

ichard Hadlee of New Zealand and Nottinghamshire.

Auckland
First-Class Matches – Batting, 1980–81

	v. Canterbury (Auckland) 27–29 December	v. Wellington (Wellington) 1–3 January	v. Otago (Auckland) 7–9 January	v. Central Districts (Napier) 12–14 January	v. Northern Districts (Hamilton) 18–20 January	v. Wellington (Auckland) 24–26 January	v. Otago (Dunedin) 30 January–1 February	Inns	NOs	Runs	HS	Av
A. E. W. Parsons	16	14 23	132 17	3 6	18 32	69 30	22* 11	13	1	393	132	32.75
T. Franklin	42	2 37	12 18	32 12	36 26	6 32	5 5	13	—	265	42	20.38
J. F. Reid	113*	56 43*	39 13	4 6*	173 9	15 25	56 15	13	3	567	173	56.70
P. N. Webb	58	119 4	15 28	1 13*	14 6*	136 16	5 16	13	2	431	136	39.18
M. D. Crowe	0	30 14	3 34*	12	75	51* 1	81	12	3	303	81	33.66
J. R. Wiltshire	48	27 20	34* 72*	77*	3	28 29	81	11	2	368	77*	40.88
J. M. McIntyre		5* 9*	21	6	9	31	4	9	4	100	31	20.00
L. W. Stott		6*	21	30	18*	0	4	7	2	83	30	16.60
N. Scott			17*	15	4*	1*	0	5	3	37	17*	18.50
J. A. J. Cushen			6*	14*			1	4	2	24	14*	12.00
J. Ackland								—				—
G. B. Troup	8*	23				1	0	3	1	2	1*	1.00
W. Linn		7		1	81		0 1*	3	1	38	23	19.00
Byes	2	14 10	3	1	9	1 7	22					
Leg byes	9	13 10	5	4		9 6	10 7					
Wides	1		1	2	1							
No balls	3	9 7	3	3	3	3	18					
Total	300	318 177	312 185	204 38	360 81	304 196	219 69					
Wickets	5	7 6	8 4	8 2	7 3	10 5	10 7					
Result	W	D	W	D	D	W						
Points	20	8	19	4	8	20	18					

Catches

14 – N. Scott (ct 10, st 4)
7 – M. D. Crowe and J. R. Wiltshire
6 – A. E. W. Parsons
5 – T. F... and P. N. W...
4 – J. A. J. Cushen
3 – L. W. Stott, W. Linn (2 as sub) and J. Ackland (2 as sub)
2 – J. M. McIntyre
1 – J. F. Reid

Auckland First-Class Matches – Bowling 1980–81

Match	J. A. J. Cushen	L. W. Stott	J. Ackland	J. M. McIntyre	J. F. Reid	M. D. Crowe	G. B. Troup	W. Linn	A. E. W. Parsons	B	Lb	W	Nb	Total	Wkt
v. Canterbury (Auckland) 27–29 December	12-4-23-3	17-4-41-5		1.3-1-0-1	2.5-0-5-2	4-2-8-2		4-0-11-0			1		1	77	9
	15-5-23-1	15-6-15-1		23-13-38-3				9-3-23-0			4		8	124	9†
v. Wellington (Wellington) 1–3 January	23.3-4-74-3	24-7-61-4		28-15-30-1				11-1-23-1		1	4		2	194	10
	16-9-26-0	32-6-95-3		30-14-57-3		7-3-19-0		11-3-28-1	1-0-12-0		6		7	251	7
v. Otago (Auckland) 7–9 January	16-3-40-0	27-9-53-5	14-5-29-0	41-19-58-2	2-0-8-1					8	6		1	203	8
	14-4-40-1	9-1-20-1	19.2-4-44-5	25-8-58-3	4-0-13-0					4	2		4	185	10
v. Central Districts (Napier) 12–14 January	15-0-33-4	9-3-29-1		10.5-0-19-1						4	3		1	89	6
v. Northern Districts (Hamilton) 18–20 January	15-3-44-2	34-13-72-2	13-4-46-0	33-12-96-3	6-3-12-0 21-4-50-2	5-0-21-0					11		2	292	7
v. Wellington (Auckland) 24–26 January	16-1-46-3	21-6-39-1		21-13-30-4			14-4-26-1			2	3			156	10
	10-1-32-2	10-2-24-0		31.1-12-39-5			11-0-25-0			1	1		1	174	10
v. Otago (Dunedin) 30 Jan–1 Feb	22-6-48-4	14-6-20-1		35-13-59-5	1-1-0-0		14.4-5-21-4			4			5	98	10
	7-1-15-0	38-9-75-2					29.1-13-35-3			5				189	10
	181.3-41- 444-23 av. 19.30	250-72- 544-26 av. 20.92	46.2-13- 119-5 av. 23.80	279.3-120- 484-31 av. 15.61	36.5-8 88-5 av. 17.60	16-5- 48-2 av. 24.00	68.5-22- 107-8 av. 13.37	35-7- 85-2 av. 42.50	1-0- 12-0 –						

† V. R. Brown, absent ill

Canterbury
First-Class Matches – Batting
1980–81

	v. Auckland (Auckland) 27-29 December	v. Northern Districts (Hamilton) 1-3 January	v. Central Districts (Christchurch) 7-9 January	v. Wellington (Christchurch) 12-14 January	v. Otago (Christchurch) 18-20 January	v. Central Districts (New Plymouth) 30 January-1 February	v. Northern Districts (Christchurch) 7-9 February	Inns	NOs	Runs	HS	Av
D. A. Dempsey	2, 10	15, 0	4, 4	22, 121	131, 29*	17, 40	49, 27	14	1	471	131	36.23
B. R. Hadlee	9, 10	76, 16	130	1	163*, 0	1, 14	44, 13	12	1	477	163*	43.36
V. R. Brown	—	78, 79	14, 0	104, 22*	37, 48*	34, 16	47, 34	12	2	513	104	51.30
C. L. Bull	19, 31	—, 14	3, 0	14	25	13, 18	22, 17*	12	1	175	31	15.90
J. Mackie	4, 10	5	0, 7	14	—	8, 0*	—	8	1	48	14	6.85
D. W. Stead	0, 17	45, 1	6, 66*	42, 1	24	2, 193*	28, 52*	13	3	477	193*	47.70
R. T. Latham	8, 1	23*, 40	40, 21	55, 63*	16	17, 10	11, 67	13	1	381	67	31.75
B. D. Ritchie	15, 30	23*, 75*	12, 2	6	2*	30, 37	61*	11	4	287	75*	41.00
R. I. Leggat	9	5	44, 23	3*	—	2, 20	32, 33	8	1	182	44	26.00
S. R. McNally	1	17	1, 36	25	5, 5	—	—	6	—	70	36	11.66
C. H. Thiele	6*, 1*	—	2*, 0	8	1	2*	2	7	5	16	6*	8.00
P. J. Rattray	—	—	—	25	—	—	—	1	—	25	25	25.00
G. C. Bateman	3, 1	5	2	8	—	7, 15	—	6	—	39	15	6.50
Byes	1	7	1, 2	1	—	—	4, 7					
Leg byes	4	8	3, 7	4	5	(13), (13)	7					
Wides	8	2	1, 2	8	1	—	1					
No balls	1	—	2	3	—	—	4					
Total	77, 124	307, 264	266, 168	253, 276	409, 83	146, 376	311, 257					
Wickets	9, 9†	6, 10	10, 10	10, 2	5, 1	10, 8	8, 5					
Result	L	W	L	W	W	L	W					
Points	2	19	7	19	22	4	20					

†V. R. Brown, absent ill

Catches
20 – J. Mackie (ct 16, st 4)
12 – B. D. Ritchie (ct 11, st 1)

4 – R. I. Leggat, S. R. McNally and C. L. Bull
3 – V. R. Brown

Canterbury First-Class Matches – Bowling 1980-81

Match	C. H. Thiele	S. R. McNally	R. T. Latham	D. A. Dempsey	D. W. Stead	V. R. Brown	R. I. Leggat	G. C. Bateman	C. L. Bull	B	Lb	W	Nb	Total	Wkts
v. Auckland (Auckland) 27-29 December	15-3-46-1	21-3-69-0	4-1-13-0		17.5-5-51-1	22.1-7-54-2		20-6-52-1		2	9	1	3	300	5
v. Northern Districts (Hamilton) 1-3 January		20-3-73-4	7-1-20-0	3-0-18-0	27-3-77-0	14-4-43-1	16-1-65-1	16-3-63-0		7	4	1	1	353	8
		14-2-52-2	1-0-4-0		13-2-72-4			14.4-4-34-3		1	4			186	10
v. Central Districts (Christchurch) 7-9 January	14-2-44-1	19-4-55-1	8-4-34-0	3-0-11-0	26-5-90-2	19-8-37-1	11-2-31-3			10	13		1	326	9
	21-5-51-3	19-5-43-0	14-1-30-1		10-3-29-0	16-8-22-2	13-2-51-2			1	4		1	232	8
v. Wellington (Christchurch) 12-14 January	18-6-47-1	16-3-43-1	9-2-21-2		24.5-3-75-3	7-3-12-0		23-6-50-2		7	6	1		262	10
	19-4-47-2	19-5-52-2	1-1-0-0		31-8-72-1	14-4-28-0		19.2-5-51-1		4	9			263	6
v. Otago (Christchurch) 18-20 January	19-8-45-3	9-4-34-0	4-1-17-0		18.2-8-49-4	5-1-13-1	12-5-24-1	13-5-24-0		12	6			224	10
	16-3-55-2	14-6-32-2			22.3-2-68-2	3-0-16-0	10-1-43-1	20-9-36-2		8	8			266	10
v. Central Districts (New Plymouth) 30 Jan-1 Feb	14-2-61-1		7-2-18-0		29.4-6-76-6	13-3-47-1	3-1-26-0	15-3-52-2	3-1-28-0		(13)			296	10
	4-0-18-1				19-3-67-1	2-0-6-0	11-1-61-1	8-0-41-4			(6)			227	7
v. Northern Districts (Christchurch) 7-9 February	12-3-37-0		2-0-9-0	4-2-6-0	28.5-3-86-5	12-4-29-0	24-7-60-3	14-5-29-2		10	9	1		270	10
	14-1-56-2				18-2-65-3		11.2-0-37-5	4-1-23-0		8	7			203	10
Totals	166-37 507-17 av. 29.82	151-35 453-12 av. 37.75	57-13 166-3 av. 55.33	10-2 35-0 —	286-53 877-32 av. 27.40	127.1-42 307-8 av. 38.37	111.2-20 398-17 av. 23.41	167-47 455-17 av. 26.76	3-1 28-0 —						

Central Districts
First-Class Matches – Batting
1980–81

	v Northern Districts (Nelson) 27–29 December	v Otago (Dunedin) 1–3 January	v Canterbury (Christchurch) 7–9 January	v Auckland (Napier) 12–14 January	v Wellington (Palmerston North) 18–20 January	v Northern Districts (Rotorua) 24–26 January	v Canterbury (New Plymouth) 30 January–1 February	v Indians (McLean Park) 17–19 February	Inns	NOs	Runs	HS	Av
R. A. Pierce	38	9 / 7	84 / 65	8	64	—	80 / 4	13 / 8*	10	1	312	84	34.66
A. H. Jones	38 / 61	25 / 9	15 / 6	7	61	7 / 77	— / 8	22 / 11*	12	1	343	77	31.18
M. H. Toynbee	20	17 / 0	58 / 33	0	177*	27 / 8	0 / 75	103	12	—	247	61	20.58
G. N. Edwards	79	96 / 9	29 / 10	2	4	8 / 39	48 / 27*	0	14	2	679	177	56.58
G. J. Langridge	1 / 50	7 / 10*	12 / 20	44*	48	37 / 62	52 / 22	8	13	2	284	62	25.81
W. G. Hodgson	31 / 21	—	21 / 10	20	35*	2 / 51	4 / 12	—	12	1	265	51	24.09
E. B. M. McSweeney	16 / 4	16	8 / 50*	—	—	0 / 56*	—	—	11	3	221	56*	27.62
D. C. Aberhart	24 / 7*	6	13 / 6	—	—	0 / 21*	—	—	7	3	77	24	19.25
D. R. O'Sullivan	2* / 0*	14	5 / 10*	—	8	0	8 / 10*	—	9	5	51	14	12.75
G. K. Robertson	3	20	56* / 16	—	—	27* / 4	65 / 24	17*	10	3	240	65	34.28
M. F. Gill	1*	1*	1*	—	—	—	6	—	4	3	9	6	9.00
R. W. Anderson	—	—	—	0	35	29 / 4	14* / 39	101	8	1	222	101	31.71
P. J. Verhoek	—	14 / 11*	—	—	—	8 / 10	—	—	4	1	43	14	14.33
M. D. Jamieson	—	—	—	—	14*	—	—	—	1	1	14	14*	—
I. D. S. Smith	—	—	—	—	—	—	—	1	1	—	1	1	1.00
Byes	1	—	10	4 / 3	1	5 / 8	(13) / (6)	5					
Leg byes	5 / 3	3 / 1	13 / 4	—	8	8 / 4	—	5					
Wides	5	—	1 / 1	1	4	—	—	—					
No balls	—	—	—	—	—	—	—	—					
Total	264 / 168	228 / 47	326 / 232	89 / 6	445 / 6	157 / 349	296 / 227	277 / 7					
Wickets	9 / 7	10 / 4	9 / 8	6	6 / 1	10 / 8	10 / 7	7					
Result	W	W	W	D	D	D	W	D					
Points	19	18	20	3	9	4	19	—					

Catches

26 – E. B. McSweeney (ct 21, st 5)
11 – G. N. Edwards
9 – W. G. Hodgson
7 – M. H. Toynbee and A. H. Jones
5 – G. J. Langridge and R. W. Anderson
4 – R. A. Pierce and D. R. O'Sullivan
3 – I. D. S. Smith and subs
2 – M. F. Gill, G. K. Robertson, M. D. Jamieson and P. J. Verhoek (as sub)

Central Districts
First-Class Matches – Bowling 1980-81

Match	M. F. Gill	G. K. Robertson	D. R. O'Sullivan	D. C. Aberhart	M. H. Toynbee	W. G. Hodgson	M. D. Jamieson	R. A. Pierce	B	Lb	W	Nb	Total	Wkts
v. Northern Districts (Nelson) 27–29 December	17-3-50-1	15-4-24-1	32-14-74-3	17-4-34-1	19-7-37-2				2	12		11	242	9
	24-6-48-1	19-6-30-2	44-15-64-4	4-1-14-0	10-4-17-1	3-1-3-0				4	1	3	186	10
v. Otago (Dunedin) 1–3 January	16.3-5-23-3	20-5-47-6	19.5-8-34-3	22-13-19-1	2-1-6-0				2	7		10	112	10
	14-2-33-2	16-4-33-1		20-6-35-4	7-1-12-0					6	1	6	162	10
v. Canterbury (Christchurch) 7–9 January	14-2-50-0	23-7-79-5	31-11-64-3	30.1-9-63-2					1	7	2		266	10
	12-3-26-2	13-3-48-4	24.4-10-33-4		10-4-24-0	7-3-29-0				3	1	2	168	10
v. Auckland (Napier) 12–14 January	16-5-48-1	15-4-39-2	29-13-50-2	18-8-36-2	13-4-21-1				1	4	2	3	204	8
	3-1-9-0	4-0-9-0		6-5-1-1	6-1-18-1							1	38	2
v. Wellington (Palmerston North) 18–20 January	17-8-42-0	24-8-59-5	30-13-70-1	16-8-26-1	10-3-25-1				3	20	1	4	250	8
	22-7-64-2	28-9-68-2	49-16-110-1	33-13-59-3	6-3-5-1	12-5-29-1			3	15		7	360	10
v. Northern Districts (Rotorua) 24–26 January		23-7-56-2	47-22-71-6	16-3-46-1	24-8-54-1				2	(8)			235	10
		10-3-16-1	37-15-54-3	6-3-9-0	27-11-60-3	4-0-31-0				2			174	7
v. Canterbury (New Plymouth) 30 Jan–1 Feb	15.4-2-53-6	13-3-46-2	11-5-18-2				7-3-16-0			(13)			146	10
	8-2-22-0	28-4-104-4	41-13-87-3		13-2-48-0	3-0-18-0	24-6-70-1	8-4-14-0		(13)			376	8
v. Indians (McLean Park, Napier) 17–19 February	15-2-61-2	15-1-55-1	29-5-89-3				16-4-51-0	16-2-46-0	3	4	3	3	312	7
	7-3-23-0	6-0-23-0	19-4-62-2				16-4-47-1	16-2-36-0		3		1	195	3
	201.1-51	272-68	443.3-164	188.1-73	147-49	29-9	63-17	40-8						
	552-20	736-38	880-40	342-16	327-11	110-1	184-2	96-0						
	av. 27.60	av. 19.36	av. 22.00	av. 21.37	av. 29.72	av. 110.00	av. 92.00	—						

Northern Districts
First-Class Matches —
Batting
1980–81

Batsman	v. CD (Nelson) 27–29 Dec	v. Canterbury (Hamilton) 1–3 Jan	v. Wellington (Wellington) 7–9 Jan	v. Otago (Whangarei) 12–14 Jan	v. Auckland (Hamilton) 18–20 Jan	v. CD (Rotorua) 24–26 Jan	v. Canterbury (Christchurch) 7–9 Feb	Inns	NOs	Runs	HS	Av
J. G. Gibson	20, 31	119, 20	16, 22	17, 4	0	10, 26	19, 45	13	—	349	119	26.84
M. J. E. Wright	46, 4	9, 5	17, 29	15, 44	55	38, 25	32, 22	13	—	341	55	26.23
C. M. Kuggeleijn	35, 8	116, 35	7, 4	21, 6	0	24, 0	14, 2	13	—	272	116	20.92
A. D. G. Roberts	12, 43	22, 29*	24, 81	14, 68	100	16, 25*	95, 12	13	2	541	100	49.18
B. G. Cooper	28, 48	28, 62	5, 105	40, 14	86	22, 39	35, 8	13	1	520	105	40.00
W. P. Fowler		6*	1, 0	34, 0			17, 0	7	1	58	34	9.66
C. W. Dickeson	58, 0	10*, 13	6, 1	26, 0	23*	9, 3	6*, 19	13	3	174	58	17.40
S. R. Gillespie	7, 2	13, 0	32, 9		2*	20, 4*	13, 20	10	2	120	32	15.00
S. J. Scott	6*, 15	10, 0	0	1		6	37, 12	9	1	87	37	10.87
P. Curtin	4*, 0*		9, 13	17, 0*		6	16	8	3	65	17	13.00
K. Treiber	4*		0*	1		6*	4, 0*	6	4	15	6*	7.50
D. J. White		10	0		6	64, 1	10, 4	7	—	95	64	13.57
R. Broughton					7	17, 47	70, 8	5	—	149	70	29.80
R. J. Griffiths						1*	12*, 0	3	2	13	12*	13.00
D. Lloyd	0, 11	4					5	4	—	20	11	5.00
Byes		2	5, 8		11	2	8					
Leg byes	12, 4	7, 4	10, 8	(15), (20)		(8)	10, 9					
Wides	11, 1	1, 1	2, 4		2	2, 2	1, 1					
No balls	3	3, 4	14, 4		2	6	8, 7					
Total	242, 186	353, 186	174, 277	200, 225	292	235, 174	270, 203					
Wickets	9, 10	8, 10	10, 10	10, 8	7	10, 7	10, 10					
Result	L	L	L	D	D	D	L					
Points	6	7	4	6	6	6	6					

Catches
13 – M. J. E. Wright (ct 11, st 2)   4 – D. J. White (one as sub) and J. G. Gibson
10 – C. M. Kuggeleijn   3 – P. Curtin, S. R. Gillespie, and R. Broughton

Northern Districts First-Class Matches – Bowling 1980-81

	K. Treiber	S. R. Gillespie	S. J. Sctoott	C. W. Dickeson	A. D. G. Roberts	P. Curtin
Central Districts	20–4–53–1	9–0–47–0	10–2–32–0	44–17–79–7		17–2–42–1
(Nelson) 27–29 December	11–6–21–3	15–2–31–1		28–7–85–3		2–1–9–0
Canterbury (Hamilton)	26–6–69–2	14–0–40–0		30–8–80–3	5–1–20–0	8–2–28–0
1–3 January	6.3–1–29–1	12–1–37–1		34–14–49–3		32–8–77–2
Wellington (Wellington)	21–2–75–2	26–5–73–1	34–9–77–2	18.5–7–63–2		
7–9 January	12–5–19–1	14–2–57–3	13–2–42–0	15–6–33–0	15–2–15–0	8–2–29–0
Otago (Whangerei)	6–3–10–0	13–4–22–1		42–20–63–3		17–5–36–2
12–14 January		11–4–18–2	15–6–46–2	25–9–70–3		8–2–29–0
Auckland (Hamilton)		29–3–78–3	15–1–69–0	31–7–76–0	7–1–24–1	
18–20 January		12–2–32–1	7–0–33–0	4–1–10–2		
Central Districts (Rotorua)		17.3–5–34–2	13–3–46–3	22–9–45–3		
24–26 January		30.4–5–65–3	16–1–52–0	44–15–104–2		
Canterbury (Christchurch)			20–1–78–2	40–13–90–3	7–1–21–0	
7–9 February			17–3–69–0	2–1–10–0		
	102.3–27	203.1–33	160–28	379.5–134	34–5	92–22
	276–10	534–18	544–9	857–34	80–1	250–5
	av. 27.60	av. 29.66	av. 60.44	av. 25.20	av. 80.00	av. 50.00

	W. P. Fowler	C. Kuggeleijn	D. J. White	R. J. Griffiths	B. G. Cooper	D. Lloyd
v. Central Districts (Nelson) 27–29 December		3–0–13–0				
v. Canterbury (Hamilton)			12–2–40–1		5–0–13–0	
1–3 January		2–2–0–0	14–2–49–3			3–0–16–0
v. Wellington (Wellington) 7–9 January	0.5–0–8–0					
v. Otago (Whangerei)	4–1–10–0	26.3–10–46–3				
12–14 January	6–3–8–0		4–0–17–1			
v. Auckland (Hamilton) 18–20 January	6–0–42–1		12–1–61–0			
v. Central Districts (Rotorua)				16–6–20–2		
24–26 January		2–1–1–0	22–2–73–2	8–1–37–1		
v. Canterbury (Christchurch)	3–2–4–0	14–5–33–2	7–0–28–1	9–1–42–0		
7–9 February		6–4–5–0	13–4–41–1	15–4–36–0	20–4–82–4	
	19.5–6	57.3–22	80–11	48–12	25–4	3–0
	72–1	115–6	292–8	135–3	95–4	16–0
	av. 72.00	av. 19.16	av. 36.50	av. 45.00	av. 23.75	—

B	Lb	W	Nb	Total	Wkts
11	5		5	264	9
6	3			168	7
7	8		2	307	6
1	2	1	3	264	10
	18		9	315	8
2	3		2	210	4
	(6)			193	10

B	Lb	W	Nb	Total	Wkts
	(8)			196	8
	9	1		360	7
	3		3	81	3
	(12)			157	10
5	8		4	349	8
4	7		4	311	8
12	1	1		257	5

Otago
First-Class Matches – Batting
1980-81

Batting Averages

	Inns	NOs	Runs	HS	Av
I. A. Rutherford	16	—	270	45	16.87
G. Blakely	16	—	291	74	18.18
B. Milburn	14	—	207	103	14.78
R. Hoskin	16	—	380	117	23.75
W. L. Blair	16	—	556	140	34.75
G. Dawson	12	2	262	61	26.20
B. R. Blair	14	—	312	65	22.28
D. Walker	10	1	119	58	11.90
J. Lindsay	6	—	82	24	16.40
S. L. Boock	12	6	60	19*	10.00
R. Webb	10	5	26	14*	5.20
G. B. Thomson	12	5	53	13	7.57
D. E. C. McKechnie	4	1	19	7	6.33
S. J. McCullum	2	—	13	8	6.50
P. W. Hills	2	—	17	10	8.50
K. Burns	4	—	4	2	1.00
W. K. Lees	2	—	0	0	—
J. G. Bracewell	2	1	56	35*	56.00
B. J. McKechnie	4	—	58	27	14.50

Match-by-Match Scores

	v Wellington (Alexandra) 27-29 December	v Central Districts (Dunedin) 1-3 January	v Auckland (Auckland) 7-9 January	v Northern Districts (Whangarei) 12-14 January	v Canterbury (Christchurch) 18-20 January	v Auckland (Dunedin) 30 January-1 February	v Wellington (Wellington) 7-9 February	v Indians (Carisbrook) 28 February-2 March
I. A. Rutherford	11, 12	25, 8	10, 6	9, 14	6, 44	4, 1	45, 39	31, 5
G. Blakely	15, 11	3, 7	74, 22	2, 8	5, 1	26, 43	33, 4	4, 33
B. Milburn	103, 0	2, 0	4, 13	21, 1	21, 6	1, 0	4, 31	16, 5
R. Hoskin	19, 4	10, 37	5, 50	57, 117	11, 9	2, 17	11, 10	10, 6
W. L. Blair	50, 49	5, 17	16, 44	14, 5	88, 140	11, 11	83, 7	6, 2
G. Dawson	0, 0		0, 6	50, 42*	0, 22	28, 35*	61, 10	65, 8
B. R. Blair		20, 57	2, 17	2, 1	45, 5	1, 57	1, 58	1
D. Walker	9, 3	22, 7	31, 2	17		2, 7	2*,	4
J. Lindsay				5,	12*, 0*	6, 5	3, 0*	
S. L. Boock	0*, 14*	0, 9*	17*, 24	0*,	0*, 0	5*, 1	5, 8	0, 35*
R. Webb	3*, 9*	9*, 4	9*, 0*	10, 0	13,	3,	7, 10	0,
G. B. Thomson								
D. E. C. McKechnie								
S. J. McCullum								
P. W. Hills								
K. Burns	0, 1	2, 1						
W. K. Lees								0, 0
J. G. Bracewell								35*, 21
B. J. McKechnie	27, 22	7, 6						0, 9
Byes	11, 13	2, 6	8, 4	(6), (8)	12, 8	4,	4, 3	3,
Leg byes	4, 7	6, 1	6, 2		6, 8	5,	10, 3	6,
Wides	1, —	1,	1, —				1, 2	
No balls	13, 4	6,	—, 4					6, 3
Total	266, 149	112, 162	203, 185	193, 196	224, 266	98, 189	271, 185	187, 117
Wickets	9	10, 10	8, 10	10, 8	10, 10	10, 10	10	10, 10
Result	W	L	L	D	L	L	D	L
Points	17	4	5	5	4	5	6	3

Catches
26 – B. Milburn (ct 21, st 5)
9 – W. L. Blair
4 – I. A. Rutherford. D. E. C. McKechnie.
B. R. Blair, R. Hoskin, G. Dawson and
G. Blakely
3 – R. Webb
2 – S. L. Boock, P. W. Hills and S. J.
McCullum
1 – B. J. McKechnie, K. Burns, J. Lindsay,
D. Walker, G. B. Thomson, J. G. Bracewell

Otago
First-Class Matches –
Bowling
1980-81

Match	R. Webb	B. R. Blair	D. Walker	S. L. Boock	J. Lindsay	W. L. Blair	G. B. Thomson	G. Dawson	D. E. C. Mckechnie	P. W. Hills	K. Burns	B. J. McKechnie
v. Wellington (Alexandra) 27-29 December	15-1-56-1	12-2-43-1			15-3-39-1		17.1-4-39-4					19-6-31-3
	20-9-42-1	12-4-21-0			12-1-40-0		26-13-41-6					28-13-37-3
v. Central Districts (Dunedin) 1-3 January	23-8-55-1	18-5-36-3			12-1-34-1		18-5-44-1		16-4-35-3		8-2-21-0	
	6.2-0-23-4						6-2-23-0					
v. Auckland (Auckland) 7-9 January	13-2-50-0	28.4-10-79-3	15-3-59-1	36-14-93-3	7.2-2-19-1	1-0-5-0						
	10-1-43-0	12-3-33-2	11-4-35-0	25-7-66-2								
v. Northern Districts (Whangerei) 12-14 January	19-6-42-3	11-4-18-0	8-5-8-0	37-11-84-7			15-6-33-0					
	20-7-49-0	9-4-20-1	3-1-14-0	46-20-62-6			12-1-40-1	9-4-20-0				
v. Canterbury (Christchurch) 18-20 January	20.4-2-88-0	20-2-88-0	19-1-70-2	30-7-125-1			10.2-4-26-0					
	3-0-23-1	5-0-23-0		6.2-3-17-0			1-0-14-0					
v. Auckland (Dunedin) 30 Jan-1 Feb	17-4-48-1	18-5-33-1		34.2-15-65-6			22-7-36-1		18-7-25-1			
	10.2-1-27-1			13-6-22-6			1-0-1-0		4-0-19-0			
v. Wellington (Wellington) 7-9 February			18-8-29-2	27-9-48-4		1-0-8-0	24-8-47-2			21-1-74-1		
			17-3-53-4	30-11-87-3		1-0-12-0	14-0-38-1			6-0-33-0		6-0-12-0
v. Indians (Carisbrook) 28 Feb-2 Mar		4-0-29-0	4-1-13-0	45-20-88-3								
Totals	177.2-2-41	149.4-37	95-26	329.4-123	46.2-7	3-0	166.3-50	9-4	38-11	27-1	8-2	53-19
	546-13	424-12	281-9	757-41	132-3	25-0	382-16	20-0	79-4	107-1	21-0	80-6
	av. 42.00	av. 35.33	av. 31.22	av. 18.46	av. 44.00	—	av. 23.87	—	av. 19.75	av. 107.00	—	av. 13.33

A. J. G. Bracewell 40.2-9-155-7

Opposition innings totals:

B	Lb	W	Nb	Total	Wkts
5	5	1		409	5
6	1			83	1
	(12)			219	10
				69	7
7	3		3	219	10
3	4		1	231	9
14	6		1	318	10 A

B	Lb	W	Nb	Total	Wkts
5	2			215	10
6	10	2		199	10
3				228	10
1				47	4
3	5	1	3	312	8
2			1	185	4
	(15)			200	10
	(20)			225	8

Wellington
First-Class Matches –
Batting
1980–81

Player	v Otago (Alexandra) 27–29 December (1)	(2)	v Auckland (Wellington) 1–3 January (1)	(2)	v Northern Districts (Wellington) 7–9 January (1)	(2)	v Canterbury (Christchurch) 12–14 January (1)	(2)	v Central Districts (Palmerston North) 18–20 January (1)	(2)	v Auckland (Auckland) 24–26 January (1)	(2)	v Otago (Wellington) 7–9 February (1)	(2)	Inns	NOs	Runs	HS	Av
P. J. Holland	—	—	0	7	38	—	9	34	33	2	55	28	32	52	11	—	290	55	26.36
G. A. Newdick	16	24	8	41	9	1	42	2	10	19	23	31	4	23	14	—	253	42	18.07
R. H. Vance	52	49	22	10	61	2	24	50	2	4	1	65	39	8	14	—	389	65	27.78
J. F. M. Morrison	33	52	10	25	36	138*	80	21	46	8	33	33*	0	84*	14	3	599	138*	54.45
E. J. Gray	55	0	77	88*	63	15	10	34*	40	42	19	2	27	1	14	2	473	88*	39.41
D. F. Oakley	1	0	9	22	9	38*	—	—	—	—	—	—	—	—	6	1	79	38*	15.80
R. Ormiston	—	—	15	1	20	9	—	—	40	85	24	0	30	18	10	—	242	85	24.20
B. W. Cederwall	16	8	17	15	16*	—	32	94	4	81	0	5*	22	10	13	2	320	94	29.09
S. B. Cater	16	8	—	—	36	—	9	—	4	4	12	2	4	6	12	—	147	36	12.25
D. Henry	—	—	17	—	—	3	0*	—	33	40*	—	0	34*	1	9	3	153	40*	25.50
P. J. Petherick	1	—	13	—	—	—	0*	—	3*	3	1*	0	10	12*	8	4	44	17	11.00
R. B. Reid	—	—	17	13	—	—	3	—	—	3	1*	—	—	—	6	—	51	28	8.50
T. Vogel	0	5*	0*	—	—	—	—	—	—	41	1	—	7	3	6	1	67	41	13.40
N. Meadows	5*	—	0*	—	—	—	—	—	3*	—	1	—	—	4	3	2	5	5*	5.00
Byes	5	6	4	2	18	9	7	6	3	3	3	2	7	3					
Leg byes	2	10	2	—	—	—	—	—	20	15	—	1	3	4					
Wides	—	—	—	—	2	—	1	—	1	—	—	—	—	—					
No balls	2	—	2	7	9	—	—	—	4	7	3	—	3	1					
Total	215	199	194	251	315	210	262	263	250	360	156	174	219	231					
Wickets	10	10	10	7	8	4	10	6	8	10	10	10	10	9					
Result	L		D		W		L		D		L		D						
Points	4		4		20		7		5		5		6						

Catches
14 – R. H. Vance (ct 11, st 3)
13 – J. F. M. Morrison
7 – R. Ormiston
6 – E. J. Gray
5 – B. W. Cederwall
4 – G. A. Newdick and S. B. Cater
3 – D. Henry
2 – R. B. Reid and P. J. Petherick
1 – D. F. Oakley and sub (Wilson)

Wellington
First-Class Matches – Bowling 1980-81

Match	S. B. Cater	B. W. Cederwall	D. Henry	P. J. Holland	E. J. Gray	P. J. Petherick	J. F. M. Morrison	T. Vogel	N. Meadows	B	Lb	W	Nb	Total	Wkts
v. Otago (Alexandra) 27–29 December	14-6-26-1	18-7-41-1	21-8-36-0		28-10-50-4	22-9-46-2			18-5-38-1	11	4	1	13	266	9
	5-1-9-0	7-3-16-2	7-3-16-2		17-1-54-2	23.1-9-46-4			6-6-0-0	13	7		4	149	9
v. Auckland (Wellington) 1–3 January	6-1-31-0	17-3-60-2		8-4-17-0	35-11-84-4	18-4-41-0			16-4-49-1	14	13		9	318	7
	27-4-71-5	32-13-64-1							6-1-22-0		10		10	177	6
v. Northern Districts (Wellington) 7–9 January	25-5-73-4	29.5-15-42-6	7-3-11-0	3-1-14-0	21.5-10-60-3	24-3-63-4				10	8	2	14	174	10
	13-2-42-1	22-8-55-0	9-2-40-1							5	8		4	277	10
v. Canterbury (Christchurch) 12–14 January	18-6-67-1	5-2-17-0	2-0-18-0	3-0-12-0	35-15-65-5	25.5-7-61-2	4-0-23-0			1	4		8	253	10
	5-0-25-0	4.2-0-41-0	12-2-54-1		22-4-62-1	7-0-55-0				7	5		3	275	2
v. Central Districts (Palmerston North) 18–20 January	25-2-124-3	7-2-20-1	16-4-50-0		37-7-159-2		2-0-11-0	13-2-68-0		1	8		4	445	6
		1-0-10-0						2-0-7-1						18	1
v. Auckland (Auckland) 24–26 January	19.2-6-39-2	10-4-15-0	12-3-41-1		21-6-66-2	27-1-88-2	3-0-9-0	6-1-33-0		1	9		3	304	10
	6-2-17-0	6-2-17-0	6-0-26-0		24-4-71-3	19-2-55-2		5-2-13-0		7	6	1		196	5
v. Otago (Wellington) 7–9 February	20-4-59-1	12-1-40-0	6-1-12-0	6-0-15-1	13-4-52-1	12.1-4-33-3		16-4-44-1		4	10	1	1	271	10
	20-6-35-3	13-9-16-1			18-12-18-0	28.5-15-48-5		17-3-60-1		3	3		2	185	10
Totals	197.2-43	177.1-66	98-26	20-5	271.5-84	207-54	9-0	59-12	46-16						
	601-21	438-12	304-5	58-1	741-27	536-24	43-0	225-3	109-2						
	av. 28.61	av. 36.50	av. 60.80	av. 58.00	av. 27.44	av. 22.33	—	av. 75.00	av. 54.50						

F

Cricket in Isolation

The Season in South Africa,
Compiled by Robert Brooke,
Chairman of the Association of
Cricket Statisticians

The departure of Zimbabwe meant changes in the set up of South African domestic cricket. The number of Castle Currie Cup teams was reduced to five, enabling a double round of 8 games per team to be completed. Changes in the Castle Bowl were more revolutionary. The competition was split into two sections of four teams each, with the winner of each section meeting in a championship play-off. The Northern section consisted of Orange Free State and Griqualand West plus the 'B' teams of Transvaal and Natal. The Southern group was Western and Eastern Province, Border and, replacing Zimbabwe 'B', Boland, situated East of Cape Town and playing its home games at Stellenbosch. Boland were the first new entries into competitive first-class cricket in South Africa for nine years.

Important cricket commenced with the Datsun Shield, with three first round matches on 25 October.

The holders Transvaal travelled to Kimberley and swept aside Griqualand West with contemptuous ease. With skipper David Dyer hitting 91 in 175 minutes, and featuring in century partnerships with Jimmy Cook and Graeme Pollock Griqualand West were set the formidable target of 283, and despite a brave 41 by Pat Symcox a superb spell of left-arm spin by Alan Kourie saw that they were never in with a real chance.

Boland made their debut with Mike Procter's Natal visiting Stellenbosch. Against the most well-equipped seam attack in the competition Boland struggled to 107 for 4 in their 60 overs, Andre du Toit carrying his bat for an unbeaten 52, and with a sound half century from Kippy Smith Natal cruised to an entirely expected easy victory.

In the third match Orange Free State entertained Western Province. The home team collapsed disastrously in the face of the left-arm seamers of Stephen Jefferies and with Allan Lamb contributing a typically cultured unbeaten 64 Western Province reached their target with 7 wickets and nearly half their overs allocation left over.

1 November saw the two remaining First round matches. At Durban Natal 'B' won the toss against Eastern Province but only a fighting innings by skipper Clive Die ensured respectability against the pace of Dave Brickett and Mike van Vuuren on a helpful wicket. When Easterns batted Geoff Cook brought all his Northants experience to bear and his 60 in $2\frac{1}{4}$ hours plus the steady supporting effort of Robbie Armitage ensured an easy win.

Meanwhile at East London Northern Transvaal, taking first innings against Border collapsed disastrously against the steady bowling and keen fielding of the home side. Border in their turn found batting tricky and soon lost three wickets but a sound stand between John Buckley and Erroll Laughlin put them into a winning position and they achieved the only 'giant-killing' act of the first round.

Datsun Shield Round One   **Griqualand West *v.* Transvaal**
25 October 1980   at Kimberley

Transvaal

D. D. Dyer	c Moore b Jesty	91
S. J. Cook	lbw b Beukes	63
H. R. Fotheringham	b Beukes	0
R. G. Pollock	c Funston b Deysel	82

C. E. B. Rice	c Rodwell b Deyzel	6
K. A. McKenzie	lbw b Deyzel	19
A. J. Kourie	not out	4
R. V. Jennings	not out	3
Extras		14

(for 6 wkts – 60 overs) 282

G. E. McMillan, R. W. Hanley, D. R. Neilson did not bat.

	O	M	R	W
Deysel	9	1	48	3
Jesty	12	0	39	1
Engelbrecht	12	1	59	0
McLaren	6	0	43	0
Funston	9	1	32	0
Beukes	12	1	47	2

Fall of Wickets
1–108, 2–108, 3–251, 4–251, 5–272, 6–278.

Griqualand West

M. J. D. Doherty	lbw b Rice	1
D. N. Martin	lbw b Kourie	4
P. Symcox	st Jennings b Kourie	41
T. E. Jesty	c McKenzie b Kourie	28
A. P. Beukes	b Kourie	10
G. Rodwell	c Jennings b Kourie	0
G. K. Funston	lbw b Rice	3
K. McLaren	c Neilson b Hanley	4
D. H. Moore	b Neilson	12
R. Engelbrecht	b Hanley	1
B. B. Deyzel	not out	2
Extras		9

115

	O	M	R	W
Neilson	8.5	4	17	1
Rice	8	3	10	2
Kourie	12	2	35	5
Hanley	9	0	25	2
McMillan	8	2	19	0

Fall of Wickets
1–2, 2–18, 3–58, 4–76, 5–89, 6–92, 7–95, 8–107, 9–111.

Transvaal won by 167 runs

Datsun Shield   Round One   **Boland *v.* Natal**
25th October 1980   **at Stellenbosch**

Boland

C. van der Merwe	b Cooper	20
A. du Toit	not out	52
D. Malan	c Procter b Cooper	8

P. H. Wallace	c Procter b Wilkins	3
J. de Villiers	c and b Procter	9
J. Kennedy	not out	6
Extras		9

(for 4 wkts – 60 overs) 107

C. Coetzee, J. Hendriks, D. Traut, van Rooyen did not bat.

	O	M	R	W
Procter	12	3	19	1
van der Bijl	12	6	12	0
Cooper	12	4	20	2
Clift	12	1	23	0
Wilkins	12	1	24	1

Fall of Wickets
1–40, 2–52, 3–63, 4–95.

Natal

C. L. Smith	not out	51
C. P. Wilkins	c and b Coetzee	1
R. M. Bentley	b J. de Villiers	23
P. W. G. Parker	not out	28
Extras		6

(for 2 wkts – 40 overs) 109

	O	M	R	W
Coetzee	10	2	15	1
Hendriks	10	1	31	1
Traut	5	1	23	0
de Villiers	10	4	15	1
Van Rooyen	5	0	19	0

Fall of Wickets
1–4, 2–38.

Natal won by 8 wickets

Datsun Shield   Round One

Orange Free State *v.* Western Province

25 October 1980   **at Bloemfontein**

Orange Free State

R. A. le Roux	c Ryall b Jefferies	2
D. P. le Roux	c Lamb b Barlow	23
L. Griessel	c Jefferies b du Toit	40
R. J. East	c Seeff b Swart	15
G. N. Lister-James	lbw b du Toit	0
L. Klopper	c Kirsten b Hobson	12
J. Strydom	lbw b le Roux	8
E. Schmidt	b Jefferies	4
S. Regenstein	c Bruce b Jefferies	9
R. Norton	b Jefferies	1
W. T. Strydom	not out	1

| Extras | | | | 16 |

| (47.3 overs) | | | | 131 |

	O	M	R	W
le Roux	11	3	23	1
Jefferies	10.3	5	14	4
Barlow	7	2	15	1
du Toit	7	1	26	2
Hobson	6	0	26	1
Swart	6	3	11	1

Fall of Wickets
1–4, 2–50, 3–80, 4–89, 5–89, 6–106, 7–114, 8–118, 9–128.

Western Province

E. J. Barlow	b R. le Roux	19
L. Seeff	c East b R. le Roux	28
P. N. Kirsten	c East b Schmidt	17
A. J. Lamb	not out	64
P. D. Swart	not out	4
Extras		3

| (for 3 wkts – 37.1 overs) | | | | 135 |

	O	M	R	W
Schmidt	8	2	31	0
Norton	8	2	27	0
R. le Roux	12	0	45	2
Strydom	6	2	11	0
Regenstein	3	0	14	0
D. le Roux	0.1	0	4	0

Fall of Wickets
1–48, 2–51, 3–113.

Western Province won by 7 wickets

Datsun Shield   Round One
1 November 1980

Natal 'B' v. Eastern Province
at Durban

Natal 'B'

B. J. Whitfield	c Richardson b van Vuuren	14
B. Plummer	run out	5
F. B. Hill	b Brickett	6
B. S. Groves	b Brickett	11
K. D. Verdoorn	c Foulkes b Brickett	0
M. M. Benkenstein	b van Vuuren	13
C. A. Gie	not out	38
Y. Omar	c Cook b van Vuuren	0
E. J. Hodkinson	c Watson b Cowley	14
I. Ebrahim	run out	3
I. R. Ault	c Armitage b Brickett	0
Extras		

| (59.1 overs) | | 121 |

	O	M	R	W
Watson	12	7	11	0
Van Vuuren	12	6	18	3
Brickett	11.1	1	19	4
Cowley	11	2	38	1
Armitage	12	6	17	0
Foulkes	1	0	1	0

Fall of Wickets
1–7, 2–22, 3–33, 4–34, 5–45, 6–79, 7–79, 8–108, 9–116.

Eastern Province

G. Cook	b Gie	60
R. L. S. Armitage	not out	44
D. J. Richardson	not out	1
Extras		18

(for 1 wkt – 41.4 overs) 123

I. Foulkes, W. K. Watson, M. K. van Vuuren, D. J. Brickett, G. S. Cowley, S. J. Beziudenhout, D. H. Howell, R. J. D. Whyte did not bat.

	O	M	R	W
Hodkinson	12	1	17	0
Ault	12	3	16	0
Omar	7.4	1	28	0
Benkenstein	3	0	14	0
Ebrahim	5	0	28	0
Gie	2	1	2	1

Fall of Wicket
1–109.

Eastern Province won by 9 wickets

Datsun Shield   Round One   Border *v.* Northern Transvaal
1 November 1980   **at East London**

Northern Transvaal

A. Barrow	b Boucher	16
V. F. du Preez	c Buckley b Hayes	10
R. C. Ontong	run out	2
E. Muntingh	c Wells b Laughlin	6
A. M. Ferreira	c Ball b Wells	14
K. G. Motley	c Schmidt b Laughlin	2
H. W. Raath	lbw b Laughlin	0
B. McBride	run out	3
W. F. Morris	c Gower b Laughlin	0
D. J. Thomas	not out	13
P. A. Robinson	c Harty b Wells	4
Extras		8

(47 overs) 78

	O	M	R	W
Boucher	12	5	20	1
Gower	6	3	5	0

Hayes	6	1	11	1
Wells	12	5	12	2
Laughlin	11	4	22	4

Fall of Wickets
1–28, 2–32, 3–32, 4–52, 5–52, 6–53, 7–53, 8–54, 9–58.

Border

I. D. Harty	b Robinson	4
R. Kent	b Thomas	4
C. M. Wells	c and b Robinson	3
J. Buckley	c Morris b Ontong	27
E. Laughlin	not out	25
G. L. Hayes	not out	4
Extras		12

(for 4 wkts – 32 overs)   79

B. Osborne, G. M. Gower, G. D. Boucher, S. J. Schmidt, T. Ball did not bat.

	O	M	R	W
Robinson	8	1	13	2
Thomsas	8	0	21	1
Ontong	8	1	17	1
Morris	7	3	10	0
Raath	1.2	0	6	0

Fall of Wickets
1–12, 2–12, 3–20, 4–62.

Border won by 6 wickets

7, 8 and 10 November 1980 SAB Currie Cup   **at Port Elizabeth**
Northern Transvaal 239 (A. M. Ferreira 106, W. K. Watson 3 for 41) and
    201 (V. E. du Preez 101, M. K. van Vuuren 5 for 42)
Eastern Province 265 (D. J. Brickett 64, G. Cook 42, P. A. Robinson 3 for 57)
    and 120 for 6 (I. Foulkes 57*)
Match drawn
Eastern Province 8 pts, Northern Transvaal 7 pts

A maiden hundred by new Northerns skipper Anton Ferreira held his side's
batting together on the first day and on the second day Easterns struggled
against a steady attack until an attacking 64 by Dave Brickett gave them a
narrow lead. Northern's second innings was another one-man effort. Vernon du
Preez emulating his skipper with a maiden century as his team mates collapsed
to Mike van Vuuren's pace but Easterns, left to make only 176 at 4 an over
never recovered from a bad start and were happy to play for a draw.

The sole Datsun Shield second round match took place on 15 November at
Durban where Natal entertained first round giant-killers Border. The visitors'
hopes of a repeat were soon dashed. Natal won the toss and a superb 121 in
165 minutes by 'Tich' Smith – his maiden hundred in the competition – plus
good batting in support from Paul Parker – 46 – and skipper Mike Procter,
58 not out in 46 minutes – enabled Natal to compile a devastating 310 for 5 in
60 overs. Proctor and van der Bijl then ripped out the first four Border batsmen
for 9 runs and although Brad Osborne, an eighteen-year-old Dale College

schoolboy fought well an overwhelming home win was inevitable, and the final margin of 247 runs was the highest ever in a Datsun Shield inter-provincial match.

Datsun Shield   Round Two
15 November 1980

Natal v. Border
at Durban

Natal

C. P. Wilkins	lbw b Boucher	32
C. L. Smith	lbw b Gower	9
A. J. S. Smith	c Boucher b Hayes	121
P. W. G. Parker	c Kent b Wells	46
P. H. Williams	b Osborne	15
M. J. Procter	not out	58
D. R. Bestall	not out	7
Extras		22

(for 5 wkts – 60 overs) 310

D. K. Pearse, V. A. P. van der Bijl, K. R. Cooper did not bat.

	O	M	R	W
Boucher	12	1	32	1
Gower	12	2	56	1
Wells	12	3	47	1
Hayes	12	1	67	1
Laughlin	5	0	32	0
Buckley	6	0	45	0
Osborne	1	0	9	1

Fall of Wickets
1–39, 2–53, 3–175, 4–218, 5–263.

Border

I. D. Harty	c A. Smith b van der Bijl	5
R. Kent	c A. Smith b Procter	5
C. M. Wells	c Parker b van der Bijl	0
J. Buckley	b Procter	14
E. Laughlin	lbw b Procter	0
G. L. Hayes	c Smith b Pearse	10
S. J. Schmidt	b Pearse	0
B. Osborne	c Williams b Pearse	22
G. M. Gower	b Procter	4
G. D. Boucher	not out	0
T. Ball	c Parker b Procter	0
Extras		5

63

	O	M	R	W
van der Bijl	8	4	9	2
Procter	7.3	5	4	5
Pearse	8	1	37	3
Cooper	6	4	8	0

Fall of Wickets
1–8, 2–8, 3–8, 4–9, 5–25, 6–25, 7–57, 8–60, 9–63.

Natal won by 247 runs

21 and 22 November   SAB Currie Cup   **at Pretoria**
Transvaal 325 for 1 dec (D. D. Dyer 164*, S. J. Cook 126)
Northern Transvaal 97 (R. W. Hanley 5 for 20, C. E. B. Rice 3 for 30) and 173
   (K. G. Motley 40, Rice 4 for 41)
Transvaal won by an innings and 55 runs
Transvaal 22 pts, Northern Transvaal 1 pt

A superb opening stand of 262 between David Dyer and Jimmy Cook, 12 short
of the Transvaal record, helped the reigning champions to a massive 325 for 1
declared in 84 overs, and before the close on the first day Hanley and Rice
had ripped out 6 Northern wickets for only 42 runs. Both Dyer and Cook
scored their seventh Currie Cup hundred, Dyer's 164* lasting 298 minutes,
Cook's 126, 47 minutes fewer. Northerns collapsed to an all out 97 on the
second morning and did little better in their second innings as they slumped to
an overwhelming two-day defeat. Two unusual incidents were a feature of the
second day's play. In the second innings Northern skipper Ferreira was
dismissed from the eighth legitimate ball of an Alan Kourie over while during
the same innings Kourie was no-balled because wicket-keeper Ray Jennings'
gloves were slightly in front of the wickets.

21, 22 and 24 November   SAB Currie Cup   **at Port Elizabeth**
Eastern Province 225 (G. Cook 61, D. J. Brickett 58, P. D. Swart 4 for 58,
   G. S. le Roux 3 for 29) and 235 (S. J. Bezuidenhout 53, G. Cook 42
   G. S. le Roux 3 for 53)
Western Province 362 (P. D. Swart 68, L. Seeff 58, A. J. Lamb 52, S. D. Bruce
   50, W. K. Watson 4 for 87) and 99 for 0 (E. J. Barlow 58*)
Western Province won by 10 wickets
Western Province 20 pts, Eastern Province 6 pts

Eastern made a poor start but Geoff Cook and Dave Brickett steered them
to a respectable total in the face of hostile seam bowling. Consistent batting by
Westerns, with four players reaching fifties ensured a good lead despite excellent
pace bowling by Ken Watson and despite a fighting opening stand by Cook
and Simon Bezuidenhout Westerns achieved a 10 wicket win on the third day,
Eddie Barlow recording their fifth half-century of the match.

21, 22 and 24 November   Castle Bowl   **at Johannesburg**
Transvaal 'B' 272 (R. F. Pienaar 56*, L. J. Barnard 54, E. Schmidt 4 for 53)
   and 174 for 7 dec (W. T. Strydom 4 for 36, R. le Roux 3 for 48)
Orange Free State 127 (A. L. M. Klopper 40, J. Fairclough 4 for 26) and 184
   (J. Fairclough 6 for 31, H. J. van der Linden 4 for 37)
Transvaal 'B' won by 135 runs
Transvaal 18 pts, Free State 4 pts

22, 24 and 25 November   Castle Bowl   **at Cape Town (Burt Oval)**
Border 111 (J. D. du Toit 6 for 37) and 205 (E. Laughlin 76*, N. Gordon
   6 for 49)
Western Province 'B' 171 (J. D. du Toit 40, G. D. Boucher 4 for 46) and 146
   for 3 (L. Seeff 57, E. Halvorsen 52*)
Western 'B' won by 7 wickets
Western Province 'B' 15 pts, Border 5 pts

Half centuries by skipper Lee Barnard and Roy Pienaar helped Transvaal 'B' to a useful first day score despite fine bowling by Ray Le Roux, the Free State seamer, at Johannesburg and then seamer John Fairclough engineered a Free State first innings collapse. Another useful innings by Pienaar enabled Transvaal to set Free State a target of 320 on the third day. Fairclough, supported by Wynand van der Linden again proved too much for the Free State batsmen and despite a stubborn innings by Louis Klopper Free State were beaten shortly after lunch on the third day.

In the Southern section match at Burt Oval Border, sent in to bat, collapsed against the left-arm seamers of Danie du Toit, who, stung at being dropped from the Western Province first team ran through the late order to finish with 6 for 37 in 21.3 overs. Province in their turn also struggled until a sixth wicket stand of 57 between Hylton Ackerman and du Toit helped them to a 60 run first innings lead. Border made a bad start in their second innings, only a well-hit unbeaten 76 by Errol Laughlin giving the home bowlers much anxiety. Left to get 139 with all wickets standing on the third day half-centuries by Jonathan Seeff and Eric Halvorsen in a third wicket stand of 109 ensured a comfortable win for Western Province.

27, 28 and 29 November   Castle Bowl   **at Kimberley**
Natal 'B', 299 for 9 dec (N. P. Daniels 75, M. M. Benkenstein 58, C. A. Gie 54, T. E. Jesty 5 for 38) and 221 for 8 dec (D. K. Pearse 59*)
Griqualand West 291 (P. Symcox 75, T. E. Jesty 56) and 61 for 1
Match drawn
Natal 'B' 6 pts, Griqualand West 5 pts

Castle Bowl   **at Stellenbosch**
Boland 281 for 8 dec (A. du Toit 102, J. Kennedy 97, A. K. Weakley 4 for 52) and 154 for 7 dec (C. van der Merwe 63, G. D. Boucher 4 for 31)
Border 235 for 8 dec (J. Buckley 108, R. Kent 56) and 187 for 5 (I. Harty 69*, G. L. Hayes 53)
Match drawn
Border 5 pts, Boland 5 pts

Martin Benkenstein and Neville Daniels put Natal 'B' in a good position with a third wicket stand of 113 in the first innings against Griqualand West before Trevor Jesty broke the stand and caused a mini-collapse. Natal declared at 299 for 9, denying Jesty the chance of a hat-trick and then saw Griqualand, thanks to Jesty's 56 and a sound 75 from Pat Symcox finish only 8 runs short of their score. The match petered out on the third day when Natal's late order took them to safety after early shocks, setting Griquas to score 230 in 75 minutes plus 20 overs – a task not attempted. Meanwhile Boland made their first-class bow against Border at Stellenbosch. The game was notable for a debut century by Boland's Andre du Toit, while forty-two-year-old Jerry Kennedy, who added 182 for the fifth wicket with du Toit was unlucky not to emulate him, falling for 97. Unfortunately the scoring was too slow to give much chance of a result. John Buckley recorded a century for Border but when set 201 the visitors fell short by 14, Ian Harty scoring a sound unbeaten 69.

29 and 30 November, 1 December   SAB Currie Cup   at Durban
Natal 250 for 9 dec (M. J. Procter 59, D. J. Brickett 4 for 79)
Eastern Province 69 (V. A. P. van der Bijl 4 for 20) and 101 (K. R. Cooper
    4 for 31)
Natal won by an innings and 80 runs
Natal 19 pts, Eastern Province 5 pts

29 November, 1 and 2 December   SAB Currie Cup   at Cape Town
Northern Transvaal 323 (V. H. du Preez 100) and 117 (A. Barrow 45, D. L.
    Hobson 4 for 31)
Western Province 251 for 6 dec (P. N. Kirsten 73) and 191 for 5 (L. Seeff 65,
    A. J. Lamb 54*)
Western Province won by 5 wickets
Western Province 17 pts, Northern Transvaal 4 pts

At Durban Natal struggled on the first morning against the tight seam bowling
of Dickie Ogilvie, back for Easterns after a serious illness and operation, and
Dave Brickett, but a lunchtime storm washed out play for the rest of the day
and a sound innings by Procter and late hitting by van der Bijl ensured a useful
total on the second day. Spineless batting against the Natal seamers, especially
van der Bijl, led to an Easterns collapse and they commenced the third day
needing 141 to make Natal bat again. Another collapse led to an innings win
for Natal with four-and-a-half hours to spare. Easterns again surrendered themselves to a fine seam attack in which Kenny Cooper, 4 for 31, emerged with
the best figures.

    At Newlands a second hundred in a month by Vernon du Preez led Northern
Transvaal's recovery after Garth le Roux had dismissed Barrow and Edwards
without a run on the board. They reached 323 on the second morning and
with three-and-a-half hours lost to rain on the second afternoon Westerns threw
the bat before declaring 72 runs in arrears. With the wicket turning Hobson
induced a late Northerns collapse on the third morning and Westerns scored
at a run a minute in the afternoon to achieve a 5 wicket victory and go to
the top of the Currie Cup log.

9, 10 and 11 December   First-class Friendly match   at Pretoria
Northern Transvaal 366 (P. Visagie 87, D. N. Edwards 84) and 222 for 7 dec
    (C. S. Stirk 108)
S.A. Universities 232 and 352
Northern Transvaal won by 4 runs

Northerns won the toss and a sixth wicket stand of 123 between Dave Edwards
and Peter Visagie put them on top on the first day. The students always struggled
against the seamers of Northern skipper Anton Ferreira, after a record sixth
wicket stand of 117 between Francois Weideman and Danie du Toit promised
a better score than was eventually obtained. In the second innings Craig Stirk
scored a maiden first-class hundred and despite a chanceless 127 by Jimmy
Furstenburg the students, set to get 357, fell five runs short of a remarkable
victory.

11, 12 and 13 December   SAB Bowl   **at Kimberley**
Transvaal 'B' 382 for 7 dec (N. T. Day 174*) and 92 for 4
Griqualand West 128 (N. V. Radford 6 for 41) and 344 (M. J. D. Doherty
   124, A. P. Beukes 59, N. V. Radford 4 for 92)
Transvaal 'B' won by 6 wickets
Transvaal 'B' 19 pts, Griqualand West 3 pts

                                                          at Bloemfontein
Natal 'B' 370 for 8 dec (C. A. Gie 90, M. M. Benkenstein 71, T. R. Madsen 57,
   W. M. van der Merwe 4 for 71) and 316 for 5 dec (N. P. Daniels 104, B. J.
   Whitfield 71, T. R. Madsen 58*)
Orange Free State 328 (L. W. Griessel 162, J. J. Strydom 61, J. S. Muill 4
   for 62) and 253 for 7 (R. J. East 73, J. J. Strydom 68)
Match drawn
Natal 'B' 11 pts, Orange Free State 9 pts

                                                          at Stellenbosch
Western Province 'B' 326 for 5 dec (E. Halvorsen 95, A. P. Kuiper 66*, P. M.
   Thompson 59), and 191 for 8 dec (H. M. Ackerman 55)
Boland 268 (L. L. Roberts 50) and 195 for 7 (A. du Toit 58)
Match drawn
Western Province 'B' 10 pts, Boland 4 pts

                                                          at Grahamstown
Eastern Province 'B' 303 for 9 dec (K. Gradwell 68, R. J. D. Whyte 61, G. D.
   Boucher 4 for 69) and 257 for 5 (K. Gradwell 105*, T. B. Reid 65)
Border 413 (R. A. Stretch 168, R. Kent 55, G. L. Hayes 51)
Match drawn
Border 9 pts, Eastern Province 'B' 7 pts

12, 13 and 15 December   SAB Currie Cup   **at Johannesburg**
Natal 256 for 9 dec (R. M. Bentley 68, M. J. Procter 61, C. P. Wilkins 52,
   A. J. Kourie 5 for 56) and 153 for 4 dec (C. P. Wilkins 75)
Transvaal 109 (K. A. McKenzie 40, K. R. Cooper 5 for 32) and 167 for 5
   (R. G. Pollock 71, V. A. P. van der Bijl 5 for 27)
Match drawn
Natal 7 pts, Transvaal 4 pts

Transvaal 'B' scored their second Northern section Bowl win at Kimberley.
On the first day they owed much to Noel Day's career best 174 not out. His
side were struggling at 109 for 4 when he arrived at the crease but with support
from the tail enders he enabled Transvaal to declare at 382 for 7 and had
enough time to send Griquas reeling at 23 for 3 by the close. Griquas found
the pace of Neal Radford, whose figures of 6 for 41 were a career best too
much for them on the second morning but improved somewhat in the follow
on, an unbeaten 110 by Mike Doherty enabling them to finish the day 201
for 4, but still 53 behind. A seventh wicket stand of 83 between Alan Beukes
and Athol Methven forced Transvaal to bat again on the third afternoon but
their win was a formality.
   Meanwhile at Bloemfontein consistent middle order batting by Natal 'B'

against some sometimes loose Free State bowling enabled them to declare at
370 for 8, giving Free State over an hour's batting in which time they scored
68 for 2. A superb maiden hundred by Lloyd Griessel on the second morning
– his 162 included 18 fours and 3 sixes in 260 minutes – seemed to make a
first innings lead likely until a late collapse against the spin of John Muil and
then a whirlwind 104 in only 80 minutes by Neville Daniels saw Natal finish
the second day in a very strong position, 251 ahead with 7 wickets remaining.
The declaration saw Free State needing 359. A fourth wicket stand of 103
between Bob East and eighteen-year-old Joubert Strydom suggested a surprise
but once this stand was broken Free State began to falter and Clive Gie's
spinners finally ran through the tail.

In the Bowl Southern Section newcomers Boland entertained competition
favourites Western Province 'B' and it was no surprise when the visitors' batting
made light of the toiling Boland attack on the first day. Despite brave batting
by Leon Roberts, Boland were 58 behind on first innings and Westerns then
increased their lead to 249 with some rapid third morning batting before setting
Boland a target which was, predictably, beyond them. The home side however
comfortably held out for a creditable draw.

Another draw was taking place in this section at Grahamstown. Sparkling
sixties by Keith Gradwell and Bob Whyte were the basis of Eastern Province's
303 for 9 declared. A superb career best of 168 by Richard Stretch was the
main contribution to Border's 413, their best ever total against Easterns, but
their victory hopes were dashed on the third day by a solid unbeaten 105 by
Keith Gradwell. He hit 11 fours and a six in a six hour stay which ensured
a draw.

In the battle of the Currie Cup 'giants' at Johannesburg Transvaal skipper
David Dyer sent Natal in on a green pitch and when a mini-collapse brought
the visitors to 103 for 4 he seemed justified. However a stand of 97 between
Rob Bentley and skipper Mike Procter enabled a recovery to be effected and
after a declaration at 256 for 9 Vince van der Bijl removed Jimmy Cook to
leave Transvaal 9 for 1 at the close. The seamers found conditions perfect
on the second morning and a devastating pre-lunch spell by Cooper, and equally
effective bowling in the afternoon by Procter saw Transvaal collapse to an
all out 109, with only a brave two hour innings of 40 by Keith McKenzie
preventing a rout. With the weather uncertain Natal achieved a lead of 300
on the third morning but despite inspired bowling by van der Bijl a third wicket
stand of 91 between skipper Dyer and a limping Grahame Pollock earned
Transvaal a gallant draw. An interesting innovation was seen when entertainment at the intervals was provided by the pop group 'Clout'.

The first legs of the Datsun Shield semi-finals were due to be played on
20 December, but rain caused the postponement of the Eastern *v.* Western
Province game until the 21st.

At Kingsmead Transvaal made a shaky start after taking first knock against
Natal. David Dyer and Henry Fotheringham fell cheaply but Jimmy Cook
stayed to complete an invaluable half-century and with Alan Kourie, Doug
Neilson and a limping Graham Pollock weighing in with useful knocks they
finished with 212 for 9 in their 60 overs, against a steady and experienced
seam attack in which Vintcent van der Bijl was the most economical with

figures of 1 for 29 in 12 overs. Natal made a flying start with a quick-fire half-century from Chris Wilkins but with the exception of Peter Williams, top scorer with 59, the middle order lacked resolution. Although keeping up with the run rate, wickets fell steadily and despite the gallant efforts of Williams and the tail-enders Natal fell 11 runs short.

On the following day at Newlands Western Province's blond seamer Danie du Toit took 5 wickets in blustery conditions as Eastern Province struggled to 101 in 46 overs, with only Simon Bezuidenhout, 26 in 99 minutes offering much resistance. In deteriorating conditions, poor light having joined the strong wind, Westerns in their turn struggled to reach the modest victory target. Ken Watson quickly removed Eddie Barlow, Lawrence Seeff and Peter Kirsten but the cool head of Allan Lamb (46*) saw Westerns to an ultimately comfortable victory with 22 overs and 6 wickets to spare.

Datsun Shield   Semi-Finals – First Leg   **Natal v. Transvaal**
20 December 1980   **at Durban**

Transvaal

D. D. Dyer	c A. Smith b Cooper	7
S. J. Cook	c and b Wilkins	55
H. R. Fotheringham	c Bestall b Wilkins	4
R. G. Pollock	b Clift	29
C. E. B. Rice	c and b Procter	3
K. A. McKenzie	c A. Smith b Clift	4
A. J. Kourie	not out	43
R. L. Jennings	lbw b Clift	0
D. R. Neilson	c Clift b Procter	27
G. E. McMillan	b van der Bijl	11
R. W. Hanley	not out	1
Extras		28
	(for 9 wkts – 60 overs)	212

	O	M	R	W
Procter	12	4	38	2
van der Bijl	12	3	29	1
Cooper	12	3	30	1
Wilkins	10	2	38	2
Clift	11	2	47	3
Pearse	3	1	2	0

Fall of Wickets
1–26, 2–54, 3–93, 4–109, 5–110, 6–115, 7–117, 8–180, 9–208.

Natal

C. P. Wilkins	c Dyer b Kourie	56
A. J. S. Smith	c Jennings b Rice	17
R. M. Bentley	run out	1
P. W. G. Parker	c Jennings b Hanley	10
P. H. Williams	lbw b Rice	59
M. J. Procter	b McMillan	5
D. R. Bestall	c Cook b Hanley	11
P. B. Clift	c Jennings b Neilson	0

V. A. P. van der Bijl	b McMillan	13
D. K. Pearse	b Rice	21
K. R. Cooper	not out	2
Extras		6

| | (53.2 overs) | 201 |

	O	M	R	W
Neilson	11	1	49	1
McMillan	9	2	30	2
Kourie	12	2	45	1
Rice	11.2	2	24	3
Hanley	10	2	47	2

Fall of Wickets
1–56, 2–74, 3–76, 4–90, 5–104, 6–138, 7–138, 8–158, 9–188.

Transvaal won by 11 runs

Datsun Shield   Semi-Finals – First Leg
Western Province v. Eastern Province

21 December 1980   at Cape Town

Eastern Province

G. W. Cook	c Ryall b Swart	19
R. L. S. Armitage	c Bruce b Barlow	9
S. J. Bezuidenhout	b du Toit	26
D. J. Richardson	run out	1
I. Foulkes	b du Toit	2
D. H. Howell	c Ryall b Swart	1
R. J. D. Whyte	lbw b du Toit	17
D. J. Brickett	b Barlow	11
W. K. Watson	c Ryall b du Toit	8
J. D. Ogilvie	not out	0
M. K. van Vuuren	b du Toit	0
Extras		7

| | (46 overs) | 101 |

	O	M	R	W
le Roux	7	3	12	0
Jefferies	7	1	14	0
Barlow	11	2	20	2
Swart	9	4	12	2
du Toit	12	1	36	5

Fall of Wickets
1–32, 2–34, 3–34, 4–48, 5–49, 6–74, 7–89, 8–95, 9–101.

Western Province

E. L. Barlow	b Watson	4
L. Seeff	lbw b Watson	16
P. N. Kirsten	b Watson	4
A. J. Lamb	not out	46
P. D. Swart	lbw b van Vuuren	18
S. D. Bruce	not out	5

Extras   9
                                           ——
                          (for 4 wkts – 38 overs)   102
R. J. Ryall, G. S. le Roux, S. T. Jefferies, J. D. du Toit, A. D. Kuiper did not bat.

	O	M	R	W
Watson	12	4	15	3
Brickett	9	0	24	0
Ogilvie	7	3	28	0
van Vuuren	10	3	26	1

Fall of Wickets
1–10, 2–24, 3–25, 4–82.

Western Province won by 6 wickets

26, 27 and 28 December   SAB Currie Cup   at Durban
Northern Transvaal 130 and 230 (P. J. A. Visagie 52, V. A. P. van der Bijl
   4 for 45, K. R. Cooper 4 for 77)
Natal 316 (C. P. Wilkins 102) and 46 for 3
Natal won by 7 wickets
Natal 21 pts, Northern Transvaal 5 pts

                                                       at Johannesburg
Transvaal 322 for 8 dec (R. G. Pollock 166*)
Western Province 128 (A. J. Kourie 3 for 12) and 172 (P. N. Kirsten 68,
   C. E. B. Rice 5 for 47)
Transvaal won by an innings and 22 runs
Transvaal 21 pts, Western Province 4 pts

SAB Bowl   at Cape Town
Boland 110 (L. L. Roberts 35, R. R. Lawrenson 6 for 24) and 125 (C. van der
   Merwe 32, D. L. Hobson 4 for 22)
Western Province 'B' 313 for 7 dec (P. H. Thompson 67, T. Clarke 54)
Western Province won by an innings and 78 runs
Western Province 21 pts, Boland 4 pts

                                                        at East London
Eastern Province 'B' 273 for 9 dec (J. M. Winstanly 112) and 155 (T. Reid 34,
   G. L. Hayes 6 for 44, A. K. Weakley 4 for 54)
Border 341 for 9 dec (G. L. Hayes 88, I. D. Harty 78) and 88 for 4
Border won by 6 wickets
Border 18 pts, Eastern Province 'B' 7 pts

Early Currie Cup stragglers Northern Transvaal were put in on a fiery Kingsmead strip and not surprisingly found the superbly equipped Natal seamers
too much for them, but after their dismissal for 130 Natal's batsmen found
things far easier as they finished the day 28 ahead and only two wickets down.
Chris Wilkins, 84 overnight, soon completed his hundred on the second morning
but he was then run out after some confusion with his skipper, Procter, and
the later Natal batsmen struggled to reach 316. 186 in arrears, Northerns made
another bad start, quickly losing both openers, but useful thirties from Edwards

and Motley plus an aggressive half-century by Visagie forced Natal to bat again, though the 45 they then needed was a mere formality. This game left Northerns rooted firmly to the bottom and put Natal top, albeit temporarily since on the following day Transvaal defeated early leaders Western Province to join Natal.

The outstanding feature of this match was a superb unbeaten 166 by Grahame Pollock, which put Transvaal on top on the first day, scored out of 322 for 8 declared, it was his twenty-ninth in the Currie Cup, and the fifty-third of his career. He was in for 286 minutes and hit 25 fours and a six. Every other batsman struggled throughout the match. Western's reply was a miserable 128 and following on they made little improvement as they slumped to an innings defeat, only Peter Kirsten putting up much resistance in the second innings against the pace of Rupert Hanley and Clive Rice.

In the SAB Bowl Southern section Western Province 'B' took a clear lead with a crushing victory over Boland. Boland batted first but put up a dismal performance against the pace of Bob Lawrenson, only Leon Roberts batting with any resolution. Fifties by Peter Thompson and Bossie Clarke were the backbone of the Western Province reply and after their declaration at 313 for 7 another dismal Boland collapse, with skipper Jerry Kennedy obtaining his third successive 'duck', and excellent spin bowling by Denys Hobson ensured an innings win for Westerns which consolidated their position at the top of the Southern log, and rooted Boland to the bottom.

In the other Southern section match a sound 112 in 164 minutes by John Winstanley, ensured a fairly healthy total of 273 for 9 for Eastern Province 'B' – an innings marred by a collision between batsmen Emslie and Cresswell which cost the latter his wicket and saw the former concussed and taken to hospital. Border more than matched them, Ian Harty (78) and Greg Hayes (88) being chief contributors to their 341 for 9 declared. Easterns then showed a disappointing lack of enterprise against medium pacers Kim Weakley and Greg Hayes as they collapsed on the third morning, leaving Border to make 88 for victory – a target which they reached, but not without some early discomfort, against the accurate seamers of Clive Wulfsohn and Mike van Vuuren.

1, 2 and 3 January 1981   SAB Currie Cup   **at Port Elizabeth**
Transvaal 273 (D. D. Dyer 64, H. R. Fotheringham 55, W. K. Watson 4 for 47) and 162 (H. R. Fotheringham 63, W. K. Watson 4 for 59)
Eastern Province 303 (R. L. S. Armitage 148, G. Cook 68, R. W. Hanley 5 for 57, C. E. B. Rice 4 for 56) and 135 for 6 (A. J. Kourie 5 for 71)
Eastern Province won by 4 wickets
Eastern Province 18 pts, Transvaal 6 pts

                                                                    at Cape Town
Western Province 132 (A. J. Lamb 54, V. A. P. van der Bijl 4 for 35) and 213 (A. J. Lamb 50, G. S. le Roux 50, P. B. Clift 5 for 46)
Natal 287 (C. P. Wilkins 109, N. P. Daniels 56*, D. L. Hobson 5 for 88) and 62 for 0 (C. P. Wilkins 45*)
Natal won by 10 wickets
Natal 17 pts, Western Province 4 pts

SAB Bowl **at Bloemfontein**
Griqualand West 273 (A. P. Beukes 89, A. D. Methuen 63, J. R. Gray 57*,
 E. Schmidt 4 for 43) and 162 for 9 (P. L. Symcox 54)
Orange Free State 252 for 8 dec (R. J. East 77, L. W. Griessel 71, T. E. Jesty
 4 for 81) and 147 for 9 (L. W. Griessel 47, T. E. Jesty 5 for 37)
Match drawn
Orange Free State 9 pts, Griqualand West 8 pts

at Durban
Transvaal 'B' 357 for 8 dec (N. T. Day 136*, I. R. Ault 4 for 83) and 172
 for 5 dec (W. van der Linden 54*)
Natal 'B' 266 (F. B. Hill 96) and 254 for 7 (K. D. Verdoorn 94, F. B. Hill 63)
Match drawn
Transvaal 'B' 7 pts, Natal 'B' 5 pts

at East London
Border 193 (R. R. Lawrenson 4 for 56) and 128 (R. R. Lawrenson 6 for 42)
Western Province 'B' 361 (O. Henry 105*, T. A. Clarke 100, G. M. Gower
 4 for 88)
Western Province 'B' won by an innings and 40 runs
Western Province 'B' 19 pts, Border 4 pts

The new year started with struggling Eastern Province entertaining the defending champions, Transvaal. Transvaal won the toss but were soon struggling
against the pace of Ken Watson. Only half-centuries by David Dyer and Henry
Fotheringham which owed more to application than flair enabled them to reach
a reasonable score. Fotheringham's 55 was specially welcome in that it signalled
the end of a lean period and rarely had his runs been more welcome. Easterns
maintained the pressure on the second day, Geoff Cook contributed a sound
68 but the main architect of their 30 run lead was Rob Armitage. The left-
hander's 148, his maiden first-class hundred, included seventeen fours and four
sixes in a 240 minute stay which left the spectators so excited that he was
chaired from the field. On his dismissal at 264 for 3 Rice and Hanley engineered
a collapse so that only 39 further runs were added but Easterns stayed on
top when Transvaal lost Dyer and McKenzie for 35 at the day's end. On the
third morning only a dogged 63 saved the Champions from disaster. Easterns
never found the task of scoring 134 in 140 minutes an easy one but finally
achieved their target with nine balls and four wickets left. This was their first
Currie Cup win over Transvaal for twelve years and Transvaal's first defeat
for four years.
   Meanwhile at Newlands Western Province batted first against Natal but
found Natal's seamers in great form again. Despite a determined 54 by Alan
Lamb Western were all out for 132, van der Bijl, 4 for 35 and Cooper, 3 for
40, being the main wicket-takers. Chris Wilkins' 109, with fifteen fours and
a six was the foundation of Natal's reply but it was only due to Neville Daniels'
unbeaten 56 that a lead of 155 was attained. Westerns finished the second
day still 67 behind with 3 second innings wickets down and despite fifties by
Lamb and Garth le Roux they finally crushed Easterns by 10 wickets with
over two hours left and took a clear lead at the top of the log.

At Bloemfontein Free State entertained Griqualand West in the Northern section of the Bowl. Half-centuries by Alan Beukes, Atholl Methuen and Jim Gray helped Griquas to a good recovery after Etienne Schmidt had swept away their first four batsmen for only 25, and Free State also recovered after early shocks had seen them 29 for 3, a fourth wicket stand of 129 between Lloyd Griessel and Robert East getting them back on the right lines. In a match of poor starts Griquas lost 2 for 19 in their second innings before Pat Symcox came to the rescue with a half-century and they were able to give Free State the task of scoring 184 in 3 hours plus 20 overs. They started the last 20 overs needing four an over with 6 wickets left but in indifferent light Trevor Jesty took 3 wickets in 15 balls and Free State were glad to hold out for the draw, with one wicket left.

In the other Northern game leaders Transvaal took on second club Natal. Transvaal won the toss and thanks to an unbeaten 136 in three-and-a-half hours from Neville Day reached an impressive 357 for 8. Despite a career best 96 by Forest Hill Natal always struggled and finished 91 short on first innings. Transvaal pushed the score along on the third morning to leave Natal a target of 264. A heroic 94 in 137 minutes by Kevin Verdoorn plus another, good, though more sedate, innings from Forest Hill. With Transvaal playing their part by keeping up a good over rate Natal found themselves just 10 short with one ball left when the umpires called it a day. Despite the draw Transvaal took two points more than Natal so increased their lead at the top.

In the Southern section runaway leaders Western Province 'B' soon got on top of a Border side which had shown some promise in previous games. Bob Lawrenson bowled well as Border struggled to a disappointing first innings 193 and then centuries by Bossie Clarke and Omar Henry – the first in big cricket for both players – helped establish a big first innings lead. Border again batted poorly, finding Bob Lawrenson particularly difficult to combat and they collapsed most disappointingly to an innings defeat, with Lawrenson having match figures of 10 for 98.

Before a full house of more than eight thousand Eastern Province again did battle with their Western counterparts at Port Elizabeth to decide who challenged the holders Transvaal in the final. Westerns batted first and made a steady start but at 41 they lost Barlow, brilliantly caught at point by Foulkes when trying to push the score along. This was the signal for a collapse. Western's much vaunted numbers 3 and 5, Lamb Kirsten and Swart amassing only 6 runs between them and despite some spirited swinging by le Roux Westerns managed only 116 from 54.5 overs. Needing less than 2 an over Easterns naturally took no risks and cruised into the final for the loss of only 3 wickets and with 13 overs remaining.

The second legs of the Datsun Shield semi-finals took place on 10 January. At the Wanderers Ground, Johannesburg Transvaal, the holders who narrowly won the first leg were hoping for a repeat, with the home ground advantage. Procter won the toss for Natal and an opening stand of 78 in 26 overs gave them the start they had prayed for. Kourie then struck, dismissing both openers, Smith and Wilkins, at the same score and with Parker falling cheaply the good start was largely dissipated. Led by Bentley and skipper Procter the middle order restored their position with some positive batting in mid-afternoon but the late order were guilty of recklessness as the overs ran out, and the last 5 wickets fell for 16 runs, with three run outs. Natal made a splendid start in the Transvaal innings when van der Bijl removed Cook in the third over and Dyer also went cheaply. Fortunately for the home team Day then got his head down while Pollock stroked his way to 33 in 50 minutes. Rice and Fotheringham also played their part but wickets fell steadily and the last ball came with Transvaal requiring 4 for a tie, and number 11 Neilson at the crease, facing Mike Procter. Neilson heaved the Natal skipper for 4 and the holders went through to another final – albeit by the skin of their teeth.

The other semi-final took place at St George's Park, Port Elizabeth. Western Province, who had won their home leg, batted first but immediately struck trouble, losing three wickets for 29. Fortunately Allan Lamb restored their fortunes with a stylish 63, but only a hard hit unbeaten 41 by Garth le Roux enabled them to top the 200. Easterns started badly, losing Bezuidenhout for a duck and managing only 19 from the first 10 overs. Le Roux was specially hard to score from but upon his removal the batsmen accelerated and a third wicket stand of 106 in excellent time between Armitage and Whyte set them on course for a seemingly comfortable win. On the fall of the fourth wicket only 49 runs were needed in 30 overs. With the return of le Roux however runs again became difficult to score and with wickets also falling the last over was commenced by Eddie Barlow with Easterns still requiring 10 runs to win, and their last men at the wicket. With a six and a four from the first three balls however Mick van Vuuren put the result beyond doubt and ensured a deciding match be played the following Wednesday, by the luck of the toss at the same ground.

Datsun Shield   Semi-Finals – Second Leg   **Transvaal *v*. Natal**
10 January 1981   **at Johannesburg**

Natal

A. J. S. Smith	b Kourie	38
C. P. Wilkins	c Dyer b Kourie	39
R. M. Bentley	run out	54
P. W. G. Parker	c McKenzie b Neilson	6
M. J. Procter	c Day b McMillan	20
P. H. Williams	c Neilson b Rice	22
N. P. Daniels	run out	28
V. A. P. van der Bijl	run out	0
D. K. Pearse	b Rice	0
P. B. Clift	run out	6
K. R. Cooper	not out	0
Extras		13
	(60 overs)	226

	O	M	R	W
Rice	12	2	45	2
McMillan	12	4	26	1
Kourie	12	3	25	2
Neilson	12	1	58	1
Hanley	12	2	59	0

Fall of Wickets
1–78, 2–78, 3–98, 4–123, 5–180, 6–210, 7–210, 8–214, 9–226.

Transvaal

D. D. Dyer	b Cooper	15
S. J. Cook	c Smith b van der Bijl	6
N. Day	c Smith b Clift	53
R. G. Pollock	c Wilkins b Clift	33
C. E. B. Rice	run out	22
H. R. Fotheringham	run out	46
K. A. McKenzie	lbw b Procter	9
A. J. Kourie	run out	20
G. E. McMillan	run out	0
D. R. Neilson	not out	5
R. W. Hanley	not out	0
Extras		17
	(for 9 wkts – 60 overs)	226

	O	M	R	W
Procter	12	3	36	1
van der Bijl	12	1	25	1
Cooper	12	2	47	1
Wilkins	7	0	19	0
Clift	11	0	60	2
Pearse	6	2	22	0

Fall of Wickets
1–8, 2–34, 3–78, 4–131, 5–137, 6–163, 7–221, 8–221, 9–221.

Match tied; Transvaal go through to final on first leg victory

Datsun Shield   Semi-Finals – Second Leg
Eastern Province *v.* Western Province

15 January 1981   **at Port Elizabeth**

Western Province

L. Seeff	c Richardson b Watson	8
P. M. Thompson	lbw b Ogilvie	7
P. N. Kirsten	c Ogilvie b Brickett	3
A. J. Lamb	c Foulkes b Brickett	63
P. D. Swart	c Richardson b van Vuuren	31
A. D. Kuiper	b Watson	16
E. J. Barlow	b van Vuuren	9
G. S. le Roux	not out	41
O. Henry	c Richardson b Watson	9
S. T. Jefferies	not out	4
Extras		10
	(for 8 wkts – 60 overs)	201

R. R. Lawrenson did not bat.

	O	M	R	W
Watson	12	4	23	3
Ogilvie	12	3	31	1

Brickett	12	2	65	2
Foulkes	12	1	44	0
van Vuuren	12	2	28	2

Fall of Wickets
1–9, 2–18, 3–29, 4–99, 5–125, 6–131, 7–145, 8–175.

Eastern Province

G. Cook	c Kirsten b Barlow	25
S. Bezuidenhout	c Kirsten b le Roux	0
R. L. S. Armitage	c Seeff b Jefferies	71
R. J. D. Whyte	lbw b Jefferies	52
D. H. Howell	b Barlow	13
D. J. Brickett	c and b le Roux	5
I. Foulkes	c Barlow b Jefferies	0
D. J. Richardson	c Thompson b le Roux	0
W. K. Watson	c Thompson b Barlow	5
M. van Vuuren	not out	10
J. D. Ogilvie	not out	6
Extras		15

| (9 wkts – 59.3 overs) | | | **202** |

	O	M	R	W
le Roux	12	7	12	3
Lawrenson	7	1	31	0
Jefferies	12	0	41	3
Barlow	11.3	0	42	3
Henry	10	0	32	0
Swart	5	0	16	0
Kirsten	2	0	13	0

Fall of Wickets
1–1, 2–44, 3–150, 4–153, 5–169, 6–170, 7–174, 8–174, 9–188.

Eastern Province won by 1 wicket. A play-off to be held on 19 January. By the toss of a coin the venue was decided upon as Port Elizabeth

Datsun Shield   Semi-Finals – Play-Off
Eastern Province *v.* Western Province

19 January 1981   **at Port Elizabeth**

Western Province

E. J. Barlow	c Foulkes b Ogilvie	19
L. Seeff	c Richardson b Brickett	9
P. N. Kirsten	lbw b Ogilvie	2
A. J. Lamb	run out	4
P. D. Swart	b Brickett	0
A. D. Kuiper	c Watson b Foulkes	11
G. S. le Roux	b van Vuuren	23
O. Henry	run out	10
R. J. Ryall	lbw b van Vuuren	1
S. T. Jefferies	not out	7
D. L. Hobson	c Richardson b van Vuuren	10

Extras				20

(54.5 overs)   116

	O	M	R	W
Watson	12	5	8	0
Ogilvie	12	1	28	2
Brickett	9	5	12	2
van Vuuren	10.5	2	19	3
Foulkes	7	1	17	1
Armitage	4	0	12	0

Fall of Wickets
1–32, 2–41, 3–46, 4–47, 5–49, 6–65, 7–81, 8–94, 9–97.

Eastern Province

G. Cook	run out		15
S. J. Bezuidenhout	c sub b Jefferies		35
R. L. S. Armitage	not out		33
R. J. D. Whyte	lbw b Kuiper		23
D. H. Howell	not out		0
Extras			11

(for 3 wkts – 46.4 overs) 117

I. Foulkes, J. D. Ogilvie, D. J. Richardson, D. J. Brickett, W. K. Watson, M. van Vuuren did not bat.

	O	M	R	W
le Roux	6	1	9	0
Jefferies	12	4	14	1
Barlow	8	0	20	0
Hobson	12	3	31	0
Henry	6	1	20	0
Kuiper	2.4	1	12	1

Fall of Wickets
1–50, 2–62, 3–111.

Eastern Province won by 7 wickets

15, 16 and 17 January   SAB Bowl   at Port Elizabeth
Eastern Province 'B' 349 (R. G. Fensham 145, T. B. Reid 47, R. J. Bowley
    4 for 64) and 226 for 7 dec (R. G. Fensham 58)
Western Province 'B' 240 (T. A. Passmore 73, R. P. Martin 51, H. M. Ackerman
    47, G. Long 6 for 60, C. Wulfsohn 4 for 74) and 60 for 1
Match drawn
Eastern Province 'B' 9 pts, Western Province 'B' 4 pts

16, 17 and 19 January   SAB Currie Cup   at Cape Town
Western Province 234 (E. J. Barlow 99, W. K. Watson 4 for 43) and 285 for
    3 dec (A. J. Lamb 95*, L. Seeff 81, P. D. Swart 63*)
Eastern Province 317 for 6 dec (D. J. Richardson 77*, S. J. Bezuidenhout 76,
    J. M. Winstanley 48*) and 166 for 5 (G. Cook 63, R. L. S. Armitage 41)
Match drawn

Western Province 4 pts, Eastern Province 5 pts

17, 18 and 19 January   SAB Currie Cup   **at Durban**
Transvaal 201 (S. J. Cook 58, H. R. Fotheringham 56, K. R. Cooper 6 for 68)
  and 22 for 0
Natal 225 for 6 dec (C. P. Wilkins 71, B. J. Whitfield 52)
Match drawn
Natal 8 pts, Transvaal 5 pts

19, 20 and 21 January   SAB Bowl   **at Johannesburg**
Transvaal 'B' 228 for 9 dec (B. Deyzel 5 for 68) and 285 for 9 dec (R. V.
  Jennings 82*, M. K. Venter 76, W. J. van der Linden 54)
Griqualand West 234 (A. D. Methuen 62, M. J. D. Doherty 50) and 156 (T. E.
  Jesty 40)
Transvaal 'B' won by 123 runs
Transvaal 'B' 16 pts, Griqualand West 7 pts

22, 23, and 24 January   SAB Bowl   **at Bloemfontein**
Transvaal 'B' 292 (M. S. Venter 71, R. F. Pienaar 71, N. E. Wright 53, A. M. L.
  Klopper 5 for 66) and 2 for 0
Orange Free State 99 and 194 (E. Schmidt 41, H. J. van der Linden 4 for 55,
  K. J. Kerr 4 for 84)
Transvaal 'B' won by 10 wickets
Transvaal 'B' 20 pts, Orange Free State 5 pts

On 15 January Southern section Bowl leaders Western Province travelled to
Port Elizabeth to take on their disappointing Eastern counterparts. A sparkling
maiden hundred by Russell Fensham helped Easterns total 349 on the opening
day, an advantage emphasized when Westerns lost two cheap wickets before
the close. Westerns sagged to 79 for 6 on the second day before half-centuries
by Tom Passmore and seventeen-year-old schoolboy Brian Martin enabled
them to reach 240. Surprisingly Easterns adopted a defensive attitude on the
third morning before leaving Westerns the very hard task of scoring 336 in
108 minutes plus 20 overs. Since this would have been nearly three times their
own rate they could hardly have been surprised when Westerns played out
for a draw. Such negative tactics from a side in the driving seat the whole
of the match are, to put it mildly, hard to comprehend.
  16 January saw Eastern Province visit Cape Town for their Currie Cup clash
with Westerns. The highlight of a slow first day was a gritty 99 by Westerns
captain Eddie Barlow, the highest of the season for the forty-year-old who
thus confounded those who thought him over the hill. Apart from Alan Lamb
and Omar Henry, Barlow received little support and it was entirely due to
him that his side eventually crawled to 234. Simon Bezuidenhout dominated
the early part of the Westerns reply with a sound 76 but the innings of the
day was by twenty-one-year-old wicket-keeper David Richardson who scored
77 in an unbroken seventh wicket stand of 122 with John Winstanley.
Richardson scored his runs in ninety-nine minutes, and hit ten fours and a
six and he confirmed his skipper Geoff Cook's opinion of him as one of the

best of the younger South Africans. Westerns showed much better form in the second innings, only the unfortunate Peter Kirsten failing, and there was never much chance of Easterns obtaining the 203 they required for victory.

On 17 January the 'match of the season' started. Against the brilliant Natal seamers Transvaal made a poor start, losing 3 wickets, including that of Pollock, for 61, but half-centuries from Jim Cook and Henry Fotheringham carried them to 148 before another collapse saw them all out for a disappointing 201. Rain curtailed the first day and washed out the second day completely. The only interest was in bonus points and on the third day Natal declared to deny Transvaal the chance of two and so despite the disappointment with the weather Natal were able to increase their lead at the top of the log.

23, 24 and 26 January   SAB Currie Cup   **at Port Elizabeth**
Eastern Province 34 (V. A. P. van der Bijl 4 for 8) and 69 (M. J. Procter 4 for 33)
Natal 148 for 6 dec (B. J. Whitfield 42)
Natal won by an innings and 45 runs
Natal 15 pts, Eastern Province 3 pts

SAB Currie Cup   **at Johannesburg**
Northern Transvaal 99 (A. J. Kourie 6 for 34, C. E. B. Rice 4 for 30) and 113 (K. G. Motley 45*, C. E. B. Rice 4 for 27)
Transvaal 179 for 9 dec (K. A. McKenzie 53, R. G. Pollock 48) and 34 for 2
Transvaal won by 8 wickets
Transvaal 16 pts, Northern Transvaal 5 pts

23, 24 and 25 January   SAB Bowl   **at Pietermaritzburg**
Natal 'B' 169 (H. Liebenberg 4 for 47) and 126 (F. B. Hill 45, H. Liebenburg 4 for 26)
Griqualand West 115 (D. K. Pearse 5 for 43) and 140 (J. S. Muil 5 for 41, D. K. Pearse 4 for 36)
Natal 'B' won by 40 runs
Natal 'B' 15 pts, Griqualand West 5 pts

24, 26 and 27 January   SAB Bowl   **at East London**
Boland 161 (E. T. Laughlin 5 for 49)
Border 33 for 3
Match drawn – bad weather
Border 5 pts, Boland 2 pts

Bowl Northern section leaders Transvaal 'B' began a busy week at Kimberley against struggling Griqualand West. A sparse crowd at the Wanderers stadium saw them struggle against Griquas seamer Brian Deyzel. No one was able to play a dominating innings as they scrambled to 228 for 9 on the rain effected first day. Griquas, showing more aggression just headed Transvaal on first innings, owing much to fifties from Mike Doherty and Atholl Methuen but late on the second day a splendidly aggressive 76 from Mark Venter enabled Transvaal to finish the day with a lead of 151 runs with 7 wickets left. On the third morning Ray Jennings, dropped from the first team due to poor batting, struck an invaluable 83 and Griquas, losing wickets steadily, never looked likely to save the game, let alone win it.

Transvaal 'B' then travelled straight to Bloemfontein knowing that another win would make their appearance in the final virtually certain. Again their first innings was disapr ointing. After an opening stand of 116 by Mark Venter and Neville Wright they struggled against occasional bowler Louis Klopper who took 5 for 66 in his first bowl in first-class cricket and totalled only 292. Free State in their turn batted appallingly, averaging little more than a run an over in their first innings 99 all out. Their middle order showed more aggression, and obtained more success, in the second innings after the early batsmen had surrendered to nineteen-year-old off-spinner Kevin Kerr but their total of 194 left Transvaal to score only 2 for victory.

On 23 January Currie Cup leaders Natal commenced their away match with the improving Eastern Province; improving that is until this game. Sent in to bat on a rain effected pitch only skipper Geoff Cook reached double figures. Most of their batsmen found the seamers unplayable – 3 wickets going down for 11, 7 for 27, and finally 10 for 34 for their lowest ever Currie Cup score. Natal in their turn hardly had things their own way but with Brian Whitfield playing a watchful 42 for the highest score of the match they finished the day in a very strong position. A blank second day decided Natal to declare at their first day score and after another delay on the third morning more batting remarkable only for its ineptness and timidity saw a collapse to 69 all out and a humiliating defeat for the home team – and a win for Natal which put them very firmly on top of the Currie Cup log.

Natal's only possible Currie Cup rivals, defending champions Transvaal, had a home game with the weak Northern Transvaal outfit. On a miserable, rain-marred first day Northerns scored 19 for one in 11.1 overs and on the second day collapsed rapidly to the pace of Clive Rice and the left-arm spin of Alan Kourie. Transvaal in their turn struggled to 48 for 4 by the close. On the third morning they moved somewhat painfully to 179 for 9 when they declared at lunch. In the afternoon Northerns batted stubbornly but without much conviction and despite a brave innings from Kevin Motley Transvaal needed only 34 to win, and maintain their slight hopes of retaining the title.

In the Northern section of the Bowl Natal 'B', striving to catch leaders Transvaal 'B', entertained Griqualand West at Pietermaritzburg. Natal won the toss but their batsmen struggled badly against pacemen Deyzel and Lieben-berg on the rain effected first day. More rain handicapped the batsmen on day two when only brave deeds from the tail enabled Griquas to struggle to 115. Forest Hill's 45 enabled Natal to reach a reasonable score against the Griqualand seamers and then with the pitch still effected by the damp weather Muil and Pearse put Griquas to flight as they attempted to score 181 to win. In such conditions however to finish only 40 short was an achievement.

The Southern section Bowl match between Border and Boland was ruined when bad weather prevented play on the first two days. When they finally started Border captain Ian Harty asked Boland to bat, hoping to salvage some bonus points from what remained of the game. The seamers were ineffective but spinners Chris Davies and Errol Laughlin managed to restrict the Boland batsmen to less than two an over while steadily chipping their way through the innings. The Boland seamers soon sent back three Border batsmen but further rain during tea-time finally caused proceedings to be abandoned. Border thus ended a disappointing season on a typically unsatisfactory note.

29, 30 and 31 January   SAB Bowl **at Port Elizabeth**
Boland 301 for 9 dec (P. H. J. Wallace 103) and 133 (G. Long 7 for 16)
Eastern Province 'B' 167 (L. L. Roberts 5 for 39) and 192 (T. C. Seaman 78, J. Hendriks 6 for 58)
Boland won by 75 runs
Boland 15 pts, Eastern Province 'B' 3 pts

Young left-hander Paul Wallace obtained a maiden first-class hundred as Boland plodded to a first innings score of 301 in seven hours on the first day against steady but by no means vicious Eastern bowling but a devastating spell on the second afternoon by left-arm seamer Leon Roberts put Boland into a strong position. This was dissipated somewhat when they collapsed on the third morning in face of a magnificent spell of medium pace swing bowling by Grant Long but the task of scoring 268 at about one a minute proved too much for Easterns and in an atmosphere of mounting expectation John Hendriks cut through the Eastern batting to give the 'Wine farmers' their first win in first-class cricket.

Datsun Shield: Final

David Dyer won the toss and asked Geoff Cook to take first innings on a pitch which showed early life but which soon became somewhat benign in character.

Easterns soon lost Simon Bezuidenhout but Robbie Armitage played an important, though junior role in a second wicket stand of 85 with Geoff Cook. Bob Whyte then came in and showed aggressive intentions but Easterns suffered a big blow when losing Cook at 122 and although the later batsmen all struck some useful blows while scoring 41 runs from the last 6 overs Easterns' final score – 224 for 8 – never appeared sufficient.

Transvaal made a steady start, but lost skipper Dyer at 23. Clive Rice, recently struggling for form, then joined Jimmy Cook, also enduring an indifferent spell, but both chose the right time to find their touch as they effectively won the match for their side with a superb stand of 132 in 112 minutes. Rice was then stumped off Armitage, coming down the wicket but with Pollock, unusually, playing a minor role Cook took his side to the verge of victory with a splendid 108 in a little over 3 hours. It was Cook's second hundred in successive Datsun finals and when he finally left his side was 17 runs from its third consecutive final victory with 7 wickets and 9 overs remaining. The Transvaal star was undoubtedly Cook but Rice's support with the bat was invaluable while early in the match they owed much to the steady bowling and superb fielding at crucial times, of Doug Neilson. For the losers skipper Geoff Cook played his part admirably as the back-bone of the early batting but was let down by his specialist colleagues – Bob Whyte excepted – while none of his bowlers was able to perform with sufficient economy when Cook and Rice started to look for runs.

Datsun Shield   Final   **Transvaal *v*. Eastern Province**
31 January 1981   **at Wanderers, Johannesburg**

Eastern Province

G. Cook	c Day b Hanley	75
S. J. Bezuidenhout	b McMillan	5
R. L. S. Armitage	c Day b Rice	23
R. J. D. Whyte	c Day b McMillan	39
D. H. Howell	run out	13
D. J. Richardson	c Neilson b Rice	0
I. Foulkes	c Kourie b Hanley	17
D. J. Brickett	c Day b Rice	15
W. K. Watson	not out	12
J. D. Ogilvie	not out	12
Extras		13

(for 8 wkts – 60 overs) 224

M. K. van Vuuren did not bat.

	O	M	R	W
Rice	12	2	29	3
McMillan	12	1	60	2
Neilson	12	3	18	0
Kourie	12	2	40	0
Hanley	12	0	64	.2

Fall of Wickets
1–8, 2–93, 3–122, 4–147, 5–148, 6–181, 7–200, 8–204.

Transvaal

D. D. Dyer	c Richardson b Watson	13
S. J. Cook	b Armitage	108
C. E. B. Rice	st Richardson b Armitage	58
R. G. Pollock	not out	31
H. R. Fotheringham	not out	6
Extras		9

(for 3 wkts – 53.2 over) 225

G. E. McMillan, R. W. Hanley, D. R. Neilson, A. J. Kourie, N. T. Day, K. A. McKenzie did not bat.

	O	M	R	W
Watson	9	2	30	1
Ogilvie	7	0	24	0
Brickett	5	0	35	0
Foulkes	11	0	53	0
van Vuuren	11	0	36	0
Armitage	10	1	34	2
Cook	0.2	0	4	0

Fall of Wickets
1–23, 2–155, 3–208.

Transvaal won by 7 wickets

5, 6 and 7 February   SAB Bowl   **at Johannesburg**
Transvaal 'B' 264 for 3 dec (N. E. Wright 128*, N. T. Day 52*) and 98 for 1
(M. S. Venter 51*)
Natal 'B' 162 (M. B. Logan 45, M. D. Tramontino 41, F. Weideman 4 for 51)
Match drawn
Transvaal 9 pts, Natal 2 pts (bad weather)

6, 7 and 9 February   SAB Currie Cup   **at Cape Town**
Transvaal 310 for 6 dec (D. D. Dyer 131, S. J. Cook 69, C. E. B. Rice 50)
and 225 for 4 dec (S. J. Cook 78, R. G. Pollock 50*)
Western Province 375 (A. J. Lamb 130, L. Seeff 71, P. N. Kirsten 62, A. J. Kourie
8 for 113) and 145 for 7 (P. N. Kirsten 43, A. J. Kourie 5 for 44)
Match drawn
Transvaal 8 pts, Western Province 6 pts

A career best unbeaten 128 by Neville Wright in five hours had put Transvaal
'B' in a good first day position when rain curtailed play and then in helpful
conditions their youthful seamers Francois Weideman and Neal Radford
initiated a Natal 'B' middle order collapse before a tail end flourish brought
respectability. Wright and Mark Venter had put Transvaal into a match winning
position when rain washed out play on the third day and so Transvaal topped
the Northern section and went through to the final. Meanwhile in the Currie
Cup Transvaal, fighting to catch log leaders Natal batted steadily on the first
day of their match with Western Province. An opening stand of 135 in two-
and-a-half hours between David Dyer and Jimmy Cook gave them a solid
base and Dyer went on to reach 131 in 197 minutes – a real captain's innings.
With the wicket still good Westerns made a splendid reply. Lamb's magnificent
130 in four-and-a-quarter hours delighted the home supporters and with Laurie
Seeff and Peter Kirsten offering sound support Westerns established a healthy
first innings lead on the second day. Transvaal, desperate for a result batted
with a strange lack of aggression on the third day, their scoring rate of well
under 3 an over being incomprehensible having regard to the fact that a draw
was of no use to them. They set Westerns a target of 161, with 70 minutes
and 20 overs remaining and although Allan Kourie again bowled splendidly,
adding 5 more wickets to the 8 he obtained in the first innings – his match
figures of 13 for 157 were the best for Transvaal for twenty-seven years –
Westerns were finally nearer to victory, finishing only 16 runs short with 3
wickets left. At the completion of this match Transvaal, with one game remaining were still 5 points behind leaders Natal who, with two games left, seemed
assured of their first title for four years.

14, 15 and 17 February   SAB Bowl   **at Durban**
Natal 'B' 233 (T. R. Madsen 75, P. H. Williams 46, W. M. van der Merwe
4 for 64) and 300 for 4 dec (F. B. Hill 105, M. A. Tramontino 72, D.
Bestall 50*)
Orange Free State 129 (E. J. Hodkinson 5 for 53) and 162 (J. J. Strydom 70*,
D. K. Pearse 5 for 41)
Natal 'B' won by 242 runs
Natal 'B' 18 pts, Orange Free State 5 pts

SAB Bowl **at Stellenbosch**

Eastern Province 'B' 314 for 7 dec (N. Mandy 65, G. S. Cowley 61, T. B. Reid 47, T. G. Shaw 45) and 245 for 6 dec (T. B. Reid 59, D. H. Howell 54, T. G. Shaw 50*, J. Hendriks 4 for 48)

Boland 278 (P. B. J. Wallace 68, C. van der Merwe 50, A. Odendaal 43) and 155 (P. B. J. Wallace 55)

Eastern Province 'B' won by 126 runs
Eastern Province 'B' 15 pts, Boland 5 pts

15, 17 and 18 February SAB Currie Cup **at Pretoria**

Eastern Province 264 (G. Long 60, I. Foulkes 56) and 208 for 5 dec (R. Whyte 61, I. Foulkes 41*)

Northern Transvaal 198 (A. M. Ferreira 65, A. Barrow 53, W. K. Watson 4 for 34) and 179 (A. M. Ferreira 45, I. Foulkes 4 for 65)

Eastern Province won by 66 runs
Eastern Province 18 pts, Northern Transvaal 5 pts

With Transvaal 'B' already in an unassailable position at the top of the Bowl Northern section the remaining two matches had little but academic interest, though a win for Natal would make them runners-up for certain. In their final match, with Free State at Durban they won the toss and in a dull day lightened by a sparkling 75 by Trevor Madsen scored 233 all out before rain curtailed play. Free State struggled against the pace of Evan Hodkinson on the second morning, only spirited work by the tail ensuring reasonable respectability. Natal openers Forest Hill and Mickey Tramontino then laid about the Free State bowlers with gay abandon, adding 151 for the first wicket in 45 overs as the fieldsmen wilted in the steamy heat. Hill completed a brilliant hundred and after being set 405 to win Free State, despite a gallant unbeaten 70 by 18-year-old Joubert Strydom – his last wicket stand of 57 with his uncle Willie was the only redeeming feature for them – were never really in with a hope of saving the game, unless with help from the weather.

The Southern section of the Bowl was also virtually a forgone conclusion, with Western Province certain champions barring miracles. Easterns travelled to Stellenbosch still believing in miracles however. Winning the toss a middle order collapse threatened to embarrass them but Gavin Shaw (61) spearheaded a recovery, enabling them to declare at 314 for 7. A third wicket stand of 90 between Cassie van der Merwe and Oxford Blue Andre Odendaal plus a solid 68 from Paul Wallace enabled Boland to make a most respectable reply. Easterns batted aggressively in their second innings to set Boland a target of 282 at about one a minute. Despite another half-century by Wallace – son of former SACA president Boon Wallace – wickets fell steadily and Easterns gained victory with 6 overs remaining.

Eastern Province and Northern Transvaal, Currie Cup sides whose season was turning sour, met at Pretoria. Easterns batted first and struggled somewhat against accurate seam bowling until Ivor Foulkes and Grant Long showed some aggression in recording half-centuries, during an eighth wicket stand of 98. Replying to Eastern's 264 Northerns decided that a no risk policy was the order of the day, Barrow and du Preez taking 46 overs for a first wicket stand of 79. Skipper Ferreira struck some hard blows in his 65 but there was no aggression from the middle batting and their total of 198 barely exceeded two runs per over. Without dominating Easterns scored steadily on the third morning before setting Northerns to score 275 at one a minute. Ferreira supplied a quick 45 but on his dismissal Northerns steadily subsided into a disappointing defeat.

19, 20 and 21 February   SAB Bowl   **at Kimberley**
Orange Free State 170 (G. G. Deyzel 4 for 30) and 299 for 8 (R. J. East 85,
   J. J. Strydom 55, S. Regenstein 43*)
Griqualand West 362 (T. E. Jesty 95, P. L. Symcox 54, M. J. D. Doherty
   50, A. P. Beukes 50, W. Dobson 48*)
Match drawn
Griqualand West 8 pts, Orange Free State 3 pts

SAB Bowl   **at Cape Town (Burt Oval)**
Eastern Province 'B' 128 (T. G. Shaw 41*, M. J. Taljaard 4 for 37) and 207
   (T. B. Reid 78, R. R. Lawrenson 6 for 72)
Western Province 'B' 241 (M. J. Nel 73, J. Seeff 50, C. Wulfsohn 6 for 46)
   and 96 for 3 (M. J. Nel 43)
Western Province 'B' won by 7 wickets
Western Province 'B' 18 pts, Eastern Province 'B' 5 pts

The final match of the Northern section of the SAB Bowl was to decide whether Griqualand West or Free State would take the wooden spoon. Free State batted poorly in the face of steady bowling, and at the end of the opening day Mike Doherty and Pat Symcox pulled Griquas around from a disastrous start, taking the score from 2 for 2 to 64 for 2. Splendid batting on the second day by Trevor Jesty and Alan Beukes helped Griquas to a first innings lead of 192 but with Robbie East adding 125 for the fourth wicket with young Joubert Strydom – emphasising his promise once again – Free State managed to hold out for a draw. With Griquas taking 8 points to Free State's 3 the two shared the Northern section wooden spoon – as fair a result as could have been desired after a mutually disappointing season.

   The last Southern section game saw champions Western Province 'B' at home to their Eastern counterparts. Easterns batted without assurance or enterprise, Tim Shaw alone doing himself justice and when Westerns replied former Currie Cup player John Nel partnered Jonathan Seeff in a second wicket stand which took them into the lead. A mid-innings collapse foiled Westerns hopes of a big score but with only Terry Reid able to cope with the pace of Western's Bob Lawrenson Westerns were required to score only 95 for victory, which was duly achieved by lunch on the third day.

21, 22 and 23 February   SAB Currie Cup   **at Durban**
Natal 176 (C. P. Wilkins 63, B. J. Whitfield 50, E. J. Barlow 5 for 29, P. D.
   Swart 4 for 42) and 165 for 8 dec (N. P. Daniels 73)
Western Province 106 (L. Seeff 41, V. A. P. van der Bijl 5 for 43) and 94
   (V. A. P. van der Bijl 6 for 30)
Natal won by 141 runs
Natal 16 pts, Western Province 5 pts

Currie Cup leaders Natal lost the toss but started splendidly against Western Province at Kingsmead, Brian Whitfield and Chris Wilkins putting on 113 for the first wicket in miserable, damp conditions. The dismissal of Wilkins however, heralded a collapse. In conditions made to measure Eddie Barlow ran through the middle order for his best figures of the season and with steady support from Peter Swart, who gained the prize wickets of the two openers, he saw Natal lose all their wickets for only 63 runs and must have been glad he chose to field. Unfortunately for Barlow Natal's seamers used the conditions equally successfully and only Laurie Seeff stood firm as Westerns slumped to 106 all out against the three pronged attack of van der Bijl, Procter and Cooper.

Natal in their turn slumped to a potentially disastrous 50 for 6 in their second innings before Neville Daniels saved the day with a splendid 73 and with van der Bijl again irresistible Westerns found the victory target of 235 way beyond their capabilities.

Natal's win put them 21 points clear of defending champions Transvaal and gave them an almost unassailable lead with only one game remaining. Western's 5 points seemed to guarantee the wooden spoon to Northern Transvaal once again.

27, 28 February and 2 March   SAB Currie Cup   at Pretoria

Western Province 237 (A. J. Lamb 43, H. W. Raath 4 for 49) and 119 (E. J. Barlow 53, F. E. Joubert 4 for 31)

Northern Transvaal 191 (A. Barrow 57, P. D. Swart 4 for 40) and 120 (K. G. Motley 41*, D. L. Hobson 7 for 49)

Western Province won by 45 runs
Western Province 18 pts, Northern Transvaal 6 pts

A match with nothing at stake except Northern's faint chances of avoiding the wooden spoon. Ferreira won the toss and invited Westerns to bat on a green but not very lively pitch. Westerns made a steady start, Barlow and Seeff adding 70 for the first wicket but the middle batsmen lost their wickets when seemingly well set and a late collapse rounded off a disappointing innings. Left-arm seamer Hein Raath bowled effectively in his first Currie Cup game of the season. Steady bowling by Swart and Hobson was mainly instrumental in limiting Northerns to a somewhat anonymous 191 but when the early Western batting collapsed in the second afternoon to pace bowler Frankie Joubert the pendulum swung towards Northerns. They were finally given a target of 166 in three-and-a-half hours plus 20 overs. Modest indeed, but seeming to panic, Northerns snatched defeat from the jaws of victory. Only Kevin Motley kept his head in the face of some splendid bowling by leg-spinner Denys Hobson and after 235 minutes of struggle Northerns finally succumbed, still 46 short of that elusive victory.

6, 7 and 9 March   SAB Currie Cup   at Johannesburg

Transvaal 262 for 9 dec (K. A. McKenzie 105, S. J. Cook 96, W. K. Watson 6 for 47) and 172 for 3 dec (R. G. Pollock 59*, S. J. Cook 53)

Eastern Province 138 (I. Foulkes 41, A. J. Kourie 4 for 44) and 140 (R. J. B. Whyte 55, A. J. Kourie, 4 for 46)

Transvaal won by 156 runs
Transvaal 18 pts, Eastern province 4 pts

Needing 22 points to have the slightest chance of retaining the title Transvaal gave a disappointing batting display, so that despite splendid innings by Jim Cook and Keith McKenzie they gained only 3 batting points and so surrendered the title. Easterns, with nothing to play for, gave a spiritless display against good bowling by Frank Weideman and Alan Kourie but despite a substantial first innings lead Transvaal also showed a sad lack of enterprise as they built themselves into an impregnable position. Finally set to score 297 on the third day Easterns disappointed once again, limping without purpose or enterprise to a 156 run defeat, Kourie again doing the main damage, with his four wickets taking his season's total to 52, equalling the fifty-four-year-old Transvaal record held by ex-Springbok Alf Hall. For Eastern Province a sadly suitable ending to a season of high promise which went off the boil.

13, 14, 16 and 17 March   SAB Bowl Final   at Johannesburg
Western Province 'B' 203 (T. A. Clarke 96, F. Weideman 4 for 50) and 299
   (A. P. Kuiper 81, M. J. Nel 48, N. V. Radford 4 for 50)
Transvaal 'B' 284 (N. T. Day 71, R. F. Pienaar 57, N. V. Radford 45, R. R.
   Lawrenson 5 for 81) and 85 (M. B. Taljaard 5 for 18, R. R. Lawrenson
   4 for 23)
Western Province 'B' won by 133 runs

Before a very small crowd Westerns batted first and were saved from disaster by a career best 96 by Bossie Clarke, better known as left-wing threequarter for his province. Dismissed for 203 Westerns hit back and at the close Transvaal had lost 3 wickets for 60, and honours were even. On the second day wicket-keeper Noel Day and Roy Pienaar added 84 for the fifth wicket and with a brisk 45 from Neal Radford Transvaal achieved a first innings lead of 81. Westerns made a poor start and seemed doomed to a three day defeat but a determined 81 from Adrian Kuiper plus useful supporting efforts from several later batsmen ensured the match would go into a fourth day. Transvaal were still favourites but were utterly confounded by the left-arm spinner Marius Taljaard. In the performance of a lifetime Taljaard broke the back of the Transvaal batting finally finishing with 5 for 18 in 18 overs, and with fine support from Bob Lawrenson, who rounded off a splendid season with 4 for 23 Westerns dismissed Transvaal for 85 to run out surprising but deserved bowl winners, with the bemused Transvaal players wondering just what had gone wrong.

13, 14 and 16 March   SAB Currie Cup   at Pretoria
Natal 296 (B. J. Whitfield 81, P. W. G. Parker 74, K. R. Cooper 43*) and
   38 for 0
Northern Transvaal 128 (N. P. Daniels 4 for 41, V. A. P. van der Bijl 4 for
   51) and 205 (L. Coetzee 51, M. J. Procter 4 for 96)
Natal won by 10 wickets
Natal 17 pts, Northern Transvaal 4 pts

New champions Natal made a flying start and with Brian Whitfield and Paul Parker adding 114 for the third wicket a big score seemed likely. Unfortunately a mid-order collapse foiled their hopes but tail enders Clift and Cooper ensured respectability. Northerns made a feeble reply, being dismissed just after lunch on the second day. Their second innings saw a more positive approach but the lack of importance seemed to cause losses of concentration and given 38 to win Natal took the extra half hour to wind up a most successful season in victorious style at the end of the second day. During the Northern second innings van der Bijl took his fifty-fourth wicket of the season. This is a personal best and only 5 short of the all-time record for a Currie Cup season, held by Mike Procter since 1976/77. Van der Bijl has taken 474 wickets in his Currie Cup career, 48 ahead of Mike Procter, lying second and the only other man over 400.

21 March   Connoisseur Challenge Match   **at Johannesburg**
Transvaal (Datsun Shield winners) 174 for 8 (50 overs) (R. G. Pollock 43,
    V. A. P. van der Bijl 3 for 26)
Rest of South Africa 178 for 9 (L. Seeff 65, A. J. Lamb 51, D. R. Neilson
    4 for 32)

Transvaal won the toss but made heavy weather of scoring at the required rate against an expert seam attack in which van der Bijl and Cooper were outstanding. Pollock and Fotheringham worked hard to add 77 for the fourth wicket but it was not until Jennings and McMillan took 17 from van der Bijl's last over that real aggression was shown. A splendid innings by Laurie Seeff – who is a twenty-one-year-old with ambitions to play in England – set The Rest on the victory road and in his stand of 87 with Lamb the best batting of the match was seen. However a magnificent spell of 4 wickets in 4 overs by Doug Neilson (he had announced his retirement before the match) put everything back into the melting pot and only achieved victory with 9 wickets down and 8 balls left when a throw by Kevin McKenzie missed the stumps and went for four byes. Had it hit the result would have been reversed.

During this match, which rounded off the season, a 'semi-official' South African team was chosen, to represent its country should the impossible suddenly happen and South Africa be re-admitted to Test cricket. The team, in probable batting order, was: C. P. Wilkins (Natal), S. J. Cook (Transvaal), P. N. Kirsten (Western Province and Derbyshire), R. G. Pollock (Transvaal), A. J. Lamb (Western Province and Northants), C. E. B. Rice (Transvaal and Notts), M. J. Procter (Captain, Natal and Glos), A. J. Kourie (Transvaal), R. V. Jennings (Transvaal), V. A. P. van der Bijl (Natal), W. K. Watson (Eastern Province and Notts), K. R. Cooper (Natal) (12th man).

Thus another season in isolation, and, in some respects, not such a happy one. Perhaps the long-predicted decline in standards had at last started. Certainly there were some outstanding performances but the gap between The Best and The Rest seemed often to be very large and the cricket seemed untidy and inconsistent. On the other hand some young players of great apparent potential made their mark, while as usual one or two English county players of repute retired from the fray with egg on their faces. T. E. Jesty exceeded his county reputation in 1980–81, as did another unsung Englishman, T. A. Lloyd, in the previous season. Otherwise in recent seasons it has been a case of tattered reputations and cynical thoughts among home supporters about the actual standard of county cricket.

What of the progress towards multi-racial cricket, so dear to the hearts of all progressive commentators? Of that I do not know – my own ideal is non-racialism at all levels. What can be said is that Mashwabadi 'Shakes' Groot-boom became the first 'Black' boy to represent Transvaal in the Nuffield Week. Nor was he a 'token' black – he was in on merit. His next ambition is the Transvaal senior team and then, who knows? If players like 'Shakes' are to progress they must have the highest peaks to aim at. In cricket that is to represent their country in Test matches. At present that peak does not exist – so the only sure thing is that development will be stunted – the development what is more of *all* South Africans, whatever race or colour.

On the current first-class scene non-whites are gradually making their presence felt. Omar Henry scored his first first-class century, and is gaining a reputation as a coach. Henry's was the first hundred by a non-white in the South African first-class game, and went almost unnoticed in the cricket world at large. For Western Province 'B' the coloured Jack Mahoney is establishing himself as a regular bowler, Ronnie Engelbrecht is still hoping for a regular spot in the Griqualand West side despite a shoulder injury which hindered him last season. Yusuf Rubidge was tried for Transvaal 'B' – without much success but he had his chance and was worth it on merit. Natal have given a chance to Yacoob Omar and Baboo Ebrahim, Keith Hartzenburg and Yassiem Snyders have played for Griqualand West, and Kenny Postman for Border. An outstanding Border schoolboy is Britan Ndzundzu. So it goes on – they will get their chance domestically – will the world at large give them similar opportunities?

Finally, some happier memories of the season. Jerry Kennedy, making his first-class debut aged forty-two for Boland – and the Stellenbosch vine grower scored 97. Dickie Ogilvie, stricken with cancer aged twenty-two, and only eight months later playing first-class cricket again for Eastern Province. Finally the legendary fast bowler Bob Crisp re-appeared in his native country on holiday from his home in a hut in Mani, Greece. Eight years ago Crisp was given six months to live when also suffering from cancer. A long six months.

SAB Currie Cup   Final Table

	P	W	D	L	*Bonus Pts*	*Total Pts*
Natal	8	6	2	0	60	120
Transvaal	8	4	3	1	60	100
Western Province	8	3	2	3	48	78
Eastern Province	8	2	2	4	47	67
Northern Transvaal	8	0	1	7	37	37

SAB Bowl   Final Table

Northern Section

	P	W	D	L	Bonus Pts	Total Pts
Transvaal 'B'	6	4	2	0	49	89
Natal 'B'	6	3	3	0	36	66
Griqualand West	6	0	3	3	36	36
Orange Free State	6	0	2	4	36	36

Southern Section

	P	W	D	L	Bonus Pts	Total Pts
Western Province 'B'	6	4	2	0	47	87
Eastern Province 'B'	6	1	2	3	36	46
Border	6	1	3	2	31	41
Boland	6	1	3	2	23	33

First-class Averages

Batting

	Inns	NOs	Runs	HS	Average
N. T. Day (Transvaal)	11	4	496	174*	70.86
R. G. Pollock (Transvaal)	12	4	488	166*	61.00
C. P. Wilkins (Natal)	12	1	595	109	54.09
N. P. Daniels (Natal)	10	3	351	104	50.14
P. B. J. Wallace (Boland)	7	1	293	103	48.83
T. A. Clarke (Western Province 'B')	7	1	284	100	47.33
F. B. Hill (Natal 'B')	8	0	373	105	46.63
M. J. D. Doherty (Griqualand West)	9	1	386	124	46.00
S. J. Cook (Transvaal)	14	1	581	126	44.69
A. J. Lamb (Western Province)	15	2	578	130	44.46
J. M. Winstanley (Eastern Province)	7	2	214	112	42.80
R. G. Fensham (Eastern Province)	8	1	287	145	41.00
B. J. Whitfield (Natal)	12	2	409	81	40.90
N. E. Wright (Transvaal 'B')	14	4	399	128*	39.90
D. D. Dyer (Transvaal)	14	2	460	164*	38.33
M. S. Venter (Transvaal 'B')	12	1	408	76	37.09
G. L. Hayes (Border)	7	0	259	88	37.00
D. K. Pearse (Natal 'B')	9	3	222	50*	37.00
L. Seeff (Western Province)	16	1	549	81	36.60
M. J. Nel (Western Province)	6	0	211	73	35.17
R. F. Pienaar (Transvaal 'B')	11	2	306	71	34.00
J. J. Strydom (Orange Free State)	10	1	397	70*	33.00
H. M. Ackerman (Western Province 'B')	7	1	196	55	32.67
R. A. Stretch (Border)	10	0	326	168	32.60
H. R. Fotheringham (Transvaal)	12	3	293	63	32.56
P. Visagie (Northern Transvaal)	6	0	194	87	32.33
R. V. Jennings (Transvaal)	10	4	193	82*	32.17
T. B. Reid (Eastern Province)	14	0	449	78	32.07
A. P. Beukes (Griqualand West)	10	0	311	89	31.10
A. P. Kuiper (Western Province)	11	1	310	81	31.00
R. J. East (Orange Free State)	12	0	370	85	30.83
Y. A. Omar (Natal 'B')	9	3	183	39	30.50
R. J. D. Whyte (Eastern Province)	14	1	391	61	30.08

O. Henry (Western Province)	12	2	300	105*	30.00
T. E. Jesty (Griqualand West)	10	0	299	95	29.90
E. J. Barlow (Western Province)	16	2	416	99	29.72
K. W. Gradwell (Eastern Province 'B')	12	1	319	105*	29.00
N. V. Radford (Transvaal 'B')	9	1	232	45	29.00
L. W. Griessel (Orange Free State)	12	0	345	162	28.75
A. D. Methuen (Griqualand West)	9	1	228	63	28.50
E. Halvorsen (Western Province 'B')	10	2	225	95	28.13
K. A. McKenzie (Transvaal)	9	0	249	105	27.67
P. L. Symcox (Griqualand West)	8	0	220	75	27.50
R. L. S. Armitage (Eastern Province)	14	0	383	148	27.36
C. van der Merwe (Boland)	11	0	296	63	26.91
I. D. Harty (Border)	10	1	238	78	26.44
J. Seeff (Western Province 'B')	12	1	289	57	26.27
K. G. Motley (Northern Transvaal)	16	3	339	45*	26.08
P. N. Kirsten (Western Province)	13	0	337	73	25.92
W. Dobson (Griqualand West)	9	3	155	48*	25.83
M. J. Procter (Natal)	11	1	257	61	25.70
A. M. Ferreira (Northern Transvaal)	18	0	458	106	25.44
I. Foulkes (Eastern Province)	13	2	279	57*	25.36
D. J. Richardson (Eastern Province)	18	6	300	77*	25.00
C. S. Stirk (Northern Transvaal)	10	0	250	108	25.00
C. I. Gie (Natal 'B')	11	1	248	90	24.80
E. T. Laughlin (Border)	10	3	172	76*	24.57
M. D. Tramontino (Natal 'B')	11	0	269	72	24.45
D. G. Emslie (Eastern Province 'B')	8	2	146	39	24.33
R. A. Smith (Natal 'B')	7	1	145	36*	24.17
V. F du Preez (Northern Transvaal)	18	0	426	101	23.67
W. J. van der Linden (Transvaal 'B')	13	2	260	54*	23.64
M. M. Benkenstein (Natal 'B')	6	0	141	71	23.50
P. M. Thompson (Western Province 'B')	10	0	233	67	23.30
J. W. Furstenburg (Eastern Province)	12	0	277	127	23.08
G. Cook (Eastern Province)	16	0	367	68	22.94
G. S. Cowley (Eastern Province)	8	0	183	61	22.88
R. Kent (Border)	9	1	183	56	22.88
J. D. du Toit (Western Province)	12	1	251	79	22.82
R. M. Bentley (Natal)	10	1	205	68	22.78
G. S. le Roux (Western Province)	7	2	113	50	22.60
A. du Toit (Boland)	11	0	239	102	21.73
P. W. G. Parker (Natal)	11	1	216	74	21.60
L. L. Roberts (Boland)	11	1	216	50	21.60
C. E. B. Rice (Transvaal)	11	1	215	50	21.50
J. Kennedy (Boland)	6	0	129	97	21.50
S. Regenstein (Orange Free State)	8	1	146	43*	20.86
P. D. Swart (Western Province)	15	1	291	68	20.79
J. Buckley (Border)	9	1	165	108	20.63
S. J. Bezuidenhout (Eastern Province)	10	0	199	76	19.90
D. N. Edwards (Northern Transvaal)	16	0	315	84	19.69
T. C. Seaman (Eastern Province 'B')	6	0	117	78	19.50
A. Barrow (Northern Transvaal)	16	0	311	57	19.44
L. J. Barnard (Transvaal 'B')	12	0	232	54	19.33
E. Schmidt (Orange Free State)	10	1	170	41	18.89
D. Bestall (Natal)	9	1	150	50*	18.75

J. R. Gray (Griqualand West)	7	1	111	57*	18.50
D. J. Brickett (Eastern Province)	11	1	181	64	18.10
A. L. M. Klopper (Orange Free State)	12	0	214	42	17.83
G. Long (Eastern Province)	11	0	193	60	17.55
P. B. Clift (Natal)	7	1	105	28	17.50
N. Mandy (Eastern Province 'B')	6	0	104	65	17.33
N. Jurgensen (Transvaal 'B')	8	0	138	39	17.25
S. D. Bruce (Western Province)	13	1	202	50	16.83
J. P. Hosking (Border)	6	0	97	36	16.17
A. J. Kourie (Transvaal)	9	3	94	21	15.67
E. Grobler (Orange Free State)	6	0	93	35	15.50
D. H. Howell (Eastern Province)	17	0	253	54	14.88
C. Wulfsohn (Eastern Province)	12	7	74	26	14.80
G. Rodwell (Griqualand West)	9	0	132	34	14.67
A. J. S. Smith (Natal)	10	1	128	32	14.22
R. A. Woolmer (Western Province)	6	0	81	28	13.50
V. G. Cresswell (Eastern Province 'B')	7	1	81	32	13.50
F. Weideman (Transvaal)	8	1	94	38	13.43
C. J. Coetzee (Boland)	9	4	64	13*	12.80
B. McBride (Northern Transvaal)	18	2	202	42	12.63
D. R. Neilson (Transvaal)	6	1	61	35	12.20
S. A. Jones (Western Province)	7	2	59	15*	11.80
R. C. Schultz (Boland)	11	1	117	29	11.70
F. E. Joubert (Northern Transvaal)	9	3	68	33*	11.33
P. H. Williams (Natal)	13	3	108	46	10.80
D. L. Hobson (Western Province)	8	4	42	22*	10.50
D. J. Thomas (Northern Transvaal)	15	5	103	16*	10.30
J. van Heerden (Orange Free State)	8	0	82	29	10.25
W. M. van der Merwe (Orange Free State)	8	3	51	15*	10.20
Y. Rubidge (Transvaal 'B')	8	1	71	21	10.14
D. P. le Roux (Orange Free State)	6	0	60	26	10.00

Bowling

	Overs	Mds	Runs	Wkts	Average
V. A. P. van der Bijl (Natal)	290.5	109	513	54	9.50
R. R. Lawrenson (Western Province)	191.1	54	434	37	11.73
T. E. Jesty (Griqualand West)	179.3	63	364	31	11.74
K. R. Cooper (Natal)	224	79	495	38	13.03
J. Fairclough (Transvaal 'B')	254.5	114	386	28	13.79
A. J. Kourie (Transvaal)	288.4	71	734	52	14.12
E. S. Gordon (Western Province 'B')	152.1	49	297	21	14.14
N. P. Daniels (Natal)	67.2	22	156	10	15.60
G. Long (Eastern Province)	160.4	54	332	21	15.81
C. E. B. Rice (Transvaal)	251.3	78	609	38	16.03
M. B. Taljaard (Western Province 'B')	133	39	251	15	16.73
W. K. Watson (Eastern Province)	278.2	82	677	40	16.93
R. W. Hanley (Transvaal)	207.2	64	444	26	17.08
F. Weideman (Transvaal)	137	29	377	22	17.14
D. K. Pearse (Natal 'B')	149.1	41	344	20	17.20
J. Hendriks (Boland)	83	19	296	17	17.41
J. D. du Toit (Western Province 'B')	155	47	310	17	18.24
P. D. Swart (Western Province)	191.1	44	509	27	18.85
N. V. Radford (Transvaal 'B')	209.2	60	537	28	19.18

M. J. Procter (Natal)	201.1	65	462	24	19.25
D. L. Hobson (Western Province)	274.5	89	683	35	19.51
P. B. Clift (Natal)	122	42	254	13	19.54
G. S. le Roux (Western Province)	137	42	322	16	20.13
G. D. Boucher (Border)	151	40	365	17	21.47
E. Schmidt (Orange Free State)	127	37	322	15	21.47
H. J. van der Linden (Transvaal 'B')	132.4	30	449	20	22.45
C. Wulfsohn (Eastern Province)	283.2	64	747	33	22.63
K. J. Kerr (Transvaal 'B')	98.5	30	252	11	22.91
R. F. Pienaar (Transvaal 'B')	123.4	32	298	13	22.92
C. A. Gie (Natal 'B')	96.4	9	325	14	23.21
J. D. du Toit (Western Province)	202	57	468	20	23.40
F. E. Joubert (Northern Transvaal)	138.3	30	412	17	24.24
G. L. Hayes (Border)	161.1	41	365	15	24.33
B. B. Deyzel (Griqualand West)	193.1	54	572	23	24.87
R. C. Ontong (Northern Transvaal)	180	44	529	21	25.19
J. S. Muil (Natal 'B')	236	73	612	24	25.50
R. A. le Roux (Orange Free State)	149.1	35	498	19	26.21
A. M. Ferreira (Northern Transvaal)	235.3	64	604	23	26.26
H. Liebenberg (Griqualand West)	149.2	39	398	15	26.53
L. L. Roberts (Boland)	146.4	34	456	17	26.82
E. J. Barlow (Western Province)	101.3	27	269	10	26.90
D. J. Brickett (Eastern Province)	237.3	61	524	19	27.58
K. J. Kerr (Transvaal)	140.5	38	378	13	29.08
W. M. van der Merwe (Orange Free State)	125	19	420	14	30.00
M. K. van Vuuren (Eastern Province)	181.3	42	521	17	30.65
A. K. Weakley (Border)	125	52	309	10	30.90
I. Foulkes (Eastern Province)	139.5	33	407	13	31.31
C. J. Coetzee (Boland)	147.5	36	435	13	33.46
E. T. Laughlin (Border)	116.3	27	370	11	33.64
A. L. Beukes (Griqualand West)	206	85	426	12	35.50
S. T. Jefferies (Western Province)	239	54	579	15	38.60
W. F. Morris (Northern Transvaal)	144	33	478	12	39.83
D. J. Thomas (Northern Transvaal)	226.5	51	679	15	45.27

Most dismissals in the field – wicket-keepers and others

32 – D. J. Richardson (Eastern Province)
28 – R. V. Jennings (Transvaal) (ct 24, st 4)
26 – B. McBride (Northern Transvaal) (ct 23, st 3)
24 – A. J. S. Smith (Natal)
22 – R. J. East (Orange Free State)
21 – N. T. Day (Transvaal) (ct 19, st 2)
19 – P. M. Thompson (Western Province 'B') (ct 16, st 3)
18 – R. C. Schultz (Boland)
     R. A. Stretch (Border) (ct 16, st 2)
16 – D. H. Howell (Eastern Province)
14 – W. Dobson (Griqualand West)
     R. J. Ryall (Western Province) (ct 12, st 2)
13 – H. M. Ackerman (Eastern Province 'B')
12 – N. Daniels (Natal)
11 – R. G. Pollock (Transvaal)
10 – G. Cook (Eastern Province)
     M. Madsen (Natal 'B') (ct 8, st 2)

Clive Rice. Dominating in England and South Africa. A leader by example.

Eastern Province Batting 1980/81	v. Northern Transvaal (Port Elizabeth) 7, 8, 10 November		v. Western Province (Port Elizabeth) 21, 22, 24 November		v. Natal (Durban) 29,30 November– 1 December		v. Transvaal (Port Elizabeth) 1, 2, 3, January		v. Western Province (Cape Town) 16, 17, 19 January		v. Natal (Port Elizabeth) 23, 24, 26 January	
G. Cook	42	0	61	42	1	17	68	27	5	63	12	1
R. L. S. Armitage	9	0			2	19	148	23	39	41	2	3
D. J. Richardson	24	1	9	39	18	16	4	4*	77*	0*	0	13
I. Foulkes	26	57*	1	31	0	1	0	6	9			
D. H. Howell	29	9	24	17	5	6	0	24	30		5	2
R. J. D. Whyte	17	9					34	33	20	18*	1	4
G. S. Cowley	20	25	14	10								
D. J. Brickett	64	11*	58	11	6	0	10		—	8	0	13
W. K. Watson	6		12*	6	9*	6	11		—		5	2
M. K. Van Vuuren	1		17	0*	2	0	2*		—	2	0	9
C. Wulfsohn	2*											
S. J. Bezuidenhout			8	53	2	17	8	7	76	19	0	9
A. L. Biggs			0	1								
R. G. Fensham			10	4	14	2*						
J. D. Ogilvie					5	0					1*	2*
J. M. Winstanley							11	6*	48*		2	9
J. W. Furstenburg												
G. Long												
T. B. Reid												
Extras	25	8	11	21	5	17	7	4	13	15	6	2
Total	265	120	225	235	69	101	303	134	317	166	34	69
Wickets	10	6	10	10	10	10	10	6	6	5	10	10
Result	D		L		L		W		D		L	
Points	8		6		5		18		5		3	

v. Northern Transvaal	Transvaal (Pretoria) 6, 7, 9 February	v. Transvaal (Johannesburg) 6, 7, 9 March		Inns	NOs	Runs	HS	Av
0	13	15	0	16	0	367	68	22.94
32	39	3	23	14	0	383	148	27.36
21	9*	24*	0	16	5	259	77*	23.55
56	41*	41	10	13	2	279	57*	25.36
				11	0	151	30	13.73
20	61	10	55	12	1	282	61	25.64
0				4	0	69	25	17.25
2*		3	1	11	1	181	64	18.10
12		5	0	11	3	63	12*	7.88
		1	1*	12	2	50	17	5.00
				3	2	4	2*	—
18	36			10	0	199	76	19.90
				2	0	1	1	0.50
				6	1	84	36	16.80
23	0	11	16	4	2	8	5	4.00
60		10	10	5	2	76	48*	25.33
		7	10	4	0	50	23	12.50
				3	0	80	60	26.67
				2	0	17	10	8.50

20	9	8	14

264	208	138	140
10	5	10	10
W		L	
18		4	

F42

Eastern Province Bowling 1980/81	W. K. Watson	M. K. van Vuuren	D. J. Brickett	C. Wulfsohn	R. I. S. Armitage	G. S. Cowie
v. Northern Transvaal (Port Elizabeth) 7, 8, 10 November	19.5–7–41–3 21–4–42–2	19–8–31–2 21.3–7–42–5	21–8–46–2 19–5–27–1	10–2–42–2 6–2–20–1	11–5–23–0 23–11–39–0	12–3–32–1 3–1–2–0
v. Western Province (Port Elizabeth) 21, 22, 24 November	32–5–87–4 8–2–26–0	23–2–84–1 7–1–23–0	26–4–79–2 4–1–8–0			5–1–22–1 3–1–3–0
v. Natal (Durban) 29, 30 November–1 December	26.2–10–93–3	7–1–30–0	29–5–79–4			
v. Transvaal (Port Elizabeth) 1, 2, 3 January	27.7–47–4 73.2–5–59–4	10–3–40–1 13–2–24–1	24.3–5–57–3 24–6–54–3		19–0–67–2 4–2–5–0	
v. Western Province (Cape Town) 16, 17, 19 January	25–10–43–4 13–1–50–2	18–5–44–2 10–1–54–0	22–6–40–1 18–4–62–0		72–6–51–1 11–0–54–0	
v. Natal (Port Elizabeth) 23, 24, 26 January	16–7–35–3	13–3–31–2	15–4–20–0		7–2–17–0	
v. Northern Transvaal (Pretoria) 6, 7, 9 February	20.5–8–34–4 11–5–31–1	12–1–35–1 8–1–35–1	25–10–35–1 10–3–17–2		9–3–20–0 11–4–23–2	
v. Transvaal (Johannesburg) 6, 7, 9 March	20–7–47–6 20–4–42–0	12–3–36–0 8–4–12–1		14.4–3–43–1 20–2–69–1	23–6–48–0 7–4–26–0	
	278.2–82– 677–40 av. 16.93	181.3–42– 521–17 av. 30.65	237.3–61– 524–19 av. 27.58	50.4–9– 174–5 av. 34.80	147–43– 373–5 av. 74.60	23–6– 59–2 av. 29.50

A. L. Biggs	J. D. Ogilvie	I. Foulkes	G. Long	Extras	Total	Wickets
				24	239	10
		3–1–10–0		19	201	10
4.2–0–20–1		16–3–54–1		16	362	10
3–0–13–0		5.2–0–18–0		8	99	0
	16–9–31–2			17	250	9
		16–2–54–0		8	273	10
		9–5–11–2		9	162	10
		16–4–46–1		10	234	10
		15–3–55–1		10	285	3
	18–5–35–0			10	148	6
		16–3–46–3	13–6–19–0	9	198	10
		24.3–6–65–4		8	179	10
		13–2–43–1	7–1–25–0	20	262	9
		6–4–5–0		18	172	3
4.2–0–	34–14–	139.5–33–	20–7–			
33–1	66–2	407–13	44–0			
—	av. 33.00	av. 31.31	—			

F44

Natal Batting 1980/81	v. Eastern Province (Durban) 29, 30 November– 1 December	v. Transvaal (Johannesburg) 12, 13, 15 December		v. Northern Transvaal (Durban) 26, 27, 28 December		v. Western Province (Cape Town) 1, 2, 3 January		v. Transvaal (Durban) 17, 18, 19 January	v. Eastern Province (Port Elizabeth) 23, 24, 26 January
C. P. Wilkins	8	52	75	102	12	109	45*	71	22
C. L. Smith	12	16	10	1					
R. M. Bentley	19	68	11	39	1*			8	3
P. W. G. Parker	41	0	21*	11	2	21		31	14
P. H. Williams	3	1	15*	5	5*	0		0	8*
D. Bestall	23	6		22		1			
A. J. S. Smith	9	17		21	13	10		26*	32
P. B. Clift	19	18		1		11		—	—
M. J. Procter	59	61	19	31	11*	19		21	17
V. A. P. van der Bijl	37*	8*		23		7		—	—
K. R. Cooper	3*	—		22*		15		—	—
B. J. Whitfield						19	9*	52	42
N. P. Daniels						56*		2*	0*
Extras	17	9	2	38	2	19	8	14	10
Total	250	256	153	316	46	287	62	225	148
Wickets	9	9	4	10	3	10	0	6	6
Result	W	D		W		W		D	W
Points	19	7		21		17		8	15

v. Western Province (Pietermaritzburg) 21, 22, 23 February		v. Northern Transvaal (Pretoria) 13, 14, 16 March		Inns	NOs	Runs	HS	Av
63	17	19		12	1	595	109	54.09
		11	9*	6	1	59	16	11.80
0	35	21		10	1	205	68	22.78
0	1	74		11	1	216	74	21.60
9	0			10	3	46	15*	6.72
				4	0	52	23	13.00
0	0	0		10	1	128	32	14.22
20	8*	28		7	1	105	28	17.50
10	8	1		11	1	257	61	25.70
2	9*	7		7	3	93	37*	23.25
0*		43*		5	4	83	43	—
50	2	81	26*	8	2	281	81	46.83
1	73	1		6	3	133	73	44.33
21	12	10	3					
176	165	296	38					
10	8	10	0					
W		W						
16		17						

Natal Bowling 1980/81	M. J. Procter	V. A. P. van der Bijl	K. R. Cooper	P. B. Clift	R. M. Bentley	P. H. Williams
v. Eastern Province (Durban) 29, 30 November–1 December	11.3–4–26–2 10–3–19–7	14–7–20–4 16.2–4–28–3	4–0–11–1 18–6–31–4	5–2–7–2 7–4–6–0		
v. Transvaal (Johannesburg) 12, 13, 15 December	16–10–20–2 9–1–38–0	18–7–18–3 20–8–27–5	17.1–7–32–5 18–3–57–0	5–1–28–0 16–8–29–0	1–0–4–0	
v. Northern Transvaal (Durban) 26, 27, 28 December	11.4–5–20–3 14–3–65–1	16–6–48–3 20–6–45–4	12–4–28–2 21–6–77–4	12–4–19–2 12–4–27–1		
v. Western Province (Cape Town) 1, 2, 3 January	7–2–13–1 19–4–48–0	20–7–35–4 33.4–12–68–2	16.1–4–40–3 21–8–50–2	10–1–33–0 22–6–36–5		
v. Transvaal (Durban) 17, 18, 19 January	16–5–29–2	28–7–59–2	24–6–68–6	10–3–26–0	4–0–5–0	4–1–7–0
v. Eastern Province (Port Elizabeth) 23, 24, 26 January	3–2–1–0 24–9–33–4	12–5–8–4 18–10–18–3	10–6–9–2 10.4–7–12–3	8–2–10–2		
v. Western Province (Pietermaritzburg) 21, 22, 23 February	13–4–29–2 14–6–20–2	23.2–8–43–5 21.3–12–30–6	20–10–23–3 16–7–19–1	4–2–4–0 8–5–12–1		
v. Northern Transvaal (Pretoria) 13, 14, 16 March	2–0–5–0 31–7–96–4	19–5–51–4 11–5–15–2	11–3–29–2 5–2–9–0	3–0–17–0	2–0–8–0	
	201.1–65– 462–24 av. 19.25	290.5–109– 513–54 av. 9.50	224–79– 495–38 av. 13.03	122–42– 254–13 av. 19.54	7–0– 17–0 —	4–1– 7–0 —

N. P. Daniels	P. W. G. Parker	A. J. S. Smith	C. P. Wilkins	Extras	Total	Wickets
				5	69	10
				17	101	10
				11	109	10
				12	167	5
				15	130	10
				16	230	10
				11	132	10
				14	216	10
				19	201	10
–2–2–0	2–1–4–0	1–0–2–0		2	22	0
				6	34	10
		1–0–4–0		2	69	10
				7	106	10
				13	94	10
8.4–8–41–4				2	128	10
2.3–7–49–3				11	205	10
5.1–17–	2–1–	1–0–	1–0–			
2–7	4–0	2–0	4–0			
13.14	—	—	—			

Northern Transvaal
Batting 1980/81

	v. Eastern Province (Port Elizabeth) 7, 8, 10 November		v. Transvaal (Pretoria) 21, 22 November		v. Western Province (Cape Town) 29 November, 1, 2 December		v. South African Universities (Pretoria) 9, 10, 11 December		v. Natal (Durban) 26, 27, 28 December		v. Transvaal (Johannesburg) 23, 24, 26 January	
A. Barrow	16	1	0	21	0	45	21	9	3	12		
F. J. le Roux	12	5										
V. F. du Preez	36	101	0	0	100	4	47	6	12	5	33	9
E. Muntingh	6	5									2	2
R. C. Ontong	4	16	3	0	21	0			24	20	0	7
A. M. Ferreira	106	15	19	11	39	22	1	39	27	3	10	9
K. G. Motley	15	1	12	40	36	22*			10	37	0	45*
B. McBride	8	1	2	6	42	0	23	1*	0	22*	7	17
W. F. Morris	9	29	15*	26	20	0	0		5	3	3	0
D. J. Thomas	0	3*	23	6	16*	4	13		1*	7	3*	16
P. A. Robinson	3*	5	0	21*	11	0						
D. N. Edwards			3	20	0	3	84	15	1	36	22	2
C. S. Stirk			17	13	32	3	32	108	22	17	6	0
P. J. A. Visagie							87	10	10	52		
C. van Rensburg							16	27				
F. E. Joubert							33*				0	0
L. Coetzee												
H. W. Raath												
P. Marnewick												
Byes	24	19	3	9	6	14	9	7	15	16	13	6
Leg byes												
Wides												
No balls												
Total	239	201	97	173	323	117	366	222	130	230	99	113
Wickets	10	10	10	10	10	10	10	7	10	10	10	10
Result	D		L		L		W		L		L	
Points	7		1		4		—		5		5	

v. Eastern Province (Pretoria) 6, 7, 9 February		v. Western Province (Pretoria) 27, 28 February, 2 March		v. Natal (Pretoria) 13, 14, 16 March		Inns	NOs	Runs	HS	Av
53	8	57	17	19	29	16	0	311	57	19.44
						2	0	17	12	8.50
25	9	8	16	15	0	18	0	426	101	23.67
				2	1	6	0	18	6	3.00
0	11	10	9	2	0	16	0	127	24	7.94
65	45	0	2	11	34	18	0	458	106	25.44
5	31	19	41*	0	25	16	3	339	45*	26.08
4	10	37	13	0	9	18	2	202	42	12.63
1	8					13	1	119	29	9.92
9	2*	0	0			15	5	103	16*	10.30
						6	2	40	21*	10.00
0	28	32	3	27	39	16	0	315	84	19.69
						10	0	250	108	25.00
19	16					6	0	194	87	32.33
						2	0	43	27	21.50
8*	3	8*	4	6	6	9	3	68	33*	11.33
		9	10	29*	51	4	1	99	51	33.00
		1	0			2	0	1	1	0.50
				15	0*	2	1	15	15	—
9	8	10	5	2	11					
198	179	191	120	128	205					
10	10	10	10	10	10					
L		L		L						
5		6		4						

Northern Transvaal Bowling 1980/81	D. J. Thomas	P. A. Robinson	R. C. Ontong	A. M. Ferreira	W. F. Morris	A. Barrow
v. Eastern Province (Port Elizabeth) 7, 8, 10 November	19–5–44–0 10–3–19–2	22.3–4–57–3 7–2–29–2	15–3–39–2 7–1–19–1	14–2–51–1 11–5–22–0	19–5–49–3 7–1–23–1	
v. Transvaal (Pretoria) 21, 22 November	15–0–78–0	10–1–48–1	23–4–87–0	21–6–32–0	15–3–63–0	
v. Western Province (Cape Town) 29 November, 1, 2 December	17–1–74–1 9–2–37–0	5–0–33–1 7–1–21–0	7–1–45–2 8–4–25–2	11–3–39–1 12–3–42–1	6–0–41–1 12–5–30–1	3.3–0–8–1
v. South African Universities (Pretoria) 9, 10, 11 December	18–6–39–1 21–3–73–1			24–7–57–5 16–1–55–0	17–6–30–0 22–5–67–2	
v. Natal (Durban) 26, 27 28 December	26–4–104–2 5.5–4–8–1		24.3–4–59–2 6–0–36–2		12–3–38–2	6–3–12–1
v. Transvaal (Johannesburg) 23, 24, 26 January	16–5–43–3 4–1–16–0		3.2–0–10–1 2–1–1–1	13–2–33–2	8–0–45–1	
v. Eastern Province (Pretoria) 6, 7, 9 February	19–5–46–3 15–3–37–0		19–8–34–2 10–1–36–0	21–5–60–3 22–8–52–2	15–3–55–0 11–2–37–1	
v. Western Province (Pretoria) 27, 28 February, 2 March	15–4–39–0 17–5–22–1		20–6–44–2 12–9–8–2	17–4–43–2 24.3–10–38–3		
v. Natal (Pretoria) 13, 14, 16 March			23.1–2–86–2	29–8–80–3		
	226.5–51– 679–15 av. 45.27	51.3–8– 188–7 av. 26.86	180–44– 529–21 av. 25.19	235.3–64– 604–23 av. 26.26	144–33– 478–12 av. 39.83	9.3–3– 20–2 av. 10.00

P. J. A. Visagie	F. E. Joubert	V. F. du Preez	H. W. Raath	P. Marnewick	K. G. Motley	Extras	Total	Wickets
						25	265	10
						8	120	6
						17	325	1
						19	251	6
						28	191	5
	15–6–64–1	6.4–0–19–3				23	232	10
3–3–49–1	16.4–3–50–4	10–0–34–0				24	352	10
5–2–65–2						38	316	10
						2	46	3
	13–3–42–2					6	179	9
	5.5–1–16–1					1	34	2
	14–2–49–1					20	264	10
	13–3–37–2					9	208	5
	17–4–50–1		17–1–49–4			12	237	10
	21–4–31–4		5–1–8–0			12	119	10
	20–4–66–1	16–7–17–2		10–4–28–1	3–1–9–1	10	296	10
	3–0–7–0	2.3–0–19–0		3–1–3–0	3–1–6–0	3	38	0
8–5–	138.3–30–	35.1–7–	22–2–	13–5–	6–2–			
14–3	412–17	89–5	57–4	31–1	15–1			
av. 38.00	av. 24.24	av. 17.80	av. 14.25	—	—			

Transvaal Batting 1980/81

	v. Northern Transvaal (Pretoria) 21, 22, 24 November	v. Natal (Johannesburg) 12, 13, 15 December		v. Western Province (Johannesburg) 26, 27, 29 December	v. Eastern Province (Port Elizabeth) 1, 2, 3 January		v. Natal (Durban) 17, 18, 19 January		v. Northern Transvaal (Johannesburg) 23, 24, 26 January	
D. D. Dyer	164*	6	42	13	64	1	4	4*	0	14
S. J. Cook	126	6	13	32	6	12	58	16*	4	12
H. R. Fotheringham	18*	9	0	15	55	63	56		11	
R. G. Pollock	—	2	71	166*	42	21	15		48	0*
C. E. B. Rice	—	11	22*	16	29	10	19		21	
K. A. McKenzie	—	40	0	6	11	17	1		53	
A. J. Kourie	—	21	7*	16	6	3	17*		18	
R. V. Jennings	—	1		11	14	9				
D. R. Neilson	—	2		17	35	3	4		0*	
G. E. McMillan	—	0		5*	3	14	1		11	
R. W. Hanley	—	0*		—	0*	0*	0		—	
N. T. Day							7		7	7*
K. J. Kerr										
F. Weideman										
Extras	17	11	12	25	8	9	19	2	6	1
Total	325	109	167	322	273	162	201	22	179	34
Wickets	1	10	5	8	10	10	10	0	9	2
Result	W	D		W	L		D		W	
Points	22	4		21	6		5		16	

v. Western Province (Cape Town) 6, 7, 9 February		v. Eastern Province (Johannesburg) 6, 7, 9 March		Inns	NOs	Runs	HS	Av
131	10	0	7	14	2	460	164*	38.33
69	78	96	53	14	1	581	126	44.69
8	23*	16	19*	12	3	293	63	32.56
8	50*	6	59*	12	4	488	166*	61.00
50	20	1	16	11	1	215	50	21.50
16		105		9	0	249	105	27.67
6*		0		9	3	94	21	15.67
0*	31	7		7	1	73	31	12.17
				6	1	61	35	12.20
				6	1	34	11	6.80
—		—		4	3	0	0*	—
—				3	1	21	7*	10.50
		7		1	0	7	7	—
		4*		1	1	4	4*	—
22	13	20	18					
310	225	262	172					
6	4	9	3					
	D	W						
	8	18						

Transvaal Bowling 1980/81	C. E. B. Rice	R. W. Hanley	D. R. Neilson	G. E. McMillan	A. J. Kourie	K. A. McKenzie
v. Northern Transvaal (Pretoria) 21, 22, 24 November	14–6–30–3 18–6–41–4	14–5–20–5 12–7–19–2	14–5–28–0 15–7–23–1	6–0–15–0 12–1–26–0	12–0–1–2 20.2–5–55–3	
v. Natal (Johannesburg) 12, 13, 15 December	19.1–1–56–2 9–1–29–0	19–3–48–2 10–3–31–1	24–5–66–0 10–1–43–1	10–5–21–0	28–7–56–5 12–2–48–2	
v. Western Province (Johannesburg) 26, 27, 29 December	12–4–29–2 14.1–3–47–5	10–5–26–2 18–3–31–3	17–6–25–1 11–3–33–1	6–0–27–2 10–2–30–1	6.3–2–12–3 15–5–22–0	
v. Eastern Province (Port Elizabeth) 1, 2, 3 January	24–10–56–4 15–3–34–1	23.2–4–57–5 8–2–10–0	18–3–57–0 2–0–6–0	8–1–13–0 6–2–8–0	22–6–82–1 16.3–3–72–5	1–0–4–0
v. Natal (Durban) 17, 18, 19 January	18.2–4–56–3	14–3–34–0	13–3–32–1	13–6–26–1	21–2–63–1	
v. Northern Transvaal (Johannesburg) 23, 24, 26 January	21–9–30–4 17.5–8–27–4	13–6–16–0 11–6–13–3	6–2–5–0	1–0–1–0 8–2–25–0	19.4–7–34–6 16–6–42–3	
v. Western Province (Cape Town) 6, 7, 9 February	21–3–72–1 13–2–48–2	20–4–52–0 11–1–42–0		8–2–27–0	49.4–10–113–8 10–0–44–5	
v. Eastern Province (Johannesburg) 6, 7, 9 March	18–11–20–2 17–7–34–1	11–6–21–0 13–6–24–3			23.3–7–44–4 27–1–9–46–4	
	251.3–78– 609–38 av. 16.03	207.2–64– 444–26 av. 17.08	130–35– 318–5 av. 63.60	88–21– 219–4 av. 54.75	288.4–71– 734–52 av. 14.12	1–0– 4–0 —

H. R. Fotheringham	K. J. Kerr	F. Weideman			*Extras*	*Total*	*Wickets*
					3	97	10
					9	173	10
					9	256	9
					2	153	4
					9	128	10
					9	172	10
6–2–27–0					7	303	10
					4	134	6
					14	225	6
					13	99	10
					6	113	10
	29–3–94–1				17	375	10
					11	145	7
	11–5–26–1	9–2–19–3			8	138	10
	2–0–6–0	10–4–16–1			14	140	10
6–2–	42–8–	19–6–					
27–0	126–2	35–4					
—	av. 63.00	av. 8.75					

Western Province
Batting
1980/81

	v. Eastern Province (Port Elizabeth) 21, 22, 24 November		v. Northern Transvaal (Cape Town) 29 November, 1, 2 December		v. Transvaal (Johannesburg) 26, 27, 29 December		v. Natal (Cape Town) 1, 2, 3 January		v. Eastern Province (Cape Town) 16, 17, 19 January		v. Transvaal (Cape Town) 6, 7, 9 February	
E. J. Barlow	7	58*	6	37	0	38*	9	24	99	36	0	8
L. Seeff	58	33*	26	65	29	13	11	36	15	81	71	23
P. N. Kirsten	35		73	3	18	68	12	15	2	0	62	43
A. J. Lamb	52		23	54*	4	6	54	50	38	95*	130	26
P. D. Swart	68		37	1	21	14	0	10	9	63*	3	7
S. D. Bruce	50		0	1	5	15						
G. S. le Roux	9		31*	2*	21	0	0	50				
O. Henry	44		36*		2	4			35		16	10
D. L. Hobson	10		—				1	0	3		3*	3*
S. T. Jefferies	6		—		8	0	18	0	7		13	
R. J. Ryall	7*		—		0*	5	2*	9*	14		16	
J. D. du Toit					11	0	2	7				
A. P. Kuiper							12	1	0			
R. Lawrenson									2*			
R. A. Woolmer											15	14
E. Halvorsen											29	0*
S. A. Jones												
M. J. Nel												
Extras	16	8	19	28	9	9	11	14	10	10	17	11
Total	362	99	251	191	128	172	132	216	234	285	375	145
Wickets	10	0	6	5	10	10	10	10	10	3	10	7
Result	W		W		L		L		D		D	
Points	20		17		4		4		4		6	

v. Natal (Pietermaritzburg) 21, 22, 23 February		v. Northern Transvaal (Pretoria) 27, 28 February, 2 March		Inns	NOs	Runs	HS	Av
				16	2	416	99	29.72
9	1	31	53	16	1	549	81	36.60
41	11	36	0	13	0	337	73	25.92
4	2			15	2	578	130	44.46
2	1	43	0	15	1	291	68	20.79
19	16	21	2	5	0	71	50	14.20
				7	2	113	50	22.60
0	7	16	25	11	1	195	44	19.50
		22*	0*	8	4	42	22*	10.50
5*	8*	0	6	11	2	71	18	7.89
3	0	0	0	11	4	56	16	8.00
				4	0	20	11	5.00
				3	0	13	12	4.33
				1	1	2	2*	—
10	28	14	0	6	0	81	28	13.50
4	6			4	1	39	29	13.00
2	1	6	15	4	0	24	15	6.00
		36	6	2	0	42	36	21.00
7	13	12	12					
106	94	237	119					
10	10	10	10					
	L		W					
	5		18					

Western Province Bowling 1980/81	G. S. le Roux	S. T. Jefferies	P. D. Swart	O. Henry	D. L. Hobson	E. J. Barlow
v. Eastern Province (Port Elizabeth) 21, 22, 24 November	18–7–29–3 25–6–53–3	18–6–28–2 23–7–43–2	16–3–58–4 14–7–19–1	17–6–60–1 14–2–38–1	11–0–39–0 23–5–61–2	
v. Northern Transvaal (Cape Town) 29 November, 1, 2 December	25–7–69–3 18–10–25–2	26–8–47–1 11–3–27–3	23.1–5–46–4 6–0–20–0	21–4–54–2	28–10–82–0 11.2–5–31–4	3–0–14–0
v. Transvaal (Johannesburg) 26, 27, 29 December	23–6–58–2	21–2–84–3	15–2–58–1			15–4–52–2
v. Natal (Cape Town) 1, 2, 3 January	24–6–66–3 4–0–22–0	24–5–60–1	6–1–28–1		37–14–88–5 4–0–24–0	10–3–22–0
v. Eastern Province (Cape Town) 16, 17, 19 January		19–4–58–0 9–1–31–0	18–3–50–1 6–0–32–0	14–5–38–2 7–1–20–1	21–6–50–1 6–2–14–1	13–4–24–0 15–2–42–2
v. Transvaal (Cape Town) 6, 7, 9 February		15–6–30–0 22–6–45–0	13–2–27–2 10–1–34–0	23–2–77–1 18–5–30–0	21–5–84–3 28–6–70–3	12–1–44–0 1–0–6–0
v. Natal (Pietermaritzburg) 21, 22, 23 February		18–2–40–0 14–1–39–2	20–8–42–4 11–2–32–2			15.3–6–29–5 8–4–15–1
v. Northern Transvaal (Pretoria) 27, 28 February, 2 March		10–1–29–1 9–2–18–0	18–5–40–4 15–5–23–3	6–4–8–0 3–1–5–0	25.2–10–43–3 27–14–49–7	9–3–21–0
	137–42– 322–16 av. 20.13	239–54– 579–15 av. 38.60	191.1–44– 509–27 av. 18.85	123–30– 330–8 av. 41.25	242.4–77– 635–29 av. 21.90	101.3–27– 269–10 av. 26.90

a L. Seeff 2–1–7–0 (2nd inns)
A. J. Lumb 1.3–1–1–0 (2nd inns)

J. D. du Toit	R. Lawrenson	R. A. Woolmer	P. N. Kirsten	S. A. Jones	A. P. Kuiper	*Extras*	*Total*	*Wickets*
						11	225	10
						21	235	10
			1–0–5–0			6	323	10
						14	117	10
6–4–45–0						25	322	8
						19	287	10
–3–4–0						8	62	0a
	18–4–66–2				5–0–18–0	13	317	6
	5–1–12–0					15	166	5
		11–5–26–0				22	310	6
		6–0–23–0	2–0–4–0			13	225	4
			7–1–15–0	11–2–29–1		21	176	10
			4–1–13–2	13–1–54–1		12	165	8
				19–6–40–2		10	191	10
				12–4–20–0		5	120	10
0–7–	23–5–	28–7–	3–0–	55–13–	5–0–			
9–0	78–2	77–2	9–0	143–4	18–0			
—	av. 39.00	av. 38.50	—	av. 35.75	—			

F60

Griqualand West
Batting
1980/81

	v. Natal (Kimberley) 27, 28, 29 November		v. Transvaal (Kimberley) 11, 12, 13 December		v. Orange Free State (Bloemfontein) 1, 2, 3 January		v. Transvaal 'B' (Johannesburg) 19, 20, 21 January		v. Natal 'B' (Pietermaritzburg) 23, 24, 25 January		v. Orange Free State (Kimberley) 19, 20, 21 February
P. L. Symcox	75				2	54	21	8	6	0	54
H. E. van der Merwe	10	9									
R. Moult	17		3	0							
M. J. D. Doherty	46	28*	13	124			50	30	23	4	50
W. Schonegevel	21										
T. E. Jesty	56		4	18	17	16	18	40	0	35	95
H. Liebenberg	8	18*	5	0			17	6	6	1	14
A. P. Beukes	6		26	59	89	26	12	27	8	8	50
D. N. Moore	1		6	4*							
B. B. Deyzel	15		11*	0	13	5	0	0	10	1*	1
C. Engelbrecht	15*										
D. N. Martin			0	27	1						
G. Rodwell			29	34	11	34	4	6	6	8	0
W. Dobson			8	16	7	11*	25	8	19*	13	48*
A. D. Methuen			12	41	63	0	62	21*	4	20	5
T. van Remburg					3	2					
J. R. Gray					49*	5	10	0	9	30	0
K. McLaren					4	1					
N. J. Fairweather							7*	0			
K. R. Hartzenberg									12	4	
R. Engelbrecht											22
Extras	21	5	11	21	6	8	8	10	12	16	23
Total	291	60	128	344	273	162	234	156	115	140	362
Wickets	10	1	10	10	10	9	10	10	10	10	10
Result	D		L		D		L		L		D
Points	5		3		8		7		5		8

Inns	NOs	Runs	HS	Av
8	0	220	75	27.50
2	0	19	10	9.50
3	0	20	17	6.67
9	1	368	124	46.90
1	0	21	21	—
10	0	299	95	29.90
9	1	75	18*	9.38
10	0	311	89*	31.10
3	1	11	6	5.50
10	2	56	15	7.00
1	1	15	15*	—
3	0	28	27	9.33
9	0	132	34	14.67
9	3	155	48*	25.83
9	1	228	63*	28.50
2	0	5	3	2.50
7	1	111	57*	18.50
2	0	5	4	2.50
2	1	7	7*	—
2	0	16	12	8.00
1	0	22		—

Griqualand West Bowling 1980/81	B. B. Deyzel	R. Moult	T. E. Jesty	C. Engelbrecht	A. L. Beukes	H. Liebenberg
v. Natal "B" (Kimberley) 27, 28, 29 November	24–5–74–1 22–8–54–2	15–1–55–1 15.2–2–49–2	22.3–11–38–5 10–7–4–2	23–9–42–1 9–3–13–0	16–3–56–0 18–7–34–0	6–1–23–0 5–1–22–0
v. Transvaal "B" (Kimberley) 11, 12, 13 December	21–6–62–0 12–4–36–2	13–0–64–1 2–0–13–0	20–5–53–1		17–8–37–3 9–3–20–0	20–4–74–1
v. Orange Free State (Bloemfontein) 1, 2, 3 January	14–3–38–2 10–2–28–1		25–7–81–4 21–8–37–5		19–9–35–2 16–1–46–1	
v. Transvaal "B" (Johannesburg) 19, 20, 21 January	26.4–9–68–5 11–0–84–1		18–8–32–2 9–0–24–3		20–9–43–1 9–0–22–1	20–7–50–0 15–0–76–2
v. Natal "B" (Pietermaritzburg) 23, 24, 25 January	12.5–3–29–3 4–2–9–0		7–1–13–1 12–4–18–4		24–13–29–1 23–10–50–2	24–7–47–4 15.2–7–26–4
v. Orange Free State (Kimberley) 19, 20, 21 February	16.4–6–30–4 19–6–60–2		14–5–25–2 21–7–39–2	15–2–37–2 22–5–54–1	12–8–20–1 23–14–34–0	20–4–35–1 24–8–45–3
	193.1–54– 572–23 av. 24.87	45.2–3– 181–4 av. 45.25	179.3–63– 364–31 av. 11.74	69–19– 146–4 av. 36.50	206–85– 426–12 av. 35.50	149.2–39– 398–15 av. 26.53

a second innings: W. Dobson 3–2–9–1; G. Rodwell 4–2–6–1
b first innings: T. van Remburg 12–3–41–0

P. L. Symcox	M. J. D. Doherty	A. D. Methuen	N. Fairweather	K. McLaren	K. Hartzenberg	Extras	Total	Wickets
2–2–0–1						11	299	9
9–6–9–0	7–1–20–1					16	221	8
	10–2–48–0	4–0–26–0				18	382	7
						8	92	4 a
5–0–30–0				7–3–22–0		5	252	8 b
				6–1–20–1		16	147	9
			8–3–16–0			19	228	9
			11–0–68–2			11	285	9
		2–1–6–0			10–4–30–1	15	169	10
						23	126	10
						9	170	10
5–1–14–0	1–1–0–0					17	299	8
8–2–14–0	14–4–29–0	3–0–7–0						
29–11–	32–8–	9–1–	19–3–	13–4–	10–4–			
67–1	97–1	39–0	84–2	42–1	30–1			
—	—	—	av. 42.00	—	—			

Natal 'B' Batting 1980/81

	v. Griqualand West (Kimberley) 27, 28, 29 November		v. Orange Free State (Bloemfontein) 11, 12, 13 December		v. Transvaal 'B' (Durban) 1, 2, 3 January		v. Griqualand West (Pietermaritzburg) 23, 24, 25 January		v. Transvaal 'B' (Johannesburg) 5, 6, 7 February	v. Orange Free State (Durban) 12, 13, 14 February	
B. J. Whitfield	33	18	6	71							
F. B. Hill	23	23			96	63	11	45			
M. M. Benkenstein	58	0	71	0	6	6				7	105
N. P. Daniels	75	12	27	104							
M. D. Tramontino	0	7	47	35	33	5	16	5	41	10	72
C. A. Gie	54	41	90	32*	12	0	6	1	8	0	4
Y. A. Omar	8	39	6*		38	35*	14	19*	17	7	
D. K. Pearse	37	50*	37	2	11*	21*	35	3		26	
I. R. Ault	0*	14			0		1*	6			
J. S. Muil	0	1*	—		0		1	2	11	9	
M. Davis	—		—								
K. D. Verdoorn					6	94	27	0			
R. A. Smith					16	15	27	5	11	35	36*
T. R. Madsen			57	58*	24	0				75	
N. D. Matthews			15								
D. Bestall							13	16	16	3	50*
J. A. O'Donoghue							3	1	1	46	15
P. H. Williams									1		
P. J. Allan									2		
M. B. Logan									45		
E. J. Hodkinson									1*	1*	
Extras	11	16	16	14	24	15	15	23	8	14	18
Total	299	221	370	316	266	254	169	126	162	233	300
Wickets	9	8	8	5	10	7	10	10	10	10	4
Result	D		W		D		W		D	W	
Points	6		20		5		15		2	18	

Inns	NOs	Runs	HS	Av
4	0	128	71	32.00
8	0	373	105	46.63
6	0	141	71	23.50
4	0	218	104	54.50
11	0	269	72	24.45
11	1	248	90	24.80
9	3	183	39	30.50
9	3	222	50*	37.00
5	2	21	14	7.00
7	1	24	11	4.00
—	—	—	—	—
4	0	127	94	31.75
7	1	145	36*	24.17
5	1	214	75	53.50
1	0	15	15	—
5	1	98	50*	24.50
3	0	5	3	1.67
3	0	62	46	20.67
1	0	2	2	—
1	0	45	45	—
2	2	2	1*	

Natal 'B' Bowling 1980/81	I. R. Ault	M. Davies	D. K. Pearse	J. S. Muil	Y. A. Omar	C. A. Gie
v. Griqualand West (Kimberley) 27, 28, 29 November	18–2–61–2 5–0–23–0	10–0–30–0 7.5–3–23–1	24.4–5–50–2	33–10–66–3 2–1–9–0	6–1–23–0	14–0–40–3
v. Orange Free State (Bloemfontein) 11, 12, 13 December		11–2–23–1 4–1–20–0	13–2–41–0 13–3–37–2	22–6–62–4 33–7–88–1	17–5–44–2 8–1–44–1	16.4–1–68–1 15–4–28–4
v. Transvaal "B" (Durban) 1, 2, 3 January	24–3–83–4 10–4–32–0		28–6–87–1 7–3–7–0	33–12–82–1 13–1–49–2	13–4–42–1 7–0–17–0	9–0–36–0 17–2–63–3
v. Griqualand West (Pietermaritzburg) 23, 24, 25 January	7–1–18–0 5–2–6–0		24–9–43–5 16.3–5–36–4	21–11–32–3 25–12–41–5	3–1–4–0	3.2–0–10–2 3–0–20–0
v Transvaal "B" (Johannesburg) 5, 6, 7 February				23–5–101–1 9–3–16–1	10–3–18–1	7–0–31–0 8–2–12–0
v. Orange Free State (Durban) 12, 13, 14 February			7–5–2–1 16–3–41–5	9–3–23–2 13–2–43–1	4–1–7–0	3.4–0–17–1
	69–12–223–6 av. 37.17	32.5–6–96–2 av. 48.00	149.1–41–344–20 av. 17.20	236–73–612–24 av. 25.50	68–16–199–5 av. 39.80	96.4–9–325–14 av. 23.21

N. Matthews	N. P. Daniels	J. A. O'Donoghue	E. J. Hodkinson	P. H. Williams	P. J. Allan	Extras	Total	Wickets
						21	291	10
						5	60	1
6.2–0–39–0	5–0–28–1					23	328	10
	17.1–5–36–2					21	274	10
						27	357	8
						4	172	5
						12	115	10
		7–1–17–1				16	140	10
		3–0–17–0	14–3–40–0	6–2–11–0	12–5–29–1	17	264	3
			6–0–20–0	7–2–24–0	3–0–21–0	5	98	1
			17–3–53–5	15–5–29–2		15	129	10
			10–3–28–2	4–0–22–0		11	162	10
6.2–0– 39–0 —	22.1–5– 64–3 av. 21.33	10–1– 34–1 —	47–9– 141–7 av. 20.14	32–9– 86–2 av. 43.00	15–5– 50–1 —			

Orange Free State Batting 1980/81

	v. Transvaal 'B' (Johannesburg) 21, 22, 24 November		v. Natal 'B' (Bloemfontein) 11, 12, 13 December		v. Griqualand West (Bloemfontein) 1, 2, 3 January		v. Transvaal 'B' (Bloemfontein) 22, 23, 24 January		v. Natal 'B' (Durban) 12, 13, 14 February		v. Griqualand West (Kimberley) 19, 20, 21 February	
D. P. le Roux	8	26	6	12	5	3						
R. A. le Roux	2	21	27	39	21	6	34	13	20	1	29	18
L. W. Griessel	2	8	162	0	71	47	12	0	8	7	28	0
G. M. Lister-James	0	0										
R. J. East	20	0	21	73	77	43	0	39	1	0	11	85
A. L. M. Klopper	40	27	0	24	42	2	10	22	4	8	34	1
E. Schmidt	0	2			19*	8	6	41	30	23	21	20
S. Regenstein	16	28	5	31	12	0					11	43*
P. Grobler	7	9*										
W. S. Norton	1*	13			—	0*						
W. T. Strydom	9	23	2*	1					2	11	0	
J. J. Strydom			61	68	0	15	9	8	11	70*	0	55
D. Jacobs			9	4	0*	6*	4	13	0	0		
W. M. van der Merwe			10	1			4	0	15*	2	7*	12*
R. G. Norton			2	0*			2*	1*				
J. van Heerden					0	1	6	13	7	29	13	13
E. G. Robler							1	34	16	0	7	35
Extras	22	27	23	21	5	16	11	10	15	11	9	17
Total	127	184	328	274	252	147	99	194	129	162	170	299
Wickets	10	10	10	10	8	9	10	10	10	10	10	8
Result	L		L		D		L		L		D	
Points	4		10		9		5		5		3	

Inns	NOs	Runs	HS	Av
6	0	60	26	10.00
12	0	231	39	19.25
12	0	345	162	28.75
2	0	0	0	0.00
12	0	370	85	30.83
12	0	214	42	17.83
10	1	170	41	18.89
8	1	146	43*	20.86
2	1	16	9*	—
3	2	14	13	—
7	1	48	23	8.00
10	1	297	70*	33.00
8	2	36	13	6.00
8	3	51	15*	10.20
4	3	5	2*	—
8	0	82	29	10.25
6	0	93	35	15.50

Orange Free State Bowling 1980/81	E. Schmidt	W. S. Norton	P. Grobler	W. T. Strydom	R. A. le Roux	S. Regenstein
v. Transvaal "B" (Johannesburg) 21, 22, 24 November	21.5–9–53–4 15–6–42–0	13–3–39–0 5–0–16–0	8–2–30–0 4–0–16–0	15–2–43–0 20–11–36–4	21–6–66–5 17.4–8–48–3	12–6–33–1
v. Natal "B" (Bloemfontein) 11, 12, 13 December				20–5–66–1 8–0–62–0	14–2–48–1 10–3–38–1	14–1–63–0 3–0–23–0
v. Griqualand West (Bloemfontein) 1, 2, 3 January	19–5–43–4 9–1–35–2	16–4–58–0 12–3–25–2			20–3–63–2 16–4–53–3	9–3–20–0
v. Transvaal "B" (Bloemfontein) 22, 23, 24 January	15–4–27–1				15.3–3–43–3	
v. Natal "B" (Durban) 12, 13, 14 February	13.2–2–51–2 11.1–2–28–0			18–9–32–2 5–1–13–0	7–2–30–0 11–1–35–0	
v. Griqualand West (Kimberley) 19, 20, 21 February	24–8–43–2			23–8–41–2	17–3–73–1	22–8–76–1
	127–37– 322–15 av. 21.47	46–10– 138–2 av. 69.00	12–2– 46–0 —	109–36– 293–9 av. 32.55	149.1–35– 498–19 av. 26.21	60–18– 215–2 av. 107.50

D. Jacobs	J. van Heerden	W. M. van der Merwe	R. Norton	A. M. L. Klopper	R. J. East	Extras	Total	Wickets
						8	232	10
						16	174	7
1-4-50-1		19-3-71-4	17-4-56-1			16	370	8
		22-2-84-1	21-3-95-3			14	316	5
20.4-3-65-3	6-1-18-1					6	273	10
13.1-0-41-2						8	162	9
7-1-34-0		16-3-50-1	8-0-56-0	21-5-66-5		15	292	10
					0.1-0-2-0	0	2	0
15-2-38-1	1-0-4-0	20-0-64-4				14	233	10
13-0-65-1	5-0-36-0	22-3-79-2		6-0-26-0		18	300	4
	9.4-2-32-1	26-8-72-2		2-1-2-0		23	362	10
79.5-10-293-8 av. 36.63	21.4-3-90-2 av. 45.00	125-19-420-14 av. 30.00	46-7-207-4 av. 51.75	29-6-94-5 av. 18.80	0.1-0-2-0 —			

Transvaal 'B'
Batting
1980/81

	v. Orange Free State (Johannesburg) 21, 22, 24 November		v. Griqualand West (Kimberley) 11, 12, 13 December		v. Natal 'B' (Durban) 1, 2, 3 January		v. Griqualand West (Johannesburg) 19, 20, 21 January		v. Orange Free State (Bloemfontein) 22, 23, 24 January		v. Natal 'B' (Johannesburg) 5, 6, 7 February	
N. E. Wright	19	44			15	30	35*	12	53	0*	128*	38*
M. S. Venter	40	18	48	14			26	76	71	2*	18	51
W. J. van der Linden	1	5	21	21	41	54*	12	54	17		14	4*
L. J. Barnard	54	17	14	4	28	15	35	0	14		35	
Y. Rubidge	1	7	10	5*	17		21	6	4		—	
N. T. Day	32	0	174*		136*	4					52*	
R. F. Pienaar	56*	44	37	5*	1	8	8	16	71		—	
M. C. van Wyk	10	23*										
N. V. Radford	29		41		39	33*	17	12	1		—	
K. J. Kerr	11		—						11		—	
J. Fairclough	11		—		—		4*	5*	5*		—	
N. Jurgensen			7	35	39	24	15	8				
K. A. Barlow			12*		11*							
K. P. Skjoldhammer					3							
R. V. Jennings							36	82*	2		28	
F. Weideman							0	3	28			
Extras	8	16	18	8	27	4	19	11	15	—	17	5
Total	272	174	382	92	357	172	228	285	292	2	264	98
Wickets	10	7	7	4	8	5	9	9	10	0	3	1
Result	W		W		D		W		W		D	
Points	18		19		7		16		20		9	

v. Western Province 'B' (Johannesburg) 13, 14, 16, 17 March		Inns	NOs	Runs	HS	Av
21	0	12	4	395	128*	49.38
27	23	12	1	408	76	37.09
15	1	13	2	260	54*	23.64
14	2	12	0	232	54	19.33
		8	1	71	21	10.14
71	6	8	3	475	174*	95.00
57	3	11	2	306	71	34.00
		2	1	33	23*	—
45	15	9	1	232	45	29.00
10	18	4	0	50	18	12.50
1*	0*	6	5	26	11	—
8	2	8	0	138	39	17.25
		2	2	23	12*	—
		1	0	3	3	—
		3	1	120	82*	60.00
2	2	5	0	35	28	7.00

19	13

284	85
10	10
	L
	—

Transvaal 'B' Bowling 1980/81	N. V. Radford	J. Fairclough	R. F. Pienaar	K. J. Kerr	H. J. van der Linden	L. J. Barnard
v. Orange Free State (Johannesburg) 21, 22, 24 November	17.2–5–32–2 10–3–36–0	19–10–26–4 15–5–31–6	9–1–28–2	7–2–19–2 13–2–26–0	15–4–37–4	1–0–5–0
v. Griqualand West (Kimberley) 11, 12, 13 December	17–6–41–6 27–5–92–4	15–5–25–1 34–14–47–1	4–2–8–0 16–4–43–0	21.3–9–44–2	10.4–3–32–3 20–3–60–2	12–8–23–0
v. Natal "B" (Durban) 1, 2, 3 January	21–6–74–1 8–0–31–2	26–8–44–3 13.5–3–44–3	7–3–17–3 8–2–37–1		18–4–62–2 11–0–39–1	8–1–25–0
v. Griqualand West (Johannesburg) 19, 20, 21 January	17–6–34–1 11–1–30–0	21–9–28–2 13–2–48–2	12–1–36–0 4–1–8–2		11–2–66–2 7–1–37–1	7.4–0–17–3 6.2–3–3–1
v. Orange Free State (Bloemfontein) 22, 23, 24 January	22–14–20–3 4–1–11–0	24–16–18–3 7–5–3–0	12–4–13–1	15.5–9–20–2 24–5–84–4	8–5–8–0 14–4–55–4	1–1–0–0
v. Natal "B" (Johannesburg) 5, 6, 7 February	16–4–46–3	14–7–17–0	8.4–5–12–2		7–2–17–1	3–1–11–0
v. Western Province 'B' (Johannesburg) 13, 14, 16, 17 March	19–5–40–2 20–4–50–4	21–12–21–2 32–18–34–1	15–4–32–1 28–5–64–1	9–2–29–0 8.3–1–30–1	5–1–26–0 6–1–10–0	
	209.2–60– 537–28 av. 19.18	254.5–114– 386–28 av. 13.79	123.4–32– 298–13 av. 22.92	98.5–30– 252–11 av. 22.91	132.4–30– 449–20 av. 22.45	39–14– 84–4 av. 21.00

K. A. Barlow	K. P. Skjoldhammer	F. Weideman	M. C. van Wyk	Extras	Total	Wickets
				22	127	10
			13–5–22–0	27	184	10
5–2–11–0				11	128	10
8–3–14–0				21	344	10
13–2–26–0	10–2–19–0			24	266	10
6–0–18–0	9–1–45–0			15	254	7
		14–0–45–2		8	234	10
		6–1–20–2		10	156	10
		7–4–9–1		11	99	10
		10–2–31–2		10	194	10
		18–6–51–4		8	162	10
		17–4–50–4		5	203	9
		29–5–89–1		22	299	10
32–7–	19–3–	101–22–	13–5–			
69–0	64–0	295–16	22–0			
—	—	av. 18.44	—			

Boland
Batting
1980/81

	v. Border (Stellenbosch) 27, 28, 29 November		v. Western Province 'B' (Stellenbosch) 12, 13, 15 December		v. Western Province 'B' (Cape Town) 26, 27 December		v. Border (East London) 24, 26, 27 January	v. Eastern Province 'B' (Port Elizabeth) 29, 30, 31 January		v. Eastern Province 'B' (Stellenbosch) 14, 16, 17 February	
C. van der Merwe	27	63	37	12	1	32	35	19	12	50	8
F. V. Moolman	5	2									
D. Malan	4	22									
L. L. Roberts	4	11	50	10*	35	22	9	15	28	8	24
A. du Toit	102	1	7	58	11	2	21	16	0	16	5
J. Kennedy	97	1	31	0	0	0					
R. C. Schultz	3	26*	29	29	1	0	5	2	4	4	14
E. E. van Rooyen	12	14									
C. J. Coetzee	13*		10*		12	11	3	13*	0	1	1*
J. Hendriks	0*						10	11*	2*	2*	1
E. Kasner	–				8	0					
H. N. Basson			18	49						19	7
R. A. Bath			9	11	0	17					
D. Traut			36	5	16	11		31	6	1	7
C. Viljoen			30	5*			28*				
A. H. Potgieter			0		4*	0					
P. B. J. Wallace					5	11*	20	103	31	68	55
A. Wasserfall							11	21	5		
A. Odendaal							3	20	30	43	5
C. Hendrickse							7	19	0	20	2
Extras	14	14	11	16	17	19	9	31	15	46	26
Total	281	154	268	195	110	125	161	301	133	278	155
Wickets	8	7	10	7	10	10	10	9	10	10	10
Results	D		D		L		D	W		L	
Points	5		10		4		2	15		5	

Inns	NOs	Runs	HS	Av
11	0	296	63	26.91
2	0	7	5	3.50
2	0	26	22	13.00
11	1	216	50	21.60
11	0	239	102	21.73
6	0	129	97	21.50
11	1	117	29	11.70
2	0	26	14	13.00
9	4	64	13*	12.80
6	4	26	11*	13.00
2	0	8	8	4.00
4	0	93	49	23.25
4	0	37	17	9.25
4	0	68	36	17.00
7	2	108	31	21.60
3	1	4	4*	2.00
7	1	293	103	48.83
3	0	37	21	12.33
5	0	101	43	20.20
5	0	48	20	9.60

Boland Bowling 1980/81	C. J. Coetzee	J. Hendriks	S. van Rooyen	E. Kasner	L. L. Roberts	D. Traut
v. Border (Stellenbosch) 27, 28 29 November	13.2–6–36–3 13–1–38–1	16–4–60–3 4–0–26–0	7–1–34–0 4–0–37–2	31–13–46–1 7–1–41–1	13–5–36–0 9–0–34–1	
v. Western Province 'B' (Stellenbosch) 12, 13, 15 December	17.3–3–47–1 15–2–53–1				20–2–92–2 7–1–34–2	18–4–62–1 18–3–62–2
v. Western Province 'B' (Cape Town) 26, 27 December	12–3–47–1			20–4–66–1	15–3–54–2	21–3–70–2
v. Border (East London) 24, 26, 27 January	5–1–17–2	4–1–7–1				
v. Eastern Province 'B' (Port Elizabeth) 29, 30, 31 January	21–10–32–2 22–6–54–2	9–2–22–1 12–4–58–6			24.4–12–39–5 9–0–33–1	
v. Eastern Province 'B' (Stellenbosch) 14, 16, 17 February	14–1–50–0 11–3–61–0	22–5–75–2 16–3–48–4			38–10–93–3 11–1–41–1	
	147.5–36– 435–13 av. 33.46	83–19– 296–17 av. 17.41	11–1– 71–2 av. 35.50	58–18– 153–3 av. 51.00	146.4–34– 456–17 av. 26.82	57–10– 194–5 av. 38.80

A. H. Potgieter	C. Viljoen	C. Hendrickse		*Extras*	*Total*	*Wickets*
				23	235	8
				11	187	5
18–3–81–1	8–1–25–0			19	326	5
10.3–3–34–3				6	189	8
18–5–54–1				22	313	7
				9	33	3
	29–13–42–1	8–2–18–0		14	167	10
	6–0–32–0			15	192	10
	26–9–56–1	5–0–28–0		12	314	7
	21–8–75–1			20	245	6
46.3–11–	90–31–	13–2–				
169–5	230–3	46–0				
av. 33.80	av. 76.67	—				

F80

Border Batting 1980/81

	v. Western Province 'B' (Constantia) 22, 24, 25 November		v. Boland (Stellenbosch) 27, 28, 29 November		v. Eastern Province 'B' (Grahamstown) 11, 12, 13 December		v. Eastern Province 'B' (East London) 26, 27, 29 December		v. Western Province 'B' (East London) 1, 2, 3 January		v. Boland (East London) 24, 26, 27 January
I. D. Harty	9	5	6	69*	23		78	13	4	10	21
R. A. Stretch	16	31	6	19	168		38	7	31	9	1
R. Kent	4	1	56	8	55		27	14*	18	0	
J. Buckley	5	26	108	4*	1		5	8	7	1	—
C. M. Wells	11	0	0	0							
G. L. Hayes	7	33	9	53	51		88	18			—
E. T. Laughlin	6	76*	14	23	5		14	7*	5	20	2*
J. P. Hosking	23	0			2		22		36	14	—
G. D. Boucher	0	0	4		21		8		8	1	—
A. K. Weakley	14*	4	—		10*		14*		2	3*	
S. J. Ker-Fox	4	16					—				
G. M. Gower			0		11				15*	16	
T. Ball			—								
B. Osborne					45		11		20	8	—
R. E. Frisch									17	32	
N. Thompson											0
R. B. C. Ranger											—
C. Davies											—
Extras	12	13	23	11	21		36	21	31	14	9
Total	111	205	235	187	413		341	88	194	128	33
Wickets	10	10	8	5	10		9	4	10	10	3
Results	L		D		D		W		L		D
Points	5		5		9		18		4		5

Inns	NOs	Runs	HS	Av
10	1	238	78	26.44
10	0	326	168	32.60
9	1	183	56	22.88
9	1	165	108	20.63
4	0	20	11	5.00
7	0	259	88	37.00
10	3	172	76*	24.57
6	0	97	36	16.17
7	1	42	21	7.00
6	4	47	14*	23.50
2	0	20	16	10.00
4	1	42	16	14.00
—	—	—	—	—
4	0	84	45	21.00
2	0	49	32	24.50
1	0	0	0	—
—	—	—	—	—
—	—	—	—	—

Border Bowling 1980/81	G. D. Boucher	S. J. Ker-Fox	C. M. Wells	G. L. Hayes	A. K. Weakley	J. P. Hosking
v. Western Province 'B' (Constantia) 22, 24, 25 November	22–4–46–4 14–5–28–1	18–4–33–3 3–2–1–0	10–3–32–1 4–0–18–0	12.2–4–26–2 10–3–27–0	8–3–26–0 20–8–34–1	4–0–14–0
v. Boland (Stellenbosch) 27, 28, 29 November	21–5–48–1 19–8–31–4		18–6–25–0 6–2–10–0	22–9–44–1 12–4–33–1	23–8–52–4 8–4–16–0	
v. Eastern Province 'B' (Grahamstown) 11, 12, 13 December	20–6–69–4 10–2–32–1			27–5–60–0 17–4–39–1	10–3–36–1 14–11–14–0	2–0–18–0
v. Eastern Province 'B' (East London) 26, 27, 28 December	15–0–51–1 7–2–9–0	13–7–13–0 9–3–10–0		27–5–63–3 24.5–6–44–6	3–1–22–0 28–13–54–4	
v. Western Province 'B' (East London) 1, 2, 3 January	19–5–50–1				11–1–55–0	
v. Boland (East London) 24, 26, 27 January	4–3–1–0			9–1–29–1		
	151–40– 365–17 av. 21.47	43–16– 57–3 av. 19.00	38–11– 85–1 —	161.1–41– 365–15 av. 24.33	125–52– 309–10 av. 30.00	6–0– 32–0 —

a R. C. B. Ranger 7–2–17–1

E. T. Laughlin	I. D. Harty	G. M. Gower	G. Osborne	R. Frisch	C. Davies	Extras	Total	Wickets
						8	171	10
7.3–3–15–1	1–0–2–0					7	146	3
7–0–32–1		27–8–66–1				14	281	8
10–3–25–0	2.3–1–5–1	13–5–20–1				14	154	7
13–1–52–2		23–6–61–1	2–0–4–0			21	303	9
21–4–70–0	5–1–17–0	16–4–35–1	5–0–16–2			16	257	5
13–1–53–2			14–2–47–1			24	273	9
6–0–21–0						17	155	10
11–3–53–0		40–4–88–4	26–3–78–3	5–2–16–1		21	361	10
28–12–49–5			8–4–6–0		26–11–50–2	9	161	10a
116.3–27–370–11	8.3–2–24–1	119–27–270–8	55–9–151–6	5–2–16–1	26–11–50–2			
av. 33.64	—	av. 33.75	av. 25.13	—	av. 25.00			

F84

Eastern Province 'B' Batting 1980–81

	v. Border (Grahamstown) 11, 12, 13 December		v. Border (East London) 26, 27, 29 December		v. Western Province 'B' (Port Elizabeth) 15, 16, 17 January		v. Boland (Port Elizabeth) 29, 30, 31 January		v. Boland (Stellenbosch) 14, 16, 17 February		v. Western Province 'B' (Constantia) 19, 20, 21 February	
K. P. Reid	0	0										
K. W. Gradwell	68	105*	17	19	20	24	27	9	11	2	8	9
G. Long	18	19	31	0	1	7	33	4				
R. J. D. Whyte	61	48										
T. B. Reid	18	65	21	34	47	25	26	12	47	59	0	78
G. C. G. Fraser	23	3			4	34*						
D. G. Emslie	35	1*	35*	10	39	3	10	13				
V. G. Cresswell	24		4	7*	32	11	3	0				
M. K. van Vuuren	29		13	5								
C. R. Kelbrick	6*											
K. Tessendorf	—		0	0	10							
J. W. Furstenberg			7	11	3	36	13	17				
J. M. Winstanley			112	26	2	6*						
M. J. Burkett			9	0	2	6*						
C. Wulfsohn			0*	26	20*		2*	1*	—		15	3*
R. G. Fensham					145	58						
T. C. Seaman							9	78	6	16	2	6
T. G. Shaw							6	1	45	50*	41*	17
A. C. Procter							10	36	29*	4*	17	19
N. Mandy							14	6	65	18	1	0
D. H. Howell									0	54	20	13
G. S. Cowley									61	22	13	18
J. W. Stephenson									38*		5	33
J. D. Ogilvie									—			
M. Basson											0	2
Extras	21	16	24	17	26	22	14	15	12	20	6	9
Total	303	257	273	155	349	226	167	192	314	245	128	207
Wickets	9	5	9	10	10	7	10	10	7	6	10	10
Result	D		L		D		L		W		L	
Points	7		7		9		3		15		5	

Inns	NOs	Runs	HS	Av
2	0	0	0	0.00
12	1	319	105*	29.00
8	0	113	33	14.13
2	0	109	61	54.50
12	0	432	78	36.00
4	1	64	34*	21.33
8	2	146	39	24.33
7	1	81	32	13.50
3	0	47	29	15.67
1	1	6	6*	—
3	0	10	10	3.33
6	0	87	36	14.50
2	0	138	112	69.00
4	1	17	9	5.67
7	5	67	26	33.50
2	0	203	145	101.50
6	0	117	78	19.50
6	2	160	50*	40.00
6	2	115	36	28.75
6	0	104	65	17.33
4	0	87	54	21.75
4	0	114	61	28.50
3	1	76	38*	38.00
—	—	—	—	—
2	0	2	2	1.00

Eastern Province "B" Bowling 1980/81	M. K. van Vuuren	G. Long	G. C. G. Fraser	K. Tessendorf	C. Wulfsohn	M. J. Burkett
v. Border (Grahamstown) 11, 12, 13 December	29.1–3–76–2	27–10–72–3	14–3–35–1	21–4–94–3		
v. Border (East London) 26, 27, 29 December	13–2–29–0 10–4–26–1	23–5–71–3 4–1–7–1		18.4–5–39–3	29–3–95–1 9–3–26–2	34–11–71–1 6–3–8–0
v. Western Province 'B' (Port Elizabeth) 15, 16, 17 January		33–11–60–6 10–3–17–0	10–2–28–0	20–6–41–0 11–7–17–1	32.2–8–74–4 8–4–9–0	7–4–12–0
v. Boland (Port Elizabeth) 29, 30, 31 January		30–9–45–1 13.4–8–16–7			26–9–47–3 21–4–63–2	
v. Boland (Stellenbosch) 14, 16, 17 February					22–8–50–3 18–2–38–3	
v. Western Province 'B' (Constantia) 19, 20, 21 February					25–7–46–6 7–3–10–0	
	52.1–9– 131–3 av. 43.67	140.4–47– 288–21 av. 13.72	24–5– 63–1 —	70.4–22– 191–7 av. 27.29	197.2–51– 458–24 av. 19.08	47–18– 91–1 —

a C. R. Kelbrick 24–2–84–0; K. P. Reid 9–1–31–0
b J. W. Furstenberg (2nd inns) 1–1–0–0
c J. D. Ogilvie (1st inns) 28–8–63–1
d T. B. Reid (2nd inns) 0.5–0–6–0

N. Mandy	A. C. Procter	T. Shaw	G. S. Cowley	K. W. Gradwell	J. W. Stephenson	*Extras*	*Total*	*Wickets*
						21	413	10a
						36	341	9
						21	88	4
						25	240	10
			1–0–6–0			11	60	1b
9–6–31–0	17–4–49–1	32–8–78–2		6–1–20–0		31	301	9
2–3–27–0	7–1–12–0					15	133	10
–1–16–0	9–5–11–2	30.2–11–69–3	14–5–23–0			46	278	10c
–4–16–1	9–3–27–2	10–6–7–1	10–2–30–0		10.1–6–11–2	26	155	10
1–4–99–4		7–0–30–0	12–2–37–0		4–0–11–0	18	241	10
–2–16–1		4–1–23–1	8–1–35–1			6	96	3d
7–20–	42–13–	83.2–26–	44–10–	7–1–	14.1–6–			
05–6	99–5	207–7	125–1	26–0	22–2			
v. 34.17	av. 19.80	av. 29.57	—	—	av. 11.00			

Western Province 'B' Batting 1980/81

	v. Border (Constantia) 22, 24, 25 November		v. Boland (Stellenbosch) 11, 12, 13 December		v. Boland (Cape Town) 26, 27, 29 December	v. Border (East London) 1, 2, 3 January	v. Eastern Province 'B' (Port Elizabeth) 15, 16, 17 January		v. Eastern Province 'B' (Constantia) 19, 20, 21 February	
A. D. Green	10	5								
J. B. Ackermann	18	13								
E. Halvorsen	13	52*	95	6						
J. Seeff	10	57	22	22	43	20	10	17*	50	21
H. M. Ackerman	36	12*	19	55	18	9	47			
A. P. Kuiper	4		66*	10					13	
J. D. du Toit	40		1*	26					7	
E. S. Gordon	3		—	17*	47	7				
M. B. Minnaar	9									
R. Whittingdale	14*		—	—						
J. A. Carse	6									
P. M. Thompson			59	27	67	26	1	10	0	14
S. D. Bruce			45	11		29	8		0	1*
R. J. Bowley			—	9	16*		14*			
M. B. Taljaard			—	—					36	
J. W. Bristow					9	29	1	22*		
T. A. Clarke					54	100	0		15	11*
L. Fairweather					2					
B. P. Martin					35*	0	51			
D. L. Hobson					—					
R. R. Lawrenson					—	15			12	
O. Henry						105*				
J. E. Mahoney						0	0		8*	
T. A. Passmore							73		9	
S. A. Jones							10			
M. J. Nel									73	43
Extras	8	7	19	6	22	21	25	11	18	6
Total	171	146	326	189	313	361	240	60	241	96
Wickets	10	3	5	8	7	10	10	1	10	3
Result	W		D		W	W	D		W	
Points	15		7		21	19	4		18	

		v. Transvaal 'B' (Johannesburg) 13, 14, 16, 17 March		Inns	NOs	Runs	HS	Av
				2	0	15	10	7.50
				2	0	31	18	15.50
2	18			6	1	186	95	37.20
3	14			12	1	289	57	26.27
				7	1	196	55	32.67
38	81			6	1	212	81	42.40
4	28			6	1	106	40	21.20
				4	1	74	47	24.67
				1	0	9	9	—
				1	1	14	14*	—
				1	0	6	6	—
25	4			10	0	233	67	23.30
2	35			8	1	131	45	18.72
				3	2	39	16*	—
2*	7			3	1	45	36	22.50
				4	1	61	29	20.33
96	8			7	1	284	100	47.33
				1	0	2	2	—
				3	1	86	51	43.00
				—	—	—	—	—
6	24			4	0	57	24	14.25
				1	1	105	105*	—
				3	1	8	8*	4.00
				2	0	82	73	41.00
5*	10*			3	2	35	15*	—
5	48			4	0	169	73	42.25
5	22							
203	299							
9	10							
W								

— No bonus pts

Western Province 'B' Bowling 1980/81	E. S. Gordon	J. D. du Toit	H. M. Ackerman	R. Bowley	M. B. Taljaard	S. D. Bruce
v. Border (Constantia) 22, 24, 25 November	18–5–36–3 25–8–49–6	21.4–7–37–6 19.2–6–42–2	5–2–5–0			
v. Boland (Stellenbosch) 11, 12, 13 December	26–7–49–2 16–4–35–2	19–4–44–2 13–2–22–1	3–0–23–0 1–0–6–0	27–7–54–3 22–5–54–1	25–6–59–1 12–6–16–1	15–5–28–2 4–1–23–0
v. Boland (Cape Town) 26, 27, 28 December	12–5–20–2 18–5–46–3			7–0–21–0 6–1–18–0		
v. Border (East London) 1, 2, 3 January	16–6–21–2 21.1–9–41–1					
v. Eastern Province 'B' (Port Elizabeth) 15, 16, 17 January			7–3–11–0	22–6–64–4		2–0–10–0
v. Eastern Province 'B' (Constantia) 19, 20, 21 February		10–3–23–2 20–7–37–0			23–6–37–4 25–3–62–3	
v. Transvaal "B" (Johannesburg) 13, 14, 16, 17 March		35–12–74–3 17–6–31–1			30–10–59–1 18–8–18–5	
	152.1–49– 297–21 av. 14.14	155–47– 310–17 av. 18.24	16–5– 45–0 —	84–19– 211–8 av. 26.38	133–39– 251–15 av. 16.73	21–6– 61–2 av. 30.50

a J. A. Carse 10–2–26–1 (1st inns); J. A. Carse 11–2–24–1 (2nd inns); J. B. Ackermann 11–2–26–1; M. B. Minnaar 9–2–26–0

b D. L. Hobson 13.1–3–26–2 (1st inns); D. L. Hobson 19–9–22–4 (2nd inns)

c O. Henry 10–5–28–9 (1st inns)

R. R. Lawrenson	B. P. Martin	J. Mahoney	S. H. Jones	T. A. Passmore	A. P. Kuiper	Extras	Total	Wickets
						12	111	10a
					7–2–20–0	13	205	10
						11	268	10
					4–0–23–0	16	195	7
)–7–24–6	2–1–2–0					17	110	10b
2–7–15–2	4–3–5–1					19	125	10
3–3–58–4	9.5–4–17–1	14–3–39–3				31	194	10c
3–8–42–6	6–0–21–1	8–5–10–1				14	128	10
	21–5–87–2	19–1–68–1	25–6–54–1	6.5–0–29–1		26	349	10
	32–5–86–3	14–1–38–0	22–8–36–2	15–3–44–2		22	226	7
9–6–41–2		10.2–6–12–2			2–0–9–0	6	128	10
7.1–8–72–6		16–7–27–1				9	207	10
8–3–81–5					21–5–51–1	19	284	10
0–7–23–4						13	85	10
68.1–49–	74.5–18–	81.2–23–	47–14–	21.5–3–	34–7–			
56–35	218–8	195–8	90–3	73–3	103–1			
v. 10.17	av. 27.25	av. 24.38	av. 30.00	av. 24.33	—			

G

A Thing of Shreds and Patches

The England tour of the West Indies

Few England sides can ever have set out on tour with their supporters in such a state of gloom as that which set out for the West Indies in 1981.

Of the sixteen players in the party only Gooch, Boycott and Gower of the batsmen, and possibly Miller of the bowlers, seemed undisputed Test class. Botham had been a world class all-rounder, but since his ascendancy to the captaincy, he had lost form, popularity and even credibility. His cause was not helped by the fact that he flew to the West Indies knowing that he would face a court case for alleged assault on his return.

The appointment of Willis as vice-captain was totally incomprehensible. His selection for the tour could only have been based on sentiment for as a performer he was now struggling at county level and had limped his way through the Australian tour of the previous winter. Without question, Bob Willis had been one of the very finest of England's fast bowlers, a loyal and good man, but after a decade in international cricket he could no longer be considered a serious challenger for a place in the Test side.

To make matters worse those chosen to support Willis were all of doubtful quality. Dilley promised much, but he had been ill and neither his true worth, nor his real fitness for the difficult tour, could be taken as proven. Old had rarely survived any series without breaking down and Stevenson's inconsistency made him a very dubious choice at international level.

Willey had given no indication that he was of Test standard with bat or ball. He had had an extended run in the Test side, but the bulk of his hundred against the West Indies at the Oval in 1980 had come when the game was 'dead'.

The spin bowling was left entirely to Emburey and Miller, both capable performers, but the absence of any bowler who could turn the ball from leg was a dreadful omission. The West Indies would not be beaten by our inadequate pace attack, but they might be troubled by a spin attack which included Edmonds and one of the off-break bowlers in harmony.

It can be argued that Edmonds had been unfit towards the end of the English season, but then so had Willey, Willis, Botham and Dilley, and they had been chosen. The ever fit Jackman and Lever had not been included, and in the case of Jackman, in particular, this seemed a rank injustice. If a man's achievements at county level go unrecognised, what meaning has the first-class game?

The batting had given little indication that it would be able to withstand the West Indian pace attack in the Caribbean. Rose had batted well against the West Indies in England, but there were many who believed, on the evidence of his last tour as an England player, that his technique would not see him safely through the islands. Butcher, the first West Indian to be selected for England, had played some exciting innings, but his achievement had been too limited to be very optimistic of any great success on his return home. The promising Athey was most unlucky not to be chosen, though another school of thought insisted that it was better for his career for him to remain in England.

Gatting had a chunky confidence that asserted that he may yet reach his potential at Test level, but it would not be easy against the finest Test side that any country had put into the arena since 1948.

Indeed, it would not be easy for even the most tried and tested of the England party, but as most England supporters feared a five-nil drubbing in the series, anything better than that would come as a welcome bonus.

23, 24, 25 and 26 January 1981   **at Pointe-a-Pierre**
England XI 483 for 6 dec (D. I. Gower 187, M. W. Gatting 94, G. Boycott
87, R. Harper 5 for 142) and 208 for 5 dec (G. Boycott 87)
President's Young West Indies XI 320 (J. Dujon 105 not out) and 181
(G. Miller 6 for 70)
England XI won by 190 runs

Having survived two fierce deliveries from Marshall, Rose was caught at
short-leg off the third so giving England an ominously bad start to the tour. It
proved a false alarm. Boycott and Gower weathered the early aggression of
Marshall and Alleyne and then, in the afternoon, moved into full flow to add 198
for the second wicket before Boycott played on to the eighteen-year-old
off-spinner Harper, the first of his five wickets. Gatting showed immediate
confidence and he and Gower shared another stand of 198. With Butcher hitting
well, England concluded a splendid first innings in time to take four Young West
Indian wickets before the close. The home side were 193 for 6, but a fine innings
from Jeff Dujon of Jamaica, who came in at number seven, lifted them to 320.
It was an excellent innings from the twenty-four-year-old Dujon and underlined
the wealth of talent to be found in the West Indies. Boycott again batted
admirably, this time without offering the chances that both he and Gower had
offered in the first innings, but the game seemed certain to end in a draw.
Astoundingly, England snatched victory on the last afternoon with twenty
minutes to spare when the combined off-spin of Miller and Willey bamboozled
the later West Indian batsmen who seemed intent on self-destruction in a game
which they had no hope of winning. Miller flighted the ball cleverly and spun it
appreciably and though Willey was hardly in the same class, he gave good
support and kept a consistent length. For England it was a surprising and
confidence boosting victory.

1 February 1981   **at St Vincent**
England XI 166 for 9
Windward Islands 150 for 9
England XI won by 16 runs

Incessant rain washed out the first two days of the scheduled first-class match
with Windward Islands and two one-day, forty over matches were arranged on
what would have been the third and fourth days of the original game. As
England were already desperately short of match practice before the First Test,
this restriction by the weather was most unwelcome. Rose again failed and
Gooch was laborious, but Butcher, playing a little riskily, plundered some useful
runs and Botham, looking more assured, batted well. Downton also made a very
useful late contribution, but the home side looked to be winning when they
reached 76 in the twenty-third over with only two men out. It was Emburey
who curtailed the batsmen, his eight overs yielding only 18 runs. The later order
now found themselves under unexpected pressure and with Botham and Dilley
at last establishing length, England snatched victory. Willis bowled seven rather
uncomfortable overs before leaving the field with a knee strain.

2 February 1981 **at St Vincent**
Windward Islands 183 (L. John 58)
England XI 184 for 4 (G. Boycott 85 not out, G. A. Gooch 50)
England XI won by 6 wickets

With the wicket now drier and a little faster, it was possible to extend the second one-day game to fifty-five overs. In the end England won with thirteen balls to spare and owed much to a well judged innings from Geoff Boycott and a fine all-round performance from Graham Gooch who took three of the first five wickets, held two catches and scored a brisk fifty. That the match became 55 overs was due to an oversight by Botham. The match began as 50 overs an innings, but Botham gave Willey an eleventh over, one more than his quota, and to save argument five overs were added to the innings, one more for each bowler. Emburey failed to exert the restrictions of the previous day, but Willey bowled tightly. Brian Rose once more failed, scoring only three runs in ten overs before playing on.

First One-Day International

None could say the preparations for the first international contest had been adequate from the English point of view, but the side had acquitted itself competently and had won matches against opposition lacking the great names of West Indian cricket. Two of those great names were missing from the West Indian side for the first one-day international, for both Richards and Greenidge were out through injury. English hopes were high and soared higher when Old dismissed Bacchus in the fifth over, mis-hooking to mid-on when only five had been scored. The pitch was of uneven bounce and gave encouragement to spin so that runs were never easy to obtain, but Haynes batted with a majesty that has grown upon him over the past two seasons until brilliantly caught by Emburey at square-leg. He covered much ground and held the ball two-handed. The bowler was Stevenson who bowled most economically and added Lloyd to the wicket of Haynes. Mattis played with great determination while the innings crumbled around him. At lunch he was one short of his fifty and the West Indies were 110 for 7. The innings lasted for six overs and two balls after lunch, Mattis, run out by Boycott's throw from long leg, scoring thirteen of the seventeen runs scored and being last out. The England bowlers could well be proud of their splendid effort and it seemed that careful application was all that was needed to bring victory. Within minutes the England innings was in shreds. Fifteen runs were on the board, Gooch, Boycott, Willey and Butcher were back in the pavilion, and Croft was rampant. Botham then joined Gower and played better than he had done for a very long time. He took on the responsibility of the innings, blending caution with aggression and steering England closer to their target. Gower gave good support and they had reached 80 before Gower drove Kallicharran hard and low to extra cover where Haynes took a diving catch. Shortly after tea Gatting was bowled by another fine delivery from Croft, but Bairstow stayed while 23 were added before Croft again produced a vicious and seemingly unplayable delivery. Three runs later Botham's mighty and courageous knock came to an end when he was caught behind to give Croft his sixth wicket for only 15 runs. West Indies now seemed certain of victory, but Emburey and Stevenson took England to within five of the required total and while Stevenson had strike there was still some hope. Holding's pace was too much for Old, however, and England had let a glorious chance of victory slip away. One wondered ruefully if they would ever come so close to beating West Indies again on the tour. To add to the England disappointment the reports on the injury to Bob Willis suggested that his part in the tour was at an end.

First One-Day International: West Indies v. England
4 February 1981   **at St Vincent**

West Indies

D. L. Haynes	c Emburey, b Stevenson	34
S. F. A. Bacchus	c Stevenson, b Old	1
E. H. Mattis	run out	62
A. I. Kallicharran	b Emburey	2
C. H. Lloyd (capt)	c Willey, b Stevenson	2
H. A. Gomes	b Willey	8
*D. A. Murray	b Gooch	1
A. M. E. Roberts	st Bairstow, b Gooch	
J. Garner	run out	4
M. A. Holding	b Botham	1
C. E. H. Croft	not out	2
Extras	lb 4, w 1, nb 3	8
		127

	O	M	R	W
Old	5	4	8	1
Botham	8	1	32	1
Stevenson	8.2	2	18	2
Emburey	10	4	20	1
Willey	10	1	29	1
Gooch	6	1	12	2

Fall of Wickets
1–5, 2–48, 3–51, 4–58, 5–89, 6–90, 7–102, 8–110, 9–120.

England

G. Boycott	c Mattis, b Croft	2
G. A. Gooch	c Lloyd, b Roberts	11
P. Willey	c Murray, b Croft	0
D. I. Gower	c Haynes, b Kallicharran	23
R. O. Butcher	c Murray, b Croft	1
I. T. Botham (capt)	c Murray, b Croft	60
M. W. Gatting	b Croft	3
*D. L. Bairstow	b Croft	5
J. E. Emburey	b Holding	5
G. B. Stevenson	not out	6
C. M. Old	b Holding	1
Extras	lb 8	8
		125

	O	M	R	W
Roberts	10	1	30	1
Holding	9.2	2	30	2
Croft	9	4	15	6
Garner	10	2	17	—
Kallicharran	10	3	25	1

Fall of Wickets
1–14, 2–14, 3–14, 4–15, 5–80, 6–88, 7–111, 8–114, 9–123.

West Indies won by 2 runs

7, 8, 9 and 10 February 1981   **at Port of Spain**
England XI 355 (G. A. Gooch 117, D. I. Gower 77, G. Boycott 70, H. J. Joseph
   5 for 116)
Trinidad and Tobago 392 for 8 (H. A. Gomes 75, D. L. Murray 75, R. Nanan 66
   not out, T. Cuffy 61)
Match drawn

With rain having played havoc with England's preparations for the First Test,
the game against Trinidad on the ground where the First Test was to be played
found four of the England party playing their first first-class game of the tour,
a totally unsatisfactory state of affairs. The position was worsened when, having
been put in to bat, England were denied yet another day's cricket by torrential
rain after only ten minutes at the wicket. There was cheer on the second day
when Gooch and Boycott opened with a stand of 173 and Gooch reached a
sparkling hundred, full of powerful shots and certainty. As the wicket deterior-
ated Gower showed a most welcome sense of application and there seemed hope
that England might even snatch victory. These hopes were soon dispelled by
a mature innings from the left-handed Gomes and the inability of the spinners
to make any impression on the later Trinidad batting. Cuffy hit lustily and
then Deryck Murray and Nanan put on 122 for the seventh wicket. There had
been much agitation locally because the Trinidad captain had been left out of the
Test side in favour of his namesake, David, and Deryck Murray's knock was
further ammunition for his supporters some of whom threatened to disrupt
the Test if he did not play. Kallicharran was also missing from the West Indian
party, having broken a finger when batting against Andy Roberts.

First Test Match – West Indies v. England

The annoyance at the omission of Deryck Murray from the West Indian side
that was felt by some Trinidadians was manifested in an ugly way when it was
discovered that there had been some possible sabotaging of the Test wicket. No
start could be made until repairs had been effected and play did not begin until
after lunch by which time the crowd was growing very angry. Inevitably, the
West Indies omitted the off-spinner Nanan from their side and played the four
quick bowlers; amazingly, England preferred Rose to Gatting. Botham won
the toss and asked West Indies to bat. There was a little uncertainty about the
wicket and this was probably the motive for Botham's decision, but it appeared
a defensive rather than an attacking gesture. Greenidge and Haynes made

mockery of the decision by reaching 144 before the close and, in so doing, they eased the tensions of the crowd who had not enjoyed being kept waiting. It was Emburey who bowled England back into the contention the following morning when he dismissed both openers and Mattis, out for nought on his Test debut. Richards and Lloyd were both given angry receptions by the local crowd and Richards fell to Miller, caught at square-leg. The success of the English spinners reinforced the opinion that many held that England would have been far better to have relied more positively on the spin in which they were strong, rather than on the pace in which their attainment was mediocre. Gomes provided Downton with his first victim in his debut Test, but Lloyd was badly missed by Willey and he and David Murray restored West Indian authority with a stand of 75 and though both fell to Emburey before the close, the score had by then reached 365. Emburey had taken five of these wickets for 112, but he was removed from the attack early on the third day's play and Botham took over. The captain dismissed both Holding and Garner with indifferent deliveries which they heaved at and missed. Roberts was more successful, however, and took 24 from five successive deliveries by Botham and the West Indies, now beyond defeat, declared in search of victory. Boycott and Gooch began with confident aggression and thirty runs came in six overs, but the advent of Croft completely changed the situation. Gooch was dropped at slip by Mattis, having an unhappy debut, and became becalmed. Boycott was caught at slip in the second over after lunch and Gooch, now struggling, was bowled by Roberts. He had survived until after tea, but the manner of his survival was at times miraculous. Rose had been less fortunate and had succumbed off bat and pad after fifty uncomfortable minutes. Gower alone played with anything approaching ease, and the wayward youth who had lost his Test place a few months before now seemed a far distant unhappy memory. Miller, batting higher for England than for Derbyshire, was caught behind and in the next over from Croft Botham was lbw. Willey was helped by a lucky snick and a loose delivery, but missed a full toss. Downton had forty minutes to survive. He succeeded against the pace men but was bowled by a Gomes off-break.

At 159 for 7, England's plight was desperate and Botham's prediction, made on the rest day, that they would survive with ease to draw the game, now seemed ludicrous. Sadly, Gower fell to Croft early on the fourth day and England followed on 248 runs behind. Gooch and Rose went with only 25 scored, but Gower and Boycott, aided by the loss of two and a half hours through rain, gave England hope of saving the game. It was not to be. West Indies won with an hour to spare in spite of a brave innings from Geoff Boycott with lasted for over five hours. Gower could not recapture his form of the previous day, and he was caught behind on the leg side. Miller was out of his depth at number five and Botham, after a disciplined period, was out in the most inexcusable manner, trying to hit Richards out of the ground. There was a flicker from Willey and Downton, but West Indies moved remorselessly to victory and England's spirits were left very low.

First Test Match   West Indies *v.* England
13, 14, 16, 17 and 18 February 1981   at Port of Spain

West Indies	*First Innings*	
C. G. Greenidge	c Botham, b Emburey	84
D. L. Haynes	c and b Emburey	96
I. V. A. Richards	c Gower, b Miller	29
E. H. Mattis	c Miller, b Emburey	0
H. A. Gomes	c Downton, b Old	5
C. H. Lloyd (capt)	b Emburey	64
*D. A. Murray	c Botham, b Emburey	46
A. M. E. Roberts	not out	50
M. A. Holding	lbw, b Botham	26
J. Garner	lbw, b Botham	4
C. E. H. Croft	not out	4
Extras	lb 15, nb 3	18
	(for 9 wkts, dec)	426

	O	M	R	W
Dilley	28	4	73	—
Botham	28	6	113	2
Old	16	3	49	1
Emburey	52	16	124	5
Miller	18	4	42	1
Gooch	2	—	3	—
Willey	3	1	4	—

Fall of Wickets
1–168, 2–203, 3–203, 4–215, 5–257, 6–332, 7–348, 8–383, 9–393.

England	*First Innings*		*Second Innings*	
G. A. Gooch	b Roberts	41	lbw, b Holding	5
G. Boycott	c Richards, b Croft	30	c Haynes, b Holding	70
B. C. Rose	c Haynes, b Garner	10	c Murray, b Holding	5
D. I. Gower	lbw, b Croft	48	c Murray, b Roberts	27
G. Miller	c Murray, b Croft	3	c Greenidge, b Croft	8
I. T. Botham (capt)	lbw, b Croft	0	c Holding, b Richards	16
P. Willey	lbw, b Garner	13	c Lloyd, b Garner	21
*P. R. Downton	b Gomes	4	c Lloyd, b Roberts	5
J. E. Emburey	not out	17	b Roberts	1
G. R. Dilley	b Croft	0	not out	1
C. M. Old	b Roberts	1	c sub (Bacchus) b Garner	0
Extras	b 4, lb 4, nb 3	11	b 1, lb 3, nb 6	10
		178		169

	O	M	R	W		O	M	R	W
Roberts	13	3	41	2		21	7	41	3
Holding	11	3	29	—		18	6	38	3
Croft	22	6	40	5		16	5	26	1
Garner	23	8	37	2		25	10	31	2
Richards	7	2	16	—		10	6	9	1
Gomes	2	1	4	1		9	4	14	—

Fall of Wickets
1–45, 2–63, 3–110, 4–121, 5–127, 6–143, 7–151, 8–163, 9–167.
1–19, 2–25, 3–86, 4–103, 5–134, 6–142, 7–163, 8–167, 9–169.

West Indies won by an innings and 79 runs

The days that followed the crushing defeat in the First Test were not easy ones
for the England party. As had been suspected, Willis's part in the tour was
over and he returned to England for a knee operation. His breakdown
emphasised the stupidity of his appointment as vice-captain for, however sad the
fact, it had to be faced that his Test career was at an end. The happy outcome of
the injury to Willis was that Robin Jackman was asked to join the party and
so gain an honour that should have been his in the first place. The departure
of Willis led to speculation as to who would take over as vice-captain. With
Botham's position as captain totally insecure, the appointment of the vice-
captain took on the importance comparable to that of the vice-presidency of the
United States when the president is aged or infirm. It was not surprising that
Boycott, who had made public criticisms of the leadership before the party left
England, was once more passed over for the deputy leadership. Miller had led
Derbyshire with intelligence, but his place in the England side was far from
secure. With Boycott having been deemed unsuitable, he appeared the obvious
choice, however. His only rivals for the post could have been Old, the captain
elect of Yorkshire, and Rose, the Somerset skipper. Rose had played poorly
on the tour and now came the unexpected news that he, too, was to return to
England as he was suffering from eye trouble. Athey, who was unlucky not to
be in the original party, was named as replacement, but in the meantime the
England party had other problems. The first-class game with Guyana was
abandoned because of torrential rain and the cricketers were imprisoned
without practice in their hotel. On the eve of the second one-day international
the Guyanese government decided that Robin Jackman was unwelcome in their
country as he had played cricket in South Africa and his visa was to be revoked.
The fact that several other members of the England party had also played
cricket in South Africa seemed to have gone unnoticed. It was all very sad –
for cricket, and for humanity.

Second One-Day International

The second one-day international was played in an air of unreality. The tourists
had had little practice and the banning of Jackman had put the rest of the tour
in jeopardy. The game itself was all in favour of the West Indies. The England
innings was a thing of rags and patches. Gatting tried to state that he should
have been in the Test side and Botham batted better than he had done in Port
of Spain, but, in spite of Greenidge and Richards being out with only eleven
scored, the issue was never in doubt and West Indies won with six wickets
and nearly eleven overs to spare. All this was dwarfed by the action of the
Guyanese government's ban on Jackman and the Cricket Council's correct
retort in withdrawing England from the Second Test in Guyana. Cricket was
suspended while the politicians attempted to salvage something from the mess
that they had created.

Second One-Day International: West Indies v. England
26 February 1981   **at Berbice**

England

G. Boycott	b Richards	7
G. A. Gooch	c Murray, b Roberts	11
M. W. Gatting	c Mattis, b Gomes	29
D. I. Gower	b Gomes	3
R. O. Butcher	c Haynes, b Gomes	5
I. T. Botham (capt)	b Roberts	27
P. Willey	b Croft	21
*D. L. Bairstow	b Croft	16
J. E. Emburey	c Croft, b Holding	0
G. B. Stevenson	not out	8
G. R. Dilley	b Croft	3
Extras	b 4, lb 2, nb 1	7
		137

	O	M	R	W
Roberts	7	—	17	2
Holding	7	1	13	1
Richards	10	—	26	1
Croft	6.2	2	9	3
Gomes	10	2	30	3
Garner	7	2	35	—

Fall of Wickets
1–16, 2–27, 3–34, 4–59, 5–62, 6–108, 7–112, 8–119, 9–132.

West Indies

C. G. Greenidge	run out	2
D. L. Haynes	c Gooch, b Emburey	48
I. V. A. Richards	c Stevenson, b Dilley	3
E. H. Mattis	b Emburey	24
H. A. Gomes	not out	22
C. H. Lloyd (capt)	not out	25
Extras	b 4, lb 8, nb 2	14
	(for 4 wkts)	138

*D. A. Murray, A. M. E. Roberts,
M. A. Holding, J. Garner and
C. E. H. Croft did not bat

	O	M	R	W
Dilley	5	—	21	1
Botham	7	1	24	—
Stevenson	6	—	21	—
Emburey	10	4	22	2
Gooch	2	—	8	—
Willey	9	—	23	—
Gower	0.3	—	5	—

Fall of Wickets
1–6, 2–11, 3–85, 4–90.

West Indies won by 6 wickets

The England players, happy to leave the politics of Guyana and the weather, flew to Barbados and a state of limbo. The remainder of the tour hung in the balance as ministers met to decide whether or not to follow the lead of Guyana and forbid entry to Jackman as he had played cricket in South Africa. The fact that several of the West Indian players had played with South Africans, and that the great Gary Sobers, among others, had played in Rhodesia, as it then was, did not seem to trouble the authorities who seemed unable to understand the freedom of the individual as practised in England. The ministers were meeting, not simply to discuss whether the tour would continue with England playing those men whom they chose to play, but, in effect, to decide if Test cricket was to be continued in the West Indies. This was not the first threat to Test cricket in the Caribbean. The riots which had developed over the years when the home side seemed in danger of defeat on occasions was a factor which did not make the lot of the tourist an easy one, nor was the fact that in Guyana, after dark, and in Jamaica, all day, it was unwise to leave one's hotel alone. In this climate the West Indian cricket authorities struggled to offer hospitality, which they managed admirably, and to maintain economic stability, which they found less easy. In the end, after days of speculation, the cricket authorities were helped by the good sense of the politicians who allowed the tour to go ahead without provisos. The politicians were motivated in no small measure by their own economic considerations for to deny tourism was to deny an important contributor to the economy of the islands. So Athey flew to replace Rose and wives flew to join husbands, and, thankfully, cricket took over from the politics.

5 March 1981   **at Bridgetown**
England XI 207 for 6 (G. A. Gooch 84)
Barbados 196 (G. Reifer 55, I. T. Botham 4 for 30, G. B. Stevenson 4 for 38)
England XI won by 11 runs

To compensate for the time lost through rain and the conference table, an extra one-day match in Bridgetown was arranged with each side limited to fifty overs. It proved an excellent work-out for England who were confronted by an attack consisting of Daniel, Garner, Clarke, King and Padmore. Boycott and Gooch made a cautious start, but Gatting quickened the pace with some lusty blows after Boycott had been caught behind off Collis King. This inspired Gooch who, with Gower in good support, launched a violent attack on the Barbadian bowling. Off-spinner Padmore, the home skipper, was hit for two fours and two mighty sixes in one over and England eventually passed 200 which, at one time, had looked far from possible. Stevenson and Botham reduced Barbados to 25 for 3 and though there was a rally by the middle order, the home side fell behind the required scoring rate and lost wickets in the scamper for runs. When Old began the last over 20 were needed for victory. Padmore hit a straight six, but was bowled by the third ball and England had won.

7, 8, 9 and 10 March 1981   **at Bridgetown**
England XI 298 (G. Boycott 77, P. Willey 51, A. L. Padmore 4 for 71) and
   219 for 6

Barbados 334 (C. L. King 76, G. N. Reifer 71, J. E. Emburey 5 for 92,
R. D. Jackman 4 for 68)
Match drawn

A solid innings by Boycott when England had once more looked on the edge of
trouble and some later resistance from Botham, Willey and Bairstow brought
the visitors a much bigger score than they could have expected on the opening
day. Once more the Barbadian attack was a formidable one and though Daniel
was wicketless, Marshall and Clarke caused early problems and the wily off-spin
of Padmore accounted for Boycott, Butcher, Botham and Jackman. In his first
first-class match of the tour Jackman, the cause of controversy, proved right
those who felt that he should never have been omitted from the original selection. He bowled with fire and that nagging accuracy which, allied to late swing,
makes him a fine competitor. He dismissed Haynes on the second day and
added the Reifer brothers and Clarke. It was Emburey, however, who was the
pick of the England bowlers, for whom Stevenson again disappointed, and his
varied flight and intelligent probing at the batsmen won him respect. There
was little to admire in the batting of either side which was woefully stolid
and generally strokeless. There was one brief flurry from King and George
Reifer, but little else in the first three days. When England batted out for the
draw which ended a run of five Barbados victories only Botham failed to get
in valuable batting practice.

Third Test Match – West Indies *v.* England

There was a reward for patience when Robin Jackman took the field with
the England side after years of waiting and endeavour. Jackman replaced Old
and the other changes in the England side brought in Gatting for Rose, Bairstow
for Downton, presumably in hope of crumbs of runs rather than a concern
for the standard of wicket-keeping, and Butcher for Miller. So Roland Butcher
became the first West Indian to play for England, and, appropriately, his Test
debut was on the island of his birth. Not surprisingly the West Indies were
unchanged. Once more Botham won the toss and, as there was some moisture
in the wicket, his decision to put the West Indies in seemed justified. In the first
forty-five minutes England had their best moments of the tour. Coming on at
first change, Jackman immediately found length and a line which troubled the
batsman. His fifth delivery in Test cricket moved away late, found the edge and
Greenidge was caught at first slip. In the next over Dilley dismissed the mighty
Richards for nought, well caught at second slip by Botham. Haynes and
Mattis appeared to have steered West Indies away from trouble for the wicket
had now lost its early fire, but with half an hour to go to lunch Jackman had
Haynes caught behind off a wider ball and then Mattis was adjudged lbw to
Botham. 72 for 4, the back of the West Indian batting broken, England lunched
in good spirits. It was almost their last joy of the match. In the afternoon Lloyd
batted in a manner to suggest that the years have only added to his lustre and
that the lumbering, feline power was as effective and as entertaining as ever.
He was magnificent and was ably supported by his fellow left-hander, Gomes.
England bowled well and their ground fielding was good, but Bairstow had a
dreadful day behind the stumps. He dropped Gomes off Botham, a bad miss,

and then missed a catch and stumping off Emburey who bowled a containing spell of disciplined accuracy. Both Lloyd and Gomes were out before the close and on the second morning the West Indians added only another twenty-seven. England began badly and became worse. Boycott was devastated by Holding's speed and Gatting made a very brief appearance before being caught at slip off Roberts, once more we had a batsman batting higher for his country than for his county. The stand of 29 for the third wicket between Gooch and Gower was the highest of a dismal innings and by tea on the second day England were a beaten side. That night came the saddest news of a troubled tour; Ken Barrington, assistant manager, kind and gentle man, zestful enthusiast for the game he loved, died of a heart attack in his hotel. The English party and, indeed, the cricket world, was desolated. The world itself had lost a joy. The players lined in tribute and the game began again, as Barrington would have wished, but, inevitably, a vitality had gone from the England players. Gooch was off the field with an injured hand. The lead grew bigger and bigger and Viv Richards, after his lean spell in his first three innings of the series, moved with remorseless power to his century. Lloyd again plundered runs and Richards now looked immovable, particularly as Botham decided to operate unchanged on the fourth morning. England were set to get 523 in ten hours. Their hopes of survival were completely shattered when Boycott received a vicious lifter from Holding which lobbed up to gully. Gatting was bowled first ball. Gooch and Gower then added 120 in good style and growing confidence. Gower was bowled by Richards after tea. The spinner was bowling round the wicket into the rough outside the left-hander's off stump and the ball just floated past Gower as he tried to push out on the off-side. It was an ironic dismissal after playing the pace quartet so well. Butcher and Botham went quickly and England finished the day at 166 for 5. The next morning Gooch completed his second century in Test cricket. It was a splendid innings, full of determination, technical application and a variety of fiercely executed shots of high quality. He was caught in the gully by Garner, a wonderful catch off a full-blooded drive. It was the end of England, but it was an innings that did much to lift morale and to show that the West Indian bowling, like any other, could be hit.

Third Test Match   West Indies v. England
13, 14, 15, 17 and 18 March 1981   **at Bridgetown**

West Indies	*First Innings*		*Second Innings*	
C. G. Greenidge	c Gooch, b Jackman	14	lbw, b Dilley	0
D. L. Haynes	c Bairstow, b Jackman	25	lbw, b Botham	25
I. V. A. Richards	c Botham, b Dilley	0	(4) not out	182
E. H. Mattis	lbw, b Botham	16	(5) c Butcher, b Jackman	24
C. H. Lloyd (capt)	c Gooch, b Jackman	100	(7) lbw, b Botham	66
H. A. Gomes	c Botham, b Dilley	58	(6) run out	34
*D. A. Murray	c Bairstow, b Dilley	9	(9) not out	5
A. M. E. Roberts	c Bairstow, b Botham	14	(8) c Bairstow, b Botham	0
J. Garner	c Bairstow, b Botham	15		
M. A. Holding	c Gatting, b Botham	0		

C. E. H. Croft	not out	0	(3) c Boycott, b Jackman	33
Extras	b 4, lb 6, w 2, nb 2	14	b 3, lb 7	10
		265	(for 7 wkts, dec)	379

	O	M	R	W		O	M	R	W
Dilley	23	7	51	3		25	3	111	1
Botham	25.1	5	77	4		29	5	102	3
Jackman	22	4	65	3		25	5	76	2
Emburey	18	4	45	—		24	7	57	—
Gooch	2	—	13	—					
Willey						6	—	23	—

Fall of Wickets
1–24, 2–25, 3–47, 4–65, 5–219, 6–224, 7–236, 8–258, 9–258.
1–0, 2–57, 3–71, 4–130, 5–212, 6–365, 7–365.

England	*First Innings*		*Second Innings*	
G. A. Gooch	b Garner	26	c Garner, b Croft	116
G. Boycott	b Holding	0	c Garner, b Holding	1
M. W. Gatting	c Greenidge, b Roberts	2	b Holding	0
D. I. Gower	c Mattis, b Croft	17	b Richards	54
R. O. Butcher	c Richards, b Croft	17	lbw, b Richards	2
I. T. Botham (capt)	c Murray, b Holding	26	c Lloyd, b Roberts	1
P. Willey	not out	19	lbw, b Croft	17
*D. L. Bairstow	c Mattis, b Holding	0	c Murray, b Croft	2
J. E. Emburey	c Lloyd, b Roberts	0	b Garner	9
R. D. Jackman	c Roberts, b Croft	7	b Garner	7
G. R. Dilley	c Gomes, b Croft	0	not out	7
Extras	b 1, lb 1, nb 6	8	b 1, lb 3, nb 4	8
		122		224

	O	M	R	W		O	M	R	W
Roberts	11	3	29	2		20	6	42	1
Holding	11	7	16	3		19	6	46	2
Croft	13.5	5	39	4		19	1	65	3
Garner	12	5	30	1		16.2	6	39	2
Richards						17	6	24	2

Fall of Wickets
1–6, 2–11, 3–40, 4–55, 5–72, 6–92, 7–94, 8–97, 9–122.
1–2, 2–2, 3–122, 4–134, 5–139, 6–196, 7–198, 8–201, 9–213.

West Indies won by 298 runs

21, 22, 23 and 24 March 1981   **at Montserrat**
Leeward Islands 161 (A. L. Kelly 72, G. R. Dilley 5 for 48, G. B. Stevenson
5 for 50) and 263 (S. I. Williams 62, V. A. Amory 56)
England XI 252 (G. Miller 91 not out, G. Boycott 72, N. Guishard 4 for 34)
and 174 for 5 (R. O. Butcher 77 not out)
England XI won by 5 wickets

England gained an uneasy, if welcome, win over the weakest opposition of the tour. Botham stood down for the first time so allowing Geoff Miller his first opportunity to lead an England side. Gooch and Gower were also missing so that Athey, Gatting and Butcher were contesting for places in the Test side. Once more the tourists encountered a delayed start and wet weather, but when play got under way Kelly and Amory opened with a stand of 102. It was Stevenson who broke the stand and he and Dilley then routed the remainder of the Islands' batting. Taking his Middlesex place as opener, Downton was out for nought, but Athey joined Boycott in a fine stand of 110 in two and three quarter hours. Athey's technique and form came as a great encouragement to the battle-scarred party. Sadly, there was a collapse, four wickets falling for 14 runs in the twenty minutes before tea. Boycott ran himself out after a good innings and it was left to Miller to save the side. Once more he came tantalisingly close to his maiden century in first-class cricket, but ran out of partners. As a player he remains an enigma. So often he looks a batsman of the very highest quality and a spinner of the very top class, yet his achievement over the years has fallen short of expectations. At the end of the third day, with the home side at 235 for 9 in their second innings, England looked poised for an easy victory. There was unexpected resistance on the last morning and England were set 174 to win, more than expected. Downton, Boycott and Gatting went for 45 and Athey left at 73. Butcher started uneasily, but suddenly hit the ball with that ferocious power he had exhibited against Warwickshire and Yorkshire the previous summer and England had won. It was a startling and breathtaking innings and assured him of retention in the Test side. Athey, too, found a place in the England eleven on the strength of his 41 and 37. Though Athey had shown undoubted promise in his first match, it showed the state of the English batting that he could win a Test place with two such insignificant scores. He replaced Gatting who had lost all confidence and, rightly, Downton, by far the better wicket-keeper, replaced Bairstow. The other change was forced upon England as Jackman was not fully fit. Stevenson came in to the side and one felt that the England attack looked far from formidable. The West Indies were expected to bring Bacchus in to their side, but in the end they fielded the eleven that had won the first two Tests.

Fourth Test Match – West Indies *v.* England

Once more Botham won the toss and this time decided to bat. It was a great and festive occasion for Antigua, joyfully welcoming their first Test match. The ground had been well prepared for the famous occasion and the wicket was good. Boycott and Gooch took advantage of the conditions and Gooch, in particular, seemed keen to continue in his Bridgetown vein.

The morning went well for England and after ninety minutes sixty runs were on the board and the openers in command. Gooch then drove Croft straight and unwisely hurried for a third run. Holding swooped and returned to the bowler and Gooch was run out – a terrible waste. Athey was never at ease and edged Croft to slip and the same bowler accounted for Boycott with a short, lifting delivery on off stump which took the edge and was well caught by Murray in front of slip. Having twice been dropped at slip, Butcher was caught there off Croft and Botham suffered a similar fate. Gower then played loosely at Holding and was taken at fourth slip and England's fine start was now a faded memory as they writhed at 138 for 6. It was now that Willey played his finest innings and justified the faith of the selectors who had persevered with him so long when many of us doubted that he was Test player standard. First with Downton and Emburey and then into second day with Dilley, Willey repaired the England innings and hit with a panache that mocked the tribulations of those who had preceded him. He cut Croft for six, if the shot can be so described, and hooked viciously and safely at anything short. His innings lasted three hours and forty minutes and the West Indian pace attack was mastered. The courageous help he was given by the three batsmen mentioned above made his century possible. When Dilley joined him he had scored only 69, but Dilley stayed for seventy minutes and Willey scored all but three of their last wicket stand of 36. It was a memorable innings. England had an early success when Haynes was brilliantly caught low down to his right by Downton off a Botham out-swinger in the second over. Then came Richards. That the man would hit a Test century on his own ground to mark its use as an international arena for the first time was one of cricket's more predictable happenings. He began in dominant mood, rested a while, then flourished again before easing to his hundred and the acclaim of his countrymen and all who love great batting. It was his first week of married life, his home ground and his fourteenth Test hundred. It took him four hours. He was out off the fourth ball of the third morning. His stop and start tactics had not always been easy to understand, but he had only once come close to being out. He was sensationally caught on the leg-side by Downton off Dilley when he was 32, but a no-ball had been signalled. Suddenly the West Indies slumped to 296 for 7 and England were right back in the game, but the tail wagged fiercely and the lead mounted to 197 before Lloyd declared. The West Indian collapse had seen Botham take three wickets in five balls, but, of the England bowlers, Emburey was in many ways the most impressive and was desperately unlucky to have two easy chances missed. England had a rest day to contemplate their task and then rain made no play possible on the scheduled fourth day. An opening stand of 144 in three hours made England safe. Gooch had a Test hundred within his grasp, but lost concentration against Richards to whom he had dealt some severe blows. He became tied up when Richards floated one at his leg-stump and lofted to Greenidge at mid-on. Athey failed as he had done in the first innings and Gower lost interest when the game was safe, but Boycott passed serenely on to his twentieth Test century, yet another model of application, determination and technique.

Fourth Test Match   West Indies *v.* England
27, 28, 29, 31 March and 1 April 1981   **at Antigua**

England	First Innings		Second Innings	
G. A. Gooch	run out	33	c Greenidge, b Richards	83
G. Boycott	c Murray, b Croft	38	not out	104
C. W. J. Athey	c Lloyd, b Croft	2	c Richards, b Croft	1

D. I. Gower	c Mattis, b Holding	32	c Murray, b Croft	22
R. O. Butcher	c Greenidge, b Croft	20		
I. T. Botham (capt)	c Lloyd, b Croft	1		
P. Willey	not out	102	(5) not out	1
*P. R. Downton	c Murray, b Garner	13		
J. E. Emburey	b Croft	10		
G. B. Stevenson	b Croft	1		
G. R. Dilley	c Murray, b Holding	2		
Extras	b 6, lb 7, w 1, nb 3	17	b 11, lb 3, nb 9	23
		271	(for 3 wkts)	234

	O	M	R	W		O	M	R	W
Roberts	22	4	59	—		17	5	39	—
Holding	18.2	4	51	2		9	2	21	—
Garner	16	5	44	1		15	3	33	—
Croft	25	5	74	6		16	4	39	2
Richards	9	4	26	—		22	7	54	1
Gomes						13	5	21	—
Mattis						1	—	4	—

Fall of Wickets
1–60, 2–70, 3–95, 4–135, 5–138, 6–138, 7–176, 8–233, 9–235.
1–144, 2–146, 3–217.

West Indies

	First Innings	
C. G. Greenidge	c Athey, b Stevenson	63
D. L. Haynes	c Downton, b Botham	4
I. V. A. Richards	c Emburey, b Dilley	114
E. H. Mattis	c Butcher, b Botham	71
H. A. Gomes	c Gower, b Botham	12
C. H. Lloyd (capt)	c Downton, b Stevenson	58
*D. A. Murray	c Boycott, b Botham	1
A. M. E. Roberts	b Stevenson	13
J. Garner	c Butcher, b Dilley	46
M. A. Holding	not out	58
C. E. H. Croft	not out	17
Extras	b 1, lb 7, w 1, nb 2	11
	(for 9 wkts, dec)	468

	O	M	R	W
Dilley	25	5	99	2
Botham	37	6	127	4
Stevenson	33	5	111	3
Emburey	35	12	85	—
Willey	20	8	30	—
Gooch	2	2	0	—
Boycott	3	2	5	—

Fall of Wickets
1–12, 2–133, 3–241, 4–268, 5–269, 6–271, 7–296, 8–379, 9–401.

Match drawn

4, 5, 6 and 7 April 1981   **at Kingston**
England XI 413 (G. Boycott 98, M. W. Gatting 93) and 294 for 8 (G. A. Gooch
    122, R. O. Butcher 51, E. H. Mattis 4 for 22)
Jamaica 368 (L. G. Rowe 116, M. Neita 67, R. B. Austin 62, J. E. Emburey
    6 for 92)
Match drawn

The Test arena at Sabina Park was in a state of semi-construction which should
have at least made the England party feel at home. Miller withdrew from the
side with influenza on the morning of the match. Since being appointed vice-
captain he had been little more than a shadowy figure on the tour. Downton
also was unwell for part of the match and Old retired on the second day with
torn thigh muscles. As Boycott, with laryngitis, and Emburey were indisposed,
England at one time fielded four substitutes. The batting was positive and
Gatting ended his miserable spell with a fine knock which, as Athey again
failed, seemed destined to win him back his Test place. Boycott and Gooch
began brightly and Boycott again demonstrated his tenacity of perpetual
application. The finest batting, however, came from Rowe. The Jamaican
captain batted in a manner that has been equalled only by Richards among
his contemporaries. Elegance, power and authority were all his and it is a
great sadness that this batsman, undeniably one of the world's greatest, has
been plagued by so many misfortunes that his true worth remains unrecognised
outside the West Indies. Emburey's off-spin bowled England to a first innings
lead and then Gooch savaged the home attack for his third century of the tour.
The ball was turning appreciably, but Gooch was fierce in his treatment of
spin and pace. Gatting and Butcher played minor innings of worth, but Athey
laboured and Botham, having opted for practice rather than for a chance of
forcing victory, was out for 14, one of the four men to fall to Mattis. Botham's
position as leader was once more brought under scrutiny and he was subjected
to the most severe criticism. The trouble for Botham had begun when Hendrick
declined to make the tour. Many believed that the Derbyshire bowler was
unwilling to serve any longer under Botham. There had certainly been strain
between them during the Centenary Test at Lord's. On the eve of the tour
Boycott had asserted on television that Botham had never sought his advice
and the England captain's dictatorial and tactless attitude had certainly lost him
some friends. As a strategist he was weak and he had earned the reputation of
being non-appreciative and having favourites. Above all he tried to take too
much on himself at a time when his own ability was in question. The terrible
loss of Ken Barrington had left its mark on Botham and the party and the
England captain had faced a difficult time since then with courage and honesty.
He had learned much, but whether he had the sagacity to reshape his captaincy
from that learning and to rekindle his own performance to its former glories
while burdened by the leadership remained a most debatable question.

Fifth Test Match – West Indies *v.* England

In spite of Gatting's sparkling display against Jamaica, Athey was retained in
the England side which showed only one change from the Fourth Test, Jackman,

fit again, for Stevenson. The West Indies, unwilling to be caught in the sentiment that had permeated English selections for a couple of years, brought in Marshall to replace Roberts whose Test career was obviously drawing to a close. It was their first change of the series. Lloyd won the toss and asked England to bat. Gooch and Boycott countered his decision with a fine opening stand. They put on 93 before Boycott fell to a Garner outswinger. Athey stayed for fifty minutes and scored three out of a stand of 55. Gooch was totally dominant as he played the finest attacking innings that an English batsman has played in a Test match for many a series. It was glorious stuff. His fifty came with a six over third man. Croft, who had been the scourge of the England batsmen throughout the series, was savaged mercilessly as Gooch rocked onto the back foot and drove him fiercely through the off-side or hit him straight. He straight drove Holding for four to reach his hundred out of 155. When Gower lost his leg-stump just before tea England were 196 for 3 and Gooch was 124. He was finally out for 153 when he attempted to drive Holding and got an inside edge which Murray, who did not have one of his best games, took very low down, one-handed, far to his left. Gooch's innings was the best of the series and the most heartening thing that happened to English cricket during the whole of the tour. For a moment it seemed as though England might reach a total which would give them a chance of victory, but Butcher, after promising much, left his leg-stump unguarded and on the second morning Holding, bowling at a fearsome pace, removed the last three batsmen while only seven runs were scored. After the magnificence of Gooch it was bitterly disappointing. Jackman, who had been booed to the wicket, bowled tidily and Dilley strove hard, but the England attack posed few problems to the openers who allied solidity to aggression. Richards did not last long and once more Mattis promised more than he achieved, but any hopes that England had of bowling themselves back in to the game were shattered by Lloyd and Gomes. The form of Lloyd in all the Tests had been quite remarkable. He had shuffled from the field at The Oval with a muscle injury and many believed he had played his last Test, but here he was batting as well as ever and displaying vastly improved captaincy. His first fifty contained ten fours and it is a testimony to his splendour that his lowest score in the series was 64. England had not really expected to encounter him in this mood. Gomes, slim and graceful, hit straight and hard and was most unlucky to be denied a century. He is the most self-effacing of the West Indian batsmen, but he is a lovely cricketer and a young man of charm. The charm and shyness combine in his batting. West Indies were all out at the end of the third day and England had a rest day in which to lick their wounds.

England could not have begun their efforts at salvation in a more depressing way on the fourth morning. Gooch was taken at first slip. Poor Athey, totally out of his depth, a boy among men, was caught behind. Boycott took a lifter on the glove and the ball looped up to Garner in the gully. In twelve overs England were 32 for 3. Willey, ruggedly and determinedly, and Gower, with lazy elegance, repaired the situation and stayed until rain brought play to an early close. England began the last day at 134 for 3 and Willey and Gower continued their resistance. Willey surprisingly fell to Richards after a most commendable innings. Butcher was lbw without playing a shot and Botham was mightily lucky to escape the same fate. West Indies scented victory when Botham was caught in the gully immediately after lunch, but Downton played with great courage and stayed with Gower throughout the afternoon. Having often thrown away his wicket when seemingly set for a good score, Gower did not allow his concentration to waver for a second and his century ensured England of safety. It was an innings of grit and grace and he became the third Englishman in the series to cut a six. So England had only lost two–nil, but the gap between the sides often looked far wider than that. There were some terrible holes in the England side, some technical, some psychological. The biggest void of all was at number three where only 24 runs were scored. It was a sad tour in many ways, but sadness should be a teacher.

Fifth Test Match   West Indies *v.* England
10, 11, 12, 14 and 15 April 1981   **at Kingston**

England	First Innings		Second Innings	
G. A. Gooch	c Murray, b Holding	153	c Lloyd, b Marshall	3
G. Boycott	c Murray, b Garner	40	c Garner, b Croft	12
C. W. J. Athey	b Holding	3	c Murray, b Holding	1
D. I. Gower	b Croft	22	not out	154
P. Willey	c Murray, b Marshall	4	c Greenidge, b Richards	67
R. O. Butcher	b Garner	32	lbw, b Croft	0
I. T. Botham (capt)	c Greenidge, b Marshall	13	c Garner, b Holding	16
*P. R. Downton	c Croft, b Holding	0	not out	26
J. E. Emburey	b Holding	1		
R. D. Jackman	c Haynes, b Holding	0		
G. R. Dilley	not out	1		
Extras	b 8, nb 8	16	b 6, lb 13, nb 4	23
		285	(for 6 wkts)	302

	O	M	R	W		O	M	R	W
Holding	18	3	56	5		28	7	58	2
Marshall	16	2	49	2		5	—	15	1
Croft	17	4	92	1		29	7	80	2
Garner	20	4	43	2		24	7	46	—
Richards	12	2	29	—		23	8	48	1
Gomes						13	3	18	—
Mattis						5	1	10	—
Haynes						1	—	4	—

Fall of Wickets
1–93, 2–148, 3–196, 4–210, 5–249, 6–275, 7–283, 8–283, 9–284.
1–5, 2–10, 3–32, 4–168, 5–168, 6–215.

West Indies	First Innings	
C. G. Greenidge	c Botham, b Dilley	62
D. L. Haynes	b Willey	84
I. V. A. Richards	c Downton, b Dilley	15
E. H. Mattis	c sub (Gatting), b Dilley	34
C. H. Lloyd (capt)	c Downton, b Jackman	95
H. A. Gomes	not out	90

*D. A. Murray	c Gooch, b Emburey	14
M. D. Marshall	b Emburey	15
J. Garner	c sub (Bairstow), b Dilley	19
M. A. Holding	c Downton, b Botham	0
C. E. H. Croft	c sub (Gatting), b Botham	0
Extras	lb 8, w 1, nb 5	14
		442

	O	M	R	W
Dilley	29.4	6	116	4
Botham	26.1	9	73	2
Jackman	26.2	6	57	1
Gooch	8	3	20	—
Emburey	56	23	108	2
Willey	18	3	54	1

Fall of Wickets
1–116, 2–136, 3–179, 4–227, 5–345, 6–372, 7–415, 8–441, 9–442.

Match drawn

West Indies *v.* England – Test Match Averages
West Indies Batting

	M	Inns	Nos	Runs	HS	Average	100s	50s
I. V. A. Richards	4	5	1	340	182*	85.00	2	
C. H. Lloyd	4	5		383	100	76.60	1	4
H. A. Gomes	4	5	1	199	90*	49.75		2
D. L. Haynes	4	5		234	96	46.80		2
C. G. Greenidge	4	5		223	84	44.60		3
E. H. Mattis	4	5		145	71	29.00		1
M. A. Holding	4	4	1	84	58*	28.00		1
A. M. E. Roberts	3	4	1	77	50*	25.66		1
J. Garner	4	4		84	46*	21.00		
D. A. Murray	4	5	1	75	46	18.75		
C. E. H. Croft	4	5	2	54	33	18.00		

Also batted: M. D. Marshall 15 (one Test).

West Indies Bowling

	Overs	Mdns	Runs	Wkts	Average	Best	5/inn
M. A. Holding	132.2	38	315	17	18.52	5–56	1
C. E. H. Croft	158.5	37	455	24	18.96	6–74	2
J. Garner	151.2	48	303	10	30.30	2–31	
A. M. E. Roberts	104	28	251	8	31.38	3–41	
I. V. A. Richards	100	35	206	5	41.20	2–24	
H. A. Gomes	37	13	57	1	57.00	1–4	

Also bowled: M. D. Marshall 21–2–64–3 (one Test); D. L. Haynes 1–0–4–0 (one Test); E. H. Mattis 6–1–14–0 (two Tests).

West Indies Catches
13 – D. A. Murray; 7 – C. H. Lloyd; 6 – C. G. Greenidge; 4 – J. Garner; 3 – I. V. A. Richards, D. L. Haynes and E. H. Mattis; 1 – M. A. Holding, A. M. E. Roberts, H. A. Gomes, C. E. H. Croft and sub (S. F. A. Bacchus).

England Batting

	M	Inns	Nos	Runs	HS	Average	100s	50s
G. A. Gooch	4	8		460	153	57.50	2	1
D. I. Gower	4	8	1	376	154*	53.71	1	1
P. Willey	4	8	3	244	102	48.40	1	1
G. Boycott	4	8	1	295	104*	42.14	1	1
R. O. Butcher	3	5		71	32	14.20		
P. R. Downton	3	5	1	48	26*	12.00		
I. T. Botham	4	7		73	26	10.42		
J. E. Emburey	4	6	1	38	17*	7.60		
R. D. Jackman	2	3		14	7	4.66		
G. R. Dilley	4	6	3	11	7*	3.66		
C. W. J. Athey	2	4		7	3	1.75		

Played in one Test: B. C. Rose 10 and 5; M. W. Gatting 2 and 0; D. L. Bairstow 0 and 2; G. Miller 3 and 8; C. M. Old 1 and 0; G. B. Stevenson 1.

England Bowling

	Overs	Mdns	Runs	Wkts	Average	Best	5/inn
I. T. Botham	145.2	31	492	15	32.80	4–77	
R. D. Jackman	73.2	15	198	6	33.00	3–65	
G. R. Dilley	130.4	25	450	10	45.00	4–116	
J. E. Emburey	185	62	419	7	59.86	5–124	1
P. Willey	47	12	111	1	111.00	1–54	

Also bowled: C. M. Old 16–3–49–1; G. Miller, 18–4–42–1; G. B. Stevenson 33–5–111–3; G. Boycott 3–2–5–0 (all bowled in one Test); G. A. Gooch 14–5–36–0 (four Tests).

England Catches

6 – P. R. Downton and D. L. Bairstow (inc. one as sub); 5 – I. T. Botham; 3 – R. O. Butcher, G. A. Gooch and M. W. Gatting (inc. two as sub); 2 – D. I. Gower, J. E. Emburey and G. Boycott; 1 – G. Miller and C. W. J. Athey.

England in West Indies, 1981
First-Class Matches – Batting

	v. President's Young West Indies XI (at Point-à-Pierre) 23–26 Jan.		v. Trinidad (Port of Spain) 7–10 February		First Test Match (Port of Spain) 13–18 February		v. Barbados (Bridgetown) 7–10 March		Third Test Match (Bridgetown) 13–18 March		v. Leeward Islands (Montserrat) 21–24 March	
G. Boycott	87	87	70	—	30	70	77	13	0	1	72	15
B. C. Rose	0	43	11	—	10	5						
D. I. Gower	187	—	77	—	48	27	18	44	17	54		
M. W. Gatting	94	—					11	22	2	0	4	0
R. O. Butcher	42	20*					43	32	17	2	5	77*
I. T. Botham	11	33	0	—	0	16	40	0	26	1		
P. Willey	16*	10	28	—	13	21	51	34*	19*	17		
D. L. Bairstow		0					22	26*	0	2	0	14*
G. Miller	12*	4*	19	—	3	8					91*	14
C. M. Old		—			1	0					4	
G. R. Dilley		—	15*	—	0	1*			0	7*	0	—
G. A. Gooch			117	—	41	5	18	29	26	116		
P. R. Downton			10	—	4	5					0	9
J. E. Emburey			1	—	17*	1	0*	—	0	9		
G. B. Stevenson			0	—			2	—			3	—
R. D. Jackman							5	—	7	7	17	—
C. W. J. Athey											41	37
Byes	7		4		4	1	2	9	1	1	6	5
Leg-byes	7	5	2		4	3	2	9	1	3	3	1
Wides	2	3	1								1	
No-balls	18	3			3	6	7	1	6	4	4	2
Total	483	208	355		178	169	298	219	122	224	251	174
Wickets	6	5	10		10	10	10	6	10	10	10	5
Result	W		D		L		D		L		W	

† P. R. Downton, absent ill.

Catches

14 – P. R. Downton (ct 11, st 3)
10 – D. L. Bairstow (ct 9, st 1)
 8 – I. T. Botham
 7 – R. O. Butcher
 5 – C. M. Old
 4 – G. Miller, D. I. Gower, G. A. Gooch and substitutes
 3 – M. W. Gatting and J. E. Emburey
 2 – G. Boycott
 1 – G. B. Stevenson and C. W. J. Athey

Fourth Test Match (Antigua) 27 March–1 April		v. Jamaica (Kingston) 4–7 April		Fifth Test Match (Kingston) 10–15 April		Inns	NOs	Runs	HS	Av
38	104*	98	4*	40	12	17	2	818	104*	54.53
						5	—	69	43	13.80
32	22	24	0	22	154*	14	1	726	187	55.84
		93	42			9	—	268	94	29.77
20	—	44	51	32	0	13	2	385	77*	35.00
1	—	26	14	13	16	14	—	197	40	14.07
102*	1*			4	67	13	5	383	102*	47.87
						7	2	64	26*	12.80
						7	3	151	91*	37.75
		8	—			4	—	13	8	3.25
2	—			1*	—	8	4	26	15*	6.50
33	83	31	122	153	3	13	—	777	153	59.76
13	—	—	0	0	26*	9	1	67	26*	8.37
10	—	34	1	1	—	10	2	74	34	9.25
1	—					4	—	6	3	1.50
		0*	11*	0	—	7	2	47	17	9.40
2	1	11	25	3	1	8	—	121	41	15.12
6	11	8	16	8	6					
7	3	21	4		13					
1			1							
3	9	14	4	8	4					
271	234	413	294	285	302					
10	3	9†	8	10	6					
D		D		D						

England in West Indies, 1981 First-Class Matches – Bowling	G. R. Dilley	C. M. Old	I. T. Botham	G. Miller	P. Willey	J. E. Emburey
v. President's Young West Indies XI (Point-à-Pierre) 23–26 Jan.	22–1–104–1 10–3–18–0	13.3–4–34–1 4–0–27–0	12–0–43–3 4–0–21–0	26–8–69–3 26.2–9–70–6	16–3–54–1 17–6–29–3	
v. Trinidad and Tobago (Port of Spain) 7–10 Feb.	21–8–63–1		16–4–44–2	25–6–65–1	20–3–61–2	32–11–72–0
First Test Match (Port of Spain) 13–18 Feb.	28–4–73–0	16–3–49–1	28–6–113–2	18–4–42–1	3–1–4–0	52–16–124–5
v. Barbados (Bridgetown) 7–10 March			24–6–79–1		10–4–14–0	49.4–13–92–5
Third Test Match (Bridgetown) 13–18 Mar.	23–7–51–3 25–3–111–1		25.1–5–77–4 29–5–102–3		6–0–23–0	18–4–45–0 24–7–57–0
v. Leeward Islands (Montserrat) 21–24 March	13.4–2–48–5 16–5–50–3	5–2–18–0 18–3–60–3		2–0–11–0 12–2–42–3		
Fourth Test Match (Antigua) 27 March–1 April	25–5–99–2		37–6–127–4		21–7–31–0	34–12–84–0
v. Jamaica (Kingston) 4–7 April		6–1–20–0	23–2–111–2			34–9–92–6
Fifth Test Match (Kingston) 10–15 April	29.4–6–116–4		26.1–9–73–2		18–3–54–1	56–23–108–2
	213.2–44– 733–20 av. 36.65	62.3–13– 208–5 av. 41.60	224.2–43– 790–23 av. 34.34	109.2–29– 299–14 av. 21.35	111–27– 270–7 av. 38.57	299.4–95– 674–18 av. 37.44

G. B. Stevenson	G. A. Gooch	R. D. Jackman	G. Boycott	M. W. Gatting	B	Lb	W	Nb	Total	Wkts
					7	4		5	320	10
					8	4		4	181	10
7–4–46–1	12–6–14–1				2	13		12	392	8
	2–0–3–0					15		3	426	9
3–2–66–0		25–6–68–4			2	8	1	4	334	10
	2–0–13–0	22–4–65–3			4	6	2	2	265	10
		25–5–76–2			3	7			379	7
5–5–50–5		5–0–22–0			2	4		6	161	10
1–1–64–0		12–2–35–1				6		6	263	10
33–5–111–3	2–2–0–0		3–2–5–0		1	7	1	2	468	9
	16–3–58–0	21–6–57–1		3–1–10–0	1	3		16	368	10
	8–3–20–0	26.2–6–57–1				8	1	5	442	10
89–17–	42–14–	136.2–29–	3–2–	3–1–						
337–9	108–1	380–12	5–0	10–0						
av. 37.44	av. 108.00	av. 31.66	—	—						

England in West Indies, 1981 One-day Matches – Batting	v. Windward Islands (St Vincent) 1 February	v. Windward Islands (St Vincent) 2 February	First One-Day International (St Vincent) 4 February	Second One-Day International (Berbice) 26 February	v. Barbados (Bridgetown) 5 March	Inns	NOs	Runs	HS	Av
G. A. Gooch	13	50	11	11	84	5	—	169	84	33.80
B. C. Rose	1	3				2	—	4	3	2.00
R. O. Butcher	44	—	1	5	9	4	—	59	44	14.75
I. T. Botham	31	—	60	27	12	4	—	130	60	32.50
D. I. Gower	14	6	23	3	39	5	—	85	39	17.00
M. W. Gatting	16		3	29	25	4	—	73	29	18.25
G. B. Stevenson	0	19*	6*	8*	—	4	3	33	19*	33.00
P. R. Downton	23*					1	1	23	23*	—
J. E. Emburey	3	—	5	0	—	3	—	8	5	2.66
G. R. Dilley	7			3		2	—	10	7	5.00
R. G. D. Willis	0*					1	1	0	0*	—
G. Boycott		85*	2	7	14	4	1	108	85*	36.00
P. Willey		11	0	21	1*	4	1	33	21	11.00
D. L. Bairstow		—	5	16	6*	3	1	27	16	13.50
C. M. Old		—	1		—	1	—	1	1	1.00
Byes	5	1		4	5					
Leg-byes		2	8	2	11					
Wides	1	1								
No-balls	8	6		1	1					
Total	166	184	125	137	207					
Wickets	9	4	10	10	6					
Result	W	W	L	L	W					

Catches

4 – I. T. Botham and G. A. Gooch

2 – D. L. Bairstow (ct 1, st 1), P. Willey, J. E. Emburey and G. B. Stevenson

1 – D. I. Gower, B. C. Rose, C. M. Old, M. W. Gatting and sub.

England in West Indies, 1981 One-day Matches – Bowling

	R. G. D. Willis	G. R. Dilley	G. B. Stevenson	I. T. Botham	G. A. Gooch	J. E. Emburey	C. M. Old	P. Willey	D. I. Gower
v. Windward Islands (St Vincent) 1 Feb.	7-0-30-1	8-0-28-3	8-1-22-1	8-0-30-3	1-0-2-1	8-1-18-0			
v. Windward Islands (St Vincent) 2 Feb.			9.2-0-25-1	7-1-21-1	6-1-23-3	11-0-41-0	9-0-34-2	11-1-23-1	
First One-Day International (St Vincent) 4 Feb.			8.2-2-18-2	8-1-32-1	6-1-12-2	10-4-20-1	5-4-8-1	10-1-29-1	
Second One-Day International (Berbice) 26 Feb.		5-0-21-1	6-0-21-0	7-1-24-0	2-0-8-0	10-4-22-2		9-0-23-0	0.3-0-5-0
v. Barbados (Bridgetown) 5 Mar.			10-2-38-4	10-2-30-4	6-0-31-0	9-2-40-0	5.3-0-29-1	9-3-23-1	
	7-0- 30-1 av. 30.00	13-0- 49-4 av. 12.25	41.4-5- 124-8 av. 15.50	40-5- 137-9 av. 15.2;	21-2- 76-6 av. 12.66	48-11- 141-3 av. 47.00	19.3-4- 71-4 av. 17.75	39-5- 98-3 av. 32.66	0.3-0- 5-0 —

	B	Lb	W	Nb	Total	Wkts
v. Windward Islands (St Vincent) 1 Feb.	1	8	1	10	150	9
v. Windward Islands (St Vincent) 2 Feb.	3	8		5	183	10
First One-Day International (St Vincent) 4 Feb.		4	1	3	127	10
Second One-Day International (Berbice) 26 Feb.	4	8		2	138	4
v. Barbados (Bridgetown) 5 Mar.		3		2	196	10

The king in his kingdom. (left) Viv Richards in action in the Test in Barbados and (right) surveying his kindom in the Benson and Hedges Final at Lord's.

Robin Jackman claims his first Test wicket. Greenidge caught Gooch (Third Test, Barbados).

H

Calypso Cricket

The West Indian Domestic Season
The Shell Shield and the Geddes Grant/
Harrison Line Limited Over Cup

The collation of scores from the West Indies is not the easiest of tasks and the editor is greatly indebted once more to the work of CLAYTON GOODWIN, Caribbean and Commonwealth News Service, and BERNARD PANTIN, Trinidad and Tobago Television.

Shell Shield Competition

10, 11, 12 and 13 January   **at Chedwin Park, Jamaica**
Trinidad and Tobago 365 (D. L. Murray 82, A. Logie 56, A. G. Burns 53, A. Rajah 50, M. A. Holding 5 for 96)
Jamaica 200 (E. H. Mattis 56, A. Daniel 4 for 62) and 189 for 2 (R. A. Austin 87 not out, E. H. Mattis 71)
Match drawn
Trinidad and Tobago 20 pts, Jamaica 6 pts

17, 18, 19 and 20 January   **at Kensington Oval, Barbados**
Guyana 184 (S. T. Clarke 4 for 46) and 108 (M. Harper 52, H. L. Alleyne 4 for 27)
Barbados 552 for 7 dec (D. L. Haynes 160, L. N. Reifer 153 not out, E. Trotman 94, T. R. O. Payne 53)
Barbados won by an innings and 260 runs
Barbados 27 pts, Guyana 3 pts

                       at Queen's Park Oval, Trinidad
Combined Islands 317 (I. V. A. Richards 168 not out, H. Joseph 6 for 105) and 170 for 4 dec (A. L. Kelly 53, E. E. Lewis 53 not out)
Trinidad and Tobago 172 (H. A. Gomes 68 not out, A. M. E. Roberts 6 for 38) and 143 for 2 (K. Bainey 55)
Match drawn
Combined Islands 17 pts, Trinidad 5 pts

23, 24, 25 and 26 January   **at Warner Park, St Kitts**
Jamaica 167 (L. G. Rowe 76, A. M. E. Roberts 7 for 30) and 218 (M. Neita 90, A. M. E. Roberts 4 for 71)
Combined Islands 481 (I. V. A. Richards 106, D. R. Parry 92, A. L. Kelly 84, A. Barrett 5 for 81)
Combined Islands won by an innings and 96 runs
Combined Islands 32 pts, Jamaica 3 pts

                            at Bourda, Guyana
Guyana 439 (A. I. Kallicharran 184, C. H. Lloyd 144, R. R. Jumadeen 4 for 137) and 123 for 2 (T. Etwaroo 69)
Trinidad and Tobago 338 for 9 dec (T. Cuffy 88, A. Logie 64)
Match drawn
Guyana 15 pts, Trinidad and Tobago 11 pts

30 and 31 January, 1 and 2 February   **at Albion Ground, Berbice**
Jamaica 307 (E. H. Mattis 92, H. S. Chang 53, L. G. Rowe 51, C. E. H. Croft 7 for 64) and 183 for 5 (E. H. Mattis 64, L. G. Rowe 58 not out)

Guyana 296 (C. H. Lloyd 117 not out, M. A. Holding 4 for 80)
Match drawn

at Queen's Park Oval, Trinidad
Barbados 234 (G. Reifer 53, R. Nanan 5 for 65) and 169 (A. T. Greenidge
74 not out)
Trinidad and Tobago 357 (A. Logie 125, J. Garner 4 for 68, S. T. Clarke 4
for 68) and 48 for 2
Trinidad and Tobago won by 8 wickets
Trinidad and Tobago 25 pts, Barbados 3 pts

7, 8, 9 and 10 February **at St George's, Grenada**
Combined Islands 196 (I. T. Shillingford 63, R. Joseph 4 for 49) and 293 for
8 dec (A. M. E. Roberts 63, A. L. Kelly 59, C. Butts 5 for 71)
Guyana 96 and 228 (S. F. A. Bacchus 86, A. M. E. Roberts 4 for 22)
Combined Islands won by 165 runs
Combined Islands 22 pts, Guyana 5 pts

at Chedwin Park, Jamaica
Jamaica 263 (J. Dujon 135 not out, R. A. Austin 50, M. D. Marshall 6 for
75) and 264 for 4 dec (M. Neita 56 not out)
Barbados 196 and 176 for 5 (C. G. Greenidge 82, D. Malcolm 4 for 53)
Match drawn
Jamaica 8 pts, Barbados 6 pts

21, 22, 23 and 24 February **at Kensington Oval, Barbados**
Combined Islands 139 (W. W. Daniel 4 for 38) and 236 (D. R. Parry 55)
Barbados 391 (E. Trotman 167, D. A. Murray 92, N. Guishard 4 for 101)
Barbados won by an innings and 16 runs
Barbados 26 pts, Combined Islands 3 pts

Combined Islands won the Shell Shield for the first time with a total of 74 points,
Barbados were second with 62, one point ahead of Trinidad and Tobago.

Geddes Grant/Harrison Line Limited Over Competition

7 January **at Alpart Club, Jamaica**
Jamaica 158 (J. Dujon 53)
Trinidad and Tobago 148 for 8 (A. Logie 50)
Trinidad and Tobago won on faster run rate

11 January **at Arnos Vale, St Vincent**
Guyana 161 for 8 (K. Hobson 4 for 41)
Windward Islands 118 for 7
Guyana won by 43 runs

14 January   **at Kensington Oval, Barbados**
Guyana 176 (S. F. A. Bacchus 56)
Barbados 178 for 4 (D. L. Haynes 73 not out)
Barbados won by 6 wickets

7 March   **at Queen's Park Oval, Trinidad**
Leeward Islands 156 for 9 (A. G. Burns 4 for 30)
Trinidad and Tobago 160 for 5 (R. S. Gabriel 57)
Trinidad and Tobago won by 5 wickets

21 March   **at Queen's Park, Grenada**
Windward Islands 187 (L. John 50)
Barbados 188 for 9 (T. R. O. Payne 67, A. T. Greenidge 58)
Barbados won by 1 wicket

Winners of Group A (Barbados) met Winners of Group B (Trinidad and Tobago) in the Final at Kensington Oval, Barbados on 25 April.

Barbados 127 (D. A. Murray 30 not out, W. W. Daniel 34 put on 58 for the last wicket, H. Joseph 10–5–7–3)
Trinidad and Tobago 129 for 6 (R. S. Gabriel 47, D. L. Murray 36, A Padmore 3 for 24)
Trinidad and Tobago won by 4 wickets
Man of the Match – H. Joseph

In their final year as a united team, Combined Islands won the Shell Shield for the first time. Next year they compete as Windward Islands and Leeward Islands. Viv Richards led by example, hitting centuries in the first two Shield matches and handling the side well, but the major contribution to the team's success came from Andy Roberts. Roberts has not always given a hundred per cent in Shield matches, but the loss of his place in the West Indian side spurred him to great efforts. Wicket-keeper Ignatious Cadette, opening bat Luther Kelly and all-rounder Derek Parry made useful contributions in a good team victory, but, perhaps, the most acclaim should go to Irving Shillingford who has been playing Shell Shield cricket for 15 years and for whom this triumph was particularly gratifying. Barbados were a pale copy of the side that won the Shield so convincingly the previous season though they did overwhelm Combined Islands in the last match. Their fast bowlers were still a force, but their middle order batting in particular was weak and they were in a mist against the spin of Trinidad. Trinidad were unbeaten and though they lacked power in all departments, they unearthed the sensation of the season in Harold Joseph, a mystery spinner, named the 'new Ramadhin'. The diminutive Augustine Logie was the best of their batsmen. Jamaica once more failed to play to their potential. Mattis and wicket-keeper Dujon batted well, but only Holding and 36-year-old leg-spinner Arthur Barrett, returning to the side after an absence of three years, were effective with the ball. In spite of the fine performances of Lloyd, Alvin Kallicharran and Croft, Guyana struggled for another season. There was encouragement in the performance of new off-spinner Clive Butts, but young Roger Harper fell away somewhat.

Barbados
Shell Shield – Batting
1981

	v. Guyana (Kensington Oval) 17–20 January	v. Trinidad and Tobago (Queen's Park Oval) 30 January–2 February		v. Jamaica (Chedwin Park) 7–10 February		v. Combined Islands (Kensington Oval) 21–24 February	Inns	NOs	Runs	HS	Av
D. L. Haynes	160	32	4	34	43	31	6	—	304	160	50.66
A. T. Greenidge	4	46	74*	10	0		5	1	134	74*	33.50
T. R. O. Payne	53	5	7	6	0	22	6	—	93	53	15.50
E. Trotman	94	0	20			167	4	—	281	167	70.25
C. L. King	1	26	22	1			4	—	50	26	12.50
L. N. Reifer	153*	1	9	4	41	19	6	1	227	153*	45.40
D. A. Murray	32			17	1*	92	4	1	142	92	47.33
M. D. Marshall	33	48	1	49*		6	5	1	137	49*	34.25
S. T. Clarke	15*	7	3			1	4	1	26	15*	8.66
A. L. Padmore		5	18	39		1*	4	1	63	39	21.00
H. L. Alleyne				0		11	2	—	11	11	5.50
J. Garner		6*	5				2	1	11	6	5.50
G. Reifer		53	0				2	—	53	53	26.50
C. G. Greenidge				8	82	18	3	—	108	82	36.00
T. F. Foster				15	1*		2	1	16	15	16.00
W. W. Daniel						9	1	—	9	9	9.00
Byes	2	1		2		4					
Leg byes	5	3		6	5	5					
Wides		1			1						
No balls				5	2						
Total	552	234	169	196	176	391					
Wickets	7	10	10	10	5	10					
Result	W		L		D	W					
Points	27		3		6	26					

Catches

8 – D. A. Murray
6 – L. Reifer
5 – T. R. O. Payne
4 – A. L. Padmore
3 – C. G. Greenidge
2 – M. D. Marshall, D. L. Haynes, T. F. Foster, S. T. Clarke and E. Trotman (one as sub)
1 – C. L. King, H. L. Alleyne and A. T. Greenidge

Barbados
Shell Shield –
Bowling
1981

	H. L. Alleyne	S. T. Clarke	M. D. Marshall	A. L. Padmore	C. L. King	J. Garner	T. F. Foster	W. W. Daniel	B	Lb	W	Nb	Total	Wkts
Guyana (Kensington Oval) 7–20 January / 17–20 January	12–2–49–2	17–4–46–4	13–3–39–2	7.2–4–15–2	3–1–6–0				6	3	1	19	184	10
	9.4–2–27–4	12–3–28–1	14–4–24–3	12–3–19–1						8		2	108	9†
Trinidad and Tobago (Queen's Park Oval) 30 January–2 February		23.2–7–68–4	16–4–40–0	40–5–120–2	10–4–22–0	40–9–68–4			3	12		24	357	10
		8.5–1–31–1				9–2–13–0			3			1	48	2
Jamaica (Chedwin Park) 7–10 February	27–7–65–1		27.1–8–75–6	41–7–85–3	10–5–10–0		9–1–23–0			2		3	263	10
	20–4–51–1		17–2–49–1	24–3–69–1	1–0–10–0		27–6–73–1		4	5		3	264	4
Combined Islands (Kensington Oval) 21–24 February	7–1–23–1	12.3–4–40–2	9–1–29–3					10–2–38–4		1		8	139	10
	8–1–35–2	15–3–64–2	15.5–3–52–2	6–1–12–1				11–2–48–1		15		10	236	10
	83.4–17	88.4–22	112–25	130.2–23	24–10	49–11	36–7	21–4						
	250–11	277–14	308–17	320–10	48–0	81–4	96–1	86–5						
	av. 22.72	av. 19.78	av. 18.11	av. 32.00	—	av. 20.25	av. 96.00	av. 17.20						

†T. Etwaroo, absent injured

Combined Islands
Shell Shield – Batting
1981

	v. Trinidad and Tobago (Queen's Park Oval) 17–20 January		v. Jamaica (Warner Park) 23–26 January	v. Guyana (Grenada) 7–10 February		v. Barbados (Kensington Oval) 21–24 February		Inns	NOs	Runs	HS	Av
A. L. Kelly	30	53	84	20	59	6	30	7	—	282	84	40.28
L. John	4	26	1					3	—	31	26	10.33
E. E. Lewis	18	53	26	7	48	1	25	7	—	178	53	25.42
J. C. Allen	12	6	81					3	—	99	81	33.00
I. V. A. Richards	168*	1	106	14	17	4	13	7	1	323	168*	53.83
I. T. Shillingford	29			63	43	8	4	5	—	147	63	29.40
S. Williams	13		22	19	13	37	26	6	1	131	37	26.20
D. R. Parry	13		92	21	2	18*	55	6	1	201	92	40.20
A. M. E. Roberts	23		1	0	63	5	4	6	—	96	63	16.00
W. Davis	1			16*		9	2*	5	2	43	16*	14.33
J. Harris	3							1	—	3	3	3.00
N. Guishard		23	15	20	32*			6	1	75	32*	15.00
U. V. C. Lawrence			12					1	—	12	12	12.00
I. Cadette			14*	0		26	33	4	1	73	33	24.33
V. Amory				6	6	15	19	4	—	46	19	11.50
Byes	1	1	10	2	3	1	15					
Leg byes	2	7	7	3	2							
Wides			1		1							
No balls			10	4	4	8	10					
Total	317	170	481	196	293	139	236					
Wickets	10	4	10	10	8	10	10					
Result	D		W	W		L						
Points	17		32	22		3						

Catches

6 – N. Guishard
5 – E. E. Lewis and I. Cadette
4 – A. M. E. Roberts and I. T. Shillingford
3 – J. C. Allen and D. R. Parry
2 – A. L. Kelly, L. John and I. V. A. Richards
1 – U. V. C. Lawrence

Combined Islands
Shell Shield –
Bowling
[19]81

	A. M. E. Roberts	W. Davis	J. Harris	D. R. Parry	I. V. A. Richards	J. C. Allen
Trinidad and Tobago (Queen's Park Oval) 17–20 January	19–6–38–6	12–1–47–2	10–3–27–0	27.3–10–50–2	2–2–0–0	
	4–0–9–0	10–2–29–0	8–2–22–0	21–3–48–2	13–4–26–0	2–1–1–0
Jamaica (Warner Park) 3–26 January	16.2–5–30–7	6–1–35–0		11–4–33–1		
	17–3–71–4	11–1–36–1		27.4–4–50–3	5–1–20–0	
Guyana (Grenada) –10 February	13–3–25–3	12–5–16–3		14–4–27–0	8.1–5–4–2	
	18.5–6–22–4	13–1–62–0		24–9–57–2	12–2–28–0	
Barbados (Kensington Oval) 21–24 February	16–5–48–1	15–1–83–2		35–5–107–3	10–2–38–0	
	104.1–28	69–12	18–5	160.1–39	50.1–16	2–1
	243–25	308–8	49–0	372–13	116–2	1–0
	av. 9.72	av. 38.50	–	av. 28.61	av. 58.00	–

	U. V. C. Lawrence	N. Guishard	B	Lb	W	Nb	Total	Wkts
Trinidad and Tobago (Queen's Park Oval) 17–20 January			1			9	172	10
			4			4	143	2
Jamaica (Warner Park) 3–26 January	6–1–30–1	13–4–35–1			3	1	167	10
	3–1–10–0	12–5–17–1			8	6	218	10
Guyana (Grenada) –10 February		6–1–9–0		6	4	5	96	9‡
		24–7–44–3	10		3	2	228	9
Barbados (Kensington Oval) 21–24 February		31–3–101–4	4		5	5	391	10
	9–2	86–20						
	40–1	206–9						
	av. 40.00	av. 22.88						

‡ A. I. Kallicharran retired hurt

Guyana
Shell Shield –
Batting
1981

	v. Barbados (Kensington Oval) 17–20 January	v. Trinidad and Tobago (Bourda) 23–26 January	v. Jamaica (Berbice) 30 January–2 February	v. Combined Islands (Grenada) 7–10 February	Inns	NOs	Runs	HS	Av
S. F. A. Bacchus	28, 15	11, 41	16	7, 86	7	—	204	86	29.14
T. Etwaroo	22	7, 69	8	0, 13	6	—	119	69	19.83
T. Mohammed	43	4	34	0, 5	5	—	83	43	16.60
M. Harper	4, 52	8, 1*	18	2, 27	7	1	112	52	18.66
M. R. Pydanna	4, 3	12, 2	0	6, 14	7	1	41	14	6.83
R. Gomes	0, 3				2	—	3	3	1.50
S. Shivnarine	3, 7				2	—	10	7	5.00
D. I. Kallicharran	18	27	37	0	4	—	93	37	23.25
R. Harper	18	2	3	26	5	—	49	26	9.80
K. Persaud	15	0	1		3	—	16	15	5.33
R. Joseph	0*	2	1	13*, 5	6	2	23	13*	5.75
A. I. Kallicharran		184	8	0*	3	1	192	184	96.00
C. H. Lloyd		144	117*	49, 35*	4	2	345	144	172.50
C. E. H. Croft		20	8	2, 0	4	—	30	20	7.50
C. Butts		11*	8	2, 2	3	1	15	11*	7.50
Byes	6	15	30	10					
Leg byes	3, 8	7	8	3					
Wides	1, 2		8	4					
No balls	19, 2	2	8	5, 2					
Total	184, 108	439, 123	296, 10	96, 228					
Wickets	10, 9†	10, 2	10	9‡, 9					
Result	L	D	D	L					
Points	3	15	5	5					

† T. Etwaroo, absent injured.
‡ A. I. Kallicharran, retired hurt.

Catches
9 – M. R. Pydanna (ct 7, st 2)
5 – C. H. Lloyd and R. Harper
3 – S. F. A. Bacchus and A. I. Kallicharran
2 – S. Shivnarine and subs (Lyte and Hewitt), M. Harper
1 – T. Etwaroo and C. Butts

Guyana
Shell Shield –
Bowling
1981

	R. Joseph	R. Gomes	R. Harper	D. I. Kallicharran	K. Persaud	S. Shivnarine
v. Barbados (Kensington Oval) 17–20 January	13–1–71–0	4–1–20–1	48–7–185–3	35–3–143–0	12–0–58–1	26–2–68–1
v. Trinidad and Tobago (Bourda) 23–26 January	17–4–65–1			17–0–68–2	12–3–35–0	
v. Jamaica (Berbia) 30 Jan–2 Feb	16–0–64–1		38.4–8–80–2	19–3–64–0		
	11–1–33–1		16–4–30–2	6–0–28–0		
v. Combined Islands (Grenada) 7–10 February	19–4–49–4		19–1–45–0			
	16–0–62–1		27–3–75–0			
	92–10	4–1	148.4–23	77–6	24–3	26–2
	344–8	20–1	415–7	303–0	93–0	68–1
	av. 43.00	av. 20.00	av. 59.28	—	—	av. 68.00

	C. E. H. Croft	C. Butts	M. Harper	A. I. Kallicharran	S. F. A. Bacchus	T. Etwaroo
v. Barbados (Kensington Oval) 17–20 January						
v. Trinidad and Tobago (Bourda) 23–26 January	25–7–71–3	31.3–10–60–3	4–1–14–0			
v. Jamaica (Berbia) 30 Jan–2 Feb	26–3–64–7		2–0–13–0	9–3–17–0		
	3–0–20–0		16–3–32–1	15–0–24–1	3–1–2–0	2–0–6–0
v. Combined Islands (Grenada) 7–10 February	22–4–59–3	15–4–33–3				
	16–2–47–2	28–5–71–5	7–2–28–0			
	92–16	74.3–19	29–6	24–3	3–1	2–0
	261–15	164–11	87–1	41–1	2–0	6–0
	av. 17.40	av. 14.90	av. 87.00	av. 41.00	—	—

B	Lb	W	Nb	Total	Wkts
2	5			552	7
3	7	1	14	338	9
2	1	1	1	307	10
4	1		3	183	5
2	3	1	4	196	10
4	2		4	293	8

Jamaica
Shell Shield – Batting
1981

	v. Trinidad and Tobago (Chedwin Park) 10-13 Jan		v. Combined Islands (St Kitts) 23-26 Jan		v. Guyana (Berbia) 30 Jan-2 Feb		v. Barbados (Chedwin Park) 7-10 Feb		Inns	NOs	Runs	HS	Av
R. A. Austin	19	87*			7	27	50	36	6	1	226	87*	45.20
A. B. Williams	6	24	4	0	4	8			6	—	46	24	7.66
E. H. Mattis	56	71			92	64	47	2	6	—	332	92	55.33
L. G. Rowe	4	—	76	0	51	58*	10	45*	7	1	230	76	38.33
H. S. Chang	34	—	5	30*	53	5	4	29	7	1	147	53	24.50
J. Dujon	16	—			4	13*	135*		4	2	168	135*	84.00
B. M. Tucker	35	0*	0	33			20		5	2	70	35	35.00
A. Barrett	23*	—	9*	6			2		5	2	65	23*	21.66
J. Williams	0	—	19*	3	34		1		5	1	44	33	11.00
M. A. Holding	1	—	0	9*			8	34	5	—	51	34	10.20
C. U. Thompson	0	—							1	—	0	0	—
C. Fletcher			20	1			8	39	4	—	68	39	17.00
C. Baugh			14	30					2	—	44	30	22.00
M. Neita			16	90	48		0	56*	5	1	210	90	52.50
D. Malcolm			0	3	0	0	26		5	—	29	26	5.80
Byes	6		3	8	2	1	2	4					
Leg byes	5												
Wides	1		1		1		2	5					
No balls	1		1	6	1	3	3	3					
Total	200	189	167	218	307	183	263	264					
Wickets	10	2	10	10	10	4	10	4					
Result	D		L		D		D						
Points	6		3		4		8						

Catches

6 – J. Dujon (ct 5, st 1)
5 – M. Neita
4 – L. G. Rowe and R. A. Austin
3 – A. Barrett
2 – A. B. Williams, H. S. Chang and E. H. Mattis
1 – J. Williams, C. Fletcher and M. A. Holding

Jamaica
Shell Shield –
Bowling
1981

	M. A. Holding	J. Williams	C. U. Thompson	B. M. Tucker	A. Barrett	R. A. Austin
v. Trinidad and Tabago (Chedwin Park) 10–13 Jan	28–5–96–5	26–9–59–3	15–0–72–0	10–2–26–1	13–3–38–0	12–2–48–0
v. Combined Islands (St Kitts) 23–26 Jan	22–3–80–1	19–1–89–1		24–1–92–2	23.1–2–81–5	
v. Guyana (Berbia) 30 Jan–2 Feb	28–3–80–4	16–5–28–1			20–1–75–2	26.1–9–34–3
v. Barbados (Chedwin Park) 7–10 Feb	15–1–59–3	14–3–45–1			8–3–12–1	12–3–52–3
	6–1–17–0	7–0–31–1			8–1–19–0	10–0–48–0
	99–13	82–18	15–0	34–3	72.1–10	60.1–14
	332–13	252–7	72–0	118–3	225–8	182–6
	av. 25.53	av. 36.00	—	av. 39.33	av. 28.12	av. 30.33

	D. Malcolm	B	Lb	W	Nb	Total	Wkts
v. Trinidad and Tobago (Chedwin Park) 10–13 Jan		10	9	6	1	365	10
v. Combined Islands (St Kitts) 23–26 Jan	26–3–112–1	10	7		10	481	10
v. Guyana (Berbia) 30 Jan–2 Feb	11–3–33–0	30	8		8	296	10
v. Barbados (Chedwin Park) 7–10 Feb	3–0–15–1	2	6		5	196	10
	19–6–53–4		5	1	2	176	5
	59–12						
	213–6						
	av. 35.50						

Trinidad and Tobago
Shell Shield – Batting
1981

	v. Jamaica (Chedwin Park) 10–13 January	v. Combined Islands (Queen's Park Oval) 17–20 January		v. Guyana (Bourda) 23–26 January	v. Barbados (Queen's Park Oval) 30 January–2 February		Inns	NOs	Runs	HS	Av
R. S. Gabriel	22	17	29	—	13	28	5	—	109	29	21.80
K. Bainey	39	7	55	15	17	2	6	—	135	55	22.50
A. Rajah	50	1	32*	10	13		5	1	106	50	26.50
H. A. Gomes		68*	19*	26	45	11*	5	3	169	68*	84.50
A. Logie	56	10		64	125	3	5	—	258	125	51.60
D. L. Murray	82	6		19	15		4	—	122	82	30.50
A. G. Burns	53	16		45	25		4	—	139	53	34.75
A. Daniel	0				16		2	—	16	16	8.00
H. Joseph	6	12		0*	8*		4	2	26	12	13.00
R. R. Jumadeen	4	1		4*			3	1	9	4*	4.50
E. Audain	23*	0					2	1	23	23*	23.00
R. Nanan		24		36	3		3	—	63	36	21.00
T. Cuffy				88	38		2	—	126	88	63.00
C. Murray				6			1	—	6	6	6.00
S. Gomes	4						1	—	4	4	4.00
Byes	10			3	3						
Leg byes	9	1		7	12						
Wides	1			1							
No balls	6	9	4	14	24	1					
Total	365	172	143	338	357	48					
Wickets	10	10	2	9	10	2					
Result	D	D		D	W						
Points	20	5		11	25						

Catches

8 – D. L. Murray (ct 4, st 4)
5 – R. S. Gabriel
4 – A. Rajah
3 – R. R. Jumadeen, T. Cuffy and K. Bainey
2 – A. G. Burns and H. Joseph
1 – S. Gomes, E. Audain, H. A. Gomes and A. Logie

Trinidad and Tobago
Shell Shield –
Bowling
1981

	A. G. Burns	E. Audain	R. R. Jumadeen	A. Daniel	H. Joseph	A. Logie
. Jamaica (Chedwin Park)	9–4–18–0	8.4–2–16–2	19–7–36–1	16–1–62–4	20–2–62–3	
10–13 January	10–3–28–0	8–2–32–0	16–4–28–0	11–1–34–0	15–4–38–2	6–0–22–0
. Combined Islands (Queen's	4–1–13–0	12–5–27–0	30–7–70–0		38–11–105–6	
Park Oval) 17–20 January	12–6–17–0	5–0–25–0	22–10–32–1		18–3–53–2	
. Guyana (Berbia)	17–2–46–1		41.5–6–137–4		29–3–106–0	
23–26 January	8–1–20–0		12–3–21–1		16.5–3–32–1	
. Barbados (Queen's Park	18–6–46–2			13–4–36–0	32.4–13–59–3	
Oval) 30 Jan–2 Feb	3–0–9–0			17–4–63–3	23.1–6–41–1	
	81–23	33.4–9	140.5–37	57–10	192.4–45	6–0
	197–3	100–2	324–7	195–7	496–18	22–0
	av. 65.66	av. 50.00	av. 46.28	av. 27.85	av. 27.55	—

	R. Nanan	H. A. Gomes	C. Murray	B	Lb	W	Nb	Total	Wkts.
. Jamaica (Chedwin Park)					6			200	10
10–13 January				5	1	1		189	2
. Combined Islands (Queen's	37–11–99–3			1	2			317	10
Park Oval) 17–20 January	22–10–25–1	8–4–10–0		1	7			170	4
. Guyana (Berbia)	46–19–83–1	17–4–41–3	2–0–9–0		15		2	439	10
23–26 January	11–1–34–0	7–3–9–0			7			123	2
. Barbados (Queen's Park	25–8–65–5	8–2–23–0		1	3		1	234	10
Oval) 30 Jan–2 Feb	25–9–41–1	3–0–9–1			6			169	10
	166–58	43–13	2–0						
	347–11	92–4	9–0						
	av. 31.54	av. 23.00	—						

Holding's hundredth Test wicket. Rose caught Murray in the First Test in Trinidad.

Clive Lloyd reigns supreme (Third Test, Barbados).

I

Australia in Sri Lanka

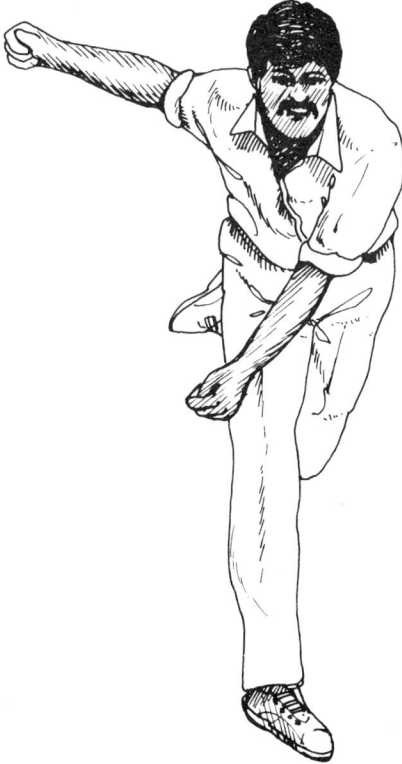

The Australian team to tour England broke their journey to play four matches in Sri Lanka. The matches were of vital importance to Sri Lanka who were intent on attaining Test status and were determined to prove that they could compete on equal terms with the best in world cricket. The three one-day matches were excitingly contested, Australia winning two of them narrowly and Sri Lanka winning the second with some ease. The four day match was halted by rain when Sri Lanka had every reason to believe that they were in a winning position.

Limited Over Matches

2 May 1981   **at Colombo**
Sri Lanka 218 for 4 (H. Devapriya 78)
Australia 164 for 7 (J. Dyson 67)
Australia won on faster scoring rate

3 May 1981   **at Colombo**
Australia 188
Sri Lanka 189 for 4 (B. Warnapura 106)
Sri Lanka won by 6 wickets

5 May 1981   **at Colombo**
Australia 242 for 6 (A. R. Border 63, M. F. Kent 62)
Sri Lanka 236 for 9 (A. Ranasinghe 61, R. S. Madugalle 55)
Australia won by 6 runs

Sri Lanka v. Australians

7, 8, 9 and 10 May 1981   **at Colombo**

Australians	*First Innings*		*Second Innings*	
J. Dyson	c Kaluperuma,		(2) c Gunatilleke,	
	b de Silva	22	b Ranasinghe	68
G. M. Wood	c Gunatilleke,		(1) c Kaluperuma,	
	b Kaluperuma	28	b de Silva	26
M. F. Kent	c and b de Silva	6	b Kaluperuma	4
K. J. Hughes (capt)	b de Silva	0	b Kaluperuma	15
A. R. Border	b de Silva	19	c Warnapura,	
			b Kaluperuma	0
G. N. Yallop	st Gunatilleke,			
	b de Silva	25	lbw, b Kaluperuma	13
G. R. Beard	st Gunatilleke,			
	b Kaluperuma	4	lbw, b Kaluperuma	9
*S. J. Rixon	c Kaluperuma,		c de Mel,	
	b de Silva	4	b Ranasinghe	14
R. J. Bright	run out	1	b de Silva	0
G. F. Lawson	not out	2	not out	9
R. M. Hogg	b Kaluperuma	1	c Mendis, b de Silva	6
Extras	b 7, lb 1, w 1, nb 3	12	b 3, lb 7, nb 4	14
		124		178

	O	M	R	W		O	M	R	W
de Mel	6	2	19	—		1	—	2	—
Guneratne	6	1	16	—		2	—	17	—
Ranasinghe	3	1	6	—		9	7	7	2
de Silva	27	14	36	6		40.1	17	64	3
Kaluperuma	24.1	11	35	3		33	11	74	5

Fall of Wickets
1–45, 2–56, 3–56, 4–70, 5–97, 6–114, 7–114, 8–121, 9–123.
1–53, 2–64, 3–93, 4–95, 5–121, 6–131, 7–162, 8–162, 9–162.

Sri Lanka	*First Innings*	
B. Warnapura (capt)	b Lawson	8
S. Wettimuny	c Dyson, b Beard	14
R. L. Dias	c Rixon, b Lawson	64
R. D. Mendis	c Hughes, b Beard	10
R. S. Madugalle	c Rixon, b Hogg	25
A. Ranasinghe	c Rixon, b Beard	8
L. Kaluperuma	b Beard	11
A. de Mel	b Lawson	19
*M. Gunatilleke	b Lawson	0
G. R. A. de Silva	st Rixon, b Beard	4
K. Guneratne	not out	0
Extras	b 3, lb 3, nb 8	14
		177

	O	M	R	W
Hogg	8	—	33	1
Lawson	10.3	4	14	4
Bright	12	3	34	—
Beard	19	3	69	5
Border	3	—	4	—
Yallop	2	—	9	—

Fall of Wickets
1–21, 2–28, 3–46, 4–120, 5–131, 6–150, 7–162, 8–162, 9–171.

Match drawn

J

The English Season

The State of Cricket by Tony Pawson;
John Arlott on the future of the game;
Secretary of the M.C.C. by Jack Bailey;
the Schweppes County Championship;
the Benson and Hedges Cup;
the John Player League;

the National
Westminster Bank Trophy,
the Prudential one-day
internationals;
the Cornhill Test Series;
form charts and averages

.

The England team returned from the West Indies a little less bruised and battered than many had expected, but the events in cricket all round the world had given cause for some concern. As Jim Swanton wrote some twenty years ago – 'Cricket achieved its unique place in the English scene because its champions were admired for themselves. They were men of dignity who stood in the eyes of their countrymen for a code of conduct.' What those who love the game wish to preserve above all else is that dignity, and that should be preserved in any class of cricket whatever the number of overs played or the distance of fielding circles from the wicket.

The state of the game is a point of annual debate, but, in a world of changing values, it is essential that we make this constant assessment. In the following pages, TONY PAWSON, a writer and player of distinction, looks at the state of cricket today, and JOHN ARLOTT, whose compassion and understanding for more than cricket has become legendary, looks at the future.

The State of Cricket (TONY PAWSON)

The response to that underarm grub which Greg Chappell instructed his brother to bowl to ensure victory in an international against New Zealand was as expressive as the action itself of the current state of cricket. The massive interest in the game was clear enough from the headline reporting and the flood of outraged comments. The most entertaining, but least perceptive of these was Keith Miller's to the effect that the grub had killed off one-day international cricket and Chappell ought to be buried with it. As any advertising man could have told him publicity, however adverse, is always good for promoting the product. Cricket was again in the limelight as it had recently been over the Packer affair, and even if it was black limelight in both cases it still made cricket a focus of attraction.

The underhand tactic was a source of argument in pub and club, and not least in the highest offices of state. What other game could stimulate a couple of Prime Ministers to pronounce weightily on the validity of a cunning little tactical ploy? Mr Muldoon indeed went to the extreme of calling Australia yellow because of it, which seemed to indicate as peculiar a view of their character as of the laws of the game. These make it quite clear that the sole judges of fair and unfair play are the two umpires, not the Prime Ministers of the countries concerned. Since it was passed by umpires Cronin and Weser as fair, the few million of the rest of us cricket lovers can't make it unfair, not even as Heads of State.

Theirs was however a welcome intervention in practical terms, since it highlighted the decline in standards by the win-at-all-costs attitude being taken to extremes at the top level of the game. Partly this has been due to a general hardening of attitude, partly to the large sums of money now at stake, partly to the scope given by the complex rules of one-day competitions to the dressing-room lawyers. Certainly the trend has grown, is growing, and needs to be rapidly diminished.

It's easy to glamorise the past at the expense of the present, and all periods of the game have had their murky incidents. But in former years the excesses were isolated, like the body-line series, and the tactical gambits less overtly contemptuous of the spirit of cricket. They were offset too by more of those generous gestures like Lindsay Hassett *not* throwing in the ball when Denis Compton had slipped in mid-pitch in the Oval Test of 1948.

What positive action can administrators take to minimise the unpleasantness of disputes which have ranged from Somerset's disqualification from the Benson and Hedges competition for exploiting the rules to win by not playing, to Chappell's equally legitimate, but equally unworthy victory tactic? The essential is that they are dealt with at the time. That can be achieved simply enough by strengthening Law 42 and urging umpires to enforce it. For that law already makes them sole arbiters of fair and unfair play and gives them the right to intervene without appeal. They may then call 'dead ball', but should also be empowered to impose penalties up to forfeiture of the match if warnings are ignored.

Sadly spectator conduct has given problems too. The inconceivable became reality in the Centenary Test when M.C.C. members physically assaulted umpires for delaying the restart. The perpetrators would no doubt have been vociferous about dissent in players. Yet the standard excuses were to be heard for their behaviour – pressure situation, intolerable provocation, heat of the moment – and though several must have been easily identifiable in the available 'action replays', no public disciplinary action was ever taken. Any future flare-ups require firmer handling than this.

The change for the worse in modern attitudes is summed up for me in one feature of play. In the forties and fifties if a wicket-keeper threw the ball up when appealing, you knew he was certain he had made a catch. Now it is done as often as not just to put pressure on the umpires. But there have of course been changes for the better too. These are best exemplified by 'consensus' captaincy which demands more involvement from the whole team, and by unstinting effort in one-day games so demanding of concentration and athletic effort. 'Progress' is usually an unequal mix of good and bad, and that is as true of cricket as of the rest of life. Two developments which have had a profound effect on the game recently can now be seen in perspective and evaluated with reasonable detachment. These are the closely related events of Kerry Packer's attempted take-over and the growth of sponsorship until it underpins the whole structure of English cricket from the Test arena to the village green.

The passions which Packer aroused stemmed from the intensity of feeling which so many people have for the game. To propose such traumatic change inevitably polarised opinion with instant hostility the predominant reaction. And though in the long run his intervention has proved salutary for the game that is *only* because he was opposed so strongly that his plans were abandoned before they undermined the existing structure.

To sustain his challenge Packer encouraged creative thinking on the presentation of cricket. Several of these novel ideas have now been absorbed into our cricket such as the new Lambert and Butler floodlit competition, the new regulations for Benson and Hedges of a minimum of close fielders within a marked zone, or improved techniques of pitch preparation.

These are gains positively attributable to Packer, and because his commercial venture was fought to the point of abandonment there have been no lasting ill-effects of consequence. There was also to his credit the financial benefits for his own players, and indirectly the pressure of his intervention has helped raise the standard of payment to first-class cricketers to a proper level. The general increase however was no thanks to him, but to those players and administrators who were prepared to battle against a development which might have helped the few, but harmed the many.

But how did his World Series Cricket affect the individuals involved? Those who stayed aloof have been all-round gainers. Those who joined had mixed fortune. Mike Procter has recently recorded his pleasure in a type of cricket which improved his game and brought him back into top-level competition. To prove how 'real' that competition was he instanced Joel Garner coming in to bat for West Indies with a broken finger and the bowler successfully aiming to hit it again to force him to retire. That certainly says something about the present concept of 'real' competition! And undoubtedly Packer was a boon to South African cricketers such as Procter, or the likes of John Snow, deserving the extra money in the twilight of a distinguished career.

For the English Test players who signed the effect on their cricket, however, was uniformly depressing. Tony Greig's lapsed until he was a cipher on the field. Knott and Underwood left as the world's leading players of their type, but returned with so little appetite for the game that they could no longer command a place in some of our weakest post-war Test teams. For Bob Woolmer the setback has been even more marked. But for World Series Cricket he should have established himself as indispensable to our Test team and might have been a candidate for the captaincy when dearth of alternatives led to Botham's premature appointment. The effects of Packer on performance weighed most heavily on Kent, the county which contributed most players to him and went into startling decline during their difficult readjustment period in 1980.

That Packer was resisted without major disruption to English cricket was due in part to the influx of sponsorship money boosting payments, particularly to Test cricketers. Cornhill Insurance played the major part in this. Happily their gamble paid off so well in business terms that it enhanced the whole value of cricket sponsorship to the point that over £1.5 million comes annually into the game. The Cornhill experience was uniquely assessable because it was the company's only major promotion with effects easy to isolate. Before having their name linked to Tests there was only a two per cent spontaneous awareness of the company, which soon increased to the very high peak of seventeen per cent. That in turn improved their market share with an attributable increase in premium income of £10,000,000 a year.

Cricket has taken trouble to control sponsorship centrally and ensure a good return for the sponsor. An important element of this is the extended TV coverage the game attracts. In 1980 BBC showed 370 hours of cricket – twenty per cent of all sport coverage on all three main channels. That left horse-racing trailing with fifteen per cent and soccer with eleven and a half per cent while all other sports were also-rans. No wonder the competition Gillette first sponsored for £6,500 in 1963 has a value to cricket of £250,000 in its new form of the Nat West Bank Trophy!

Cricket has benefitted greatly from happy and stable relationships with its main sponsors, who have also had value for money. In particular it has been a model to other sports in ensuring a fair proportion of sponsorship money goes to the grass-roots of the game. This year the TCCB has passed on £100,000 to the National Cricket Association and The Lord's Taverners will have raised a similar sum for the benefit of school and club cricket. Some of the lesser sponsorships are also of great value in ensuring a sound base to the pyramid. Wrigley and Commercial Union have both contributed to improved coaching and youth facilities, while Haig and Whitbread have sponsored the important competitions for clubs and villages.

Because of sponsorship there is no lack now of opportunity for talented youngsters and a promising and profitable career for the best of them. All of which leaves one mystery. Why are we not producing a stream of gifted young players like those South Africans who so dominate county cricket? Gower and Botham stood out for that natural ability, which no systems can produce. We are overdue for a larger crop of talent.

The future of English cricket (JOHN ARLOTT)

The future of English cricket, like its present, will be shaped by financial pressures. They are the root of all the difficulties – and the benefits – of the game here. It is simple to point to apparently separate grounds for anxiety – declining standards at representative level: the dominance of overseas players; the schizophrenia induced by the varying types of play – one-day (in three different forms), three-day and five-day; high organisational, promotional and administrative costs. All, however, stem directly from the game's need for more money.

This is a money-conscious age. That is not necessarily an indictment. It is a fact apparent throughout the modern field of business. Hotels used to be controlled by hoteliers; the booktrade by booksellers; car manufacture by engineers; shipping by sailors. Now, though, business is increasingly directed by men – whether they are called accountants, actuaries, or financiers – whose expertise is in money.

That is the explanation of Mr Packer. As Mr Justice Slade observed: he was inevitable: surprising only in that he – or his kind – did not emerge earlier. Cricket traditionally was run by cricketers. Mr Packer took it over as part of his business, which is not simply that of a television channel and magazine publication, but the manipulation of finance. Thus one of his companies now arranges and markets Australian representative cricket: and their Board of Control seems satisfied. It must be hoped, though, that they recognise the situation. Despite his declared enthusiasm for it, cricket is a facet of Mr Packer's business. That is why he has increased the intensity of international matches in Australia to a point which cricketers regard as too great, while, to his mind, a reasonable maximum of revenue is being achieved. If one of his television programmes or magazines began to make an uncompensated loss, though, he would, presumably, as a business man, divest himself of it. We must hope Australian cricket continues in profit.

The acceptance of Sri Lanka into Test play might help the world game financially but that would be a slow process. Their entry as full members of the ICC would, of course, create a majority, with India, Pakistan and West Indies, which would affectively block the readmission of South Africa so long as apartheid is practised there.

First-class cricket has a different financial climate in every country where it is played. India and Pakistan are solvent through their vast captive audiences; South Africa is wealthy enough for its amateur game to flourish; New Zealand, also amateur, has worked out an effective *modus vivendi*; West Indies, on the other hand, are desperately hard up. Indeed, their players cannot earn a living from cricket there; and the reduction of the number of overseas players in the English domestic game could have damaging effects on the strength of West Indies cricket.

There is no doubt that the problem of playing strength in England stems from the lifting of the maximum wage in soccer at the end of 1960. Until then cricket was slightly better paid than football and made a greater social appeal. Of course the effect, at the intake end, took time to work through; but within a decade it was plain to be seen. The subsequent reduction in top talent is unmistakable. Most English boys used to grow up playing football and cricket; and the athletically talented tended to be good at both. Some played both professionally; but that possibility is ended. Nowadays a considerable number of state schools play no cricket at all. It poses problems of space, pitch preparation, time, gear, and coaching – and their cost – which are more easily avoided by switching to other games than overcome. Thus, many potential cricketers are lost simply because they never play. For those with the opportunity to play one or the other at professional level, a parent or schoolmaster can hardly advise cricket in the material interest of the boy. In terms of income and security, football has vast advantages. English cricket conceded its bare 160 capped players a minimum wage of £5,450, plus bonus and prize monies. The basic for the 140 uncapped varies between £1,950 and £3,250. Some counties find it difficult to meet these figures.

Yet there are British footballers earning as much as £50,000 a year from their clubs. If that peak represents an inducement; there is also a vast fail-safe system. As opposed to 300 cricketers, there are 2000 players with Football League clubs; while, for those who do not climb so high, a number of lesser clubs pay appreciably more than pocket money for match play.

If they were seventeen-years-old today, such international cricketers, of varying but positive footballing talents, as Jack Hobbs, Walter Hammond, Patsy Hendren, Denis Compton, Bill Edrich, Fred Trueman, Leslie Compton and Brian Close would find it extremely financially disadvantageous to play county cricket in preference to professional soccer.

The counties search anxiously for increased revenue. The one-day competitions have been profitable. An extra Test match – along the Australian line – should prove worthwhile. England, though, lacks the major Australian asset. There, television companies competing for rights force up the price. In England commercial television are not interested, so the fee eventually paid is a toothless compromise between cricket and a financially straitened BBC.

South African cricketers, deprived of international competition, move into the English counties in numbers which reflect the changed status of the over-seas players since the idea was first conceived. Originally such as Richards, Lloyd and Procter were recruited as stars, box-office attractions who would in-crease gates. Since then the imported cricketers have become necessities, to make good the dearth of home talent.

In the attempt to increase revenue, counties which house Test Matches can take financial advantage of that fact by increasing membership subscriptions. Others must weigh the dangers of pensioners' inability to pay much more; and of estranging goodwill members.

They should, too, exploit their real estate; cricket grounds in desirable situations could yield considerable gains if sold; or produce greater revenue if more extensively used. Some have developed catering facilities; squash courts or driving ranges; other opportunities ought to be taken.

To remove the fear of insolvency, though, English cricket needs more money than it can envisage finding; essentially to buy back the talent now locked up in highly paid footballers.

22, 23 and 24 April   **at Cambridge**
Cambridge University 146 (S. Turner 4 for 20) and 204 for 6 (D. R. Pringle 66)
Essex 240 (M. S. A. McEvoy 53, D. R. Pringle 4 for 56)
Match drawn

The 1981 English season began in sensational, if somewhat gloomy, fashion. Peter Mills played forward to the first ball of the season, bowled by John Lever, missed, and was lbw. In dull weather Cambridge were out by early afternoon, mainly through a four wickets in 29 balls spell from Turner. McEvoy, for whom the season was most crucial, reached the first fifty. The second came from Pringle, the Cambridge acting captain, who also bowled impressively. Rain ended play early on the last day and just after twelve the players had left the field because of the intense cold. The English season had begun.

25, 26 and 27 April   **at Cambridge**
Hampshire 176 for 3 dec (T. M. Tremlett 62)
Cambridge University 117 for 5 dec
Match drawn

25, 27 and 28 April   **at Oxford**
Oxford University 171 (N. V. H. Mallett 52, R. N. S. Hobbs 4 for 50)
Glamorgan 108 for 7 (N. V. H. Mallett 5 for 52)
Match drawn

The rain which had brought an early end to the first game of the season ruined the second and third games. There was enough time, however, for Tim Tremlett to give a reminder of his promise and for Robin Hobbs to display the forgotten art of leg-spin. Oxford slumped to 115 for 8 against Hobbs after new fast medium bowler Barwick had made the first inroads into the batting. Then Mallett, recovered from injury, hit a maiden fifty and followed this with a career best bowling performance which reduced Glamorgan to 62 for 7 before Nash, Holmes and rain ended Oxford's hopes of early season glory.

29 and 30 April, 1 May **at Lord's**

Middlesex 269 for 6 dec (M. W. Gatting 101 not out) and 149 for 3 dec
M.C.C. 210 for 7 dec (D. I. Gower 108) and 101 for 2 (D. I. Gower 51 not
out)
Match drawn

at Cambridge

Cambridge University 133 (P. Willey 5 for 46) and 187 (P. Willey 5 for 72)
Northamptonshire 362 for 7 dec (G. Cook 131, W. Larkins 117)
Northamptonshire won by an innings and 42 runs

at Oxford

Oxford University 63 (H. R. Moseley 4 for 16) and 100 (D. Breakwell 6 for
38)
Somerset 209 for 5 dec (P. A. Slocombe 62 not out, S. P. Sutcliffe 4 for 86)
Somerset won by an innings and 46 runs

The traditional opening to the season at Lord's, M.C.C. versus the champion
county, was, in the main, a dull affair in gloomy weather. It did, however, produce the first century of the season, Mike Gatting on the opening day, and the
second, David Gower on the Thursday. Both were good innings and England
supporters were grateful for them. On the last day Gower alone seemed to be
enjoying the events as the game drawled to its close, he played a superb little
knock in the final hour. Both universities suffered defeat by an innings. The
off-spin of Willey, ably supported by Williams, overwhelmed the Cambridge
batsmen and Cook and Larkins, helped by some very poor catching and fielding, put on 207 for the first Northants wicket. Moseley's pace in the first
innings and the spin of Breakwell and Lloyds in the second routed Oxford
on a doubtful wicket. The University opened their bowling with off-spinner
Sutcliffe who enjoyed the conditions almost as much as the Somerset bowlers.
Somerset's fielding was of a high standard, and, though they had some leading
players missing, and the opposition was not strong, they contrived to look a
good side.

2, 4 and 5 May **at Cambridge**

Lancashire 314 for 5 dec (G. Fowler 143, A. Kennedy 65)
Cambridge University 234 for 5 dec (R. J. Boyd-Moss 84, S. J. G. Doggart
69 not out)
Match drawn

at Oxford

Yorkshire 278 for 6 dec (D. L. Bairstow 79 not out, R. G. Lumb 63, A.
Sidebottom 52 not out, G. Boycott 51)
Oxford University 120 (J. P. Whiteley 4 for 50) and 123 for 6
Match drawn

Rain had ruined both matches in which the Universities were involved, but there
was still time for three career best performances at Cambridge. Fowler, on the
first day, and Boyd-Moss, ending a lean spell, and Doggart on the last day
were the celebrants. The confident Yorkshire batting display at Oxford was

marred by the injury to Lumb which would keep him out of the side for at
least a fortnight.

6, 7 and 8 May   **at Cardiff**
Glamorgan *v* Gloucestershire, match abandoned without a ball being bowled.
No points

at Southampton
Hampshire 299 for 8 dec (D. R. Turner 106, N. G. Cowley 52) and 7 for 0
Somerset 255 (P. M. Roebuck 75, D. Breakwell 53)
Match drawn
Hampshire 6 pts, Somerset 4 pts

at Canterbury
Nottinghamshire 293 for 7 dec (B. Hassan 97 not out, D. W. Randall 81) and
     198 for 6 dec (C. E. B. Rice 84)
Kent 250 for 8 dec (C. J. Tavare 66) and 192 for 9 (M. Benson 81, E. E.
     Hemmings 6 for 80)
Match drawn
Kent 5 pts, Nottinghamshire 5 pts

at Leicester
Leicestershire 300 for 6 dec (N. E. Briers 101 not out, P. B. Clift 73, M.
     Hendrick 4 for 86)
Derbyshire 119 (L. B. Taylor 7 for 28) and 315 for 4 dec (B. Wood 123 not
     out, G. Miller 67, P. N. Kirsten 64)
Match drawn
Leicestershire 8 pts, Derbyshire 2 pts

at Lord's
Middlesex 153 (N. Phillip 6 for 40) and 116 for 5
Essex 250 for 8 dec (K. R. Pont 56, J. R. Thomson 4 for 66)
Match drawn
Essex 7 pts, Middlesex 4 pts

at Northampton
Northamptonshire 141 (P. J. W. Allott 8 for 48) and 253 for 4 dec (A. J. Lamb
     133 not out)
Lancashire 184 and 28 for 1
Match drawn
Lancashire 5 pts, Northamptonshire 4 pts

at Edgbaston
Yorkshire 396 (J. D. Love 161, J. H. Hampshire 64, R. G. D. Willis 5 for
     60) and 112 for 1 (G. Boycott 51 not out)
Warwickshire 260 (C. Lethbridge 69, D. L. Amiss 53)
Match drawn
Yorkshire 8 pts, Warwickshire 5 pts

at Worcester
Sussex 252 for 8 dec (J. D. Inchmore 4 for 65) and 163 for 2 dec (G. D.
     Mendis 79 not out, J. R. T. Barclay 55)

Worcestershire 158 for 0 dec (G. M. Turner 104 not out) and 145 for 4
Match drawn
Worcestershire 4 pts, Sussex 3 pts

at Cambridge

Surrey 257 for 8 dec (G. S. Clinton 123, D. R. Pringle 4 for 39) and 237 for
   2 dec (A. R. Butcher 133 not out, G. P. Howarth 75)
Cambridge University 240 (R. J. Boyd-Moss 50, S. T. Clarke 4 for 47) and
   126 for 5 (D. R. Pringle 55 not out)
Match drawn

As in 1980, the first round of matches in the Schweppes County Championship
was mutilated by rain. There was no play at all at Cardiff and no one was able
to force a result in any of the other games. The match which came closest to
providing a definite result was that at Canterbury. Randall and Tavare, two of
England's forgotten men, batted well in the first innings as did the veteran
Basharat Hassan who missed his century when Rice declared in order to try to
capture a Kent wicket on the first evening. It was Rice's superbly aggressive
batting which enabled Notts to set Kent a target of 242 in three-and-a-quarter
hours. Quick wickets to Hadlee did not help Kent's cause, but Mark Benson
played a career best innings in every respect, with a six and eleven fours in his
81. Nevertheless Kent had to hang on grimly at the end as Hemmings' off-
spin bemused all but Benson and Asif. There was no such excitement at
Southampton where Turner hit a century, but tedium generally ruled. Nigel
Briers was another centurion as Leicestershire took maximum points against
Derbyshire. Les Taylor had a career best 7 for 28, so outshining Andy Roberts,
and Derbyshire had to follow on. Wood and Kirsten put on 96 for the second
wicket and Miller gave an elegant display, causing one to sigh for the hundredth
time for what might, or should, be with this man's batting. Barry Wood
reached his highest score for Derbyshire. Another West Indian bowler to be
outshone was Michael Holding who was making his debut for Lancashire.
Northants were destroyed by the fast medium accuracy of Paul Allott whose 8
for 48 was easily his best ever performance in first-class cricket. Lancashire fared
little better against an all-round attack in which young Neil Mallender was again
prominent. Holding threatened to destroy Northants at the second attempt, but
Allan Lamb played an innings of great majesty which strengthened the argument of those who maintained that he was currently the best batsman in
England. Jeff Thomson made a good start for Middlesex who fielded eleven
Test players. He was top scorer with 35 and with Mike Selvey saved his side
from complete ignominy against the pace of Norbert Phillip. Keith Pont gave
promise of a better season ahead than he had enjoyed in 1980 and the honours
were very much with Essex in spite of Thomson's four wickets. Edmonds
bowled disappointingly for Middlesex, but Mike McEvoy, bowling his occasional medium pace as the game was dying, dismissed Radley, Butcher and
Barlow for 20 runs, a remarkable first three wickets in first-class cricket. There
was some high scoring at Edgbaston where Love led the Yorkshire spree. Bob
Willis showed a fine return to fitness with five wickets, but overshadowing all
was nineteen-year old Chris Lethbridge. With his first delivery in first-class
cricket, medium pace, he had the mighty Boycott caught at slip. He then hit

an accomplished 69 and thwarted Yorkshire's ambition of asking the home side to follow on. Sussex recovered from 95 for 6 to reach 252 for 8, thanks mainly to an unbeaten ninth wicket stand of 99 by Arnold and Le Roux. Turner and Ormrod put on an unbeaten 158 for the first Worcestershire wicket, the new skipper reaching the ninetieth century of his career, but the weather was the only winner in the end. Although Clinton and Butcher hit centuries, the most encouraging batting from Surrey's point of view was Geoff Howarth's second innings 75. He had had such a lean season in 1980 and Surrey supporters hoped that this innings promised better things for 1981. Derek Pringle again showed splendid all-round form, containing Surrey with economical bowling in the first innings and saving his side with a fine fifty after they had slumped to 36 for 4 in the second innings.

Benson and Hedges Cup

9 May   **at Swansea**
Glamorgan 206 for 9 (Javed Miandad 67, N. G. Featherstone 51)
Essex 124 (R. C. Ontong 4 for 41)
Glamorgan (2 pts) won by 82 runs

                                                                              at Leicester
Leicestershire 256 for 6 (J. C. Balderstone 113 not out)
Gloucestershire 195 for 7
Leicestershire (2 pts) won by 61 runs

                                                                              at Lord's
Middlesex 175 (C. T. Radley 50, K. Stevenson 4 for 18)
Hampshire 176 for 9 (D. R. Turner 69, J. R. Thomson 7 for 22)
Hampshire (2 pts) won by 1 wicket

                                                                      at Northampton
Northamptonshire 152 (A. J. Lamb 54, C. E. B. Rice 6 for 22)
Nottinghamshire 155 for 9 (D. W. Randall 61 not out)
Nottinghamshire (2 pts) won by 1 wicket

9 and 11 May   **at Derby**
Derbyshire 202 for 8 (P. N. Kirsten 65)
Yorkshire 203 for 9 (D. L. Bairstow 103 not out, C. J. Tunnicliffe 5 for 24)
Yorkshire (2 pts) won by 1 wicket

In spite of the weather, the opening matches in the Benson and Hedges tournament produced cricket that was both stimulating and attractive. At Lord's, Jeff Thomson, whose signing was still producing adverse criticism around the counties, bowled with fire and splendour for Middlesex. Middlesex batted meanly, but when Thomson had reduced Hampshire, without a win in the Benson and Hedges cup for two seasons, to 38 for 4, victory for the team of all stars looked certain. Turner and Rice added 76, but the return of Thomson brought further devastation. He took seven wickets in his eleven overs, but Hampshire held out beyond his quota and Stevenson saw them to an unexpected, and remarkable, victory with three balls left. This was the same margin by which Notts gained victory at Northampton where Clive Rice bowled with Thomson's success, but managed to finish on the winning side thanks to Hadlee's cool batting and Randall's energetic running and stroke play. Glamorgan were put in to bat at Swansea and lost three wickets for 67 before Javed Miandad and Norman Featherstone came together in a match winning stand of 113. Reduced to 15 for 3, Essex never recovered and sank without trace. An innings of mighty foundation by opener Chris Balderstone, his highest in the competition, gave Gloucestershire a task which they found insurmountable. The same seemed to be true of Yorkshire. Weather had affected matches throughout the country, the game at Lord's did not finish until 8.25, and on the Saturday, Derbyshire reached 202 in their fifty-five overs and Yorkshire had scored 12 in 4 overs before the game was halted to be restarted on the Monday. Yorkshire were soon in trouble, even though Old was recalled after being bowled by Wood because Derbyshire had one fielder too few inside the thirty yard circle. At 123 for 9 the visitors seemed well beaten. Tunnicliffe had bowled with economy and hostility and the last Yorkshireman was debutant Johnson who had bowled Kirsten on the Saturday. There were nine overs remaining and 80 runs were needed for victory. Bairstow had gone in with the score at 64 for 5 and he now jettisoned all caution as he violently attacked the bowling. His 50 occupied twenty-one overs, and with only six overs remaining, 49 were still required for victory. Johnson was batting with solid discretion and Bairstow hit Steele for 26 in one over. It was a brave and match-winning gesture. Miller bowled the fifty-fourth over with only seven runs needed for a Yorkshire win. Bairstow swung him over mid-wicket for his ninth, glorious six. It brought one of the very great centuries of the Benson and Hedges competition, and Yorkshire's victory, founded on a record last wicket stand of 80, of which the tenacious Johnson had scored 4, was accomplished with eight balls to spare. It was one of the mighty county's mightiest triumphs.

John Player League

10 May   **at Abergavenny**
Worcestershire 170 for 7
Glamorgan 152
Worcestershire (4 pts) won by 18 runs

                                   at Moreton-in-Marsh

Match abandoned
Gloucestershire 2 pts, Leicestershire 2 pts

                                   at Old Trafford

Derbyshire 163 for 9 (P. G. Lee 4 for 28)
Lancashire 138 for 7
Derbyshire (4 pts) won on faster scoring rate

                                   at Lord's

Match abandoned
Middlesex 2 pts, Hampshire 2 pts

at Northampton

Match abandoned
Northamptonshire 2 pts, Nottinghamshire 2 pts

at Taunton

Essex 139 for 8
Somerset 130 for 7
Essex (4 pts) won by 9 runs

at Hove

Match abandoned
Sussex 2 pts, Surrey 2 pts

at Edgbaston

Match abandoned
Warwickshire 2 pts, Yorkshire 2 pts

The rain reduced the programme of the opening day of the John Player League to three matches and of those three only the game at Abergavenny went the full quota of forty overs. The Lancashire innings was brought to a halt after thirty-five overs which left the brisk scoring of Kirsten, Steele and Barnett as the decisive factor in giving Derbyshire victory. Glamorgan started confidently in answer to Worcestershire's solid 170, but the spin of Jack Birkenshaw, rarely used by Leicestershire towards the end of his days with them in limited over matches, turned the game in Worcestershire's favour. He bowled Alan Jones and Francis, caught and bowled Javed for nought, and conceded only 17 runs in his eight overs. Gooch failed again for Essex, but McEwan, Phillip and Turner struck some mighty blows and, although Botham took 3 for 11 in six overs, Essex reached 139 runs in thirty overs. Somerset lost Rose and Denning for six, and when Richards skied Turner to McEwan after a couple of massive hits, Essex were winning. Botham batted well for 32, but sixteen were needed from the last over, and Lever made sure that Somerset would not score them.

Benson and Hedges Cup

11 May   **at Old Trafford**
Lancashire 288 for 9 (C. H. Lloyd 124)
Warwickshire 291 for 5 (G. W. Humpage 87 not out)
Warwickshire (2 pts) won by 5 wickets

at Canterbury

Combined Universities 104 (G. R. Dilley 4 for 14)
Kent 108 for 2 (R. A. Woolmer 56 not out)
Kent (2 pts) won by 8 wickets

at Hove

Surrey 142 for 7
Sussex 143 for 7
Sussex (2 pts) won by 3 wickets

The match at Old Trafford, which had been postponed on the Saturday, provided a contest of excitement and surprise. Hogg had placed his old county in jeopardy by dismissing Fowler and Hayes with only 17 scored, but Clive Lloyd then played an innings of magnificent power. He hit five sixes and twelve fours, and when he reached his century in the forty-fourth over, victory for Lancashire seemed assured. Facing Holding and a total of 288, Warwickshire could have been expected to have surrendered lamely, but Lancashire displayed an incapacity to field to Holding's bowling, catches being dropped at regular intervals of the West Indian. Warwickshire benefitted from these errors and 81 for the first wicket came from Smith and Amiss, but it was Geoff Humpage who was to be the Warwickshire hero. He drove with sense and power and his innings rightly won him the gold award, for he had nursed Warwickshire to an improbable victory with seven balls to spare, and they had achieved the highest winning total in the history of the competition. There were no such tensions at Canterbury where the Universities performed with mediocrity and Woolmer's fifty won him the gold award. At Hove, Clinton batted with a resolution that gained him the gold award, but his effort on an uncertain wicket could not bring his side victory. Jackman gave Surrey hope when he dismissed Mendis and Parker with successive deliveries and Imran a few balls later. Wells and Barclay, who had bowled well, batted with sense and Sussex eventually edged home. Wells was ordered to change his pads when Surrey complained that they had been treated with a substance that was spoiling the ball.

Benson and Hedges Cup

13 May   **at Southampton**

Minor Counties 182 for 7 (T. E. Jesty 4 for 22)
Hampshire 179
Minor Counties (2 pts) won by 3 runs

Cricket is ever a corrective. Four days before their match with Minor Counties, Hampshire had gained a totally unexpected victory over Middlesex. They had won through perseverance which was tempered by confidence and humility. Sadly, the second of these qualities seemed to desert them when they returned to Southampton. Jesty's late swing brought three wickets in twenty-one deliveries and reduced Minor Counties to 76 for 5. At this point they found their hero in the former Essex player Steve Plumb, now of Norfolk, who added 26 with O'Brien, 53 in eleven overs with Collyer, and 27 off the last sixteen balls with Holder. Plumb showed a wide range of strokes while never violating correct technique and finished on 48 not out. Greenidge treated the target of 183 with disdain as he slogged Holder and Jesty, too, was at his most aggressive, but wickets were falling and at 112 for 5, Hampshire suddenly realised the game was in the balance. Minor Counties gnawed away and when gold award winner Steve Plumb dismissed Cowley, victory seemed a possibility. It became a reality when Stevenson miss-hit to fine leg and Greensword took the catch and the plaudits of his side.

13, 14 and 15 May   **at Old Trafford**

Somerset 309 for 3 dec (J. W. Lloyds 127, I. V. A. Richards 82) and 89 (M. A. Holding 5 for 37, P. J. W. Allott 4 for 23)

Lancashire 244 (D. P. Hughes 87, D. Lloyd 66, J. Garner 5 for 59) and 121
(J. Garner 5 for 57, I. T. Botham 4 for 62)
Somerset won by 33 runs
Somerset 24 pts, Lancashire 3 pts

at Trent Bridge
Leicestershire 170 (B. F. Davison 57, K. E. Cooper 4 for 52) and 195
Nottinghamshire 279 (P. A. Todd 81, C. E. B. Rice 66, R. J. Hadlee 66) and
90 for 2
Nottinghamshire won by 8 wickets
Nottinghamshire 23 pts, Leicestershire 5 pts

at The Oval
Surrey 258 (G. S. Clinton 123, C. J. Richards 62, M. Hendrick 4 for 43) and
181 for 6 dec (G. R. J. Roope 55 not out)
Derbyshire 233 for 6 dec (B. Wood 53, A. Hill 54 not out) and 31 for 1
Match drawn
Derbyshire 6 pts, Surrey 5 pts

at Hove
Glamorgan 230 (A. Jones 109) and 119 (G. G. Arnold 6 for 39, G. S. Le Roux
4 for 38)
Sussex 195 (E. A. Moseley 4 for 44) and 155 for 3
Sussex won by 7 wickets
Sussex 21 pts, Glamorgan 6 pts

at Nuneaton
Kent 323 for 6 dec (M. R. Benson 114, Asif Iqbal 108) and 218 for 2 dec (R. A.
Woolmer 119 not out, C. J. Tavare 96)
Warwickshire 217 for 7 dec (G. W. Humpage 58) and 325 for 6 (A. I. Kalli-
charran 135)
Warwickshire won by 4 wickets
Warwickshire 20 pts, Kent 7 pts

at Leeds
Middlesex 329 for 4 dec (M. W. Gatting 158, G. D. Barlow 73 not out) and
142 for 9 dec (C. M. Old 5 for 52)
Yorkshire 207 (C. W. J. Athey 72, M. W. W. Selvey 5 for 91) and 183 (W. W.
Daniel 6 for 64)
Middlesex won by 81 runs
Middlesex 24 pts, Yorkshire 3 pts

at Cambridge
Cambridge University 281 for 7 dec (D. R. Pringle 127 not out, N. Russom
65, J. Cumbes 5 for 69) and 220 for 4 dec (D. R. Pringle 61 not out, J. P. C.
Mills 50)
Worcestershire 225 for 4 dec (J. A. Ormrod 100 not out, D. J. Humphries 64
not out)
Match drawn

at Oxford
Oxford University 114 (R. P. G. Ellis 50, D. A. Graveney 4 for 9) and 291
(R. S. Cowan 113, K. A. Hayes 59, R. P. G. Ellis 58)

Gloucestershire 340 for 5 dec (A. J. Hignell 102 not out, B. Dudleston 99)
and 97 for 0 (A. W. Stovold 61 not out)
Gloucestershire won by 10 wickets

A sudden burst of summer weather encouraged a flurry of centuries and of the
Schweppes County Championship matches, only the miserable game at the Oval
failed to produce a positive result. Hendrick had made a sorry mess of the
early Surrey batting on the opening morning, but Clinton, with his customary
resolution, batted bravely and found an able partner in Richards, with whom
he shared a stand of 119 for the seventh wicket. Richards reached 62, his
highest score in first-class cricket. Miller declared 25 short of the Surrey total,
but the Surrey second innings was a moribund affair, and tedium was its only
characteristic. There was brighter fare at Old Trafford where Jeremy Lloyds hit
a maiden century and shared a second wicket partnership of 166 with Viv
Richards who in no way overshadowed the young all-rounder. Lancashire
stuttered a reply and would have been overwhelmed by Garner but for David
Lloyd and the ferocious David Hughes who kindled memories of a great occasion when he hit a six and fifteen fours in his 87. Holding, in his first
championship game, and Allott then destroyed Somerset and at lunch on the last
day, Lancashire needed only 136 more for victory with all their wickets in
hand. Within two hours after lunch they had been beaten by 33 runs. Garner and
Botham bowled unchanged and, with the aid of an uncertain pitch and some
very fragile batting, they seized a victory for Somerset which had looked very
unlikely in the morning. Nottinghamshire's win was more easily accomplished
early on the last day. Leicestershire gave two poor batting displays against
an accurate and varied attack and Notts, for whom Hadlee once more made
a late and valuable batting contribution, swept to an impressive victory. Sussex's
win at Hove was less predictable for, after Barclay had put Glamorgan in, Alan
Jones, the constant reminder of a talent that England has neglected, hit the
fifty-first century of his career. Moseley bowled the Welshman to a first innings
lead, but this was nullified by some splendid seam bowling from Arnold and
Le Roux. Imran, though not taking a wicket, gave good support, and Sussex
had given early indication that they could be among the leading counties at the
end of the season.

There was a maiden century at Nuneaton where a magnificent wicket fostered
four players to the hundred and Tavare to 96. On the opening day, Mark
Benson, who had reached a career best in the previous match, hit a most
impressive maiden century and was concerned in a fourth wicket stand of 185
in 144 minutes with Asif Iqbal who showed his form had improved with the
responsibility of captaincy with a sparkling knock, so different to the player of
1980 whose highest score had been 41. The Warwickshire bowling was un-
relieved monotony, for, incomprehensibly, Ferreira had been preferred to Doshi
as the second overseas player. Their batting was a little more colourful, but
with rain interruptions, Willis declared more than a hundred behind. Woolmer
and Tavare, in pre-England form, then savaged a Warwickshire attack in which
Willis was unable to perform. When Tavare was out Asif declared and left
the home side 305 minutes in which to score 325, a task which, on the evidence
of their first innings, they looked unlikely to accomplish. That they won was
due to some sound batting and a brilliant innings of 135 in three-and-three-

quarter hours by Alvin Kallicharran. He hit a six and seventeen fours and Warwickshire won with twenty-two balls to spare. At Headingley Mike Gatting enhanced his claim to return to the England side with a forceful innings on the opening day which brought him his second hundred of the season and the highest score of his career. It was also remarkable that though this was only the sixth century of Gatting's career, three of them had been scored against Yorkshire. Selvey bowled Middlesex into a commanding position on the second day and though Old gave hint that Yorkshire were still in contention, Brearley declared his second innings with a lead of 264 so leaving his bowlers just over four hours in which to dismiss the home side. They needed less time than this, in fact, for when Daniel had Whiteley caught by Gatting, thirteen overs still remained. The Middlesex bowling and fielding were most impressive and the batting of Gatting and Barlow in both innings were decisive. Rain hindered progress at Cambridge, but Derek Pringle played two good innings and Ormrod reached a welcome century. Oxford's troubles continued as they were lashed by Dudleston, his best for his new county, and Hignell. They gained some consolation as Ralph Cowan hit a maiden hundred and Kevin Hayes a career best. They shared a sixth wicket stand of 136.

16 May   **at Arundel**
Australians 106
Lavinia, Duchess of Norfolk's XI 107 for 7
Duchess of Norfolk's XI won by 3 wickets

Benson and Hedges Cup

at Oxford
Match abandoned
Combined Universities 1 pt, Glamorgan 1 pt

at Chelmsford
Essex 278 for 5 (G. A. Gooch 138, K. W. R. Fletcher 62)
Somerset 240 (D. J. S. Taylor 54 not out, S. Turner 4 for 51)
Essex (2 pts) won by 38 runs

at Bristol
Match abandoned
Gloucestershire 1 pt, Northamptonshire 1 pt

at Bournemouth
Hampshire 143 for 5 (C. G. Greenidge 50) *v.* Surrey
Match abandoned
Hampshire 1 pt, Surrey 1 pt

at Slough
Match abandoned
Minor Counties 1 pt, Middlesex 1 pt

at Trent Bridge
Worcestershire 214 for 8 (P. A. Neale 73)

Nottinghamshire 217 for 4 (R. T. Robinson 77 not out)
Nottinghamshire (2 pts) won by 6 wickets

at Edgbaston

Derbyshire 23 for 1 *v.* Warwickshire
Match abandoned
Warwickshire 1 pt, Derbyshire 1 pt

17 May   **at Glasgow (Titwood)**
Scotland 112 for 7
Lancashire 116 for 4
Lancashire (2 pts) won by 6 wickets

In a May which was becoming increasingly, and depressingly, the dampest on record, the Australians opened their tour at Arundel. Their gravest concern was over the health of Dennis Lillee who had been taken to hospital with a bronchial condition and was already deemed as unlikely to play in the First Test. The Australians performed indifferently with the bat and Kim Hughes was lbw to Intikhab first ball. Mike Denness was able to make the winning hit and gain belated, and justified, consolation for the sufferings of a decade ago. Elsewhere the weather was dreadful and only at Chelmsford and Trent Bridge were the Benson and Hedges games completed. Lancashire were able to beat Scotland on the Sunday in a game reduced to 48 overs. David Hughes steadied Lancashire when they threatened to flounder and won the Man of the Match award. The winner at Chelmsford was Graham Gooch who had returned from the West Indies a hero, but whose early season form in all competitions had been poor. He survived an early difficult chance to Botham at slip to play an innings of controlled splendour and power. He shared a third wicket stand of 158 in 29 overs with Keith Fletcher whose quiet efficiency once more hid his rapidity of run getting. One of the most proficient of English batsmen of the past twenty years, the man has never received the acclaim he has deserved. Gooch's 138 equalled his highest in the Benson and Hedges competition. Somerset began badly, losing Denning lbw to Phillip for nought. Rose and Richards put on 75 in 18 overs, but both fell to Turner, and the innings disintegrated. Taylor and Moseley bravely added fifty for the last wicket, but Essex were easy winners and had blunted Somerset for the second time in a week. Botham has an X-ray on a damaged finger and was hit for 74 runs in his ten overs and one ball. At Trent Bridge Nottinghamshire continued their impressive form, beating Worcestershire with two overs, one ball and six wickets to spare. Hadlee and Rice again bowled well and Hadlee confirmed his all-round status with a late flourish that insured victory. Neale, enjoying some luck, was Worcester's top scorer, but the hero of the day was Tim Robinson who won the gold award in his first Benson and Hedges match with an innings of good sense that steered his side to victory. Victory, in fact, came from an Alleyne bouncer which went for four wides. The matches abandoned meant that Middlesex, the favourites, and Northants, the holders, would be unlikely to qualify for the quarter finals, but that Minor Counties had a real chance of reaching that stage.

John Player League

17 May   **at Bournemouth**
Hampshire 112 for 2
Glamorgan 91 for 7
Hampshire (4 pts) won by 21 runs

                                                          at Northampton

Gloucestershire 113 for 4 (Zaheer Abbas 55)
Northamptonshire 108 for 8
Gloucestershire (4 pts) won by 5 runs

                                                          at Trent Bridge

Nottinghamshire 107 for 5
Somerset 96 for 2
Somerset (4 pts) won on faster scoring rate

                                                          at the Oval

Surrey 167 for 6 (M. W. W. Selvey 4 for 36)
Middlesex 110 for 5
Middlesex (4 pts) won on faster scoring rate

                                                          at Edgbaston

Match abandoned
Warwickshire 2 pts, Leicestershire 2 pts

                                                          at Worcester

Worcestershire 93 for 7
Sussex 96 for 2 (G. D. Mendis 56 not out)
Sussex (4 pts) won by 8 wickets

                                                          at Huddersfield
Kent 223 for 6 (C. J. Tavare 97)
Yorkshire 79 for 7 (D. L. Underwood 4 for 22)
Kent (4 pts) won on faster scoring rate

Somehow the weather was defeated for all but one of the Sunday League matches to be played though all were curtailed. The one casualty was, sadly, at Edgbaston where engineers struggled to rectify faults in the covering system which would enable cricket to be played at all times when it was not actually raining. Everyone hoped that Warwickshire's brave instigation would succeed. Hampshire and Glamorgan played an 18 over match and Jesty and Cowley smote some mighty blows to give the home side a winning total. Zaheer and Broad started with a stand of 104 in 13.2 overs and so put Gloucestershire on the way to a victory in their 15 over match at Northampton. Rain reduced Somerset's target at Trent Bridge and they won with three overs to spare. They were mainly indebted to the relentless accuracy of Garner's bowling which made scoring very difficult for Notts. Middlesex also had their target reduced by rain and won with seven balls to spare. The ever dependable Radley was the foundation of the victory with the bat and Selvey, who took three wickets in five balls, took the bowling honours. Worcestershire made 93 in their fifteen overs against Sussex, being cut down by Imran Khan who took three wickets and ran out top scorer Neale. Sussex lost 2 for 22, but Imran and Mendis reached the target with ten balls remaining. The performance of the day, however, was at Huddersfield where Kent scored 223 in 33 overs, 6.75 runs per over. Chris Tavare missed a century for the second time in three days by a narrow margin, but he hit 97 in 53 minutes and his innings included four sixes and ten fours. He had been a sad sight at Lord's the previous summer when he had appeared strokeless against the West Indian attack in the second Test, but, with confidence regained, he had made an early season assertion that he should play against Australia. Benson was also in good form, being run out for 49. Yorkshire passed into oblivion though their innings was reduced to 21 overs.

Benson and Hedges Cup

19 May   **at Cambridge**
Combined Universities 111 for 9
Somerset 114 for 3
Somerset (2 pts) won by 7 wickets

                                                at Derby

Scotland 97 (M. Hendrick 4 for 18)
Derbyshire 98 for 3
Derbyshire (2 pts) won by 7 wickets

                                                at Lord's

Match abandoned
Middlesex 1 pt, Sussex 1 pt

                                          at Northampton

Leicestershire 20 for 2 *v.* Northamptonshire
Match abandoned
Northamptonshire 1 pt, Leicestershire 1 pt

                                              at Edgbaston

Yorkshire 221 (J. D. Love 84, R. G. D. Willis 7 for 32)
Warwickshire 211 (G. W. Humpage 93)
Yorkshire (2 pts) won by 10 runs

                                               at Worcester

Gloucestershire 247 for 6 (Sadiq Mohammad 91, A. J. Hignell 51 not out)
Worcestershire 178 (A. H. Wilkins 4 for 35)
Gloucestershire (2 pts) won by 69 runs

20 May   **at Cardiff**
Kent 80 for 8 (E. A. Moseley 4 for 8)
Glamorgan 71 for 9
Kent (2 pts) won by 9 runs

The rain so devastated the country once more as to wash out the games in which both Middlesex and Northamptonshire were involved and so ensure their elimination from the competition. Somerset quickly disposed of a lustreless Universities side, Garner's bowling earned him the gold award, and Hend-rick and Derbyshire were too much for Scotland who, for the second year, had failed to reveal their true ability. Sadiq was another gold award winner in a game in which Gloucestershire's batting was always too strong for the limited Worcestershire bowling. It was good to see that Alastair Hignell once more revealed the batting form which had eluded him in 1980. Kent and Glamorgan had to be content with a fifteen over thrash; the game could not start until 5.40 on the Wednesday. Ezra Moseley did the first hat-trick of his career when he dismissed Knott, Shepherd and Dilley, and he finished with 4 for 8 in his three overs, but Glamorgan lost openers Hopkins and Javed for 8 and were always struggling. Alan Jones came in at number five and hit two sixes and two fours in the match top score of 25, but the rest was silence. By far the finest game, however, was at Edgbaston. Willis won the toss and asked Yorkshire to bat. His gesture was rewarded with the wickets of Boycott and Athey, but the preference of Ferreira to Doshi again looked unwise as Love and Hampshire effected a Yorkshire recovery. Willis returned to destroy the remainder of the batting and return the remarkable figures of 7 for 32, a feat which won him the gold award, but could not win his side the match. Warwickshire started badly, Amiss and Lloyd were out for 13, but Humpage played another storming innings. He had good support from Kallicharran and young Asif Din, but he was caught by Love off Hartley seven short of his hundred and Warwickshire died bravely by 10 runs.

Benson and Hedges Cup

21 May   **at Taunton**
Kent 172 (R. A. Woolmer 64)
Somerset 173 for 5 (I. T. Botham 57 not out)
Somerset (2 pts) won by 5 wickets

                                                                          at The Oval
Middlesex 54 for 5 *v.* Surrey
Match abandoned
Surrey 1 pt, Middlesex 1 pt

21 and 22 May   **at Chelmsford**
Combined Universities 120 (S. Turner 4 for 19)
Essex 121 for 2 (A. Lilley 63 not out)
Essex (2 pts) won by eight wickets

                                                                          at Gloucester
Nottinghamshire 191 for 9 (C. E. B. Rice 96)
Gloucestershire 127 (Sadiq Mohammad 57)
Nottinghamshire (2 pts) won by 64 runs

                                                                          at Old Trafford
Lancashire 179 for 7 (J. Simmons 59 not out, S. P. Hughes 52, M. Hendrick
   4 for 42)
Derbyshire 181 for 8 (G. Miller 74)
Derbyshire (2 pts) won by 2 wickets

at Slough

Sussex 154 for 5 (P. W. G. Parker 58)
Minor Counties 108
Sussex (2 pts) won by 46 runs

at Leicester

Leicestershire 238 for 7 (J. C. Balderstone 87)
Worcestershire 190 (G. J. Parsons 4 for 33)
Leicestershire (2 pts) won by 48 runs

at Bradford

Yorkshire 228 for 6 (J. D. Love 118 not out, C. M. Old 78 not out)
Scotland 186 (M. Johnson 4 for 18)
Yorkshire (2 pts) won by 42 runs

20, 21 and 22 May   **at Southampton**
Hampshire 176 for 3 dec (M. C. J. Nicholas 58)
Australians 237 for 7 (R. W. Marsh 72 not out, J. Dyson 60)
Match drawn

When Yorkshire stood at 25 for 5, having been put in to bat, it seemed that the Scots would achieve the sensation of the competition. The position improved only slightly to 79 for 6, but then Old joined Love and mayhem followed. They added a record seventh wicket stand for the competition of 149 in only 16 overs and completely reversed the course of the game. Both reached their best scores in Benson and Hedges matches. Old, who took 17 from one over by left-arm spinner Scarff, hit five sixes and four fours; Love hit two sixes and thirteen fours. The next day Mark Johnson took four wickets and Yorkshire were through to the quarter finals. Derbyshire kept alive their hopes of joining them by beating Lancashire, who were saved from humiliation by veterans Simmons and Hughes. Derbyshire struggled to get the runs. They were 34 for 3 on the Thursday evening, closing at 52 for 3, but Miller played a fine innings the next day and they won with three balls to spare. Somerset, too, kept their hopes alive with a good win in difficult conditions at Taunton. Woolmer batted creditably, but four Kent batsmen were run out in a lemming like rush for runs. Somerset started solidly in reply and then Botham hit his first fifty of the season when it was most needed and gave his side victory. It was an innings of calm among much frenzy.

The other victors in Section C were Essex who owed much to the fire brigade for making Chelmsford playable on the Friday. Combined Universities had started unusually well, but Stuart Turner altered the game with some fine bowling, dismissing Cowan and Ellis in one over and finishing with 4 for 19 in his eleven overs. Essex, in a hurry to win before the return of rain, lost Gooch early, but Alan Lilley, who had spent 1980 in the shadows, hit finely and the target was reached in 23 overs. The gold award went to Turner, his first in the competition, and one that was richly deserved by one of the very best of one-day cricketers. He has served Essex and cricket splendidly for over a decade and many lesser men have earned more reward and acclaim. Nottinghamshire and Leicestershire both reached the quarter finals from Group A.

Gloucestershire transferred their game from Bristol to Gloucester and were encouraged by the restrictions that Childs placed on Notts, but Rice flourished and, ultimately, the victory for Notts was an easy one. So, too, was Leicestershire's win. Balderstone anchored the Leicester innings and though several Worcester batsmen promised much, none accomplished the size of innings that was needed. Sussex and Minor Counties were reduced to 23 overs which was asking too much of the part-timers, and Middlesex finished their unhappy series with their third abandonment. The Australians opening first-class game against Hampshire was put back one day, and then the new first day was lost to rain. Eventually Nicholas, Dyson and Marsh batted agreeably, and nobody learned very much. Whatever happened to those days in the sun at Worcester?

23, 24 and 25 May   **at Taunton**
Australians 232 for 8 dec
Somerset 25 for 0
Match abandoned

23, 25 and 26 May   **at Cardiff**
Kent 44 for 5 *v.* Glamorgan
Match abandoned
No points

         at Old Trafford
Yorkshire 348 for 9 dec (J. D. Love 154, P. J. W. Allott 6 for 105)
Lancashire 310 for 8 dec (F. C. Hayes 126, G. B. Stevenson 4 for 78)
Match drawn
Yorkshire 7 pts, Lancashire 6 pts

         at Edgbaston
Warwickshire 185 for 9 dec
Worcestershire 187 for 4 (Younis Ahmed 106 not out)
Worcestershire won by 6 wickets in match restricted to one day
Worcestershire 12 pts, Warwickshire 0 pts

The matches – Derbyshire *v.* Nottinghamshire (Derby); Essex *v.* Gloucestershire (Chelmsford); Middlesex *v.* Sussex (Lord's); Northamptonshire *v.* Leicestershire (Northampton); Surrey *v.* Hampshire (The Oval) were all abandoned without a ball being bowled.

The very wettest of weather ruined the holiday fixtures. Play was limited at Old Trafford but at least Yorkshire and Lancashire were able to contest bonus points. The marvellous form of Jim Love continued and there was more encouraging bowling from Allott. On the last day it was Frank Hayes, once a golden hope for English cricket, who played with assurance and charm. Warwickshire and Worcestershire contrived a game at Edgbaston where Younis won the points for the visitors with one of those innings which he produces every so often and against which there is seemingly no defence. Dyson, Trevor Chappell and Yallop all got into the forties for the Australians in the brief amount of batting time allowed them at Taunton. It was some compensation. Distressingly, Wood was again dismissed without scoring. Botham was appointed captain of England for the Prudential matches, an announcement which was greeted with few cheers.

John Player League

24 May   **at Derby**
Match abandoned
Derbyshire 2 pts, Nottinghamshire 2 pts

                                                                           at Chelmsford

Essex 28 for 2 *v.* Gloucestershire
Match abandoned
Essex 2 pts, Gloucestershire 2 pts

                                                                           at Cardiff

Glamorgan 64 for 3 *v.* Kent
Match abandoned
Glamorgan 2 pts, Kent 2 pts

                                                                           at Old Trafford

Lancashire 144 for 8
Northamptonshire 96 for 9
Lancashire (4 pts) won on faster scoring rate

                                                                           at Lord's

Match abandoned
Middlesex 2 pts, Sussex 2 pts

                                                                           at Edgbaston

Warwickshire 224 for 4 (G. W. Humpage 71, T. A. Lloyd 63)
Worcestershire 222 (E. J. O. Hemsley 67, G. M. Turner 56)
Warwickshire (4 pts) won by 2 runs

                                                                           at Leeds

Yorkshire 147 for 8
Leicestershire 142
Yorkshire (4 pts) won by 5 runs

The weather was a little kinder to the Sunday league than to the Schweppes County Championship and there was some excitement in the three games that were completed. Geoff Humpage was again in splendid aggressive form for Warwickshire and shared a second innings stand of 93 with Lloyd. Worcestershire's reply was founded on good knocks by Turner and Hemsley, but when the ninth wicket went down they were still 17 short of victory. Twelve were needed from Hogg's last over, and Gifford and Cumbes ran singles on the first three balls. Then Cumbes hit a mighty six, only to be bowled next ball so that Worcestershire slumped to their fifth successive defeat in one-day matches. The match at Headingley was curtailed to 33 overs and Yorkshire owed much to the hitting of Bairstow and Sidebottom after Boycott had been bowled for one. The asking rate of four and a half an over was always a little too much for Leicestershire. Rain reduced Northants target at Old Trafford to 99 in 24 overs. They needed 10 from Allott's last over. Cook was run out off the first ball when going for a second run, Carter was lbw to the next and Tim Lamb caught behind off the third. Mallender hit a four and was then bowled. Griffiths needed to hit the last ball for four, but he could only manage two.

27, 28 and 29 May   **at Swansea**
Australians 147 (E. A. Moseley 6 for 23)
Glamorgan 84 for 4
Match drawn

at Chelmsford
Surrey 300 for 6 dec (R. D. V. Knight 96, A. R. Butcher 73) and 221 for 7 dec (R. D. V. Knight 84)
Essex 247 (K. S. McEwan 106, M. S. A. McEvoy 56, S. T. Clarke 5 for 36) and 163 for 6 (G. A. Gooch 50)
Match drawn
Surrey 8 pts, Essex 4 pts

at Bristol
Gloucestershire *v.* Surrey
Match abandoned
No points

at Dartford
Kent 200 for 6 dec (Asif Iqbal 64 not out, J. N. Shepherd 59 not out) and 191 for 6 dec (C. J. C. Rowe 54, P. Carrick 4 for 76)
Yorkshire 164 for 5 dec (J. D. Love 53 not out) and 112 for 5
Match drawn
Kent 4 pts, Yorkshire 3 pts

at Leicester
Leicestershire 224 (D. I. Gower 109, B. F. Davison 60, M. D. Marshall 6 for 57) and 23 for 0 dec
Hampshire 0 for 0 and 160 for 9
Match drawn
Hampshire 4 pts, Leicestershire 2 pts

at Uxbridge
Nottinghamshire 258 for 3 dec (C. E. B. Rice 117 not out, P. A. Todd 61) and 0 for 0
Middlesex 0 for 0 and 180 for 6 (J. M. Brearley 53)
Match drawn
Nottinghamshire 3 pts, Middlesex 1 pt

at Northampton
Northamptonshire 170 for 8 dec (A. J. Lamb 51, G. Cook 51, C. J. Tunnicliffe 5 for 34)
Derbyshire 261 for 6 (K. J. Barnett 67 not out, A. Hill 60 not out, B. Wood 58)
Match drawn
Derbyshire 6 pts, Northamptonshire 3 pts

at Worcester

Worcestershire 183 for 5 dec (Younis Ahmed 83 not out, J. D. Inchmore 63 not out)

Lancashire 185 for 3 (G. Fowler 105 not out)

Lancashire won by 7 wickets in match restricted to one day

Lancashire 12 pts, Worcestershire 0 pts

at Oxford

Warwickshire *v.* Oxford University

Match abandoned

29 May **at Edgbaston**

Warwickshire 229 for 7 (K. D. Smith 101)

Oxford University 231 for 5 (K. A. Hayes 106)

Oxford University won by 5 wickets

The rain relented a little though not enough to allow any match to produce a result. At Worcester play was only possible on the last day and, in spite of another fine innings from Younis and some whirlwind hitting by Inchmore, Lancashire won the one innings contest due to a splendid hundred from Graeme Fowler who hit two sixes and eleven fours. The Australians were in terrible trouble at Swansea where they were 16 for 5. Dyson batted with grim, and necessary, determination for 166 minutes to score 44 before he became another Ezra Moseley victim. Alderman and Lawson added 44 valuable runs for the last wicket. Ray Bright took three wickets to keep Australia in the game before the rain returned. The best news for the tourists was of the improving health of Dennis Lillee. Poor Gloucestershire suffered their third wash-out, but Surrey and Essex were luckier. Fletcher put Surrey in and must have regretted his decision when Clinton and Butcher put on 120 for the first wicket. Gooch then took 3 wickets in 8 balls, but Knight, surviving early alarms, scored 96 and Surrey took four points. Gooch was out third ball and it was left to the solid McEvoy and the exuberant McEwan to bolster Essex. They reached 241 for 6, obviously intent on three batting points, but even though they forced Hardie in to service at number eleven with his two broken fingers strapped, they fell to Clarke. Hardie had broken fingers in fielding. Knight again batted well, but, as against Derbyshire, he was far too cautious in his declaration and the game petered to a draw, lightened only by Gooch's first first-class fifty of the season. Kent were much more adventurous in their quest to beat the weather, but without avail. The success of Love continued. Gower scored a fine hundred for Leicestershire who made a valiant effort to beat Hampshire. Hampshire were positive in their desire to win and forfeited their first innings, but they fell to an all-round attack and were in terrible trouble at 78 for 8, but Marshall, who had bowled splendidly, and Southern took the score to 141 and then Stevenson joined Southern in an unbroken, match-saving last wicket stand of 19. Notts forfeited their second and Middlesex their first innings in an attempt to force a result at Uxbridge, but to no avail. Notts had the better of the conditions and Clive Rice once more emphasised his claim to be the most valuable player in county cricket with a brisk and immaculate century. Tunnicliffe had another impressive bowling spell for Derbyshire at Northampton and Hill joined Barnett in an undefeated seventh wicket partnership of 126 in 106 minutes on the last afternoon to add two valuable batting points. Warwickshire at Oxford University beat the weather by moving to Edgbaston for a 45 over game on the Friday. Surprisingly, the University won with four balls to spare, and, encouragingly, Hayes hit a century, as Smith had done for Warwickshire.

Benson and Hedges Cup

30 May   **at Dartford**
Essex 161 (K. W. R. Fletcher 51)
Kent 162 for 2 (R. A. Woolmer 79 not out)
Kent (2 pts) won by 8 wickets

                                                    at Trent Bridge
Leicestershire 114 for 8
Nottinghamshire 117 for 4
Nottinghamshire (2 pts) won by 6 wickets

                                                    at Glasgow (Titwood)
Warwickshire 221 for 5 (K. D. Smith 50)
Scotland 203
Warwickshire (2 pts) won by 18 runs

                                                    at Taunton
Glamorgan 169 for 8
Somerset 170 for 6
Somerset (2 pts) won by 4 wickets

                                                    at The Oval
Surrey 226 (B. G. Collins 4 for 44)
Minor Counties 98 (N. T. O'Brien 51 not out)
Surrey (2 pts) won by 128 runs

                                                    at Worcester
Worcestershire 123
Northamptonshire 127 for 1 (G. Cook 71 not out)
Northamptonshire (2 pts) won by 9 wickets

                                                    at Leeds
Match abandoned
Yorkshire 1 pt, Lancashire 1 pt

30 May and 1 June   **at Hove**
Hampshire 194 (C. G. Greenidge 60, I. A. Greig 5 for 35)
Sussex 198 for 7 (J. R. T. Barclay 59, I. A. Greig 51)
Sussex (2 pts) won by 3 wickets

The final round of matches in the qualifying round of the Benson and Hedges Cup failed to produce quite the excitement that had been expected. Warwickshire needed to beat Scotland and to take nine wickets to reach the quarter-finals in front of Derbyshire. This was a task they accomplished with a little more anxiety than they would have wished for, particularly as Scotland were 4 for 2 at the beginning of their innings. Notts and Leicester had already qualified, but Notts maintained their one hundred per cent record when they won with 18½ overs to spare. The Leicestershire innings was painful, Bore, who conceded only 7 runs in his 11 overs, was a particular problem for them. Northants also had an easy victory. They beat Worcestershire, perpetual losers in limited over cricket, with nine wickets and nearly nine overs left. Surrey's pace attack overwhelmed Minor Counties for whom O'Brien played a valiant innings and won the gold award. Surrey's win gave them a chance of qualifying if Sussex could beat Hampshire in the game which was held over to Monday. Hampshire started wonderfully, Greenidge and Rice put on 105 for the first wicket. Then came some woeful batting against the seam of Ian Greig who had his best figures in the competition, 5 for 35, and Hampshire were all out for 194. Marshall gave them renewed hope with hostile and relentlessly accurate bowling, but Barclay batted soundly, Greig with the flair of one about to receive the gold award, and Sussex won with one ball to spare. That Hampshire failed to win could be attributed to an injury to Rice which prevented him from bowling, their batting collapse on the Saturday, and some poor fielding in the early stages of the Sussex innings. They must have rued, too, their defeat at the hands of Minor Counties for it was that which cost them their place in the quarter-finals. The fireworks that were promised in Group C turned out to be the dampest of squibs. Jones and Hopkins started with a stand of 95 for Glamorgan against Somerset, but the innings never increased in momentum and the strong Somerset batting brought victory with nearly five overs left. Having been criticised for putting Surrey in to bat in the Schweppes County Championship match, Fletcher gained further criticism when he elected to bat at Dartford. He could hardly have foreseen, however, that his side would play so dreadfully. Fletcher and Pont apart, they batted badly, and, Phillip and Turner apart, they did not bowl too well. They also missed a couple of chances, had some cause for grievance about a couple of umpiring decisions and, all in all, had a thoroughly miserable day. Kent did everything right. Woolmer took the gold award, but it could have gone to Jarvis, Dilley, Shepherd, Asif, Knott or Benson.

Benson and Hedges Tournament Final
Tables – Qualifying Round

Group A	*P*	*W*	*L*	*NR*	*Pts*
Nottinghamshire	4	4	—	—	8
Leicestershire	4	2	1	1	5
Northamptonshire	4	1	1	2	4
Gloucestershire	4	1	2	1	3
Worcestershire	4	—	4	—	0
Group B	*P*	*W*	*L*	*NR*	*Pts*
Yorkshire	4	3	—	1	7
Warwickshire	4	2	1	1	5
Derbyshire	4	2	1	1	5
Lancashire	4	1	2	1	3
Scotland	4	—	4	—	0

Group C	P	W	L	NR	Pts
Kent	4	3	1	—	6
Somerset	4	3	1	—	6
Essex	4	2	2	—	4
Glamorgan	4	1	2	1	3
Combined Universities	4	—	3	1	1

Group D	P	W	L	NR	Pts
Sussex	4	3	—	1	7
Surrey	4	1	1	2	4
Hampshire	4	1	2	1	3
Minor Counties	4	1	2	1	3
Middlesex	4	—	1	3	3

Civil War at Lord's. Jeff Thomson, for Middlesex against his fellow Australians.

Combined Universities of Oxford and Cambridge 1981
Benson and Hedges
Batting

	v. Kent (Canterbury) 11 May	v. Glamorgan (Oxford) 16 May	v. Somerset (Cambridge) 19 May	v. Essex (Chelmsford) 21 and 22 May	Inns	NOs	Runs	HS	Av
J. P. C. Mills	19		0	3	3	—	22	19	7.33
R. P. Ellis	0		0	32	3	—	32	32	10.66
R. J. Boyd-Moss	5		37	11	3	—	53	37	27.66
D. R. Pringle	18		12	15	3	—	45	18	15.00
J. O. D. Orders	10				1	—	10	10	—
R. P. Moulding	7				1	—	7	7	—
N. Russom	22		1		2	—	23	22	11.50
S. J. G. Doggart	7		3	6	3	—	16	7	5.33
J. M. Knight	3		4*	6	3	1	13	6	6.50
K. I. Hodgson	0		16*	0	3	1	16	16*	8.00
I. G. Peck	4*		19	11*	3	2	34	19	34.00
R. S. Cowan			11	13	2	—	24	13	12.00
K. Hayes			5	17	2	—	22	17	11.00
N. V. H. Mallett				0	1	—	0	0	—
Byes	6		2	1					
Leg byes	1			3					
Wides	2		1	1					
No balls				1					
Total	104		111	120					
Wickets	10		9	10					
Result	L	Ab	L	L					
Points	0	1	0	0					

Catches
2 – J. P. C. Mills and K. I. Hodgson
1 – I. G. Peck and N. V. H. Mallett

Combined Universities of Oxford and Cambridge 1981 Benson and Hedges Bowling

	J. M. Knight	D. R. Pringle	N. Russom	K. I. Hodgson	S. J. G. Doggart	N. V. H. Mallett	B	Lb	W	Nb	Total	Wkts
v. Kent (Canterbury) 11 May	5-0-24-0	11-1-36-1	7-2-14-0	3-0-15-1	2-0-12-0			4	3		108	2
v. Somerset (Cambridge) 19 May	5-2-13-1	11-1-25-1	8-2-25-1	6-3-15-0	3-0-20-0		5	5	6		114	3
v. Essex (Chelmsford) 21 and 22 May	9-0-41-1	5-0-25-0		2-0-15-0		7-2-30-1	5	2	2	1	121	2
	19-2-78-2 av. 39.00	27-2-86-2 av. 43.00	15-4-39-1 av. 39.00	11-3-45-1 av. 45.00	5-0-32-0 —	7-2-30-1 av. 30.00						

Minor Counties 1981
Benson and Hedges
Batting

	v. Hampshire (Southampton) 13 May	v. Middlesex (Slough) 16 May	v. Sussex (Slough) 22 May	v. Surrey (The Oval) 30 May	Inns	NOs	Runs	HS	Av
R. V. Lewis	11		9	6	3	—	26	11	8.66
J. G. Tolchard	36		11	0	3	—	47	36	15.66
S. Greensword	9		15	11	2	—	24	15	12.00
D. Bailey	1		15	1	3	—	27	15	9.00
N. A. Riddell	7		9		3	—	17	9	5.66
S. G. Plumb	48*		14	2	3	1	64	48*	32.00
N. T. O'Brien	10			51*	2	1	61	51*	61.00
F. E. Collyer	21		1		2	1	22	21	11.00
V. A. Holder	22*		6	6	2	1	28	22*	28.00
B. G. Collins			0*	6	1	1	6	6	6.00
A. W. Allin					1	—	10	10	—
B. L. Cairns			10	0	2	—	7	7	3.50
I. Gemmill			7	7	1	—	7	7	—
G. I. Burgess				6	1	—	6	6	—
A. Griffiths									
Byes	8		2	1					
Leg byes	9		6	1					
Wides			3						
No balls									
Total	182		108	98					
Wickets	7		10	10					
Result	W	Ab.	L	L					
Points	2	1	0	0					

Catches
3 – N. A. Riddell
2 – D. Bailey and N. T. O'Brien
1 – V. A. Holder, S. Greensword, I. Gemmill, G. I. Burgess.
R. V. Lewis and A. Griffiths (st 1)

Minor Counties 1981
Benson and Hedges
Bowling

	V. A. Holder	B. G. Collins	S. Greensword	A. W. Allin	D. Bailey	N. T. O'Brien
v. Hampshire (Southampton) 13 May	7-1-46-1	9-2-25-2	11-4-20-2	11-3-27-0	1-0-3-0	8.3-1-19-3
v. Sussex (Slough) 22 May	5-0-32-1	5-0-14-1	3-0-29-1			
v. Surrey (The Oval) 30 May		10.4-2-44-4		11-2-39-0	2-0-10-1	4-0-19-0
	12-1-78-2 av. 39.00	24.4-2-83-7 av. 11.85	14-4-49-3 av. 16.33	22-5-66-0 —	3-0-13-1 av. 13.00	12.3-1-38-3 av. 12.66

	S. G. Plumb	B. L. Cairns	I. Gemmill	G. I. Burgess
v. Hampshire (Southampton) 13 May	7-0-27-2			
v. Sussex (Slough) 22 May	2-0-19-1	5-0-19-0	3-0-27-1	
v. Surrey (The Oval) 30 May	8-1-38-0		8-3-29-1	11-4-25-3
	17-1-84-3 av. 28.00	5-0-19-0 —	11-3-56-2 av. 28.00	11-4-25-3 av. 8.33

	B	Lb	W	Nb	Total	Wkts
v. Hampshire (Southampton) 13 May	2	3		7	179	10
v. Sussex (Slough) 22 May	8	3		3	154	5
v. Surrey (The Oval) 30 May	8	6			226	10

Scotland 1981
Benson and Hedges
Batting

	v. Lancashire (Glasgow) 17 May	v. Derbyshire (Derby) 19 May	v. Yorkshire (Bradford) 21 and 22 May	v. Warwickshire (Glasgow) 30 May	Inns	NOs	Runs	HS	Av
W. R. Scarff	14	21	28	0	4	—	63	28	15.75
T. B. Racionzer	20	3	8	2	4	—	33	20	8.25
R. C. Swan	6	2	35	20	4	—	63	35	15.75
C. J. Warner	25	19	20	33	4	—	97	33	24.25
A. Brown	20	11	32	29	4	—	92	32	23.00
H. G. F. Johnston	3	11	23	30	4	—	67	30	16.75
W. A. Donald	3	9	0	14	4	1	26	14	6.50
J. E. Ker	10*	2	2	31	4	2	45	31	15.00
G. F. Goddard	2*	1*	1*	14	4	2	18	14	9.00
F. Robertson		6*	2	0*	3	2	8	6*	8.00
J. Clark		11			1	—	11	11	—
W. D. W. Lauden			22	12	2	—	34	22	17.00
Byes	3		7	4					
Leg byes	6	1	3	4					
Wides			3	4					
No balls				6					
Total	112	97	186	203					
Wickets	7	10	10	10					
Result	L	L	L	L					
Points	0	0	0	0					

Catches
5 – A. Brown (ct 4, st 1)
3 – C. J. Warner and R. C. Swan
2 – H. G. F. Johnston
1 – W. R. Scarff and T. B. Racionzer

Scotland 1981
Benson and Hedges
Bowling

	F. Robertson	J. Clark	H. G. F. Johnston	G. F. Goddard	W. R. Scarff	J. E. Ker	W. D. W. Lauden	W. A. Donald	B	Lb	W	Nb	Total	Wkts
v Lancashire (Glasgow) 17 May	7-1-20-0	2-0-16-0	10-4-16-1	10-0-25-2	9-2-15-0	5.1-0-19-1			3	2			116	4
v Derbyshire (Derby) 19 May	4-1-15-0		9.2-3-20-0	8-0-34-2	8-3-17-1	3-0-12-0							98	3
v Yorkshire (Bradford) 21 and 22 May	11-2-52-2		6-3-22-0	6-0-16-0	8-1-37-1	6-1-15-0	8-2-40-0	10-2-37-2	4	4		1	228	6
v Warwickshire (Glasgow) 30 May	11-3-34-2		11-1-30-1	8-0-38-2	11-0-49-0	9-0-51-0	5-1-10-0		3	6			221	5
	33-7-121-4 av. 30.25	2-0-16-0 —	36.2-11-88-2 av. 44.00	32-0-113-6 av. 18.83	36-6-118-2 av. 59.00	23.1-1-97-1 av. 97.00	13-3-50-0 —	10-2-37-2 av. 18.50						

Chris Tavare of Kent who was later to be back in the England side.

John Player League

31 May   **at Chelmsford**
Kent 49 for 2
Essex 33 for 3
Essex (4 pts) won on faster scoring rate

                                              at Basingstoke
Hampshire 163 for 6 (T. E. Jesty 62)
Sussex 164 for 3 (I. J. Gould 69 not out)
Sussex (4 pts) won by 7 wickets

                                              at Old Trafford
Lancashire 92 for 7
Somerset 49 for 2
Somerset (4 pts) won on faster scoring rate

                                              at Northampton
Northamptonshire 116 for 9
Leicestershire 118 for 5 (D. I. Gower 54)
Leicestershire (4 pts) won by 5 wickets

                                              at the Oval
Derbyshire 139 for 6
Surrey 140 for 7
Surrey (4 pts) won by 3 wickets

                                              at Bradford
Middlesex 85 for 6
Yorkshire 45 for 4
Match abandoned
Yorkshire 2 pts, Middlesex 2 pts

Rain brought curtailment everywhere. At Bradford the floods returned to save Yorkshire who were chasing Middlesex's 85 at six and a half an over and not succeeding. It brought Essex victory at Chelmsford. Kent had scored 49 for 2 in sixteen overs when a storm hit the ground. The match was reduced to ten overs, leaving Essex a meagre 31 in 10. They reached the target in 8, but without much conviction. Nevertheless, they joined Middlesex on ten points, two behind Sussex who were inspired to victory by a superb knock from Ian Gould. He hit a six and four fours and reached his first fifty in the competition. Somerset's game at Old Trafford was also reduced to ten overs. Somerset needed 47, but they reached 49 in under six overs, thanks to Richards and Botham. Botham had also bowled most tightly and productively. At Northampton there was a thirty over match and Gower and Briers appeared to have given Leicester an easy victory with an opening stand of 91. Gower's last three innings against Northants had seen him lbw to Tim Lamb for 0, but this time he batted with his customary panache to reach 54. There then came a mild panic as five wickets fell for twenty runs and when the last over started five were still needed. Davison put aside frivolities by hoisting Griffiths' first ball for six. The hero of the day was Surrey's David Thomas. At The Oval Derbyshire had made 139 in their thirty-seven overs and seemed to have victory assured when Richards was seventh out at the end of the thirty-sixth over so leaving Surrey needing fifteen from the last over. Oldham, who had disposed of Roope, Lynch and Knight at a personal cost of 29 runs, was bowling. Clarke took a single from the first ball. Thomas drove the second over long on for six, sliced the third to third man for two, and drove the fourth mightily into the distance for a winning six. Story book stuff for the young left-hander! The England thirteen for the Prudential Cup matches included Love, Humpage and Randall. Dilley and Tavare were the surprising omissions.

31 May, 1 and 2 June   **at Bristol**
Australians 278 for 7 dec (T. M. Chappell 91, G. M. Wood 81)
Gloucestershire 80 for 2 (Zaheer Abbas 60 not out)
Match abandoned as a draw

Once more the weather ruined efforts for the Australians to achieve some worthwhile match practice. There was play only on the Monday at Bristol though efforts had been made to play on the two preceding days. The Australians took advantage of the solitary day of fine weather to show that once their limbs had been oiled by a little sunshine they could disprove their label as the weakest team to be sent from their country. Wood scored his first runs of the tour and Trevor Chappell, though as yet lacking the elegance and fluency of his brothers, grafted dourly to enhance his chances of a Test place. In the late evening Zaheer playing a scintillating innings as he reached his fifty in as many minutes with eleven fours and then the rain returned.

3, 4 and 5 June   **at Basingstoke**
Hampshire 211 (C. G. Greenidge 96, M. W. W. Selvey 5 for 79) and 261 for 9 (C. G. Greenidge 57, T. E. Jesty 57)
Middlesex 322 for 6 dec (J. M. Brearley 135)
Match drawn
Middlesex 8 pts, Hampshire 4 pts

at Old Trafford
Lancashire 332 for 7 dec (C. H. Lloyd 74, A. Kennedy 64, D. Lloyd 63) and
199 for 5 dec (G. Fowler 75, B. W. Reidy 55)
Surrey 254 (S. T. Clarke 79) and 156 for 8 (G. S. Clinton 79 not out, M. A.
Holding 5 for 60)
Match drawn
Lancashire 8 pts, Surrey 4 pts

at Trent Bridge
Gloucestershire 200 (K. Saxelby 4 for 64) and 152 (Zaheer Abbas 72, E. E.
Hemmings 6 for 21)
Nottinghamshire 262 (P. A. Todd 96, R. T. Robinson 60, J. H. Childs 5 for 73,
M. J. Procter 4 for 45) and 93 for 1
Nottinghamshire won by 9 wickets
Nottinghamshire 23 pts, Gloucestershire 6 pts

at Hove
Sussex 360 for 6 dec (P. W. G. Parker 108, T. D. Booth-Jones 95, Imran
Khan 74) and 164 for 8 dec
Somerset 272 for 9 dec (P. W. Denning 72, J. Garner 52) and 152 for 5
Match drawn
Sussex 6 pts, Somerset 4 pts

at Edgbaston
Warwickshire 237 (C. Maynard 70, R. G. Williams 4 for 32) and 233 for 8 dec
(A. I. Kallicharran 59, S. J. Rouse 55 not out)
Northamptonshire 325 for 7 dec (W. Larkins 157)
Match drawn
Northamptonshire 7 pts, Warwickshire 5 pts

at Hereford
Glamorgan 234 (A. Jones 63, Javed Miandad 52) and 180 for 8 dec
Worcestershire 229 (Younis Ahmed 80, R. N. S. Hobbs 5 for 67) and 183 for 9
(Younis Ahmed 74)
Match drawn
Glamorgan 6 pts, Worcestershire 5 pts

at Leeds
Essex 354 for 8 dec (K. R. Pont 89, A. Sidebottom 4 for 44)
Yorkshire 129 (J. K. Lever 8 for 49) and 357 for 4 (M. D. Moxon 116, C. W. J.
Athey 57, R. G. Lumb 53, D. L. Bairstow 53 not out)
Match drawn
Essex 8 pts, Yorkshire 3 pts

at Oxford
Leicestershire 240 for 4 dec (B. F. Davison 75 not out, J. F. Steele 56) and 178
for 7 dec (R. W. Tolchard 55, N. E. Briers 51, N. V. H. Mallett 4 for 104)
Oxford University 165 and 142 (J. C. Balderstone 4 for 17)
Leicestershire won by 111 runs

With the weather showing an unexpected kindness, cricketers emerged from
the pavilion and performed some notable deeds. In the Schweppes County
Championship, however, only Nottinghamshire could force a victory. They
had a comfortable win early on the last day over a Gloucestershire side who

had become unaccustomed to playing first-class cricket. Gloucestershire started badly and that they reached 200 was due to some aggression from Procter, some sound defence by Hignell, and a little fortune for Graveney. The medium pace of Kevin Saxelby ended any real hopes of recovery and Todd, the most consistent and under-praised opening batsman in the country, and Robinson, quickly put Notts into a strong position. John Childs checked the advance with some fine left-arm spin bowling which accounted for both openers plus Dexter, Rice and French. The lead of 62 was a disappointment for Notts, but it assumed greater proportions when the beautifully controlled off-spin of Hemmings routed Gloucestershire in the second innings as they slipped from 117 for 3 to 152 all out, their last six wickets falling for eight runs. Notts fielded well and their lead in the championship was increased to seventeen points. They had a compact and balanced side which was capable of carrying off English cricket's highest honour. One doubted only their belief in themselves. The reigning champions, Middlesex, were in second place, having been thwarted by Hampshire who were saved by Greenidge when they were put in to bat. Brearley scored his first hundred of the season in a rather restrained manner, and Hampshire batted bravely on the last day to save the game. Parks played out the last eighty minutes to score 33 not out. An interesting debutant for Middlesex was the thirty-seven-year-old Irish spinner Dermot Monteith. He held three catches and in the second innings dismissed Turner. Yorkshire ended the first day at Leeds in total disarray against Essex. Hardie made a surprisingly rapid return to the Essex side in spite of his broken fingers and he and McEvoy gave the side a brisk start. Sidebottom apart, the Yorkshire bowling reached the depths it had reached in the Gillette Cup semi-final of 1980, perhaps it sank even lower, and Essex prospered. Keith Fletcher, who was being advocated for the England captaincy from many quarters, became the first Essex player to score 30,000 runs in first-class cricket, and Keith Pont, one of several Essex players to benefit from missed chances, hit a fine 89. Satisfied with his side's score, Fletcher declared and left Yorkshire fifty minutes batting at the end of the first day during which time Lever and Turner reduced them to 16 for 5. Lever took all the wickets to fall on the second day to finish with 8 for 49 so equalling his career best. Yorkshire followed on 225 runs behind. The game was saved. Lumb and Moxon put on 122 for the first wicket. Moxon and Athey 99 for the second. Martyn Moxon was making his debut for Yorkshire and he reached his century in 313 minutes. He was the first Yorkshire player since Cecil Tyson in 1921 to score a hundred on his debut for the county.

There was a career best at Hove where Paul Parker and Tim Booth-Jones put on 177 for the third wicket. Parker, all grace and charm, emphasised his claim to a place in the England side, an honour which should have already come his way, and Booth-Jones, a latecomer to county cricket, hit a career best. Somerset were saved by a late fifty from Garner and a purposeful innings from the ever busy Denning. Richards made a late flourish in the second innings, but the match was drawn and Sussex looked a match for anybody in the country. As Humpage was on duty with the England Prudential side, Maynard came into the Warwickshire side for first time in the season and saved his team with an innings of 70. Northamptonshire enjoyed themselves against a moderate attack. Cook and Larkins began with a stand of 112, and Larkins and Williams who had bowled well, added 123 for the second wicket. Larkins was third out, having scored 157 out of 240 and given a gentle reminder of his class as a batsman. A solid innings by Rouse saved Warwickshire when defeat had looked a possibility. Surrey were very much in the wars at Old Trafford. Lancashire built a sound score on the opening day and on the gloomy second they dismissed Surrey batsmen with frequency. Butcher was injured and when Sylvester Clarke came in the score was 166 for 7. He lightened the gloom with an innings of 79 out of 85 in 15 overs. He hit six sixes and seven fours and followed this with two quick wickets to put Surrey back in the game. In the end, however, Holding had Surrey struggling to avoid defeat and that they managed a draw was due to the redoubtable Clinton and the brave Butcher who survived the last eleven balls with his injured hand. There was a thrilling finish at Hereford, a delightful place for a meeting between Worcestershire and Glamorgan. Glamorgan took a narrow lead in the first innings through some fine leg-spin bowling by Robin Hobbs who returned his best figures since joining Glamorgan. Nash made a sporting and well judged declaration and the last twenty overs were reached with Glamorgan seven wickets and Worcester 92 runs. Younis, who had batted brilliantly in both innings, and Humphries were both stumped off Hobbs, and the game flowed first one way and then the other. With two balls to go and one wicket to fall Pridgeon swung wildly at Hobbs and narrowly escaped being another stumping victim, and his efforts to hit a winning boundary off the last ball only produced one to mid-wicket. The only consolation for Oxford in The Parks was that Taylor became the first of the university bowlers to hit the stumps when he bowled Chris Balderstone. Balderstone later wreaked revenge and Leicestershire were ample winners. For the third season in succession it seemed apparent that Oxford were the weaker of the two university sides.

Prudential Trophy

First One-Day International

That the first of the international matches was upon us seemed to take most of us by surprise, not least the Australians themselves who had had so little practice as to make it appear that their tour had not yet started. There was, too, the absence of fanfare surrounding the arrival of the Australian party due, no doubt, to the fact that they were now frequent visitors and the mystique which had once surrounded their visits every four years had gone. It was sad that Greg Chappell had found himself unable to make the trip and surprising that Doug Walters, so successfully recalled to the colours, had not been chosen. The other main surprise was in the choice of Bright as spinner ahead of Higgs or Yardley. Bright bore a charmed life as far as Australian selectors were concerned, frequently gaining preference over players whose records were more impressive. The amazing fitness of Dennis Lillee was never better illustrated than by the fact that he reported fit for this first one-day international in spite of being stricken with bronchial pneumonia only a fortnight earlier when fears as to his ability to continue the tour were expressed. He would not, of course, be partnered by Jeff Thomson, a controversial omission from the party and a controversial signing by Middlesex. It needed all Mike Brearley's eloquent powers at the Middlesex A.G.M. to convince the members that Middlesex had acted wisely and not in a manner detrimental to the game. England omitted Emburey and Randall, both of whom had been expected to play. Love and Humpage gained their first experience at international level. It was not a memorable match. Dyson was lbw second ball of the day. Wood ran himself out in his customary bizarre fashion and Chappell was unluckily run out when Jackman diverted a ball onto the stumps with the batsman out of his ground. Border played with confidence and aggression, and on a slow wicket the Australians laboured a little against a moderate, if adequate attack in which Hendrick and Jackman were the best performers. Gooch and Boycott gave England a match winning start and then Gower played an innings of brief charm and graceful power, and the match was won. Boycott won the Man of the Match award for his chanceless 75. England had won comfortably yet one was left with the suspicion that this was far from being the weakest Australian side to visit these shores. The batting looked potentially formidable. Yallop was not playing in this match, but he, with Wood, Hughes and Border formed a strong nucleus whilst Kent had played some impressive shots in his innings of 28. It was felt that spin would give the Australians most trouble, but, as against the West Indies, England seemed committed, wrongly, to be trying to beat the visitors at their own game.

First Prudential One-Day International: England v. Australia
4 June 1981   at Lord's

Australia

J. Dyson	lbw, b Willis	2
G. M. Wood	run out	22
T. M. Chappell	run out	16
K. J. Hughes (capt)	lbw, b Jackman	12
A. R. Border	not out	73
M. F. Kent	c Gooch, b Botham	28
* R. W. Marsh	b Botham	18
R. J. Bright	b Willis	18
G. F. Lawson	not out	12
D. K. Lillee		
R. M. Hogg		
Extras	b 1, lb 8	9
		—
	(for 7 wkts)	210

	O	M	R	W
Willis	11	—	56	2
Botham	11	1	39	2
Hendrick	11	2	32	—
Jackman	11	1	27	1
Willey	6	1	26	—
Gooch	5	1	21	—

Fall of Wickets
1–2, 2–36, 3–48, 4–60, 5–134, 6–162, 7–189.

England

G. A. Gooch	c Kent, b Lillee	53
G. Boycott	not out	75
M. W. Gatting	lbw, b Lillee	0
D. I. Gower	c Kent, b Chappell	47
J. D. Love	c Bright, b Lawson	15
I. T. Botham (capt)	not out	13
P. Willey		
* G. W. Humpage		
R. D. Jackman		
R. G. D. Willis		
M. Hendrick		
Extras	b 5, lb 4	9
	(for 4 wkts)	212

	O	M	R	W
Hogg	11	1	36	—
Lillee	11	3	23	2
Lawson	9	—	51	1
Chappell	11	1	50	1
Bright	9.4	—	43	—

Fall of Wickets
1–86, 2–86, 3–172, 4–199.

England won by 6 wickets

Prudential Trophy

Second One-Day International

On a rain interrupted, and mostly cold, day, Australia beat England at 8.35 in the evening by two runs. It was a fine game of cricket, but for England it was something of a disaster. The Australians made two changes, Yallop and Alderman replacing Dyson and Bright; England played the same team as at Lord's. Once more Botham asked Australia to bat when he won the toss, and once more there was an early success when Botham had Trevor Chappell caught behind. Wood and Yallop quickly repaired the damage, and after Wood was well caught at long-leg off Jackman, Hughes joined Yallop in authoritative stand. Hughes was close to the majesty he had shown in the Centenary Test, the one golden memory of that bleak occasion, and at one time he and Yallop were scoring at six an over. Hendrick, far and away the best of the England bowlers, bowled Yallop leg stump, and Hughes and Border were needlessly run out. Marsh made some lusty clouts and Botham had erred in his allotments to his bowlers. England's fifth bowler was a combination of Gooch and Willey; they conceded 74 runs between them. Gooch found himself, unaccountably, bowling the penultimate over and Lawson took fourteen from it, including two sixes. England were quickly in disarray with Gooch, Boycott and Gower, the best of their batting, out for only 36. Gatting was dropped twice by Marsh, one the simplest of catches before he had scored. He responded with a violent innings which grew in stature as it lengthened. Love gave him able support and then Willey matched him run for run. Botham, too, seemed in good form and England were moving to victory. When the captain was caught at mid-on by Hughes, running back, England needed 26 to win with five overs remaining and four wickets left. Humpage fretted and was bowled. Sixteen runs were needed off two overs. Gatting hit two fours off Hogg, and England needed six off Lillee's last over. Jackman was run out in spite of Australia's over-excitement in the field and then Gatting drove high to mid-off for what looked another certain four and one which would bring him his century. Lawson sprinted round the boundary, dived and held the ball one handed, an historic and brilliant catch. Willis and Hendrick provided light comedy at the moment of high drama, and Hendrick was caught behind off the penultimate ball to the joy of the Australians.

Second Prudential One-Day International: England v. Australia
6 June 1981   **at Edgbaston**

Australia

G. M. Wood	c Willis, b Jackman	55
T. M. Chappell	c Humpage, b Botham	0
G. N. Yallop	b Hendrick	63
K. J. Hughes (capt)	run out	34
A. R. Border	run out	17
*R. W. Marsh	c Love, b Botham	20
M. F. Kent	lbw, b Willis	1
G. F. Lawson	not out	29
D. K. Lillee	run out	8
R. M. Hogg	not out	0
T. M. Alderman		
Extras	b 1, lb 18, w 1, nb 2	22
	(for 8 wkts)	249

	O	M	R	W
Willis	11	3	41	1
Botham	11	1	44	2
Hendrick	11	2	21	1
Jackman	11	—	47	1
Willey	6	—	36	—
Gooch	5	—	38	—

Fall of Wickets
1–10, 2–96, 3–160, 4–171, 5–183, 6–193, 7–213, 8–248.

England

G. A. Gooch	b Hogg	11
G. Boycott	b Lawson	14
M. W. Gatting	c Lawson, b Lillee	96
D. I. Gower	b Alderman	2
J. D. Love	b Lawson	43
P. Willey	c Wood, b Chappell	37
I. T. Botham (capt)	c Hughes, b Lawson	24
*G. W. Humpage	b Lillee	5

R. D. Jackman	run out	2
R. G. D. Willis	not out	1
M. Hendrick	c Marsh, b Lillee	0
Extras	lb 12	12
		247

	O	M	R	W
Hogg	11	2	42	1
Lillee	10.5	2	36	3
Alderman	11	1	46	1
Lawson	11	2	42	3
Chappell	11	—	69	1

Fall of Wickets
1–20, 2–27, 3–36, 4–111, 5–177, 6–224, 7–232, 8–244, 9–244.

Australia won by 2 runs

6, 8 and 9 June   **at Derby**
Warwickshire 247 (D. L. Amiss 109) and 270 (D. L. Amiss 127, D. S. Steele
   6 for 77)
Derbyshire 300 for 5 dec (J. G. Wright 75, A. Hill 56 not out, G. Miller 51
   not out, S. P. Perryman 4 for 60) and 109 for 1 (J. G. Wright 54 not out)
Match drawn
Derbyshire 7 pts, Warwickshire 4 pts

                                            at Swansea
Surrey 131 (M. A. Nash 7 for 62) and 317 for 8 dec (S. T. Clarke 100 not
   out, G. P. Howarth 77, C. J. Richards 53)
Glamorgan 132 (S. T. Clarke 6 for 66) and 192 (J. A. Hopkins 53, P. I. Pocock
   4 for 54)
Surrey won by 124 runs
Surrey 20 pts, Glamorgan 4 pts

                                            at Bristol
Gloucestershire 172 (Zaheer Abbas 71, B. C. Broad 50, C. M. Old 4 for 41)
   and 268 (Zaheer Abbas 74, B. C. Broad 71, A. Sidebottom 5 for 68)
Yorkshire 130 (A. H. Wilkins 4 for 40) and 193 (A. Ramage 52, J. H. Childs
   5 for 61)
Gloucestershire won by 117 runs
Gloucestershire 21 pts, Yorkshire 4 pts

                                            at Lord's
Somerset 324 for 9 dec (I. V. A. Richards 92, P. M. Roebuck 68, P. W. Denning
   63) and 166 for 4 dec (P. W. Denning 75 not out)
Middlesex 265 for 4 dec (R. O. Butcher 106 not out, C. T. Radley 87)
Match drawn
Middlesex 6 pts, Somerset 4 pts

                                        at Northampton
Kent 293 for 6 dec (G. W. Johnson 107, M. R. Benson 82) and 258 for 2 dec

(C. J. Tavare 135 not out, R. A. Woolmer 63, M. R. Benson 51 not out)
Northamptonshire 306 for 8 dec (W. Larkins 77, A. J. Lamb 65) and 224 for 7
(W. Larkins 74, T. J. Yardley 55 not out)
Match drawn
Kent 6 pts, Northamptonshire 5 pts

at Hove

Sussex 397 for 7 dec (P. W. G. Parker 136, I. A. Greig 71, C. P. Phillipson
56 not out)
Lancashire 131 (B. W. Reidy 50, Imran Khan 4 for 50) and 204 (N. V. Radford
75 not out, I. A. Greig 6 for 21)
Sussex won by an innings and 62 runs
Sussex 24 pts, Lancashire 2 pts

at Worcester

Essex 308 for 4 dec (K. W. R. Fletcher 127, B. R. Hardie 76, K. S. McEwan
51) and 187 for 4 dec (N. Phillip 80 not out)
Worcestershire 221 (J. A. Ormrod 84 retired hurt, D. L. Acfield 4 for 34) and
276 for 4 (G. M. Turner 101, Younis Ahmed 65)
Worcestershire won by 6 wickets
Worcestershire 19 pts, Essex 8 pts

at Cambridge

Cambridge University 126 (N. Russom 51, P. J. Hacker 4 for 34) and 224 (N.
Russom 58, T. D. W. Edwards 57)
Nottinghamshire 298 for 6 dec (B. Hassan 91 not out, R. T. Robinson 77,
R. E. Dexter 57) and 53 for 0
Nottinghamshire won by 10 wickets

Some sunshine allowed matches to be completed in spite of the inevitable
interruptions for rain. Sussex routed Lancashire and moved to the top of the
table alongside Notts who were engaged in completing a very easy win over
a strangely lack-lustre Cambridge side. Clive Lloyd had asked Sussex to bat,
but Mendis and Barclay gave the innings a solid foundation and then Paul
Parker played with vigour to reach a hundred full of rich strokes. He and
Ian Greig added 158 for the fifth wicket in a stirring partnership; both batsmen
recorded their highest scores in the county championship. From Parker it was
another reminder to the selectors that here was a batsman of the highest class
who was long overdue for Test honours. The Lancashire fielding was poor,
the bowling moderate; their batting was even worse. Reidy alone saved them
from total disgrace in the first innings, and a late, brave career best from
Radford saved them for further humiliations in the second innings. Greig
completed a memorable match with his best bowling figures for Sussex who,
under Barclay's astute and virile leadership, looked capable of winning
everything. The same could not be said of Somerset who threw away an early
advantage given to them by Viv Richards at his sparkling best. He was brilliantly
caught behind by Paul Downton, diving to his right, when eight short of his
hundred. Roebuck then occupied the crease for most of the remainder of the
day, leaving the memory of not a single shot. Somerset continued on the
Monday, and, anxious to force a result, Brearley declared 59 runs behind. He

was helped by a brisk knock from Radley and an even brisker hundred from Butcher who displayed that exciting range of shots that earned him selection for the England side the previous summer. Rose refused any challenge and batted out time. The bright aspect for Somerset was the batting of Denning in both innings. Here is a player who goes for his shots in a cultured and aggressive manner. He is always busy and cricket is the better for him. Like Rose, Knight had been mentioned as a likely England captain, but, like Rose, he had received criticism for recent ultra caution. There seemed good need for caution at Swansea on the Saturday when Malcolm Nash bowled with the experience of fifteen years in the first-class game and routed Surrey on a doubtful wicket. Sadly, Glamorgan fared no better themselves, managing a lead of only one run, and that entirely due to the top score of 20 not out by Robin Hobbs who went in at number eleven. Glamorgan still seemed set for victory when, in spite of a fine innings from Geoff Howarth, desperately in need of form and some luck, Surrey were 166 for 7. Sylvester Clarke, who had earlier been Glamorgan's destroyer, now joined Richards. By the close the score was 264 for 7. Their stand was eventually worth 147 and it was made in 59 minutes. Richards, who broke a toe during his innings, an injury to keep him out of the Surrey side in the coming weeks, was out for 53, but Clarke hit seven sixes and eight fours in his maiden hundred which came in 62 minutes, the season's fastest to date. In one over he hit Nash for 23. Glamorgan began a difficult task well. Allan Jones and Hopkins put on 106 for the first wicket, then Pocock and, surprisingly, Monty Lynch extracted turn from the pitch and Glamorgan crumbled. Lynch, a very occasional off-break bowler, returned a career best 3 for 6.

There were no such fireworks at Derby where Amiss, acting captain, hit a century in each innings, Wright showed improving form, and David Steele spun his left-arm well, but all ended in stalemate. There was a draw, too, at Northampton where Graham Johnson, returning to opener in the absence of Rowe, hit a hundred on the Saturday. He was out for nought in the second innings, but Benson played with his joyful aggression on both occasions. Tavare was again in fine form as was Woolmer. For Northants Wayne Larkins produced that streak of elegant batsmanship which, to the chagrin of his many admirers, he had never produced for England. Like Tavare, he seemed worthy of another chance. The end was thrilling. Northants had needed 246 in 160 minutes and had accepted the challenge, but it was Kent who nearly snatched victory in the end. Worcestershire did snatch victory from Essex after they had been outplayed for most of the match. Fletcher, at his most fluent, and with cries for him to be named as England's captain growing every minute, hit a splendid century though he injured a hand in the process. He was given able support from Brian Hardie, returning to the side with fingers strapped. Acfield brought about a middle order collapse on the second day, and, with Ormrod having his arm broken by a ball from Phillip, Worcester were struggling. Phillip and Turner hit lustily in the second innings and Worcester were set 275 in 205 minutes. Lever dismissed Patel early, but Glenn Turner gave the innings a firm and fierce foundation in company with the irrepressible Younis. Hemsley hit the fifth ball of Lever's last over for six to bring a startling victory. Worcester could reflect that their bowlers had taken only eight wickets during the match. Essex could reflect that for the second time they had thrown away a match that they had been winning. Bowlers dominated the game at Bristol where only the reliable Broad and the immaculate Zaheer rose above the norm of the batting. On the last afternoon it was the left-arm of Childs, an ever improving player, that spun Yorkshire to defeat. Ramage scored a late fifty to save Yorkshire from complete disgrace. Their own spinners had not seemed in the Gloucestershire class.

John Player League
7 June   at Swansea
Surrey 43 for 1 *v.* Glamorgan
Match abandoned
Glamorgan 2 pts, Surrey 2 pts

                                                                    at Bristol
Gloucestershire 216 for 4 (Zaheer Abbas 58, B. C. Broad 56, M. J. Procter 52 not out) *v.* Yorkshire
Match abandoned
Gloucestershire 2 pts, Yorkshire 2 pts

                                                                 at Maidstone
Northamptonshire 154 for 5 (W. Larkins 64)
Kent 49 for 2
Northamptonshire (4 pts) won on faster scoring rate

                                                                   at Lord's
Middlesex 170 for 9 (G. D. Barlow 52, C. H. Dredge 5 for 35)
Somerset 51 for 1
Somerset (4 pts) won on faster scoring rate

                                                              at Trent Bridge
Nottinghamshire 182 for 6
Essex 41 for 3
Nottinghamshire (4 pts) won on faster scoring rate

                                                                      at Hove
Lancashire 181 for 7 (D. Lloyd 76)
Sussex 160 for 2 (G. D. Mendis 69 not out, Imran Khan 63 not out)
Sussex (4 pts) won on faster scoring rate

Rain interrupted everybody, which was particularly hard on Gloucestershire who had been scoring at six and a half an over against Yorkshire. Kent could not match Larkins scoring rate for Northants, and some accurate bowling from Dredge (his best Sunday League figures) saw Somerset to an easy win at Lord's. They scored at 5.1 an over to the 4.47 of Middlesex. Notts were equally impressive against Essex, and Sussex overwhelmed Lancashire by scoring at 6.67 an over. Mendis could not hit a ball wrong and Imran played an innings of characteristic fire. Sussex stayed top of the league.

Prudential Trophy
Third One-Day International

England once more omitted Emburey and Randall, a strange decision, and Australia brought back Dyson for Kent. Australia outclassed England more comprehensively than one can recall England ever being outclassed in a one-day international. Wood and Dyson started solidly. Yallop once more brought panache, and then Wood scampered for every run to reach a hundred which was founded on sheer determination. Hendrick once more was the pick of the England bowlers. Hogg dismissed Boycott second ball and then roused the crowd with his tantrums. Gooch was circumspect and patently out of form. Gatting was more assured – he had brilliantly caught Hughes on the boundary first ball. Willey and Jackman batted bravely at the close, but, in truth, England were overwhelmed. Botham was appointed captain for the First Test and England had lost to Australia in a one-day series for the first time. It is worth recalling that only two years previously when we had been beaten by the West Indies in the Prudential World Cup Final, many felt that England were close to becoming a very great side. Somewhere in the next two seasons we lost our direction.

Third Prudential One-Day International: England v. Australia
8 June 1981   **at Headingley, Leeds**

Australia

G. M. Wood	run out	108
J. Dyson	c Gooch, b Hendrick	22
G. N. Yallop	run out	48
K. J. Hughes (capt)	c Gatting, b Jackman	0
A. R. Border	c Jackman, b Willis	5
* R. W. Marsh	c Humpage, b Botham	1
T. M. Chappell	c Gooch, b Willis	14
G. F. Lawson	run out	8
D. K. Lillee	not out	0
R. M. Hogg		
T. M. Alderman		
Extras	lb 27, w 1, nb 2	30
	(for 8 wkts)	236

	O	M	R	W
Willis	11	1	35	2
Botham	11	2	42	1
Hendrick	11	3	31	1
Gooch	11	—	50	—
Jackman	11	1	48	1

Fall of Wickets
1–43, 2–173, 3–173, 4–187, 5–189, 6–216, 7–236, 8–236.

England

G. A. Gooch	c Marsh, b Lawson	37
G. Boycott	c Marsh, b Hogg	4
M. W. Gatting	c Marsh, b Hogg	32
D. I. Gower	b Alderman	5
J. D. Love	b Chappell	3
P. Willey	c Marsh, b Hogg	42
I. T. Botham (capt)	c Hughes, b Chappell	5
*G. W. Humpage	c Border, b Alderman	6
R. D. Jackman	b Chappell	14
R. G. D. Willis	not out	2
M. Hendrick	c Marsh, b Hogg	0
Extras	b 10, w 1, nb 4	15
		165

	O	M	R	W
Hogg	8.5	1	29	4
Lillee	7	—	37	—
Lawson	11	3	34	1
Alderman	11	3	19	2
Chappell	9	—	31	3

Fall of Wickets
1–5, 2–71, 3–80, 4–89, 5–95, 6–106, 7–133, 8–160, 9–164.

Australia won by 71 runs

10, 11 and 12 June   **at Bristol**
Gloucestershire 356 for 8 dec (B. C. Broad 94, P. Bainbridge 84 not out,
   A. W. Stovold 57) and 363 (D. A. Graveney 105 not out, Zaheer Abbas 50)
Northamptonshire 348 (T. J. Yardley 96 not out, P. Willey 79, A. J. Lamb
   78, M. J. Procter 5 for 80)
Match drawn
Gloucestershire 8 pts, Northamptonshire 7 pts

at Bournemouth
Glamorgan 281 for 7 dec (N. G. Featherstone 113 not out, K. Stevenson 5 for
   94) and 17 for 3 dec
Hampshire 0 for 0 and 301 for 5 (C. G. Greenidge 115, T. M. Tremlett 83,
   R. N. S. Hobbs 4 for 84)
Hampshire won by 5 wickets
Hampshire 19 pts, Glamorgan 3 pts

at Tunbridge Wells
Leicestershire 308 for 8 dec (D. I. Gower 115, N. E. Briers 50) and 0 for 0
Kent 0 for 0 and 233 for 7 (J. N. Shepherd 56 not out, N. G. B. Cook 4 for
   84)
Match drawn
Leicestershire 3 pts, Kent 1 pt

at Old Trafford
Lancashire 352 for 9 dec (D. P. Hughes 126, G. Fowler 72) and 124 for 2 dec
   (G. Fowler 65 not out)

Warwickshire 135 for 3 dec (K. D. Smith 56) and 218 for 4 (G. W. Humpage
81 not out, K. D. Smith 56)
Match drawn
Lancashire 5 pts, Warwickshire 3 pts

at The Oval
Worcestershire 273 (Younis Ahmed 116, Intikhab Alam 5 for 66) and 168 for 2
dec (G. M. Turner 73, M. S. Scott 52)
Surrey 170 (A. P. Pridgeon 4 for 49) and 274 for 6 (G. S. Clinton 69, R. D. V.
Knight 62)
Surrey won by 4 wickets
Surrey 21 pts, Worcestershire 7 pts

at Derby
Derbyshire 218 for 9 dec (J. G. Wright 144, T. M. Alderman 4 for 38) and
163 for 5 dec
Australians 190 for 8 dec (J. Dyson 61, I. S. Anderson 4 for 35)
Match drawn

at Cambridge
Sussex 348 for 9 dec (C. M. Wells 79, A. P. Wells 63, C. E. Waller 51 not
out, I. A. Greig 50, K. I. Hodgson 4 for 77)
Cambridge University 165 (D. C. Holliday 57, I. A. Greig 5 for 45) and 143
(I. A. Greig 7 for 43)
Sussex won by an innings and 40 runs

at Oxford
Oxford University 263 (R. S. Cowan 62) and 208 (R. G. P. Ellis 63, J. E.
Emburey 7 for 88)
Middlesex 287 (W. N. Slack 65, T. J. Taylor 5 for 81, S. P. Sutcliffe 4 for 130)
and 39 for 1
Match drawn

Conditions were once more unfavourable for cricket and it took the ingenuity
and bravery of captains to contrive a contest. There was no excitement at Bristol
where over a thousand runs were scored in three innings as the match became
moribund. There were two performances of note by Gloucestershire batsmen;
Philip Bainbridge hit a career best in the first innings and David Graveney
a maiden championship hundred in the second. At Bournemouth Featherstone,
who, when he first played for Middlesex, had looked one of the most exciting
and beautiful of players, hit his second hundred for his new county Glamorgan
on the opening day. Then came rain and Hampshire forfeited their innings
and Glamorgan's second innings lasted only half an hour. Hampshire had to
score 299 in 324 minutes to win. Gordon Greenidge and Tim Tremlett launched
them with a devastating opening stand of 180 in 152 minutes. Eventually
Hampshire won their first championship game of the season by five wickets
with nearly fourteen overs to spare. They had managed only one win in the
Schweppes County Championship in the whole of the 1980 season. Four of
the Hampshire wickets to fall were taken by Robin Hobbs and the other leg-
spinner still operating, Intikhab Alam, had five wickets in Worcestershire's

first innings. Younis Ahmed ravished the Surrey attack and when Glenn Turner declared setting the home side 272 at five an over. Victory would have taken Worcestershire to the top of the table, but it was Surrey who snatched the points and the lead in the championship race. When the last twenty overs began Surrey still needed 127 to win. To their eternal credit both sides maintained their desire to win and amid the cascade of runs, wickets tumbled. Clinton and Knight had made victory possible with a second wicket stand of 119, but it was Thomas and Smith who snatched the final glory. They came together at 220 for 6 and scored the last 54 runs in 8 overs. Victory came with eight balls to spare.

Kent were less successful at Tunbridge Wells where, after a blank second day and a fine century from David Gower, Kent were asked to make 309 in five hours. They finished 76 runs short and only the hitting of Shepherd and Dilley saved them from defeat and denied Leicestershire the points. Warwickshire gave up the chase at Old Trafford and the match ended predictably in a draw. Fowler batted well in both innings, but the honours of the game went to David Hughes. He came to the wicket with Lancashire at 99 for 4. In under three hours he reached his first championship century in fourteen years as a professional cricketer. A wonderful celebration for his testimonial year. John Wright became the first batsman to take a hundred off the Australian tourists' bowling, but the match, bedevilled by rain and a grotesquely slow wicket, dragged to a draw. It was Dennis Lillee's first first-class game of the tour. Oxford, mainly through their spinners, showed greatly improved form in their match against Middlesex who were captained by Phil Edmonds. John Emburey, opening the bowling in the second innings, gave a reminder to the England selectors that spin can be an attacking weapon. Cambridge were submerged by Sussex after having the better of the opening exchanges, Sussex were 47 for 3 at one time. Colin Wells, a prospective England player in 1980, unable to command a regular place in the Sussex side in 1981, played a fine knock as did his younger brother Alan, and Greig and Waller hit fifties. For Waller it was his first in first-class cricket. Hodgson had career best bowling figures for Cambridge, but the rest of the match belonged to Ian Greig. He had match figures of 12 for 88, including a career best 7 for 43 in the second innings. It completed a memorable week which had brought him his highest score in first-class cricket and 18 wickets for 109 runs. It all added to the growing Sussex confidence. Off the field the Australians announced that they could not agree to the hundred overs a day suggestion and Northants announced that Kapil Dev was joining them.

13, 14 and 15 June   **at Lord's**
Middlesex 150 (D. K. Lillee 5 for 41) and 261 for 5 dec (J. M. Brearley 132 not out, M. W. Gatting 75)
Australians 146 and 144 for 4 (G. N. Yallop 52 not out)
Match drawn

13, 15 and 16 June   **at Derby**
Derbyshire 289 (P. N. Kirsten 95, G. Miller 50, J. K. Lever 4 for 62) and 188 for 9 dec (P. N. Kirsten 90, J. K. Lever 4 for 36)

Essex 156 (P. G. Newman 5 for 51) and 250 for 5 (G. A. Gooch 78, S. Turner 58 not out, B. R. Hardie 55 not out)
Match drawn
Derbyshire 7 pts, Essex 5 pts

at Tunbridge Wells
Kent 250 for 8 dec (Asif Iqbal 76, A. P. E. Knott 52) and 270 for 5 dec (N. Taylor 99, C. J. Tavare 88)
Sussex 301 for 5 dec (J. R. T. Barclay 65, P. G. W. Parker 60 not out, T. D. Booth-Jones 60, G. D. Mendis 55) and 182 (G. D. Mendis 80, K. B. S. Jarvis 5 for 82)
Kent won by 37 runs
Kent 20 pts, Sussex 7 pts

at Leicester
Leicestershire 251 (J. C. Balderstone 91) and 276 for 5 dec (B. F. Davison 86, J. F. Steele 65)
Glamorgan 309 (J. A. Hopkins 111, N. G. Featherstone 58, L. B. Taylor 4 for 45) and 103 for 4
Match drawn
Glamorgan 5 pts, Leicestershire 3 pts

at Bath
Gloucestershire 361 for 4 dec (Zaheer Abbas 215 not out, A. J. Hignell 55) and 303 for 4 dec (Zaheer Abbas 150 not out)
Somerset 316 (J. Garner 90, D. Breakwell 58) and 245 for 9 (B. C. Rose 85 not out, D. Breakwell 53, P. Bainbridge 5 for 68)
Match drawn
Gloucestershire 8 pts, Somerset 5 pts

at Worcester
Worcestershire 115 (T. E. Jesty 4 for 28, M. D. Marshall 4 for 46) and 194 (M. S. Scott 50, T. E. Jesty 5 for 56, K. Stevenson 4 for 63)
Hampshire 337 (D. R. Turner 73, H. L. Alleyne 4 for 79)
Hampshire won by an innings and 28 runs
Hampshire 24 pts, Worcestershire 4 pts

at Bradford
Nottinghamshire 322 for 8 dec (R. J. Hadlee 142 not out, C. E. B. Rice 67)
Yorkshire 78 (R. J. Hadlee 4 for 16, E. E. Hemmings 4 for 31) and 355 for 7 (G. Boycott 124, J. D. Love 97)
Match drawn
Nottinghamshire 8 pts, Yorkshire 3 pts

at Oxford
Combined Universities of Oxford and Cambridge 309 (J. P. C. Mills 111, A. Ranasinghe 5 for 65) and 82 (R. G. Wijesuriva 5 for 35)
Sri Lankans 211 (T. J. Taylor 4 for 62) and 165 for 9 (S. P. Sutcliffe 4 for 54)
Match drawn

The Queen's Birthday List brought honours to Dennis Lillee and Bob Taylor.

At Lord's, Lillee celebrated his M.B.E. by routing Middlesex in mid-afternoon on the Saturday. There were further sensations after tea when Dyson was out for nought and Wood retired hurt after being struck on the cheek by a ball from Thomson whose fire had been kindled by playing against his former colleagues. Yallop played the only memorable shot of the day, a straight drive off Edmonds, but he went early on the Sunday when the Australians collapsed against a fierce attack. Mike Brearley then batted Middlesex to a position of command with an innings of authority which heartened many outside Middlesex, but, on the eve of the First Test, the Australians declined any dramatics and the match was drawn. Bob Taylor was cheered by the Essex players at Derby where Derbyshire recovered from John Lever's early burst and seized the initiative. Kirsten, searching for form, Miller and Tunnicliffe gave them respectability with the bat and then pace bowler Paul Newman returned a career best which had Essex struggling to save the follow-on. Essex were without Keith Fletcher who missed his first county game through injury in his nineteen-year career. Lever gave Essex renewed hope, but Kirsten again batted solidly and Essex were set 322 to win, a task, in their recent form, which was obviously beyond them, particularly as McEwan was hampered by injury. Gooch gave sign of return to form after which the game drifted to a draw. The other England opener, Geoff Boycott hit his first century of the summer. His innings lasted for just over seven hours and though he and Love and Hampshire saved Yorkshire from defeat and ignominy, they could not hide the fact that Yorkshire cricket was in an unhealthy state, with growing rumours of more political unrest. Richard Hadlee had resurrected the Notts innings on the Saturday. He came in at 120 for 5 and hit a career best, underlining the paucity of the Yorkshire spin attack. Then he and Hemmings conjured life from a dead pitch and for the second time in the season Yorkshire were routed before their own crowd. In the end Notts had to be content with eight points, but it was enough to take them to the top of the table, one point ahead of Sussex who lost an incredible match at Tunbridge Wells.

Sussex outplayed Kent for most of the game and on the last day Kent batted miserably. They scored at 2.41 an over against an enterprising spin attack. In the end, Barclay resorted to wicket-keeper Gould and Paul Parker as his bowlers. Taylor was bowled by Waller when one short of his first championship century. Having lumbered throughout the day, Kent then invited Sussex to score 220 in 25 overs. To their credit, Sussex tried to win and refused to call off the chase when wickets tumbled. The last over began with Sussex 182 for 8; Mendis, who had batted magnificently, was 80 not out. He played the first three deliveries from Underwood and went back to the fourth and was bowled. Waller survived the fifth and was yorked by the last to give Kent a dramatic and totally undeserved victory. It was Barclay's first defeat as the Sussex skipper, but he did not lose any friends, and there was a growing conviction that Sussex would take at least one of the four trophies for which they were competing. There was more jubilation on the south coast at Hampshire's second victory of the season. Twice their pace attack shot out Worcestershire. The Hampshire fielding was keen and Parks performed well behind the stumps. They batted efficiently and the match was over by lunch on the last day. Worcestershire were ordered to use the afternoon in batting practice.

Glamorgan promised for a time at Leicester, but the game fizzled to a draw. There was a draw of a different sort at Bath where Rose and Roebuck, batting at ten and eleven because of injury, survived the final fourteen overs to save the match. The game was a triumph for Zaheer Abbas who, for the fourth time, hit a double century and a century in the same match, so improving on his own record. Garner's late spirited knock saved Somerset in the first innings, but Gloucestershire had looked certain winners of the splendid contest until the dramatic last wicket stand. As well as Zaheer's regal batting, Gloucestershire could be well pleased with the fine all round form of Bainbridge. The Sri Lankans opened their tour with a match against a combined team from Oxford and Cambridge and their last pair survived the last fifteen overs to draw the match. Only 30 runs were needed, in fact, from these overs, but discretion prevailed.

John Player League

14 June   **at Derby**
Hampshire 179 for 7
Derbyshire 180 for 5 (P. N. Kirsten 55)
Derbyshire (4 pts) won by 5 wickets

                                                                at Leicester
Glamorgan 207 for 4 (Javed Miandad 107 not out, J. A. Hopkins 55)
Leicestershire 150 (E. A. Moseley 4 for 22)
Glamorgan (4 pts) won by 57 runs

                                                                 at Bath
Somerset 212 for 7 (P. M. Roebuck 73 not out)
Gloucestershire 192 (M. J. Procter 91, A. W. Stovold 54, J. Garner 4 for 21)
Somerset (4 pts) won by 20 runs

                                                              at The Oval
Northamptonshire 221 for 4 (A. J. Lamb 83, G. Cook 65)
Surrey 129
Northamptonshire (4 pts) won by 92 runs

                                                             at Worcester
Worcestershire 149 for 7
Essex 151 for 5 (K. W. R. Fletcher 61 not out)
Essex (4 pts) won by 5 wickets

The sun shone on the Sunday League. Kirsten confirmed his return to form as Derbyshire beat Hampshire with ease and Allan Lamb inspired Northants at The Oval with a scintillating innings. Cook gave good support and then Surrey rushed recklessly to defeat – all ten wickets falling to catches. Fletcher, though injured, steered Essex to an easy win at Worcester. The home side had started well, but Stuart Turner dismissed Scott and the prolific Younis and conceded only 12 runs in his eight overs. East also bowled economically and Essex faced an easy task. Javed Miandad scored his maiden century in the John Player League and with Hopkins also in good form, Glamorgan swept to their first Sunday win of the season. With so much already achieved, it was hard to realise that Javed was only two days past his twenty-fourth birthday. He is a giver of joy. The innings of the day, however, was played by Mike Procter at Bath. Somerset batted first and Peter Roebuck batted with charm and aggression, so different from his innings at Lord's, but was hurt in the course of his knock. Marks gave good support though of a more rustic nature and Gloucester faced a stiff task. The loss of Zaheer for 8 posed great problems and though Stovold stayed, he was never in touch and missed many opportunities of quickening the scoring rate. Procter played an innings of heroic proportions. He was suffering from a pinched nerve in the neck, but he dealt blows of massive power. Sadly, when Stovold left, the rest of the Gloucester batting disintegrated against Garner – six men failed to score. Procter was stumped off the first ball of the last over, a glorious death for a glorious innings.

17, 18 and 19 June   **at Ilford**

Essex 305 (A. W. Lilley 90, K. R. Pont 87) and 218 for 9 dec (B. R. Hardie 70, J. D. Monteith 5 for 60)

Middlesex 263 (J. M. Brearley 113, M. W. W. Selvey 57, S. Turner 4 for 44, J. K. Lever 4 for 75) and 163 (C. T. Radley 54, D. L. Acfield 5 for 58, R. E. East 4 for 56)

Essex won by 95 runs

Essex 23 pts, Middlesex 7 pts

at Cardiff

Warwickshire 247 (D. L. Amiss 103, E. A. Moseley 4 for 56) and 100 (M. A. Nash 4 for 20)

Glamorgan 408 (Javed Miandad 105, J. A. Hopkins 93, E. A. Moseley 50)

Glamorgan won by an innings and 61 runs

Glamorgan 24 pts, Warwickshire 4 pts

at Northampton

Northamptonshire 300 for 2 dec (G. Cook 146 not out, R. G. Williams 133) and 252 for 6 dec (A. J. Lamb 102 not out)

Sussex 250 for 7 dec (J. R. T. Barclay 107 not out) and 111 for 3 (P. W. G. Parker 53 not out)

Match drawn

Northamptonshire 7 pts, Sussex 3 pts

at Bath

Nottinghamshire 222 (J. D. Birch 63) and 97 (J. Garner 6 for 29)

Somerset 380 for 9 dec (I. V. A. Richards 106, V. J. Marks 70, P. A. Slocombe 50)

Somerset won by an innings and 61 runs

Somerset 24 pts, Nottinghamshire 3 pts

at The Oval

Lancashire 266 (C. H. Lloyd 84, S. T. Clarke 5 for 80) and 144 (R. D. Jackman 4 for 25, S. T. Clarke 4 for 41)

Surrey 290 (Intikhab Alam 79, D. M. Smith 76, P. J. W. Allott 5 for 94) and 124 for 6

Surrey won by 4 wickets

Surrey 22 pts, Lancashire 6 pts

at Sheffield

Yorkshire 374 for 9 dec (R. G. Lumb 145, M. D. Moxon 111, P. G. Newman 4 for 100)

Derbyshire 480 (A. Hill retired hurt 101, R. W. Taylor 100, J. G. Wright 65, B. Wood 53)

Match drawn

Yorkshire 6 pts, Derbyshire 5 pts

at Bristol

Sri Lankans 246 (D. Mendis 75, J. H. Childs 6 for 61) and 398 (D. S. De Silva 97, A. De Mel 94, B. Warnapura 70, M. Whitney 4 for 86)

Gloucestershire 416 for 2 dec (Sadiq Mohammad 203, P. Bainbridge 100 not out, B. C. Broad 70) and 3 for 0

Match drawn

at Leicester

Cambridge University 183 (J. P. C. Mills 63, L. B. Taylor 4 for 30, J. F. Steele 4 for 31) and 98 for 2 (J. P. C. Mills 55 not out)

Leicestershire 249 for 8 dec (J. F. Steele 83)

Match drawn

at Oxford

Oxford University 155 (G. W. Johnson 5 for 30) and 183 (D. L. Underwood 4 for 51)

Kent 233 for 8 dec (C. S. Cowdrey 70, S. P. Sutcliffe 4 for 74) and 107 for 0 (C. J. Tavare 63 not out)

Kent won by 10 wickets

Whilst Sussex maintained their determination to win the Schweppes County Championship with a spirited reply to Northants challenge that they should make 303 in 2¾ hours, a response that was ended by rain, Nottinghamshire showed an acute lack of confidence by collapsing to Joel Garner and losing to Somerset by an innings and 61 runs. Somerset owed much to some fine batting by Viv Richards, Vic Marks and Phil Slocombe, who was making a welcome return to the Somerset side. Slocombe made a competent fifty and fielded quite splendidly throughout the match. Notts never recovered from finishing the second day at 12 for 3 and only 'Pasty' Harris showed the necessary application against Garner and Moseley. Sussex suffered a second wicket stand of 280 by Geoff Cook and Richard Williams, a partnership full of majestic shots on a superb wicket. Northants reached 300 in under 75 overs and then John Barclay and Allan Lamb both hit good centuries before rain spoiled an exciting finish. With Sussex and Notts taking only six points between them, Surrey consolidated their lead at the top of the table with an unexpected win over Lancashire. Lancashire batted dourly on the opening day, but still were having the best of the match until Smith and Intikhab came together at 153 for 6. They added 119 and then Jackman and Clarke put out Lancashire for 144. This left Surrey needing 121 to win in 27 overs. Holding and Allott bowled unchanged and Surrey won off the third ball of the last over. There were no such eccentricities at Sheffield where Yorkshire and Derbyshire completed only one innings each. There were moments to savour, however. Martyn Moxon and Richard Lumb, who chipped a bone in his finger, put on 218 for the first wicket. Moxon reached his second century in first-class cricket in only his third game. Praise was tempered by the memory of former Yorkshire starlets and one hoped that Yorkshire would not once more turn a beautiful duckling into an ugly swan, as Robin Marlar so memorably worded it. Moxon's headlines were stolen on the last day by Bob Taylor who hit his maiden hundred in first-class cricket at the age of thirty-nine. As he was still unquestionably the best wicket-keeper in the country one wondered why he was not at Trent Bridge. Glamorgan recorded their first win of the season and their biggest for twelve years. Amiss hit another hundred for Warwickshire, but good all-round bowling and more fine batting from Javed and Hopkins gave Glamorgan the foundation for victory. As Hobbs was injured the much travelled A. A. Jones was brought in to the Glamorgan side. There are many who believe that he could have been an England quick bowler of quality and he raised fond memories when he dismissed Asif Din, Kallicharran and Small in one over on the last day. There was also a first victory of the season for Essex. Keith Pont and the aggressive Alan Lilley, a batsman of much promise who all too rarely is used in the championship side, rallied Essex on the opening day and Turner and Lever blunted the Middlesex batting on the Thursday after Brearley had hit his second century in successive innings. Essex scored briskly on the last morning with Brian Hardie as cornerstone. Dermot Monteith took five wickets and Phil Edmonds three, but it was the Essex spinning combination of East and Acfield that won the game on the last afternoon. The last eight Middlesex wickets fell for 62 runs.

At Bristol, Sri Lanka were spun out by Childs, a rapidly maturing player, on the opening day, and then came a feast of runs from Broad, Sadiq and Bainbridge. Sadiq hit the first double century of his career and Phil Bainbridge his maiden first-class hundred. Sri Lanka batted well on the last day to save the game and win esteem. There was no play on the last day at Leicester, but Cambridge had already gained satisfaction from the batting of Mills who followed his maiden first-class hundred for the Combined Universities against Sri Lanka with fifty in each innings against Leicestershire. Kent beat Oxford with ease, but they suffered injuries on the way and Benson's hand injury made it seem unlikely that he would be fit for the Benson and Hedges quarter final with Warwickshire.

First Cornhill Test Match

There were doubts about the wicket at Trent Bridge which made it somewhat surprising that England omitted Emburey from their team. Australia left out Bright so that once more we were confronted by a spinless Test. Woolmer returned to the England side in spite of the more substantial claims of Tavare, Parker and Larkins. Jackman could find no place now that Hendrick was back and it would be sad if this fine cricketer's Test appearances were to be restricted to his controversial replacement flight to the West Indies. Willis returned to the England side and one could only admire the man's phoenix-like qualities. Hughes won the toss and asked England to bat. His decision received quick justification when Gooch edged across the line at Lillee and Wood at first slip took the catch. Woolmer flashed frighteningly and then gave Wood his second catch. Alderman took his first wicket when he had Boycott taken at second slip, but Gower batted with good sense and Gatting with grit and pugnacity. Then Gower was caught in the gully, Botham bowled playing across the line, Gatting lbw playing a grotesque swipe, Willis' first ball caught behind on the leg side, and Willey caught at second slip. Concentrated Australian bowling, accurate, aggressive and remorseless in its determination, was backed by superb catching. Dilley hit some brave and important blows, but England were out for 185. Dilley struck a further blow for England when he had Wood lbw second ball and when Willis had Hughes lbw on the last ball of the day, his two hundredth Test wicket, Australia were 33 for 4 and England back in the hunt.

England's position would have been even better had they held the chances that came their way. This malaise became more deep rooted on the second day and was unquestionably the main contributory factor to England's defeat. Botham missed three straightforward catches, Gooch one, Woolmer a skier running back to mid-wicket, Downton dropped Border at ten off the easiest of catches from Hendrick's bowling, and one lost count of the catalogue. Border survived to take Australia to within six of the England total, and he was well aided by some sensible knocks from Marsh, Lawson, Lillee and Alderman. When England batted again Gooch was brilliantly caught in the gully by Yallop, Boycott and Woolmer were caught behind off Alderman, and Gatting was lbw to Lillee. Marsh's catch to dismiss Woolmer for a 'pair' looked spectacular, but, in truth, Marsh moved to the ball later than of yore. 33 for 4, and it was all like intruding upon someone's private grief. Botham, given a warm and sympathetic reception, mixed some fine shots and some airy swipes, but he was responsible for giving Australia some sort of target. Australia won late on the Sunday afternoon after grinding their way to the 132 they needed. Trevor Bailey had described them as the worst Australian batting side he had ever seen, and that may well be true, but their spirit and tenacity were undeniable. Lillee and Alderman had complemented each other admirably and the Australian fielding had been magnificent. England could contemplate the belief that catches win matches.

First Cornhill Test Match: England v. Australia

18, 19, 20 and 21 June 1981 at Trent Bridge, Nottingham

England	First Innings		Second Innings	
G. A. Gooch	c Wood, b Lillee	10	c Yallop, b Lillee	6
G. Boycott	c Border, b Alderman	27	c Marsh, b Alderman	4
R. A. Woolmer	c Wood, b Lillee	0	c Marsh, b Alderman	0
D. I. Gower	c Yallop, b Lillee	26	c sub(Kent), b Lillee	28
M. W. Gatting	lbw, b Hogg	52	lbw, b Alderman	15
P. Willey	c Border, b Alderman	10	lbw, b Lillee	13
I. T. Botham (capt)	b Alderman	1	c Border, b Lillee	33
*P. R. Downton	c Yallop, b Alderman	8	lbw, b Alderman	3
G. R. Dilley	b Hogg	34	c Marsh, b Alderman	13
R. G. D. Willis	c Marsh, b Hogg	0	c Chappell, b Lillee	1
M. Hendrick	not out	6	not out	0
Extras	lb 6, w 1, nb 4	11	lb 8, nb 1	9
		185		**125**

	O	M	R	W		O	M	R	W
Lillee	13	3	34	3		16.4	2	46	5
Alderman	24	7	68	4		19	3	62	5
Hogg	11.4	1	47	3		3	1	8	—
Lawson	8	3	25	—					

Fall of Wickets
1–13, 2–13, 3–57, 4–67, 5–92, 6–96, 7–116, 8–159, 9–159.
1–12, 2–12, 3–13, 4–39, 5–61, 6–94, 7–109, 8–113, 9–125.

Australia	*First Innings*		*Second Innings*	
G. M. Wood	lbw, b Dilley	0	c Woolmer, b Willis	8
J. Dyson	c Woolmer, b Willis	5	c Downton, b Dilley	38
G. N. Yallop	b Hendrick	13	c Gatting, b Botham	6
K. J. Hughes (capt)	lbw, b Willis	7	lbw, b Dilley	22
T. M. Chappell	b Hendrick	17	not out	20
A. R. Border	c and b Botham	63	b Dilley	20
*R. W. Marsh	c Boycott, b Willis	19	lbw, b Dilley	0
G. F. Lawson	c Gower, b Botham	14	not out	5
D. K. Lillee	c Downton, b Dilley	12		
R. M. Hogg	c Boycott, b Dilley	0		
T. M. Alderman	not out	12		
Extras	b 4, lb 8, w 1, nb 4	17	b 1, lb 6, nb 6	13
		179	(for 6 wkts)	132

	O	M	R	W		O	M	R	W
Dilley	20	7	38	3		11.1	4	24	4
Willis	30	14	47	3		13	2	28	1
Hendrick	20	7	43	2		20	7	33	—
Botham	16.5	6	34	2		10	1	34	1

Fall of Wickets
1–0, 2–21, 3–21, 4–33, 5–64, 6–89, 7–110, 8–147, 9–153.
1–20, 2–40, 3–77, 4–80, 5–122, 6–122.

Australia won by 4 wickets

20, 22 and 23 June   **at Derby**
Derbyshire 252 for 2 dec (J. G. Wright 110, P. N. Kirsten 59 not out) and
  257 for 5 dec (P. N. Kirsten 114, A. Hill 74)
Northamptonshire 234 for 9 dec (A. J. Lamb 91) and 279 for 1 (W. Larkins
  126, G. Cook 120 not out)
Northamptonshire won by 9 wickets
Northamptonshire 18 pts, Derbyshire 7 pts

                                                                 at Ilford
Sussex 436 for 4 dec (P. W. G. Parker 132, G. D. Mendis 119, Imran Khan 98
  not out)
Essex 169 (J. R. T. Barclay 4 for 47) and 246 (A. W. Lilley 61, C. E. Waller
  4 for 86, J. R. T. Barclay 4 for 90)
Sussex won by an innings and 21 runs
Sussex 24 pts, Essex 2 pts

at Southampton
Hampshire 349 for 3 dec (C. G. Greenidge 140, T. E. Jesty 81 not out, D. R.
Turner 55 not out) and 249 for 3 dec (M. C. J. Nicholas 101 not out,
C. G. Greenidge 73)
Gloucestershire 277 for 5 dec (Zaheer Abbas 101 not out, Sadiq Mohammad
100) and 270 for 6 (M. J. Procter 53)
Match drawn
Hampshire 6 pts, Gloucestershire 4 pts

at Liverpool
Nottinghamshire 329 for 3 dec (D. W. Randall 162 not out, C. E. B. Rice 102)
Lancashire 179 (B. W. Reidy 55, R. J. Hadlee 7 for 25) and 320 for 3 (D.
Lloyd 128 not out, F. C. Hayes 98)
Match drawn
Nottinghamshire 8 pts, Lancashire 2 pts

at Worcester
Somerset 246 (I. V. A. Richards 63) and 331 for 4 (I. V. A. Richards 118,
B. C. Rose 107)
Worcestershire 431 for 6 dec (D. N. Patel 105 not out, P. A. Neale 101, Younis
Ahmed 87)
Match drawn
Worcestershire 8 pts, Somerset 3 pts

at Lord's
Oxford University 222 (K. A. Hayes 56, J. J. Rogers 54) and 274 for 4 dec
(R. A. B. Ezekowitz 93, R. S. Cowan 87)
Cambridge University 236 for 7 dec. (C. F. E. Goldie 77, R. J. Boyd-Moss 58,
S. P. Sutcliffe 4 for 91) and 155 for 3
Match drawn

at Edgbaston
Warwickshire 274 for 7 dec (A. I. Kallicharran 121 not out, G. W. Humpage
73) and 268 for 3 dec (S. H. Wootton 77, Asif Din 70 not out)
Sri Lankans 335 (D. Mendis 90, Y. Gunesekera 56, A. Ranasinghe 50, S. P.
Perryman 5 for 52) and 91 for 2 (R. Devapriya 68)
Match drawn

With the wicket at Trent Bridge far below the standard expected for a Test
match, there was some conjecture that a Test could be played at Derby where
over a thousand runs were scored and only seventeen wickets fell in the three
days. For Derbyshire Wright and Kirsten hit hundreds and Alan Hill, who
had forced his way back in to the side after missing most of 1980, again played
well, following his century against Yorkshire. Inevitably, Allan Lamb held
Northants together in the first innings and eventually the visitors were set to
make 276 at just under 90 an hour. Larkins and Cook opened with a stand
of 239 and the game was won. The pair batted with exuberance and dignity
and the Derbyshire bowling was powerless to halt the flow of majestic shots.
Runs came at over five an over, and victory was achieved with four overs
to spare. There were no such finishes at Worcester and Liverpool. Somerset

trailed badly on the first innings to Worcester for whom Patel and Neale recaptured lost form, but then Richards and Rose reached hundreds and batted Somerset to safety. Lancashire were in a worse plight. Randall staked an England claim with a magnificent 162 not out. He and Rice added 229 for the third wicket, and then Hadlee, on a placid wicket, conjured evil for Lancashire with hostile and relentless bowling. Without help from the conditions, though with some from the Lancashire batting, his 7 for 25 was a performance of outstanding quality. The Lancashire second innings was a different affair. David Lloyd and Frank Hayes reaffirmed basic principles and the game was saved. Hampshire's rejuvenation continued with more fine batting. Mark Nicholas hit the third century of his career and there was some brilliant stroke play from Greenidge in the first innings. Sadiq and Zaheer both hit centuries for Gloucestershire who found the ultimate target of 322 in 295 minutes beyond them. Zaheer's total for the season had now reached 865 at an average of 123.57. Sri Lanka had the better of the game with Warwickshire but they, too, found the final task beyond them as did Cambridge in a disappointing varsity match. Pringle had Oxford in trouble early on, but he strained a groin muscle and Cambridge failed to capitalise on their early break-through. The Cambridge hero was night-watchman Goldie who hit his highest score in first-class cricket, but the Cambridge lead was slender and was nullified by a career best from Ezekowitz. The Oxford declaration was unrealistic and Cambridge were curbed by the Oxford spin attack. Pringle and Ellis were elected captains for 1982. At Ilford Sussex had a riot of runs on the Saturday. Mendis, a reliable, stylish and rapid scoring opener, and Parker, surely a cricketer of Test class, hit excellent centuries, and Imran a whirlwind 98 before he was hurt. Sussex batted for one ball on the Monday so that they could use the heavy roller and Essex soon disintegrated. Turner in both innings, Lilley, emphasising his right to a regular place, in the second, and McEwan and Phillip tried to stave off defeat, but the Sussex spinners triumphed just after lunch on the last day and the southern county went to the top of the Schweppes County Championship.

John Player League
21 June   **at Ilford**
Essex 215 for 8 (B. R. Hardie 58)
Sussex 216 for 7 (G. D. Mendis 60)
Sussex (4 pts) won by 3 wickets

                                                            at Portsmouth

Gloucestershire 180 for 8 (Zaheer Abbas 51)
Hampshire 184 for 3 (D. R. Turner 59 not out)
Hampshire (4 pts) won by 7 wickets

                                                          at Old Trafford

Nottinghamshire 139 for 6
Lancashire 143 for 3 (A. Kennedy 62)
Lancashire (4 pts) won by 7 wickets

at Lord's

Leicestershire 135 for 8
Middlesex 136 for 5
Middlesex (4 pts) won by 5 wickets

at Bath

Somerset 132 (L. Potter 4 for 27)
Kent 134 for 6
Kent (4 pts) won by 4 wickets

at Edgbaston

Derbyshire 233 for 7 (J. G. Wright 62, A. M. Ferreira 4 for 39)
Warwickshire 191 (D. L. Amiss 80, G. Miller 4 for 35)
Derbyshire (4 pts) won by 42 runs

at Worcester

Northamptonshire 255 for 3 (A. J. Lamb 127 not out, R. G. Williams 81)
Worcestershire 259 for 7 (Younis Ahmed 71)
Worcestershire (4 pts) won by 3 wickets

at Hull

Glamorgan 153 for 8
Yorkshire 139
Glamorgan (4 pts) won by 14 runs

In their determination to win everything Sussex restricted Essex to 215 at Ilford.
Mendis once more anchored the Sussex innings, but when the last over began
8 were needed for victory. Barclay produced a cover drive and a sweep off
Acfield and the last four balls were not necessary. This put Sussex four points
ahead of Somerset who were surprisingly beaten by Kent at Bath. Eldine
Baptiste, from Antigua, bowled Viv Richards for nought in his debut game,
and Laurie Potter, also a debutant and born in Australia, took four good
wickets. Derbyshire moved into third place by crushing Warwickshire who,
inevitably, were well served by Amiss. Miller had a splendid all-round match
for Derbyshire. Hampshire's ring of confidence swept them to victory with
three overs to spare at Portsmouth, and Middlesex, for whom the season had
so far been one of low profile, founded their victory on tight bowling and
an opening stand of 62 by Radley and Brearley. Metson made his debut for
Middlesex behind the stumps and took two catches. Lancashire revived
memories of former glories with a last over win against Notts, but the White
Rose, depleted by injury, lost ingloriously to Glamorgan who were beginning
to enjoy winning. The saddest aspect for Yorkshire was that Kevin Sharp, a
superb young cricketer who has had an unhappy time, was recalled to the
side and run out for nought. The most incredible game was at Worcester where
Allan Lamb (seven sixes, and ten fours) and Richard Williams hit a League
record stand for the third wicket of 188. Facing a massive 255, Worcestershire
were given a splendid start by Turner and Younis of 107. Inchmore slashed
forcefully at number three and the target came within bounds. When Griffiths
bowled the last ball the scores were level and Humphries thrashed it to the
boundary for a memorable victory.

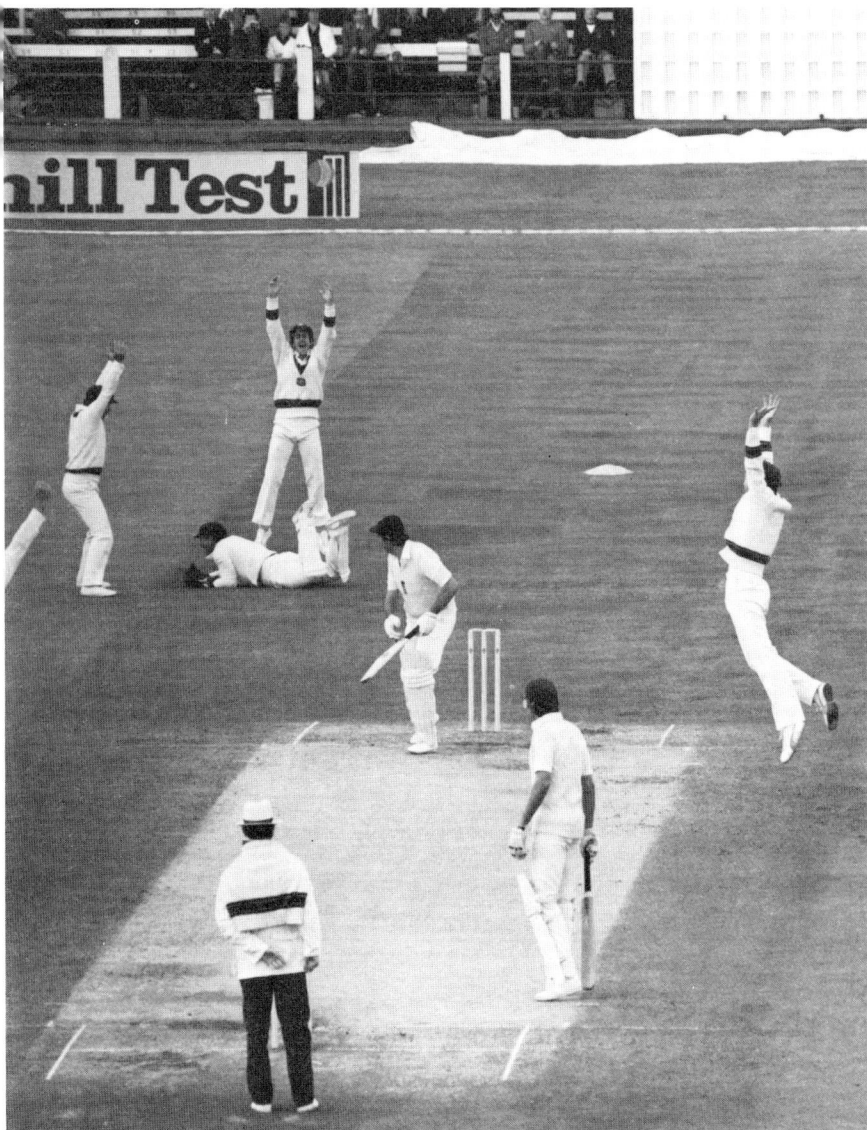

Woolmer caught Marsh, bowled Alderman at Trent Bridge.

Cambridge University First-Class Matches – Batting 1981

	v. Essex (Cambridge) 22–24 April		v. Hampshire (Cambridge) 25–27 April		v. Northamptonshire (Cambridge) 29 April–1 May		v. Lancashire (Cambridge) 2–5 May		v. Surrey (Cambridge) 6–8 May		v. Worcestershire (Cambridge) 13–15 May	
J. P. C. Mills	0	43	37	—	25	11	8	—	47	0	7	50
A. J. Murley	14	15			1	48	29	—	5	1		
T. D. W. Edwards	36	2	6	—	41	11	12	—	6	3	33	49
R. J. Boyd-Moss	1	0	0	—	1	19	84	—	50	27	6	2
D. R. Pringle	3	66	21	—	14	11	1	—	17	55*	127*	61*
N. Russom	32	47*	14*	—					1	22*	65	10*
S. J. G. Doggart	5	1*	—	—			69*	—	26	9	0	—
D. C. Holliday	32	—	—	—	0	13			29*	—	5	—
K. I. Hodgson	6	—	—	—	1	29			26	—	14*	—
C. F. E. Goldie	3	13	—	—	13	17			2	—	—	—
R. S. Dutton	0*	—	—	—	7*	0*	—	—				
I. G. Peck			22	—	23	0	11*	—	19	—	9	45
P. D. Hemsley					0	10						
R. Palmer												
H. Torkington												
R. Compton-Burnett												
A. Clarke												
D. Varey												
R. Huxter												
Byes	1	2	9		2	5	5		6	3	6	
Leg byes	3	6	2		4	9	8		6	6	5	3
Wides			4				3				1	
No balls	10	5	6		1	4	4				3	
Total	146	204	117		133	187	234		240	126	281	220
Wickets	10	6	5		10	10	5		10	5	7	4
Result	D		D		L		D		D		D	

Catches

8 – C. F. E. Goldie (ct 6/st 2)

6 – D. C. Holliday

4 – T. D. W. Edwards

2 – R. S. Dutton, N. Russom, K. I. Hodgson, A. J. Murley, J. P. C. Mills, D. Varey, R. J. Boyd-Moss and I. G. Peck

1 – D. R. Pringle, P. D. Hemsley, S. J. G. Doggart, R. Palmer and H. Torkington

v. Nottinghamshire (Cambridge) 6–9 June		v. Sussex (Cambridge) 10–12 June		v. Leicestershire (Leicester) 17–19 June		v. Oxford University (Lord's) 20–23 June		Inns	NOs	Runs	HS	Av
		0	2	63	55*	2	34	16	1	384	63	25.60
0	17			5	17			11	—	152	48	13.81
4	57	2	37	11	5	21	30*	18	1	366	57	21.52
		10	23	0	12*	58	27	16	1	320	84	21.33
		5	17			2	—	13	3	400	127*	40.00
51	58	0	1	10	—	3	—	13	4	314	65	34.88
				16	—	13*	—	8	3	139	69*	27.80
21	25	57	0	9	—	13*	—	11	2	204	57	22.66
		28	10*	4	—	—	30*	9	3	148	30*	24.66
4	2	30*	7	2*	—	77	—	11	2	170	77	18.88
								3	3	7	7*	—
		11	14			30	29	11	1	213	45	21.30
4	0*							4	1	14	10	4.66
								—				
9	0							2	—	9	9	4.50
5	18							2	—	23	18	11.50
12	1							2	—	13	12	6.50
12*	27	3	0	39	—			5	1	81	39	20.25
0	4	2	20	8	—	—	—	5	—	34	20	6.80
	5		7	3		10						
4	9	5		8	7	3	5					
				4		1						
	1	12	5	1	2	3						
126	224	165	143	183	98	236	155					
10	10	10	10	10	2	7	3					
	L		L		D		D					

Cambridge University First-Class Matches – Bowling 1981	D. R. Pringle	N. Russom	R. S. Dutton	S. J. G. Doggart	K. I. Hodgson	D. C. Holliday
v. Essex (Cambridge) 22–24 April	21–8–56–4	18–1–60–2	11–0–45–1	11–3–22–0	8–0–33–3	2–1–1–0
v. Hampshire (Cambridge) 25–27 April	8–1–25–0	24–9–49–2	2–0–22–0	6–1–8–0	20.5–6–58–1	
v. Northamptonshire (Cambridge) 29 April–1 May	32–7–89–3		6–0–41–0		23–2–79–3	
v. Lancashire (Cambridge) 2–5 May	25–9–65–2		7–2–23–0	32–13–76–0	13–4–52–1	
v. Surrey (Cambridge) 6–8 May	21–6–39–4 16–4–54–0	22–2–66–1 18–3–64–1		30–9–64–1 18–7–35–0	17–4–52–2 20–2–76–1	
v. Worcestershire (Cambridge) 13–15 May	16–4–50–1	22–5–49–2		9.4–1–29–0	14–4–40–0	
v. Nottinghamshire (Cambridge) 6–9 June		29.3–7–91–2 5–1–11–0				23–3–71–1
v. Sussex (Cambridge) 10–12 June	20–3–51–1	27–8–87–1			20–4–77–4	5–0–24–0
v. Leicestershire (Leicester) 17–19 June		17–5–38–0		23.3–7–66–3	13–1–39–3	
v. Oxford University (Lord's) 20–23 June	28–9–64–3 22–2–59–2	20–9–45–2 15–0–56–0		17–7–29–2 15–3–35–0	14–2–37–1 12.2–0–54–1	
	209–53– 552–20 av. 27.60	217.3–50– 616–13 av. 47.38	26–2– 131–1 av. 131.00	162.1–51– 364–6 av. 60.66	175.1–29– 597–20 av. 29.85	30–4– 96–1 av. 96.00

P. D. Hemsley	R. J. Boyd-Moss	R. Palmer	R. Huxter	A. J. Murley	T. D. W. Edwards	B	Lb	W	Nb	Total	Wkts
						3	3		17	240	10
							5	1	8	176	3
15–2–40–0	27–8–92–1					1	5	1	14	362	7
	21–7–74–2						3	1	20	314	5
	5–2–23–0					2	7		4	257	8
	1–0–1–0					1	4	1	1	237	2
	3–0–17–0	7–1–30–1				2	6	1	1	225	4
11–3–23–0			27–4–76–2		14–5–25–0	1	9		2	298	6
7.5–1–27–0			10–5–12–0	2–1–1–0			2			53	0
	7–1–25–0		13–4–49–2		4–2–17–1	9	2		7	348	9
	14–3–45–2		11–3–32–0		2–0–16–0	7	2		4	249	8
			19.3–5–30–1			8	1		8	222	10
	10–2–24–1		8–0–25–0			3	12		6	274	4
33.5–6– 90–0 —	88–23– 301–6 av. 50.16	7–1– 30–1 av. 30.00	88.3–21– 224–5 av. 44.80	2–1– 1–0 —	20–7– 58–1 av. 58.00						

Oxford University
First-Class Matches –
Batting
1981

	v. Glamorgan (Oxford) 25–28 April	v. Somerset (Oxford) 29 April–1 May		v. Yorkshire (Oxford) 2–5 May		v. Gloucestershire (Oxford) 13–15 May		v. Leicestershire (Oxford) 3–5 June		v. Middlesex (Oxford) 10–12 June	
R. A. B. Ezekowitz	12 —	0	8	0	45	22	8	27	35	5	12
R. P. G. Ellis	34 —	3	0	8	36	50	58	46	7	45	63
J. O. D. Orders	1 —	2	9	9	0	8	7	21	13	30	18
R. P. Moulding	5 —	20	4	0	23	15	0	0	18	5	0
R. S. Cowan	28 —	2	3	19	1	4	113	10	4	62	17
J. J. Rodgers	13 —	3	28	0	3	22	0	5	28	48	35
N. V. H. Mallett	52 —	0	7	19	0*	7	23*	2	4		
J. M. Knight	0 —	24	20	41*	3*	2	5			4	37
S. P. Sutcliffe	1 —	6	1*	2	—	0	4			0	1
I. J. Curtis	7 —	0	0	0	—						
P. N. Huxford	0* —	0*	5							7	0
R. A. Gordon-Walker				1	—	0*	2	12	4		
K. A. Hayes						8	59	11	17	9	6
S. P. Ridge								7*	0		
T. J. Taylor								10	2*	20*	6*
Byes	4	1	6	3	2		3	4	4	8	1
Leg byes	9	2	9	12	6	6	4	3	2	14	12
Wides			1				4	1		1	
No balls	5			5	4		1	6	4	4	
Total	171	63	100	120	123	144	291	165	142	262	208
Wickets	10	10	10	10	6	10	10	10	10	10	10
Result	D	L		D		L		L		D	

The match v. Warwickshire (Oxford) 27–29 May was abandoned.

Catches
11 – R. S. Cowan (ct 10/st 1)
7 – R. P. G. Ellis
6 – R. A. B. Ezekowitz
5 – P. N. Huxford (ct 3/st 2) and R. A. Gordon-Walker (ct 3/st 2)
2 – N. V. H. Mallett and I. J. Curtis
1 – J. O. D. Orders, R. P. Moulding, J. M. Knight, J. J. Rogers, K. A. Hayes, S. P. Sutcliffe and substitute.

v. Kent (Oxford) 17–19 June		v. Cambridge University (Lord's) 20–23 June		Inns	NOs	Runs	HS	Av
9	1	18	93	15	—	295	93	19.66
11	46	6	26	15	—	439	63	29.26
7	38	25	9*	15	1	197	38	14.07
4	13	23	—	14	—	130	23	9.28
18	23	15	87	15	—	406	113	27.06
14	0	54	—	14	—	253	54	18.07
4	20	1	—	12	2	139	52	13.90
				9	2	136	41*	19.43
1	6	2	—	11	1	24	6	2.40
				4	—	7	7	1.75
10	1*	0*	—	8	4	23	10	5.75
				5	1	19	12	4.75
42	16	56	38	10	—	262	59	26.20
				2	1	7	7*	7.00
28*	5	5	—	7	4	76	28*	25.33
4	1	8	3					
	6	1	12					
1	1							
2	6	8	6					
155	183	222	274					
10	10	10	4					
L		D						

Oxford University First-Class Matches – Bowling 1981	J. M. Knight	N. V. H. Mallett	I. J. Curtis	S. P. Sutcliffe	J. O. D. Orders	K. A. Hayes
v. Glamorgan (Oxford) 25–28 April	22–9–44–2	24.5–7–52–5	3–2–4–0			
v. Somerset (Oxford) 29 April–1 May	6–1–16–0	7–0–22–0	40–16–70–1	41–12–86–4		
v. Yorkshire (Oxford) 2–5 May	21–7–68–0	15–2–45–0	33–12–58–4	34–10–69–2	7–1–17–0	
v. Gloucestershire (Oxford) 13–15 May	26–4–94–1 8–1–28–0	18–1–77–0 4–1–20–0		31–8–87–1 7–0–29–0	16–2–44–2	3.2–1–12–0
v. Leicestershire (Oxford) 3–5 June		22–10–42–0 27–6–104–4			12–1–46–1	
v. Middlesex (Oxford) 10–12 June	11–3–31–1 4–0–10–1			40–7–130–4	8–1–29–0 5–1–14–0	
v. Kent (Oxford) 17–19 June		19–5–48–1 4–1–10–0		34.5–5–74–4 14–3–35–0	13–3–38–1 4–2–9–0	3–0–21–0
v. Cambridge University (Lord's) 20–23 June		7–1–22–1 5–1–13–0		38–8–91–4 19–2–67–1	7–1–17–0 5–0–14–0	
	98–25– 291–5 av. 58.20	152.5–35– 455–11 av. 41.36	76–30– 132–5 av. 26.40	258.5–55– 668–20 av. 33.40	77–12– 228–4 av. 57.00	6.2–1– 33–0 —

R. S. Cowan	S. P. Ridge	T. J. Taylor	B	Lb	W	Nb	Total	Wkts
			2	3	1	2	108	7
			9	5		1	209	5
			5	4	2	10	278	6
7–1–16–0			4	6	8	4	340	5
				2	6			97	0
14–6–30–0	20–6–50–1	27–11–54–2	4	7	7		240	4
	3–0–15–0	24–8–54–3		2		3	178	7
		32.4–8–81–5	3	4	9		287	10
3–1–10–0		1–0–3–0		2			39	1
3–0–9–1		30–13–55–1	1	4		4	233	8
4–1–9–0		14–6–21–0		2			107	0
10–3–20–0		29–7–69–2	10	3	1	3	236	7
		19–4–56–2		5			155	3
41–12–	23–6–	176.4–57–						
94–1	65–1	393–15						
av. 94.00	av. 65.00	av. 26.20						

Benson and Hedges Cup Quarter Finals

24 June   **at Trent Bridge**
Surrey 226 for 7 (R. D. V. Knight 70)
Nottinghamshire 179 (D. W. Randall 62, R. D. Jackman 4 for 24)
Surrey won by 47 runs

                                                                                      at Leeds
Yorkshire 221 for 9 (C. W. J. Athey 58, J. H. Hampshire 58)
Somerset 223 for 7 (B. C. Rose 68, P. W. Denning 66)
Somerset won by 3 wickets

24 and 25 June   **at Hove**
Sussex 196 for 9 (C. P. Phillipson 59)
Leicestershire 199 for 6 (J. C. Balderstone 67)
Leicestershire won by 4 wickets

26 June   **at The Oval**
Kent 193 for 8 (C. J. Tavare 76)
Warwickshire 179 (T. A. Lloyd 60)
Kent won by 14 runs

Once again the rain hampered cricket. The match between Kent and Warwick-shire was completely washed out at Canterbury and it was not until noon on the Friday that the game, reduced to fifty overs, began under dark clouds at The Oval which Surrey had kindly offered. Chris Tavare played a patient and solid innings of 76 which, it transpired, won Kent the match. Warwickshire reached 133 for 2 and appeared to be strolling to victory, but their last eight wickets went down for 46 runs, some of them fretfully and suicidally, and Kent won with ease. Somerset should have beaten Yorkshire with ease but a late panic came close to costing them the match. Yorkshire, in spite of good innings from Athey and Hampshire, never scored fluently. Marks dismissed Boycott and proved surprisingly restrictive. Rose and Denning began the Somerset reply with a stand of 135 and Viv Richards then dealt some characteristic lusty blows. Somerset were strolling to victory, but, in wild panic Popplewell and Marks were run out as three wickets went down for 5 runs. In the end Taylor restored sanity with an edged four to win the match. Clive Rice asked Surrey to bat at Trent Bridge, but Roger Knight played a noble innings and once more the Nottinghamshire batting showed fragile tendencies. Clarke and Jackman bowled frugally and Surrey won with five overs to spare. Sussex never really recovered from losing 5 wickets for 48. The start was delayed and the match went into the second day. Phillipson, having a wonderfully effective season, gave Sussex some hope in a stand with Le Roux, but Balderstone and Gower added 88 for the Leicestershire second wicket after Steele had been run out and then Garnham hit well after the middle order had faltered. In the end Leicester won with five balls to spare.

24 June **at Old Trafford**

Lancashire 275 for 3 (A. Kennedy 115 not out, D. Lloyd 63, C. H. Lloyd 58)

Australians 197 for 4 (G. M. Wood 50)

Lancashire won on faster scoring rate

25 June **at Watford**

Sri Lankans 211 (R. D. Mendis 64)

Middlesex 209 for 9 (K. P. Tomlins 58, D. S. De Silva 4 for 28)

Sri Lankans won by 2 runs

With Rodney Hogg suffering injury that would keep him out of the Test and Andrew Kennedy in devastating form, the Australians suffered badly at Manchester. The Sri Lankans, on the other hand, gained a memorable victory over Middlesex. The champion county needed only five to win off the last over bowled by leg-spinner D. S. De Silva. Singles were pushed off the first two deliveries and then De Silva had Downton and Selvey caught off successive balls before he bowled Merry with the last ball of the match.

27, 28 and 29 June **at Canterbury**

Kent 147 for 6 dec (G. F. Lawson 5 for 72)

Australians 283 for 6 (K. J. Hughes 61)

Match drawn

27, 29 and 30 June **at Swansea**

Glamorgan 301 for 4 dec (Javed Miandad 137 not out, N. G. Featherstone 63) and 247 for 5 dec (Javed Miandad 106, G. C. Holmes 50 not out)

Somerset 303 for 9 dec (I. T. Botham 123 not out, P. M. Roebuck 51) and 46 for 2

Match drawn

Glamorgan 8 pts, Somerset 5 pts

at Gloucester

Warwickshire 325 for 6 dec (G. W. Humpage 146, T. A. Lloyd 78) and 257 for 8 dec (G. W. Humpage 110)

Gloucestershire 301 for 8 dec (Zaheer Abbas 100, G. C. Small 4 for 70) and 198 for 6 (Zaheer Abbas 51)

Match drawn

Warwickshire 7 pts, Gloucestershire 6 pts

at Old Trafford

Lancashire 349 for 6 dec (D. P. Hughes 85, C. H. Lloyd 80, M. D. Marshall 4 for 82) and 123 (K. Stevenson 4 for 56)

Hampshire 260 for 3 dec (M. C. J. Nicholas 94, T. M. Tremlett 88, C. G. Greenidge 57) and 213 for 8 (C. G. Greenidge 58, P. J. W. Allott 4 for 80)

Hampshire won by 2 wickets

Hampshire 21 pts, Lancashire 5 pts

at Leicester

Essex 387 for 4 dec (G. A. Gooch 164, K. R. Pont 72 not out, N. Phillip 60 not out, K. S. McEwan 54) and 273 for 5 dec (K. S. McEwan 109 not out, G. A. Gooch 87)

Leicestershire 319 for 1 dec (D. I. Gower 156 not out, J. C. Balderstone 127 not out) and 235 for 7 (D. I. Gower 67, N. E. Briers 65)

Match drawn

Leicestershire 5 pts, Essex 4 pts

at Trent Bridge

Middlesex 151 (R. O. Butcher 58, M. W. W. Selvey 55, R. J. Hadlee 4 for 57) and 396 (J. M. Brearley 131, P. H. Edmonds 93, R. O. Butcher 53, M. K. Bore 4 for 121)

Nottinghamshire 309 (R. J. Hadlee 82, S. P. Hughes 6 for 102, W. W. Daniel 4 for 89) and 126 (J. E. Emburey 5 for 30)

Middlesex won by 112 runs

Middlesex 21 pts, Nottinghamshire 8 pts

at The Oval

Surrey 320 for 9 dec (R. D. V. Knight 77, Intikhab Alam 71, T. M. Lamb 4 for 77) and 200 for 4 dec (G. R. J. Roope 96 not out)

Northamptonshire 224 (Intikhab Alam 4 for 50) and 230 for 6 (R. G. Williams 77, W. Larkins 55 not out)

Match drawn

Surrey 8 pts, Northamptonshire 6 pts

at Worcester

Yorkshire 319 for 7 dec (J. H. Hampshire 94, C. W. J. Athey 64) and 251 (D. L. Bairstow 73 not out, C. M. Old 55, N. Gifford 4 for 82)

Worcestershire 303 for 3 dec (G. M. Turner 168, P. A. Neale 102) and 271 for 7 (M. S. Scott 68, P. A. Neale 65)

Worcestershire won by 3 wickets

Worcestershire 22 pts, Yorkshire 4 pts

at Hastings

Sussex 161 and 228 for 6 dec (J. R. P. Heath 101 not out)

Sri Lankans 158 (H. Devapriya 56, C. M. Wells 4 for 48) and 149 (N. D. P. Hettiartchy 57, C. E. Waller 4 for 43, J. R. T. Barclay 4 for 75)

Sussex won by 82 runs

The Schweppes County Championship moved into its most exciting position for four years when Surrey's failure to clinch the match against Northants brought them equal with Sussex at the top of the table. Surrey had gained a good position through the reliability of Knight, the all-round ability of the veteran Intikhab, who had announced that he was retiring at the end of the season, and the hostility of Clarke. In the end Northants were set 297 in fours to win. They rushed at the target and lost wickets rather quickly so that the injured Larkins had to restore sanity. Graham Roope showed a welcome return to form with a sound knock in the second innings; he was denied his hundred by Knight's lunch-time declaration. Sussex were engaged in beating the Sri Lankans who had held the upper hand, but threw away their advantage by missing catches. One to profit from being missed was Jerry Heath and the left-hander went on to record a maiden century. The Sri Lankans succumbed to the spin of Waller and Barclay after impressive young pace bowler Jones had taken the first two wickets. The most exciting event was that Hampshire moved into third place with a thrilling, if nervous, victory at Old Trafford. Lancashire had prospered on the Saturday, but Nicholas was again in fine form and with Tremlett reaching a career best, Pocock declared 89 runs behind. Nagging medium pace from Jesty and Stevenson troubled Lancashire in the second innings. Hayes was unable to bat because of a strained shoulder and three wickets went down in half an hour after lunch on the last afternoon for only 16 runs. This left Hampshire 205 minutes in which to get 213 runs. Greenidge scored briskly, but wickets fell to the persistent Allott on a deteriorating wicket. Nicholas, Jesty and Turner all played sensibly in the middle order and Turner stayed until the end which came with nine balls and two wickets to spare. It was Hampshire's third win of the season. A third win of the season for Worcester moved them into fourth place. Yorkshire had not scored briskly enough in their first innings although it was good to see Athey among the runs again showing confidence completely restored after recently being dropped from the side. The second day belonged entirely to Turner and Neale who added 231 for the second wicket. Gifford posed problems for Yorkshire in the second innings and Worcestershire were left needing 268 to win, a task they accomplished with one ball to spare. It was a fine match and a good team performance by the home county who had obviously recovered from the traumas imparted on them by Hampshire. They owed much to Scott and Neale who laid the foundation of victory with a second wicket stand of 115. Scott, in the side since Ormrod's injury, played most commendably, but once more it must be said that Yorkshire's spin attack was below the standard of their opponents. Notts again faltered and suddenly, and unexpectedly, Middlesex were in contention for the title. With Thomson in hospital and unlikely to have recovered from his operation in time to play again during the season, Middlesex wilted badly on the Saturday before the marvellous Hadlee. They were 97 for 8, but reached 151 thanks to the whirling bats of Butcher and Selvey. Notts themselves were in some trouble, but it was Richard Hadlee who led them to a big score with some lusty blows. Middlesex appeared to be facing an innings defeat when they slipped to 49 for 3, but Butcher again batted well and then Brearley, who batted for $6\frac{1}{2}$ hours, and Edmonds added 155. Notts needed 239 in 205 minutes, but their batting, which had taken on a nervous and fragile look in recent weeks, succumbed to Embury's spin. Simon Hughes who had taken six first innings wickets took the first three wickets. It was a sensational win for Middlesex, not the least because, following treatment to Hemmings on the pitch after he had edged a ball into his mouth, the last hour was not deemed to have begun until 5.05 so that the 22nd and final over was being bowled after six p.m. The Notts members were not pleased. Neither were the Australians who, once more, had only a few hours play. Lawson did enough to keep his Test place and Kim Hughes had useful batting practice. Javed

Miandad hit a century in each innings at Swansea so bringing three hundreds in succession. There was some brilliant hitting from Botham, too, which brought him his first hundred of the season and more than doubled his season's aggregate. Bowlers had a hard time and the match was drawn. The most memorable batting came from Zaheer Abbas. This was hard on Geoff Humpage who scored a century in each innings at Gloucester, but Zaheer hit 100 and 51 so bringing his total number of runs scored in June to 1016 at an average of 112.88. It placed him alongside W. G. Grace and Wally Hammond in the Gloucestershire record books. He became only the third batsman since the Second World War to score a thousand runs in a month. He also took 3 for 32 in the Warwickshire second innings. June belonged to Zaheer Abbas. Graham Gooch hit a hundred before lunch on the Saturday at Leicester. Essex flayed the Leicestershire bowling with Pont and Philip scoring 99 in 25 overs. Leicestershire responded in kind. Balderstone and Gower put on 289 for the second wicket, a county record. It beat the record of Watson and Wharton set up in 1961. Essex again hit merrily through Gooch and McEwan and Leicestershire were set 342 to win in four hours on the superb Grace Road wicket. After Gower had been dismissed they lost their way and some wickets and Briers steered them to a draw. Essex could reflect on the fact that their last two matches had produced only one bowling point.

John Player League

28 June   at **Swansea**
Glamorgan 224 for 8 (J. A. Hopkins 75, Javed Miandad 73)
Warwickshire 209 for 9 (T. A. Lloyd 73, Asif Din 51, M. A. Nash 4 for 31)
Glamorgan (4 pts) won by 15 runs

                                                              at **Gloucester**
Gloucestershire 150 for 7
Derbyshire 151 for 1 (J. G. Wright 76, B. Wood 58 not out)
Derbyshire (4 pts) won by 9 wickets

                                                              at **Old Trafford**
Lancashire 151 for 9 (T. M. Tremlett 4 for 22)
Hampshire 152 for 8
Hampshire (4 pts) won by 8 wickets

                                                              at **Leicester**
Leicestershire 121 for 9
Essex 125 for 6
Essex (4 pts) won by 4 wickets

                                                              at **Trent Bridge**
Middlesex 246 for 6 (C. T. Radley 93, R. O. Butcher 56)
Nottinghamshire 212 for 9 (C. E. B. Rice 105, J. E. Emburey 4 for 41)
Middlesex (4 pts) won by 34 runs

at Hastings

Northamptonshire 218 for 7 (W. Larkins 68, G. Cook 58, C. P. Phillipson
4 for 34)

Sussex 196 for 8

Northamptonshire (4 pts) won on faster scoring rate

at Worcester

Worcestershire 212 for 6 (E. J. O. Hemsley 74 not out)

Yorkshire 215 for 1 (G. Boycott 91 not out, C. W. J. Athey 79 not out)

Yorkshire (4 pts) won by 9 wickets

Having lost their first limited over match of the season when they were beaten
by Leicestershire in the quarter final of the Benson and Hedges Cup, Sussex
lost their unbeaten John Player League record three days later when they lost
by six runs to Northants. Cook and Larkins launched Northants with a stand
of 109. Bad light reduced Sussex's overs to 36 and, in spite of noble efforts
from Barclay and Alan Wells, they failed in their quest. Derbyshire moved
into second place when they routed Gloucestershire with four overs to spare.
Level with them on 18 points were Essex who restricted Leicestershire to 121
and appeared to be strolling to victory. They became bogged down and it was
only a last over flourish from Phillip and Turner that brought victory.
Middlesex were also on 18 points. Radley, Butcher and Edmonds batted finely,
but Clive Rice played an heroic, if unavailing, innings for Notts for whom
the season that had promised so much was suddenly trembling. Emburey once
more proved that spin has a place on Sunday. Hampshire and Glamorgan
maintained their appetites for Sunday wins and, at Worcester, Geoff Boycott
paced Yorkshire to an easy win. He was aided by Athey who was not only
back to his best with the bat, but shone in the field for Yorkshire whose out-
cricket was not of the highest quality. Hartley looked the most efficient of
their bowlers.

1, 2 and 3 July **at Chesterfield**

Lancashire 380 for 5 dec (A. Kennedy 180, C. H. Lloyd 56, G. Fowler 54)
and 232 for 2 dec (D. Lloyd 86 not out, G. Fowler 58)

Derbyshire 303 for 4 dec (B. Wood 127, J. G. Wright 60) and 149 for 9
(J. Simmons 5 for 39)

Match drawn

Derbyshire 5 pts, Lancashire 5 pts

at Chelmsford

Nottinghamshire 348 for 5 dec (C. E. B. Rice 166 not out, J. D. Birch 111,
J. K. Lever 4 for 81) and 147 for 5 dec

Essex 272 (K. W. R. Fletcher 61, R. J. Hadlee 6 for 60) and 152 for 7
K. W. R. Fletcher 55, M. S. A. McEvoy 50)

Match drawn

Nottinghamshire 8 pts, Essex 4 pts

at Swansea

Glamorgan 317 for 9 dec (R. C. Ontong 151 not out) and 283 for 4 dec (J. A. Hopkins 135, R. C. Ontong 50)

Hampshire 340 (C. G. Greenidge 109, N. E. J. Pocock 61, M. A. Nash 4 for 67) and 111 for 2

Match drawn

Glamorgan 8 pts, Hampshire 8 pts

at Maidstone

Kent 120 and 182 (A. P. E. Knott 51 not out, W. W. Daniel 4 for 48)

Middlesex 209 (G. D. Barlow 101) and 97 for 9 (D. L. Underwood 6 for 29)

Middlesex won by 1 wicket

Middlesex 22 pts, Kent 4 pts

at Northampton

Northamptonshire 312 (A. J. Lamb 162, D. A. Graveney 5 for 44) and 344 for 7 dec (G. Cook 84, R. G. Williams 80, A. J. Lamb 79)

Gloucestershire 301 (Zaheer Abbas 135 not out, A. J. Hignell 72) and 224 for 5 (Zaheer Abbas 128, P. Bainbridge 53 not out)

Match drawn

Gloucestershire 8 pts, Northamptonshire 6 pts

at Taunton

Surrey 275 (G. S. Clinton 66) and 219 for 7 dec (M. A. Lynch 66 not out, R. D. V. Knight 57)

Somerset 190 (P. W. Denning 65, R. D. Jackman 6 for 70) and 200 for 5 (I. V. A. Richards 68, P. W. Denning 50)

Match drawn

Surrey 7 pts, Somerset 5 pts

at Bradford

Leicestershire 249 (A. M. E. Roberts 52, C. M. Old 4 for 65) and 194 (J. C. Balderstone 73)

Yorkshire 358 (J. H. Hampshire 112, D. L. Bairstow 84, J. P. Agnew 5 for 72) and 89 for 3

Yorkshire won by 7 wickets

Yorkshire 24 pts, Leicestershire 4 pts

at Worcester

Worcestershire 301 (D. S. De Silva 6 for 100) and 225 for 6 dec (M. S. Scott 73, D. N. Patel 72)

Sri Lankans 350 (S. Wettimuny 89, R. D. Mendis 66, D. N. Patel 5 for 76)

Match drawn

Against a backcloth which would have been an admirable setting for Lear's madness, Middlesex beat Kent by one wicket and, to the surprise of all, suddenly appeared in second place in the championship table. On a wicket which always gave the bowlers some encouragement Barlow played an innings of great concentration and good sense which, in the end, was the decisive batting of the match. Knott batted courageously for Kent, but Middlesex needed only 94 to win. At lunch they were 66 for 5, and Downton fell to the first ball of the afternoon. Underwood was at his best, Radley at his most determined. The ninth wicket went down with 5 runs still needed and lightning flashing dramatically over Maidstone where, in the town centre, heavy rain was already falling. Daniel and Merry gave Middlesex their nail-biting win. Surrey held first place with a draw at Taunton where Jackman compensated for the absence of Clarke to give Surrey a first innings advantage, but, in the end, the game died. Honours were even at Swansea where Hampshire had reduced Glamorgan to 177 for 9 in their first innings. Robin Hobbs then joined Rodney Ontong in a last wicket stand of 140 which was unbroken. It was a new last wicket record stand for the county, the previous record having stood for 46 years. Ontong reached his highest score in the county championship and Hobbs was 49 not out. Greenidge and Pocock gave Hampshire a first innings lead, but then Hopkins hit the second highest score of his career and Hampshire declined Nash's invitation to score 261 in 155 minutes. There were off-field incidents at Chesterfield when Clive Lloyd delayed his declaration and annoyed local inhabitants. Kennedy hit his first championship century of the season and Wood replied with a hundred against his former county, sharing a century opening stand with Wright. The Derbyshire supporters were upset that Lloyd asked the home side to get 310 in 195 minutes. The game seemed destined for a limp draw until Derbyshire contrived to collapse and Jack Simmons took five wickets. In the end Oldham held out with fielders clustered round the bat. Yorkshire gained their first win of the season when they hit 89 in 16 overs to beat bottom of the table Leicestershire. Hampshire and Bairstow batted splendidly in spite of Agnew returning a career best and though Balderstone held out for $4\frac{3}{4}$ hours, Yorkshire were not to be denied. There was a cascade of runs and an inevitable draw at Northampton. Zaheer Abbas hit a hundred in each innings, but 365 was too great a target for Gloucestershire. Allan Lamb hit a six and 27 fours on the opening day when David Graveney took the last five Northants wickets. Essex started well against Notts who were 75 for 3 before Rice and Birch both hit fine centuries and added 209 for the fourth wicket. Essex struggled badly. Only Fletcher of the earlier batsmen batted with any determination and it was left to Turner, East and Smith to banish the humiliation of the follow-on. Rice made what seemed a generous declaration when he asked Essex to make 224 in 168 minutes. McEvoy and Fletcher gave Essex hope, but whereas in the first innings it had been the incomparable Hadlee who had troubled Essex, now it was Bore. He sent back Hardie, Pont, Turner and East and Essex were thankful to hang on. D. S. De Silva had caused great consternation with his leg-spin at Worcester, but the match ended in batting practice as Mark Scott recorded a best of his brief career.

Second Cornhill Test Match

England brought in Emburey for Hendrick and Bob Taylor returned at the expense of Downton. Downton had had a poor game in the first Test. He had dropped a simple catch, but so had several others, and his judgement of where to position himself had seemed badly at fault and had caused the slips to be wrongly positioned. Nevertheless, the England selectors had a poor record in their selection and treatment of wicket-keepers. Taylor had had a mediocre time in Australia, but had had a memorable game in the Jubilee Test in India. Then he had been dropped. Knott had returned to Test cricket, but his batting form had deserted him. Bairstow came next, but his wicket-keeping had been well below Test standard so the promising Downton had replaced him, and now he had given way to the veteran Taylor who was still the best keeper in England. Bright replaced the injured Hogg in the Australian side. Hughes won the toss and, without the same justification that he had had at Nottingham, asked England to bat. Gooch began briskly and confidently and then mispulled a ball from Alderman. What followed was pretty dreary stuff. Woolmer was struck on the arm and retired hurt, resuming on the second day. Gatting played some aggressive shots as, ultimately, did Willey. Emburey batted on after coming in as night-watchman and then ran himself out. Botham played across the line and was one of the magnificent Lawson's seven victims. Indeed, Lawson's career best performance was the one bright light of the first two days. The scoring rate was slow and at the close we were left with memories of players sprinting off the field to avoid playing at the earliest opportunity. The umpires became confused over the rules and the players were in the showers anyway so that when the light was good at the end of the second day no play was taking place. As England had taken two days to score 311, a draw seemed inevitable. The brightest cricket came before lunch on the third day when Wood played excitingly and England took four wickets. Taylor caught Wood one handed, a wonderful effort, and but for the waywardness of their bowling and a plethora of no-balls, England could have been in an even better position. Border and Hughes promised much in the early afternoon, but Hughes drove wildly in Emburey's first over and Border was becalmed. Lillee lifted Australia to a first innings lead and England again batted doggedly and then made a late flourish. Bright was turning the ball appreciably and this encouraged people to think that Emburey might spin England to victory. Australia slumped to 17 for 3, but the game had been drawn since Friday evening. In truth, it is difficult to write of this match for, having watched Test cricket for 35 years, one could not recall the standard ever being so low. At the end of the match Botham resigned the England captaincy. It was said that he wished to end the uncertainty and felt, with justification, that a captain should be appointed for the series. The next morning the selectors announced that Mike Brearley had been recalled to captain England in the next three Tests. Like a character from Browning, the lost leader was being sought to recapture past glories. One wondered how much help he would get from the selectors whose lack of planning, method and foresight had brought England to a sorry state.

Second Cornhill Test Match   England v. Australia
2, 3, 4, 6 and 7 July   at Lord's

England	*First Innings*		*Second Innings*	
G. A. Gooch	c Yallop, b Alderman	44	lbw, b Lawson	20
G. Boycott	c Alderman, b Lawson	17	c Marsh, b Lillee	60
R. A. Woolmer	c Marsh, b Lawson	21	lbw, b Alderman	9
D. I. Gower	c Marsh, b Lawson	27	c Alderman, b Lillee	89
M. W. Gatting	lbw, b Bright	59	c Wood, b Bright	16
P. Willey	c Border, b Alderman	82	(7) c Chappell, b Bright	12
J. E. Emburey	run out	31		
I. T. Botham (capt)	lbw, b Lawson	0	(6) b Bright	0
* R. W. Taylor	c Hughes, b Lawson	0	b Lillee	9
G. R. Dilley	not out	7	(8) not out	27
R. G. D. Willis	c Wood, b Lawson	5		
	b 2, lb 3, w 3, nb 10	18	b 2, lb 8, nb 13	23
		311	(for 8 wkts, dec)	265

	O	M	R	W		O	M	R	W
Lillee	35.4	7	102	—		26.4	8	82	3
Alderman	30.2	7	79	1		17	2	42	1
Lawson	43.1	14	81	7		19	6	51	1
Bright	15	7	31	1		36	18	67	3

Fall of Wickets
1–60, 2–65, 3–134, 4–187, 5–284, 6–293, 7–293, 8–293, 9–298
1–31, 2–55, 3–178, 4–217, 5–217, 6–217, 7–242, 8–265

Australia	*First Innings*		*Second Innings*	
G. M. Wood	c Taylor, b Willis	44	not out	62
J. Dyson	c Gower, b Botham	7	lbw, b Dilley	1
G. N. Yallop	b Dilley	1	c Botham, b Willis	3
K. J. Hughes (capt)	c Willis, b Emburey	42	lbw, b Dilley	4
T. M. Chappell	c Taylor, b Dilley	2	c Taylor, b Botham	5
A. R. Border	c Gatting, b Botham	64	not out	12
* R. W. Marsh	lbw, b Dilley	47		
R. J. Bright	lbw, b Emburey	33		
G. F. Lawson	lbw, b Willis	5		
D. K. Lillee	not out	40		
T. M. Alderman	c Taylor, b Willis	5		
	b 6, lb 11, w 6, nb 32	55	w 1, nb 2	3
		345	(for 4 wkts)	90

	O	M	R	W		O	M	R	W
Willis	27.4	9	50	3		12	3	35	1
Dilley	30	8	106	3		7.5	1	18	2
Botham	26	8	71	2		8	3	10	1
Gooch	10	4	28	—					
Emburey	25	12	35	2		21	10	24	—

Fall of Wickets
1–62, 2–62, 3–69, 4–81, 5–167, 6–244, 7–257, 8–268, 9–314
1–2, 2–11, 3–17, 4–62

Match drawn

4, 6 and 7 July **at Chesterfield**
Derbyshire 248 (G. Miller 81, A. P. Pridgeon 5 for 63) and 337 for 4 dec
(B. Wood 153, J. G. Wright 141)
Worcestershire 307 for 7 dec (D. N. Patel 100 not out) and 275 (Younis
Ahmed 107, G. M. Turner 67, P. A. Neale 52, M. Hendrick 5 for 41)
Derbyshire won by 3 runs
Derbyshire 21 pts, Worcestershire 6 pts

at Bournemouth
Nottinghamshire 143 (C. E. B. Rice 105 not out, M. D. Marshall 4 for 32,
K. Stevenson 4 for 86) and 99 (K. Stevenson 5 for 32, M. D. Marshall 5
for 64)
Hampshire 190 (C. E. B. Rice 4 for 50, R. J. Hadlee 4 for 59) and 53 for 1
Hampshire won by 9 wickets
Hampshire 21 pts, Nottinghamshire 4 pts

at Maidstone
Lancashire 203 (E. Baptiste 5 for 37) and 318 for 7 dec (J. Simmons 65 not out,
J. Abrahams 59 not out, D. P. Hughes 54)
Kent 250 for 8 dec (Asif Iqbal 112) and 123 for 3
Match drawn
Kent 7 pts, Lancashire 5 pts

at Leicester
Leicestershire 116 (J. Garner 7 for 41) and 290 (J. C. Balderstone 71, J. Garner
5 for 65)
Somerset 356 (I. V. A. Richards 196, J. W. Lloyds 73, G. J. Parsons 4 for 115)
and 53 for 0
Somerset won by 10 wickets
Somerset 24 pts, Leicestershire 4 pts

at Northampton
Northamptonshire 243 (W. Larkins 57) and 331 for 3 dec (R. G. Williams
142 not out, A. J. Lamb 76, G. Cook 59)
Glamorgan 105 (B. J. Griffiths 8 for 50) and 212
Northamptonshire won by 257 runs
Northamptonshire 22 pts, Glamorgan 4 pts

at Hove
Sussex 304 (G. D. Mendis 78) and 197 for 3 dec (G. D. Mendis 95, P. W. G.
Parker 50 not out)
Gloucestershire 285 (Zaheer Abbas 145, C. E. Waller 4 for 94) and 159 for 8
(A. W. Stovold 57)
Match drawn
Sussex 7 pts, Gloucestershire 6 pts

at Edgbaston
Warwickshire 289 for 8 dec (T. A. Lloyd 94) and 296 for 3 dec (G. W. Humpage
119 not out, Asif Din 73 not out)

Essex 303 for 7 dec (K. W. R. Fletcher 123 not out, K. R. Pont 56) and 282
  for 2 (B. R. Hardie 111 not out, N. Phillip 66 not out, K. W. R. Fletcher 52)
Essex won by 8 wickets
Essex 23 pts, Warwickshire 6 pts

at Harrogate
Surrey 192 (G. R. J. Roope 63) and 246 (D. M. Smith 84 not out, R. D. Jackman
  51, A. Ramage 5 for 65)
Yorkshire 157 (R. D. Jackman 5 for 47, Intikhab Alam 5 for 65) and 283 for 5
  (J. H. Hampshire 127, S. N. Hartley 63)
Yorkshire won by 5 wickets
Yorkshire 21 pts, Surrey 5 pts

The match at Bournemouth was all over on the second afternoon and
Hampshire, bottom of the Schweppes County Championship in 1980, with only
one victory to their credit, had gained their fourth win of the season and gone
top of the table. On the Saturday Marshall and Stevenson had bowled out
Notts for 143 and determined Hampshire batting had given them the lead with
only four wickets down. Smith was in the side for the first time in the season,
replacing the injured Greenidge. The remarkable thing about the Notts innings
was that Clive Rice hit 105 not out, 73.4 percent of the innings total. Only sixteen
players have bettered this percentage in the history of first-class cricket. Rice
followed this with four wickets, but Notts collapsed a second time before the
Hants opening bowlers and this time Hadlee scored 40 out of 99. Leicestershire
were overwhelmed by the combined might of Viv Richards and Joel Garner
and Somerset moved ominously into second place. Without ever displaying
their real might Somerset were in the last stages of the Benson and Hedges
Cup and well placed in the John Player League, and they were now threatening
in the championship which remained a very open contest. Sussex, who were
without Le Roux as well as Imran, survived another century from the majestic
Zaheer and then, with the confidence born of success, set Gloucestershire 217
in three hours and ten minutes. There was no need to hurry, but Gloucestershire floundered against spin and were struggling for survival at the close. It
was no more than Sussex's due that Barclay should be appointed captain of
the representative side to play Sri Lanka and that Parker and Mendis should
be in the side with him. Greig, too, must have come under consideration.
Surrey's chance of going top of the league was blighted at Harrogate where
Yorkshire won their second match in succession. Smith and Jackman had
effected a Surrey recovery with a ninth wicket stand of 87 in the second innings
and Surrey had had a grip on the match for most of the time. Yorkshire's
final task of 282 in 275 minutes seemed well beyond them, particularly when
Thomas reduced them to 21 for 3. Surrey missed some chances. Hampshire
was again magnificent and Hartley, in the side for the injured Lumb, gave
good support. They added 179 in $2\frac{3}{4}$ hours and then Old and Bairstow hit
lustily to finish the job. Having been bowled out on a good wicket on the
opening day, Northants overwhelmed Glamorgan. The Welshmen were 71 for
6 on Saturday evening. They had been 6 for 4, all to Jim Griffiths who finished
with a career best 8 for 50. The Northants batting might then played to its

potential for the first time in the season. Richard Williams reminded us that he had been considered on the verge of the England side only a few months previously with a powerful display and Glamorgan surrendered quietly. There was a much closer contest at Chesterfield. Derbyshire had batted indifferently on the first day and owed much to Geoff Miller, an astute captain, who had been having a bad time with the ball, but a better one with the bat. Pridgeon bowled well for Worcestershire and Patel nursed them to a first innings lead. Then Wood and Wright put on 283 for the first wicket and Worcestershire were left three hours in which to make 279. Turner gave them a wonderful start with 67 off 35 balls. Younis was quite brilliant, hitting both Miller and Hendrick for sixes. Only 112 were needed from the last 20 overs and there were seven wickets in hand. Various forms of panic then manifested themselves against some relentlessly accurate bowling from Hendrick. It was Hendrick who bowled the last over and he yorked Birkenshaw with the fifth delivery. As Gifford had been detained in hospital with a chicken bone lodged in his throat and could not bat, Derbyshire had won by three runs, their first championship win of the season. At Maidstone, Baptiste bowled splendidly on the Saturday to take a career best of 5 for 37, his victims including Clive and David Lloyd. Asif then hit a fine hundred, but Kent lost their grip on the match and a draw became inevitable. Andy Lloyd provided the substance to the Warwickshire first innings after Essex had invited them to bat. Warwickshire finished the first day in a good position, Essex being 28 for 2 in reply to the home side's 289 for 8. Ferreira's late hitting had boosted the Warwickshire total. Essex had sprung two surprises in that Acfield, rightly, was preferred to Ray East for the spinner's position and Smith was dropped as wicket-keeper and replaced by David East. East had shown promise in the second team, but this seemed very harsh on Neil Smith who was among the leading wicket-keepers in the country and appeared to be the scape-goat for Essex's failure to take wickets. All was forgotten by the end of the match, however, for Fletcher and Pont salvaged Essex's first innings and took them to four batting points and Humpage hit furiously, albeit against McEwan and McEvoy's bowling at the end, and with Asif Din added 125 in 45 minutes. Essex were set to make 283 in 200 minutes. They won by 8 wickets with 6 overs to spare and the gloom around Chelmsford was lightened. Norbert Phillip reached his fifty in 27 minutes and Hardie's hundred came in 118 minutes. Fletcher and McEvoy had provided a good foundation and the third wicket stand between Phillip and Hardie produced 126 in under an hour.

John Player League

5 July   **at Chesterfield**
Worcestershire 160 for 9
Derbyshire 163 for 2 (J. G. Wright 87 not out)
Derbyshire (4 pts) won by 8 wickets

at Portsmouth

Nottinghamshire 123 for 8
Hampshire 125 for 2 (N. G. Cowley 64 not out)
Hampshire (4 pts) won by 8 wickets

at Maidstone

Kent 221 for 7 (C. J. Tavare 59, M. R. Benson 50)
Lancashire 221 (A. Kennedy 59)
Match tied. Kent 2 pts, Lancashire 2 pts

at Leicester

Leicestershire 164 for 8 (A. M. E. Roberts 59 not out)
Somerset 151 for 9
Leicestershire (4 pts) won by 13 runs

at Luton

Northamptonshire 174 for 7 (G. Cook 54)
Glamorgan 179 for 4 (A. Jones 50)
Glamorgan (4 pts) won by 6 wickets

at Hove

Sussex 287 for 4 (G. D. Mendis 125 not out, I. J. Gould 57)
Gloucestershire 236 for 6 (Zaheer Abbas 53)
Sussex (4 pts) won by 51 runs

at Edgbaston

Essex 239 for 4 (K. S. McEwan 83 not out, K. R. Pont 55 not out)
Warwickshire 136 (K. R. Pont 4 for 22)
Essex (4 pts) won by 103 runs

at Scarborough

Surrey 243 for 3 (G. S. Clinton 105 not out, M. A. Lynch 70)
Yorkshire 228 (D. L. Bairstow 78)
Surrey (4 pts) won by 15 runs

The John Player League took positive shape as the top sides gained victories. Sussex scored far too many for Gloucestershire. Their victory was founded on an opening stand of 119 between Gould and Mendis. Mendis, emerging as the leading batsman in the league, hit a brilliant century which included three sixes and ten fours. Derbyshire and Essex both won with ease. Pont had a wonderful all-round match at Edgbaston. His 55 not out was his highest score in the competition. Glamorgan moved into fourth place with a comfortable win at Luton and Hampshire demolished Notts for the second day in succession. Somerset were the only one of the top sides to lose ground when they were surprisingly beaten at Leicester. Their tormentor was Andy Roberts who hit a late, brisk fifty and then bowled tightly to put Somerset behind the asking rate. Graham Clinton hit two sixes and ten fours in his hundred and was given fine support from Monty Lynch, but Yorkshire, mainly through Bairstow and

Hampshire, reacted bravely and the margin of Surrey's victory was less than expected. The great excitement was at Maidstone. Put into bat, Kent scored 221 which was founded on an opening stand of 112 by Tavare and Benson. Lancashire had not reached a score as high as 221 for two seasons, but Kennedy gave them a vigorous start. Lancashire needed eleven off the last over. Abrahams, who batted very well, hit a single off the first ball, then Allott struck two fours. Abrahams was run out and two were needed off the last ball. Allott pushed the ball into the covers. Asif's underarm throw missed the wicket, but Johnson hit the wicket when Holding went for the overthrow and the match was tied.

Benson and Hedges Cup Semi-Finals

8 July   at The Oval
Surrey 191 for 9 (G. R. J. Roope 55 not out)
Leicestershire 188
Surrey won by 3 runs

at Taunton
Kent 154
Somerset 157 for 5 (P. M. Roebuck 51 not out)
Somerset won by 5 wickets

Surrey gained a very surprising victory at The Oval to enter one of the two limited over knock-out competition finals for the third year running. Surrey's total had seemed inadequate and it would have been indefensibly low but for the determination of Roope and the earlier efforts of Knight and Richards. Leicestershire bowled tightly and fielded well and when Balderstone and Steele passed fifty for the first wicket, they appeared to be strolling to victory. They lost their way dreadfully when Payne dismissed Gower and Davison in three balls and Steele also went with the score at 84. Garnham played encouragingly, but suddenly his side had a lot to do. It was Andy Roberts who made victory a possibility with some scorching hits, but the ninth wicket went down with 27 still needed. Bulging with experience, Ken Higgs cajoled Parsons into believing these runs could be obtained and Surrey looked strained. Jackman bowled the last over with 12 needed. The third ball was pulled over mid-wicket by Parsons for 6. The next went for two, but an unwise attempt to run off the fifth ball saw Higgs run out at the bowler's end and Surrey were victorious. There was no such excitement at Taunton where Kent never recovered from Botham's opening blast which removed Woolmer and Benson. Popplewell dismissed Tavare and Ealham and it was he who joined Roebuck in a match-winning stand of 67 for the fifth wicket. At one stage he took 16 runs in an over from Woolmer. He was rightly given the gold award as was Payne at The Oval.

Tilcon Trophy

8 July at Harrogate

Northamptonshire 336 (G. Cook 126, T. J. Yardley 73, A. J. Lamb 55)
Glamorgan 175 (Javed Miandad 59)
Northamptonshire won by 161 runs

9 July

Nottinghamshire 221 for 7 (C. E. B. Rice 58, D. W. Randall 55)
Worcestershire 222 for 6 (P. A. Neale 57)
Worcestershire won by 4 wickets

Final

10 July

Worcestershire 236 (T. M. Lamb 5 for 42)
Northamptonshire 135 (J. Birkenshaw 6 for 46)
Worcestershire won by 101 runs

9 July at Edgbaston

Warwickshire 127 for 8
v. Australians
Match abandoned

8, 9 and 10 July at Trent Bridge

T. C. B. XI 259 for 4 dec (M. W. Gatting 82 not out, G. D. Mendis 65) and
   140 for 3 dec (W. Larkins 78)
Sri Lanka 203 (R. L. Dias 50) and 199 for 7 (R. D. Mendis 66 not out,
   P. J. W. Allott 4 for 42)
Sri Lanka won by 3 wickets

The Tilcon Trophy at Harrogate again produced a most entertaining festival.
On the opening day Northants hit the highest score in the history of the
competition, but they were beaten in the final by Worcestershire for whom
Jack Birkenshaw, back on native soil, took six wickets in succession and had
one spell of 5 for 12 in six overs. Northants' score was the lowest in the history
of the competition. Many of their batsmen died bravely on the boundary. Sri
Lanka faced an exciting young England eleven at Trent Bridge. In spite of
some poor weather, the game was most entertaining and there were impressive
performances by several young men. Barclay was generous in his declaration,
Sri Lanka being allowed three hours in which to make 197. They won with
time to spare, but the game was encouraging in every respect. Larkins, Allott,
Barclay, Mendis and Gatting all acquitted themselves well.

National Westminster Bank Trophy Round One

11 July at Southampton

Cheshire 137 (S. J. Malone 5 for 34, T. E. Jesty 4 for 31)
Hampshire 138 for 4 (C. G. Greenidge 56)
Hampshire won by 6 wickets

at Hitchin

Essex 306 for 8 (G. A. Gooch 101, B. R. Hardie 81, K. W. R. Fletcher 51 not out)

Hertfordshire 115

Essex won by 191 runs

at Dublin

Gloucestershire 246 for 8 (A. W. Stovold 70, P. Bainbridge 61 not out, Sadiq Mohammad 50)

Ireland 75 (D. A. Graveney 5 for 11)

Gloucestershire won by 171 runs

at Canterbury

Yorkshire 222 for 6 (J. H. Hampshire 63, D. L. Bairstow 52 not out, C. S. Cowdrey 4 for 41)

Kent 223 for 4 (C. J. Tavare 118, M. R. Benson 57)

Kent won by 6 wickets

at Oxford (Christchurch)

Oxfordshire 150 (M. D. Nurton 70, M. A. Nash 5 for 31)

Glamorgan 154 for 2 (R. C. Ontong 53 not out)

Glamorgan won by 8 wickets

at Bury St Edmunds

Derbyshire 270 for 6 (D. S. Steele 89 not out, G. Miller 57)

Suffolk 99

Derbyshire won by 171 runs

11 and 13 July   ·   **at Old Trafford**

Durham 187 (S. R. Atkinson 80)

Lancashire 190 for 2 (A. Kennedy 102 not out)

Lancashire won by 8 wickets

The first round of the new National Westminster Bank Trophy produced no surprises. The minnows were swallowed as expected. Steve Malone had his best figures for Hampshire and then saw Gordon Greenidge get the Man of the Match award. 'After all, he was only a bowler.' Gooch devastated Herts as he and Brian Hardie hit 184 for the first wicket. The minor county were beaten before they had batted. Gloucestershire had a fright in Dublin, being 25 for 3, including Zaheer for 7. Thereafter the Irishmen wilted before the Gloucestershire batting and the left-arm spin of David Graveney. Spin also had the last say at Bury St Edmunds where David Steele turned in a good all round performance. Nurton won some consolation for the Minor Counties when his brave innings earned the gold award at Oxford. Rain delayed the inevitable for Durham and they succumbed on the Monday to a splendid innings from Kennedy and a totally efficient one from Clive Lloyd. The main excitement was at Canterbury. Yorkshire lost Moxon early and became a little bogged down, but Athey, Hampshire and the aggressive Bairstow who could, perhaps, have come in sooner all batted well. The revelation for Kent who were without the injured Dilley was Chris Cowdrey who bowled Boycott and Hartley and also dismissed Athey and Love. Kent lost Woolmer and Johnson for 19, but a marvellous stand of 144 between Benson and Tavare won them the match. Tavare was out when only three were needed for victory after an innings of splendour and fluency.

11, 12 and 13 July   **at Northampton**
Northamptonshire 252 (R. M. Hogg 6 for 87) and 167 for 7 (R. J. Bright 5 for 57)
Australians 415 for 8 dec (D. M. Welham 135 not out, T. M. Chappell 71, K. J. Hughes 51)
Match drawn

                                             at Leicester
Leicestershire 303 for 6 dec (R. W. Tolchard 104 not out, B. F. Davison 60) and 232 for 8 dec (D. A. Wenlock 62)
Sri Lankans 304 (R. L. Dias 127, A. De Mel 56, J. P. Agnew 4 for 83) and 143 for 1 (S. Wettimuny 95 not out)
Match drawn

11, 13 and 14 July   **at Trent Bridge**
Worcestershire 132 (G. M. Turner 51, K. E. Cooper 4 for 13) and 282 (Younis Ahmed 80, D. J. Humphries 61)
Nottinghamshire 402 (C. E. B. Rice 152, D. W. Randall 65, A. P. Pridgeon 4 for 82) and 13 for 0
Nottinghamshire won by 10 wickets
Nottinghamshire 24 pts, Worcestershire 2 pts

                                           at Taunton
Somerset 104 (G. G. Arnold 4 for 30, I. A. Greig 4 for 33) and 367 (B. C. Rose 82, I. T. Botham 72, J. W. Lloyds 68, P. W. Denning 61, G. S. Le Roux 8 for 107)
Sussex 233 (G. S. Le Roux 65, I. T. Botham 6 for 90) and 242 for 4 (P. W. G. Parker 105 not out, T. D. Booth-Jones 75)
Sussex won by 6 wickets
Sussex 22 pts, Somerset 4 pts

                                           at The Oval
Surrey 300 for 4 dec (A. R. Butcher 93, G. P. Howarth 90) and 264 for 9 dec (G. P. Howarth 110 not out, G. C. Small 6 for 76)
Warwickshire 300 for 5 dec (G. W. Humpage 126, D. L. Amiss 110) and 104 for 6
Match drawn
Surrey 6 pts, Warwickshire 5 pts

A fine, youthful hundred by Welham was the highlight of the Australians' game at Northampton. The tourists were almost spun to victory by Ray Bright on the last day, but Yardley and Sarfraz stayed firm. Rodney Hogg gave full evidence of his return to fitness with some fierce bowling on the Saturday. There was welcome news for Leicestershire, too, as skipper Roger Tolchard returned from injury and hit a century against Sri Lanka. Roy Dias played a brilliant knock for the tourists on the Sunday when he and De Mel added 109 in 22 overs for the eighth wicket. The Sri Lankans scored at nearly five an over throughout their innings which made their non-acceptance of Leicestershire's challenge to score 232 in 2½ hours very strange. David Wenlock hit a career best 62 for Leicestershire in the second innings. Once more Clive Rice was in dominant mood for Notts and their win over Worcestershire put them level at the top of the table with Sussex who had a splendid victory in a superb game of cricket at Taunton. Arnold and the consistently impressive Greig routed Somerset on the first day, but Botham, with new found fire, bowled Somerset back into contention. Waller and Le Roux added 79 for the last wicket to reassert the Sussex advantage, but Rose and Lloyds began the Somerset second innings with a stand of 151. Le Roux worked away at the determined Somerset batting and finished with a career best, and a very well earned, 8 for 107. Sussex needed 239 in 4½ hours and though they lost both openers quickly, Booth-Jones first and then the immaculate and gracefully powerful Parker, who took 14 in one over from Richards, saw them purposefully to victory. No such luxury at The Oval where Warwickshire's plans went astray. The highlights were another thumping Humpage century, and an innings of distinct charm from Amiss; Gladstone Small's career best; and, perhaps most welcome of all to those who love elegant batting, two innings from Geoff Howarth which showed recaptured form and were a delight. Butcher, too, showed some of his old magic.

John Player League

12 July   **at Canterbury**
Nottinghamshire 164 for 8 (C. E. B. Rice 52, D. L. Underwood 4 for 25)
Kent 168 for 4 (M. R. Benson 62)
Kent (4 pts) won by 6 wickets

                                                at Old Trafford
Middlesex 218 for 7 (G. D. Barlow 52)
Lancashire 221 for 7 (C. H. Lloyd 105 not out)
Lancashire (4 pts) won by 3 wickets

                                                at Taunton
Sussex 154 (J. Garner 4 for 23)
Somerset 155 for 6
Somerset (4 pts) won by 4 wickets

                                                at The Oval
Surrey 195 for 9 (M. A. Lynch 80 not out)
Warwickshire 196 for 3 (D. L. Amiss 84)
Warwickshire (4 pts) won by 7 wickets

at Worcester

Hampshire 213 for 8 (C. G. Greenidge 50)
Worcestershire 214 for 4 (G. M. Turner 57)
Worcestershire (4 pts) won by 6 wickets

With their closest rivals not playing, Sussex lost ground badly when they were well beaten at Taunton. Garner and Marks restrained Sussex and the home side's strong batting found the task of reaching 155 an easy one. Kent, too, won easily. Underwood and Jarvis were in restrictive form and the Notts batting looked far from impressive. Rice, far from his best, still managed fifty, but the exuberant Benson and the dependable Woolmer opened briskly, and Asif and Cowdrey finished the job. By one of the oddities of cricket, Tavare, so brilliant the previous day, found it hard to make contact and was out for one. Warwickshire, the champions, who had had a very lean time, beat Surrey in grand style. Monty Lynch maintained his improvement with a hard hit 80, but Amiss and Lloyd passed the hundred for the first wicket and though Kallicharran, who had been dropped from the county championship side, went quickly, Warwickshire strolled to victory. Hampshire's winning run was ended by some consistently fierce hitting from the Worcestershire batsmen. The match of the day was at Old Trafford. Chasing 219 for victory, a formidable task for a side who had not shown the best of form, Lancashire looked well beaten when they were 87 for 5, three of them to Daniel. Clive Lloyd then found an able partner in Jack Simmons and they added 94 in 14 overs. Clive Lloyd was at his most masterly and he hit six sixes and four fours in his hundred which came in 98 minutes. Two runs were needed for victory off the last ball of the match and Lloyd drove Hughes for four for a memorable win.

15, 16 and 17 July   **at Southend**
Essex 196 (K. S. McEwan 71, N. A. Mallender 4 for 45, Sarfraz Nawaz 4 for 54) and 108 (B. J. Griffiths 4 for 27, N. A. Mallender 4 for 42)
Northamptonshire 86 (J. K. Lever 6 for 47) and 163 (R. G. Williams 60, W. Larkins 55, D. L. Acfield 5 for 32)
Essex won by 55 runs
Essex 21 pts, Northamptonshire 4 pts

at Cardiff
Glamorgan 343 for 6 dec (J. A. Hopkins 116, G. C. Holmes 70 not out) and 49 for 0
Yorkshire 185 and 205 (J. H. Hampshire 75, E. A. Moseley 6 for 63)
Glamorgan won by 10 wickets
Glamorgan 24 pts, Yorkshire 3 pts

at Bristol
Worcestershire 316 for 5 dec (M. S. Scott 109, Younis Ahmed 83 not out) and 186 for 4 dec (G. M. Turner 57)
Gloucestershire 251 (Zaheer Abbas 71, A. W. Stovold 67) and 87 for 2
Match drawn
Worcestershire 7 pts, Gloucestershire 5 pts

at Portsmouth

Derbyshire 104 (T. M. Tremlett 4 for 11, K. Stevenson 5 for 49) and 209 (D. S. Steele 55)

Hampshire 345 for 8 dec (C. G. Greenidge 109)

Hampshire won by an innings and 32 runs

Hampshire 24 pts, Derbyshire 3 pts

at Lord's

Middlesex 167 (W. N. Slack 56, J. N. Shepherd 5 for 61) and 367 for 0 dec (W. N. Slack 181 not out, G. D. Barlow 174 not out)

Kent 284 (C. S. Cowdrey 60, Asif Iqbal 55, W. W. Daniel 4 for 74) and 67 for 2

Match drawn

Kent 7 pts, Middlesex 5 pts

at Hove

Surrey 175 (R. D. V. Knight 61, I. A. Greig 4 for 41) and 90 for 3

Sussex 289 (I. A. Greig 78 not out, P. W. G. Parker 58, I. J. Gould 52, Intikhab Alam 5 for 44)

Match drawn

Sussex 6 pts, Surrey 4 pts

at Coventry

Warwickshire 136 (L. B. Taylor 4 for 26, G. J. Parsons 4 for 44) and 160

Leicestershire 357 for 9 dec (T. J. Boon 83, J. F. Steele 64, D. R. Doshi 4 for 90)

Leicestershire won by an innings and 61 runs

Leicestershire 23 pts, Warwickshire 2 pts

at Old Trafford

Lancashire 183 (D. S. De Silva 7 for 55)

Sri Lankans 184 for 3 (B. Warnapura 75 not out)

Match abandoned as a draw

Derbyshire must have regretted their decision to bat on a green wicket at Portsmouth, for they were routed by Stevenson and, especially, by Tremlett who took four wickets in 13 overs before lunch. Greenidge soon gave Hampshire the ascendancy and they never lost their grip on the game, dismissing Derbyshire cheaply a second time. The neat, and most promising, Bob Parks held six catches in the first innings, a Hampshire record, and four more in the second. Hampshire returned to the top of the championship table. Sussex, for whom Ian Greig gave another splendid all-round performance, were thwarted by rain, as were the Sri Lankans who had Lancashire in a strangle-hold after some spectacular leg-break bowling by Somachandra De Silva. Leicestershire gained their first championship win of the season when they outplayed a limp Warwickshire side. Good seam bowling by Taylor and Parsons was followed by a career best from Tim Boon. Warwickshire sank without a murmur for the second time and manager David Brown was vehement in his criticism of his team's inept performance. There was a maiden century for Mark Scott as he and Younis shared a third wicket stand of 113. Left-arm quick bowler Whitney from New South Wales took three wickets for Gloucestershire and Zaheer became the first batsman to reach 1500 runs in the season, but the match dwindled to a draw. There was a draw, too, at Lord's where the weather was the final winner. Middlesex never recovered from 15 for 3 and only Wilf Slack and Paul Downton offered any resistance to Jarvis and Shepherd. Kent consolidated a lead with Chris Cowdrey again showing good form and confidence. When Middlesex batted again Graham Barlow and Wilf Slack, the two left-handers, both reached their highest scores in first-class cricket and their unbeaten 367 constituted a new record for the Middlesex first wicket. They were encouraged towards the close by some generous Kent bowling, aimed at forcing a declaration and a result, but the achievement was still a notable one. Glamorgan took pride in destroying a Yorkshire side a little thin in determination. Yorkshire put Glamorgan in, but Alan Jones and John Hopkins quickly proved this decision wrong. On the second day Yorkshire fell to the all-round abilities of the home attack, and only Hampshire saved some dignity when they followed on. Ezra Moseley was their chief tormentor. After their two successive wins Yorkshire appeared to be in the doldrums once more. Essex clambered into fifth place with a good win over Northants. The ball was seaming disconcertingly under heavy cloud on the first two days and only Ken McEwan batted with confidence. Northants crumpled before Lever, but Essex, in their turn, found runs hard to get. Northants were left needing 219 to win and, though Cook went for 0, they began to look like winners when Larkins and Williams took the score past the hundred. They lost their last eight wickets to Turner and Acfield for 34 runs, however, and Essex won by 55 runs.

Third Cornhill Test Match

The match was preceded by arguments about the regularity with which fast bowlers were leaving the field, a custom initiated by the West Indies, but this was amicably settled. The Australians were unchanged, not surprisingly, but England brought in Old for Emburey and one wondered again why four pace bowlers were necessary. If three could not do the job, four would not be able to. Brearley was back to lead England and, as expected, it was Woolmer who made way for him. Hughes won the toss and Australia batted. Dyson and Wood began confidently with Dyson attempting more shots than at Lord's. At 55, Botham bowled for the first time and had Wood lbw with his third ball. It signalled a rejuvenated Botham. As many of us had hoped, without the burden of captaincy, he was a different player, running in with all his old determination and moving the ball late to cause many problems for the batsmen. That they survived for two days was due to their determined application, the paucity of the support for Botham and the poor English catching. Dyson reached his maiden Test hundred and was a model of responsible batting. Hughes and Yallop gave ample support and there was an inevitability that the Australians would reach 400. The pitch was always favouring the bowler, but, Botham apart, the England attack failed to exploit the conditions. They erred in line and length and Dilley, who captured the wickets of Dyson and

Bright, seemed too concerned with gesticulating his contempt for the crowd, energy which would have been better employed on the basics of his bowling technique. Hughes declared and England faced two rather wild overs on the Friday evening. It was Boycott's 101st Test match. He had reached the century at Lord's and was anxious to do well on his own ground, but it was not to be. Gooch was out on Saturday morning to the first ball that he received, playing across the line. Brearley was caught behind, as was Gower the ball after he had been dropped at slip. Boycott had his leg stump knocked back by a ball from Lawson that came back at him. Gatting was dropped off a straight forward chance at slip and was then lbw pushing half way forward, bat and legs in discord. Willey was yorked inelegantly. Taylor hung his bat out. Botham cheered England with a counter attack of uncompromising belligerence, but he received a vicious lifter from Lillee and Marsh took the catch to break Alan Knott's Test record of victims. Dilley lobbed a caught and bowled and England were asked to follow on 227 runs behind. Gooch was caught at slip off Lillee third ball and they came off bad light. It was Lillee's birthday and the Australians were celebrating. Although the light was perfectly playable at six o'clock, indeed the best of the day, play did not resume. Once more the rules had defied interpretation. The paying customers were angry. Cricket stood alienated from its supporters, arrogant and aloof. England's cricket team was at its lowest in public regard. The Monday appeared a formality. Brearley went at slip, as did Gower. Boycott and Gatting were lbw though, for a time, Boycott had looked as if he might save something from the wreck. By mid-afternoon England were 135 for 7 and sinking fast. Botham was at the wicket with Dilley. Dilley played a courageous innings, but if it becomes forgotten, along with Chris Old's determined knock on his home ground, it is because of the magnitude of Botham's performance. This was one of the great innings of Test cricket. Seemingly bereft of care, the man did what he does best – he played it simply and without inhibition. He lifted on his toes and crashed the ball through the off-side. He advanced down the wicket and drove Alderman high for six. Occasionally there was a slice over the slips for four, but this was no blemish. The power of the man and the purposefulness defied contradiction. The Australian bowling never wilted, but who could contain this? Jessop's name was conjured from the past, but there should be no comparisons; Botham stood and smote in his own right. He reached his hundred in $2\frac{1}{2}$ hours. He and Dilley, a brave youth, added 117 in 80 minutes, and with Old, Botham added 67 in 55 minutes, and suddenly Australia had to bat again. They went in on the last morning needing 130 to win. Two deliveries from Botham, one a no-ball, produced 8 runs and they were on their way. Wood left at 13, but the fifty was passed without further loss and Australia were cruising to victory. Chappell received a violent lifter from Willis and the ball lobbed to Taylor. In the last over before lunch Willis had Hughes brilliantly caught at slip by Botham and Yallop taken bat-pad. Border played on to Old. Dyson, who had played with composure, mis-hooked and was caught behind on the leg side. Marsh swung terrifyingly and Dilley took a superb catch at fine leg from a ball that would have carried for six. Lawson hung his bat out. Bright and Lillee countered with pugnacious batting. They brought Australia within 20 of victory before Willis deceived

Lillee and had him caught, well, by Gatting running in at mid-on. Alderman was twice dropped in the slips by Old and the tension was acute. Willis ended all uncertainty when he knocked Bright's middle stump out of the ground. It was the first time for 87 years that a Test side had won after being asked to follow on. It was an heroic performance. Within 48 hours England's cricket prestige had been transformed. Once again Brearley had raised his side in the field. Under Brearley's leadership, Botham was once more a cricketer of determination and glorious belligerence. Botham was named Man of the Match, but on the last day Bob Willis had taken 8 for 43. He had bowled like a man possessed. There was fire in his eyes and in his heart. This was one of the most monumental pieces of bowling in Test history and it was accomplished by a man whom many of us had considered to be no longer of Test standard. It was a performance that transcended records for it was of the spirit and of a human endeavour that cannot be measured by statistics.

Third Cornhill Test Match   **England v. Australia**
16, 17, 18, 20 and 21 July   at Headingley, Leeds

Australia	*First Innings*		*Second Innings*	
J. Dyson	b Dilley	102	c Taylor, b Willis	34
G. M. Wood	lbw, b Botham	34	c Taylor, b Botham	10
T. M. Chappell	c Taylor, b Willey	27	c Taylor, b Willis	8
K. J. Hughes (capt)	c and b Botham	89	c Botham, b Willis	0
R. J. Bright	b Dilley	7	(8) b Willis	19
G. N. Yallop	c Taylor, b Botham	58	(5) c Gatting, b Willis	0
A. R. Border	lbw, b Botham	8	(6) b Old	0
*R. W. Marsh	b Botham	28	(7) c Dilley, b Willis	4
G. F. Lawson	c Taylor, b Botham	13	c Taylor, b Willis	1
D. K. Lillee	not out	3	c Gatting, b Willis	17
T. M. Alderman			not out	0
	b 4, lb 13, w 3, nb 12	32	lb 3, w 1, nb 14	18
	(for 9 wkts dec)	401		111

	O	M	R	W		O	M	R	W
Willis	30	8	72	—		15.1	3	43	8
Old	43	14	91	—		9	1	21	1
Dilley	27	4	78	2		2	—	11	—
Botham	38.1	11	95	6		7	3	14	1
Willey	13	2	31	1		3	1	4	—
Boycott	3	2	2	—					

Fall of Wickets
1–55, 2–149, 3–196, 4–220, 5–332, 6–354, 7–357, 8–396, 9–401
1–13, 2–56, 3–58, 4–58, 5–65, 6–68, 7–74, 8–75, 9–110

England	*First Innings*		*Second Innings*	
G. A. Gooch	lbw, b Alderman	2	c Alderman, b Lillee	0
G. Boycott	b Lawson	12	lbw, b Alderman	46
J. M. Brearley (capt)	c Marsh, b Alderman	10	c Alderman, b Lillee	14
D. I. Gower	c Marsh, b Lawson	24	c Border, b Alderman	9
M. W. Gatting	lbw, b Lillee	15	lbw, b Alderman	1

P. Willey	b Lawson	8	c Dyson, b Lillee	33
I. T. Botham	c Marsh, b Lillee	50	not out	149
*R. W. Taylor	c Marsh, b Lillee	5	c Bright, b Alderman	1
G. R. Dilley	c and b Lillee	13	b Alderman	56
C. M. Old	c Border, b Alderman	0	b Lawson	29
R. G. D. Willis	not out	1	c Border, b Alderman	2
	b 6, lb 11, w 6, nb 11	34	b 5, lb 3, w 3, nb 5	16
		174		356

	O	M	R	W		O	M	R	W
Lillee	18.5	7	49	4		25	6	94	3
Alderman	19	4	59	3		35.3	6	135	6
Lawson	13	3	32	3		23	4	96	1
Bright						4	—	15	—

Fall of Wickets
1–12, 2–40, 3–42, 4–84, 5–87, 6–112, 7–148, 8–166, 9–167
1–0, 2–18, 3–37, 4–41, 5–105, 6–133, 7–135, 8–252, 9–319

England won by 18 runs

18, 20 and 21 July   **at Southend**
Essex 308 (B. R. Hardie 129, S. Turner 73 not out, C. Gladwin 53, N. V. Radford 4 for 71)
Lancashire 111 (N. Phillip 4 for 33) and 245 for 7 (C. H. Lloyd 65)
Match drawn
Essex 8 pts, Lancashire 4 pts

                                    at Bristol
Gloucestershire 421 for 9 dec (Zaheer Abbas 159, A. W. Stovold 104, P. Bainbridge 72, M. A. Nash 4 for 114) and 245 for 6 dec (A. W. Stovold 65 not out, B. J. Lloyd 4 for 110)
Glamorgan 379 for 3 dec (Javed Miandad 152, R. C. Ontong 116 not out, A. Jones 50) and 113 for 1 (A. Jones 64 not out)
Match drawn
Glamorgan 8 pts, Gloucestershire 4 pts

                                    at Portsmouth
Surrey 204 (T. E. Jesty 4 for 38) and 181 (M. D. Marshall 5 for 60)
Hampshire 164 (S. T. Clarke 5 for 41) and 91 (R. D. Jackman 5 for 30)
Surrey won by 130 runs
Surrey 22 pts, Hampshire 5 pts

                                    at Leicester
Kent 224 (C. J. Tavare 62, L. B. Taylor 4 for 64) and 319 (R. A. Woolmer 87, C. J. Tavare 69, J. P. Agnew 4 for 64)
Leicestershire 266 (N. E. Briers 89, B. F. Davison 82, G. J. Parsons 50, K. B. S. Jarvis 7 for 78) and 166 (M. A. Garnham 74, J. N. Shepherd 4 for 42, K. B. S. Jarvis 4 for 69)
Kent won by 111 runs
Kent 22 pts, Leicestershire 7 pts

at Lord's

Middlesex 108 (R. O. Butcher 54, H. L. Alleyne 8 for 43) and 444 for 7 dec (W. N. Slack 248 not out, R. O. Butcher 66, K. P. Tomlins 57)

Worcestershire 345 (G. M. Turner 61, M. S. Scott 59, D. J. Humphries 58, W. W. Daniel 4 for 91) and 103 for 4

Match drawn

Worcestershire 8 pts, Middlesex 4 pts

at Trent Bridge

Yorkshire 104 (R. J. Hadlee 4 for 26) and 364 (S. N. Hartley 106, J. H. Hampshire 82, R. J. Hadlee 4 for 90)

Nottinghamshire 354 (C. E. B. Rice 172, D. W. Randall 87, G. B. Stevenson 5 for 58, A. Ramage 4 for 117) and 115 for 2 (J. D. Birch 50 not out)

Nottinghamshire won by 8 wickets

Nottinghamshire 24 pts, Yorkshire 4 pts

at Taunton

Somerset 335 for 8 dec (P. M. Roebuck 91, P. W. Denning 71) and 337 for 3 dec (I. V. A. Richards 130, J. W. Lloyds 98)

Derbyshire 495 for 7 dec (P. N. Kirsten 228, D. S. Steele 137)

Match drawn

Derbyshire 5 pts, Somerset 4 pts

at Hove

Warwickshire 249 (T. A. Lloyd 89, Asif Din 57) and 126 (D. L. Amiss 58, G. S. le Roux 6 for 36)

Sussex 208 (W. Hogg 4 for 54) and 169 for 5 (P. W. G. Parker 50)

Sussex won by 5 wickets

Sussex 22 pts, Warwickshire 6 pts

18, 19 and 20 July   **at Northampton**

Northamptonshire 328 for 7 dec (Sarfraz Nawaz 90, J. P. C. Mills 68, G. Cook 60) and 205 for 4 dec (G. Cook 78, A. J. Lamb 56 not out)

Sri Lankans 292 for 6 dec (N. Hettiarachi 80, S. Wettimuny 68) and 134 for 1 (N. Hettiarachi 58 not out, S. Wettimuny 51 not out)

Match drawn

Sussex moved back to the top of the championship table when they beat Warwickshire with a fine display on the last day when Garth le Roux did the hat-trick in a splendidly fiery spell. Paul Parker again paced Sussex to victory after they had stuttered following a good opening stand. Hampshire, having asked Surrey to bat, bowled well enough, but found the reunited Clarke and Jackman too much for them on a wicket that was never easy. Jackman took four wickets in eight balls on the last day and to add to Hampshire's woe Pocock was injured again. Notts maintained a challenge by crushing Yorkshire. The Notts bowlers demoralised and destroyed Yorkshire on the Saturday and inevitably Rice and Randall batted Notts to a big lead. Notts then showed their usual failing in having difficulty dismissing a side for the second time. Once more Hampshire batted well for Yorkshire, but it was Neil Hartley with a maiden hundred who took the honours. His innings lasted five and a half hours and included a six and ten fours. Notts were left 20 overs in which to score 115 and they achieved their target with 11 balls to spare. In the west country there were many runs and few wickets. Peter Kirsten, who hit a career best, and David Steele added a record 291 for the Derbyshire third wicket at Taunton, and Javed Miandad and Rodney Ontong set a Glamorgan third wicket record of 270 at Bristol. Without Brain and Procter the Gloucestershire attack looked very weak, but Andy Stovold and Zaheer emphasised the batting strength with a third wicket stand of 162. Bowlers had a better time at Lord's, initially, where Hartley Alleyne combined fire and accuracy to return the best figures of the season. Worcestershire's batsmen capitalised on Alleyne's performance to build a commanding lead and an innings victory seemed certain when Middlesex were 0 for 2. Then Wilf Slack played a remarkable innings which lasted ten minutes under seven hours. He was helped by the fact that Alleyne was unable to bowl, but he did not give a chance as he hit a five and 32 fours in the highest score of the season and the highest at Lord's for thirty-three years. It had been a remarkable five days for the Middlesex reserve. An accomplished fifty in his first match by young Chris Gladwin, a fine hundred by the dependable Brian Hardie and some ferocious hitting from Stuart Turner gave Essex four batting points in a rain interrupted match at Southend. Lancashire folded limply before Phillip and Lever, but when they followed on a solid knock from Clive Lloyd and missed chances by Essex ensured a draw. Kent reversed their fortunes well at Leicester to snatch a splendid victory. Kent trailed on the first innings in spite of heroic bowling by Kevin Jarvis, enjoying an excellent season. Then Woolmer, captaining Kent for the first time, and Tavare batted well. Cowdrey, Knott and Baptiste added a few brisk runs and Leicestershire needed 278 to win in over four hours. They found survival difficult against Shepherd and Jarvis, and later impossible. Garnham batted extremely well and showed strokes of rich promise, but he fell to Underwood and Kent had gained a surprisingly easy victory. Viv Richards' hundred took him past his thousand for the season and meant that he has scored a century against every county, including Somerset.

John Player League

19 July   **at Southend**
Essex 217 for 5 (K. W. R. Fletcher 56, K. R. Pont 50 not out)
Lancashire 153 for 6 (D. Lloyd 59, J. K. Lever 4 for 28)
Essex (4 pts) won by 64 runs

                                                                at Bristol
Gloucestershire 192 for 6 (A. W. Stovold 58)
Glamorgan 194 for 3 (Javed Miandad 63 not out, J. A. Hopkins 51)
Glamorgan (4 pts) won by 7 wickets

                                                            at Southampton
Surrey 167 for 8 (M. A. Lynch 56 not out)
Hampshire 171 for 6 (N. G. Cowley 52)
Hampshire (4 pts) won by 4 wickets

at Leicester

Kent 177 for 6
Leicestershire 60 for 4
Leicestershire (4 pts) won on faster scoring rate

at Lord's

Worcestershire 160 for 8
Middlesex 165 for 4 (R. O. Butcher 77 not out)
Middlesex (4 pts) won by 6 wickets

at Trent Bridge

Yorkshire 154 (K. Saxelby 4 for 37)
Nottinghamshire 85 for 2
Nottinghamshire (4 pts) won on faster scoring rate

at Taunton

Derbyshire 184 for 5 (P. N. Kirsten 63, J. G. Wright 50)
Somerset 188 for 3 (I. V. A. Richards 86 not out)
Somerset (4 pts) won by 7 wickets

at Horsham

Sussex 198 for 9 (P. W. G. Parker 54, A. M. Ferreira 4 for 26)
Warwickshire 200 for 3 (D. L. Amiss 117 not out)
Warwickshire (4 pts) won by 7 wickets

Having refound their appetite for the Sunday League, Warwickshire destroyed Sussex in majestic fashion. Ferreira swung the ball appreciably, but the victory rested on a mighty and elegant innings by Dennis Amiss who hit seven sixes and took Warwickshire to victory with more than six overs to spare. Kent and Yorkshire both lost in cloudy conditions to considerably faster scoring rates, and Essex, fearing curtailment hit some violent runs at Southend. Fletcher, Pont and Phillip brought about the Essex recovery and then Pont and Turner hit 60 from the last 7 overs. Lancashire showed no interest in trying to match this and Essex went top of the league. The were followed by Glamorgan and Somerset, both of whom won in style thanks to their overseas Test batsmen, and Hampshire who gave another impressively confident display. Middlesex gained revenge for their humiliation of the previous day when Butcher and Barlow added 98 for the third wicket in 50 minutes and saw their side to an easy win.

National Westminster Bank Trophy – Round Two

22 July   **at Cardiff**
Hampshire 176 for 7 (T. E. Jesty 67, S. R. Barwick 4 for 14)
Glamorgan 146 (Javed Miandad 64)
Hampshire won by 30 runs

at Northampton

Somerset 202 (N. F. M. Popplewell 57)
Northamptonshire 204 for 3 (W. Larkins 59, G. Cook 50)
Northamptonshire won by 7 wickets

22 and 23 July   **at Canterbury**
Kent 154
Nottinghamshire 156 for 6
Nottinghamshire won by 4 wickets

                                                at Edgbaston
Sussex 274 for 8 (I. A. Greig 82)
Warwickshire 150 (I. A. Greig 4 for 31)
Sussex won by 124 runs

                                                at Worcester
Worcestershire 228 (G. M. Turner 59, C. J. Tunnicliffe 5 for 50)
Derbyshire 229 for 6 (P. N. Kirsten 84 not out, J. G. Wright 50)
Derbyshire won by 4 wickets

22, 23 and 24 July   **at Bristol**
Essex 207
Gloucestershire 85
Essex won by 122 runs

24 July   **at Old Trafford**
Lancashire 231 for 8 (D. Lloyd 81, W. W. Daniel 4 for 28)
Middlesex 189 (W. N. Slack 53)
Lancashire won by 42 runs

23 and 24 July   **at The Oval**
Leicestershire 261 (B. F. Davison 137 not out, M. A. Garnham 58, D. J. Thomas
    4 for 60)
Surrey 12 for 0
Match abandoned
Leicestershire 104 for 5
Surrey 88 for 2
Leicestershire won by 16 runs

22, 23 and 24 July   **at Sheffield**
Yorkshire 275 for 5 dec (K. Sharp 116)
v. Sri Lankans
Match abandoned

23 July   **at Glasgow**
Australians 135 for 9 (J. Clark 4 for 28)
Scotland 125 for 9
Australians won by 10 runs

So poor was the weather that only two matches in the second round of the
National Westminster Bank Trophy could be completed on the scheduled day.
Somerset surrendered to Northants with surprising ease. A fifth wicket stand
of 63 between Botham and Popplewell gave Somerset some hope, but Geoff
Cook and Wayne Larkins began the Northants innings with a stand of 111
and the Northants display was their most accomplished of the season. Another
skipper to win a Man of the Match award was Trevor Jesty who was leading
Hampshire in the absence of Nick Pocock. He steadied the Hampshire innings

and then handled his bowlers and fielders astutely in defending a not very big score. Ian Greig gave a splendid all-round display at Edgbaston. He batted superbly and, in conjunction with Waller, bowled Warwickshire to extinction. Only 23 minutes, 35 balls, were needed to complete the game on the second day. There was an upset at Canterbury where Kent were contained on the first day, but reduced Notts to 79 for 6 and looked likely winners. Underwood bowled his 12 overs for 12 runs, but the honours went to Hadlee and French who added 77 in 22 overs and won the match. Hadlee took the individual award. Worcestershire and Derbyshire seemed well balanced at the end of the first day's play, but Kirsten was at his best, he had hit his career highest two days previously and he and Barnett added 62 in 12 overs. Taylor also proved a reliable partner and Derbyshire won with 10 balls to spare.

The Essex and Gloucestershire game spread over three days though only four overs were bowled on the Thursday. Lilley, Gooch, Turner and Ray East batted well in difficult conditions. Surprisingly, the wicket favoured the spin, but none believed that the Essex total would provide them with such a wide margin of victory, particularly as, unwisely, they had omitted Acfield. Gloucestershire, however, crumpled badly. Broad was caught behind off Lever's fourth delivery. Stovold was leg-before in the England bowler's third over and then Phillip and David East decided the match. Zaheer was caught by the wicket-keeper diving to his right and Hignell was taken next ball, brilliantly, by David East diving to his left. The young wicket-keeper who had made an immense impression since surprisingly being preferred to Smith was given the Man of the Match award, and rightly so. Middlesex had a splendid start when Fowler went to Daniel for 0, but Kennedy and David Lloyd then added 100 and the last Gillette Cup winners were struggling ever afterwards. Justice was done at The Oval where Brian Davison played an exciting innings which was declared null and void when the teams were forced into a ten over slog by the weather. Davison then proved his point again by taking 22 from Jackman's first over and 43 from the 18 balls he faced. Surrey were asked to score at more than ten and a half an over, which was well beyond them. In the other matches Kevin Sharp, to the delight of all who love graceful batting, restored himself with a century before the rain and Rodney Marsh bowled a maiden over in which he took three wickets against Scotland.

Benson and Hedges Cup Final

Both sides had been knocked out of the National Westminster Bank Cup earlier in the week so that the incentive to succeed was even greater than it might have been normally, but, as it transpired, this was one of the poorest of finals. Surrey left out Butcher and promoted Richards to open the innings. This proved to be an unwise decision. Richards was totally out of his depth and struggled embarrassingly against Garner and Botham before, rather unluckily, he played on. Sadly for Surrey, Clinton was also unable to find his touch and batted with growing frustration until he drove Marks to mid-off where Roebuck took an easy catch. After an hour's play and sixteen overs Surrey had lost both openers and scored only 16 runs. Howarth and Knight did their best to rectify matters. Howarth went for the big hits, not always connecting, and

Knight began to gather runs unobtrusively. Howarth went at 63 and there was a brief aggressive flourish from Lynch which lifted Surrey spirits but was ended by a Garner catch in the deep. Knight moved unobtrusively to 92 before a ball looped off his glove to Taylor and Surrey had totalled 194 in their fifty-five overs. Momentarily, the match was alive when Jackman and Clarke bowled Rose and Denning. Then came Richards. He was in his clouting mood. Roebuck gave sensible support and 105 were added in 107 minutes. The Surrey bowling and fielding declined, and the usually competent Jack Richards added to his batting failure with a lethargic display behind the stumps. Thomas had a nightmare. Botham joined Richards and the power of England and the West Indies bludgeoned Somerset to victory with nearly eleven overs to spare. It was not one of Viv Richards' best innings (it did not have to be), but it was the highest recorded in a Benson and Hedges Final and it won him the gold award. There should be an award, too, for Joel Garner whose 5 for 14 in 11 overs was as devastating as those figures suggest.

Benson and Hedges Cup Final   Surrey *v.* Somerset
25 July 1981   at Lord's

Surrey

G. S. Clinton	c Roebuck, b Marks	6
* C. J. Richards	b Garner	1
R. D. V. Knight (capt)	c Taylor, b Garner	92
G. P. Howarth	c Roebuck, b Marks	16
M. A. Lynch	c Garner, b Popplewell	22
D. M. Smith	b Garner	7
S. T. Clarke	c Popplewell, b Garner	15
G. R. J. Roope	not out	14
D. J. Thomas	b Garner	0
R. D. Jackman	not out	2
P. I. Pocock	did not bat	
Extras	b 2, lb 14, w 2, nb 1	19
	(for 8 wkts)	194

	O	M	R	W
Garner	11	5	14	5
Botham	11	2	44	—
Dredge	11	—	48	—
Marks	11	5	24	2
Popplewell	11	—	45	1

Fall of Wickets
1–4, 2–16, 3–63, 4–98, 5–132, 6–166, 7–182, 8–183.

Somerset

B. C. Rose (capt)	b Jackman	5
P. W. Denning	b Clarke	0
I. V. A. Richards	not out	132
P. M. Roebuck	c Smith, b Knight	22
I. T. Botham	not out	37
Extras	nb 1	1
	(for 3 wkts)	197

V. J. Marks, N. F. M. Popplewell, D. Breakwell, *D. J. S. Taylor, J. Garner and C. H. Dredge did not bat.

	O	M	R	W
Clarke	8	1	24	1
Jackman	11	1	53	1
Thomas	5.3	—	32	—
Pocock	11	1	46	—
Knight	9	—	41	1

Fall of Wickets
1–5, 2–5, 3–110.

Somerset won by 7 wickets

25 July   **at Chelmsford**
Essex 213 for 9 (G. A. Gooch 59, A. Ranasinghe 4 for 50)
Sri Lankans 214 for 6 (S. Wettimuny 64)
Sri Lankans won by 4 wickets

25, 26 and 27 July   **at Worcester**
Worcestershire 189 and 344 for 8 dec (P. A. Neale 145 not out, J. Birkenshaw 54)
Australians 293 (A. R. Border 115, M. F. Kent 92, J. Cumbes 4 for 62) and 241 for 3 (A. R. Border 70 not out, G. M. Wood 59, D. M. Welham 54 not out)
Australians won by 7 wickets

at Dublin
Scotland 210 (D. L. Bell 60, R. Torrens 6 for 42) and 137 for 2 (A. B. M. Ker 65)
Ireland 331 for 9 dec (I. J. Anderson 99)
Match drawn

25, 27 and 28 July   **at Derby**
Kent 348 for 3 dec (C. J. Tavare 156, M. R. Benson 108, C. S. Cowdrey 56 not out) and 139 (A. P. E. Knott 50, C. J. Tavare 57, D. S. Steele 7 for 53)
Derbyshire 297 (D. S. Steele 67) and 191 for 1 (J. G. Wright 88, B. Wood 85 not out)
Derbyshire won by 9 wickets
Derbyshire 19 pts, Kent 8 pts

at Trent Bridge
Lancashire 150 (C. H. Lloyd 50, R. J. Hadlee 5 for 47) and 209 (J. Abrahams 74)
Nottinghamshire 167 (C. E. B. Rice 80, N. V. Radford 5 for 107) and 193 for 2 (P. A. Todd 112, D. W. Randall 52 not out)
Nottinghamshire won by 8 wickets
Nottinghamshire 21 pts, Lancashire 5 pts

The Sri Lankans celebrated their elevation to Test status with a victory in the one-day match at Chelmsford, and Australia improved morale with a fine performance at Worcester. There was excellent batting from Border and Kent, and then Phil Neale, acting captain, hit the highest score ever recorded by a Worcestershire player against the Australians. He and Jack Birkenshaw added 122 in 77 minutes and Australia were set to score 241 in 130 minutes. They accomplished the task with 32 balls to spare, and Border and Welham, pressing for a Test place, scored the last 128 runs in 58 minutes. At Derby, Geoff Miller, whose eleven first-class wickets had cost more than fifty runs each, resigned the captaincy and Barry Wood took over. He had a terrible first day when Kent ravaged the Derbyshire bowling and the home side were wilting at 76 for 4. David Steele and the tail raised them to within 51 of Kent. Then Steele's left-arm spin reduced Kent to tatters, in spite of more fine batting from Tavare, and Wood and Wright put on 162 for the first wicket to assure Derbyshire of a victory, which had been totally unexpected. Lancashire and Notts were honours even on the first innings on the Trent Bridge wicket which was becoming notorious as a bowler's paradise. Notts seemed set for victory when Lancashire were at 128 for 8 in their second innings. Abrahams and Scott batted bravely and added 67 for the last wicket. Todd and Weightman, in his first championship match, started the Notts bid for victory with a stand of 94, and Paul Todd, with determined professionalism, reached a splendid hundred and Notts were 17 points clear at the top of the Schweppes County Championship.

John Player League

26 July   **at Derby**
Derbyshire 187 for 9 (D. L. Underwood 4 for 23)
Kent 169 for 9
Derbyshire (4 pts) won by 18 runs

                                                                    at Chelmsford
Essex 250 for 3 (B. R. Hardie 108 not out, G. A. Gooch 100)
Yorkshire 177
Essex (4 pts) won by 73 runs

                                                                     at Ebbw Vale
Sussex 241 for 7 (Imran Khan 60 not out, G. D. Mendis 55)
Glamorgan 153 (G. G. Arnold 4 for 22)
Sussex (4 pts) won by 88 runs

                                                                      at Leicester
Leicestershire 214 for 7 (N. E. Briers 80, E. E. Hemmings 4 for 44)
Nottinghamshire 200 for 7 (C. E. B. Rice 101 not out)
Leicestershire (4 pts) won by 14 runs

                                                                          at Tring
Northamptonshire 200 for 6 (R. G. Williams 55 not out, W. Larkins 50)
Middlesex 196 (R. O. Butcher 64, C. T. Radley 62, N. A. Mallender 5 for 34, Sarfraz Nawaz 5 for 31)
Northamptonshire (4 pts) won by 4 runs

at The Oval

Lancashire 162 for 7 (A. Kennedy 61)
Surrey 163 for 2 (A. R. Butcher 82 not out, R. D. V. Knight 51)
Surrey (4 pts) won by 8 wickets

at Edgbaston

Hampshire 242 for 8 (N. G. Cowley 74, A. M. Ferreira 4 for 42)
Warwickshire 246 for 4 (D. L. Amiss 108)
Warwickshire (4 pts) won by 6 wickets

Essex celebrated their leadership of the league in magnificent style. Put in to bat, Gooch and Hardie hit 180 for the first wicket at six an over, both reached maiden hundreds in the competition. Gooch's century came in 86 minutes off 92 balls. It included four sixes and six fours. Hardie hit seven fours and reached his hundred off 119 balls. Yorkshire had no answer and some spectacular Essex catching saw them romp to victory. Sussex maintained their challenge with an equally convincing win at Ebbw Vale where Imran and the consistent Mendis gave Glamorgan an impossible target. Derbyshire bowled too tightly for Kent and stayed in third place. Kent made a late, brave flourish from Underwood and Dilley, but they were always being asked a scoring rate beyond their capabilities. Warwickshire climbed up the table with a splendid win over Hampshire. Facing a total of 242, Warwickshire lost Lloyd at 3, but Amiss and Kallicharran added 107 for the second wicket, and Amiss reached his second hundred in successive Sundays. Asif Din finished the job as the home side won with nine balls to spare. Surrey recovered from the Lord's blues to trounce Lancashire and Butcher made his point with 82 not out. Once more the mighty Clive Rice found himself valiant in defeat. His unbeaten century failed to bring Notts victory. There was high drama at Tring where Middlesex needed six to win off the last over. Butcher was caught on the boundary as he tried to make the winning hit and then Mallender bowled Selvey and Daniel to give Northants a startling victory.

29, 30 and 31 July   **at Derby**

Gloucestershire 91 (A. W. Stovold 50, C. J. Tunnicliffe 5 for 40, P. G. Newman
    4 for 11) and 150
Derbyshire 267 (G. Miller 62, D. S. Steele 58, B. Wood 54, J. H. Childs 5
    for 43)
Derbyshire won by an innings and 26 runs
Derbyshire 23 pts, Gloucestershire 4 pts

at Canterbury

Essex 310 (K. S. McEwan 102, B. R. Hardie 71, S. Turner 51, D. L. Under-
    wood 7 for 93) and 122 for 6 dec (D. L. Underwood 5 for 61)
Kent 166 (M. R. Benson 57, D. L. Acfield 8 for 55) and 126 (R. E. East 7
    for 49)
Essex won by 140 runs
Essex 23 pts, Kent 4 pts

at Southport

Lancashire 244 (C. H. Lloyd 91, S. P. Hughes 6 for 75) and 241 (C. H. Lloyd 69, G. Fowler 51, W. W. Daniel 5 for 82)
Middlesex 366 for 9 dec (G. D. Barlow 177, C. R. Cook 79) and 120 for 2
Middlesex won by 8 wickets
Middlesex 23 pts, Lancashire 4 pts

at Hinckley

Leicestershire 431 for 8 dec (B. F. Davison 123 not out, J. F. Steele 116, J. C. Balderstone 100) and 124 for 6
Nottinghamshire 200 (D. W. Randall 76, A. M. E. Roberts 4 for 55) and 334 (N. I. Weightman 105, D. W. Randall 101, N. G. B. Cook 5 for 92)
Leicestershire won by 4 wickets
Leicestershire 23 pts, Nottinghamshire 2 pts

at Taunton

Glamorgan 336 for 9 dec (Javed Miandad 200 not out, I. V. A. Richards 4 for 55) and 157 (N. G. Featherstone 68 not out, C. H. Dredge 4 for 41)
Somerset 172 (E. A. Mosley 6 for 37) and 121 for 2
Match drawn
Glamorgan 8 pts, Somerset 4 pts

at Guildford

Sussex 302 (Imran Khan 92) and 127 (D. J. Thomas 5 for 31)
Surrey 311 (M. A. Lynch 75, G. S. Clinton 60) and 119 for 5
Surrey won by 5 wickets
Surrey 23 pts, Sussex 8 pts

at Stourbridge

Worcestershire 376 for 5 dec (G. M. Turner 161, P. A. Neale 125) and 317 for 6 dec (G. M. Turner 101, D. N. Patel 87)
Northamptonshire 359 for 6 dec (A. J. Lamb 86, Kapil Dev 79, G. Cook 52) and 199 for 8 (T. J. Yardley 65 not out, W. Larkins 58)
Match drawn
Worcestershire 6 pts, Northamptonshire 6 pts

at Scarborough

Warwickshire 288 (P. R. Oliver 122, M. Johnson 4 for 48) and 296 (P. R. Oliver 67, G. P. Thomas 52, G. B. Stevenson 4 for 103)
Yorkshire 384 (D. L. Bairstow 62, S. N. Hartley 59, K. Sharp 51, D. R. Doshi 5 for 73)
Match drawn
Yorkshire 7 pts, Warwickshire 4 pts

at Bournemouth

Hampshire 330 for 5 dec (R. E. Hayward 101 not out, C. G. Greenidge 80, N. G. Cowley 67) and 189 for 8 (R. E. Hayward 53, D. S. de Silva 4 for 67)
Sri Lankans 370 for 7 dec (R. D. Mendis 99, R. L. Dias 78)
Match drawn

Derbyshire's success continued when, after Stovold and Broad had opened with a stand of 64, Gloucestershire were bowled out by the seamers for 91. Geoff Miller batted at his elegant best until he was run out, and then Gloucestershire succumbed a second time. At Canterbury, Hardie, Lilley, McEwan and Turner sparked Essex to three hundred in spite of Underwood's spin, and then Acfield and East twice destroyed Kent. Acfield's 8 for 55 in the first innings was the best of his career, a splendid way to celebrate a benefit year. Essex were able to narrow the gap on Notts who lost to bottom of the table Leicester at Hinckley. On a placid pitch the Notts bowlers toiled as Balderstone and Steele made their contribution to Royal Wedding Day with an opening stand of 206. Davison added to the Notts misery which was completed when they were bowled out for 200 in 68.4 overs. Following on, they fared much better with centuries from Randall, who was recalled by Tolchard after he had been given run out when backing up, and Neil Weightman, his first in first-class cricket. It was a brave recovery by Notts and Leicestershire were set 124 in 14 overs. They attacked furiously and the target came down to 6 off the last over. There was a boundary to Steele, Balderstone was run out, Boon hit a single, and then the batsman ran a leg-bye to give Leicester victory with a ball to spare. Sussex were also beaten after they surrendered meekly in their second innings to the accuracy of Thomas's left-arm medium. Worcestershire were without Younis, suspended for one match for dissent, and were denied victory by a stubborn innings from Jim Yardley. The game was saturated with runs until Northants crumpled in their second innings. Turner batted quite remarkably as he and Scott put on 198 for the first wicket in 46 overs. Turner had scored 147 of them. He hit a century in the second innings too. Neale also batted well and in spite of some whirlwind hitting from Kapil Dev, the edge was with Worcestershire. Yorkshire created a surprise, and some consternation in their own camp, when they appointed Neil Hartley, an uncapped player, captain against Warwickshire. The honours of the match belonged to Phil Oliver who, returning after a long absence through injury, hit a maiden hundred in the first innings and then saved his side with a defiant innings in the second. Richard Hayward hit a century on his first-class debut at Bournemouth, but rain brought the match to a premature close. There was also an early closure at Taunton where Javed Miandad played magnificently on the opening day and Viv Richards had a career best with the ball. Somerset then collapsed to Ezra Moseley, at one time they were 90 for 7, and the initiative was now with the bowlers. Featherstone batted well as Glamorgan struggled at their second attempt, they were 11 for 4, but weather deemed a draw. Simon Hughes bowled well for Middlesex and it was only a dour knock from Clive Lloyd that gave Lancashire any respectability. Graham Barlow, surviving several chances, reached a career best for Middlesex and there was an encouragingly bright innings from debutant Colin Cook. The two shared a stand of 148 for the third wicket. Wayne Daniel performed the first hat-trick of his career – Kennedy, O'Shaughnessy and Hughes – and though Lancashire recovered from 17 for 3 with some resolute batting, Middlesex were left with 120 to get in 76 minutes. Lancashire bowled only four overs in the first 16 minutes, but 20 had to be bowled in the last hour, but Middlesex needed only 16.1 of them.

Fourth Cornhill Test Match

Kent came into the Australian side to mark the only change in the teams.
Brearley opened with Boycott, Gooch dropping to number four. Boycott was
the first to go when he hung his bat out to the splendidly aggressive Alderman.
Gower went for nought, skying a mis-hook. Gooch moved away to cut Bright
and Marsh took the catch. Gatting and Brearley were taken at slip, driving
firm footed. Willey was bowled behind his legs and Botham through the gate,
and though there were some rustic swipes from Old and Willis, England were
out for a miserable 189. Alderman had claimed five wickets. The Australian
buoyancy was quietened when Old, bowling very fiercely, dismissed both Dyson
and Border before the close of the first day. The second day saw them move
into a lead of 69 and claim the wicket of Brearley before the arrears had been
cleared. Much of the Australian batting promised more than it achieved and
there was a lot of temperament from both sides which was all rather childish,
but it was the bowling of Emburey which really kept England in the game.
He is not a great spinner of the ball, but with the names of Acfield and
Hemmings being suggested as replacements for him, he varied his flight and
bowled with intelligence. England proceded at funereal pace, leaden against
the spin of Bright. One longed for them to take the advice that Alan
Ayckbourn's elderly doctor in *Sisterly Feelings* had given to his patients, 'Talk
to your feet'. Seventeen maiden overs were bowled before lunch when Boycott
was 28 off 45 overs. It was not until one o'clock that England had cleared
the deficit. Gower had gone to a catch at silly point and Gooch played
uncharacteristically until, trying to change gear, he was bowled by Bright.
Gatting and Willey suffered the same fate. Boycott, pushing forward, was
caught behind and he, more than anyone, must take the blame for England's
total lack of progress. At 116 for 6, England were once more in ruins. Chris
Old was promoted to attack Bright. He did and in 27 minutes plundered 23
runs before the returning pace of Alderman accounted for him. Gatting fell
and England were 167 for 8. Taylor and Emburey now joined in a stand of
courage and determination and no little skill. They added 50 in 73 minutes
of good sense and application. Taylor defended in the main part while Emburey
swept successfully against Bright in a way that had escaped the main batsmen.
Theirs was the crucial batting of the match. Taylor was adjudged lbw and
Willis was caught behind two runs later. Australia needed only 151 to win
and England needed another miracle. Old had Wood lbw on the Saturday
evening and Australia needed 142 on the Sunday with nine wickets in hand.
The crowd was once more baying as at a gladiatorial combat and they were
rewarded with blood. Dyson lbw to Willis after twenty minutes, Hughes
hooking high to Emburey who had been placed at long leg for the very shot.
Australia were 29 for 3 and England were again coming back from the dead.
Yallop and Border steadied the innings and the score at lunch was 62 for
3. Willis's return made no impact on Yallop except to increase the run rate,
but Emburey, with yet another vital contribution to the match, had Yallop
taken bat-pad and Border off his glove. 105 for 5. Then, inevitably, came
Botham. He took the last five wickets for one run in 26 balls. The sheer physical
power of the man dominated the ground. 'He doth bestride the narrow world

/ Like a Colossus; and we petty men / Walk under his huge legs, and peep about.'

Shattered Australia moved to Old Trafford 2–1 down in the series when, in truth, they should have been leading 3–0.

Fourth Cornhill Test Match   England *v.* Australia
30 and 31 July, 1 and 2 August   **at Edgbaston, Birmingham**

England	First Innings		Second Innings	
G. Boycott	c Marsh, b Alderman	13	c Marsh, b Bright	29
J. M. Brearley (capt)	c Border, b Lillee	48	lbw, b Lillee	13
D. I. Gower	c Hogg, b Alderman	0	c Border, b Bright	23
G. A. Gooch	c Marsh, b Bright	21	b Bright	21
M. W. Gatting	c Alderman, b Lillee	21	b Bright	39
P. Willey	b Bright	16	b Bright	5
I. T. Botham	b Alderman	26	c Marsh, b Lillee	3
J. E. Emburey	b Hogg	3	(9) not out	37
*R. W. Taylor	b Alderman	0	(10) lbw, b Alderman	8
C. M. Old	not out	11	(8) c Marsh, b Alderman	23
R. G. D. Willis	c Marsh, b Alderman	13	c Marsh, b Alderman	2
Extras	b 1, lb 5, w 1, nb 10	17	lb 6, w 1, nb 9	16
		189		219

	O	M	R	W		O	M	R	W
Lillee	18	4	61	2		26	9	51	2
Alderman	23.1	8	42	5		22	5	65	3
Hogg	16	3	49	1		10	3	19	—
Bright	12	4	20	2		34	17	68	5

Fall of Wickets
1–29, 2–29, 3–60, 4–101, 5–126, 6–145, 7–161, 8–161, 9–165.
1–18, 2–52, 3–89, 4–98, 5–110, 6–116, 7–154, 8–167, 9–217.

Australia	First Innings		Second Innings	
G. M. Wood	run out	38	(2) lbw, b Old	2
J. Dyson	b Old	1	(1) lbw, b Willis	13
A. R. Border	c Taylor, b Old	2	c Gatting, b Emburey	40
R. J. Bright	lbw, b Botham	27	(8) lbw, b Botham	0
K. J. Hughes (capt)	lbw, b Old	47	(4) c Emburey, b Willis	5
G. N. Yallop	b Emburey	30	(5) c Botham, b Emburey	30
M. F. Kent	c Willis, b Emburey	46	(6) b Botham	10
*R. W. Marsh	b Emburey	2	(7) b Botham	4
D. K. Lillee	b Emburey	18	c Taylor, b Botham	3
R. M. Hogg	run out	0	not out	0
T. M. Alderman	not out	3	b Botham	0
Extras	b 4, lb 19, nb 21	44	b 1, lb 2, nb 11	14
		258		121

	O	M	R	W		O	M	R	W
Willis	19	3	63	—		20	6	37	2
Old	21	8	44	3		11	4	19	1
Botham	20	1	64	1		14	9	11	5
Emburey	26.5	12	43	4		22	10	40	2

Fall of Wickets
1–5, 2–14, 3–62, 4–115, 5–166, 6–203, 7–220, 8–253, 9–253.
1–2, 2–19, 3–29, 4–87, 5–105, 6–114, 7–114, 8–120, 9–121.

England won by 29 runs

1, 3 and 4 August   **at Chelmsford**
Essex 296 (B. R. Hardie 96, K. S. McEwan 64)
Derbyshire 93 (D. L. Acfield 4 for 21) and 143 (D. L. Acfield 4 for 56,
   R. E. East 4 for 56)
Essex won by an innings and 60 runs
Essex 23 pts, Derbyshire 3 pts

                                                              at Canterbury
Kent 315 (Asif Iqbal 73, R. M. Ellison 55 not out, C. S. Cowdrey 53,
   D. L. Underwood 50, T. E. Jesty 5 for 53) and 205 for 7 dec
Hampshire 217 (M. C. J. Nicholas 88 not out, D. L. Underwood 5 for 72) and
   122 (G. W. Johnson 6 for 33, D. L. Underwood 4 for 58)
Kent won by 181 runs
Kent 24 pts, Hampshire 5 pts

                                                              at Old Trafford
Lancashire 358 for 8 dec (C. H. Lloyd 97, B. W. Reidy 70 not out, G. Fowler
   66, D. N. Patel 5 for 118)
Worcestershire 138 (J. Simmons 4 for 21) and 175 (D. P. Hughes 4 for 40)
Lancashire won by an innings and 45 runs
Lancashire 23 pts, Worcestershire 2 pts

                                                              at Leicester
Leicestershire 358 for 8 dec (N. E. Briers 116, J. F. Steele 97, G. S. Le Roux 5
   for 83) and 155 for 3 dec (J. F. Steele 51)
Sussex 250 for 7 dec (J. R. T. Barclay 101) and 260 (G. D. Mendis 137,
   N. G. B. Cook 7 for 81)
Leicestershire won by 3 runs
Leicestershire 22 pts, Sussex 4 pts

                                                              at Lord's
Middlesex 302 for 3 dec (K. P. Tomlins 77 not out, W. N. Slack 74,
   C. T. Radley 69 not out, G. D. Barlow 58) and 202 for 4 dec (W. N. Slack 81)
Gloucestershire 201 for 1 dec (P. Bainbridge 105 not out, Sadiq Mohammad
   78 not out) and 176 for 6 (B. C. Broad 51, P. H. Edmonds 4 for 43)
Match drawn
Middlesex 4 pts, Gloucestershire 3 pts

                                                              at Northampton
Northamptonshire 223 (A. J. Lamb 79, W. Hogg 4 for 46) and 342 for 6 dec
   (W. Larkins 130, A. J. Lamb 88, R. G. Williams 64, W. Hogg 4 for 65)
Warwickshire 201 (A. M. Ferreira 67, B. J. Griffiths 4 for 64) and 365 for 9
   (P. R. Oliver 171 not out, Sarfraz Nawaz 6 for 84)
Warwickshire won by 1 wicket
Warwickshire 22 pts, Northamptonshire 6 pts

at Sheffield

Somerset 183 (P. M. Roebuck 50, S. J. Dennis 5 for 35) and 349 for 6 dec
(I. V. A. Richards 153, V. J. Marks 58, N. F. M. Popplewell 51 not out)
Yorkshire 180 (H. R. Moseley 4 for 44) and 185 (D. L. Bairstow 70, J. D. Love
51, C. H. Dredge 6 for 43)
Somerset won by 167 runs
Somerset 21 pts, Yorkshire 5 pts

1, 2 and 3 August **at Cardiff**

Glamorgan 168 (N. G. Featherstone 83, L. W. Kaluperuma 5 for 34) and 240
(A. L. Jones 81, N. G. Featherstone 55, A. de Silva 4 for 41)
Sri Lankans 190 (R. C. Ontong 6 for 62) and 185 for 7 (A. N. Ranasinghe 54
not out, R. C. Ontong 4 for 45)
Match drawn

1 and 3 August **at Trent Bridge**

Surrey 175 (G. R. J. Roope 94 not out) and 103 (C. E. B. Rice 6 for 44)
Nottinghamshire 293 (R. J. Hadlee 98, B. Hassan 61, S. T. Clarke 5 for 81)
Nottinghamshire won by an innings and 15 runs
Nottinghamshire 23 pts, Surrey 5 pts

Victory in two days over the team in second place was emphatic championship
form by Nottinghamshire. A brave innings by Graham Roope saved Surrey
from disgrace on the Saturday, but Notts struggled to gain the lead and once
more it was the violent batting of Richard Hadlee, the outstanding all-rounder
of the season, which gave them a considerable first innings advantage. Then,
late on the Monday, Clive Rice and Hadlee destroyed the Surrey batting again
with only Roope and Clarke reaching double figures. Essex moved into second
place with a resounding win over a surprisingly limp Derbyshire side. Rain
restricted play on the Saturday when David Steele was banned from bowling
for running on the pitch. He completed an unhappy match when he was lbw
not playing a shot in the first innings and bowled not playing a shot in the
second. John Wright had three ducks in twenty-four hours and the spin of
Acfield and Ray East was too much for the visitors. Hardie, Fletcher and
McEwan were the backbone of the Essex innings. Hampshire's challenge
faltered as Kent, having been put in, recovered strongly and then spun the
visitors out twice. The main batting heroes were Richard Ellison and Derek
Underwood. Ellison was making his debut and he and Underwood put on
108 in 32 overs for the ninth wicket. Nicholas alone offered any real resistance
to the wiles of Johnson and Underwood. There was a run saturated wicket
at Lord's, but no result. The highlight of the match was a career best from
Phil Bainbridge, celebrating the award of his county cap.
  Lancashire gained their second win of the season when some solid, if
unspectacular, batting in the early stages was supplemented by some accurate
slow bowling which was good enough to see Worcestershire twice bowled out
for under two hundred. Somerset wilted against Simon Dennis at Sheffield,
but Hallam Moseley denied Yorkshire a first innings advantage, and then Viv
Richards took over. Revelling in the sunshine, he hit 153 in 162 minutes, seven
sixes and twenty-two fours. Yorkshire were powerless to halt his attack on

Sri Lankans First-class Matches – Batting, 1981

	v. Combined Universities (Oxford) 13–16 June		v. Gloucestershire (Bristol) 17–19 June		v. Warwickshire (Edgbaston) 20–23 June		v. Sussex (Hastings) 27–30 June		v. Worcestershire (Worcester) 1–3 July		v. T.C.C.B. Select XI (Trent Bridge) 8–10 July		v. Leicestershire (Leicester) 11–13 July	
B. Warnapura	5	16	38	70	21	—	4	2	42	—	19	18	0	31
S. Wettimuny	16	5	6	16					89	—	25	5	10	95*
R. L. Dias	24	29	34	1	41	8*	14	43	36	—	50	22	127	11*
R. D. Mendis	23	20	75	2	90	—	14	22	66	—	29	66*	27	—
R. S. Madugalle	46	4	35	9	20	—	0	0					7	—
A. Ranasinghe	3	40	7	25	50	—	20	4	34	—	6	27	15	—
L. Kaluperuma	18	9	4	40	6	—	14*	5	0	—	6*	3*	14*	—
A. De Mel	31	3	3	94			22	0			8	1	56	—
M. Gunatilleke	24	10*	6	5*					2	—			15	—
R. J. Wisesuriva	5	6*												
R. Ratnayake	0*	10					0	4*	4*	—	1			
D. S. De Silva			7	97					9	—	24	20		
A. De Silva			4*	7	4	—	0	0			0		7	—
N. Hettiaratchy					0	13	1	57	16	—			10	—
Y. Gunesekera					56	0*			23	—				
H. Devapriya					20	68	56	5			22	29		
L. Fernando					7*	—								
Byes	9	7	7	9	8		2	1	1		3	2	1	1
Leg byes	3	4	11	17	6		5	3	13		1	4	8	3
Wides	1	1	4	3	1			1	3				4	2
No balls	3	1	5	3	5	2	6	2	12		9	2	3	
Total	211	165	246	398	335	91	158	149	350		203	199	304	143
Wickets	10	9	10	10	10	2	10	10	10		10	7	10	1
Result	D		D		D		L		D		W		D	

Catches

19 – M. Gunatilleke (ct 11/st 8)

12 – H. Devapriya (ct 9/st 3)

11 – N. Hettiaratchy

8 – R. S. Madugalle

7 – R. D. Mendis

6 – R. L. Dias and L. Kaluperuma

4 – A. Ranasinghe and A. De Silva

3 – S. Wettimony, R. J. Wijesuriva, A. De Mel and Y. Gunesekera

2 – L. Fernando, D. S. De Silva and subs.

1 – R. Ratnayake

v. Lancashire (Old Trafford) 15–17 July		v. Northamptonshire (Northampton) 18–20 July		v. Yorkshire (Sheffield) 22–24 July		v. Hampshire (Bournemouth) 29–31 July		v. Glamorgan (Cardiff) 1–3 August		v. Minor Counties (Reading) 4–6 August		Inns	NOs	Runs	HS	Av
75*	—	22	—					23	22			16	1	408	75*	27.20
46	—	68	51*	—	—	4	—			91	—	14	2	527	95*	43.21
15	—	30	—			78	—			44	—	17	2	607	127	40.46
9*	—					99	—			3	—	14	2	545	99	45.41
—	—	47	—	—	—	43	—	27	1	8	—	13	—	247	47	19.00
				—	—	37	⌐	18	54*			14	1	340	54*	26.15
—	—			—	—			29	1	40	—	14	4	189	40	18.90
		0*	—	—	—			4	7	0	—	13	1	229	94	19.08
—	—			—	—	1*	—	3	2*	10	—	10	4	78	24	13.00
—	—					—	—	3	—			3	1	14	6*	7.00
						—	—			9*	—	7	4	28	10	9.33
—	—			—	—	29*	—					6	1	186	97	37.20
								2*	—	11	—	9	2	35	11	5.00
27	—	80	58*	—	—	24	—	49	42	23	—	13	1	400	80	33.33
				—	—	44	—	7	23	63	—	7	1	216	63	36.00
		11	8					13	15			10	—	247	68	24.70
—	—					—	—					1	1	7	7*	—
4		7	9			8		1	4	6						
4		13	8			3		3	9	10						
								2	2							
4		14						6	3							
184		292	134			370		190	185	318						
3		6	1			7		10	7	10						
D		D		D		D		D		D						

Sri Lankans First-class Matches – Bowling, 1981	A. De Mel	R. Ratnayaka	R. J. Wijesuriva	A. Ranasinghe	L. Kaluperuma	D. S. Silva
v. Combined Universities (Oxford) 13–16 June	21–3–63–1 5–4–1–0	14–4–33–0 3–0–3–1	26–10–61–0 22–9–35–5	35–13–65–5 12–8–12–1	28.2–5–66–3 10–3–16–3	
v. Gloucestershire (Bristol) 17–19 June	23–2–83–0			8–1–31–0	24–6–69–0	25.1–5–105–1
v. Warwickshire (Edgbaston) 20–23 June				19–5–50–0 16–2–58–0	28–6–84–0 36–13–67–0	
v. Sussex (Hastings) 27–30 June	21–3–72–3 15–3–62–0	11–2–38–3 18–6–51–2		3–0–12–0 3–1–12–0	1.4–0–4–1 22–7–50–1	
v. Worcestershire (Worcester) 1–3 July		14–2–57–0 19–4–83–3		13–5–41–3 20–1–71–1	27–7–75–1	39.5–13–100–6 24–9–54–2
v. T.C.C.B. Select XI (Trent Bridge) 8–10 July	9–1–28–0 8–1–35–1	7–1–30–0 4–1–11–0			17–3–51–1 1–1–0–0	34–10–82–1 24–2–42–2
v. Leicestershire (Leicester) 11–13 July	22–1–85–2 23–7–70–3			20–4–55–0 7–2–9–1	18–2–45–0 28–6–69–2	
v. Lancashire (Old Trafford) 15–17 July	7–0–32–0		26–7–51–3			28–13–55–7
v. Northamptonshire (Northampton) 18–20 July	15–3–41–1 7–0–27–0		35–7–109–1 21–5–58–2		34–5–92–3 20–5–74–1	
v. Yorkshire (Sheffield) 22–24 July	21–3–70–0	9–0–37–0		9–0–30–1	26–8–58–2	32–8–67–2
v. Hampshire (Bournemouth) 29–31 July			29–7–64–1 22–10–49–3	20–5–78–2 13–2–42–1		37–6–109–0 28–7–67–4
v. Glamorgan (Cardiff) 1–3 August	17–6–37–3 11–2–37–0		4–0–23–0 9–2–17–0	7–3–14–0 23–6–44–2	12.5–3–34–5 27–6–84–3	
v. Minor Counties (Reading) 4–6 August	16–3–49–1 4–0–24–0	7–0–27–0 5–2–18–0			23.4–1–83–3 9–1–24–2	
	245–42– 816–15 av. 54.40	111–22– 388–9 av. 43.11	194–57– 467–15 av. 31.13	228–58– 624–17 av. 36.70	393.3–88– 1045–31 av. 33.70	272–73– 681–25 av. 27.24

A. De Silva	B. Warnapura	R. L. Dias	L. Fernando	S. Wettimuny	Y. Gunesekera	B	Lb	W	Nb	Total	Wkts
						5	9	3	4	309	10
						5	7		3	82	10
19–4–68–0	5–0–33–1					14	6	1	6	416	2
		1–0–3–0								3	0
24–8–53–3	9–0–33–2		19–4–37–1				11	5	1	274	7
25–11–56–1	20.2–9–47–1		6–1–27–0			10	2		1	268	3
14–5–24–3	3–2–1–0					5	4		1	161	10
27–10–42–3							8	2	1	228	6
	4–0–22–0					4	1	1		301	10
						3	14			225	6
25–7–58–2						3	2		5	259	4
9–3–36–0	3–1–5–0					2	7		2	140	3
31–6–88–3	2–0–18–0					4	6	2		303	6
19–7–49–2	7–3–19–0					7	8	1		232	8
	5–0–17–0		7–1–21–0				3		4	183	10
14–4–41–1			6–1–33–0			5	2		5	328	7
			8–2–26–0			12	5		3	205	4
							7	2	4	275	5
			20–1–68–0				6	1	4	330	5
			5–1–22–0	1–0–2–0			4	1	2	189	8
23–11–32–1	5–2–20–1					6	1	1		168	10
33–15–41–4						5	12			240	10
27–10–46–3			7–4–7–1			6	9	1	6	234	10
11–5–12–0				2–1–9–0	1–0–5–0		3		1	96	2
301–106–646–26 *av.* 24.84	63.2–17–215–5 *av.* 43.00	1–0–3–0 —	71–11–234–1 *av.* 234.00	10–5–18–1 *av.* 18.00	1–0–5–0 —						

their bowling, as indeed are any team once he is in full flow. On the last day Colin Dredge completed Somerset's victory when he returned a career best 6 for 43. There was a career best too for Phil Oliver in a remarkable game at Northampton. Good innings from Larkins and Allan Lamb had put Northants in a commanding position and Warwickshire were set 365 in 5¾ hours. At tea, Warwickshire were 208 for 5 and a draw the most likely result. Then Oliver began his onslaught, but Warwickshire were 277 for 8 before Hogg and Oliver added 77 in 12 overs. Victory finally came with seven overs to spare. Oliver's 171 included seven sixes and twenty fours. His innings lasted 196 minutes and was a memorable achievement. Sussex died bravely at Leicester in their effort to maintain their challenge on Notts. Sussex needed 264 in 3 hours 10 minutes. Leicestershire had accumulated runs efficiently rather than quickly in both their innings, a fine century from Briers being the highlight. Barclay made an elegant hundred for Sussex and Mendis set them on the road to victory with a sparkling 137 before being stumped. Nick Cook, with the best figures of his career, took the last seven wickets. The seventh was off the last ball of the match when, with Sussex needing four to win, Geoff Arnold swung and missed and was bowled.

4, 5 and 6 August   **at Reading**
Minor Counties 234 (P. D. Johnson 66) and 96 for 2
Sri Lankans 318 (S. Wettimuny 91, Y. Gunasekera 63)
Match drawn

There was no play on the third day and the Sri Lankan tour came to a damp end. One can only wish this happy band of cricketers well. They will give much joy. They need a stronger opening attack and more courage when chasing a target.

John Player League
2 August   **at Chelmsford**
Essex 142
Derbyshire 110
Essex (4 pts) won by 32 runs

                                                                 at Canterbury
Kent 230 for 4 (C. J. Tavare 99 not out, C. S. Cowdrey 57)
Hampshire 140
Kent (4 pts) won by 90 runs

                                                                at Old Trafford
Worcestershire 213 for 5 (P. A. Neale 53 not out, Younis Ahmed 50)
Lancashire 214 for 7 (G. Fowler 65)
Lancashire (4 pts) won by 3 wickets

                                                                    at Lord's
Middlesex 213 for 6 (G. D. Barlow 77, C. R. Cook 73)
Gloucestershire 215 for 2 (Zaheer Abbas 129 not out)
Gloucestershire (4 pts) won by 8 wickets

at Northampton

Warwickshire 245 for 9 (T. A. Lloyd 63, D. L. Amiss 60)
Northamptonshire 223 for 9 (R. J. Boyd-Moss 62)
Warwickshire (4 pts) won by 22 runs

at Trent Bridge

Nottinghamshire 155 for 7 (R. J. Hadlee 67 not out)
Surrey 159 for 6
Surrey (4 pts) won by 4 wickets

at Scarborough

Yorkshire 230 for 3 (G. B. Stevenson 56, K. Sharp 54)
Somerset 210 for 8 (P. M. Roebuck 79, B. C. Rose 63)
Yorkshire (4 pts) won by 20 runs

at Leicester

Leicestershire 158 for 9 (G. S. Le Roux 4 for 26)
Sussex 162 for 7 (A. M. E. Roberts 4 for 27)
Sussex (4 pts) won by 3 wickets

The top of the table clash at Chelmsford turned out to be a most disappointing affair. Both sides batted very badly. Essex were lifted from the despair of 68 for 7 by an innings of 42 not out by Pringle who forsook his usual introspection to clout the ball. He then took 2 for 8 in his 8 overs as Derbyshire slumped from 54 for 1 to 110 all out. Sussex maintained their challenge with victory off the penultimate ball at Leicester although they always seemed very likely winners. They owed much to Le Roux and a disciplined innings from Mendis. Barclay and Waller proved that spin could be effective on Sundays. Lancashire beat Worcestershire off the last ball when O'Shaughnessy lofted Pridgeon over mid-wicket. Chris Tavare produced another sparkling innings and Hampshire were routed. Amiss and Lloyd opened with a stand of 118 at Northampton and Asif Din and Ferreira built on this so that the total became too much for the home side in spite of Boyd-Moss' best John Player League score. There were plenty of runs at Scarborough too where Stuchbury had Viv Richards lbw for 2, a dismissal which probably clinched the game for Yorkshire. There was some good all-round batting from the home side and defeat was a set-back for Somerset who had been climbing the table. Surrey won a rather mediocre game at Trent Bridge where Notts efforts were being concentrated on the Schweppes County Championship. Zaheer pounded Middlesex to defeat with a marvellously exciting hundred at Lord's, three sixes and eleven fours.

National Westminster Bank Trophy Third Round

at Derby

Derbyshire 164
Nottinghamshire 141 (P. A. Todd 62)
Derbyshire won by 23 runs

at Southampton

Hampshire 167 for 9
Lancashire 169 for 7 (C. H. Lloyd 82 not out)
Lancashire won by 3 wickets

at Hove

Essex 195 for 9 (G. S. Le Roux 5 for 35)
Sussex 170
Essex won by 25 runs

at Northampton

Leicestershire 227 (R. W. Tolchard 70, B. F. Davison 67)
Northamptonshire 207 for 4 (W. Larkins 81 not out, G. Cook 63)
Northamptonshire won on faster scoring rate

With the skies at Northampton threatening not only the end of play, but seemingly the end of the world, the match was halted and rain prevented resumption on the next two days. Thanks to a graceful and brisk innings by Wayne Larkins, Northants went through on the faster scoring rate. They needed 21 for victory off 9.1 overs when play was called off. Such a target was too much for Nottinghamshire however. They bowled Derbyshire out for 164 and appeared to be strolling to victory at 75 for 1. Then Wood dismissed Randall and Hassan and some guileful spin from David Steele completely unsettled the middle order. He bowled Rice for 1 and had Birch caught for 0, conceding only 23 runs in his 12 overs – and 14 of these runs came in a one over slash by Hadlee. Man of the Match Todd was ninth out, one of Newman's three victims, and Derbyshire snatched an improbable victory. There was some appalling cricket at Southampton. Hampshire batted dreadfully against bowling that, for the most part, had the sole merit of being straight. Hayward and Cowley roused them from the despair of 69 for 5, and then they bowled well, especially Steve Malone, but caught badly, except Bobbie Parks. Lloyd was twice missed off easy chances and the West Indian captain steered Lancashire to an unconvincing victory. In glorious sunshine at Hove, Essex and Sussex contrived a most exciting game. Essex won the toss and batted first. They appeared to be cruising to a big score and reached 63 without loss, but then Imran dismissed Gooch, Hardie and Fletcher in 28 balls. Lilley batted very well, but McEwan could never get his timing right and Le Roux's bowling completed the strangulation of Essex. They were 174 for 9, but David East and John Lever had an invaluable last wicket stand of 21. Essex needed a quick breakthrough to give them a chance and a spectacular diving catch on the leg-side to dismiss Barclay in Lever's first over provided the tonic they needed. Mendis and Parker tried to repair matters, but Mendis skied the ball and David East took another fine catch. It was Imran who provided the necessary injection of strokes into the Sussex innings, but Stuart Turner returned to take the wickets of Imran and Gould in one over and Sussex were struggling. David East ran out two batsmen and Lever bowled Arnold and Waller in the final over. John Jameson gave the individual award to John Lever – perhaps he hadn't been watching David East.

8, 9 and 10 August   **at Chelmsford**
Essex 216 for 7 dec (G. A. Gooch 86, G. N. Yallop 4 for 63) and 270 for 8 dec
  (A. W. Lilley 64, K. S. McEwan 50, G. R. Beard 4 for 92)
Australians 240 for 5 dec and 237 for 8 (G. M. Wood 60, G. N. Yallop 59
  not out)
Match drawn

8, 10 and 11 August   **at Derby**
Leicestershire 196 (D. S. Steele 7 for 85)
Derbyshire 62 (L. B. Taylor 6 for 19) and 107 (B. Wood 53 not out, N. G. B.
  Cook 4 for 25)
Leicestershire won by an innings and 27 runs
Leicestershire 21 pts, Derbyshire 4 pts

                                                          at Cardiff
Lancashire 249 (B. W. Reidy 96, C. H. Lloyd 65, J. G. Thomas 4 for 65) and
  231 (B. J. Lloyd 8 for 70)
Glamorgan 162 (N. G. Featherstone 62, P. G. Lee 4 for 49) and 252 (Javed
  Miandad 72, E. A. Moseley 57, P. G. Lee 6 for 44)
Lancashire won by 66 runs
Lancashire 22 pts, Glamorgan 5 pts

                                                      at Cheltenham
Surrey 160 (J. H. Childs 6 for 69, D. A. Graveney 4 for 18) and 170 (A. R.
  Butcher 90, D. A. Graveney 6 for 54)
Gloucestershire 166 (Intikhab 4 for 69) and 168 for 2 (B. C. Broad 76 not out,
  P. Bainbridge 75)
Gloucestershire won by 8 wickets
Gloucestershire 21 pts, Surrey 5 pts

                                                          at Lord's
Middlesex 284 (W. N. Slack 130, J. M. Brearley 58, W. Hogg 4 for 50, D. R.
  Doshi 4 for 97) and 184 for 2 dec (J. M. Brearley 100, W. N. Slack 65)
Warwickshire 154 (K. D. Smith 58 not out, J. E. Emburey 5 for 52, P. H.
  Edmonds 4 for 57) and 196 (D. L. Amiss 53, P. H. Edmonds 5 for 53,
  J. E. Emburey 5 for 80)
Middlesex won by 118 runs
Middlesex 23 pts, Warwickshire 5 pts

                                                  at Weston-super-Mare
Somerset 169 (T. M. Lamb 4 for 50) and 236 (T. M. Lamb 4 for 31)
Northamptonshire 201 (A. J. Lamb 58, T. J. Yardley 53, N. F. M. Popplewell
  5 for 33) and 205 for 8 (G. Cook 75)
Northamptonshire won by 2 wickets
Northamptonshire 22 pts, Somerset 5 pts

                                                      at Eastbourne
Sussex 310 for 9 dec (I. A. Greig 86, J. R. T. Barclay 79, G. D. Mendis 61,
  K. B. S. Jarvis 6 for 60) and 51 for 2

Kent 104 (G. G. Arnold 4 for 26) and 254 (C. S. Cowdrey 97, C. J. Tavare 72, Imran Khan 4 for 51)
Sussex won by 8 wickets
Sussex 24 pts, Kent 4 pts

at Worcester

Nottinghamshire 170 for 9 dec (N. Gifford 4 for 64) and 214 for 4 dec (J. D. Birch 65 not out, D. W. Randall 55, B. Hassan 51 not out)
Worcestershire 146 (E. E. Hemmings 6 for 66) and 132 (E. E. Hemmings 4 for 64)
Nottinghamshire won by 106 runs
Nottinghamshire 21 pts, Worcestershire 4 pts

at Middlesbrough

Yorkshire 205 for 6 dec (D. L. Bairstow 71, C. W. J. Athey 64 not out) and 208 for 3 dec (J. H. Hampshire 118 not out)
Hampshire 150 for 0 dec (J. M. Rice 56 not out, C. G. Greenidge 53 retired hurt) and 130 for 7 (G. B. Stevenson 5 for 41)
Match drawn
Hampshire 3 pts, Yorkshire 2 pts

The rain returned to interfere with the start of most matches. Essex and the Australians still contrived an entertaining social game in which Yallop had a career best with the ball, Rob Leiper made 49 on his first-class debut and Gooch and Lilley swatted merrily. Wood and Yallop nearly hit the tourists to victory, but Essex bowlers gave as good as they got. Yallop, Marsh and Rixon all kept wicket during the match. In more serious matters, Sussex, after a week of disappointment, showed great character in overwhelming Kent. In spite of another fine performance from Jarvis, Sussex accumulated runs quickly in an even batting performance and then Geoff Arnold led the rout of Kent. Following-on, Kent were 60 for 3 before a spirited reply from Tavare and Chris Cowdrey gave Sussex their only problems of the match. Notts, however, remained firmly in first place. There were only four overs possible on the Saturday, but Notts still forced a resounding victory. Brisk scoring by Randall and Birch, ever reliable batting from Hassan and the spin of Eddie Hemmings were key factors in their win. Hemmings had 10 for 130 in the match and was now firmly established as the season's outstanding spinner. Somewhat untidy in action, he spins the ball appreciably and is quick to take advantage of any help that the pitch offers. His eagerness and determination mark him as a great club man. It is ironic that Warwickshire, so weak in bowling, felt that they could do without him. Rain also affected the game at Middlesbrough where, in spite of some scintillating batting and brave declarations, the match was drawn. Both Greenidge and Bairstow were injured.

The Cheltenham Festival brought the Gloucestershire spinners to their haven. Graveney and Childs responded happily and Surrey, with Mickey Stewart's son making his debut behind the stumps, were well beaten in spite of a fine knock by Alan Butcher. David Graveney was doing well as Gloucestershire skipper in the absence of Procter whose county career, sadly, was at an end. There was no play on the first day at Derby and when play did start Les Taylor dominated the match. Coming in at 172 for 9, he swung his bat to a career best 22 before being the last of David Steele's seven victims. Then he bowled Wood with the first ball of the innings and took a wicket with the first ball of the last morning. He had 6 for 19 and Derbyshire followed-on to be beaten by an innings. Glamorgan surrendered a first innings lead of 87 to Lancashire and when they appeared to be bowling their way back into the game they allowed the last three Lancashire second innings wickets to add 98 runs. The Welshmen seemed well beaten when, in spite of Javed's 72, they were 159 for 9, chasing 319. Ezra Moseley and Geoff Holmes staged a valiant last wicket stand of 93 before Moseley was caught at short-leg off Simmons. Peter Lee had by far his best match of the season for Lancashire with figures of 10 for 93. With Wilf Slack in continuing good form and Mike Brearley hitting a good hundred, Middlesex were too strong for Warwickshire for whom the most interesting contribution came from Doshi. David Smith, back in the side after injury, had batted heroically for the visitors, but when Doshi joined him they were 112 for 9 and the follow-on seemingly a formality. Doshi batted for 50 minutes and reached his highest score in England, 35, and the follow-on was avoided. Slack reached his thousand runs for the season and Emburey and Edmonds, back to his best, spun Middlesex to victory. Northants and Somerset contrived a fine game of cricket which Northants won with twelve overs and two wickets to spare. They owed much to Geoff Cook, who was dropped at slip early on. Willey broke his thumb, a cruel blow to one who had just lost his place in the England side.

John Player League

9 August   **at Derby**
Derbyshire 178 for 6 (G. Miller 52 not out, P. N. Kirsten 50)
Leicestershire 155 for 9
Derbyshire (4 pts) won by 23 runs

                                                       at Cardiff
Glamorgan 188 for 6 (Javed Miandad 96)
Lancashire 189 for 8
Lancashire (4 pts) won by 2 wickets

                                                     at Cheltenham
Gloucestershire 127
Surrey 128 for 7 (M. A. Lynch 69)
Surrey (4 pts) won by 3 wickets

                                                       at Lord's
Middlesex 186 for 9
Warwickshire 161 for 4 (T. A. Lloyd 62)
Warwickshire (4 pts) won on faster scoring rate

                                                at Weston-super-Mare
Northamptonshire 106 for 6
Somerset 108 for 3 (P. W. Denning 65)
Somerset (4 pts) won by 7 wickets

at Eastbourne

Kent 164 for 9
Sussex 147
Kent (4 pts) won on faster scoring rate

at Worcester

Nottinghamshire 150 for 7 (C. E. B. Rice 74)
Worcestershire 107
Nottinghamshire (4 pts) won by 43 runs

at Middlesbrough

Yorkshire 117 for 6
Hampshire 81 for 6
Yorkshire (4 pts) won by 36 runs

With Essex not playing, Sussex had every opportunity of moving to the top
of the table, but they lost at Eastbourne in most bizarre fashion. Rain reduced
their target to 148 in 35 overs, but they were all out for 147 in 34.5 and the
next day the T.C.C.B. ruled that they had lost so Essex stayed clear. The rise
of Warwickshire continued and they moved to within six points of Essex with
some brisk scoring at Lord's. Somerset were on the same number of points,
28, after their easy win over Northants. A third wicket stand of 82 between
Roebuck and Denning was the basis of their victory. Derbyshire moved back
into contention when their bowling proved to be too tight for Leicester. David
Steele again showed his value as a bowler in limited over competitions. In
a match restricted to 15 overs, Yorkshire were far too good for Hampshire.
Yorkshire omitted Boycott and Hampshire from their side as they wished to
retain the 'young' players who had done well in the John Player League. In
a low scoring game on a difficult wicket at Cheltenham, Surrey owed much
to the aggression of Monty Lynch. Notts won the bottom of the table battle
with Worcestershire and moved up two places. Glamorgan appeared to be
winning easily when they had Lancashire at 135 for 8, chasing 189 at Cardiff.
Javed Miandad had again batted brilliantly for Glamorgan, but it was Neal
Radford who stole the game for Lancashire. He hit four sixes and three fours
as he scored an undefeated 48 off 24 balls to give Lancashire victory with
an over to spare.

12, 13 and 14 August   **at Chelmsford**
Essex 453 for 5 dec (K. W. R. Fletcher 165 not out, A. W. Lilley 67, S. Turner
    62 not out, K. S. McEwan 59, L. J. Wood 4 for 124)
Kent 216 (R. A. Woolmer 73, Asif Iqbal 58, R. E. East 5 for 68) and 170
    (Asif Iqbal 52, R. E. East 7 for 55)
Essex won by an innings and 67 runs
Essex 24 pts, Kent 3 pts

at Cheltenham
Gloucestershire 381 for 7 dec (A. J. Hignell 97, Zaheer Abbas 68, P.
    Bainbridge 61, M. J. Bailey 4 for 138)

Hampshire 174 (T. E. Jesty 84, J. H. Childs 5 for 67, D. A. Graveney 4 for 53) and 121 (D. A. Graveney 4 for 18)
Gloucestershire won by an innings and 86 runs
Gloucestershire 24 pts, Hampshire 4 pts

at Northampton
Northamptonshire 344 for 7 dec (A. J. Lamb 159) and 166 (G. Cook 51, P. H. Edmonds 5 for 57, J. D. Monteith 5 for 68)
Middlesex 252 (W. N. Slack 64, G. D. Barlow 54, R. G. Williams 4 for 64) and 203 for 9 (W. N. Slack 67, R. G. Williams 5 for 88)
Match drawn
Northamptonshire 8 pts, Middlesex 4 pts

at Weston-super-Mare
Worcestershire 188 (D. J. Humphries 53) and 198 (Younis Ahmed 60, C. H. Dredge 4 for 53)
Somerset 282 (I. V. A. Richards 150, J. D. Inchmore 5 for 85) and 107 for 5
Somerset won by 5 wickets
Somerset 23 pts, Worcestershire 5 pts

at The Oval
Surrey 334 (M. A. Lynch 118, A. R. Butcher 67, C. J. Richards 63) and 185 (G. S. Clinton 79, J. C. Balderstone 4 for 30)
Leicestershire 235 (J. C. Balderstone 82, T. J. Boon 56, P. I. Pocock 4 for 99) and 195 for 6 (B. F. Davison 72)
Match drawn
Surrey 8 pts, Leicestershire 5 pts

at Eastbourne
Derbyshire 256 (P. N. Kirsten 85, J. G. Wright 73, I. A. Greig 4 for 75) and 227 (P. N. Kirsten 68, D. S. Steele 59, Imran Khan 5 for 52)
Sussex 250 for 7 dec (P. W. G. Parker 82 not out, P. G. Newman 4 for 73) and 235 for 5 (Imran Khan 107 not out)
Sussex won by 5 wickets
Sussex 23 pts, Derbyshire 6 pts

at Edgbaston
Glamorgan 409 for 6 dec (Javed Miandad 153 not out, A. Jones 84, N. G. Featherstone 54) and 289 for 4 dec (N. G. Featherstone 109 not out, Javed Miandad 96)
Warwickshire 315 for 2 dec (D. L. Amiss 132, T. A. Lloyd 100) and 348 (G. W. Humpage 102, K. D. Smith 93, Asif Din 54, J. G. Thomas 4 for 92)
Glamorgan won by 35 runs
Glamorgan 20 pts, Warwickshire 6 pts

Sussex closed the gap on Notts to four points when a thrilling all-round display by Imran Khan took them to victory over Derbyshire. Sussex had been left 145 minutes in which to make 234. That they had reached this position was due to Imran who had returned to the attack when Derbyshire were dozing at 193 for 3 and had bowled fiercely to have them out for 227. He then hit 107 not out, his hundred coming in 88 minutes, and hit three sixes and eleven fours. Parker also had a fine match and he and Gould started the Sussex challenge with 74 in 15 overs, but 143 were needed in the last twenty. It was then that Imran attacked and Sussex won with five balls to spare. Essex also maintained their challenge, 21 points behind the leaders with a game in hand. They savaged the weakened Kent attack on the opening day. Fletcher was the main prop of the innings, but there was some violent hitting from Lilley and Turner. In his first match Lindsay Wood, slow left-arm, took 4 for 124 in 43 overs. As at Canterbury, Kent were dismissed twice by the Essex spinners although this time it was Ray East who did most of the damage. Top of the John Player League, in the semi-final of the NatWest Trophy and threatening in the Schweppes County Championship, Essex were looking the most formidable combination in the country. In spite of a maiden championship century from Monty Lynch and a career best from Jack Richards, Surrey could not force a win over Leicestershire, Somerset were again indebted to the brilliance of Viv Richards and though they faltered a little in reaching a meagre target, Marks and Russom, playing his first game of the season for Somerset, stayed calm and saw them to victory.

Middlesex's championship hopes diminished when limp batting saw them thankful to hang on for a draw at Northampton. There was another display of elegant power from Allan Lamb, more runs from Slack and Barlow and then some fine spin bowling from Phil Edmonds and Dermot Monteith. Middlesex needed 259 to win in 185 minutes and were 129 for 3 when the last 20 overs began. Sharp was injured and Allan Lamb kept wicket. Substitute Peter Mills held three fine catches and Middlesex slumped so badly that Daniel and Downton had to play out the last 9.4 overs to save the game. Once more the Gloucestershire spinners enjoyed Cheltenham after their batsmen had exploited the wicket when it was at its best on the first day. Hampshire, since Pocock's injury, and without Tremlett and Greenidge, had lost their way, but were still a remarkably improved side. There was a feast of runs at Edgbaston where Javed Miandad narrowly missed two centuries in the match. Norman Featherstone batted beautifully in the second innings and fielded superbly. Amiss and Lloyd shared a second wicket stand of 172 in 145 minutes as Warwickshire declared with only two men out. In the end Warwickshire were left 275 minutes in which to score 384 runs, a mammoth task. They were 16 for 2, but still chased the runs. Humpage scored 102 in 105 minutes. They stayed on target, but lost bravely in the twelfth over of the last hour by 35 runs. Greg Thomas again showed considerable promise in the Glamorgan attack.

Fifth Cornhill Test Match

There were three changes in the England twelve for the fifth Test. Tavare, Knott and Underwood replaced Willey, Taylor and Dilley. The inclusion of Tavare had been expected and Dilley had fallen out of serious contention, but the exclusion of Taylor was unforgivably cruel and the autocracy of Brearley's captaincy was clearly seen. In many quarters it was a very unpopular decision. Paul Allott came in to the side when Old was deemed unfit. In the event Underwood was made twelfth man. The Australians also caused a major surprise. With Hogg and Lawson unfit, they called upon Mike Whitney who had made his debut for New South Wales only a few months earlier and was in England playing for Fleetwood in the Northern League as well as assisting Gloucestershire. It made one wonder as to the original selection of the Australian party. Why was Beard chosen if there was no intention of playing him? England elected to bat first and under a lowering sky they scored 175 for 9 in 74 overs on the first day. It was miserable stuff. Alderman passed Lillee's record of 32 wickets in a series in England and Whitney had Gower as his first Test victim, caught at slip where he had already been dropped. Disasters came in battalions, but Tavare stood resolute if strokeless, his fifty coming in four hours. Border broke a finger catching Emburey and Gatting, like Gower, was out to a dreadful shot. It was a dismal day. The second day started most unexpectedly with Allott and Willis not surrendering immediately, but taking their last wicket stand to 56 with Allott reaching the first fifty of his career in his first Test. Then Australia followed a familiar pattern as Willis and Allott reduced them to 24 for 4, Wood being lbw to the Lancastrian to complete a memorable morning. Willis was again irresistible, bowling with the fire of possession that is only conjured from the innermost depths of a man's soul. There were some brave flourishes, but on a wicket which Hughes had described as a beauty, Australia, inexcusably, were bowled out for 130. Lillee had started the day with his 150th wicket against England. Willis took his 100th wicket against Australia and bowled his 100th no-ball of the series. Boycott had passed Cowdrey's record aggregate for England, Gooch lost his leg stump before the end of the day, but Boycott and Tavare played out time sedately and with some profit. Quite conclusively, England were winning.

The Saturday morning produced one of the worst batting displays in Test history as England added only 28 runs and lost Boycott, Gower (caught mis-hooking) and Gatting, lbw after having been dropped. When Brearley was out in the early afternoon, Botham came in and the score was 104 for 5. What followed was one of the most glorious episodes in the history of cricket. The bare facts are that Tavare and Botham added 149 of which Botham had scored 118. His runs came in 123 minutes off 102 deliveries. He hit six sixes and thirteen fours. What can never be recorded on paper is the thrill that reverberated round the ground as Botham first played himself in and then began his onslaught on the Australian bowling. When Lillee tried a bouncer he was hooked into the crowd. Bright was driven straight back over his head and pulled lustily. Whitney should have caught Botham when he was 32, but what pleasure that would have denied us. This was no slog, but two hours of sustained aggression which comprised shots of majesty and infinite power. In size it was breathtaking, in its mightiness it was almost frightening. He was finally caught behind off Whitney and though Knott plundered runs from a battered attack and Tavare reached his second half century of the match, a most commendable perform- ance, what could bear comparison with this? Emburey also reached fifty and Australia needed 506 to win and save The Ashes. 24 for 2 was not a good beginning, but Hughes suggested something of his former charm with an innings of 43 which supported Yallop who was in magnificent form, reminding us of his impressive Test record. He was out at 198, bowled by Emburey after a superb 114, an innings of both grit and power. Sadly Kent went quickly

so that the hope that Yallop had given faded. It flickered again on the final
day with an innings of great courage, determination and technical skill from
Allan Border. Nursing a broken finger, he carried out his bat for 123 and
first with Marsh and then with Lillee, he made stands which made Australians
believe that the impossible might be achieved. A brilliant slip catch by Botham
accounted for Lillee and the end came swiftly after that though Whitney survived
for a while, but England had retained The Ashes.

Fifth Cornhill Test Match   England *v.* Australia
13, 14, 15, 16 and 17 August   **at Old Trafford, Manchester**

England	*First Innings*		*Second Innings*	
G. A. Gooch	lbw, b Lillee	10	b Alderman	5
G. Boycott	c Marsh, b Alderman	10	lbw, b Alderman	37
C. J. Tavare	c Alderman, b Whitney	69	c Kent, b Alderman	78
D. I. Gower	c Yallop, b Whitney	23	c Bright, b Lillee	1
J. M. Brearley (capt)	lbw, b Alderman	2	(6) c Marsh, b Alderman	3
M. W. Gatting	c Border, b Lillee	32	(5) lbw, b Alderman	11
I. T. Botham	c Bright, b Lillee	0	c Marsh, b Whitney	118
*A. P. E. Knott	c Border, b Alderman	13	c Dyson, b Lillee	59
J. E. Emburey	c Border, b Alderman	1	c Kent, b Whitney	57
P. J. W. Allott	not out	52	c Hughes, b Bright	14
R. G. D. Willis	c Hughes, b Lillee	11	not out	5
Extras	lb 6, w 2	8	b 1, lb 12, nb 3	16
		231		**404**

	O	M	R	W		O	M	R	W
Lillee	24.1	8	55	4		46	13	137	2
Alderman	29	5	88	4		52	19	109	5
Whitney	17	3	50	2		27	6	74	2
Bright	16	6	30	—		26.4	11	68	1

Fall of Wickets
1–19, 2–25, 3–57, 4–62, 5–109, 6–109, 7–131, 8–137, 9–175.
1–7, 2–79, 3–80, 4–98, 5–104, 6–253, 7–282, 8–356, 9–396.

Australia	*First Innings*		*Second Innings*	
G. M. Wood	lbw, b Allott	19	c Knott, b Allott	6
J. Dyson	c Botham, b Willis	0	run out	5
K. J. Hughes (capt)	lbw, b Willis	4	lbw, b Botham	43
G. N. Yallop	c Botham, b Willis	0	b Emburey	114
M. F. Kent	c Knott, b Emburey	52	(6) c Brearley, b Emburey	2
A. R. Border	c Gower, b Botham	11	(5) not out	123
*R. W. Marsh	c Botham, b Willis	1	c Knott, b Willis	47
R. J. Bright	c Knott, b Botham	22	c Knott, b Willis	5
D. K. Lillee	c Gooch, b Botham	13	c Botham, b Allott	28
M. R. Whitney	b Allott	0	(11) c Gatting, b Willis	0
T. M. Alderman	not out	2	(10) lbw, b Botham	0
Extras	nb 6	6	lb 9, w 2, nb 18	29
		130		**402**

	O	M	R	W	O	M	R	W
Willis	14	—	63	4	30.5	2	96	3
Allott	6	1	17	2	17	3	71	2
Botham	6.2	1	28	3	36	16	86	2
Emburey	4	—	16	1	49	9	107	2
Gatting					3	1	13	—

Fall of Wickets
1–20, 2–24, 3–24, 4–24, 5–58, 6–59, 7–104, 8–125, 9–126.
1–7, 2–24, 3–119, 4–198, 5–206, 6–296, 7–322, 8–373, 9–378.

England won by 103 runs

15, 17 and 18 August   **at Swansea**
Derbyshire 320 (K. J. Barnett 64 not out, R. C. Ontong 4 for 61, B. J. Lloyd
   4 for 98)
Glamorgan 131 (G. Miller 4 for 27, D. S. Steele 4 for 28) and 182 (Javed
   Miandad 79, D. S. Steele 5 for 62)
Derbyshire won by an innings and 7 runs
Derbyshire 24 pts, Glamorgan 4 pts

         at Cheltenham
Kent 310 for 6 dec (Asif Iqbal 93, M. R. Benson 87, N. Taylor 60) and 276
   for 6 dec (R. Ellison 59 not out, N. Taylor 51)
Gloucestershire 336 for 3 dec (Zaheer Abbas 136 not out, P. Bainbridge 81)
   and 121 for 5 (P. Bainbridge 57 not out)
Match drawn
Gloucestershire 6 pts, Kent 4 pts

         at Southampton
Hampshire 340 for 7 dec (M. D. Marshall 75 not out, J. M. Rice 63, D. R.
   Turner 53, R. E. East 4 for 64) and 180 for 7 dec (D. L. Acfield 4 for 52)
Essex 279 (K. S. McEwan 103, M. D. Marshall 4 for 67) and 105 (T. E. Jesty
   6 for 25, M. D. Marshall 4 for 39)
Hampshire won by 136 runs
Hampshire 23 pts, Essex 6 pts

         at Leicester
Leicestershire 322 for 2 dec (J. C. Balderstone 150 not out, N. E. Briers 103)
   and 248 for 4 dec (B. F. Davison 74, J. C. Balderstone 50)
Worcestershire 268 (E. J. O. Hemsley 73 not out, G. M. Turner 56) and 175 for
   4 (Younis Ahmed 83 not out)
Match drawn
Leicestershire 8 pts, Worcestershire 3 pts

         at Wellingborough
Northamptonshire 156 and 207 (A. J. Lamb 73, G. Cook 66, A. Sidebottom
   6 for 62)
Yorkshire 238 (C. W. J. Athey 123 not out, N. A. Mallender 6 for 37) and 115
   for 4 (K. Sharp 79)
Yorkshire won by 6 wickets
Yorkshire 22 pts, Northamptonshire 5 pts

at Trent Bridge

Sussex 208 (G. D. Mendis 65, E. E. Hemmings 5 for 94) and 144 (E. E. Hemmings 4 for 57)

Nottinghamshire 102 (B. Hassan 58 not out, C. E. Waller 5 for 36) and 223 for 9 (B. Hassan 79, C. E. B. Rice 58)

Match drawn

Sussex 6 pts, Nottinghamshire 4 pts

at The Oval

Middlesex 139 (Intikhab Alam 4 for 26) and 144 (C. T. Radley 51, Intikhab Alam 4 for 63)

Surrey 259 (D. M. Smith 71, J. D. Monteith 4 for 85) and 25 for 0

Surrey won by 10 wickets

Surrey 23 pts, Middlesex 4 pts

at Edgbaston

Lancashire 326 (D. Lloyd 108, G. Fowler 55, A. Kennedy 53, W. Hogg 4 for 56, G. C. Small 4 for 76) and 299 for 5 dec (G. Fowler 141, F. C. Hayes 61, W. Hogg 4 for 92)

Warwickshire 301 for 5 dec (A. I. Kallicharran 91 not out, T. A. Lloyd 74) and 125 for 5

Match drawn

Warwickshire 7 pts, Lancashire 6 pts

16, 17 and 18 August   **at Portadulas**

Ireland 338 for 6 dec and 253 for 3 dec

Wales 296 for 8 dec and 166

Ireland won by 129 runs

The top of the table clash at Trent Bridge produced a dour and tense struggle. Rice won the toss and put Sussex in, but the visitors, led by Mendis, showed the utmost resolution and had grasped the advantage by the end of the first day. Notts trailed by 106 on the first innings, but Hemmings and Bore bowled them back into contention. Notts needed 251 to win and although they lost 3 for 75, a fourth wicket stand of 101 between the cool Hassan and Rice gave them every hope of success. Barclay used delaying tactics and the crowd became angry, but suddenly wickets fell and the game swung dramatically in favour of Sussex. Notts needed 62 in the last 20 overs. Hadlee and French were dismissed. 205 for 7 and the Notts batsmen gladly came off for bad light. When they returned Birch and Cooper fell to Le Roux. Amid continuous cheers, Hemmings and Bore played out the last 28 balls with straight, defensive bats. This draw was just the result that Essex could have wished for, but, weakened by some incomprehensible team selection, they failed at Southampton where Malcolm Marshall hit a career best and Essex collapsed dreadfully against Jesty in the second innings. Hampshire batted solidly and McEwan sparkled for Essex, but all the honours went to Hampshire and a deflated Essex trailed to Derby. Derbyshire, with Steele spinning subtly and Kim Barnett showing a return to form and confidence, accounted for Glamorgan in two days and the leg-spin of Intikhab brought a two day victory over Middlesex at The Oval. After a very lean season, Smith was among the runs for Surrey.

Cheltenham disappointed the spinners and the batsmen enjoyed themselves, Zaheer becoming the first man to reach 2000 runs for the season. There was a plethora of runs at Leicester too, where Chris Balderstone and Nigel Briers put on 209 for the second wicket, and a draw became inevitable. As ever Edgbaston provided another batsmen's paradise. Fowler showed his continued progress with his third century of the season and there were fine innings from David Lloyd and, happily, Alvin Kallicharran, whose omission from the West Indies party to tour Australia seemed to suggest his international career was at an end. In their bid for victory, Warwickshire stumbled to 84 for 5, but Din and Oliver saved the day. There was a surprising win for Yorkshire at Wellingborough. They bowled out Northants for 156, but were wilting at 103 for 7. Bill Athey took charge with a chanceless century which lifted them to 236, a wonderful effort, and then Sidebottom bowled Northants out again, only Lamb and Cook offering any resistance. Kevin Sharp set off as if he intended getting the required runs single handed and victory was obtained with ease. The Northants consolation was Neil Mallender's career best 6 for 37 and Tim Lamb's bowling on the last afternoon when he gave Yorkshire a small fright.

John Player League

16 August   **at Swansea**
Glamorgan 132 for 9 (A. Jones 66 not out)
Derbyshire 134 for 5 (J. G. Wright 66 not out)
Derbyshire (4 pts) won by 5 wickets

                                                                    at Cheltenham
Kent 182 for 7
Gloucestershire 183 for 5 (A. W. Stovold 55 not out)
Gloucestershire (4 pts) won by 5 wickets

                                                                   at Southampton
Essex 194 for 4 (B. R. Hardie 87, K. S. McEwan 67)
Hampshire 198 for 3 (C. L. Smith 65)
Hampshire (4 pts) won by 7 wickets

                                                                      at Leicester
Leicestershire 168 for 7 (N. E. Briers 74)
Worcestershire 169 for 4 (Younis Ahmed 65 not out)
Worcestershire (4 pts) won by 6 wickets

                                                                 at Wellingborough
Yorkshire 132 (D. L. Bairstow 53)
Northamptonshire 126 (G. Cook 50)
Yorkshire (4 pts) won by 6 runs

                                                                   at Trent Bridge
Sussex 160 for 8
Nottinghamshire 164 for 6 (Imran Khan 5 for 36)
Nottinghamshire (4 pts) won by 4 wickets

at The Oval

Somerset 220 for 7 (B. C. Rose 79)
Surrey 171
Somerset (4 pts) won by 49 runs

at Edgbaston

Lancashire 178 for 9 (A. M. Ferreira 4 for 42)
Warwickshire 180 for 7 (A. I. Kallicharran 51, Asif Din 51)
Warwickshire (4 pts) won by 3 wickets

Essex frittered away their overall leadership of the League in a sorry fashion. Hardie and McEwan added 159 for the second wicket at Southampton but failed to force the pace with brisk singles or to upset the field placing. Smith and Rice gave Hampshire a fine start in reply and the Essex field setting seemed a little bizarre. After Smith, Rice and Turner had been dismissed for 135, Essex seemed to have regained control of the match, but the Essex fielding collapsed and John Lever returned for a nightmare three overs as Cowley and Jesty hit 60 runs in 7 overs. Marshall bowled very quickly and very well for Hampshire. Derbyshire drew level on points at the top with a very easy win at Swansea, and Warwickshire and Somerset both drew to within two points of the top. Warwickshire saw Din and Kallicharran add 99 for the fourth wicket which gave them the impetus needed to beat Lancashire with four balls to spare. It was their sixth win in succession. Somerset trounced Surrey at The Oval, but Sussex, in spite of some fearsome bowling by Imran Khan, lost to Notts who thereby moved off the bottom. Sussex's chances of capturing the title now seemed very remote. Yorkshire maintained their challenge with a surprise win in a low scoring game at Wellingborough. The home side disintegrated after the dismissal of Cook and Yorkshire kept cool to win by six runs. Worcestershire gained a welcome win at Leicester where the home side's batting on a good pitch was woefully weak, Briers alone batted with conviction. Gloucestershire were another of the lowly sides to give their supporters some cheer.

National Westminster Bank Trophy – Semi-Finals

19 August   **at Northampton**
Lancashire 186 for 9 (G. Fowler 57, D. Lloyd 52)
Northamptonshire 187 for 9
Northamptonshire won by 1 wicket

19 and 20 August   **at Derby**
Essex 149
Derbyshire 149 for 8 (K. J. Barnett 59)
Derbyshire won on losing fewer wickets

It would be hard to conceive of two more exciting matches than those that graced the semi-final stage of the NatWest Trophy. Northamptonshire asked Lancashire to bat and with the Red Rose 116 for 1, and Fowler and David Lloyd in command, it seemed a poor decision. Lancashire then lost 8 wickets for 45 runs, three to Tim Lamb, who also caught Hughes. Simmons and Holding added 25 for the last wicket, but 186 was a disappointing score. Northants seemed well set, but lost their way badly against Jack Simmons. Yardley and Carter rallied them, but again they faltered and when the ninth wicket fell they were 13 short of victory. Jim Griffiths, with no aspirations as a batsman, joined Tim Lamb. The improbable was accomplished. Holding was withstood, and Peter Lee had unwisely been omitted, and the last over was reached with the scores level. A bye saw Griffiths and Lamb chaired from the field as heroes of a marvellous match. Tim Lamb was Man of the Match. At Derby it was just as tense. Essex were put in on a green wicket under lowering sky. The Derbyshire seam attack exploited the conditions well and though Phillip batted with a sensible mixture of caution and aggression, Essex managed only 149. Derbyshire lost Wright and Kirsten before bad light ended play. On the second day, in far better conditions, and on a wicket that had been cut, Derbyshire were soon in trouble against Pringle and Turner. Kim Barnett batted with mature confidence, particularly good on the leg side, but he was bowled by Phillip and the score went to 133 for 8. Newman and Taylor faced the last over with ten runs needed to win. Five runs came from Phillip's first four deliveries and then he dropped woefully short and Newman pulled him for four. One run was needed to tie the scores off the last ball. Newman pushed out on the off-side and Phillip gathered the ball. He needed only to lob the ball under-arm to Hardie and the others who had run to guard the wicket and Newman would have been run out by five yards, but he threw wildly and Essex had lost the sixty over competition by losing more wickets with the scores level for the third time in four years.

20 August　　　　　　　　　　　　　　　　　　　　　　**at Leicester**
Australians 213 for 8 (T. M. Chappell 63, J. P. Agnew 4 for 58)
Leicestershire 145
Australians won by 68 runs

22, 23 and 24 August　　　　　　　　　　　　　　　　**at Hove**
Sussex 150 (M. R. Whitney 5 for 60) and 261 (J. R. P. Heath 56, T. J. Head 52 not out, R. M. Hogg 4 for 83)
Australians 236 (K. J. Hughes 52, A. N. Jones 4 for 68, I. A. Greig 4 for 76) and 176 for 3 (K. J. Hughes 70 not out, J. Dyson 65 not out)
Australians won by 7 wickets

　　　　　　　　　　　　　　　　　　　　　　　　at Chesterfield
Derbyshire 400 for 8 dec (J. G. Wright 150, P. N. Kirsten 79) and 151 for 3 dec (B. Wood 68 not out, D. S. Steele 53)
Yorkshire 252 for 4 dec (G. Boycott 122 not out, J. H. Hampshire 84) and 300 for 4 (D. L. Bairstow 88 not out, J. D. Love 84 not out, G. B. Stevenson 57)
Yorkshire won by 6 wickets
Yorkshire 22 pts, Derbyshire 5 pts

　　　　　　　　　　　　　　　　　　　　　　　　at Folkestone
Kent 316 for 7 dec (C. J. Tavare 123 not out, M. R. Benson 52) and 259 for 6 dec (C. J. Tavare 82, Asif Iqbal 81 not out)

Zaheer Abbas. A memorable year.

Wood, caught Taylor, bowled Willis; Second Test at Lord's. The rejuvenated Willis was a vital factor in England's successful summer.

The moment of glory for Jim Griffiths. The ball goes for a bye and Northants are in the NatWest Final. David Lloyd is in despair.

Surrey 295 for 8 dec (A. R. Butcher 116, G. R. J. Roope 81) and 274 for 7
   (A. R. Butcher 89, G. S. Clinton 54, G. W. Johnson 4 for 91)
Match drawn
Kent 7 pts, Surrey 6 pts

at Old Trafford

Leicestershire 111 (D. I. Gower 63, P. G. Lee 6 for 50, P. J. W. Allott 4 for
   59) and 270 for 5 dec (D. I. Gower 67, N. G. B. Cook 62, N. E. Briers 61
   not out)
Lancashire 163 (P. B. Clift 5 for 32) and 175 (I. Cockbain 50, P. B. Clift 6
   for 47)
Leicestershire won by 43 runs
Leicestershire 20 pts, Lancashire 5 pts

at Lord's

Middlesex 361 for 7 dec (M. W. Gatting 99, J. M. Brearley 72, M. A. Nash
   4 for 80)
Glamorgan 96 and 229 (P. H. Edmonds 4 for 57)
Middlesex won by an innings and 36 runs
Middlesex 24 pts, Glamorgan 3 pts

at Northampton

Essex 300 for 7 dec (G. A. Gooch 146, Sarfraz Nawaz 4 for 71) and 199 for
   8 dec (K. W. R. Fletcher 78, R. M. Carter 4 for 52)
Northamptonshire 251 for 4 dec (A. J. Lamb 117, G. Sharp 69 not out) and
   139 for 2 (R. G. Williams 72 not out)
Match drawn
Northamptonshire 6 pts, Essex 5 pts

at Taunton

Hampshire 184 (C. L. Smith 58) and 120 (T. E. Jesty 67, J. Garner 7 for 23)
Somerset 287 (J. W. Lloyds 50, M. D. Marshall 5 for 68) and 21 for 1
Somerset won by 9 wickets
Somerset 23 pts, Hampshire 5 pts

at Edgbaston

Warwickshire 331 for 9 dec (D. L. Amiss 83, G. W. Humpage 65, R. J. Hadlee
   4 for 59) and 49
Nottinghamshire 303 for 9 dec (D. W. Randall 117, C. E. B. Rice 50, D. R. Doshi
   4 for 94) and 79 for 2 (P. A. Todd 52 not out)
Nottinghamshire won by 8 wickets
Nottinghamshire 24 pts, Warwickshire 8 pts

at Worcester

Worcestershire 251 (M. S. Scott 54, D. A. Graveney 5 for 57, J. H. Childs
   4 for 91) and 277 for 6 dec (G. M. Turner 111, P. A. Neale 66 not out)
Gloucestershire 250 for 8 dec (Zaheer Abbas 76) and 279 for 3 (Zaheer Abbas
   103 not out, Sadiq Mohammad 61, A. J. Hignell 54 not out)
Gloucestershire won by 7 wickets
Gloucestershire 23 pts, Worcestershire 6 pts

Notts took a firm grip on the Schweppes title with a remarkable two-day win over Warwickshire who collapsed after tea on the second day for the season's lowest total. Until then all had been even. Notts were now playing with great spirit and team confidence. Sussex, criticised for leaving out so many regulars, showed spirit against the Australians, but a lively knock by Kim Hughes brought the tourists victory. Jones bowled well for Sussex, a pace man of promise, and it was good to have Pigott back in action. Garner destroyed Hampshire to give Somerset victory in two days, and Middlesex needed only a short while on the third morning to beat a rather lustreless Glamorgan side. Some fine bowling from Paddy Clift and a career best of 62 from Nick Cook saw Leicestershire to victory at Old Trafford with eleven balls to spare. Gooch answered the selectors who had dropped him from the Oval Test with a sparkling knock at Northampton and Allan Lamb replied with an equally impressive knock for the home side, but much else was not so sparkling and the game was drawn. In a game of much good cricket at Folkestone, Surrey were seven short of victory at the end. Tavare had two fine innings and Kent recovered from 7 for 3 in their second innings. Clinton and Butcher gave hopes of Surrey victory with an opening stand of 125. Another storming innings by Zaheer who added 150 in 79 minutes with Hignell countered Glenn Turner's sixth century of the season and gave Gloucestershire victory. There was some violent hitting by Bairstow too. He hit a six and seventeen fours as Yorkshire won, surprisingly considering Derbyshire's early dominance, with 8.3 overs to spare.

John Player League

23 August   **at Chesterfield**
Yorkshire 208 for 6 (J. D. Love 60, D. L. Bairstow 50)
Derbyshire 137 (P. N. Kirsten 63, C. W. J. Athey 5 for 35)
Yorkshire (4 pts) won by 71 runs

                                                                          at Folkestone
Kent 195 for 6 (C. J. Tavare 53, A. P. E. Knott 51 not out)
Surrey 158 for 9 (A. R. Butcher 74)
Kent (4 pts) won by 37 runs

                                                                          at Old Trafford
Leicestershire 185 for 6
Lancashire 135 (L. B. Taylor 4 for 14)
Leicestershire (4 pts) won by 50 runs

                                                                          at Lord's
Glamorgan 151 for 5 (J. A. Hopkins 63 not out)
Middlesex 114
Glamorgan (4 pts) won by 37 runs

                                                                          at Northampton
Essex 212 for 6 (N. Phillip 83 not out)
Northamptonshire 193 for 4 (G. Cook 52, A. J. Lamb 50)
Essex (4 pts) won by 19 runs

at Taunton

Somerset 286 for 7 (I. T. Botham 106, I. V. A. Richards 93)
Hampshire 137 (H. R. Moseley 4 for 25)
Somerset (4 pts) won by 149 runs

at Edgbaston

Nottinghamshire 221 for 3 (B. Hassan 120 not out, D. W. Randall 67)
Warwickshire 222 for 4 (A. I. Kallicharran 102 not out, D. L. Amiss 53)
Warwickshire (4 pts) won by 6 wickets

at Worcester

Gloucestershire 159 (J. D. Inchmore 4 for 28)
Worcestershire 161 for 3 (G. M. Turner 69)
Worcestershire (4 pts) won by 7 wickets

Essex maintained their lead at the top of the table with a comfortable win after some fireworks from Norbert Phillip. The real fireworks, however, were at Taunton where Botham and Richards added 179 for the fifth wicket. In fifteen overs they advanced by 100 and then cut loose. Botham moved from 50 to 100 in 15 balls, 9 minutes, 26 in one over from Stevenson, 20 from the next by Cowley. There was little to contest after that. Yorkshire's success continued with Athey having his best ever bowling figures and Derbyshire being dismissed in under 34 overs so losing ground in the title race. Warwickshire's run continued. Notts had an opening stand of 188 from Hassan and Randall, but Kallicharran's century still gave the home side victory with nearly three overs to spare, most impressive. Lancashire, Gloucestershire and Middlesex all wilted rather badly and Surrey found Kent's aggression too much for them.

26, 27 and 28 August   **at Colchester**
Essex 340 for 6 dec (K. S. McEwan 141, G. A. Gooch 75, L. B. Taylor
    4 for 93) and 256 for 7 dec (G. A. Gooch 105)
Leicestershire 198 (N. Phillip 4 for 46) and 259 (A. M. E. Roberts 57, S. Turner
    5 for 55)
Essex won by 139 runs
Essex 24 pts, Leicestershire 3 pts

at Swansea
Glamorgan 351 for 7 dec (J. A. Hopkins 134, Javed Miandad 59) and 160
    (J. A. Hopkins 61, N. Gifford 6 for 67, D. N. Patel 4 for 48)
Worcestershire 237 (B. J. Lloyd 4 for 33) and 275 for 5 (G. M. Turner 130
    not out)
Worcestershire won by 5 wickets
Worcestershire 20 pts, Glamorgan 8 pts

at Bournemouth
Hampshire 148 (Imran Khan 4 for 50) and 233 (D. R. Turner 64, I. A. Greig
    4 for 53)
Sussex 237 (Imran Khan 100, M. D. Marshall 6 for 62) and 135 for 2 (G. D.
    Mendis 51)
Sussex won by 8 wickets
Sussex 22 pts, Hampshire 4 pts

at Folkestone

Kent 186 (R. M. Ellison 61 not out) and 121 (V. J. Marks 5 for 34, J. Garner 4 for 37)

Somerset 309 (P. W. Denning 98, P. M. Roebuck 51, D. L. Underwood 7 for 118)

Somerset won by an innings and 2 runs
Somerset 22 pts, Kent 2 pts

at Blackpool

Derbyshire 406 for 7 dec (P. N. Kirsten 204 not out, K. J. Barnett 61)

Lancashire 190 (G. Fowler 52, P. G. Newman 4 for 34, G. Miller 4 for 62) and 408 for 6 (D. Lloyd 146 not out, D. P. Hughes 86, N. V. Radford 76 not out)

Match drawn
Derbyshire 7 pts, Lancashire 2 pts

at Lord's

Yorkshire 264 for 9 dec (J. D. Love 66, D. L. Bairstow 52 not out) and 167 (R. G. Lumb 56, J. D. Monteith 4 for 22)

Middlesex 366 for 9 dec (K. P. Tomlins 79 not out, R. O. Butcher 72, C. T. Radley 56, W. W. Daniel 53 not out, A. Sidebottom 4 for 66) and 66 for 4

Middlesex won by 6 wickets
Middlesex 23 pts, Yorkshire 6 pts

at Cleethorpes

Northamptonshire 85 (R. J. Hadlee 5 for 34, C. E. B. Rice 4 for 25) and 181 (A. J. Lamb 73)

Nottinghamshire 319 (R. T. Robinson 91, J. D. Birch 63 not out)

Nottinghamshire won by an innings and 53 runs
Nottinghamshire 24 pts, Northamptonshire 4 pts

With Northants disintegrating on the opening day before Hadlee and Rice, and Robinson and Birch leading the charge for batting points, Notts swept to a two-day victory and came closer to the title. There was no respite from their challengers. The magnificent all-round cricket of Imran Khan again inspired Sussex who convincingly beat Hants to remain close on the heels of Notts. Denning defied the spin of Underwood and then Marks and Garner brushed aside a rather spiritless Kent to hold fourth place behind Essex who took maximum points from Leicestershire. A century by McEwan in the first innings allied to a hundred in 89 minutes from Gooch in the second put pressure on the visitors and Turner and Phillip did the rest in spite of late resistance from Roberts. Yorkshire were rallied by Bairstow, inevitably, and Love, but then produced some dreadful out-cricket at Lord's to lose easily. Middlesex, after some sound first innings batting all down the order, made very hard work of victory. Lancashire once more batted through the last day to save a match, a creditable performance as they had been 114 for 5. David Lloyd and Hughes added 170, and then Lloyd and Radford an unbeaten 124. Earlier Peter Kirsten had reached a fine double hundred, there had been a good little innings from Kim Barnett, growing in confidence, and good bowling from Newman and Miller. There was a complete reversal of fortunes at Swansea where Glamorgan

Allan Border. The leading Australian batsman.

The Power and The Glory. Ian Botham at Leeds.

dominated the first half of the match with some fine batting, but then collapsed to Gifford's spin in the second innings and bowed the knee to Turner who hit yet another splendid century.

Sixth Cornhill Test Match

Gooch and Gower, the two most exciting stroke players, were omitted from the England side, and Hendrick played instead of Allott, Old having been declared unfit. Paul Parker was given a much deserved Test cap and Wayne Larkins was recalled. Dirk Welham made his debut for Australia, replacing Dyson. Brearley had been retained as captain in a gesture of thanks. He has not completely caught the imagination of the English public in spite of his succes as a leader, but the accomplishment of the man is undeniable and it would be ungenerous not to pay tribute to his magnificent achievement. At the end of the Second Test at Lord's, English cricket stood at a very low ebb and now two months later, it had scaled the heights again. Although the rubber had already been decided, people flocked to The Oval and England was alive with cricket, and for this, Brearley must take no small part of the credit. There must be supreme accolade too for Ian Botham who, like English cricket, had risen from the depths to the pinnacle of success in a matter of weeks. He is quite simply one of the very greatest of cricketers and we are lucky to have seen his like. Brearley won the toss and asked Australia to bat which, in view of the rapidity with which they scored, appeared to have been a mistake. There was a fine opening stand and then another century from the determined and pugnacious Border – here is a Test batsman in quality and temperament. The final Australian total must have disappointed them a little and once more it was Botham and Willis who retarded the progress. England looked as if they would amass a huge score. Larkins showed some fine shots as did Gatting. Boycott accumulated runs in his most obdurate manner and much of the England batting was rather painful. Then came a collapse and sadly Parker was one of those to suffer, but the innings belonged more than anyone to Dennis Lillee. That mighty figure of a man bristled with endeavour and as he returned the best figures of his Test career, he showed no sign of his appetite for the game or for English batsmen abating. Australia recovered from an uncertain start with another splendid knock from Border and a hundred in his first Test from the likeable Dirk Welham. He had a little luck, Boycott dropped him on 99, but he played some handsome shots and he will give us much trouble and pleasure in years to come. The irrepressible Marsh hit fifty and it will be hard to imagine what an Australian side will be like when he is no longer bubbling behind the stumps. Australia sensed victory when Boycott went in Lillee's first over and Alderman beat Hogg's record number of wickets in a series against England – the score was 144 for 6. Brearley joined Knott in saving the day and hit fifty in what was probably his last Test, but with him none can be sure. He has durable qualities and an acute sense of what is good for the game. So the series ended. It had been a memorable one, and if we complained occasionally about the quality, the vitality and entertainment were marvellous. Cricket won.

Sixth Cornhill Test Match   England *v.* Australia
27, 28, 29 and 31 August, 1 September   at The Oval

Australia	First Innings		Second Innings	
G. M. Wood	c Brearley, b Botham	66	c Knott, b Hendrick	21
M. F. Kent	c Gatting, b Botham	54	c Brearley, b Botham	7
K. J. Hughes (capt)	hit wkt, b Botham	31	lbw, b Hendrick	6
G. N. Yallop	c Botham, b Willis	26	b Hendrick	35
A. R. Border	not out	106	c Tavare, b Emburey	84
D. M. Welham	b Willis	24	lbw, b Botham	103
*R. W. Marsh	c Botham, b Willis	12	c Gatting, b Botham	52
R. J. Bright	c Brearley, b Botham	3	b Botham	11
D. K. Lillee	b Willis	11	not out	8
T. M. Alderman	b Botham	0		
M. R. Whitney	b Botham	4	(10) c Botham, b Hendrick	0
Extras	b 4, lb 6, w 1, nb 4	15	b 1, lb 8, w 1, nb 7	17
		352	(for 9 wkts, dec)	344

	O	M	R	W		O	M	R	W
Willis	31	6	91	4		10	—	41	—
Hendrick	31	8	63	—		29.2	6	82	4
Botham	47	13	125	6		42	9	128	4
Emburey	23	2	58	—		23	3	76	1

Fall of Wickets
1–120, 2–125, 3–169, 4–199, 5–260, 6–280, 7–303, 8–319, 9–320.
1–26, 2–36, 3–41, 4–104, 5–205, 6–291, 7–332, 8–343, 9–344.

England	First Innings		Second Innings	
G. Boycott	c Yallop, b Lillee	137	lbw, b Lillee	0
W. Larkins	c Alderman, b Lillee	34	c Alderman, b Lillee	24
C. J. Tavare	c Marsh, b Lillee	24	c Kent, b Whitney	8
M. W. Gatting	b Lillee	53	c Kent, b Lillee	56
J. M. Brearley (capt)	c Bright, b Alderman	0	(6) c Marsh, b Lillee	51
P. W. G. Parker	c Kent, b Alderman	0	(5) c Kent, b Alderman	13
I. T. Botham	c Yallop, b Lillee	3	lbw, b Alderman	16
*A. P. E. Knott	b Lillee	36	not out	70
J. E. Emburey	lbw, b Lillee	0	not out	5
R. G. D. Willis	b Alderman	3		
M. Hendrick	not out	0		
Extras	lb 9, w 3, nb 12	24	b 2, lb 5, w 2, nb 9	18
		314	(for 7 wkts)	261

	O	M	R	W		O	M	R	W
Lillee	31.4	4	89	7		30	10	70	4
Alderman	35	4	84	3		19	6	60	2
Whitney	23	3	76	—		11	4	46	1
Bright	21	6	41	—		27	12	50	—
Yallop						8	2	17	—

Fall of Wickets
1–61, 2–131, 3–246, 4–248, 5–248, 6–256, 7–293, 8–293, 9–302.
1–0, 2–18, 3–88, 4–101, 5–127, 6–144, 7–237.

Match drawn

England v. Australia – Test Match Averages

England Batting

	M	Inns	NOs	Runs	HS	Average	100s	50s
A. P. E. Knott	2	4	1	178	70*	59.33		2
C. J. Tavare	2	4	—	179	78	44.75		2
G. R. Dilley	3	6	2	150	56	37.50		1
I. T. Botham	6	12	1	399	149*	36.27	2	1
G. Boycott	6	12	—	392	137	32.66	1	1
M. W. Gatting	6	12	—	370	59	30.83		4
J. E. Emburey	4	7	2	134	57	26.80		1
D. I. Gower	5	10	—	250	89	25.00		1
P. Willey	4	8	—	179	82	22.37		1
C. M. Old	2	4	1	63	29	21.00		
J. M. Brearley	4	8	—	141	51	17.62		1
G. A. Gooch	5	10	—	139	44	13.90		
R. A. Woolmer	2	4	—	30	21	7.50		
R. G. D. Willis	6	10	2	43	13	5.37		
R. W. Taylor	3	6	—	23	9	3.83		

Played in two Tests: M. Hendrick 0*, 0* and 6*.
Played in one Test: P. J. W. Allott 52* and 14; P. R. Downton 8 and 3; W. Larkins 34 and 24; P. W. G. Parker 0 and 13.

England Bowling

	Overs	Mdns	Runs	Wkts	Av	Best	10/m	5/inn
G. R. Dilley	98	24	275	14	19.64	4/24		
I. T. Botham	272.3	81	700	34	20.58	6/95	1	3
R. G. D. Willis	252.4	56	666	29	22.96	8/43		1
J. E. Emburey	193.5	58	399	12	33.25	4/43		
C. M. Old	84	27	175	5	35.00	3/44		
M. Hendrick	100.2	28	221	6	36.83	4/82		

Also bowled: P. J. W. Allott 23–4–88–4; G. Boycott 3–2–2–0; M. W. Gatting 3–1–13–0; G. A. Gooch 10–4–28–0; P. Willey 16–3–35–1.

England Catches

13 – R. W. Taylor; 12 – I. T. Botham; 8 – M. W. Gatting; 6 – A. P. E. Knott; 4 – J. M. Brearley; 3 – D. I. Gower; 2 – G. Boycott, P. R. Downton, R. G. D. Willis and R. A. Woolmer; 1 – G. R. Dilley, J. E. Emburey, G. A. Gooch and C. J. Tavare.

Australia Batting

	M	Inns	NOs	Runs	HS	Average	100s	50s
A. R. Border	6	12	3	533	123*	59.22	2	3
M. F. Kent	3	6	—	171	54	28.50		2
G. M. Wood	6	12	1	310	66	28.18		2
G. N. Yallop	6	12	—	316	114	26.33	1	1
K. J. Hughes	6	12	—	300	89	25.00		1
D. K. Lillee	6	10	3	153	40*	21.85		
J. Dyson	5	10	—	206	102	20.60	1	
R. W. Marsh	6	11	—	216	52	19.63		1
T. M. Chappell	3	6	1	79	27	15.80		
R. J. Bright	5	9	—	127	33	14.11		

G. F. Lawson	3	5	1	38	14	9.50
T. M. Alderman	6	9	5	22	12*	5.50
M. R. Whitney	2	4	—	4	4	1.00
R. M. Hogg	2	3	1	0	0*	0.00

Played in one Test: D. M. Welham 24 and 103

Australia Bowling

	Overs	Mdns	Runs	Wkts	Av.	Best	10/m	5/in
T. M. Alderman	325	76	893	42	21.26	6/135		4
D. K. Lillee	311.4	81	870	39	22.30	7/89	1	2
G. F. Lawson	106.1	30	285	12	23.75	7/81		1
R. M. Hogg	40.4	8	123	4	30.75	3/47		
R. J. Bright	191.4	81	390	12	32.50	5/68		1
M. R. Whitney	78	16	246	5	49.20	2/50		

Also bowled: G. N. Yallop 8–2–17–0.

Australia Catches
23 – R. W. Marsh; 12 – A. R. Border; 8 – T. M. Alderman; 7 – G. N. Yallop
and M. F. Kent (one as sub); 4 – R. J. Bright and G. M. Wood; 3 – K. J.
Hughes; 2 – T. M. Chappell and J. Dyson; 1 – R. M. Hogg and D. K. Lillee.

The last contest of two giants? Boycott, lbw, bowled Lillee at The Oval.

Australians First-Class Matches – Batting, 1981

	v. Hampshire (Southampton) 20–22 May		v. Somerset (Taunton) 23–25 May		v. Glamorgan (Swansea) 27–29 May		v. Gloucestershire (Bristol) 31 May–2 June		v. Derbyshire (Derby) 10–12 June		v. Middlesex (Lord's) 13–15 June		First Test Match (Trent Bridge) 18–21 June		v. Kent (Canterbury) 27–29 June		Second Test Match (Lord's) 2–7 July	
J. Dyson	60	—	46	—	44	—			61	—	0	49	5	38	26	—	7	1
G. M. Wood	0	—	0	—			81	—			14*	9	0	8	41	—	44	62*
M. F. Kent	27	—			1	—	20	—	2	—								
K. J. Hughes	9	—	33	—			7	—	19	—	31	5	7	22	61	—	42	4
A. R. Border	5	—			0	—	24	—	5	—	5	11*	63	20	39	—	64	12*
G. N. Yallop	9	—	49*	—	0	—					16	52*	13	6	45	—	1	3
R. W. Marsh	72*	—			12	—					2	—	19	0			47	—
R. J. Bright	42	—			7	—			0	—	10	—			12*	—	33	—
R. M. Hogg	2*	—	5	—			—	—			6	—	0	—				
G. F. Lawson	—	—			38*	—	—	—	—	—	26	—	14	5*	—	—	5	—
T. M. Alderman	—	—			10	—	—	—	—	—			12*	—			5	—
T. M. Chappell			47	—	1	—	91	—	14	—	18	7	17	20*	6	—	2	5
D. M. Welham			22	—	3	—	2	—	47*	—								
G. R. Beard			4	—	12	—	20	—	2	—					27*	—		
S. J. Rixon			18	—			17*	—	24	—					—	—		
D. K. Lillee									—	—	5*	—	12	—			40*	—
M. R. Whitney																		
Byes	2		1		1		2		4			6	4	1			6	
Leg byes	6		4		10		11		5		10	5	8	6	15		11	
Wides	3		3		3						2		1				6	1
No balls					5		3		7		1		4	6	11		32	2
Total	237		232		147		278		190		146	144	179	132	283		345	90
Wickets	7		8		10		7		8		9†	4	10	6	6		10	4
Result	D		D		D		D		D		D		W		D		D	

† G. M. Wood retired hurt.

Catches

28 – R. W. Marsh (ct 26, st 2)
21 – S. J. Rixon (ct 19, st 2)
16 – A. R. Border
12 – R. J. Bright, T. M. Alderman and M. F. Kent
 8 – K. J. Hughes, G. N. Yallop and G. M. Wood
 4 – G. F. Lawson
 3 – T. M. Chappell, D. M. Welham and D. K. Lillee and substitutes
 2 – J. Dyson and R. M. Hogg
 1 – M. R. Whitney

v. Northamptonshire (Northampton) 11–13 July		Third Test Match (Leeds) 16–21 July		v. Worcestershire (Worcester) 25–27 July		Fourth Test Match (Edgbaston) 30 July–2 August		v. Essex (Chelmsford) 8–10 August		Fifth Test Match (Old Trafford) 13–17 August		v. Sussex (Hove) 22–24 August		Sixth Test Match (The Oval) 27 August–1 September		Inns	NOs	Runs	HS	Av
		102	34	9	—	1	13			0	5	16	65*			20	1	582	102	30.63
26	—	34	10	1	59	38	2	45	60	19	6	44	—	66	21	24	2	690	81	31.36
1	—			92	16	46	10	17	0	52	2			54	7	15	—	347	92	23.13
51	—	89	0	5	36	47	5			4	43	52	70*	31	6	24	1	679	89	29.52
		8	0	115	70*	2	40			11	123*			106*	84	21	5	807	123*	50.43
16	—	58	0			30	30	49	59*	0	114	13	—	26	35	22	3	624	114	32.84
		28	4			2	4	28	38	1	47			12	52	16	1	368	72*	24.53
22	—	7	19	12	—	27	0	—	20	22	5	28	—	3	11	18	1	280	42	16.47
—				2	—	0	0*					0	—			8	2	15	6	2.50
35*		13	1					—	3							9	3	140	38*	23.33
		—	0*	2*	—	3*	0			2*	0			0	—	10	5	34	12*	6.80
71	—	27	8					46	3*			10	16			18	2	409	91	25.56
135*				8	54*			37*	0			44	18	24	103	13	4	497	135*	55.22
10	—			36	—			—	9			11*	—			9	2	131	36	18.71
30	—			2	—			6*	40			9	0			9	2	146	40	20.85
		3*	17			18	3			13	28			11	8*	11	4	158	40*	22.57
										0	0	1	—	4	0	5	—	5	4	1.00
11		4		3		4	1	1				3	1	4	1					
2		13	3	6	6	19	2	3			9	1	3	6	8					
		3	1					1			2	1		1	1					
5		12	14			21	11	8	4	6	18	3	3	4	7					
415		401	111	293	241	258	121	240	237	130	402	236	176	352	344					
8		9	10	10	3	10	10	5	8	10	10	10	3	10	9					
D		L		W		L		D		L		W		D						

Australians
First-Class Matches – Bowling, 1981

	R. M. Hogg	T. M. Alderman	G. F. Lawson	R. J. Bright	G. R. Beard	D. K. Lillee
v. Hampshire (Southampton) 20–22 May	18–6–36–2	16–2–41–1	13–3–39–0	15–4–36–0		
v. Somerset (Taunton) 23–25 May	4–0–17–0	4–4–0–0			1–0–5–0	
v. Glamorgan (Swansea) 27–29 May		4–1–8–0	7–1–34–0	8–2–18–3	6–1–20–1	
v. Gloucestershire (Bristol) 31 May–2 June	9–4–37–1		6–0–27–1		7–4–12–0	
v. Derbyshire (Derby) 10–12 June		21–5–38–4		24.3–10–43–2	17–5–38–1	24–9–53–2
		13–8–18–2		25–9–55–1	9–4–15–0	19–8–38–0
v. Middlesex (Lord's) 13–15 June	15–6–19–1		15–5–34–2	11.3–2–33–2		11–1–41–5
	12–2–33–0		16–3–47–1	24–5–57–2		12–3–26–1
First Test Match (Trent Bridge) 18–21 June	11.4–1–47–3	24–7–68–4	8–3–25–0			13–3–34–3
	3–1–8–0	19–3–62–5				16.4–2–46–5
v. Kent (Canterbury) 27–29 June	8–5–9–0		21–4–72–5	1–1–0–0	14–1–55–1	
Second Test Match (Lord's) 2–7 July		30.2–7–79–1	43.1–14–81–7	15–7–31–1		35.4–7–102–0
		17–2–42–1	19–6–51–1	36–18–67–3		26.4–8–82–3
v. Northamptonshire (Northampton) 11–13 July	18.4–2–87–6		15–4–45–2	17–4–55–1	16–7–39–1	
	11–2–46–1		6–1–20–1	30–12–57–5	13.1–4–32–0	
Third Test Match (Leeds) 16–21 July		19–4–59–3	13–3–32–3	4–0–15–0		18.5–7–49–4
		35.3–6–135–6	23–4–96–1			25–6–94–3
v. Worcestershire (Worcester) 25–27 July	16–6–42–3	7–2–17–1		25–8–48–3	27–10–51–3	
	21–1–64–3	12.5–2–49–1		35–12–117–3	26–8–61–1	
Fourth Test Match (Edgbaston) 30 July–2 August	16–3–49–1	23.1–8–42–5		12–4–20–2		18–4–61–2
	10–3–19–0	22–5–65–3		34–17–68–5		26–9–51–2
v. Essex (Chelmsford) 8–10 August	5–1–14–0		6–1–25–0	22–9–49–1	17–5–61–1	
	8–1–12–1		7–1–24–1	8–4–17–0	23–2–92–4	
Fifth Test Match (Old Trafford) 13–17 August		29–5–88–4		16–6–30–0		24.1–8–55–4
		52–19–109–5		26.4–11–68–1		46–13–137–2
v. Sussex (Hove) 22–24 August	7–1–35–1			5.5–3–5–2	7–0–20–1	
	24–6–83–4			30.1–11–76–3	26–7–58–2	
Sixth Test Match (The Oval) 27 August–1 September		35–4–84–3		21–6–41–0		31.4–4–89–7
		19–6–60–2		27–12–50–0		30–10–70–4
	217.2–51–	402.5–100–	218.1–53–	473.4–177–	209.1–58–	377.4–102–
	657–27	1064–51	652–25	1056–40	559–16	1028–47
	av. 24.33	av. 20.86	av. 26.08	av. 26.40	av. 34.93	av. 21.87

a R. W. Marsh 0.2–0–0–1
b D. M. Welham 2–0–11–1; S. J. Rixon 2–0–19–0

A. R. Border	T. M. Chappell	K. J. Hughes	J. Dyson	G. N. Yallop	M. R. Whitney	Byes	Leg byes	Wides	No balls	Total	Wickets
							11	1	12	176	3
								1	2	25	0
							1		3	84	4
								1	3	80	2
5–0–13–0	4–1–18–0						5	2	8	218	9
9–5–12–1		3–2–3–0	1–0–2–0			11	5	1	3	163	5
1–0–4–0				2–0–5–0		1	3	1	9	150	10
6–1–24–1				15–1–62–0			9		3	261	5
							6	1	4	185	10
							3	1	7	147	6
							8		1	125	10
						2	3	3	10	311	10
						2	8		13	265	8
						1	7		18	252	10
		0.5–0–0–0		4–2–2–0			8		2	167	7
						6	11	6	11	174	10
						5	3	3	5	356	10
						10	4		17	189	10
3–0–12–0		2–0–11–0				5	10		15	344	8
						1	5	1	10	189	10
							6	1	9	219	10
				19–6–63–4		2			2	216	7 a
				17–2–80–1		5	8	2		270	8 b
					17–3–50–2		6	2		231	10
					27–6–74–2	1	12		3	404	10
				4–1–12–1	19–2–60–5	1			17	150	10
					5–1–21–1	8	5	1	9	261	10
					23–3–76–0		9	3	12	314	10
				8–2–17–0	11–4–46–1	2	5	2	9	261	7
24–6–	4–1–	5.5–2–	1–0–	69–14–	102–19–						
65–2	18–0	14–0	2–0	241–6	327–11						
av. 32.50	—	—	—	av. 40.16	av. 29.72						

29 and 31 August, 1 September   **at Colchester**
Essex 187 (R. C. Ontong 4 for 37) and 411 for 9 dec (G. A. Gooch 113, B. R. Hardie 114, A. W. Lilley 88, R. N. S. Hobbs 5 for 85)
Glamorgan 274 (Javed Miandad 81, N. G. Featherstone 59, D. L. Acfield 6 for 64) and 311 (Javed Miandad 200 not out, J. K. Lever 5 for 62)
Essex won by 11 runs
Essex 21 pts, Glamorgan 7 pts

at Bristol
Somerset 147 (P. Bainbridge 4 for 38, A. H. Wilkins 4 for 62) and 180 (J. W. Lloyds 75, J. H. Childs 9 for 56)
Gloucestershire 76 (C. H. Dredge 6 for 37, J. Garner 4 for 24) and 193 (Zaheer Abbas 72, J. Garner 6 for 56)
Somerset won by 58 runs
Somerset 20 pts, Gloucestershire 4 pts

at Bournemouth
Kent 323 for 6 dec (D. G. Aslett 146 not out, G. W. Johnson 70) and 112 for 2 (R. A. Woolmer 52)
Hampshire 153 (K. B. S. Jarvis 4 for 79, E. Baptiste 4 for 37) and 278 (C. G. Greenidge 69, N. E. J. Pocock 63, T. M. Tremlett 54)
Kent won by 8 wickets
Kent 23 pts, Hampshire 3 pts

at Leicester
Northamptonshire 300 for 4 dec (G. Cook 117, R. G. Williams 63) and 211 for 3 dec (A. J. Lamb 78 not out, G. Cook 71)
Leicestershire 251 for 9 dec (B. F. Davison 55, R. A. Cobb 54, D. I. Gower 53, R. G. Williams 5 for 101) and 263 for 6 (D. I. Gower 117 not out, P. B. Clift 73)
Leicestershire won by 4 wickets
Leicestershire 20 pts, Northamptonshire 8 pts

at Trent Bridge
Derbyshire 208 (A. Hill 79, E. E. Hemmings 7 for 59) and 146 (E. E. Hemmings 6 for 70)
Nottinghamshire 265 (J. D. Birch 62 not out, C. J. Tunnicliffe 5 for 75, D. S. Steele 4 for 37) and 90 for 1
Nottinghamshire won by 9 wickets
Nottinghamshire 23 pts, Derbyshire 5 pts

at Hove
Middlesex 154 (Imran Khan 4 for 41) and 157 (C. T. Radley 51, Imran Khan 6 for 52)
Sussex 252 (I. J. Gould 51, S. P. Hughes 5 for 94) and 60 for 0
Sussex won by 10 wickets
Sussex 23 pts, Middlesex 5 pts

at Worcester
Warwickshire 300 for 6 dec (D. L. Amiss 145, A. I. Kallicharran 82 not out) and 297 for 4 dec (T. A. Lloyd 120, G. W. Humpage 111)

Worcestershire 251 for 2 dec (G. M. Turner 147 not out) and 347 for 4 (G. M. Turner 139, D. N. Patel 138)
Worcestershire won by 6 wickets
Worcestershire 21 pts, Warwickshire 4 pts

at Leeds

Yorkshire 149 (S. N. Hartley 53, M. A. Holding 4 for 39, P. J. W. Allott 4 for 63) and 181 (M. A. Holding 6 for 76, P. J. W. Allott 4 for 78)
Lancashire 346 (C. H. Lloyd 145, D. P. Hughes 54, J. P. Whiteley 4 for 64)
Lancashire won by an innings and 16 runs
Lancashire 24 pts, Yorkshire 4 pts

Eddie Hemmings, with his best bowling performance in a championship match, was the hero who kept Notts 28 points clear at the top of the table. Notts now had the unenviable task of waiting for ten days before they could clinch the title. On the Saturday, Hill held Notts at bay for 84 overs while he scored 79 and it seemed Notts would be denied full bowling points, but Hemmings bowled Tunnicliffe with the last ball of the hundredth over. Then the dependable Birch saw them through. There was confidence and belief at Notts, and with their eagerness and determination, they were good to watch. So, too, were Sussex who kept hard on the heals of the leaders with a crushing victory over Middlesex. Once more Imran provided the bowling sparks, but it was a fine team performance, and one is confident that Sussex will carry off the highest honours in the next couple of years. Somerset clung on to their title hopes with a comfortable win on a bowler's paradise at Bristol – not a single batting point was gained. Defeat was hard for John Childs who, enjoying his best season, took nine for 56 with his naggingly accurate left-arm spin. It was the best Gloucestershire bowling performance for 32 years. Gloucestershire, in spite of their defeat, were showing that they were beginning to find that life without Procter was possible. Essex also maintained their challenge in a wonderful game at Colchester. They clawed their way back in the first innings with some more splendid bowling from David Acfield. How good that this wittiest and most cultured of men should enjoy such a successful benefit season. Then Gooch attacked again. His third century in eight days came in 85 minutes. Hardie, too, batted well as they added 169 for the first wicket. Appropriately, Robin Hobbs finished the innings with five wickets, but Glamorgan needed 325 in five and a half hours. Javed Miandad gave another display of verve, courage and delight and batted in a way that suggested that the visitors could win, but Lever denied them just in time for Essex. There were runs galore at Leicester where the consistent Geoff Cook furthered his claims for a place on the tour to India and David Gower hit a hundred to win the game. At Worcester, some more splendidly aggressive batting by Warwickshire was nullified once more by the limitations of their bowling. A century in each innings by Glenn Turner, the ninety-seventh and ninety-eighth of his career, set up Worcester's win. Patel batted excitingly in the second innings as Worcester, needing 347 in 210 minutes, won with 25 balls to spare. Lancashire's West Indian pair, aided by Paul Allott, cast gloom over Headingley. It was a miserable Yorkshire performance in an unhappy season. Kent won easily at Bournemouth and Derek Underwood took his two thousandth first-class wicket. The headlines were stolen, however, by Derek Aslett from Dover who, in his first first-class match, scored a hundred.

John Player League

30 August   **at Derby**
Derbyshire 190 for 5 (J. G. Wright 82)
Northamptonshire 152 (C. J. Tunnicliffe 5 for 24)
Derbyshire (4 pts) won by 38 runs

                                                        at Colchester

Glamorgan 133 for 7 (M. J. Llewellyn 50)
Essex 134 for 3
Essex (4 pts) won by 7 wickets

                                                          at Bristol
Warwickshire 201 for 7 (T. A. Lloyd 62, P. R. Oliver 58 not out)
Gloucestershire 191 for 8 (Zaheer Abbas 73)
Warwickshire (4 pts) won by 10 runs

                                                       at Canterbury
Middlesex 150 for 7 (W. N. Slack 52 not out)
Kent 151 for 5
Kent (4 pts) won by 5 wickets

                                                        at Leicester
Leicestershire 193 for 7 (D. I. Gower 64)
Surrey 194 for 5
Surrey (4 pts) won by 5 wickets

                                                        at Worcester
Somerset 163 for 9 (B. C. Rose 61)
Worcestershire 168 for 6
Worcestershire (4 pts) won by 4 wickets

                                                           at Leeds
Yorkshire 141
Lancashire 143 for 4
Lancashire (4 pts) won by 6 wickets

With Somerset suffering an unexpected reverse at Worcester, Essex and
Warwickshire now seemed in a straight fight for the title. Essex, celebrating
Fletcher's appointment as England captain, won with glorious ease at
Colchester. Glamorgan struggled with the bat except for Llewellyn who shone
in one of his rare appearances and then they were destroyed in five overs. Gooch
hit 42 off 26 balls and Essex won with 13.2 overs to spare. Derbyshire had
a confidence boosting win over their NatWest Final opponents and Warwickshire had a hard struggle to beat Gloucestershire whose hopes faded with
Zaheer's dismissal. Surrey and Kent won easily and Yorkshire received another
mauling in the Roses match.

2, 3 and 4 September   **at Leicester**
Middlesex 407 for 5 dec (G. D. Barlow 152, C. T. Radley 101 not out, J. M.
  Brearley 72)

Leicestershire 172 (J. E. Emburey 5 for 59) and 173 (J. E. Emburey 5 for 49, N. G. Cowans 5 for 58)
Middlesex won by an innings and 62 runs
Middlesex 24 pts, Leicestershire 2 pts

at The Oval
Kent 257 (Asif Iqbal 88, A. P. E. Knott 65, R. D. Jackman 4 for 90) and 204 for 8 dec (C. J. Tavare 53)
Surrey 115 (K. B. S. Jarvis 7 for 65) and 286 (A. R. Butcher 139, K. B. S. Jarvis 5 for 82)
Kent won by 60 runs
Kent 23 pts, Surrey 4 pts

at Hove
Sussex 416 for 7 dec (I. A. Greig 118 not out, C. M. Wells 111, G. D. Mendis 58) and 24 for 1
Hampshire 241 (J. M. Rice 101 not out, I. A. Greig 6 for 75) and 196 (I. A. Greig 4 for 57)
Sussex won by 9 wickets
Sussex 24 pts, Hampshire 5 pts

at Edgbaston
Somerset 300 for 6 dec (V. J. Marks 81 not out, P. M. Roebuck 72, B. C. Rose 70) and 220 for 5 dec (P. W. Denning 102 not out)
Warwickshire 225 (G. W. Humpage 59, T. A. Lloyd 51) and 253 (T. A. Lloyd 138, K. D. Smith 51, V. J. Marks 5 for 116, J. Garner 4 for 25)
Somerset won by 42 runs
Somerset 24 pts, Warwickshire 4 pts

The Schweppes County Championship reached a most exciting climax as Sussex and Somerset won victories which took them close to Notts. Sussex dwarfed Hampshire with some pulsating cricket. Put in to bat, Sussex responded with an exciting display, as Colin Wells, missed early on, hit his first hundred of the season, a lean one for him, and Ian Greig capped a marvellous year with a maiden century. There was dash from Mendis and Gould and then Hampshire succumbed twice to the buoyant Greig. Their consolation was a maiden century from Rice who was in his eleventh season with Hampshire. Sussex climbed to within four points of Notts and Somerset moved into third place with a surprise win at Edgbaston. There was a first hundred of the summer for Peter Denning after Somerset had gained a lead of 75 on the first innings. Warwickshire needed 196 in four and a half hours and with Lloyd batting brilliantly for a career best until superbly stumped off the persevering Marks, they seemed at least sure of a draw. Then Joel Garner took three wickets in four balls to bring Somerset a tense victory with three overs to spare. Middlesex piled up the runs at Leicester and dismissed the home side twice to win comfortably. Phil Edmonds did the hat-trick, John Emburey displayed his immaculate control and, in his first championship game, Cowans bowled quickly and impressively. Jarvis, in a fine year, returned his career best match figures of 12 for 147 to give Kent victory at The Oval in spite of Butcher's fine knock.

Fenner Trophy

2 September   **at Scarborough**
Essex 262 for 8 (A. W. Lilley 72, B. R. Hardie 64, K. S. McEwan 59)
Northamptonshire 252 for 7 (T. J. Yardley 68, R. J. Boyd-Moss 55)
Essex won by 10 runs

3 September
Yorkshire 245 for 7 (K. Sharp 107, J. H. Hampshire 56)
Worcestershire 224 for 9
Yorkshire won by 21 runs

Final—4 September
Yorkshire 264 for 5 (J. H. Hampshire 84 not out, K. Sharp 57)
Essex 262 for 8 (A. W. Lilley 86, B. R. Hardie 55)
Yorkshire won by 2 runs

Beautiful weather, excellent and exciting cricket watched by large crowds, provided a fitting festival and a grand finale for the last Fenner Trophy.

National Westminster Bank Trophy Final

It was not expected that the final of the new NatWest Trophy could produce a match to compare in excitement with the two semi-finals, but it did just that. Wood won the toss and asked Northants to bat, a decision which looked unwise as Cook and Larkins plundered 99 for the first wicket. Wood himself broke the stand when he had Larkins, who had batted with that mixture of belligerence and beauty that makes him such an appealing batsman, well caught at square-leg on the boundary by Miller. Allan Lamb, for whom the stage was now set, failed to exploit the situation and was narrowly run out after twelve hesitant overs. Williams was blatantly positive, but he was wonderfully caught on the boundary by the falling Alan Hill when he hit Miller back over his head. Willey was wastefully run out and the rest stuttered, particularly against Tunnicliffe who returned to bowl splendidly after a loose opening spell in which he had been savaged. He claimed Cook who had held the Northants innings together with his usual composure and certainty. His century had become axiomatic, but the final Northants total was below what had been expected after that fine start. Hill and Wright began a little circumspectly and when Hill was out 14 overs had gone for 41. Much now depended on Kirsten and Wright and they did not disappoint. Gradually the tempo increased and Wright confirmed one's opinion that off the back foot he was among the very best of players. One hundred and twenty-three had been added and Wright had just pulled Mallender into the tavern when he was lbw the same over and one run later, in the same over, Kirsten went the same way. Wood and Barnett batted with sense and vigour; Steele was out as soon as he attempted to hit the ball. Miller provided the hope and Tunnicliffe the final panache. 34 were needed off four overs. Miller deposited Sarfraz's full toss into the tavern. Twenty were needed off three overs, but Barnett had been run out. Then Tunnicliffe smashed boundaries square and straight, 12 runs came in Sarfraz's last over. Seven were needed off the last over. A two to Miller and a single, and then the realisation that only one was needed off the last ball to tie the scores and so give Derby-shire victory. The bowler was Griffiths, the hero of the semi-final. The field closed in and Tunnicliffe swung and padded away and ran. Miller dived home and then flung his arms in the air as Lord's was engulfed with excited fans and Tunnicliffe and Miller, for whom the season had been so disappointing and now so triumphant, embraced each other in the middle of the arena. Geoff Cook was named Man of the Match, but Barry Wood clasped the trophy.

National Westminster Bank Trophy Final   Derbyshire *v.* Northamptonshire

5 September   **at Lord's**

Northamptonshire

G. Cook (capt)	lbw, b Tunnicliffe	111
W. Larkins	c Miller, b Wood	52
A. J. Lamb	run out	9
R. G. Williams	c Hill, b Miller	14
P. Willey	run out	19
T. J. Yardley	run out	4
*G. Sharp	c Kirsten, b Tunnicliffe	5
Sarfraz Nawaz	not out	3
N. A. Mallender	c Taylor, b Newman	0
T. M. Lamb	b Hendrick	4
B. J. Griffiths		
Extras	b 2, lb 9, w 1, nb 2	14
	(for 9 wkts)	235

	O	M	R	W
Hendrick	12	3	50	1
Tunnicliffe	12	1	42	2
Wood	12	2	35	1
Newman	12	—	37	1
Steele	5	—	31	—
Miller	7	—	26	1

Fall of Wickets
1–99, 2–137, 3–168, 4–204, 5–218, 6–225, 7–227, 8–227, 9–235.

Derbyshire

A. Hill	b Mallender	14
J. G. Wright	lbw, b Mallender	76
P. N. Kirsten	lbw, b Mallender	63
B. Wood (capt)	b Sarfraz	10
K. J. Barnett	run out	19
D. S. Steele	b Griffiths	0
G. Miller	not out	22
C. J. Tunnicliffe	not out	15
*R. W. Taylor		
P. G. Newman		
M. Hendrick		
Extras	b 5, lb 7, w 3, nb 1	16
	(for 6 wkts)	235

	O	M	R	W
Sarfraz Nawaz	12	2	58	1
Griffiths	12	2	40	1
Mallender	10	1	35	3
Willey	12	—	33	—
T. M. Lamb	12	—	43	—
Williams	2	—	10	—

Fall of Wickets
1–41, 2–164, 3–165, 4–189, 5–191, 6–213.

Derbyshire won on losing fewer wickets

John Player League
6 September   **at Chelmsford**
Middlesex 190 for 7 (R. O. Butcher 88)
Essex 192 for 7 (K. S. McEwan 109)
Essex (4 pts) won by 3 wickets

                                                             at Cardiff

Glamorgan 159 for 8 (Javed Miandad 85)
Somerset 161 for 7 (I. T. Botham 50 not out)
Somerset (4 pts) won by 3 wickets

                                                             at Bournemouth

Leicestershire 225 for 3 (N. E. Briers 119 not out)
Hampshire 228 for 5 (J. M. Rice 58, C. L. Smith 51)
Hampshire (4 pts) won by 5 wickets

                                                             at Canterbury

Kent 96
Warwickshire 99 for 1 (T. A. Lloyd 53 not out)
Warwickshire (4 pts) won by 9 wickets

                                                             at Trent Bridge

Nottinghamshire 210 for 4 (B. Hassan 55, C. E. B. Rice 52, J. D. Birch 51)
Gloucestershire 181 for 9 (E. E. Hemmings 5 for 27)
Nottinghamshire (4 pts) won by 29 runs

                                                             at The Oval

Worcestershire 183 for 8 (D. N. Patel 82)
Surrey 185 for 2 (D. B. Pauline 92)
Surrey (4 pts) won by 8 wickets

                                                             at Hove

Derbyshire 170 for 5 (J. G. Wright 73)
Sussex 173 for 5
Sussex (4 pts) won by 5 wickets

For Derbyshire there was something of a hang-over and they fell at Hove with
Ian Greig again to the fore. A superb hundred by Nigel Briers was unable
to save Leicestershire from defeat in their last match and Duncan Pauline, back
in the Surrey side, was run out for a match-winning 92 against Worcester.

Somerset enhanced their chance of prize money with a win at Cardiff and Notts, blooding some youngsters like Ian Pont, brother of Essex's Keith, disposed of Gloucester. But these were academic exercises compared to the real contests at Canterbury and Chelmsford. Kent gave the season's most inept performance against Warwickshire for whom Steve Perryman, the old faithful, dismissed Asif and Cowdrey with successive deliveries. Woolmer hit Kent's only boundary and Warwickshire won with over eleven overs to spare. There was a sharp contrast at Chelmsford where Essex and Middlesex contrived a marvellous game. Lever had Barlow in the first over, but Radley, Gatting and then Butcher displayed fine form. Butcher was in the mood of uninhibited aggression that marked his success in 1980 and hit 88 in 24 overs. He was particularly savage on the inexperienced Pringle whom he hit for two sixes. Essex had an unhappy start, losing Hardie and Gooch for 27, but Fletcher joined McEwan in a splendid stand of 106 in 19 overs. Phillip and Lilley went quickly, but Turner and McEwan saw Essex to within sight of victory. They added 38 and McEwan hit Edmonds onto the Riverside Stand and into the pavilion to move from 97 to 109, but then he mis-hit Emburey and Essex needed 3 to win off the last over with Turner at the non-striker's end. East was caught and bowled second ball. Pringle pushed forward at the third ball of the over and edged the fourth to the vacant third man boundary and Essex had one hand on the trophy.

9, 10 and 11 September   **at Cardiff**
Glamorgan 323 for 9 dec (A. Jones 82, N. G. Featherstone 68, R. C. Ontong 54, A. M. E. Roberts 5 for 71) and 196 for 8 dec (Javed Miandad 105 not out, A. M. E. Roberts 5 for 49)
Leicestershire 282 (D. I. Gower 62, M. A. Nash 5 for 81) and 5 for 1
Match drawn
Glamorgan 8 pts, Leicestershire 7 pts

                                                                at Old Trafford
Lancashire 182 (A. H. Wilkins 8 for 57) and 230 for 8 dec (I. Cockbain 85)
Gloucestershire 219 (A. J. Hignell 80 not out) and 63 for 0
Match drawn
Gloucestershire 6 pts, Lancashire 5 pts

                                                                     at Uxbridge
Surrey 411 (G. S. Clinton 114, A. R. Butcher 75, M. A. Lynch 58, J. E. Emburey 5 for 134, P. H. Edmonds 4 for 121) and 145 (J. E. Emburey 5 for 37)
Middlesex 392 for 8 dec (M. W. Gatting 169, W. N. Slack 60, Intikhab Alam 4 for 133) and 165 for 4 (C. T. Radley 56 not out)
Middlesex won by 6 wickets
Middlesex 23 pts, Surrey 7 pts

                                                                      at Taunton
Somerset 408 (I. V. A. Richards 128, I. T. Botham 88, P. M. Roebuck 70, J. K. Lever 6 for 97)
Essex 211 (B. R. Hardie 98) and 240 for 6 (G. A. Gooch 122)
Match drawn
Somerset 8 pts, Essex 6 pts

Warwickshire 345 for 9 dec (A. M. Ferreira 67 not out) and 335 (D. L. Amiss
56, A. M. Ferreira 54, A. I. Kallicharran 54, G. W. Humpage 50, J. W.
Southern 5 for 108, N. G. Cowley 4 for 134)
Hampshire 300 for 1 dec (J. M. Rice 161 not out, C. L. Smith 81 not out)
and 334 for 8 (T. E. Jesty 99, C. G. Greenidge 64, A. M. Ferreira 4 for 73)
Match drawn
Hampshire 8 pts, Warwickshire 4 pts

Yorkshire 287 (D. L. Bairstow 62, J. D. Love 57, T. M. Lamb 4 for 68) and
236 (J. H. Hampshire 120, B. J. Griffiths 4 for 43)
Northamptonshire 232 (W. Larkins 61, A. Sidebottom 5 for 35, C. M. Old 4
for 53) and 135 (G. B. Stevenson 7 for 46)
Yorkshire won by 156 runs
Yorkshire 23 pts, Northamptonshire 6 pts

Having made a public statement that he wanted a showdown with manager
Illingworth as to why he had been omitted from Yorkshire's side for the Fenner
Trophy and for the friendly against Barbados, Geoff Boycott arrived at Scarborough to find himself ordered out of the dressing-room and suspended for
the rest of the season. The civil war and discontent which had smouldered
all season was now debate for all. John Hampshire, who had lived through
this before, scored a fine hundred and Stevenson bowled fiercely so that Yorkshire won, but it was a sorry state for this proud county. Having tasted glory,
Rice hit another hundred, a career best, for Hampshire and Warwickshire were
doomed to bottom place in the table. Rain ended play at Cardiff after some
more fine batting from Javed and career bests from Wilkins and Cockbain
were highlights of a limp draw at Old Trafford. Runs flowed and spinners
bowled mammoth spells at Uxbridge and Gatting made the best score of his
career as Middlesex won a match of great entertainment. Gooch, captaining
Essex, asked Somerset to bat and though Essex met with early success, the
flashing blades of Richards and Botham buried their championship hopes.
Gooch batted brilliantly in the second innings to save the day for Essex, who
were also helped by the weather, and only Sussex could now rob Notts of the
title.

John Player League

13 September   **at Derby**
Middlesex 218 for 7 (G. D. Barlow 71, R. O. Butcher 70)
Derbyshire 138 for 4 (J. G. Wright 64 not out)
Derbyshire (4 pts) won on faster scoring rate

at Bristol
Gloucestershire 135 for 4 (B. C. Broad 58) v. Lancashire.
Match abandoned.
Gloucestershire 2 pts, Lancashire 2 pts

at Southampton

Northamptonshire 192 for 7
Hampshire 194 for 4 (D. R. Turner 82 not out)
Hampshire (4 pts) won by 6 wickets

at Canterbury

Worcestershire 206 for 9 (Younis Ahmed 64)
Kent 149 for 7 (M. R. Benson 88)
Worcestershire (4 pts) won on faster scoring rate

at Trent Bridge

Glamorgan 145 for 7 (N. G. Featherstone, 57, N. Illingworth 4 for 39)
Nottinghamshire 146 for 3
Nottinghamshire (4 pts) won by 7 wickets

at Taunton

Somerset 211 for 6 (I. V. A. Richards 101)
Warwickshire 153 for 7 (P. R. Oliver 55)
Somerset (4 pts) won by 58 runs

at The Oval

Essex 203 for 7 (N. Phillip 80 not out)
Surrey 182 for 5 (G. R. J. Roope 60 not out)
Essex (4 pts) won by 21 runs

at Hove

Match abandoned
Sussex 2 pts, Yorkshire 2 pts

All interest was centred on the games at Taunton and The Oval. At Taunton rain delayed the start and the game was reduced to 28 overs. Somerset were 24 for 3, but Richards ended Warwickshire's dreams of glory with a century of savage power off 59 deliveries. He hit six sixes and eight fours and Warwickshire were doomed. It mattered little for Essex were in winning vein at the Oval. They were put in and lost Gooch early, but Hardie and Fletcher played well, and then came Norbert Phillip. His future with Essex had been uncertain, but he had just signed a contract for one more year and now he celebrated in magnificent fashion. He batted for 18 overs and hit four mighty sixes and two fours. He was given splendid support by the admirable Turner. Thirty-seven runs came off the last two overs, 34 of them to Phillip. Essex bowled tightly, particularly Ray East, who flighted and spun the ball appreciably, and David East had another outstanding game behind the wicket. Surrey played with determination, but the target was always just out of reach and so Essex won the title. It had evaded them so narrowly over the years and none could begrudge them what had been hard earned.

John Player League – Final Table

	P	W	L	NR	T	Pts
Essex (14)	16	12	3	1	0	50
Somerset (2)	16	11	5	0	0	44
Warwickshire (1)	16	10	4	2	0	44
Derbyshire (6)	16	10	5	1	0	42
Sussex (9)	16	8	5	3	0	38
Hampshire (11)	16	8	7	1	0	34
Kent (11)	16	7	7	1	1	32
Surrey (5)	16	7	7	2	0	32
Yorkshire (14)	16	6	6	4	0	32
Glamorgan (17)	16	6	8	2	0	28
Lancashire (13)	16	6	8	1	1	28
Nottinghamshire (14)	16	6	8	2	0	28
Worcestershire (6)	16	7	9	0	0	28
Leicestershire (4)	16	5	9	2	0	24
Middlesex (3)	16	4	9	3	0	22
Gloucestershire (10)	16	3	9	4	0	20
Northamptonshire (6)	16	4	11	1	0	18

1980 positions in brackets

12, 14 and 15 September   **at Derby**
Middlesex 372 for 3 dec (M. W. Gatting 186 not out, J. M. Brearley 145) and
152 for 7 dec (W. N. Slack 68 not out)
Derbyshire 286 (A. Hill 107, P. H. Edmonds 5 for 93, J. E. Emburey 4 for
124)
Match drawn
Middlesex 5 pts, Derbyshire 2 pts

at Bristol
Gloucestershire 281 for 9 dec (B. C. Broad 115 not out) and 0 for 0 dec
Leicestershire 0 for 0 dec and 177 for 7 (R. W. Tolchard 51 not out)
Match drawn
Leicestershire 4 pts, Gloucestershire 3 pts

at Southampton
Hampshire 305 (V. P. Terry 94 not out, C. L. Smith 68, B. J. Griffiths 6 for
73, N. A. Mallender 4 for 92)
Northamptonshire 228 for 2 dec (G. Cook 106 not out, R. G. Williams 103)
Match drawn
Northamptonshire 6 pts, Hampshire 4 pts

at Canterbury
Kent 301 for 3 dec (C. J. Tavare 135 not out, C. S. Cowdrey 72) and 0 for
0 dec
Worcestershire 38 for 2 dec and 186 for 9 (G. W. Johnson 4 for 42)
Match drawn
Kent 4 pts, Worcestershire 1 pt

at Trent Bridge

Glamorgan 60 (R. J. Hadlee 4 for 18, K. E. Cooper 4 for 25) and 149 (Javed Miandad 75, R. J. Hadlee 4 for 38, E. E. Hemmings 4 for 51)

Nottinghamshire 180 (M. A. Nash 4 for 48) and 30 for 0

Nottinghamshire won by 10 wickets

Nottinghamshire 21 pts, Glamorgan 4 pts

at Taunton

Warwickshire 375 for 6 dec (A. I. Kallicharran 119, G. W. Humpage 65) and 0 for 0 dec

Somerset 0 for 0 dec and 378 for 6 (P. M. Roebuck 89 not out, B. C. Rose 75, I. V. A. Richards 59, I. T. Botham 56)

Somerset won by 4 wickets

Somerset 18 pts, Warwickshire 4 pts

at The Oval

Essex 276 (K. S. McEwan 102, K. W. R. Fletcher 72, R. D. Jackman 5 for 83) and 252 for 3 dec (K. W. R. Fletcher 128 not out, B. R. Hardie 85 not out)

Surrey 288 for 6 dec (M. A. Lynch 120 not out, C. J. Richards 60 not out, N. Phillip 4 for 73) and 244 for 5 (A. R. Butcher 154 not out)

Surrey won by 5 wickets

Surrey 23 pts, Essex 5 pts

at Hove

Yorkshire 153 (Imran 4 for 11, A. N. Jones 4 for 33) and 198 (J. H. Hampshire 53)

Sussex 250 for 5 dec (C. M. Wells 80) and 102 for 2

Sussex won by 8 wickets

Sussex 23 pts, Yorkshire 3 pts

At 1.45 on Monday, 14 September Malcolm Nash bowled a no-ball and Notts had beaten Glamorgan by ten wickets to become county champions for the first time since 1929. On the Saturday, Rice had once more invited the opposition to bat and Glamorgan had been devastated by Hadlee and Cooper. Notts had reached a lead of 120 and then Hadlee and Hemmings put out Glamorgan for the second time in spite of resistance from the great Javed Miandad. It had been deserved triumph for Notts. They were a workmanlike side with inspiring leadership. They always played to win and if their batting was at times a little vulnerable, their bowling, both home and away, touched great heights. Hadlee was magnificent and Eddie Hemmings enjoyed a marvellously successful year which is the right of such a happy cricketer. With a fierce attack with bat and ball, Sussex clinched second place, richly deserved. Imran was again splendid and this eager side, led by the colourful, and sometimes eccentric, Barclay, must surely win the title within the next two years. It was symbolic of Yorkshire's season that they should bat two short in the second innings. In a final attempt to beat the weather innings were forfeited, but without bringing a result at Bristol and Canterbury where Tavare tuned up for the Indian tour. At Taunton, however, there was a marvellous finish to the season as Somerset reached their target of 376 with five overs to spare. They scored at seven runs an over and won third place in the table. They are a mighty side in this mood and if their attack occasionally looks thin, they are still the most fearsome of adversaries. The much improved Hampshire ended their match with Northants, a disappointing side, on a note of farce. Williams and Cook hit centuries, but Hampshire's main objective was to bowl as many overs to the hour as possible to avoid being fined. Alan Hill, that honest professional, held Middlesex at bay, but the last year's champions held fourth place as Essex were beaten at The Oval. Monty Lynch hit a career best for Surrey and was well supported by Jack Richards, celebrating his selection for the England party. Keith Fletcher then hit a superb hundred, but the final honours went to Alan Butcher who steered Surrey to a notable victory. With him at the end was Intikhab Alam who left first-class cricket at the end of this match. With him went the last exponent of leg-spin bowling and cricket is the poorer. Within days of the season's close, Yorkshire committee held an all-day meeting which failed to resolve the Illingworth–Boycott problem, an enquiry was promised. Then it was announced that Miller, Hendrick and Steele would be leaving Derbyshire. Steele was to return to Northants. Cricket Year 1982 was already beginning.

Schweppes County Championship – Final Table

	P	W	L	D	Bt	Bl	Total Pts
Nottinghamshire (3)	22	11	4	7	56	72	304
Sussex (4)	22	11	3	8	58	68	302
Somerset (5)	22	10	2	10	54	65	279
Middlesex (1)	22	9	3	10	49	64	257
Essex (8)	22	8	4	10	62	64	254
Surrey (2)	22	7	5	10	52	72	236
Hampshire (17)	22	6	7	9	45	65	206
Leicestershire (9)	22	6	6	10	45	58	199
Kent (16)	22	5	7	10	51	58	189
Yorkshire (6)	22	5	9	8	41	66	187
Worcestershire (11)	22	5	9	8	44	52	172
Derbyshire (9)	22	4	7	11	51	57	172
Gloucestershire (7)	22	4	3	15	51	55	170
Glamorgan (13)	22	3	10	9	50	69	167
Northamptonshire (12)	22	3	6	13	51	67	166
Lancashire (15)	22	4	7	11	47	57	164
Warwickshire (14)	22	2	11	9	56	47	135

1980 positions in brackets

Worcestershire and Lancashire totals include 12 points for win in a match reduced to one innings.

Perhaps we should close the section on the English season with the contribution from JACK BAILEY, Secretary of the M.C.C. His work never ceases and in the cold of winter we should reflect on those who make the game possible for us.

These days the office of the Secretary looks out onto the Ground. To anyone with cricket in the soul it is a position to be envied, and to the steady stream of visitors from all over the world who call during the summer months there is little point or profit in trying to persuade them that there is virtually no opportunity to watch the cricket. In fact, the old desk at which the work is done is so tilted away from the window as to make viewing possible only by the conscious effort of a neck-twisting exercise.

I mention this because there is often (understandably) a misconception that leads to questions such as 'is it a full-time job?' or 'what did you think of Brearley's innings today?' And while the answer to the former is often best answered by drawing an analogy with the work of the farmer, who would be put out if you assumed he only worked during the harvest, the answer to the second, alas, is often along the lines that you haven't yet had the chance to read the evening paper.

In fact, of course, it's more than a full-time job: it's a form of human bondage with the great asset of being (mostly) involved with a way of life you admire and seek to uphold, with all the advantages of friendships and rivalries in a cause you believe in and the accompanying disadvantages on a large scale of having to settle – to paraphrase a bit of Lincoln – for reconciliation to the premise that: 'You can please all the people some of the time, you can even please some of the people all the time, but you cannot please all the people all the time.'

It must ever have been thus. The other evening when Winter was turning, nominally, towards Spring and a lengthy meeting had finished around about 7 pm, and the unofficial meetings which always follow were due, I sat, reflectively, surveying the ground and the view through the trees to the Nursery beyond. The desk, my desk, with its ten drawers, two large cupboards, inlaid leather top and air of solid dependability, caused the present to dwindle in importance beside the wealth of history represented on its scratched pen and paper-worn surface.

The desk had been handed down from Secretary to Secretary, my predecessor, Billy Griffith, once informed me. First occupied by the irascible Henry Perkins who had first taken office in 1876 as the fifth Secretary of M.C.C. (though only the third to be paid) it had in turn served the needs first of Sir Francis Lacey and then, throughout its hundred year life, four further Secretaries until as only the eleventh Secretary since the Club's formation in 1787, it had fallen to me.

As I sat there, the weight of tradition, never far away when you are at Lord's, seemed embodied in that desk and my mind turned over the lore handed down imperceptibly through the ages from Secretary to Secretary and how different things were now when compared with the days of Parkino the little bearded barrister who was reputed to have handed over the reins of office with the somewhat controversial advice: 'Don't take any notice of the bloody Committee.' And of Sir Francis himself, who at a time when the Club's powers were on the threshold of their zenith innovated and consolidated its position as the world-wide headquarters of the game.

The period between 1898 and 1926 when Sir Francis Lacey served the Club was undoubtedly one of growth for cricket and for M.C.C. There must have been considerable difficulties for the Secretary of M.C.C. to overcome and he must have derived considerable pleasure from the progress made during his time at Lord's. The forming of the Advisory County Cricket Committee, the formation of the Board of Control for Test Matches and of the Imperial Cricket Conference all came about during his day and the system within M.C.C. of Committee and Sub-Committee structure is very much the same today as it was then.

As I sat pondering this I wondered what the great man would have said at the changes that have since been wrought at Lord's and indeed within the whole world of cricket. When he left office membership of M.C.C. stood at 5,500. Apart from Test Matches, Oxford *v*. Cambridge and Gentlemen *v*. Players were the two most widely followed matches. India, New Zealand and West Indies had just been admitted to Test Match Cricket. The place of M.C.C. within the structure of society as a private members' club was secure and unquestioned in the natural order of things and it was the heyday of the amateur.

It is perhaps an interesting reflection of how things have changed in general that M.C.C. should now have eighteen thousand members. The Gentlemen *v*. Players match no longer exists, although the great majority of Players are gentlemen. Oxford *v*. Cambridge is often watched by less than five per cent of the crowd that used to turn out. There would not be many now to dispute the fact that West Indies are the most powerful team in the world or that the support given in quantity and volume in this country is second only to that bestowed upon them in their native islands.

The International Cricket Conference has grown in membership from the three original founder members to twenty-three, of whom six play Test cricket and all are able to take part in the Prudential World Cup. The intermix of Television, Sponsorship and the financial and promotional benefits of both; the occasional disadvantages of ever-increasing commercialisation of the game; the ceaseless probing of our highly sophisticated media in connection with what were previously matters of fact; and the emergence of cricket as a potent political weapon have all had an impact of enormous proportions on those who serve M.C.C.

All the issues surrounding the ownership and administration of Lord's: the staging of big matches: the provision of some two hundred and fifty teams to play against clubs and schools each season: the accommodation of the Cricket Council, the Test and County Cricket Board, the National Cricket Association and the Middlesex County Cricket Club: the administration of the International Cricket Conference and the responsiblity for the Laws of Cricket have become infinitely more complex. The basic principles by which the Club has steered itself through a hundred and ninety-four years remain the same. The pressures to depart from the strait and narrow are perhaps more prevalent than at any time in the Club's history but even in his day Sir Francis Lacey was accused of being 'over-rigid in interpretation of rules and regulations' as have been several Secretaries before and since and to refer back to that paraphrase of Lincoln ...

In this increasingly consultative and bureaucratic age the proliferation of paper is said once to have caused Sir Alec Douglas-Home, now Lord Home of The Hirsel, in his year of Presidency of M.C.C. to remark that 'as much paper passed through his hands as President of M.C.C. as he ever had to read when he was Prime Minister'. Things have not changed!

And yet life has its compensations. Several disparate items come readily to mind: the sight of a full house at Lord's basking in the sunshine which is for the staff who work so hard to achieve it a cause for quiet satisfaction: the evidence of love and affection for Lord's felt by so many cricketers from all over the world and none more so than those who have represented the old enemy, Australia: and above all, the fact of being at the heart of something which is so very much a part of the traditional English way of life.

First Class Averages
Batting

	M	Inns	NOs	Runs	HS	Av	100s	50s
Zaheer Abbas	21	36	10	2306	215*	88.69	10	10
Javed Miandad	22	37	7	2083	200*	69.43	8	7
A. J. Lamb	24	43	9	2049	162	60.26	5	14
I. V. A. Richards	20	33	3	1718	196	57.26	7	5
C. E. B. Rice	21	30	4	1462	172	56.23	6	6
P. N. Kirsten	21	35	6	1605	228	55.34	3	7
G. M. Turner	24	42	4	2101	168	55.28	9	6
M. W. Gatting	19	33	6	1492	186*	55.25	4	7
A. I. Kallicharran	13	23	6	923	135	54.29	3	4
C. J. Tavare	22	40	7	1770	156	53.63	4	12
Younis Ahmed	22	39	8	1637	116	52.80	3	9
P. R. Oliver	8	14	3	554	171*	50.36	2	1
G. W. Humpage	23	39	5	1701	146	52.02	6	7
C. G. Greenidge	19	30	1	1442	140	49.72	4	9
D. I. Gower	19	33	4	1418	156*	48.89	5	7
R. M. Ellison	7	11	6	237	61*	47.40		3
W. N. Slack	18	32	3	1372	248*	47.31	3	9
K. W. R. Fletcher	18	29	4	1180	165*	47.20	4	5
B. Wood	22	37	6	1439	153	46.41	3	8
P. W. G. Parker	23	41	10	1416	136	45.67	4	6
C. H. Lloyd	18	31	2	1324	145	45.65	1	10
D. W. Randall	18	24	5	1093	162*	45.54	3	6
J. M. Brearley	19	33	1	1445	145	45.15	6	5
A. R. Butcher	19	38	6	1444	154*	45.12	4	5
Asif Iqbal	19	31	3	1252	112	44.71	2	9
G. Cook	24	43	3	1759	146*	43.97	5	11
G. A. Gooch	16	31		1345	164	43.38	5	5
J. H. Hampshire	20	37	4	1425	127	43.18	4	6
B. Hassan	13	20	5	641	97*	42.73		6
I. T. Botham	16	24	2	925	149*	42.04	3	4
D. L. Amiss	22	41		1722	145	42.00	6	5
G. D. Mendis	22	40	3	1522	137	41.13	2	10
Imran Khan	18	27	6	857	107*	40.80	2	3
P. Bainbridge	22	36	11	1019	105*	40.76	2	8
W. Larkins	22	39	1	1545	157	40.65	4	8
P. M. Roebuck	22	34	8	1057	91	40.65		9
J. G. Wright	20	32	1	1257	150	40.54	4	6
D. L. Bairstow	23	38	11	1083	88*	40.11		10

	M	*Inns*	*NOs*	*Runs*	*HS*	*Av*	*100s*	*50s*
G. Fowler	24	42	3	1560	143	40.00	3	9
J. M. Rice	11	19	3	639	161*	39.93	2	2
G. D. Barlow	22	38	5	1313	177	39.78	4	3
B. F. Davison	22	35	5	1188	123*	39.60	1	9
K. S. McEwan	22	37	1	1420	141	39.44	6	6
A. Hill	22	32	8	940	107	39.16	2	5
S. Turner	20	30	10	782	73*	39.10		4
G. Boycott	16	28	2	1009	124	38.80	3	3
B. R. Hardie	23	39	4	1339	129	38.25	3	7
P. W. Denning	24	36	6	1087	102*	36.23	1	8
N. E. Briers	23	36	3	1195	116	36.21	3	5
J. D. Birch	20	27	6	757	111	36.04	1	5
C. T. Radley	23	40	7	1177	101*	35.66	1	7
J. C. Balderstone	23	39	3	1266	150*	35.16	3	5
D. Lloyd	21	35	3	1122	146*	35.06	3	3
A. Hignell	22	33	5	979	102*	34.96	1	5
P. A. Neale	23	41	5	1247	145*	34.63	4	3
T. A. Lloyd	23	43	1	1445	138	34.40	3	5
R. W. Tolchard	17	24	8	535	104*	33.43	1	2
J. D. Love	23	40	4	1203	161	33.41	2	6
R. G. Williams	23	38	2	1203	142*	33.41	3	6
C. L. Smith	8	15	2	428	81*	32.92		3
C. S. Cowdrey	17	27	4	757	97	32.91		6
J. W. Southern	13	13	6	230	46	32.85		
N. G. Featherstone	23	39	5	1105	113*	32.50	2	9
A. M. Ferreira	15	24	6	585	67*	32.50		3
R. J. Hadlee	21	26	3	745	142*	32.39	1	3
M. R. Benson	21	36	3	1063	114	32.21	2	6
D. N. Patel	22	40	4	1155	138	32.08	3	2
G. P. Howarth	8	16	1	480	110*	32.00	1	3
D. S. Steele	21	32	3	902	137	31.10	1	5
B. C. Broad	22	40	4	1117	115	31.02	1	6
K. P. Tomlins	10	16	3	403	79*	31.00		3
M. A. Lynch	19	37	6	958	120*	30.90	2	3
A. W. Stovold	21	35	5	927	104	30.90	1	6
T. E. Jesty	23	35	6	891	99	30.72		5
A. Jones	23	41	2	1192	109	30.56	1	5
N. Russom	10	17	5	366	65	30.50		3
J. A. Hopkins	23	41	1	1217	135	30.42	4	3
I. A. Greig	23	34	4	911	118*	30.36	1	4
T. J. Yardley	23	35	8	803	96*	29.74		4
B. W. Reidy	15	23	2	624	96	29.71		5
Sadiq Mohammad	18	32	1	917	203	29.58	2	2
D. P. Hughes	24	39	5	1002	126	29.47	1	5
A. P. E. Knott	21	32	5	795	70*	29.44		5
R. G. Lumb	15	25	1	706	145	29.41	1	3
A. W. Lilley	12	21		616	90	29.33		5
D. R. Turner	22	30	6	704	106	29.33	1	4
I. Cockbain	6	10	1	262	85	29.11		2
K. R. Pont	16	27	3	692	89	28.83		5
B. C. Rose	23	39	4	1005	107	28.71	1	5
P. B. Clift	11	17	2	430	73	28.66		2

	M	Inns	NOs	Runs	HS	Av	100s	50s
R. E. Hayward	7	13	3	285	101*	28.50	1	1
C. M. Wells	14	22	4	513	111	28.50	1	1
D. A. Graveney	20	22	7	427	105*	28.46	1	
D. R. Pringle	18	28	7	596	127*	28.38	1	3
G. S. Clinton	22	44	2	1191	123	28.35	3	6
K. Sharp	8	14		395	116	28.21	1	2
J. P. C. Mills	13	24	1	648	111	28.17	1	4
Sarfraz Nawaz	11	16	3	366	90	28.15		1
N. E. J. Pocock	15	15	1	393	63	28.07		2
S. J. G. Doggart	7	8	3	139	69*	27.80		1
R. C. Ontong	23	40	5	968	151*	27.65	2	2
F. C. Hayes	12	20	3	470	143	27.64	1	2
N. V. Radford	15	19	7	330	76*	27.50		2
D. J. Humphries	18	28	7	575	64*	27.30		3
J. F. Steele	19	32	2	819	116	27.30	1	6
R. G. B. Ellis	9	17		464	63	27.29		3
M. D. Moxon	11	19		518	116	27.26	2	
P. A. Todd	21	37	4	899	112	27.24	1	4
R. S. Cowan	8	15		406	113	27.06	1	2
M. J. Harris	8	10	4	162	44*	27.00		
M. S. Scott	19	37	1	968	109	26.88	1	6
M. C. J. Nicholas	19	32	5	721	101*	26.70	1	3
Asif Din	21	37	4	878	73*	26.60		4
T. M. Tremlett	16	25	1	636	88	26.50		4
J. R. T. Barclay	23	38	5	874	107*	26.48	2	3
R. T. Robinson	19	33	7	687	91	26.42		3
S. T. Clarke	10	14	1	342	100*	26.30	1	1
G. C. Holmes	14	23	8	394	70*	26.26		2
G. S. Le Roux	19	20	7	340	65*	26.15		1
I. J. Gould	21	26	3	594	52	25.82		2
D. Breakwell	12	13	2	284	58	25.81		3
R. D. V. Knight	22	42	1	1045	96	25.48		6
J. W. Lloyds	21	35	2	837	127	25.36	1	5
R. A. Woolmer	21	38	1	934	119*	25.24	1	4
K. D. Smith	16	28	3	630	93	25.20		5
C. J. Richards	19	31	4	680	63	25.18		4
S. N. Hartley	18	29	3	654	106	25.15	1	3
G. R. J. Roope	20	37	4	829	96*	25.12		5
C. R. Cook	6	12	2	249	79	24.90		1
A. Kennedy	24	42		1044	180	24.85	1	3
P. Willey	13	21	1	495	82	24.75		2
K. I. Hodgson	9	9	3	148	30*	24.66		
V. J. Marks	24	31	7	591	81*	24.62		3
C. W. J. Athey	22	40	2	930	123*	24.47	1	4
D. M. Smith	17	32	4	684	84*	24.42		3
J. Abrahams	14	22	4	438	74	24.33		2
C. P. Phillipson	21	30	10	485	56*	24.25		1
G. P. Thomas	6	12	1	263	52	23.90		1
N. Smith	10	12	4	191	41	23.87		
G. R. Dilley	14	14	6	189	56	23.62		1
K. J. Barnett	17	23	4	443	67*	23.31		3
G. W. Johnson	24	38	8	698	107	23.26	1	

	M	Inns	NOs	Runs	HS	Av	100s	50s
R. O. Butcher	20	33	3	695	106*	23.16	1	5
A. M. E. Roberts	11	17	2	347	57	23.13		2
R. A. Cobb	8	12		275	54	22.91		1
K. A. Hayes	7	12		273	59	22.75		2
D. C. Holliday	10	11	2	204	57	22.66		1
G. Sharp	21	29	5	544	69*	22.66		2
S. H. Wootton	6	11	2	204	77	22.66		1
N. Taylor	11	19	2	385	99	22.64		2
T. J. Boon	15	26	2	542	83	22.58		2
S. J. Windaybank	11	12	3	203	46*	22.55		
J. D. Inchmore	18	21	2	428	63*	22.52		1
C. M. Old	18	21	6	335	55	22.33		1
N. F. M. Popplewell	17	25	2	513	51*	22.30		1
M. A. Garnham	18	27	4	512	74	22.26		1
J. N. Shepherd	15	20	6	310	52*	22.14		2
A. Sidebottom	15	21	4	376	52*	22.11		1
N. Phillip	22	37	4	720	80*	21.81		3
E. J. O. Hemsley	20	30	5	540	73	21.60		1
T. D. W. Edwards	10	18	1	366	57	21.52		1
M. D. Marshall	17	23	3	425	75*	21.25		1
J. Simmons	16	22	6	340	65*	21.25		1
R. D. Jackman	20	26	10	331	51	20.68		1
M. J. Procter	7	11		225	46	20.45		
M. W. Stovold	8	10	3	142	39	20.28		
J. Garner	18	18	2	324	90	20.25		2
R. N. S. Hobbs	15	15	10	101	49*	20.20		
T. D. Booth-Jones	16	27		541	95	20.03		3
E. Baptiste	13	22	4	359	37*	19.94		
G. Miller	21	31	3	552	81	19.71		5
R. A. B. Ezekowitz	8	15		295	93	19.66		1
J. M. Knight	5	9	2	136	41*	19.43		
J. E. Emburey	18	21	4	330	57	19.41		1
M. S. A. McEvoy	11	19		367	56	19.31		3
E. A. Moseley	15	19	3	306	57	19.12		1
R. E. Dexter	8	14	3	209	57	19.00		1
N. Gifford	24	23	8	284	37*	18.93		
A. L. Jones	6	12	1	204	81	18.54		1
J. J. Rogers	8	14		253	54	18.07		1
G. G. Arnold	18	17	7	180	46*	18.00		
R. J. Boyd-Moss	17	32	3	522	84	18.00		3
R. M. Tindall	6	8	1	126	29*	18.00		
I. G. Peck	9	15	2	233	45	17.92		
W. W. Daniel	21	22	11	195	53*	17.72		1
D. J. S. Taylor	24	28	7	370	48*	17.61		
D. J. Thomas	14	24	5	323	47	17.00		
Intikhab Alam	17	31	3	469	79	16.75		2
P. R. Downton	23	29	6	382	44	16.60		
A. Ramage	6	9	2	116	52	16.57		1
K. Stevenson	24	23	9	232	31	16.57		
J. Birkenshaw	10	10		165	54	16.50		1
C. F. E. Goldie	11	13	2	181	77	16.45		1
C. E. Waller	22	15	6	148	51*	16.44		1

	M	Inns	NOs	Runs	HS	Av	100s	50s
C. Lethbridge	8	10	1	146	69	16.22		1
N. G. Cowley	23	29	1	451	67	16.10		2
R. E. East	20	25	4	333	47	15.85		
G. J. Parsons	19	23	7	252	50	15.75		1
R. J. Parks	23	29	8	330	37*	15.71		
P. H. Edmonds	23	31	6	391	93	15.64		1
D. J. Wild	6	10	3	106	30	15.14		
J. O. D. Orders	9	17	1	241	38	15.06		
J. H. Childs	22	18	10	120	20	15.00		
M. Hendrick	13	11	6	75	21	15.00		
P. B. Fisher	6	8	3	74	28*	14.80		
D. L. Underwood	23	21	10	162	50	14.72		1
R. W. Taylor	19	22	4	259	100	14.38	1	
J. P. Agnew	12	16	6	143	26	14.30		
M. W. W. Selvey	17	18	1	242	57	14.23		2
C. J. C. Rowe	5	10		142	54	14.20		1
P. I. Pocock	18	21	10	154	46	14.00		
S. J. O'Shaughnessy	14	18	2	223	38	13.93		
N. V. H. Mallett	7	12	2	139	52	13.90		1
A. J. Murley	6	11		152	48	13.81		
J. P. Whiteley	19	23	11	164	19*	13.66		
E. E. Hemmings	22	23	4	257	44	13.52		
G. B. Stevenson	20	27		355	57	13.14		1
H. R. Moseley	20	21	8	162	36*	12.46		
P. J. W. Allott	22	28	8	243	52*	12.15		1
R. G. D. Willis	13	18	5	149	33*	11.46		
B. N. French	20	23		261	31	11.34		
A. P. Pridgeon	24	22	11	122	30	11.09		
M. A. Holding	5	8	2	66	32	11.00		
N. G. B. Cook	25	25	8	184	62	10.82		1
J. Cumbes	10	9	4	54	19*	10.80		
J. G. Thomas	5	8	3	53	13*	10.60		
M. A. Nash	23	31	5	275	36*	10.57		
L. B. Taylor	21	16	9	74	22	10.57		
S. P. Henderson	6	9	1	83	37	10.37		
D. E. East	13	17	3	144	28	10.28		
C. J. Tunnicliffe	21	25	1	246	39	10.25		
S. Oldham	15	14	5	92	33	10.22		

(Qualification 8 inns; average 10.00)

Bowling

	Overs	Mdns	Runs	Wkts	Av	Best	10/m	5/inn
R. J. Hadlee	708.4	231	1564	105	14.89	7/25		4
S. T. Clarke	359.4	98	734	49	14.97	6/66		5
J. Garner	615.4	182	1349	88	15.32	7/25	4	7
A. N. Jones	83	11	283	17	16.64	4/33		
M. A. Holding	271.1	75	715	40	17.87	6/74	1	4
E. A. Moseley	355.4	88	842	52	18.11	6/23		2
A. Sidebottom	305.5	88	899	47	19.12	6/62		3
C. E. B. Rice	494.5	142	1248	65	19.20	6/44		1
I. A. Greig	477	100	1469	76	19.32	7/43	2	4

	Overs	Mdns	Runs	Wkts	Av	Best	10/m	5/inn
M. D. Marshall	531.3	166	1321	68	19.42	6/57		5
G. S. Le Roux	599.1	135	1582	81	19.53	8/107	1	3
P. J. Hacker	175.4	52	446	23	19.39	4/34		
T. E. Jesty	437.4	136	1033	52	19.86	6/25		3
E. E. Hemmings	808.5	263	1857	90	20.63	7/59	2	5
L. B. Taylor	547.1	131	1628	75	21.70	7/28		2
D. S. Steele	403	141	1019	46	22.15	7/53		4
Imran Khan	565.1	133	1464	66	22.18	6/52		2
W. W. Daniel	514.2	103	1494	67	22.29	6/64		2
D. A. Graveney	480.3	148	1078	48	22.45	6/54	1	3
D. L. Acfield	769.5	232	1719	76	22.61	8/55	1	3
J. R. Thomson	162.3	30	522	23	22.69	4/66		
D. L. Underwood	774.3	282	1788	78	22.92	7/93	1	5
P. J. W. Allott	673.5	174	1963	85	23.09	8/48		3
K. B. S. Jarvis	586.3	137	1885	81	23.27	7/65	2	5
C. H. Dredge	493.2	129	1286	54	23.81	6/37		2
N. A. Mallender	396.5	91	1170	49	23.87	6/37		1
P. G. Newman	359.5	65	1204	50	24.08	5/51		1
C. M. Old	472.3	149	1165	48	24.27	5/52		1
R. D. Jackman	608.3	142	1606	66	24.33	6/70		4
M. A. Nash	568.5	149	1728	71	24.33	7/62		2
Intikhab Alam	560.5	153	1585	65	24.38	5/44		3
J. E. Emburey	803.4	236	1782	73	24.41	7/88	3	8
K. Saxelby	99.4	24	293	12	24.41	4/64		
S. J. Dennis	162.1	36	490	20	24.50	5ı35		1
R. G. D. Willis	391.1	85	1036	42	24.66	8/43		2
Sarfraz Nawaz	251.5	46	815	33	24.69	6/84		1
A. R. Butcher	64.3	15	247	10	24.70	2/15		
J. D. Monteith	222.3	58	596	24	24.83	5/60		2
P. H. Edmonds	909	280	1814	73	24.84	6/93		3
A. M. E. Roberts	310.1	79	923	37	24.94	5/49	1	1
K. E. Cooper	423.3	125	1081	43	25.13	4/13		
J. Simmons	331.5	111	740	29	25.15	5/39		1
I. T. Botham	574.2	156	1712	67	25.55	6/90	1	4
P. Willey	297	98	589	23	25.60	5/46	1	2
J. K. Lever	680.5	148	2049	80	25.61	8/49	1	4
S. P. Hughes	355.1	67	1132	44	25.72	6/75		3
H. L. Alleyne	324.3	63	1019	39	26.12	8/43	1	1
J. H. Childs	770.4	229	1962	75	26.16	9/56		7
J. R. T. Barclay	387.5	96	969	37	26.18	4/47		
H. R. Moseley	436	101	1291	49	26.34	4/16		
B. J. Griffiths	682.5	196	1845	70	26.35	8/50		2
M. J. Procter	172.5	45	513	19	27.00	5/80		1
T. J. Taylor	351.1	99	751	27	27.07	5/81		1
S. Turner	485	132	1203	44	27.34	5/55		1
T. M. Tremlett	196	68	383	14	27.35	4/11		
D. J. Thomas	323.5	77	933	34	27.44	5/31		1
P. B. Clift	308.2	82	799	29	27.55	6/47	1	2
G. W. Johnson	627.3	177	1572	57	27.57	6/33		2
R. C. Ontong	457.5	96	1369	49	27.93	6/62	1	1
G. G. Arnold	458.1	122	1121	40	28.01	6/39		1
M. Hendrick	426.4	119	1013	36	28.13	5/41		1

	Overs	*Mdns*	*Runs*	*Wkts*	*Av*	*Best*	*10/m*	*5/inn*
R. E. East	680.2	190	1513	53	28.54	7/49	1	3
C. E. Waller	512.2	151	1264	44	28.72	5/36		2
T. M. Lamb	673.1	184	1698	59	28.77	4/31		
W. G. Merry	125	27	378	13	29.07	2/17		
E. Baptiste	280.2	63	844	29	29.10	5/37		1
J. F. Steele	322.3	86	787	27	29.14	4/31		
K. I. Hodgson	174.1	29	597	20	29.85	4/77		
M. K. Bore	476.5	158	1075	36	29.86	4/46		
C. M. Wells	89	19	299	10	29.90	4/48		
M. W. W. Selvey	388.2	114	1054	35	30.11	5/79		2
M. R. Whitney	223	49	726	24	30.25	5/60		1
J. Cumbes	306.3	76	848	28	30.28	5/69		1
G. B. Stevenson	537.4	122	1857	61	30.44	7/46		3
A. Ramage	148	22	550	18	30.55	5/65		1
P. Bainbridge	355.1	85	1009	33	30.57	5/68		1
N. G. B. Cook	829	272	2030	63	31.25	7/81		2
S. J. O'Shaughnessy	103.2	20	345	11	31.36	3/17		
J. C. Balderstone	159.3	43	444	14	31.71	4/17		
V. J. Marks	659.5	195	1571	49	32.06	5/34		2
G. J. Parsons	462.3	94	1452	45	32.26	4/44		
J. P. Agnew	221	48	775	24	32.29	5/72		1
B. J. Lloyd	619.3	142	1717	53	32.39	8/70		1
P. G. Lee	285.1	81	816	25	32.64	6/44	1	2
P. I. Pocock	603.1	190	1511	46	32.84	4/54		
R. N. S. Hobbs	390.3	99	1151	35	32.88	5/67		2
J. P. Whiteley	392	93	1124	34	33.05	4/50		
N. F. M. Popplewell	194.2	42	598	18	33.22	5/33		1
G. R. Dilley	281.5	57	936	28	33.42	4/23		
N. Phillip	518.1	87	1725	51	33.82	6/40		1
K. Stevenson	595.5	119	1966	57	34.49	5/32		3
R. G. Williams	612.1	163	1686	48	35.12	5/88		1
A. P. Pridgeon	673.1	119	1978	56	35.32	5/63		1
J. G. Thomas	80.3	10	355	10	35.50	4/65		
W. Hogg	546.2	109	1853	51	36.33	4/46		
A. H. Wilkins	630	146	1892	52	36.38	8/57		1
S. J. Malone	147	27	578	14	37.00	3/88		
D. P. Hughes	291.5	83	780	21	37.14	4/40		
C. J. Tunnicliffe	499.2	105	1563	42	37.21	5/34		3
N. Russom	246.5	56	710	19	37.36	2/28		
Sadiq Mohammad	102.4	15	412	11	37.45	3/34		
R. M. Carter	184.4	32	676	18	37.55	3/88		
D. Breakwell	241	44	719	19	37.84	6/38		1
G. C. Small	395.5	52	1590	42	37.85	6/76		
D. R. Pringle	383	85	1138	30	37.93	4/39		
B. M. Brain	205	49	609	16	38.06	3/34		
G. Miller	464.2	137	1281	33	38.81	4/27		
J. D. Inchmore	355	63	1166	30	38.86	5/85		1
N. Gifford	963.4	253	2476	63	39.30	6/67		1
S. P. Sutcliffe	434.1	81	1281	32	40.03	4/54		
P. Carrick	532.1	171	1412	35	40.34	4/76		
J. Abrahams	202.5	49	567	14	40.50	3/27		
J. N. Shepherd	422.3	111	1136	28	40.57	5/61		1

	Overs	*Mdns*	*Runs*	*Wkts*	*Av*	*Best*	*10/m*	*5/inn*
D. N. Patel	595.3	137	1749	43	40.67	5/76		1
R. D. V. Knight	285	82	741	18	41.18	2/18		
N. V. H. Mallett	152.5	35	455	11	41.36	5/52		1
N. G. Cowley	368.5	92	1134	27	42.00	4/134		
R. J. Boyd-Moss	136	35	465	11	42.27	2/24		
D. R. Doshi	669.3	163	1950	45	43.33	5/73		1
S. P. Perryman	305.4	64	1046	24	43.58	5/52		1
S. Oldham	314.2	55	1025	23	44.56	3/35		
I. V. A. Richards	185.5	38	585	13	45.00	4/55		
J. W. Southern	352.1	98	952	20	47.60	5/108		1
B. Wood	254.3	58	815	17	47.94	2/12		
A. M. Ferreira	436.3	83	1542	32	48.18	4/73		
J. W. Lloyds	144.2	29	482	10	48.20	3/12		
D. Lloyd	205.2	49	586	12	48.83	2/18		
N. V. Radford	303.2	64	1140	21	54.28	5/107		1
J. Birkenshaw	202.5	40	644	11	58.54	3/131		

(Qualification 10 wickets)

The Ashes retained. Whitney is caught by Gatting.

English Counties Form Charts

The statistics of all limited-over cricket matches follow in J172–J239. The games covered are:

John Player League (J.P.)	Tilcon Trophy (T.T.)
Benson and Hedges Cup (B.&H.)	Fenner Trophy (F.T.)
National Westminster Bank Trophy (N.W.T.)	

Once again averages are not produced as it is felt that they have little relevance in limited-over cricket where batsmen often sacrifice their wickets for quick runs and bowlers are ordered to contain rather than capture wickets.

The statistics of all first class matches are given on pages J240–J333. The games covered are:

Schweppes County Championship.

Matches against touring and representative sides.

In the batting tables a blank indicates that a batsman did not *play* in a game, a dash (—) that he did not *bat*. A dash (—) is placed in the batting averages if a player had 2 innings or less, and in the bowling figures if no wicket was taken.

Editor's Note

The editor wishes to express his deepest thanks to VICTOR ISAACS, the Hampshire C.C.C. scorer, for his corrections and advice.

Mr Isaacs is one of the country's leading statisticians, with particular reference to limited-over cricket. His research and pursuit of accuracy are renowned and we are deeply indebted to him.

Derbyshire C.C.C. Limited-Over Matches – Batting, 1981

	v. Yorkshire (Derby) 9 and 11 May (B.&H.)	v. Lancashire (Old Trafford) 10 May (J.P.)	v. Warwickshire (Edgbaston) 16 May (B.&H.)	v. Scotland (Derby) 19 May (B.&H.)	v. Lancashire (Old Trafford) 21 and 22 May (B.&H.)	v. Nottinghamshire (Derby) 24 May (J.P.)	v. Surrey (The Oval) 31 May (J.P.)	v. Hampshire (Derby) 14 June (J.P.)	v. Warwickshire (Edgbaston) 21 June (J.P.)	v. Gloucestershire (Gloucester) 28 June (J.P.)	v. Worcestershire (Chesterfield) 5 July (J.P.)	v. Suffolk (Bury St Edmunds) 11 July (N.W.T.)
J. G. Wright	47	4	10*	47	0		13	13	62	76	87	47
G. Miller	20	5	—	3*	74		38		42	—	36	57
P. N. Kirsten	65	30	6*	5	0		4	55	16	6*	29*	36
D. S. Steele	12	30	—	11	9		25	35	34	—	0*	89*
K. J. Barnett	7	26	—	—	17		7	4	17*	—	—	3*
K. G. Brooks	3	12										
B. Wood	10	9	4	32*	30		0	31	29	58*	—	5
C. J. Tunnicliffe	10	16	—	—	11		1*	10*	0	—		0
R. W. Taylor	14*	1	—	—	16		—	—	0*	—	—	—
M. Hendrick	0*	12*	—	—	2*		—	—	—	—	—	—
S. Oldham	—	1*			—		—	—	—	—	—	—
A. Hill			—	—			33*	15*	13	—		3
P. G. Newman			—	—	5*						—	
M. J. Deakin												
I. S. Anderson												
B. J. N. Maher												
A. J. Borrington												
Byes		1			5		5		1		5	1
Leg byes	8	16	1		3		11	8	17	9	4	24
Wides					9		2	9	1	1	2	3
No balls	6		2						1	1		2
Total	202	163	23	98	181		139	180	233	151	163	270
Wickets	8	9	1	3	8		6	5	7	1	2	6
Result	L	W	Ab	W	W	Ab	L	W	W	W	W	W
Points	0	4	1	2	2	2	0	4	4	4	4	—

Catches

31 – R. W. Taylor (ct 23, st 8)

11 – G. Miller

10 – J. G. Wright

9 – C. J. Tunnicliffe, B. Wood and D. S. Steele

8 – P. N. Kirsten

6 – S. Oldham

5 – K. J. Barnett

4 – A. Hill

3 – K. G. Brooks

2 – P. G. Newman and M. J. Deakin

1 – M. Hendrick and sub.

v. Somerset (Taunton) 19 July (J.P.)	v. Worcestershire (Worcester) 22–23 July (N.W.T.)	v. Kent (Derby) 26 July (J.P.)	v. Essex (Chelmsford) 2 August (J.P.)	v. Nottinghamshire (Derby) 5 August (N.W.T.)	v. Leicestershire (Derby) 9 August (J.P.)	v. Glamorgan (Swansea) 16 August (J.P.)	v. Essex (Derby) 19 and 20 August (N.W.T.)	v. Yorkshire (Chesterfield) 23 August (J.P.)	v. Northamptonshire (Derby) 30 August (J.P.)	v. Northamptonshire (Lord's) 5 September (N.W.T.)	v. Sussex (Hove) 6 September (J.P.)	v. Middlesex (Derby) 13 September (J.P.)
50	50	12	0	42	16	66*	1	0	82	76	73	64*
	2	16	1		52*	5*	0	0	2	22*	8	24
63	84*	22	24	38	50	8	8	63	25	63	22	8
—	5			12	12	0	7	9	—	0	—	—
8*	26	13	5	29*	10	16	59	34	35	19	27	3
2	10	41	31	5	16	20	18	1	21*	10	11*	15
27	—	1	1	2	1*	—	1	5	3	15*	17*	9*
	12*	26*		12			9*	12				
—	—	3	5*				—	0*		—		
—	—	10*	14	1			0		—			
21	18	33	5	1	7	0	21		3*	14	2	—
		0	3	8			7*	7				
—												
—												
			0									
				0								
				6	1	4			2	5		6
8	20	8	14	4	12	2	12	4	15	7	5	4
4		4	7	3	1	5	3	1	1	3	4	5
1	2	2		1		8	3	1	1	1	1	
184	229	187	110	164	178	134	149	137	190	235	170	138
5	6	9	10	10	6	5	8	10	5	6	5	4
L	W	W	L	W	W	W	W	L	W	W	L	W
0	—	4	0	—	4	4	—	0	4	—	0	4

Derbyshire C.C.C. Limited-Over Matches – Bowling, 1981

	M. Hendrick	S. Oldham	C. J. Tunnicliffe	G. Miller	B. Wood	D. S. Steele
(B.&H.) v. Yorkshire (Derby) 9 and 11 May	10–1–22–0	11–1–36–0	11–3–24–5	1.4–0–18–0	11–2–24–2	9–0–70–2
(J.P.) v. Lancashire (Old Trafford) 10 May	8–2–14–2	6–0–32–2	7–0–25–1	7–0–34–1	7–3–16–0	
(B.&H.) v. Warwickshire (Edgbaston) 16 May						
(B.&H.) v. Scotland (Derby) 19 May	10.3–2–18–4		11–4–19–2	11–3–20–1		7–3–7–2
(B.&H.) v. Lancashire (Old Trafford) 21 and 22 May	11–1–42–4	11–4–33–1	11–0–46–1		11–5–21–0	
(J.P.) v. Surrey (The Oval) 31 May	7–0–17–1	6.4–1–44 3	7–0–29–1	8–1–21–1	8–0–20–1	
(J.P.) v. Hampshire (Derby) 14 June	8–0–33–2	7–0–36–0	8–1–29–3		8–1–32–0	
(J.P.) v. Warwickshire (Edgbaston) 21 June		4.2–0–38–3	8–0–27–1	6–0–35–4	8–0–39–1	
(J.P.) v. Gloucestershire (Gloucester) 28 June	8–1–31–0	8–0–37–1	8–1–32–1	8–1–16–2	8–3–20–3	
(J.P.) v. Worcestershire (Chesterfield) 5 July	8–2–21–2	7–0–45–1			8–0–38–1	8–0–24–2
(N.W.T.) v. Suffolk (Bury St Edmunds) 11 July	8–3–8–0		7–5–7–2	12–3–28–2	12–6–14–2	3.3–0–23–2
(J.P.) v. Somerset (Taunton) 19 July	8–0–31–0	6–0–44–1	8–0–27–1		8–0–44–1	1.4–0–12–0
(N.W.T.) v. Worcestershire (Worcester) 22–23 July	12–3–31–0	12–3–48–1	12–1–50–5	12–1–53–2	12–3–32–1	
(J.P.) v. Kent (Derby) 26 July	8–1–40–1	8–0–24–3	8–2–26–2		8–0–31–2	
(J.P.) v. Essex (Chelmsford) 2 August	8–0–27–1	8–0–38–1	8–1–18–3		8–0–37–1	
(N.W.T.) v. Nottinghamshire (Derby) 5 August		11–0–29–3	7–3–27–0		12–4–22–2	12–4–23–2
(J.P.) v. Leicestershire (Derby) 9 August		7–1–30–1	7–0–18–0		7–0–43–2	7–0–36–3
(J.P.) v. Glamorgan (Swansea) 16 August	8–3–10–1		3–0–26–0	8–5–6–1	8–2–19–3	
(N.W.T.) v. Essex (Derby) 19 and 20 August	12–2–20–2		12–2–21–2	3–0–16–2	12–3–24–0	9–1–35–0
(J.P.) v. Yorkshire (Chesterfield) 23 August	8–1–43–3	8–2–29–0	8–0–37–0		8–0–44–1	
(J.P.) v. Northamptonshire (Derby) 30 August		8–0–41–0	7.1–0–24–5		8–0–28–1	8–2–22–2
(N.W.T.) v. Northamptonshire (Lord's) 5 September	12–3–50–1		12–1–42–2	7–0–26–1	12–2–35–1	5–0–31–0
(J.P.) v. Sussex (Hove) 6 September		6.2–0–28–0	7–0–34–0	8–0–27–2	4–0–16–0	
(J.P.) v. Middlesex (Derby) 13 September		8–0–48–2	7–1–27–2	1–0–18–0	8–0–40–3	6–0–43–0

P. N. Kirsten	P. G. Newman	K. J. Barnett	B	Lb	W	Nb	Total	Wkts
				6	1	2	203	9
			2	9	5	1	138	7
							Abandoned	
6–0–18–0	5–2–14–1					1	97	10
	11–1–30–1		1	5	1		179	7
			2	6	1		140	7
	8–0–30–1			6	11	2	179	7
	8–0–37–0			13	2		191	10
				13		1	150	7
	8–0–24–3		2	4	2		160	9
		4–1–19–1					99	10
5–0–24–0				5		1	188	3
			1	8	1	4	228	10
	8–0–38–0		2	8			169	9
	8–0–12–2			8	2		142	10
2–0–8–0	6.4–1–23–3			3	1	5	141	10
	7–0–21–1			6	1		155	9
4–0–15–1	8–0–36–2		8	8		4	132	9
	12–2–26–3			4		3	149	10
	8–0–49–1			6			208	6
	7–0–25–2		2	6	4		152	10
	12–0–37–1		2	9	1	2	235	9
4–0–15–2	8–1–35–0			13	3	2	173	5
	8–1–29–0			6	5	2	218	7

Essex C.C.C. Limited-Over Matches – Batting, 1981

	v. Glamorgan (Swansea) 9 May (B.&H.)	v. Somerset (Taunton) 10 May (J.P.)	v. Somerset (Chelmsford) 16 May (B.&H.)	v. Combined Universities (Chelmsford) 21 and 22 May (B.&H.)	v. Gloucestershire (Chelmsford) 24 May (J.P.)	v. Kent (Dartford) 30 May (B.&H.)	v. Kent (Chelmsford) 31 May (J.P.)	v. Nottinghamshire (Trent Bridge) 7 June (J.P.)	v. Worcestershire (Worcester) 14 June (J.P.)	v. Sussex (Ilford) 21 June (J.P.)	v. Leicestershire (Leicester) 28 June (J.P.)	v. Warwickshire (Edgbaston) 5 July (J.P.)
G. A. Gooch	4	2	138	5	15*	3	2		26		33	
B. R. Hardie	1	17	21	—	0			0*	23	58	1	41
K. S. McEwan	4	43	24	28	9	12	11	19	3	46	27	83*
K. W. R. Fletcher	18	3	62	15*	—	51	6*		61*	21	23	2
A. W. Lilley	18	1	2	63*	—	7	7	2	5	5		
K. R. Pont	23	14	0*	—	—	47*	—	8*	7	15	2	55*
N. Phillip	32	24	17*	—	0*	6	5*	—	7*	12	16*	26
S. Turner	10	28	—	—	—	0	—	—	—	9*	6*	—
R. E. East	0	—	—	—	—	1	—	—	—	0	—	—
N. Smith	0	0*	—	—	—	8	—	—	—	20	10	—
J. K. Lever	2*	—	—	—	—	0	—	—	—	1*	—	—
M. S. A. McEvoy					—	13	—	9			—	13
D. L. Acfield								—		—		
D. E. East												—
D. R. Pringle												—
Byes	1		2	5	4			1	7	1	5	
Leg byes	5	4	8	2		10		2	5	18	2	11
Wides	4	2	1	2		3	2		3	7		6
No balls	2	1	3	1					4	2		2
Total	124	139	278	121	28	161	33	41	151	215	125	239
Wickets	10	8	5	2	2	10	3	3	5	8	6	4
Result	L	W	W	W	Ab	L	W	L	W	L	W	W
Points	0	4	2	2	2	0	4	0	4	0	4	4

Catches

22 – D. E. East (ct 18, st 4)

12 – R. E. East

10 – K. S. McEwan

9 – J. K. Lever

7 – K. W. R. Fletcher and B. R. Hardie

6 – S. Turner and N. Smith (ct 4, st 2)

4 – N. Phillip

3 – G. A. Gooch

2 – M. S. A. McEvoy and K. R. Pont

1 – A. W. Lilley

v. Hertfordshire (Hitchin) 11 July (N.W.T.)	v. Lancashire (Southend) 19 July (J.P.)	v. Gloucestershire (Bristol) 22-24 July (N.W.T.)	v. Yorkshire (Chelmsford) 26 July (J.P.)	v. Derbyshire (Chelmsford) 2 August (J.P.)	v. Sussex (Hove) 5 August (N.W.T.)	v. Hampshire (Southampton) 16 August (J.P.)	v. Derbyshire (Derby) 19 and 20 August (N.W.T.)	v. Northamptonshire (Milton Keynes) 23 August (J.P.)	v. Glamorgan (Colchester) 30 August (J.P.)	v. Northamptonshire (Scarborough) 2 September (F.T.)	v. Yorkshire (Scarborough) 4 September (F.T.)	v. Middlesex (Chelmsford) 6 September (J.P.)	v. Surrey (The Oval) 13 September (J.P.)
101		35	100		33		14	28	42	22	1	15	8
81	16	6	108*	6	39	87	5	26	32*	64	55	0	33
5	0	9	22	10	33	67	28	1	28	59	9	109	18
51*	56		—	14	2	9*	4	20	18	15	20	35	27
	18	40		15	34	6		15	—	72	86	2	1
31	50*	5	—			—	20	0*		4	43		
4	30	4	2	10	0	8	42	83*	2*			1	80*
7	39*	30	4*	4	5	2*	0	25	—	2	29*	14*	23
0	—	22	—	18	0	—	6		—	—	0	0	0*
		3*	—	12	10*	—	4*						
				0									
7*	—	7	—	1	8*	—	18			1*	0*	—	—
6	—	16	—	42*	17	—	1	—		13	0	4*	0
1		3	2		1	3		1	6	4	1	3	4
5	7	20	9	8	8	10	4	10	1	4	11	5	9
2	1	4		2	2	1		1			2	3	
5		3	3		3	1	3	2	5	2	5	1	
306	217	207	250	142	195	194	149	212	134	262	262	192	203
8	5	10	3	10	9	4	10	6	3	8	8	7	7
W	W	W	W	W	W	L	L	W	W	W	L	W	W
—	4	—	4	4	—	0	—	4	4	—	—	4	4

Essex C.C.C. Limited-Over Matches – Bowling, 1981	J. K. Lever	N. Phillip	K. R. Pont	S. Turner	G. A. Gooch	R. E. East
(B.&H.) v. Glamorgan (Swansea) 9 May	11–4–33–2	11–3–29–3	11–1–36–0	11–1–48–1	11–0–45–1	
(J.P.) v. Somerset (Taunton) 10 May	6–3–12–1	6–0–29–2	6–1–24–0	6–1–17–1	3–0–15–2	3–0–11–1
(B.&H.) v. Somerset (Chelmsford) 16 May	8.2–2–26–1	9–2–54–1	11–0–50–2	11–0–51–4		11–0–38–1
(B.&H.) v. Combined Univ. (Chelmsford) 21 and 22 May	9.4–2–23–3	7–1–26–0	6–1–11–2	11–2–19–4	11–3–20–1	4–0–15–0
(B.&H.) v. Kent (Dartford) 30 May	9–0–41–1	11–3–19–0		8–3–23–0	5–0–20–0	8–1–38–1
(J.P.) v. Kent (Chelmsford) 31 May	2–0–5–0	3–0–13–0	5–2–13–2	2–0–4–0	4–0–9–0	
(J.P.) v. Nottinghamshire (Trent Bridge) 7 June	8–1–41–0	8–0–20–1	7–0–36–2	8–1–31–1		
(J.P.) v. Worcestershire (Worcester) 14 June	7–1–30–0	7–0–30–2	4–0–13–1	8–2–12–2	4–0–19–1	8–2–20–1
(J.P.) v. Sussex (Ilford) 21 June	8–0–43–1	7–1–24–1	4–0–17–1	8–1–35–1		8–0–41–1
(J.P.) v. Leicestershire (Leicester) 28 June	7–1–19–3	6–3–11–1	6–1–28–1	8–0–23–2	6–0–17–0	6–1–11–1
(J.P.) v. Warwickshire (Edgbaston) 5 July	4–1–14–1	4–0–23–0	6–0–22–4	4–1–10–1		8–0–36–1
(N.W.T.) v. Hertfordshire (Hitchin) 11 July	8–3–14–2	3–0–15–0	1.5–0–2–0	5–1–26–1	10.1–3–33–2	4.1–1–5–2
(J.P.) v. Lancashire (Southend) 19 July	8–0–28–4	8–1–29–0		8–1–33–1		8–2–32–1
(N.W.T.) v. Gloucestershire (Bristol) 22–24 July	7–3–15–2	9–3–12–3		12–2–24–0		5–2–6–1
(J.P.) v. Yorkshire (Chelmsford) 26 July	7–2–22–1	6.4–0–24–3		8–0–49–2		8–0–32–3
(J.P.) v. Derbyshire (Chelmsford) 2 August	5.4–2–19–2	5–0–14–0		4–1–10–1		8–0–32–3
(N.W.T.) v. Sussex (Hove) 5 August	10–1–25–3	11–0–27–1		11–3–31–2	5–2–10–1	7–0–40–1
(J.P.) v. Hampshire (Southampton) 16 August	7–0–52–0	8–0–36–0		8–0–40–0		8–1–31–0
(N.W.T.) v. Derbyshire (Derby) 19 and 20 August	12–4–22–2	12–2–42–3		12–4–18–1	12–2–30–0	
(J.P.) v. Northamptonshire (Milton Keynes) 23 August	8–1–34–0	7–0–28–1		8–0–41–1	8–0–24–0	
(J.P.) v. Glamorgan (Colchester) 30 August	7–0–19–3	7–0–25–1		6–0–21–0	8–0–19–0	2–0–11–1
(F.T.) v. Northamptonshire (Scarborough) 2 September	10–1–66–1			10–2–22–0	10–0–51–3	10–0–53–0
(F.T.) v. Yorkshire (Scarborough) 4 September	10–3–50–0			10–0–34–1	10–1–41–1	10–2–42–2
(J.P.) v. Middlesex (Chelmsford) 6 September	7–1–35–2	8–1–24–1		8–0–37–1	3–0–23–0	4–0–14–0
(J.P.) v. Surrey (The Oval) 13 September	8–0–30–0	8–0–38–1		8–0–45–1		8–1–21–2

† K. Collyer retired hurt; B. G. Collins absent injured

K. W. R. Fletcher	D. L. Acfield	D. R. Pringle	B	Lb	W	Nb	Total	Wkts
			4	8	1	2	206	9
			1	19	2		130	7
			4	12	3	2	240	10
			1	3	1	1	120	10
0.4–0–5–0				12	3	1	162	2
				5			49	2
	8–1–38–1			14	2		182	6
			4	19	2		149	7
	4.2–1–28–2		1	21	4	2	216	7
			3	6	3		121	9
		5.3–0–13–2	1	15	1	1	136	10
		7–4–9–1	2	3	5	1	115	8†
		7–1–23–0	1	5		2	153	6
		9–2–12–3	8	4	2	2	85	10
		8–0–38–1		7	2	3	177	10
	4–1–6–2	8–3–8–2		14	7		110	10
		12–2–22–0	1	11	1	2	170	10
		8–0–29–3	1	7		2	198	3
		12–5–19–1		12	3	3	149	8
		8–1–42–0	6	13	2	3	193	4
		8–1–24–1		4	8	2	133	7
		10–0–43–3	2	9	2	4	252	7
		10–0–79–1	5	9	1	3	264	5
		8–0–50–2		7			190	7
		7–0–34–1	1	9	3	1	182	5

Glamorgan C.C.C. Limited-Over Matches – Batting, 1981	v. Essex (Swansea) 9 May (B.&H.)	v. Worcestershire (Abergavenny) 10 May (J.P.)	v. Hampshire (Bournemouth) 17 May (J.P.)	v. Combined Universities (Oxford) 18 May (B.&H.)	v. Kent (Cardiff) 20 May (B.&H.)	v. Kent (Cardiff) 24 May (J.P.)	v. Somerset (Taunton) 30 May (B.&H.)	v. Surrey (Swansea) 7 June (J.P.)	v. Leicestershire (Leicester) 14 June (J.P.)	v. Yorkshire (Hull) 21 June (J.P.)	v. Warwickshire (Swansea) 28 June (J.P.)	v. Northamptonshire (Luton) 5 July (J.P.)
A. Jones	38	23	33		25	27	49	—	6	36	23	50
J. A. Hopkins	4	20	3		6	0	36	—	55	41	75	28
D. A. Francis	9	11	4		0							
Javed Miandad	67	0	18		1	13*	24	—	107*	33	73	29
N. G. Featherstone	51	12	6		8	—	0	—	19	23	14	46*
R. C. Ontong	7	30	16*		14	5	8	—	6*		6	13*
M. A. Nash	1	0	0		2	—	4	—	—	0	2	—
E. A. Moseley	2	20	1*		4	—	0	—	4	0	3	—
E. W. Jones	11*	14	2		0	—	4	—	—	1	1*	—
B. J. Lloyd	1	5	—		2*	—	—	—	—	1*	—	—
S. R. Barwick	0*	2*	—		1*	—	—	—	—			
M. J. Llewellyn						12*	23*	—				
G. C. Holmes									—	8*	6	2
A. L. Jones										2	1*	
A. A. Jones										—		
J. G. Thomas												
S. A. B. Daniels												
Byes	4	1				2				2	5	5
Leg byes	8	9	5		4	1	16		7	3	13	5
Wides	1	3	3		4	3	4			2	2	1
No balls	2	2				1	1		3	1		
Total	206	152	91		71	64	169		207	153	224	179
Wickets	9	10	7		9	3	8		4	8	8	4
Result	W	L	L	Ab	L	Ab	L	Ab	W	W	W	W
Points	2	0	0	1	0	2	0	2	4	4	4	4

Catches

23 – E. W. Jones (ct 17, st 6)

10 – Javed Miandad

7 – R. C. Ontong

5 – N. G. Featherstone

4 – G. C. Holmes, M. A. Nash and A. Jones

3 – S. R. Barwick

2 – D. A. Francis, E. A. Moseley, J. A. Hopkins, B. J. Lloyd and S. A. B. Daniels

1 – A. L. Jones

v. Northamptonshire (Harrogate) 8 July (T.T.)	v. Oxfordshire (Oxford) 11 July (N.W.T.)	v. Gloucestershire (Bristol) 19 July (J.P.)	v. Hampshire (Cardiff) 22 July (N.W.T.)	v. Sussex (Ebbw Vale) 26 July (J.P.)	v. Lancashire (Cardiff) 9 August (J.P.)	v. Derbyshire (Swansea) 16 August (J.P.)	v. Middlesex (Lord's) 23 August (J.P.)	v. Essex (Colchester) 30 August (J.P.)	v. Somerset (Cardiff) 6 September (J.P.)	v. Nottinghamshire (Trent Bridge) 13 September (J.P.)
27	40	34	1	1	6	66*	18	5	5	11
18	18	51	1	13	0	14	63*	0	0	4
59	36*	63*	64	6	96	0	13	9	85	9
0	—	19	10	22	24	1	10	9	6	57
24	53*	—	23	38	6	7	—	22	25	40
0	—	—	0	3	10*	8	—	5	3	0
6	—	—	2	4			—			
1	—	—	15	37	—	9	—	9*	13*	3*
1	—	—	1	9	—	1	—	10*	7	2*
0*	—	—	1*	3*	—					—
								50		
32	—	0*	11	8	16	4	25		2	1
						0*				
					10*	2			0*	
					—	—		—	—	—
	1	6	6		3	8	2			4
4		14	7	4	12	8	13	4	7	9
2	3	6		3	5	4	2	8	2	4
1	3	1	4	2			5	2	4	1
175	154	194	146	153	188	132	151	133	159	145
10	2	3	10	10	6	9	4	7	8	7
L	W	W	L	L	L	L	W	L	L	L
—	—	4	0	0	0	0	4	0	0	0

Glamorgan C.C.C.
Limited-Over Matches – Bowling, 1981

	M. A. Nash	E. A. Mosley	S. R. Barwich	B. J. Lloyd	R. C. Ontong	A. A. Jones
(B.&H.) v. Essex (Swansea) 9 May	6–2–11–2	6–3–5–1	6–2–31–2	11–2–24–1	10.2–3–41–4	
(J.P.) v. Worcestershire (Abergavenny) 10 May	8–0–31–2	8–1–24–1	8–2–23–0	8–0–19–1	8–0–52–2	
(J.P.) v. Hampshire (Bournemouth) 17 May	4–0–16–1	3–0–17–0	3–0–25–0	4–0–21–1	4–0–21–0	
(B.&H.) v. Kent (Cardiff) 20 May	3–0–21–1	3–1–8–4	3–0–23–0	3–0–12–1	3–0–11–2	
(B.&H.) v. Somerset (Taunton) 30 May	11–2–29–1	11–2–22–0	10–1–38–3	10–1–45–1	8.1–3–26–0	
(J.P.) v. Surrey (Swansea) 7 June	5–1–17–0	5–1–9–1	1–0–11–0	1–0–2–0		
(J.P.) v. Leicestershire (Leicester) 14 June	7–1–13–1	6.5–0–22–4	8–1–29–2	8–3–22–1	8–0–46–2	
(J.P.) v. Yorkshire (Hull) 21 June	8–0–33–2	6.5–3–16–3		8–0–21–1		5–0–38–1
(J.P.) v. Warwickshire (Swansea) 28 June	8–0–31–4	8–0–26–2		8–1–39–1	8–0–32–1	
(J.P.) v. Northamptonshire (Luton) 5 July	8–0–31–2	8–0–21–1	4–0–12–0	6–0–39–1	7–1–25–1	
(T.T.) v. Northamptonshire (Harrogate) 8 July	11–0–80–3	10.2–1–36–3	9–1–39–0	7–0–65–2	11–0–63–1	
(N.W.T.) v. Oxfordshire (Oxford) 11 July	12–1–31–5	11.2–5–19–2	10–1–33–1	12–7–9–1	12–5–19–0	
(J.P.) v. Gloucestershire (Bristol) 19 July	8–1–28–2	8–2–31–1	8–0–43–1	8–0–33–0	8–0–44–0	
(N.W.T.) v. Hampshire (Cardiff) 22 July	12–1–35–1	12–2–39–2	9–3–14–4	12–3–20–0	9–3–27–0	
(J.P.) v. Sussex (Ebbw Vale) 26 July	8–0–57–0	8–1–26–1	8–0–39–3	7–0–55–0	8–2–35–2	
(J.P.) v. Lancashire (Cardiff) 9 August	8–0–36–3		4–1–17–1	8–3–21–2	7–1–22–0	
(J.P.) v. Derbyshire (Swansea) 16 August	6.5–0–31–1			7–1–19–2	8–1–20–0	8–4–20–2
(J.P.) v. Middlesex (Lord's) 23 August	6–1–25–2	4–1–6–2		8–3–9–2	8–1–25–2	
(J.P.) v. Essex (Colchester) 30 August	3–0–29–0			8–0–25–1	2–0–10–0	4–0–28–1
(J.P.) v. Somerset (Cardiff) 6 September	8–2–21–2			8–1–24–0	7–0–35–0	
(J.P.) v. Nottinghamshire (Trent Bridge) 13 September	6–0–25–0		8–2–37–1	8–0–21–0	6–0–21–0	

G. C. Holmes	J. G. Thomas	Javed Miandad	S. A. B. Daniels	B	Lb	W	Nb	Total	Wkts
				1	5	4	2	124	10
				4	12	5		170	7
					9	3		112	2
					5			90	8
					9	1		170	6
						2	2	43	1
					12	4	2	150	10
8–0–20–1				1	7		3	139	10
8–0–54–0				14	11	1	1	209	9
6–0–32–1					8	2	4	174	7
6–0–33–0					10	6	4	336	10
2–0–14–0				3	10	10	2	150	10
				1	9	1	2	192	6
6–1–19–0					9	6	7	176	7
1–0–9–0				1	13	3	3	241	7
6–0–30–2	5–0–36–0			9	10	8		189	8
	2–0–15–0	1–0–10–0		4	2	5	8	134	5
5.1–0–17–2			4–0–18–0	1	5	5	3	114	10
		1.4–0–5–1	6–0–25–0	6	1		5	134	3
	8–0–33–3		6.5–0–27–1		10	9	2	161	7
		0.2–0–2–0	7–0–32–0		3	2	3	146	3

Gloucestershire C.C.C. Limited-Over Matches – Batting, 1981

	v. Leicestershire (Leicester) 9 May (B.&H.)	v. Leicestershire (Moreton-in-Marsh) 10 May (J.P.)	v. Northamptonshire (Northampton) 17 May (J.P.)	v. Northamptonshire (Bristol) 16 and 18 May (B.&H.)	v. Worcestershire (Worcester) 20 May (B.&H.)	v. Nottinghamshire (Gloucester) 21 and 22 May (B.&H.)	v. Essex (Chelmsford) 24 May (J.P.)	v. Yorkshire (Bristol) 7 June (J.P.)	v. Somerset (Bath) 14 June (J.P.)	v. Hampshire (Portsmouth) 21 June (J.P.)	v. Derbyshire (Gloucester) 28 June (J.P.)	v. Sussex (Hove) 5 July (J.P.)
B. C. Broad	25		42		3	3	—	56	25	37	19	26
Sadiq Mohammad	35		—		91	57	—					
Zaheer Abbas	49		55		18	0	—	58	8	51	30	53
M. J. Procter	24		0		1	5	—	52	91	12	4	
A. J. Hignell	11		1		51*	5	—	12*	0	0	2	37
P. Bainbridge	7		—		15*	0	—	21*	0	6	2	35
A. W. Stovold	23*		4*		28	19	—	4	54	23	2	37*
D. A. Graveney	3		—		—	0	—	—	0	9		30*
A. H. Wilkins	1*		—		—	6	—	—	1		19*	—
B. M. Brain	—		—		—	23	—	—	0	3*	—	
J. H. Childs	—		—			1*	—	—				
B. Dudleston			0*		12							
S. J. Windaybank								—	0	16	44*	0
D. Surridge									0*	—	—	
M. W. Stovold										9*	14	3
M. R. Whitney											—	—
R. J. Doughty												
Byes	2		4		2	4		1				4
Leg byes	11		7		18	3		10	7	10	13	6
Wides	2				6	1		1	6	4		1
No balls	2				2			1			1	4
Total	195		113		247	127		216	192	180	150	236
Wickets	7		4		6	10		4	10	8	7	6
Result	L	Ab	W	Ab	W	L	Ab	Ab	L	L	L	L
Points	0	2	4	1	2	0	2	2	0	0	0	0

Catches

16 – A. W. Stovold (ct 13, st 3)

11 – A. J. Hignell

 5 – B. C. Broad

 4 – P. Bainbridge and A. H. Wilkins

 2 – Zaheer Abbas, M. J. Procter, D. A. Graveney and B. M. Brain

 1 – B. Dudleston, D. Surridge, M. W. Stovold and Sadiq Mohammad

v. Ireland (Dublin) 11 July (N.W.T.)	v. Glamorgan (Bristol) 19 July (J.P.)	v. Essex (Bristol) 22 July (N.W.T.)	v. Middlesex (Lord's) 2 August (J.P.)	v. Surrey (Cheltenham) 9 August (J.P.)	v. Kent (Cheltenham) 16 August (J.P.)	v. Worcestershire (Worcester) 23 August (J.P.)	v. Warwickshire (Bristol) 30 August (J.P.)	v. Nottinghamshire (Trent Bridge) 6 September (J.P.)	v. Lancashire (Bristol) 13 September (J.P.)
7	38	0	20	0	37	32	38	0	58
50									
7	14	3	129*	9	22	2	73	18	45
23	45	0	20	49	9	19	14	32	20
61*	0	10	—	25	34	3	7	1	3*
70	58	5	—	1	55*	45	0	8	2
1	—	10	—	18	—	16	0	49	—
16	—		—		—	7*	—	0*	—
6*				5	—	11			—
—	—	4	—	6			16*		
0									
	21*	18	—	0	5*	6	2	56	—
	—	0	—		—	0			
	3	17	24*	5	3	4	24*	0	0*
		2*		0*				5	0
1	1	8	3	3	1	2	3		1
4	9	4	17	6	14	9	8	10	5
	1	2	1		3	3	1	3	1
	2	2	1					4	
246	192	85	215	127	183	159	191	181	135
8	6	10	2	10	5	10	8	9	4
W	L	L	W	L	W	L	L	L	Ab
—	0	—	4	0	4	0	0	0	2

Gloucestershire C.C.C.
Limited-Over Matches – Bowling, 1981

	B. M. Brain	A. H. Wilkins	J. H. Childs	M. J. Procter	P. Bainbridge	D. A. Graveney
(B.&H.) v. Leicestershire (Leicester) 9 May	11–1–56–3	11–1–33–1	11–0–48–1	11–1–39–1	10–1–36–0	1–0–9–0
(J.P.) v. Northamptonshire (Northampton) 17 May	4–0–30–3	4–0–28–0		4–0–29–3	3–0–15–1	
(B.&H.) v. Worcestershire (Worcester) 20 May	9–2–21–0	11–3–35–4		8.2–1–21–2	11–0–45–2	11–0–46–2
(B.&H.) v. Nottinghamshire (Gloucester) 21 and 22 May	11–0–45–1	7–0–32–1	11–9–4–1	11–0–42–2	7–0–21–3	8–0–40–0
(J.P.) v. Essex (Chelmsford) 24 May	4–1–10–2	2–0–5–0			1–0–9–0	
(J.P.) v. Somerset (Bath) 14 June	8–0–42–2	8–0–56–1		8–1–28–0	8–0–32–2	
(J.P.) v. Hampshire (Portsmouth) 21 June	6–0–34–1			8–1–15–1	7–0–39–0	
(J.P.) v. Derbyshire (Gloucester) 28 June	7–0–30–1	7–0–30–0		8–2–28–0	7–0–39–0	
(J.P.) v. Sussex (Hove) 5 July		8–0–66–1			8–0–46–0	4–0–29–0
(N.W.T.) v. Ireland (Dublin) 11 July	12–5–13–1	7–1–14–1	12–5–15–2		5–2–8–1	9.5–6–11–5
(J.P.) v. Glamorgan (Bristol) 19 July		7–0–28–0	8–0–27–0		8–0–35–1	4.2–0–22–1
(N.W.T.) v. Essex (Bristol) 22 July			12–2–29–2		12–0–38–1	12–2–25–3
(J.P.) v. Middlesex (Lord's) 2 August		7–0–21–3	8–0–50–0		7–1–38–2	
(J.P.) v. Surrey (Cheltenham) 9 August	8–3–13–2		6–1–32–1		8–0–31–1	6–0–22–0
(J.P.) v. Kent (Cheltenham) 16 August	8–1–10–2	8–0–30–0			4–0–17–0	8–0–36–1
(J.P.) v. Worcestershire (Worcester) 23 August	5–0–33–0	3–0–17–0			8–2–31–2	8–0–25–0
(J.P.) v. Warwickshire (Bristol) 30 August		8–1–26–3	4–0–18–0		5–0–30–0	6–0–32–0
(J.P.) v. Nottinghamshire (Trent Bridge) 6 September		8–2–50–2			8–0–41–1	3–0–15–0

D. Surridge	B. C. Broad	Zaheer Abbas	M. R. Whitney	R. J. Doughty		B	Lb	W	Nb	Total	Wkts
						6	26	3		256	6
						1	4	1		108	8
							9	1		178	10
						3	3	1		191	9
						4				28	2
8–0–38–0							13		3	212	7
6–0–33–0	8–0–31–0	1–0–6–0				3	14	8	1	184	3
			7–3–13–0				9	1	1	151	1
8–0–61–2	4–0–22–1		8–0–44–0				13	5	1	287	4
						4	7	1	2	75	10
8–0–31–1	3–0–24–0					6	14	6	1	194	3
11.2–2–38–1			12–2–47–2			3	20	4	3	207	10
8–0–43–1	8–0–43–0						14	4		213	6
	2.3–0–12–0		8–5–9–2			4	5			128	7
8–0–41–0	4–0–32–0					1	13	1	1	182	7
6–0–22–0		7–0–25–1				4	2	1	1	161	3
	8–0–48–3			8–0–36–1			9	2		201	7
	5–0–20–1		8–0–27–0	8–0–39–0			13	4	1	210	4

Hampshire C.C.C. Limited-Over Matches – Batting, 1981

	v. Middlesex (Lord's) 9 May (B.&H.)	v. Middlesex (Lord's) 10 May (J.P.)	v. Minor Counties (Southampton) 13 May (B.&H.)	v. Surrey (Bournemouth) 16 May (B.&H.)	v. Glamorgan (Bournemouth) 17 May (J.P.)	v. Sussex (Hove) 30 May and 1 June (B.&H.)	v. Sussex (Basingstoke) 31 May (J.P.)	v. Derbyshire (Derby) 14 June (J.P.)	v. Gloucestershire (Portsmouth) 21 June (J.P.)	v. Lancashire (Old Trafford) 28 June (J.P.)	v. Nottinghamshire (Portsmouth) 5 July (J.P.)	v. Cheshire (Southampton) 11 July (N.W.T.)
C. G. Greenidge	8		37	50	26	60	18	36	17	7		56
T. M. Tremlett	7		22	29	—		—	3*	—	0		6
M. C. J. Nicholas	1		0	26	—	13	2	2				5
T. E. Jesty	15		46	5	39*	0	62	27	26	27	4*	11
D. R. Turner	69		17	12*	0	22	1	10	59*	8	37	27*
J. M. Rice	30		5	—	—	49	19	43				
N. G. Cowley	19		36	—	35*	7	9*	21	17	38	64*	—
M. D. Marshall	0		10	—	—	18	18*	7*	—	8	—	—
R. J. Parks	11		9	—	—	7	—	—	—	1	—	—
K. Stevenson	4*		5	—	—	9	—	—	—	3*	—	—
S. J. Malone	0*		0*	—	—	3*	—	—	—	—	—	—
N. E. J. Pocock				6	—	0	24	11	39*	22	—	20*
J. W. Southern							—					
Y. P. Terry									—	26*	—	
C. L. Smith											7	
R. E. Hayward												
Byes			2				2		3		4	
Leg byes	9		3	10	9	5	6	6	14	6	4	6
Wides	3			5	3		2	11	8	3	4	1
No balls			7			1		2	1	3	1	6
Total	176		179	143	112	194	163	179	184	152	125	138
Wickets	9		10	5	2	10	6	7	3	8	2	4
Result	W	Ab	L	Ab	W	L	L	L	W	W	W	W
Points	2	2	0	1	4	0	0	0	4	4	4	—

Catches

21 – R. J. Parks (ct 17, st 4)

12 – C. G. Greenidge

8 – J. M. Rice

7 – V. P. Terry

6 – D. R. Turner

4 – N. G. Cowley

3 – K. Stevenson, T. E. Jesty and N. E. J. Pocock

2 – T. M. Tremlett and M. D. Marshall

1 – M. C. J. Nicholas and R. E. Hayward

v. Worcestershire (Worcester) 12 July (J.P.)	v. Surrey (Southampton) 19 July (J.P.)	v. Glamorgan (Cardiff) 22 July (N.W.T.)	v. Warwickshire (Edgbaston) 26 July (J.P.)	v. Kent (Canterbury) 2 August (J.P.)	v. Lancashire (Southampton) 5 August (N.W.T.)	v. Yorkshire (Middlesbrough) 9 August (J.P.)	v. Essex (Southampton) 16 August (J.P.)	v. Somerset (Taunton) 23 August (J.P.)	v. Leicestershire (Bournemouth) 6 September (J.P.)	v. Northamptonshire (Southampton) 13 September (J.P.)
50	16	10	36	28	8	18			19	11
1*	—	9*								—
		6	30*	16	24	13	—	2	—	
14	24	67	46	48	9	29	35*	2	22	28
24	7	0	15	1	11	4	6	10	26*	82*
		5	4*	6	4	0	39	20	58	9
36	52	32	74	5	38	6	43*	22	13	48*
5	—	2*	13	17	16*		—	20		
0	17*	19*	7	11*	2	—	—	32	—	—
1*	0	—	5	0	6	4*	—	11*	—	—
—	—		—	2	0*	—	—	0	—	—
22	17								30*	
22	26*	4	0	0						—
							65	9	51	5
					33	3*	—	0		
8	8		2	4	1		1	1	2	6
19	1	9	10	2	10	3	7	6	5	4
5	3	6			1	1		2	1	1
6		7			4		2		1	
213	171	176	242	140	167	81	198	137	228	194
8	6	7	8	10	9	6	3	10	5	4
L	W	W	L	L	L	L	W	L	W	W
0	4	—	0	0	—	0	4	0	4	4

Hampshire C.C.C. Limited-Over Matches – Bowling, 1981

	M. D. Marshall	K. Stevenson	S. J. Malone	N. G. Cowley	T. E. Jesty	J. M. Rice
(B.&H.) v. Middlesex (Lord's) 9 May	10–3–18–0	8–1–18–4	2–0–13–0	11–2–44–2	8–2–22–0	11–0–42–3
(B.&H.) v. Minor Counties (Southampton) 13 May	11–2–37–1	10–3–42–0	7–2–18–1	10–2–19–0	11–4–22–4	6–1–27–1
(B.&H.) v. Surrey (Bournemouth) 16 May						
(J.P.) v. Glamorgan (Bournemouth) 17 May	4–1–11–0	3–0–15–0		2–0–9–3	4–0–16–1	3–0–17–1
(B.&H.) v. Sussex (Hove) 30 May and 1 June	11–5–11–3	11–1–42–1	11–1–37–2	7–0–23–0	11–1–50–1	
(J.P.) v. Sussex (Basingstoke) 31 May	7–1–24–0			7–0–34–2	4–0–20–0	5–0–28–0
(J.P.) v. Derbyshire (Derby) 14 June	8–0–28–0	7.1–0–36–0			8–0–29–1	6–0–38–2
(J.P.) v. Gloucestershire (Portsmouth) 21 June	8–1–22–0	6–0–30–0	8–1–42–2	8–0–27–2	3–0–28–0	
(J.P.) v. Lancashire (Old Trafford) 28 June	8–2–25–0	6–1–20–0	4–0–21–0	8–0–29–2	8–0–25–3	
(J.P.) v. Nottinghamshire (Portsmouth) 5 July	8–1–20–1	8–3–16–1	6–0–52–2		8–0–16–3	
(N.W.T.) v. Cheshire (Southampton) 11 July	9–1–27–0	5–1–14–0	10.5–4–34–5		12–2–31–4	
(J.P.) v. Worcestershire (Worcester) 12 July	7–0–37–1	6–0–19–0	2–0–19–0	8–0–44–2	8–0–47–1	
(J.P.) v. Surrey (Southampton) 19 July	8–0–27–3	8–1–22–0	8–1–41–2	8–1–23–3		
(N.W.T.) v. Glamorgan (Cardiff) 22 July	9.5–1–15–2	12–2–24–3		12–1–32–0	10–3–23–2	12–1–35–2
(J.P.) v. Warwickshire (Edgbaston) 26 July	7–0–47–1	7.3–0–41–1	8–0–40–1	4–0–31–0	4–0–22–1	8–0–59–0
(J.P.) v. Kent (Canterbury) 2 August	8–0–30–0	8–0–38–0	8–0–45–0	6–0–36–1	6–0–42–1	4–0–30–0
(N.W.T.) v. Lancashire (Southampton) 5 August	12–1–17–1	12–2–36–3	10–5–16–3	12–2–31–0	7 4–0–39–0	2–0–11–0
(J.P.) v. Yorkshire (Middlesbrough) 9 August	3–0–11–0	3–0–23–0	2–0–12–1	3–0–26–2	3–0–34–1	1–0–9–1
(J.P.) v. Essex (Southampton) 16 August	8–2–13–1	8–0–52–1	8–0–41–2	8–0–33–0	8–0–40–0	
(J.P.) v. Somerset (Taunton) 23 August	8–1–31–2	7–0–75–0	8–0–62–3	7–0–68–0	8–1–32–1	
(J.P.) v. Leicestershire (Bournemouth) 6 September		8–1–47–0	8–1–51–0	8–1–32–0	8–0–48–1	8–0–36–2
(J.P.) v. Northamptonshire (Southampton) 13 September		5–1–20–0	8–0–47–3	5–0–33–1	6–0–26–0	5–0–26 0

†P. J. Dunkley retired hurt

T. M. Tremlett	M. C. J. Nicholas	C. G. Greenidge	J. W. Southern	B	Lb	W	Nb	Total	Wkts
4–0–17–1					1			175	10
					8	9		182	7
						Abandoned			
2–0–15–1					5	3		91	7
	2–0–7–0	1.5–0–10–0			8	9	1	198	7
5.3–0–25–1			2–0–17–0	6	9	1		164	3
8–0–32–2					8	9		180	5
6–0–17–2					10	4		180	8
6–1–22–4					5	4		151	9
5–0–24–1				7	4	4		123	8
6–2–15–0				5	9	2		137	9†
6–0–31–0					9	8		214	4
8–0–43–0				4	2	4	1	167	8
				6	7		4	146	10
				1	5			246	4
				2	5	2		230	4
					9	8	2	169	7
					1	1		117	6
				3	10	1	1	194	4
					12	6		286	7
				2	7	2		225	3
8–0–32–1				2	5	1		192	7

Kent C.C.C.
Limited-Over Matches – Batting, 1981

	v. Combined Universities (Canterbury) 11 May (B.&H.)	v. Yorkshire (Huddersfield) 17 May (J.P.)	v. Glamorgan (Cardiff) 20 May (B.&H.)	v. Somerset (Taunton) 21 May (B.&H.)	v. Glamorgan (Cardiff) 24 May (J.P.)	v. Essex (Dartford) 30 May (B.&H.)	v. Essex (Chelmsford) 31 May (J.P.)	v. Northamptonshire (Maidstone) 7 June (J.P.)	v. Somerset (Bath) 21 June (J.P.)	v. Warwickshire (The Oval) 26 June (B.&H.)	v. Lancashire (Maidstone) 5 July (J.P.)	v. Somerset (Taunton) 8 July (B.&H.)
R. A. Woolmer	56*		14	64	—	79*		28*		38		1
C. J. C. Rowe	6	29				4	17					
C. J. Tavare	33	97	21	1	—	30	3*	11	36	76	59	44
M. R. Benson	6*	49	8	30	—	33*	22	2			50	1
Asif Iqbal	—	12	6	14	—	—	—	5*	11	22	34	11
A. P. E. Knott	—	4*	4	8	—	—	—	—	8*	0	12*	29
J. N. Shepherd	—	8	13	16	—	—	—	—	13	19	8	7
G. W. Johnson	—	2*	4*	19	—	—	—	—	5	8	9	13
G. R. Dilley	—	—	0	8	—	—	—	—		5*		8
D. L. Underwood	—	—	2*	0	—	—	—	—		0*	—	0
K. B. S. Jarvis	—	—	—	0*	—	—	—	—			—	0*
C. S. Cowdrey		14	3	5	—		2*	—	23	0	21	
L. Potter									3			
A. G. E. Ealham									29*	11	18	17
E. Baptiste									—		—	
R. M. Ellison												
N. Taylor												
S. N. V. Waterton												
D. Aslett												
Byes									4	3	1	6
Leg byes		7	5	6		12	5	1	1	6	6	8
Wides	4	1		1		3		1	1	1	3	7
No balls	3					1		1		4		2
Total	108	223	80	172		162	49	49	134	193	221	154
Wickets	2	6	8	10		2	2	2	6	8	7	10
Result	W	W	W	L	Ab	W	L	L	W	W	T	L
Points	2	4	2	0	2	2	0	0	4	—	2	—

Catches
33 – A. P. E. Knott (ct 29, st 4)
12 – C. J. Tavare
10 – Asif Iqbal
9 – C. S. Cowdrey
7 – D. L. Underwood
5 – R. A. Woolmer, G. W. Johnson and K. B. S. Jarvis
4 – J. N. Shepherd and E. Baptiste
3 – A. G. E. Ealham and M. R. Benson
1 – G. R. Dilley, C. J. C. Rowe, S. N. V. Waterton, R. M. Ellison and sub.

v. Yorkshire (Canterbury) 11 July (N.W.T.)	v. Nottinghamshire (Canterbury) 12 July (J.P.)	v. Leicestershire (Leicester) 19 July (J.P.)	v. Nottinghamshire (Canterbury) 22 July (N.W.T.)	v. Derbyshire (Derby) 26 July (J.P.)	v. Hampshire (Canterbury) 2 August (J.P.)	v. Sussex (Eastbourne) 9 August (J.P.)	v. Gloucestershire (Cheltenham) 16 August (J.P.)	v. Surrey (Folkestone) 23 August (J.P.)	v. Middlesex (Canterbury) 30 August (J.P.)	v. Warwickshire (Canterbury) 6 September (J.P.)	v. Worcestershire (Canterbury) 13 September (J.P.)
6	24	21	0			8	10	41	5	14	6
118*	1	18	2	4	99*	44		53		4	7
57	62	29	35	9	15	25	17	19		5	88
29	45*		17	4	37	2	34	3	35	3	6
—	—	22	2	35	—	3		51*		13	1
—	6	15	22	12							2
2	—	17*	35	36	—	10	0	0	26*	31*	2*
			2	16*							0*
—	—		1*	20	—	1	—	—	—	5	—
—	—		0	5*	—	1*	—	—	—	0	—
0*	18*	21	25	13	57	21	18	7	37	0	27
					13				4		
—	—	18*		5	—	10	22	—	4*	6	
	—				—	12*	16*	9*	—	6	
							49				
							—		25		
	1			2	2	1	1	2			
7	8	15	7	8	5	16	13	9	11	9	6
2	3	1	4		2	8	1	1	3		2
2			2			2	1			1	2
223	168	177	154	169	230	164	182	195	151	96	149
4	4	6	10	9	4	9	7	6	5	10	7
W	W	L	L	L	W	W	L	W	W	L	L
—	4	0	—	0	4	4	0	4	4	0	0

Kent C.C.C. Limited-Over Matches – Bowling, 1981

	G. R. Dilley	J. N. Shepherd	K. B. S. Jarvis	D. L. Underwood	R. A. Woolmer	G. W. Johnson
(B.&H.) v. Combined Univ. (Canterbury) 11 May	7.4–0–14–4	8–2–16–1	9–5–14–0	11–6–11–2	7–1–18–1	11–2–22–2
(J.P.) v. Yorkshire (Huddersfield) 17 May	4–0–12–0	7–0–33–2	4–1–7–1	6–1–22–4		
(B.&H.) v. Glamorgan (Cardiff) 20 May	3–0–16–1	3–1–6–2	3–0–10–0	1–0–3–1	3–1–6–2	
(B.&H.) v. Somerset (Taunton) 21 May	7.4–0–40–0	11–0–37–1	9–2–32–1	5–0–25–0	5–0–11–0	11–2–18–2
(J.P.) v. Glamorgan (Cardiff) 24 May	5–0–16–0	5–0–12–0	5–2–9–1		5–1–16–0	
(B.&H.) v. Essex (Dartford) 30 May	9–1–32–3	11–3–24–1	9.4–0–31–3	11–1–32–2	11–1–29–1	
(J.P.) v. Essex (Chelmsford) 31 May	4–0–14–1		4–0–17–2			
(J.P.) v. Northamptonshire (Maidstone) 7 June	6–2–12–0	8–0–26–0	8–2–12–2	6–0–37–2	8–1–30–1	
(J.P.) v. Somerset (Bath) 21 June		8–1–25–1	8–1–25–1	8–4–8–1		
(B.&H.) v. Warwickshire (The Oval) 26 June	10–1–27–2	10–3–24–3	9.1–1–34–1	10–0–46–2	10–2–33–0	
(J.P.) v. Lancashire (Maidstone) 5 July		8–0–29–2	8–0–51–2	3–0–15–1		5–0–30–1
(B.&H.) v. Somerset (Taunton) 8 July	6–0–32–0	8.3–1–30–2	7–2–16–1	11–4–1–25	6–1–27–0	10–1–28–0
(N.W.T.) v. Yorkshire (Canterbury) 11 July		12–2–65–0	9–0–33–2	12–6–10–0	6–1–21–0	
(J.P.) v. Nottinghamshire (Canterbury) 12 July		6–0–27–1	7–2–19–3	8–0–25–4	6–0–20–0	
(J.P.) v. Leicestershire (Leicester) 19 July		4.4–0–22–2	4–0–30–2	1–0–3–0		
(N.W.T.) v. Nottinghamshire (Canterbury) 22–23 July	12–2–37–2	12–2–31–0	11–3–23–2	12–8–12–0		1.3–0–7–0
(J.P.) v. Derbyshire (Derby) 26 July	8–0–40–2	6–0–35–1	6–0–25–1	8–0–23–4		
(J.P.) v. Hampshire (Canterbury) 2 August			5–0–13–1	8–0–32–1		4.5–0–17–3
(J.P.) v. Sussex (Eastbourne) 9 August			7.5–1–31–3		7–1–22–2	
(J.P.) v. Gloucestershire (Cheltenham) 16 August			7.4–0–44–0	8–1–28–1	8–0–35–1	
(J.P.) v. Surrey (Folkestone) 23 August			8–0–33–2	8–0–44–2	8–2–20–0	
(J.P.) v. Middlesex (Canterbury) 30 August			8–0–18–1	8–0–24–1	2–0–17–0	
(J.P.) v. Warwickshire (Canterbury) 6 September			4–0–9–0	8–2–18–1		8–2–29–0
(J.P.) v. Worcestershire (Canterbury) 13 September	8–0–47–2		8–0–37–2	8–0–37–3		8–1–38–0

Asif Iqbal	C. S. Cowdrey	E. Baptiste	L. Potter	R. M. Ellison	B	Lb	W	Nb	Total	Wkts
					6	1	2		104	10
						5			79	7
2–0–22–1						4	4		71	9
						8	1	1	173	5
	0.3–0–4–0				2	1	3	1	64	3
						10	3		161	10
							2		33	3
3–0–12–0	1–0–17–0					6	2		154	5
		8–1–30–2	8–0–27–4			16		1	132	10
					1	11	1	2	179	10
	7–0–44–2	8–0–42–0				5	4	1	221	10
					2	3	2	2	157	5
	12–1–41–4	9–2–35–0				8	1	8	222	6
	8–0–32–0	5–0–16–0				21	4		164	8
						5			60	4
	8–2–25–2				4	8	6	3	156	6
	4–0–20–1	8–0–34–0				8		2	187	9
	4–0–18–1	5–0–17–1		8–1–37–2	4	2			140	10
	4–0–18–0	8–0–32–3		8–0–29–2		13	2		147	10
		8–2–26–0		8–0–32–2	1	14	3		183	5
		7–1–23–2		8–1–31–2		6	1		158	9
		8–1–19–2	6–0–31–2	8–1–24–0		11	6		150	7
	1–0–7–0	4–1–18–0		3.5–1–17–0		1			99	1
	8–0–35–1					9	3		206	9

Lancashire C.C.C. Limited-Over Matches – Batting, 1981	v. Derbyshire (Old Trafford) 10 May (J.P.)	v. Warwickshire (Old Trafford) 11 May (B.&H.)	v. Scotland (Glasgow) 17 May (B.&H.)	v. Derbyshire (Old Trafford) 21 and 22 May (B.&H.)	v. Northamptonshire (Old Trafford) 24 May (J.P.)	v. Somerset (Old Trafford) 31 May (J.P.)	v. Sussex (Hove) 7 June (J.P.)	v. Nottinghamshire (Old Trafford) 21 June (J.P.)	v. Hampshire (Old Trafford) 28 June (J.P.)	v. Kent (Maidstone) 5 July (J.P.)	v. Durham (Old Trafford) 11 and 13 July (N.W.T.)	v. Middlesex (Old Trafford) 12 July (J.P.)
A. Kennedy	36	24	13	5	0	3		62	40	59	102*	38
G. Fowler	7	13	34	5	33	1	36	37	28	26	23	20
F. C. Hayes	22	0		10	16		25	0				
C. H. Lloyd	13	124	5				2	8*	14	24	46*	105*
D. Lloyd	10	42	18	1	46*	18*	76	32*	5	2	11	8
B. W. Reidy	2	21	12*	32	0	24	0	—	3	21	—	
J. Simmons	14	10	—	59*	3	4	11	—	22	15	—	24
D. P. Hughes	8*	29	29*	52	14	10	2	—	5	11	—	0
N. V. Radford	9*		—	1	7	6	13*	—	0	—	—	3
P. J. W. Allott	—	5*	—	7*	3*	—	2*	—	0*	17*	—	6*
P. G. Lee	—	0*	—				—					
M. A. Holding		1	—		—					0		
S. J. O'Shaughnessy			—		13	1*		—	9*	2	—	—
C. J. Scott			—		—	—		—				
I. Cockbain						12						
J. Abrahams									16	34	—	6
K. A. Hayes												
D. K. Beckett												
Byes	2			1	4	1	2	1			1	
Leg byes	9	10	3	5	2	7	6	1	5	5	4	10
Wides	5	3	2	1	3	2	6		4	4	2	1
No balls	1	6				3		2		1	1	
Total	138	288	116	179	144	92	181	143	151	221	190	221
Wickets	7	9	4	7	8	7	7	3	9	10	2	7
Result	L	L	W	L	W	L	L	W	L	T	W	W
Points	0	0	2	0	4	0	0	4	0	2	—	4

Catches

20 – G. Fowler (ct 17, st 3)

8 – D. P. Hughes

7 – J. Simmons

6 – A. Kennedy, D. Lloyd and C. H. Lloyd

4 – C. J. Scott

3 – B. W. Reidy, P. T. W. Allott and N. V. Radford

2 – S. J. O'Shaugnnessy and sub.

1 – F. C. Hayes, M. A. Holding, P. G. Lee and I. Cockbain

v. Essex (Southend) 19 July (J.P.)	v. Middlesex (Old Trafford) 24 July (N.W.T.)	v. Surrey (The Oval) 26 July (J.P.)	v. Worcestershire (Old Trafford) 2 August (J.P.)	v. Hampshire (Southampton) 5 August (N.W.T.)	v. Glamorgan (Cardiff) 9 August (J.P.)	v. Warwickshire (Edgbaston) 16 August (J.P.)	v. Northamptonshire (Northampton) 19 August (N.W.T.)	v. Leicestershire (Old Trafford) 23 August (J.P.)	v. Yorkshire (Leeds) 30 August (J.P.)	v. Gloucestershire (Bristol) 13 September (J.P.)
6	46	61	31	7	4	17	6	13	14	—
4	0	0	65	42	13	3	57	0	9	—
						44				
7	3	5	12	82*	25	26	4		16	—
59	81			4		9	52	16	17*	—
	16	22	12	1	2	2	0	16		
13	16	12	12	6		4	28*	16		
39	25	5	34	6	23	35	13	39	45*	—
—	7*	1*			48*	20		9		
—	—	—	12*	—	8		0	1		—
—	—	—						2		
							12*			—
1*	13*	1	15*	2*			3			
					6*					
								0		
16*	5	48*	9	0	7	0*	2	19*		—
		—								
					26			9	30	—
1	3				9	1		4		
5	10	4	10	9	10	13	7	6	7	
	6	1	2	8	8		1	1	3	
2		2		2		4	1		2	
153	231	162	214	169	189	178	186	135	143	
6	8	7	7	7	8	9	9	10	4	
L	W	L	W	W	W	L	L	L	W	Ab
0	—	0	4	—	4	0	—	0	4	2

Lancashire C.C.C. Limited-Over Matches – Bowling, 1981

	N. V. Radford	P. G. Lee	B. W. Reidy	P. J. W. Allott	J. Simmons	M. A. Holding
(J.P.) v. Derbyshire (Old Trafford) 10 May	8–1–34–2	8–2–28–4	8–0–25–0	8–1–24–1	8–0–35–1	
(B.&H.) v. Warwickshire (Old Trafford) 11 May		8.5–0–47–0	9–0–64–1	9–0–45–0	11–0–57–0	11–3–28–1
(B.&H.) v. Scotland (Glasgow) 17 May	10–3–25–0	5–0–19–0		4–1–7–0	10–3–17–2	
(B.&H.) v. Derbyshire (Old Trafford) 21 and 22 May	11–2–31–0		9–1–32–0	11–2–34–3	7.3–0–24–1	11–3–21–2
(J.P.) v. Northamptonshire (Old Trafford) 24 May	6–1–24–3		3–0–14–0	8–1–23–3	7–1–24–2	
(J.P.) v. Somerset (Old Trafford) 31 May	2–0–12–1			2.5–0–26–1	1–0–10–0	
(J.P.) v. Sussex (Hove) 7 June	5–0–42–0	4–0–28–0		5–0–21–1	8–0–46–0	
(J.P.) v. Nottinghamshire (Old Trafford) 21 June	8–0–26–2		8–0–28–1	8–1–33–0	8–1–13–1	
(J.P.) v. Hampshire (Old Trafford) 28 June	7.1–0–16–3		4–0–21–1	8–1–22–2	8–2–21–1	
(J.P.) v. Kent (Maidstone) 5 July			8–0–35–1	7–1–36–1	8–0–46–2	8–0–31–2
(N.W.T.) v. Durham (Old Trafford) 11 and 13 July	7–1–29–0		7–1–21–0	10.4–3–22–3	12–6–10–1	
(J.P.) v. Middlesex (Old Trafford) 12 July	7–1–20–2	6–0–43–1		8–2–30–2	8–0–37–1	
(J.P.) v. Essex (Southend) 19 July	8–0–48–1	8–0–24–0		8–0–42–3	7–0–45–1	
(N.W.T.) v. Middlesex (Old Trafford) 24 July	10.3–1–20–3		5–1–19–0	10–0–39–2	12–0–39–2	
(J.P.) v. Surrey (The Oval) 26 July	8–0–45–0	8–0–29–1	6–0–36–0	6–0–17–0	8–0–22–1	
(J.P.) v. Worcestershire (Old Trafford) 2 August		7–1–30–0	6–0–32–0	8–0–42–1	8–0–28–2	
(N.W.T.) v. Hampshire (Southampton) 5 August			12–2–31–2	12–3–25–1	12–2–22–1	12–1–35–3
(J.P.) v. Glamorgan (Cardiff) 9 August	5–0–28–0	8–1–25–1	8–0–35–0	7–1–37–1		
(J.P.) v. Warwickshire (Edgbaston) 16 August	8–1–31–2	8–1–29–2	8–0–38–1		7.2–0–32–1	
(N.W.T.) v. Northamptonshire (Northampton) 19 August			10–3–22–3	12–2–32–2	12–4–17–2	12–2–36–0
(J.P.) v. Leicestershire (Old Trafford) 23 August	8–0–20–0	8–0–42–2	7–0–35–1	8–0–44–2		
(J.P.) v. Yorkshire (Leeds) 30 August	7–0–31–1	8–1–22–1		7.2–1–18–2	8–0–23–2	
(J.P.) v. Gloucestershire (Bristol) 13 September		8–0–52–0		5–0–24–0	6–0–22–3	4–1–14–0

D. P. Hughes	D. Lloyd	S. J. O'Shaughnessy	J. Abrahams	A. Kennedy	D. K. Beckett	B	Lb	W	Nb	Total	Wkts
						1	16			163	9
5-0-33-2						1	14	2		291	5
10-4-8-1	9-3-27-3					3	6			112	7
5-0-22-1						5	3	9		181	8
						1	7	2	1	96	9
							1			49	2
2-0-12-0						7	2	1	1	160	2
		8-0-27-1					12			139	6
	4-0-20-0	8-0-40-0					6	3	3	152	8
3-0-24-1		5-0-39-0				1	6	3		221	7
10-2-46-2	7-1-22-3	2-0-15-0				1	19	2		187	10
	2-0-24-0	8-0-35-1				4	22	3		218	7
		8-0-50-0					7	1		217	5
2-0-15-0	5-0-18-1	4-0-27-0				1	9	1	1	189	10
			0.2-0-4-0				10			163	2
		8-0-54-1	3-0-17-0			3	6	1		213	5
		12-0-38-1				1	10	1	4	167	9
			8-0-36-1	3-1-7-1		3	12	5		188	6
				8-0-30-1			16	1	3	180	7
	9.5-0-34-1	4-0-25-1				2	16	1	2	187	9
				6-1-21-0	3-0-13-0		10			185	3
1-0-8-0					8-1-23-2	1	11	2	2	141	10
3-0-16-1						1	5	1		135	4

Leicestershire C.C.C.
Limited-Over Matches – Batting, 1981

	v. Gloucestershire (Leicester) 9 May (B.&H.)	v. Gloucestershire (Moreton-in-Marsh) 10 May (J.P.)	v. Warwickshire (Edgbaston) 17 May (J.P.)	v. Northamptonshire (Northampton) 20 May (B.&H.)	v. Worcestershire (Leicester) 21 and 22 May (B.&H.)	v. Yorkshire (Leeds) 24 May (J.P.)	v. Nottinghamshire (Trent Bridge) 30 May (B.&H.)	v. Northamptonshire (Northampton) 31 May (J.P.)	v. Glamorgan (Leicester) 14 June (J.P.)	v. Middlesex (Lord's) 21 June (J.P.)	v. Sussex (Hove) 24 and 25 June (B.&H.)	v. Essex (Leicester) 28 June (J.P.)
J. C. Balderstone	113*			10	87	0	15	0	33	28	67	15
N. E. Briers	11			5*	3	0	2	35	0	2	4	0
D. I. Gower	28			0	47	28	1	54	12		44	2
B. F. Davison	26			0*	43	23	5	15*	7	23	15	12
R. W. Tolchard	25			—	10*	3	36	1				
P. B. Clift	3			—	14							
A. M. E. Roberts	15				17						5*	
M. A. Garnham	0*			—	0	4	33*	9	7	14	47	34
J. F. Steele	—			—	1*	48	4	0*	6	8	2	10
G. J. Parsons	—			—	—	7	6*	—	5	6	—	0
L. B. Taylor	—			—	—	3*	—	—	1	—	—	
K. Higgs				—	1			—	2*	—	—	0*
D. A. Wenlock				—	10	0		—	22			
J. P. Agnew						1						
T. J. Boon									37	2		24
P. Booth										18	2*	9*
R. A. Cobb										13*		
N. G. B. Cook										13*		3
Byes	6					1					4	3
Leg byes	26				8	8	7	4	12	6	4	6
Wides	3			1	4	4	1		4	1	4	3
No balls				4	4	2	3		2	1	1	
Total	256			20	248	142	114	118	150	135	199	121
Wickets	6			2	7	10	8	5	10	8	6	9
Result	W	Ab	Ab	Ab	W	L	L	W	L	L	W	L
Points	2	2	2	1	2	0	0	4	0	0	—	0

Catches
26 – M. A. Garnham (ct 25, st 1)
10 – R. W. Tolchard
 8 – D. I. Gower and J. F. Steele
 7 – N. E. Briers and J. C. Balderstone
 5 – L. B. Taylor
 3 – G. J. Parsons and A. M. E. Roberts
 2 – K. Higgs, B. F. Davison, P. B. Clift and D. A. Wenlock
 1 – N. G. B. Cook and sub.

v. Somerset (Leicester) 5 July (J.P.)	v. Surrey (The Oval) 8 July (B.&H.)	v. Kent (Leicester) 19 July (J.P.)	v. Surrey (The Oval) 24 July (N.W.T.)	v. Nottinghamshire (Leicester) 26 July (J.P.)	v. Sussex (Leicester) 2 August (J.P.)	v. Northamptonshire (Leicester) 5 August (N.W.T.)	v. Derbyshire (Derby) 9 August (J.P.)	v. Worcestershire (Leicester) 16 August (J.P.)	v. Lancashire (Old Trafford) 23 August (J.P.)	v. Surrey (Leicester) 30 August (J.P.)	v. Hampshire (Bournemouth) 6 September (J.P.)
10	21	5*	14*	10	3	19			34		
13	14	24*	18	80	2	2	47	74	4	24	119*
	11		2	44		13	6		3	64	37
13	0	5	43	27	14	67	12	1	35	1	3
		13	12*	21*	46	70	7	26*			37*
					15	2	18	7	46	33	—
59*	29	2	0	19	15	2	7				
18	32	6	3	1	29	24	13	2	37	12	18
20	39	—	—	5	9	3	27*	12	—	1	—
0	14*	—	—	—	1*	2	7	3*	—	4*	—
0*	1	—	—	—		0*	3*		—	—	—
—	10	—	—						—	—	—
									16*	11*	—
								0			
0										39	
22	4	—		2*	16			1			
								24			
								—			—
	4		1		1	1					2
4	7	5	5	5	6	11	6	12	10	2	7
3	2	5		1	3		1	2		2	2
2		5	1		8			5			
164	188	60	104	214	158	227	155	168	185	193	225
8	10	4	5	7	9	10	9	7	6	7	3
W	L	W	W	W	L	L	L	L	W	L	L
4	—	4	—	4	0	—	0	0	4	0	0

Leicestershire C.C.C. Limited-Over Matches – Bowling, 1981

	A. M. E. Roberts	G. J. Parsons	P. B. Clift	L. B. Taylor	J. F. Steele	N. E. Briers
(B.&H.) v. Gloucestershire (Leicester) 9 May	11-1-37-1	11-1-28-1	11-1-36-0	11-0-39-3	11-1-38-2	
(B.&H.) v. Worcestershire (Leicester) 21 and 22 May	9-1-24-1	9.5-1-33-4	6-0-13-1	11-2-23-2	11-1-38-0	5-0-37-1
(J.P.) v. Yorkshire (Leeds) 24 May		7-1-26-1		6-0-43-2	7-0-27-1	
(B.&H.) v. Nottinghamshire (Trent Bridge) 30 May		7-1-23-1		11-5-23-2		
(J.P.) v. Northamptonshire (Northampton) 31 May		6-1-19-3		6-0-23-0	6-0-13-1	
(J.P.) v. Glamorgan (Leicester) 14 June		8-0-56-0		8-1-34-1	8-0-37-1	
(J.P.) v. Middlesex (Lord's) 21 June		7-0-39-0			8-0-19-1	
(B.&H.) v. Sussex (Hove) 24 and 25 June	11-1-52-2	10-2-22-2		11-5-33-2	7-1-16-0	
(J.P.) v. Essex (Leicester) 28 June		7-0-31-1			8-2-14-0	
(J.P.) v. Somerset (Leicester) 5 July	8-1-19-2	8-2-38-2		8-1-31-2	8-0-37-1	
(B.&H.) v. Surrey (The Oval) 8 July	11-2-27-2	11-2-32-2		11-0-38-2	11-0-39-0	
(J.P.) v. Kent (Leicester) 19 July	8-0-29-0	8-1-40-1		7-1-36-2	8-2-31-2	
(N.W.T.) v. Surrey (The Oval) 24 July	2-0-7-0	2-0-19-0		2-0-9-1	2-0-24-0	
(J.P.) v. Nottinghamshire (Leicester) 26 July	8-0-28-2	8-0-49-1		8-2-34-1	8-0-34-2	
(J.P.) v. Sussex (Leicester) 2 August	8-0-27-4	8-1-31-0	8-0-24-1	7.5-0-29-2	8-0-33-0	
(N.W.T.) v. Northamptonshire (Leicester) 5 August	12-2-44-0	10-0-43-1	12-0-53-0	10.5-2-39-3	6-0-18-0	
(J.P.) v. Derbyshire (Derby) 9 August	7-0-25-2	3-0-22-0	7-0-26-2	6-1-36-0	5-0-18-1	
(J.P.) v. Worcestershire (Leicester) 16 August		3-0-11-0	8-2-19-0	6-1-24-0	8-0-41-1	
(J.P.) v. Lancashire (Old Trafford) 23 August		8-3-14-1	7-0-30-0	7.5-3-14-4	8-0-35-3	
(J.P.) v. Surrey (Leicester) 30 August		8-0-32-1	8-0-29-1	7.5-0-56-1	4-1-19-1	
(J.P.) v. Hampshire (Bournemouth) 6 September		7-0-31-1	8-1-59-2	7.5-0-60-1	8-1-33-1	

K. Higgs	D. A. Wenlock	J. P. Agnew	N. G. B. Cook	P. Booth	B	Lb	W	Nb	Total	Wkts
					2	11	2	2	195	7
					9	10	2	1	190	10
8–2–20–2	5–0–18–1					11	2		147	8
	11–4–20–1	7.3–2–37–0			3	4	2	5	117	4
6–0–17–3	6–0–31–1				1	8	4		116	9
8–0–36–1	8–0–34–1					7		3	207	4
6.5–2–13–1			8–0–32–1	8–0–26–1	1	5	1		136	5
11–4–25–1				5–0–13–1	11	11	9	4	196	9
7.3–1–32–1			8–3–20–2	8–0–21–1	5	2			125	6
8–2–12–1						10	3	1	151	9
11–3–40–2						10	5		191	9
8–0–25–0						15	1		177	6
2–0–20–1					1	3	3	2	88	2
				8–0–46–0		9			200	7
						15	3		162	7
					4	3	1	2	207	4
				7–0–37–1	1	12	1		178	6
		5.3–0–38–1	8–0–29–1			6	1		169	4
8–0–31–0					4	6	1		135	10
8–0–27–0	4–0–25–1					5	1		194	5
			8–0–36–0		2	5	1	1	228	5

Middlesex C.C.C.
Limited-Over
Matches –
Batting, 1981

	v. Hampshire (Lord's) 9 May (B.&H.)	v. Hampshire (Lord's) 10 May (J.P.)	v. Surrey (The Oval) 17 May (J.P.)	v. Minor Counties (Slough) (B.&H.) 16 and 18 May	v. Sussex (Lord's) 20 May (B.&H.)	v. Surrey (The Oval) 21 May (B.&H.)	v. Sussex (Lord's) 24 May (J.P.)	v. Yorkshire (Bradford) 31 May (J.P.)	v. Somerset (Lord's) 7 June (J.P.)	v. Leicestershire (Lord's) 21 June (J.P.)	v. Nottinghamshire (Trent Bridge) 28 June (J.P.)	v. Lancashire (Old Trafford) 12 July (J.P.)
J. M. Brearley	27		0			0		4*	17	31	4	7
P. R. Downton	11		—			13		—	0		—	—
C. T. Radley	50		40			9		22	11	42	93	37
M. W. Gatting	27		6			11		8			3	25
R. O. Butcher	27					3*		14	5	8	56	44
G. D. Barlow	21		18			5		27	52		17	52
J. E. Embury	7		5*			—		0*		1*	2*	1
M. W. W. Selvey	3		—			—			8*		10	4
J. R. Thomson	0							1	2			
W. W. Daniel	0		—			—			0	—	—	—
W. G. Merry	1*		—			—			—		—	
P. H. Edmonds			15			0*		1	31	24	42*	19*
W. N. Slack			15*						35			
R. G. Ellis										9		
K. P. Tomlins									14*			
C. P. Metson										—		
S. P. Hughes												—
C. R. Cook												
J. D. Monteith												
K. D. James												
N. G. Cowans												
Byes						2				1		4
Leg byes	1		11			5		5	4	5	8	22
Wides						4		3	2	1	6	3
No Balls						2			3		5	
Total	175		110			54		85	170	136	246	218
Wickets	10		5			5		6	9	5	6	7
Result	L	Ab.	W	Ab.	Ab.	Ab.	Ab.	Ab.	L	W	W	L
Points	0	2	4	1	1	1	2	2	0	4	4	0

Catches

14 – P. R. Downton (ct 13/st 1)

8 – J. E. Embury

6 – P. H. Edmonds

4 – J. M. Brearley and G. D. Barlow

3 – M. W. Gatting

2 – C. T. Radley, C. P. Metson, W. W. Daniel and R. O. Butcher

1 – M. W. W. Selvey, J. R. Thomson, R. G. Ellis, K. P. Tomlins and W. N. Slack

v. Worcestershire (Lord's) 19 July (J.P.)	v. Lancashire (Old Trafford) 24 July (NWT)	v. Northamptonshire (Tring) 26 July (J.P.)	v. Gloucestershire (Lord's) 2 August (J.P.)	v. Warwickshire (Lord's) 9 August (J.P.)	v. Glamorgan (Lord's) 23 August (J.P.)	v. Kent (Canterbury) 30 August (J.P.)	v. Essex (Chelmsford) 6 September (J.P.)	v. Derbyshire (Derby) 13 September (J.P.)
	0	2		29	11			6
—	0	0	8	2*	5	24	5	3*
34		62	16	11	11	2	20	20
	5	26		6	7		38	14
77*	31	64		41	7	4	88	70
44	26	0	77	1	8	6	1	71
1*	25*	1		35*	1		5	19
	2	0	0*		6	1*	0*	1*
—	0	0	—	1*	1			1*
—		1*						
—	34	18	7	19	24	16	25	3
4	53		13	2		52*		
1			7			34	3	
—	1				0*	—	—	
			73					
			—	10			—	
						13		
	1	1		4	1			
2	9	10	14	16	5	11	7	6
1	1	1	4	4	5	6		5
1	1	2		2	3			2
165	189	196	213	186	114	150	190	218
4	10	10	6	9	10	7	7	7
W	L	L	L	L	L	L	L	L
4	—	0	0	0	0	0	0	0

Middlesex C.C.C. Limited-Over Matches – Bowling, 1981	W. W. Daniel	J. R. Thomson	W. G. Merry	M. W. W. Selvey	J. E. Emburey	M. W. Gatting
(B.&H.) v. Hampshire (Lord's) 9 May	11–1–34–0	11–3–22–7	10–1–39–1	11–2–30–1	10.3–2–34–0	1–0–5–0
(J.P.) v. Surrey (The Oval) 17 May	7–0–26–0		7–0–30–0	7–0–36–4	7–0–32–0	1–0–14–0
(J.P.) v. Yorkshire (Bradford) 31 May	1–0–4–0	3–0–11–2		1.5–0–10–1	2–0–17–1	
(J.P.) v. Somerset (Lord's) 7 June	5–0–12–0	2–0–13–0		3–0–23–1		
(J.P.) v. Leicestershire (Lord's) 21 June	8–1–16–1	8–0–33–2		8–2–20–1	8–0–29–2	
(J.P.) v. Nottinghamshire (Trent Bridge) 28 June	8–1–14–1		8–0–52–3	8–1–48–1	8–0–41–4	
(J.P.) v. Lancashire (Old Trafford) 12 July	8–1–43–3			7–0–58–1	8–3–18–2	
(J.P.) v. Worcestershire (Lord's) 19 July	7–0–34–1		7–1–26–2		8–0–32–2	
(N.W.T.) v. Lancashire (Old Trafford) 24 July	12–4–28–4			12–4–45–1	12–3–29–1	3–0–14–0
(J.P.) v. Northamptonshire (Tring) 26 July	8–0–39–0		8–0–44–2	4–0–30–0	8–1–31–3	4–0–22–0
(J.P.) v. Gloucestershire (Lord's) 2 August	6.4–0–41–0			6–0–23–1		
(J.P.) v. Warwickshire (Lord's) 9 August	8–0–26–0				8–2–34–0	5–1–27–1
(J.P.) v. Glamorgan (Lord's) 23 August	7–1–31–0			8–0–14–0	8–0–23–1	1–0–10–0
(J.P.) v. Kent (Canterbury) 30 August				8–3–14–2		
(J.P.) v. Essex (Chelmsford) 6 September				8–1–16–2	6–0–34–1	1–0–13–0
(J.P.) v. Derbyshire (Derby) 13 September	5.4–0–35–0			8–0–29–0	3–0–20–0	

P. H. Edmonds	S. P. Hughes	J. D. Monteith	K. D. James	K. P. Tomlins	N. G. Cowans	B	Lb	W	Nb	Total	Wkts
							9	3		176	9
5-0-16-1						1	8	3	1	167	6
							1	1	1	45	4
						1	2			51	1
8-2-29-2							6	1	1	135	8
8-1-37-0						2	14	2	2	212	9
8-0-39-1	8-0-52-0						10	1		221	7
8-1-23-1	8-0-34-2					4	5	2		160	8
9-0-37-0	12-2-59-1					3	10	6		231	8
8-0-26-1						1	5	2		200	6
8-0-58-0	5-0-29-0	8-0-42-1				3	17	1	1	215	2
7-0-31-2		3.5-0-30-1				1	12			161	4
8-0-25-0	8-0-26-1					2	13	2	5	151	4
8-0-32-1	7-1-24-1	8-1-21-1	5-0-30-0	3-0-15-0			11	3	1	151	5
6.4-0-45-1	8-0-45-2				8-1-27-1	3	5	3	1	192	7
1-0-8-1					4-0-31-1	6	4	5		138	4

Northamptonshire C.C.C.
Limited-Over Matches – Batting, 1981

	v. Nottinghamshire (Northampton) 9 May (B.&H.)	v. Nottinghamshire (Northampton) 10 May (J.P.)	v. Gloucestershire (Northampton) 17 May (J.P.)	v. Gloucestershire (Bristol) 16 and 18 May (B.&H.)	v. Leicestershire (Northampton) 20 May (B.&H.)	v. Lancashire (Old Trafford) 24 May (J.P.)	v. Worcestershire (Worcester) 30 May (B.&H.)	v. Leicestershire (Northampton) 31 May (J.P.)	v. Kent (Maidstone) 7 June (J.P.)	v. Surrey (The Oval) 14 June (J.P.)	v. Worcestershire (Worcester) 21 June (J.P.)	v. Sussex (Hastings) 28 June (J.P.)
G. Cook	28		0		—	13	71*	11	6	65	0	58
W. Larkins	0		17		—	31	23	0	64	18	18	68
R. G. Williams	19		15		—	4	31*	12	26	—	81	13
A. J. Lamb	54		36		—	7	—	0	10	83	127*	38
P. Willey	28		16		—	20	—	41		40		6
T. J. Yardley	9*		2		—	1	—	32	1	7*	1*	16
R. M. Carter	1		1		—	0	—	5*				6*
G. Sharp	1		12		—	3*	—	1	29*			1*
T. M. Lamb	4		3*		—	0	—	0				
N. A. Mallender	1		0*		—	4	—	1				
B. J. Griffiths	0		—		—	2*	—					
R. M. Tindall									10*		—	
D. J. Wild											—	
C. D. Booden										—		
R. J. Boyd-Moss												
Sarfraz Nawaz												
J. P. C. Mills												
Byes			1			1		1		1		
Leg byes	6		4			7	1	8	6	3	23	9
Wides	1		1			2		4	2	4	1	1
No balls						1	1				4	2
Total	152		108			96	127	116	154	221	255	218
Wickets	10		8			9	1	9	5	4	3	7
Result	L	Ab.	L	Ab.	Ab.	L	W	L	W	W	L	W
Points	0	2	0	1	1	0	2	0	4	4	0	4

Catches

28 – G. Sharp (ct 27/st 1)

14 – G. Cook

10 – T. M. Lamb and R. G. Williams

8 – T. J. Yardley (ct 6/st 2)

6 – R. M. Carter and A. J. Lamb

5 – W. Larkins and B. J. Griffiths

4 – Sarfraz Nawaz

3 – P. Willey

2 – C. D. Booden and N. A. Mallender

1 – R. M. Tindall, D. J. Wild and R. J. Boyd-Moss

v. Glamorgan (Luton) 5 July (J.P.)	v. Glamorgan (Harrogate) 8 July (T.T.)	v. Worcestershire (Harrogate) 10 July (T.T.)	v. Somerset (Northampton) 22 July (N.W.T.)	v. Middlesex (Tring) 26 July (J.P.)	v. Warwickshire (Northampton) 2 August (J.P.)	v. Leicestershire (Leicester) 5 August (N.W.T.)	v. Somerset (Weston-super-Mare) 9 August (J.P.)	v. Yorkshire (Wellingborough) 16 August (J.P.)	v. Lancashire (Northampton) 19 August (N.W.T.)	v. Essex (Milton Keynes) 23 August (J.P.)	v. Derbyshire (Derby) 30 August (J.P.)	v. Essex (Scarborough) 2 September (F.T.)	v. Derbyshire (Lord's) 5 September (N.W.T.)	v. Hampshire (Southampton) 13 September (J.P.)
54	126	33	50	30	6	63	12	50	31	52	0	26	111	48
0			59	50	48	81*	4	1	9	27			52	42
31	5	10	25	55*	0	1	1	14	41	—		17	14	5
21	55	9	28*	26	36	6	24	11	10	50	39	8	9	43
			32*	6		46	21					8	19	31
19	73	0	—	1	3	0*	23*	12	31	25	20	68	4	3
								9	14	—	16	17		4*
	6	36	—	21	3	—	8*		1	8*	19	11*	5	6
—	6	12	—	—	26*	—	—	1	10*	—	3	—	4	—
8*	18	10	—	—	22	—	—	6	4	—	4	—	0	—
—	2*	2*	—	—	2*	—	—	1*	1*	—	3*		—	—
11*	8	16									18			2*
16	16	0			62		4	1				55		
0	1	1	—	3*	4	—		7	14	7*	18	25*	3*	
											0			
			1	1	2	4	1		2	6	2	2	2	2
8	10	3	4	5	5	3	7	5	16	13	6	9	9	5
2	6	2	3	2	3	1	1	5	1	2	4	2	1	1
4	4	1	2		1	2		3	2	3		4	2	
174	336	135	204	200	223	207	106	126	187	193	152	252	235	192
7	10	10	3	6	9	4	6	10	9	4	10	7	9	7
L	W	L	W	W	L	W	L	L	W	L	L	L	L	L
0	—	—	—	4	0	—	0	0	—	0	0	—	—	0

Northamptonshire C.C.C. Limited-Over Matches – Bowling, 1981	B. J. Griffiths	N. A. Mallender	T. M. Lamb	P. Willey	R. G. Williams	R. M. Carter
(B.&H.) v. Nottinghamshire (Northampton) 9 May	10.3–2–42–2	11–1–30–1	11–2–27–2	11–3–13–1	11–1–34–1	
(J.P.) v. Gloucestershire (Northampton) 17 May	4–0–26–0	4–0–21–2	2–0–11–2	2–0–16–0	2–0–18–0	1–0–10–0
(B.&H.) v. Leicestershire (Northampton) 20 May	5–0–11–0	5.2–1–4–0	1–1–0–2			
(J.P.) v. Lancashire (Old Trafford) 24 May	6–0–22–1	7–1–31–1	7–2–18–2	6–0–29–2	1–0–10–0	8–2–25–2
(B.&H.) v. Worcestershire (Worcester) 30 May	10.3–2–25–3	11–4–13–3	10–3–15–0	11–2–27–0	7–3–11–2	4–1–22–0
(J.P.) v. Leicestershire (Northampton) 31 May	5.1–0–24–1	6–0–24–1	6–1–15–2	6–1–29–1	6–1–22–0	
(J.P.) v. Kent (Maidstone) 7 June			5–2–7–0			
(J.P.) v. Surrey (The Oval) 14 June	5–1–11–2		4.4–1–14–3	7–1–33–3		7–0–35–2
(J.P.) v. Worcestershire (Worcester) 21 June	8–0–35–0		8–0–52–2		8–0–56–1	8–0–46–2
(J.P.) v. Sussex (Hastings) 28 June	8–0–32–2		8–0–44–0	2–0–17–0		8–1–42–2
(J.P.) v. Glamorgan (Luton) 5 July	7.2–0–32–0	7–0–46–1	5–0–21–0		6–1–26–2	
(T.T.) v. Glamorgan (Harrogate) 8 July	6–1–19–0	6–2–28–2	11–1–47–3		4.3–1–10–3	
(T.T.) v. Worcestershire (Harrogate) 10 July	11–1–50–1	9–1–50–0	10.5–2–42–5		3–2–4–1	
(N.W.T.) v. Somerset (Northampton) 22 July	11.4–1–43–3	12–3–33–0	12–2–35–0		12–1–44–3	
(J.P.) v. Middlesex (Tring) 26 July	8–0–35–0	7.4–2–34–5	8–1–33–0	1–0–7–0	7–0–42–0	
(J.P.) v. Warwickshire (Northampton) 2 August	8–1–60–0	8–0–52–1	8–0–45–2		8–1–35–2	
(N.W.T.) v. Leicestershire (Leicester) 5 August	12–0–51–3	11.4–1–26–2	12–3–43–2	12–0–46–1		
(J.P.) v. Somerset (Weston-s-Mare) 9 August	7–1–21–1	4.2–1–16–0	6–1–20–2	4–0–24–0		
(J.P.) v. Yorkshire (Wellingborough) 16 August	8–2–22–0	8–1–25–1	7.5–0–24–1		8–3–14–3	
(N.W.T.) v. Lancashire (Northampton) 19 August	12–1–46–2	12–3–28–0	12–1–28–3		12–0–40–2	
(J.P.) v. Essex (Milton Keynes) 23 August	8–0–36–0	6–0–40–2	7.3–0–41–1		1.3–0–2–1	3–0–20–0
(J.P.) v. Derbyshire (Derby) 30 August	8–0–31–2	8–1–44–1	8–0–30–0			
(F.T.) v. Essex (Scarborough) 2 September		10–2–35–3	10–0–55–2	10–0–50–1	5–0–35–1	5–0–45–0
(N.W.T.) v. Derbyshire (Lord's) 5 September	12–2–40–1	10–1–35–3	12–0–43–0	12–0–33–0	2–0–10–0	
(J.P.) v. Hampshire (Southampton) 13 September	6.4–0–32–2		7–1–26–0	8–1–44–0	2–0–6–0	3–0–29–0

C. D. Booden	D. J. Wild	W. Larkins	Sarfraz Nawaz	B	Lb	W	Nb	Total	Wkts
					5		4	155	9
				4	7			113	4
						1	4	20	2
				4	2	3		144	8
				1	3	4	2	123	10
					4			118	5
7–1–21–2	3–0–18–0				1	1	1	49	2
8–0–32–0					3		1	129	10
8–0–58–0				1	8	3		259	7
	8–1–28–2	2–0–20–1		10		3		196	8
	4–0–24–0		8–0–19–1	5	5	1		179	4
	7–0–38–1		10–1–26–1		4	2	1	175	10
	10–1–36–2		11–2–38–1		13	1	2	236	10
			12–2–29–3	1	15	1	1	202	10
			8–0–31–5	1	10	1	2	196	10
			8–0–45–3		6	1	1	245	9
			12–2–38–2	1	11	3	8	227	10
		7–1–21–0			5	1		108	3
			8–0–37–2		5	4	1	132	10
			12–2–35–2		7	1	1	186	9
		5–0–29–0	8–0–30–1	1	10	1	2	212	6
	8–1–32–1		8–1–34–0	2	15	1	1	190	5
			10–1–32–1	4	4		2	262	8
			12–2–58–1	5	7	3	1	235	6
	8–0–46–1			6	4	1		194	4

Nottinghamshire C.C.C. Limited-Over Matches – Batting, 1981

	v. Northamptonshire (Northampton) 9 May (B.&H.)	v. Northamptonshire (Northampton) 10 May (J.P.)	v. Worcestershire (Trent Bridge) 16 May (B.&H.)	v. Somerset (Trent Bridge) 17 May (J.P.)	v. Gloucestershire (Gloucester) 21 and 22 May (B.&H.)	v. Derbyshire (Derby) 24 May (J.P.)	v. Leicestershire (Trent Bridge) 30 May (B.&H.)	v. Essex (Trent Bridge) 7 June (J.P.)	v. Lancashire (Old Trafford) 21 June (J.P.)	v. Surrey (Trent Bridge) 24 June (B.&H.)	v. Middlesex (Trent Bridge) 28 June (J.P.)	v. Hampshire (Portsmouth) 5 July (J.P.)
P. A. Todd	16		31	11	39		15	5	21	4	0	21
R. T. Robinson	5		77*	1	3		35*	17		6		2
D. W. Randall	61		26	34	6		20		18	62	42	
C. E. B. Rice	0		13	0	96		1	46	28	27	105	0
J. D. Birch	0			28*	21		0	12	20	9	22	8
M. J. Harris	15		—				—	29				2*
B. N. French	14		—	—	6		—		3*	16	0	
R. J. Hadlee	18*		27*	2*	2		32*	14	19	30	0	32
E. E. Hemmings	9		—	—	7		—	6*	1	0	3	8
P. J. Hacker	8		—									
M. K. Bore	0*		—	—	1*		—		—		—	—
B. Hassan			17	18	0				17*	5	12*	13
K. E. Cooper					3*			—	—	1*		6*
R. E. Dexter								37*			8	16
K. Saxelby									—	1	0	
N. I. Weightman												
N. Illingworth												
M. A. Fell												
P. Wood												
P. Johnson												
I. L. Pont												
Byes				1	3		3			8	2	7
Leg byes	5		11	9	3		4	14	12	6	14	4
Wides			14	2	1		2	2		2	2	4
No balls	4		1	1			5			2	2	
Total	155		217	107	191		117	182	139	179	212	123
Wickets	9		4	5	9		4	6	6	10	10	8
Result	W	Ab.	W	L	W	Ab.	W	W	L	L	L	L
Points	2	2	2	0	2	2	2	4	0	—	0	0

Catches

17 – B. N. French (ct 15, st 2)

10 – R. J. Hadlee

9 – C. E. B. Rice

6 – D. W. Randall

5 – M. K. Bore

4 – E. E. Hemmings and K. Saxelby

3 – K. E. Cooper, R. T. Robinson, J. D. Birch and B. Hassan

2 – N. I. Weightman and N. Illingworth

1 – P. J. Hacker, P. A. Todd, P. Wood and M. A. Fell

v. Worcestershire (Harrogate) 9 July (T.T.)	v. Kent (Canterbury) 12 July (J.P.)	v. Yorkshire (Trent Bridge) 19 July (J.P.)	v. Kent (Canterbury) 22–23 July (N.W.T.)	v. Leicestershire (Leicester) 26 July (J.P.)	v. Surrey (Trent Bridge) 2 August (J.P.)	v. Derbyshire (Derby) 5 August (N.W.T.)	v. Worcestershire (Worcester) 9 August (J.P.)	v. Sussex (Trent Bridge) 16 August (J.P.)	v. Warwickshire (Edgbaston) 23 August (J.P.)	v. Gloucestershire (Trent Bridge) 6 September (J.P.)	v. Glamorgan (Trent Bridge) 13 September (J.P.)
33			18			62	7	2			
										22*	48*
55	33	—	25	15	19	29	30	17	67	12	27
58	52	14*	10	101*	0	1	74	30	—	52	47*
10	21	25	4	18	6	0	3	32	—	51	1
0	4	—	33*	23	20	15	0*	6*	—		—
2	0	19*	38*	11	67*	15	15	36*	—	—	—
	6	—	—	9	9	4	0			—	
	—	2*	—		1*					—	
	—					1*					
38	17	—	1	2	10	0	9	33	120*	55	
						4				—	—
4*											
3*	2*	—			0*						
	2	17	6	11	5	1					
				—	—						
							1*	2	14		
									3		15
									3*		
									—		
			4		5				7		
15	21	5	8	9	4	3	10	3	6	13	3
2	4	5	6	9		1				4	2
1		5	3		1	5	1	3	1	1	3
221	164	85	156	200	155	141	150	164	221	210	146
7	8	2	6	7	7	10	7	6	3	4	3
I.	L	W	W	L	L	L	W	W	L	W	W
—	0	4	—	0	0	—	4	4	0	4	4

J214

Nottinghamshire C.C.C. Limited-Over Matches – Bowling, 1981	R. J. Hadlee	C. E. B. Rice	P. J. Hacker	M. K. Bore	E. E. Hemmings	K. E. Cooper
(B.&H.) v. Northamptonshire (Northampton) 9 May	10–1–28–2	10.5–1–22–6	11–2–37–1	11–1–39–0	11–2–19–1	
(B.&H.) v. Worcestershire (Trent Bridge) 16 May	11–1–38–2	11–3–50–2	11–2–43–1	11–1–25–1	11–0–36–0	
(J.P.) v. Somerset (Trent Bridge) 17 May	6.3–0–29–0	8–0–33–2	2–0–12–0	4–0–14–0		
(B.&H.) v. Gloucestershire (Gloucester) 21–22 May	8–2–18–2	8–3–24–2		11–3–27–2	11–1–24–1	11–2–26–3
(B.&H.) v. Leicestershire (Trent Bridge) 30 May	11–1–27–1	11–3–21–2		11–7–7–0	11–4–25–1	11–4–23–1
(J.P.) v. Essex (Trent Bridge) 7 June	6–3–11–1	2–0–2–0		6–2–20–1	1–0–5–0	
(J.P.) v. Lancashire (Old Trafford) 21 June	8–1–22–0			8–0–46–0	8–1–20–0	7.1–1–26–1
(B.&H.) v. Surrey (Trent Bridge) 24 June	11–0–37–2	11–2–32–2			11–3–40–1	11–1–50–1
(J.P.) v. Middlesex (Trent Bridge) 28 June	8–0–36–2	8–0–49–1		8–1–38–1	8–1–50–0	
(J.P.) v. Hampshire (Portsmouth) 5 July	6.1–4–10–1	6–1–22–0		3–0–24–0	5–0–27–0	6–0–29–0
(T.T.) v. Worcestershire (Harrogate) 9 July	9.5–0–30–2	9–1–43–1	10–1–38–1	10–1–51–1		
(J.P.) v. Kent (Canterbury) 12 July	7–0–19–1	7–0–30–0	4–0–30–0	6–0–26–1	8–1–20–1	
(J.P.) v. Yorkshire (Trent Bridge) 19 July	6–2–9–1	5–0–29–0	4–0–20–1	8–1–27–1	8–2–21–2	
(N.W.T.) v. Kent (Canterbury) 22–23 July	10.3–3–14–2	10–2–21–3		12–1–30–1	12–0–42–1	12–1–34–2
(J.P.) v. Leicestershire (Leicester) 26 July	8–0–28–2	7–0–57–0	3–0–18–0	8–0–28–0	8–1–44–4	
(J.P.) v. Surrey (Trent Bridge) 2 August	8–1–28–0	4–0–20–0		8–1–32–3	8–2–12–2	
(N.W.T.) v. Derbyshire (Derby) 5 August	12–3–28–1	11–2–35–3		12–2–18–1	12–2–31–1	12–0–38–2
(J.P.) v. Worcestershire (Worcester) 9 August	7–2–15–1	6.5–1–17–3		8–1–27–2	8–1–14–2	
(J.P.) v. Sussex (Trent Bridge) 16 August	8–0–41–1	8–0–28–3		8–2–25–0	8–1–21–2	
(J.P.) v. Warwickshire (Edgbaston) 23 August		4–0–26–1			8–0–37–1	7–0–36–0
(J.P.) v. Gloucestershire (Trent Bridge) 6 September		8–0–24–2	6–0–36–0		7–2–27–5	6–0–32–1
(J.P.) v. Glamorgan (Trent Bridge) 13 September	5–1–11–1	8–2–21–1		8–3–7–1	8–1–29–0	

K. Saxelby	N. Illingworth	B. S. Hassan	M. A. Fell	D. W. Randall	I. L. Pont	B	Lb	W	Nb	Total	Wkts
							6		1	152	10
						4	13	4	1	214	8
							4	3	1	96	2
						4	3	1		127	10
							7	1	3	114	8
						1	2			41	3
8–1–25–1						1	1		2	143	3
11–1–34–1						4	19	4	6	226	7
8–0–54–1							8	6	5	246	6
						4	4	4	1	125	2
10–1–49–0						1	6	3	1	222	6
7–0–31–1						1	8	3		168	4
6–0–37–4							4	7		154	10
							7	4	2	154	10
	6–0–34–0						5			214	7
5–0–34–1	5–0–23–0					2	5	1	2	159	6
						6	4	3	1	164	10
	8–0–28–0					1	4	1		107	10
	8–1–34–1						10		1	160	8
	8–0–49–0	4–0–33–0	6–1–35–1	0.1–0–2–0			3	1		222	4
	8–1–28–0				5–0–17–0		10	3	4	181	9
	8–0–39–4				3–0–20–0	4	9	4	1	145	7

Somerset C.C.C. Limited-Over Matches – Batting, 1981

	v. Essex (Taunton) 10 May (J.P.)	v. Essex (Chelmsford) 16 May (B.&H.)	v. Nottinghamshire (Trent Bridge) 17 May (J.P.)	v. Combined Universities (Cambridge) 19 May (B.&H.)	v. Kent (Taunton) 21 May (B.&H.)	v. Glamorgan (Taunton) 30 May (B.&H.)	v. Lancashire (Old Trafford) 31 May (J.P.)	v. Middlesex (Lord's) 7 June (J.P.)	v. Gloucestershire (Bath) 14 June (J.P.)	v. Kent (Bath) 21 June (J.P.)	v. Yorkshire (Leeds) 24 June (B.&H.)	v. Leicestershire (Leicester) 5 July (J.P.)
B. C. Rose	0	49	19	31	35	18	—	23	1	7	68	
P. W. Denning	3	0	33	11	25	16	1	25*	26	41	66	7
I. V. A. Richards	14	43	28*	4	17	47	24*	0*	21	0	47	1
P. M. Roebuck	20	7	8*	23*	10	44*	—	—	73*		10	9
I. T. Botham	32	8	—	29*	57*	20	23*		29		0	
D. Breakwell	6	7	—	—	—	1*	0	—		12		9
V. J. Marks	15	9	—	—	—	—	—	—	44	0	4	9
J. Garner	13*	12	—	—	—	—	—	—	0	0	1*	20
D. J. S. Taylor	5*	54*	—	—	14*	2	—	—	1*	20*	4*	21
C. H. Dredge	—	6	—	—	—	—	—	—		0	—	6*
H. R. Moseley	—	24	—	—	—	—	—	—	—	14	—	12*
J. W. Lloyds			—	—	5	12	—		1			
N. F. M. Popplewell								—		10	11	1
P. A. Slocombe										11		42
K. F. Jennings												
Byes	1	4		5				1			2	
Leg-byes	19	12	4	5	8	9	1	2	13	16	7	10
Wides	2	3	3	6	1	1					1	3
No-balls		2	1		1				3	1	2	1
Total	130	240	96	114	173	170	49	51	212	132	223	151
Wickets	7	10	2	3	5	6	2	1	7	10	7	9
Result	L	L	W	W	W	W	W	W	W	L	W	L
Points	0	0	4	2	2	2	4	4	4	0	—	0

Catches

31 – D. J. S. Taylor (ct 26, st 5)

9 – I. V. A. Richards

8 – I. T. Botham and P. M. Roebuck

7 – B. C. Rose and C. H. Dredge

5 – P. W. Denning

4 – J. Garner

3 – H. R. Moseley and I. V. A. Richards

2 – J. W. Lloyds and N. F. M. Popplewell

1 – V. J. Marks

v. Kent (Taunton) 8 July (B.&H.)	v. Sussex (Taunton) 12 July (J.P.)	v. Derbyshire (Taunton) 19 July (J.P.)	v. Northamptonshire (Northampton) 22 July (N.W.T.)	v. Surrey (Lord's) 25 July (B.&H.)	v. Yorkshire (Scarborough) 2 August (J.P.)	v. Northamptonshire (Weston-super-Mare) 9 August (J.P.)	v. Surrey (The Oval) 16 August (J.P.)	v. Hampshire (Taunton) 23 August (J.P.)	v. Worcestershire (Worcester) 30 August (J.P.)	v. Glamorgan (Cardiff) 6 September (J.P.)	v. Warwickshire (Taunton) 13 September (J.P.)
22	32	7*	2	5	63	—	79	0	61		4
22	27	23	23	0	22	65	21	8	4	8	1
2	46	86*	0	132*	2	8	5	93	9	6	101
51*	2	25	29	22	79	23*	7*	15	22	27	35*
2	0		45	37*		6*		106		50*	5
		41	0	—							
7*	14*	—	8	—	9	—	5	15*	15	1	3*
—	—	—	19	—	4	—	13	2*	1	14*	22
—	10*	—	1	—	7*	—	3*	—	7*	8	—
—	—	—	0*	—	—	—	—	—	0*	—	—
—	—	—					—	—	0	—	—
					1	0	33	2	5	14	
42	14	—	57	—	2	—	43	27	29	12	23
						3*					
2			1				3		1		
3	10	5	15		14	5	8	12	8	10	7
2			1		4	1		6		9	9
2		1	1	1				1		2	1
157	155	188	202	197	210	108	220	286	163	161	211
5	6	3	10	3	8	3	7	7	9	7	6
W	W	W	L	W	L	W	W	W	L	W	W
—	4	4	—	—	0	4	4	4	0	4	4

Somerset C.C.C. Limited-Over Matches – Bowling, 1981

	J. Garner	I. T. Botham	C. H. Dredge	H. R. Moseley	I. V. A. Richards	D. Breakwell
(J.P.) v. Essex (Taunton) 10 May	6–0–26–0	6–1–11–3	6–0–25–1	6–0–22–0	3–0–21–1	3–0–27–1
(B.&H.) v. Essex (Chelmsford) 16 May	11–3–44–0	10.1–1–74–1	11–0–34–1	10.5–0–60–1		1–0–2–0
(J.P.) v. Nottinghamshire (Trent Bridge) 17 May	7–3–18–3	8–1–36–2	5–0–29–0	4–0–8–0	3–0–3–0	
(B.&H.) v. Combined Univ. (Cambridge) 19 May	11–4–21–3	11–5–22–0	11–3–20–2	11–2–22–2		11–4–23–1
(B.&H.) v. Kent (Taunton) 21 May	10.1–2–18–1	11–1–32–1	11–0–42–2	11–2–36–0		11–2–37–2
(B.&H.) v. Glamorgan (Taunton) 30 May	11–2–30–1	11–2–32–1	10–1–24–1	11–1–32–0	4–1–9–1	8–2–21–1
(J.P.) v. Lancashire (Old Trafford) 31 May	4–1–7–0	4–0–19–3	4–0–20–0	4–0–12–2	4–0–21–2	
(J.P.) v. Middlesex (Lord's) 7 June	7–0–32–0		8–0–35–5	7–0–38–0		4–0–15–1
(J.P.) v. Gloucestershire (Bath) 14 June	8–1–21–4	8–1–34–1	8–0–49–1	8–1–33–0	2.1–0–18–1	
(J.P.) v. Kent (Bath) 21 June	8–1–26–2		8–1–33–0	8–0–18–3		5–0–21–0
(B.&H.) v. Yorkshire (Leeds) 24 June	11–1–33–3	11–0–34–0	11–0–72–3	11–1–31–1		
(J.P.) v. Leicestershire (Leicester) 5 July	8–1–29–0		8–0–42–1	8–1–35–0	8–2–23–2	
(B.&H.) v. Kent (Taunton) 8 July	9.1–0–24–3	10–4–23–3	10–4–31–2	11–1–22–0	1–1–0–0	
(J.P.) v. Sussex (Taunton) 12 July	7.3–1–23–4	7–0–36–1	4–0–18–2	8–0–21–1		
(J.P.) v. Derbyshire (Taunton) 19 July	8–1–24–1		8–0–28–3	8–0–45–0	3–0–21–1	
(N.W.T.) v. Northamptonshire (Northampton) 22 July	12–2–32–1	11–2–58–1	9–1–27–0		1.1–0–5–0	9–0–34–1
(B.&H.) v. Surrey (Lord's) 25 July	11–5–14–5	11–2–44–0	11–0–48–0			
(J.P.) v. Yorkshire (Scarborough) 2 August	8–1–29–1		8–0–54–0			
(J.P.) v. Northamptonshire (Weston-s-Mare) 9 August		7–0–25–1	7–0–19–1	7–0–18–1	7–0–18–1	
(J.P.) v. Surrey (The Oval) 16 August	8–2–16–3		8–1–42–2	8–0–27–1		
(J.P.) v. Hampshire (Taunton) 23 August	4–1–16–0	4–0–13–1		8–0–25–4	2–0–6–0	
(J.P.) v. Worcestershire (Worcester) 30 August	8–2–18–3		8–0–33–1	8–0–48–1	5–0–27–0	
(J.P.) v. Glamorgan (Cardiff) 6 September	8–1–25–3		8–0–32–0	8–1–30–2		
(J.P.) v. Warwickshire (Taunton) 13 September	6–0–28–3	6–0–24–0	6–0–23–1	5–0–30–3	3–0–16–0	

a. P. W. Denning 2–0–10–0

V. J. Marks	N. F. M. Popplewell	K. F. Jennings	J. W. Lloyds	B. C. Rose	P. M. Roebuck	B	Lb	W	Nb	Total	Wkts
							4	2	1	139	8
11–0–50–1						2	8	1	3	278	5
						1	9	2	1	107	5
							2		1	111	9
							6	1		172	10
							16	4	1	169	8
						1	7	2	3	92	7
8–0–24–1	4–1–17–1						4	2	3	170	9
5–0–24–1							7	6		192	10
0.3–0–6–0	7–0–24–1					4	1	1		134	6
11–3–31–1						1	16	2	1	221	9
	8–1–26–2						4	3	2	164	8
	11–0–31–2					6	8	7	2	154	10
8–0–23–2	4–0–15–0						12	5	1	154	10
8–1–22–0	5–0–31–0						8	4	1	184	5
8–0–27–0	3–1–11–0					1	4	3	2	204	3
11–5–24–2	11–0–45–1					2	14	2	1	194	8
8–1–32–1	6–0–58–1	8–0–40–0				2	11	2	2	230	3
	7–1–17–2					1	7	1		106	6
8–1–31–1	5.1–0–35–2					5	7	8		171	10
8–0–23–2	3–0–19–1		1.3–0–1–2	2–0–6–0	2–0–9–0	1	6	2		137	10 a
8–0–21–0	2–0–8–0						11			166	6
8–1–25–1	8–0–34–2						7	2	4	159	8
	2–0–23–0						5	2	2	153	7

Surrey C.C.C. Limited-Over Matches – Batting, 1981

	v. Sussex (Hove) 10 May (J.P.)	v. Sussex (Hove) 11 May (B.&H.)	v. Hampshire (Bournemouth) 16 May (B.&H.)	v. Middlesex (The Oval) 17 May (J.P.)	v. Middlesex (The Oval) 21 May (B.&H.)	v. Minor Counties (The Oval) 30 May (B.&H.)	v. Derbyshire (The Oval) 31 May (J.P.)	v. Glamorgan (Swansea) 7 June (J.P.)	v. Northamptonshire (The Oval) 14 June (J.P.)	v. Nottinghamshire (Trent Bridge) 24 June (B.&H.)	v. Yorkshire (Scarborough) 5 July (J.P.)	v. Leicestershire (The Oval) 8 July (B.&H.)
A. R. Butcher		9	—	23		33	11		22	15	14	
G. S. Clinton		46	—	42	—	42	35	3		48	105*	17
G. P. Howarth		4			—				8			
R. D. V. Knight		6	—	24*	—	1	16	27*	11	70	13	38
G. R. J. Roope		20	—	31	—	19	24	—	5	2*	—	55*
D. M. Smith		29*	—	21*	—	29	7	9*	13	25		1
D. J. Thomas		1	—	1	—	9	28*	—	9	13		0
R. D. Jackman		3	—	—	—	1	—		3*	—		1
C. J. Richards		11*	—	0	—	10	1	—		—	—	32
S. T. Clarke		—	—	—	—	9	1*	—	17	0		4*
P. I. Pocock		—	—	—	5*	—	—		0	—		4*
M. A. Lynch		—		12	—	46	8	—	4	17	70	22
I. R. Payne								—	33		—	2
Intikhab Alam										3*	33*	4
P. H. L. Wilson												
D. B. Pauline												
A. J. Stewart												
G. Monkhouse												
R. G. L. Cheatle												
K. Mackintosh												
Byes		3		1		8	2			4		
Leg-byes		8		8		8	6		3	19	4	10
Wides		1		3		6	1	2		4	4	5
No-balls		1		1				2	1	6		
Total		142		167		226	140	43	129	226	243	191
Wickets		7		6		10	7	1	10	7	3	9
Result	Ab.	L	Ab.	L	Ab.	W	W	Ab.	L	W	W	W
Points	2	0	1	0	1	2	4	2	0	—	4	—

Catches

13 – G. R. J. Roope (ct 11, st 2)
11 – C. J. Richards (ct 10 st 1)
9 – D. M. Smith
8 – M. A. Lynch
6 – P. I. Pocock and G. S. Clinton
5 – R. D. Jackman
4 – R. D. V. Knight
2 – A. R. Butcher, S. T. Clarke, D. J. Thomas and D. B. Pauline
1 – Intikhab Alam, P. H. L. Wilson and K. Mackintosh

v. Warwickshire (The Oval) 12 July (J.P.)	v. Hampshire (Southampton) 19 July (J.P.)	v. Leicestershire (The Oval) 24 July (N.W.T.)	v. Somerset (Lord's) 25 July (B.&H.)	v. Lancashire (The Oval) 26 July (J.P.)	v. Nottinghamshire (Trent Bridge) 2 August (J.P.)	v. Gloucestershire (Cheltenham) 9 August (J.P.)	v. Somerset (The Oval) 16 August (J.P.)	v. Kent (Folkestone) 23 August (J.P.)	v. Leicestershire (Leicester) 30 August (J.P.)	v. Worcestershire (The Oval) 6 September (J.P.)	v. Essex (The Oval) 13 September (J.P.)
5				82*	40	5	8	74	25	37	19
19	27	19	6	4	27	0		5			—
39	19	—	16							27	
	10	—	92	51	10	2	7	14	29	1*	29
11	18	—	14*	—	39*	14	42	2	22	—	60*
13	6	—	7	—		5	25	17	32*		24
10		10*	0	14*							
0	—	—	2*		—	1	3	11	—	—	—
1	0		1					13		—	14*
	20	45*	15								
1*	—	—	—		—	—	0*	3*	—	—	—
80*	56*	5	22	16*	7	69	38	1	44	46*	4
1	0	—					2				
				—	12	15*	0	6	9*		
				—		—	1				
					0		25			92	18
					8*						
								5*			
								—			
	4	1	2		2	4	5				1
8	2	3	14	10	5	5	7	6	5	5	9
5	4	3	2		1		8	1	1	4	3
2	1	2	1		2						1
195	167	88	194	163	159	128	171	158	194	185	182
9	8	2	8	2	6	7	10	9	5	2	5
L	L	L	L	W	W	W	L	L	W	W	L
0	0	—	—	4	4	4	0	0	4	4	0

Surrey C.C.C. Limited-Over Matches – Bowling, 1981	S. T. Clarke	R. D. Jackman	D. J. Thomas	R. D. V. Knight	P. I. Pocock	G. R. J. Roope
(B.&H.) v. Sussex (Hove) 11 May	10.4–0–28–0	11–4–22–3	11–3–30–1	11–3–21–2	7–0–27–0	2–1–4–0
(B.&H.) v. Hampshire (Bournemouth) 16 May	7–4–10–1	10–3–24–1	9–1–18–0	11–5–28–0	8–1–36–1	4–2–12–0
(J.P.) v. Middlesex (The Oval) 17 May	5.5–0–39–2	6–1–23–1	5–0–26–0	2–0–4–1	2–0–7–1	
(B.&H.) v. Middlesex (The Oval) 21 May	5–3–5–1	8–2–12–1	8–1–19–2	2–1–5–0		
(B.&H.) v. Minor Counties (The Oval) 30 May	11–4–14–3	11–4–40–3	4–2–4–0	11–2–25–3	4.2–1–13–1	
(J.P.) v. Derbyshire (The Oval) 31 May	6–0–41–0	8–2–11–0	7–2–16–2	8–0–22–2	7–0–27–1	1–0–4–1
(J.P.) v. Northamptonshire (The Oval) 14 June	8–0–38–0	8–0–57–0	8–0–42–1	7–1–39–1	8–0–37–1	
(B.&H.) v. Nottinghamshire (Trent Bridge) 24 June	8–3–26–2	9.4–3–24–4	6–0–29–1	11–0–36–2	11–1–30–0	
(J.P.) v. Yorkshire (Scarborough) 5 July			8–0–41–2		8–2–22–3	4–0–23–1
(B.&H.) v. Leicestershire (The Oval) 8 July		10.5–0–43–0	11–1–30–3	6–2–13–0	11–2–50–3	3–0–10–0
(J.P.) v. Warwickshire (The Oval) 12 July		7.3–0–36–0	7–0–37–0		8–2–36–1	6–0–37–1
(J.P.) v. Hampshire (Southampton) 19 July	7–0–15–1	4.3–0–41–0		8–0–22–2	8–1–26–2	4–0–24–0
(N.W.T.) v. Leicestershire (The Oval) 24 July	2–0–10–2	2–0–29–0	2–0–17–2	2–0–11–1	2–0–25–0	
(B.&H.) v. Somerset (Lord's) 25 July	8–1–24–1	11–1–53–1	5.3–0–32–0	9–0–41–1	11–1–46–0	
(J.P.) v. Lancashire (The Oval) 26 July			7–0–30–1	2–0–15–0	8–4–14–1	
(J.P.) v. Nottinghamshire (Trent Bridge) 2 August		8–3–20–1	7–1–27–3	8–0–38–0	8–1–22–2	
(J.P.) v. Gloucestershire (Cheltenham) 9 August		8–4–17–2		7–2–17–1	8–4–17–1	8–0–35–3
(J.P.) v. Somerset (The Oval) 16 August		8–0–52–2		4–0–29–0	8–0–38–1	
(J.P.) v. Kent (Folkestone) 23 August		8–2–25–0		8–0–44–2	7–0–50–1	
(J.P.) v. Leicestershire (Leicester) 30 August		8–1–31–1		4–0–28–1	8–0–29–1	
(J.P.) v. Worcestershire (The Oval) 6 September		8–0–33–2		8–0–46–0	8–0–38–2	
(J.P.) v. Essex (The Oval) 13 September		8–0–46–1		7–0–56–0	8–2–21–3	

a R. G. L. Cheatle 4–1–20–0

Intikhab Alam	P. H. L. Wilson	I. R. Payne	M. A. Lynch	G. Monkhouse	K. Mackintosh	B	Lb	W	Nb	Total	Wkts
						1	7	1	2	143	7
							10	5		143	5
							11			110	5
						2	5	4	2	54	5
							1	1		98	10
						5	11	2		139	6
						1	3	4		221	4
4–0–16–0						8	6	2	2	179	10
	7.3–0–52–0	8–0–32–1	4–0–38–0				17	3		228	10
2–0–9–0		11–3–20–3				4	7	2		188	10
		8–0–30–1				2	13	5		196	3
		7–1–31–0				8	1	3		171	6
						1	5	5	1	104	5
									1	197	3
8–0–29–1	8–1–31–2	7–0–36–0					4	1	2	162	7
	7–0–29–1					5	4	9	1	155	7
2–0–19–0	5.3–1–13–2					3	6			127	10
8–0–31–1	7–0–36–1	4–0–23–0				3	8			220	7
8–0–40–2				8–0–24–0		2	9	1		195	6
8–1–36–2				8–0–45–0			2	2		193	7 a
				8–2–23–2	6–0–34–1	2	6	1		183	8
				8–0–33–0	8–1–34–1	4	9			203	7

Sussex C.C.C. Limited-Over Matches – Batting, 1981	v. Surrey (Hove) 10 May (J.P.)	v. Surrey (Hove) 11 May (B.&H.)	v. Worcestershire (Worcester) 17 May (J.P.)	v. Middlesex (Lord's) 20 May (B.&H.)	v. Minor Counties (Slough) 22 May (B.&H.)	v. Middlesex (Lord's) 24 May (J.P.)	v. Hampshire (Hove) 30 May and 1 June (B.&H.)	v. Hampshire (Basingstoke) 31 May (J.P.)	v. Lancashire (Hove) 7 June (J.P.)	v. Essex (Ilford) 21 June (J.P.)	v. Leicestershire (Hove) 24–25 June (B.&H.)	v. Northamptonshire (Hastings) 28 June (J.P.)
G. D. Mendis		7	56*		16		0	30	69*	60	1	4
J. R. T. Barclay		31	—		—		59	—	—	23*	17	17
P. W. G. Parker		0	0		58		25	15	0	14	0	5
Imran Khan		4	34*		15		0	17	63*			
I. A. Greig		19	—		14		51	17*	—	40	11	28
C. M. Wells		32	—		8*		7	—	—	9	30	24
C. P. Phillipson		15	—		19*		16*	—	—	7	59	7
I. J. Gould		17*	2		10		6	69*	17	4	4	27
G. S. Le Roux		7*	—		—		16*	—	—	30	25*	16
G. G. Arnold		—	—		—		—	—	—	—	5	8*
C. E. Waller		—	—		—		—	—	—	—	—	—
T. D. Booth-Jones										1*	9	
A. P. Wells												47*
A. N. Jones												
J. R. P. Heath												
A. C. S. Pigott												
Byes		1						6	7	1	11	10
Leg-byes		7	2				8	9	2	21	11	
Wides		1			3		9	1	1	4	9	3
No-balls		2	2		3		1		1	2	4	
Total		143	96		154		198	164	160	216	196	196
Wickets		7	2		5		7	3	2	7	9	8
Result	Ab.	W	W	Ab.	W	Ab.	W	W	W	W	L	L
Points	2	2	4	1	2	2	2	4	4	4	—	0

Catches

14 – I. J. Gould (ct 12, st 2)

9 – J. R. T. Barclay

8 – P. W. G. Parker

6 – I. A. Greig

5 – C. M. Wells

4 – G. D. Mendis

3 – C. E. Waller and C. P. Phillipson

2 – G. S. Le Roux and G. G. Arnold

1 – Imran Khan, A. P. Wells, A. C. S. Pigott and sub

v. Gloucestershire (Hove) 5 July (J.P.)	v. Somerset (Taunton) 12 July (J.P.)	v. Warwickshire (Horsham) 19 July (J.P.)	v. Warwickshire (Edgbaston) 22–23 July (N.W.T.)	v. Glamorgan (Ebbw Vale) 26 July (J.P.)	v. Leicestershire (Leicester) 2 August (J.P.)	v. Essex (Hove) 5 August (N.W.T.)	v. Kent (Eastbourne) 9 August (J.P.)	v. Nottinghamshire (Trent Bridge) 16 August (J.P.)	v. Derbyshire (Hove) 6 September (J.P.)	v. Yorkshire (Hove) 13 September (J.P.)
125*	7	19	40	55	39	26	13	41	35	
—	1	20	31	1*	6	0	0		—	
36	16	54	33	10	13	45	12	13	18	
	5	18		60*	10	38	7	21	19*	
7	32	30	82	34	36	11	20	2	40*	
31	6	3	28	30	2	25	0	36*	4	
12*	13	5	1	17	24*	8*	29	20	15*	
57	7	19	10	12	6	1	21	3	24	
	18	2	3*	2	8*	1	30*	9		
—	17	19*				0	0	4*		
—	2*	1*				0	0			
—	17		0*						—	
—										
								0		
—										
				1		1				
13	12	15	22	13	15	11	13	10	13	
5	5	6	2	3	3	1	2		3	
1	1		4	3			2		1	2
287	154	198	274	241	162	170	147	160	173	
4	10	9	8	7	7	10	10	8	5	
W	L	L	W	W	W	L	L	L	W	Ab.
4	0	0	—	4	4	—	0	0	4	2

Sussex C.C.C. Limited-Over Matches – Bowling, 1981

	G. G. Arnold	G. S. Le Roux	Imran Khan	I. A. Greig	J. R. T. Barclay	C. E. Waller
(B.&H.) v. Surrey (Hove) 11 May	11–3–17–1	11–1–38–3	11–3–21–1	4–0–15–0	11–2–24–1	7–2–14–0
(J.P.) v. Worcestershire (Worcester) 17 May	3–0–11–1	3–0–28–1	3–0–12–3	3–0–18–0	2–0–11–1	
(B.&H.) v. Minor Counties (Slough) 22 May	3–0–17–0	5–0–21–2	5–1–15–1	5–0–27–1	2.2–0–11–1	2–1–6–1
(B.&H.) v. Hampshire (Hove) 30 May and 1 June	11–4–29–0	9.2–0–38–1	11–0–39–2	11–1–35–5	5–2–12–1	7–0–35–0
(J.P.) v. Hampshire (Basingstoke) 31 May	7–3–14–1	6–0–36–1	6–0–38–1	2–0–12–0	6–1–39–2	7–0–14–1
(J.P.) v. Lancashire (Hove) 7 June	8–0–21–0	7–0–29–0	7–0–21–1	8–0–38–3	2–0–20–0	
(J.P.) v. Essex (Ilford) 21 June	8–3–8–0	8–0–53–0		8–0–38–3	4–0–17–1	8–0–42–1
(B.&H.) v. Leicestershire (Hove) 24 and 25 June	11–4–20–0	11–0–41–1		10.1–0–36–1	11–0–34–3	3–1–15–0
(J.P.) v. Northamptonshire (Hastings) 28 June	8–0–39–0	6.4–0–36–0		8–0–34–1	3–0–27–0	
(J.P.) v. Gloucestershire (Hove) 5 July	8–1–34–1			8–0–36–0	8–0–39–2	
(J.P.) v. Somerset (Taunton) 12 July	8–1–27–0	7–0–38–1		7.4–0–38–2	8–2–18–0	7–1–24–2
(J.P.) v. Warwickshire (Horsham) 19 July	4–1–8–0	5–0–31–0	7–0–32–0	7.4–0–45–1	6–0–35–0	
(N.W.T.) v. Warwickshire (Edgbaston) 22–23 July		8–0–28–2	8–1–25–0	7.5–0–31–4	12–2–31–1	12–3–28–3
(J.P.) v. Glamorgan (Ebbw Vale) 26 July	8–1–22–4	5–0–33–2	7.5–0–37–1	6–1–28–1		8–0–24–2
(J.P.) v. Leicestershire (Leicester) 2 August	8–0–16–1	8–1–26–4	8–0–25–1	8–0–40–0	3–0–17–0	2–0–7–2
(N.W.T.) v. Essex (Hove) 5 August	12–0–52–0	12–4–35–5	12–1–36–3	12–4–15–0		12–0–43–1
(J.P.) v. Kent (Eastbourne) 9 August	8–2–19–0	8–1–14–2	8–0–25–2	8–0–46–2	2–0–10–0	
(J.P.) v. Nottinghamshire (Trent Bridge) 16 August	5.2–0–40–1	7–1–17–0	8–1–36–5	8–1–38–0		8–0–27–0
(J.P.) v. Derbyshire (Hove) 6 September			8–2–16–1	8–0–35–0	8–2–24–1	8–1–45–1

C. P. Phillipson	C. M. Wells	A. N. Jones	A. C. S. Pigott	B	Lb	W	Nb	Total	Wkts
				3	8	1	1	142	7
1-0-4-0				1	7	1		93	7
				2	6	3		108	10
					5		1	194	10
				2	6	2		163	6
5-0-38-2				2	6	6		181	7
4-0-29-1				1	18	7	2	215	8
	8-1-40-0			4	4	4	1	199	6
5.2-0-34-4	8-0-36-2				9	1	2	218	7
	8-0-55-0	8-0-57-1		4	6	1	4	236	6
					10			155	6
	4-1-28-2				16	5		200	3
					5	1	1	150	10
					4	3	2	153	10
	8-0-19-0			1	6	1		158	9
				1	8	2	3	195	9
	5-0-23-3			1	16	8	2	164	9
					3		3	164	6
			8-0-40-1		5	4	1	170	5

Warwickshire C.C.C.
Limited-Over Matches – Batting, 1981

	v. Yorkshire (Edgbaston) 10 May (J.P.)	v. Lancashire (Old Trafford) 11 May (B.&H.)	v. Derbyshire (Edgbaston) 16 May (B.&H.)	v. Leicestershire (Edgbaston) 17 May (J.P.)	v. Yorkshire (Edgbaston) 19 May (B.&H.)	v. Worcestershire (Edgbaston) 24 May (J.P.)	v. Scotland (Glasgow) 30 May (B.&H.)	v. Derbyshire (Edgbaston) 21 June (J.P.)	v. Kent (The Oval) 26 June (B.&H.)	v. Glamorgan (Swansea) 28 June (J.P.)	v. Essex (Edgbaston) 5 July (J.P.)	v. Surrey (The Oval) 12 July (J.P.)
D. L. Amiss		36	—		0	23	18	80	5	9	0	84
K. D. Smith		48	—		16		50					
T. A. Lloyd		32	—		5	63	36	27	60	73	31	40
G. W. Humpage		87*	—		93	71	31	17	35	4	25	21*
A. I. Kallicharran		27	—		20	31*	36*	8	4	9	6	9
Asif Din		29	—		27	15	37	3	10	51	7	22*
A. M. Ferreira		15*	—		8	—		19	3	11	10	—
S. J. Rouse		—					4*					—
R. G. D. Willis		—	—	—	1	—	—		4	2	2*	
W. Hogg		—	—		5	—	—	0	4	—	2*	
S. P. Perryman		—	—		1	—	—	0*	1		12	—
G. C. Small			—		19*	—		1	5*	6	0	
S. H. Wootton						4*		20	33	8	22	—
C. Lethbridge						—		1				
D. R. Doshi							—					
C. Maynard										9*	3	
P. R. Oliver												
Byes		1				9	3		1	14	1	2
Leg-byes		14			11	6	6	13	11	11	15	13
Wides		2			2	2		2	1	1	1	5
No-balls						3			2	1	1	
Total		291			211	224	221	191	179	209	136	196
Wickets		5			10	4	5	10	10	9	10	3
Result	Ab.	W	Ab.	Ab.	L	W	W	L	L	L	L	W
Points	2	2	1	2	0	4	2	0	—	0	0	4

Catches

24 – G. W. Humpage (ct 23, st 1)

10 – T. A. Lloyd

7 – R. G. D. Willis

6 – D. L. Amiss

5 – W. Hogg and A. I. Kallicharran

4 – S. P. Perryman, Asif Din, and A. M. Ferreira

3 – S. H. Wootton

2 – S. J. Rouse and G. C. Small

1 – K. D. Smith, C. Lethbridge and C. Maynard

v. Sussex (Horsham) 19 July (J.P.)	v. Sussex (Edgbaston) 22–23 July (N.W.T.)	v. Hampshire (Edgbaston) 26 July (J.P.)	v. Northamptonshire (Northampton) 2 August (J.P.)	v. Middlesex (Lord's) 9 August (J.P.)	v. Lancashire (Edgbaston) 16 August (J.P.)	v. Nottinghamshire (Edgbaston) 23 August (J.P.)	v. Gloucestershire (Bristol) 30 August (J.P.)	v. Kent (Canterbury) 6 September (J.P.)	v. Somerset (Taunton) 13 September (J.P.)
117*	29	108	60	5	0	53	3	32	20
21	25	2	63	62	21	26	62	53*	7
0	12	29	2	16	15	3	4	13*	3
15	9	41	3	31	51	102*	0	—	3
26*	33	40*	49	18*	51	5	40	—	17
—	9	—	43	—	16*	—	7	—	—
—	6	—	4	—					
—	0	—							5*
—	9*	—	0	—				—	
—	—	—		—	—	—	—	—	—
—	9	—	0*		4*		3*		3
—	2	20*			1	—	13	—	31*
			13	16*	1	29*	58*	—	55
		1		1					
16	5	5	6	12	16	3	9	1	5
5	1		1	1	1	1		2	2
		1		1	3				2
200	150	246	245	161	180	222	201	99	153
3	10	4	9	4	7	4	7	1	7
W	L	W	W	W	W	W	W	W	L
4	—	4	4	4	4	4	4	4	0

Warwickshire C.C.C. Limited-Over Matches – Bowling, 1981	R. G. D. Willis	W. Hogg	S. J. Rouse	S. P. Perryman	A. M. Ferreira
(B.&H.) *v.* Lancashire (Old Trafford) 11 May	11–1–43–1	11–0–49–3	6–0–32–1	11–1–34–1	8–0–70–3
(B.&H.) *v.* Derbyshire (Edgbaston) 16 May	6–3–9–0	5.1–2–11–1			
(B.&H.) *v.* Yorkshire (Edgbaston) 19 May	10.3–1–32–7	11–1–36–1		11–2–36–0	11–1–44–2
(J.P.) *v.* Worcestershire (Edgbaston) 24 May	8–0–39–2	5.5–0–31–1			8–1–32–2
(B.&H.) *v.* Scotland (Glasgow) 30 May	10–3–20–3	11–2–33–2	7.5–2–20–3	9–4–17–0	
(J.P.) *v.* Derbyshire (Edgbaston) 21 June		8–0–43–0		8–0–37–0	7–0–39–4
(B.&H.) *v.* Kent (The Oval) 26 June	10–2–33–2	10–1–46–2		10–1–41–0	10–0–38–3
(J.P.) *v.* Glamorgan (Swansea) 28 June	8–0–29–1	8–2–26–2			8–0–63–2
(J.P.) *v.* Essex (Edgbaston) 5 July		8–1–44–0		8–0–29–1	8–0–45–1
(J.P.) *v.* Surrey (The Oval) 12 July	7–1–17–2	7–0–25–2	8–0–41–1	8–0–61–0	8–0–36–2
(J.P.) *v.* Sussex (Horsham) 19 July		8–0–43–3	8–1–28–0	8–0–36–0	8–1–26–4
(N.W.T.) *v.* Sussex (Edgbaston) 22–23 July	12–2–43–2	12–1–40–0	12–0–48–2		12–1–61–1
(J.P.) *v.* Hampshire (Edgbaston) 26 July	8–0–54–2	8–2–40–1	4–0–36–0	8–0–32–1	8–0–42–4
(J.P.) *v.* Northamptonshire (Northampton) 2 August		8–0–55–2	8–0–31–3	8–1–29–2	8–0–51–1
(J.P.) *v.* Middlesex (Lord's) 9 August	8–1–19–2	8–0–24–0	6–0–50–1	8–2–28–3	8–2–28–2
(J.P.) *v.* Lancashire (Edgbaston) 16 August		8–1–44–0		8–0–24–0	8–0–42–4
(J.P.) *v.* Nottinghamshire (Edgbaston) 23 August	8–0–39–2	8–0–40–0		8–0–42–0	8–0–50–1
(J.P.) *v.* Gloucestershire (Bristol) 30 August		8–0–32–1		8–0–30–1	8–0–33–1
(J.P.) *v.* Kent (Canterbury) 6 September	7.3–0–17–1	8–1–21–1		8–0–21–3	7–2–14–3
(J.P.) *v.* Somerset (Taunton) 13 September	6–0–22–0			5–0–23–1	6–0–53–2

A. I. Kallicharran	G. C. Small	C. Lethbridge	D. R. Doshi	Asif Din	G. W. Humpage	B	Lb	W	NB	Total	Wkts
8–0–41–0							10	3	6	288	9
							1		2	23	1
	11–0–54–0					2	12	1	4	221	10
6–0–33–1	3–0–25–1	8–1–45–1				1	12	3	1	222	10
3–0–15–0			11–0–60–2	2–0–20–0		4	4	4	6	203	10
2–0–10–0	8–0–44–1	7–0–40–2				1	17	1	1	233	7
	10–2–21–1					3	6	1	4	193	8
	8–0–48–0				8–0–38–1	5	13	2		224	8
	8–1–55–1				8–0–47–1		11	6	2	239	4
							8	5	2	195	9
	8–0–44–1						15	6		198	9
	12–2–54–2						22	2	4	274	8
4–0–26–0						2	10			242	8
	8–0–46–1					2	5	3	1	223	9
1–0–11–0						4	16	4	2	186	9
	8–3–20–2	8–0–30–2				1	13		4	178	9
		8–0–36–0				7	6		1	221	3
	7–0–43–2	8–0–41–1				3	8	1		191	8
		8–1–14–1					9			96	10
	6–0–41–2	5–0–55–1					7	9	1	211	6

Worcestershire C.C.C. Limited-Over Matches – Batting, 1981

	v. Glamorgan (Abergavenny) 10 May (J.P.)	v. Nottinghamshire (Trent Bridge) 16 May (B.&H.)	v. Sussex (Worcester) 17 May (J.P.)	v. Gloucestershire (Worcester) 20 May (B.&H.)	v. Leicestershire (Leicester) 21 and 22 May (B.&H.)	v. Warwickshire (Edgbaston) 24 May (J.P.)	v. Northamptonshire (Worcester) 30 May (B.&H.)	v. Essex (Worcester) 14 June (J.P.)	v. Northamptonshire (Worcester) 21 June (J.P.)	v. Yorkshire (Worcester) 28 June (J.P.)	v. Derbyshire (Chesterfield) 5 July (J.P.)	v. Nottinghamshire (Harrogate) 9 July (T.T.)
G. M. Turner	19	30	19	21	6	56	1	24	45	32	8	
J. A. Ormrod	4	4										
Younis Ahmed	16	30	16	11	37	22	2	4	71	30	6	33
P. A. Neale	15	73	22	32	21	14	17	23*		21	20	57
E. J. O. Hemsley	43	34	9	32	4	67	32	2	34	74*	43	44*
D. J. Humphries	16	17	0	13	34	2	12	12	21*	8	3	13
J. Birkenshaw	16	0		14	6	5						
J. D. Inchmore	20*	0	8*	11	21	1	0	1	45	11	45	1*
J. Cumbes	—				1*	6	7*	—	—	—	—	
N. Gifford	—	2*	—	16	4	12*	7		3*	5*	8	
A. P. Pridgeon	—	—	—	6*			3	—	—	—	0*	—
H. L. Alleyne		2*	3	0	7	7	0	6*	1	—	18	—
S. P. Henderson			3									7
D. N. Patel			4*	12	27	13	32	12	27	22	1	18
M. S. Scott								40	0			38
T. S. Curtis												
M. Weston												
Byes	4	4	1		9	1	1	4	1	5	2	1
Leg-byes	12	13	7	9	10	12	3	19	8	2	4	6
Wides	5	4	1	1	2	3	4	2	3	2	2	3
No-balls		1			1	1	2					1
Total	170	214	93	178	190	222	123	149	259	212	160	222
Wickets	7	8	7	10	10	10	10	7	7	6	9	6
Result	W	L	L	L	L	L	L	L	W	L	L	W
Points	4	0	0	0	0	0	0	0	4	0	0	—

Catches

14 – D. J. Humphries (ct 9, st 5)

8 – J. Cumbes

7 – P. A. Neale and J. Birkenshaw

6 – G. M. Turner

5 – H. L. Alleyne

4 – J. D. Inchmore, Younis Ahmed and D. N. Patel

3 – T. S. Curtis, M. Weston and E. J. O. Hemsley

2 – N. Gifford, A. P. Pridgeon and S. P. Henderson

1 – M. S. Scott

v. Northamptonshire (Harrogate) 10 July (T.T.)	v. Hampshire (Worcester) 12 July (J.P.)	v. Middlesex (Lord's) 19 July (J.P.)	v. Derbyshire (Worcester) 22–23 July (N.W.T.)	v. Lancashire (Old Trafford) 2 August (J.P.)	v. Nottinghamshire (Worcester) 9 August (J.P.)	v. Leicestershire (Leicester) 16 August (J.P.)	v. Gloucestershire (Worcester) 23 August (J.P.)	v. Somerset (Worcester) 30 August (J.P.)	v. Yorkshire (Scarborough) 3 September (F.T.)	v. Surrey (The Oval) 6 September (J.P.)	v. Kent (Canterbury) 13 September (J.P.)
	57	27	59	38	5	42	69	18	20	12	23
21	32	32	29	50	0	65*	30*			19	64
22	5	16	53*	21	8	1		49	20	27	
34	34*				10	6*	11*	17	5	2	8
6	—	11	15	—	4	—	—	17*	8	2	9
14*											
10	42	0	10	13	8	12	—	—	9	—	44*
		0	—					—	18*	—	
		9	3		4*			17*	33	3	12
0		2*	6*		0				6*		2
7		—	—				—				—
40	—	9									
49	8*	21	42	9	21			27	44	82	21
17	24		5	11	25	29	42	10	36	17	5
		33*	29	29*	3			0	7	10*	6
	4	1	3	1			4		2	2	
13	9	5	8	6	4	6	2	11	10	6	9
1	8	2	1	1	1	1	1			1	3
2		4					1			6	
236	214	160	228	213	107	169	161	166	224	183	206
10	4	8	10	5	10	4	3	6	9	8	9
W	W	L	L	L	L	W	W	W	L	L	W
—	4	0	—	0	0	4	4	4	—	0	4

Worcestershire C.C.C. Limited-Over Matches – Bowling, 1981	J. D. Inchmore	A. P. Pridgeon	J. Birkenshaw	N. Gifford	J. Cumbes	H. L. Alleyne
(J.P.) v. Glamorgan (Abergavenny) 10 May	8–2–23–1	7.2–0–27–2	8–1–17–3	8–0–39–1	8–1–31–1	
(B.&H.) v. Nottinghamshire (Trent Bridge) 16 May	7–1–22–0	11–2–29–1	10–0–41–0	10–0–40–2		10.5–1–41–0
(J.P.) v. Sussex (Worcester) 17 May	2.2–0–26–1	3–0–28–0		3–0–18–0		3–0–10–0
(B.&H.) v. Gloucestershire (Worcester) 20 May	11–1–38–1	11–0–54–1	11–0–54–2	11–1–43–0		11–1–30–1
(B.&H.) v. Leicestershire (Leicester) 21 and 22 May	9–3–28–2		10–0–48–0	11–1–53–1	11–1–38–0	11–3–32–2
(J.P.) v. Warwickshire (Edgbaston) 24 May	7–0–54–1		8–0–42–0	8–0–47–0	8–2–35–2	8–0–29–1
(B.&H.) v. Northamptonshire (Worcester) 30 May	2–0–6–0	9.2–3–27–0		11–0–33–0	8–3–12–1	8–2–18–0
(J.P.) v. Essex (Worcester) 14 June	7.4–0–25–3	7–1–25–0			8–1–26–0	8–1–27–2
(J.P.) v. Northamptonshire (Worcester) 21 June	8–1–37–0	8–1–73–2		8–0–45–0	8–0–54–0	8–2–18–0
(J.P.) v. Yorkshire (Worcester) 28 June	8–0–36–0	8–1–28–0		4–0–29–1	8–0–43–0	8–0–44–0
(J.P.) v. Derbyshire (Chesterfield) 5 July	3–0–19–0	4–0–15–0		5–0–24–1	7–0–43–0	7–0–26–0
(T.T.) v. Nottinghamshire (Harrogate) 9 July	10–0–39–1	10–0–44–0				10–1–41–3
(T.T.) v. Northamptonshire (Harrogate) 10 July	5–0–19–1	5–0–13–0	11–1–46–6			5–3–2–0
(J.P.) v. Hampshire (Worcester) 12 July	8–0–37–2	7–0–24–2		5–0–12–0		8–0–37–1
(J.P.) v. Middlesex (Lord's) 19 July	7–1–21–2	8–1–41–1		5.3–0–29–0		8–0–29–0
(N.W.T.) v. Derbyshire (Worcester) 22–23 July	11.2–1–53–1	11–0–50–1		12–4–26–1	12–0–43–1	
(J.P) v. Lancashire (Old Trafford) 2 August	8–0–47–3	8–1–51–1		8–0–28–1	8–0–41–2	
(J.P.) v. Nottinghamshire (Worcester) 9 August	8–1–33–3	8–1–28–1		8–2–16–2		
(J.P.) v. Leicestershire (Leicester) 16 August	8–2–25–3	8–0–22–1		8–0–25–2		8–1–30–0
(J.P.) v. Gloucestershire (Worcester) 23 August	6–0–28–4	4–0–21–0		8–1–19–1		8–0–27–1
(J.P.) v. Somerset (Worcester) 30 August	8–0–45–3	8–0–27–3		8–1–31–0	8–1–28–0	
(F.T.) v. Yorkshire (Scarborough) 3 September	6–1–13–0	9–1–38–1		6–0–42–0	10–1–43–3	
(J.P.) v. Surrey (The Oval) 6 September		6.2–0–32–0		8–0–45–0	5–0–20–0	
(J.P.) v. Kent (Canterbury) 13 Septem.'	8–0–26–3	4.1–0–18–0		8–0–47–1		5–0–21–2

Younis Ahmed	E. J. O. Hemsley	D. N. Patel	B	Lb	W	Nb	Total	Wkts
			1	9	3	2	152	10
4-0-18-0				11	14	1	217	4
	2-0-10-0			2		2	96	2
			2	18	6	2	247	6
	3-0-23-2			8	4	4	238	7
				9	6	2	224	4
		8-2-29-0		1		1	127	1
3-0-17-0		3-0-12-0	7	5	3	4	151	5
				23	1	4	255	3
		3-0-21-0		10	3	1	215	1
		3.2-0-25-1	5	4	2		163	2
10-1-26-0		10-0-53-2		15	2	1	221	7
	5-1-11-2	11-1-38-1		3	2	1	135	10
3-0-31-1		8-1-34-1	8	19	5	6	213	8
		8-0-41-0		2	1	1	165	4
		12-0-35-1		20		2	229	6
		8-0-35-0		10	2		214	7
8-0-31-0		8-0-31-0		10		1	150	7
		8-0-47-0		12	2	5	168	7
	6-0-21-1	8-0-29-2	2	9	3		159	10
		8-2-22-2	1	8		1	163	9
	9-0-49-3	10-1-45-0	1	12	1	1	245	7
7-0-39-0		6-1-40-1		5	4		185	2
		8-0-27-0		6	2	2	149	7

Yorkshire C.C.C. Limited-Over Matches – Batting, 1981

	v. Derbyshire (Derby) 9 and 11 May (B.&H.)	v. Warwickshire (Edgbaston) 10 May (J.P.)	v. Kent (Huddersfield) 17 May (J.P.)	v. Warwickshire (Edgbaston) 19 May (B.&H.)	v. Scotland (Bradford) 21 and 22 May (B.&H.)	v. Leicestershire (Leeds) 24 May (J.P.)	v. Middlesex (Bradford) 31 May (J.P.)	v. Gloucestershire (Bristol) 7 June (J.P.)	v. Glamorgan (Hull) 21 June (J.P.)	v. Somerset (Leeds) 24 June (B.&H.)	v. Worcestershire (Worcester) 28 June (J.P.)	v. Surrey (Scarborough) 5 July (J.P.)
G. Boycott	31		17	9	3	1	—			21	91*	
C. W. J. Athey	4		11	16	2	21	1	—	59	58	79*	24
J. D. Love	6		3	84	118*		8		8	9		6
J. H. Hampshire	14			47			9		2	58	31	38
S. N. Hartley	1		15	17	4	6	4		30	14		7
D. L. Bairstow	103*		19	1	0	48	19*		3	0		78
P. Carrick	3			9	14	1			14	4		
C. M. Old	15		2	6	78*	8	1*			8		
G. B. Stevenson	13		4*	13					2	7*		
A. Sidebottom	0		—	0		26*			6*			
M. Johnson	4*		—	0*					2			15*
K. Sharp			0		0					0		8
P. G. Ingham			3*			23						
S. J. Dennis							0*		2			0
R. G. Lumb								—				
M. D. Moxon										22		20
J. P. Whiteley												3
A. Ramage												9
S. Stuchbury												
P. Jarvis												
Byes					2				1	1		
Leg-byes	6		5	12	4	11	1		7	16	10	17
Wides	1		1	4	2		1			2	3	3
No-balls	2			4	1		1		3		1	1
Total	203		79	221	228	147	45		139	221	215	228
Wickets	9		7	10	6	8	4		10	9	1	10
Result	W	Ab.	L	W	W	W	Ab.	Ab.	L	L	W	L
Points	2	2	0	2	2	4	2	2	0	—	4	0

Catches

12 – D. L. Bairstow (ct 11, st 1)
10 – S. N. Hartley
7 – P. Carrick
5 – J. D. Love and C. W. J. Athey
4 – C. M. Old and K. Sharp
3 – G. Boycott, A. Sidebottom, and M. D. Moxon
2 – M. Johnson and G. B. Stevenson
1 – S. J. Dennis, J. H. Hampshire, A. Ramage, J. P. Whiteley and R. G. Lumb

v. Kent (Canterbury) 11 July (N.W.T.)	v. Nottinghamshire (Trent Bridge) 19 July (J.P.)	v. Essex (Chelmsford) 26 July (J.P.)	v. Somerset (Scarborough) 2 August (J.P.)	v. Hampshire (Middlesbrough) 9 August (J.P.)	v. Northamptonshire (Wellingborough) 16 August (J.P.)	v. Derbyshire (Chesterfield) 23 August (J.P.)	v. Lancashire (Leeds) 30 August (J.P.)	v. Worcestershire (Scarborough) 3 September (F.T.)	v. Essex (Scarborough) 4 September (F.T.)	v. Sussex (Hove) 13 September (J.P.)
32		22								
40	27	25	45	48	3	28	4	4		
1	5	6	19*	2	23	60	16	1	0	
63	19	18						56	84*	
15	0	46	—	12	1	0	28	5	36	
52*	27	11	39*	19	53	50	3	27	30	
			—	2*	4	1*		—	—	
1*		19*	56	12*		10*		—	—	
	38	7		2	6		2	20*	15*	
					13*	—	29	—	—	
	2	11	—							
	21	0	54	18	4	14	17	107	57	
—	2*		—	—						
								10	24	
1			—	—	10	—	7		—	
—	1				1		14			
—	1	0			4	—	0			
							5*			
			2				1	1	5	
8	4	7	11	1	5	6	11	12	9	
1	7	2	2	1	4		2	1	1	
8		3	2		1		2	1	3	
222	154	177	230	117	132	208	141	245	264	
6	10	10	3	6	10	6	10	7	5	
L	L	L	W	W	W	W	L	W	W	Ab.
—	0	0	4	4	4	4	0	—	—	2

Yorkshire C.C.C. Limited-Over Matches – Bowling, 1981	C. M. Old	G. B. Stevenson	M. Johnson	A. Sidebottom	S. N. Hartley	G. Boycott
(B.&H.) v. Derbyshire (Derby) 9 and 11 May	11–0–33–3	11–0–43–1	11–0–33–1	10–0–33–1	5–0–14–0	3–0–16–0
(J.P.) v. Kent (Huddersfield) 17 May	7–0–39–1	7–0–31–2	6–0–41–0	7–0–58–1	4–0–31–0	2–0–15–1
(B.&H.) v. Warwickshire (Edgbaston) 19 May	10.3–2–20–2	10–3–41–1	11–1–32–1	9–0–55–1	3–0–16–2	
(B.&H.) v. Scotland (Bradford) 21 and 22 May	8–3–23–1	9.3–3–28–1	6–1–18–4		7–1–32–2	5–0–20–0
(J.P.) v. Leicestershire (Leeds) 24 May	8–2–31–3	8–0–33–1	8–0–32–1	8–1–26–2	0.5–0–5–1	
(J.P.) v. Middlesex (Bradford) 31 May	3–0–23–0	3–0–19–2	2–1–8–1		2–0–10–2	
(J.P.) v. Gloucestershire (Bristol) 7 June	4.4–1–26–0		8–0–60–1	5–0–27–0		
(J.P.) v. Glamorgan (Hull) 21 June		6–1–10–2	7–0–28–1	8–0–27–0	8–0–36–1	
(B.&H.) v. Somerset (Leeds) 24 June	11–4–19–1	11–1–50–1	11–0–55–1		11–0–33–2	7–0–37–0
(J.P.) v. Worcestershire (Worcester) 28 June	6–1–33–1	8–0–34–0	2–0–22–0		8–0–35–3	
(J.P.) v. Surrey (Scarborough) 5 July			8–0–32–0		7–1–54–1	
(N.W.T.) v. Kent (Canterbury) 11 July	11–3–33–2				12–2–41–1	
(J.P.) v. Nottinghamshire (Trent Bridge) 19 July		5–0–30–0	2–0–9–0			
(J.P.) v. Essex (Chelmsford) 26 July	8–0–33–2	8–0–56–0	8–1–45–0		8–0–55–0	
(J.P.) v. Somerset (Scarborough) 2 August		8–1–28–1	8–0–40–1		4–0–29–1	
(J.P.) v. Hampshire (Middlesbrough) 9 August	3–0–15–0	3–0–16–0			3–0–11–1	
(J.P.) v. Northamptonshire (Wellingborough) 16 August		8–0–23–3		8–0–26–1	3.5–0–15–2	
(J.P.) v. Derbyshire (Chesterfield) 23 August	7–0–15–1	5–0–14–0		8–1–36–2	2–0–14–0	
(J.P.) v. Lancashire (Leeds) 30 August		7–2–21–0		7.3–0–27–0		
(F.T.) v. Worcestershire (Scarborough) 3 September	10–3–23–1	10–0–45–1		10–0–59–1	10–0–37–3	
(F.T.) v. Essex (Scarborough) 4 September	10–0–33–2	10–1–40–1		10–0–53–2	10–0–63–0	

a P. Jarvis 7–0–24–1

P. Carrick	S. J. Dennis	C. W. J. Athey	J. P. Whiteley	A. Ramage	S. Stuchbury	B	Lb	W	Nb	Total	Wkts
4–0–16–0							8		6	202	8
							7	1		223	6
11–2–31–2							11	2	3	211	10
9–2–25–1	7–1–27–1						7	3	3	186	10
						1	8	4	2	142	10
	3–0–17–0						5	3		85	6
2–0–17–1	8–1–30–1	6–0–43–1				1	10	1	1	216	4
5–0–24–1	4–0–20–0					2	3	2	1	153	8
2.5–0–17–0						2	7	1	2	223	7
	8–0–46–2		8–0–33–0			5	2		2	212	6
	8–2–30–1	2–0–16–0	7–0–54–0	8–0–49–1			4	4		243	3
	10.2–0–48–1		12–3–48–0	12–1–42–0			7	2	2	223	4
	3–0–13–1			6.3–2–23–1			5	5		85	2
				8–0–47–1		2	9		3	250	3
3–0–19–0	8–1–43–1				7–0–33–2		14	4		210	8
	3–0–19–3				3–0–16–1		3	1		81	6
8–1–17–1			6–0–27–1		5–2–5–1		5	5	3	126	10
		7.5–0–35–5			4–0–17–0		4	1	1	137	10
			8–0–33–1		8–1–26–1		7	3	2	143	4a
4–1–13–0		6–0–29–2				2	10		6	224	9
			10–0–54–2			1	11	2	5	262	8

Derbyshire C.C.C. First-Class Matches – Batting, 1981

	v. Leicestershire (Leicester) 6–8 May		v. Surrey (The Oval) 13–15 May		v. Northamptonshire (Northampton) 27–29 May		v. Warwickshire (Derby) 6–9 June		v. Australians (Derby) 10–12 June		v. Essex (Derby) 13–16 June	
B. Wood	8	123*	55	15*	58	—	29	37	2	25	1	14
J. G. Wright	4	8	2	11	8	—	75	54*	144	3	26	23
P. N. Kirsten	37	64	12	1*	1	—	45	8*	1	41	95	90
D. S. Steele	6	10	20	—	12	—	12	—	20	46*	21	0
G. Miller	15	67	19	—	17	—	51*	—	14	—	50	5
K. J. Barnett	23	22*	15	—	67*	—	2	—	2	28	16	0
A. Hill	0	—	54*	—	60*	—	56*	—	4	0	1	39
R. W. Taylor	0	—	22*	—	—	—	—	—	5*	—	5	2
C. J. Tunnicliffe	4	—	—	—	29	—	—	—	7	—	32	2
M. Hendrick	14*	—	—	—	—	—	—	—			13*	—
S. Oldham	0	—	—	—	—	—	—	—				
P. G. Newman							—	—			0	4*
I. S. Anderson									4	0*		
M. J. Deakin												
B. J. N. Maher												
D. G. Moir												
Byes		5	10	1			2			11	7	1
Leg byes	7	9	13		4		10	6	5	5	14	5
Wides		5	4		1		1	2	2	1		
No balls	1	2	7	3	4		17	2	8	3	8	3
Total	119	315	233	31	261		300	109	218	163	289	188
Wickets	10	4	6	1	6		5	1	9	5	10	9
Result	D		D		D		D		D		D	
Points	2		6		6		7		—		7	

The match v. Nottinghamshire (Derby) was abandoned without a ball being bowled.

	v. Yorkshire (Sheffield) 17-19 June		v. Northamptonshire (Derby) 20-23 June		v. Lancashire (Chesterfield) 1-3 July		v. Worcestershire (Chesterfield) 4-7 July		v. Hampshire (Portsmouth) 15-17 July		v. Somerset (Taunton) 18-21 July		v. Kent (Derby) 25-28 July		v. Gloucestershire (Derby) 29-31 July	
	53	—	40	10	127	19	8*	153	14	38	62	—	0	85*	54	—
	65	—	110	—	60	30	15	141	6	3	12	—	27	88	38	—
	31	—	59*	114	35	21	0	15*	12	36	228	—	23	14*	8	—
	0	—	30*	28	49*	25	44	—	7	55	137	—	67	—	58	—
	5	—	—	12*	0	8	81	6	2	10			1	—	62	—
	25	—	—	7*							—					
	101*	—	—	74	25*	21	12	2*	33*	3	23*	—	47	—	5	—
	100	—	—	—									26	—		
	28	—	—	0	—	6			0	1	0	—	39	—	6	—
							0	—	1	21	—	—	2*	—		
	22*	—	—	—	—	0*	3	—	5	3*	—	—	33	—	3	—
	23	—	—	—	—	0	27	—							3	—
					—	8*	44	—	3	22	0	—	0	—	0	—
					—	7	3	8	9	3	15	—			4*	—
	5						2	2	1	1	4		4	2	8	
	9		5	1	5	3	5	9	4	11	9		17	2	7	
			3		1		1				1		3		7	
	13		5	11	1	1	3	1	7	1	5		8		4	
	480		252	257	303	149	248	337	104	209	495		297	191	267	
	9†		2	5	4	9	10	4	10	10	7		10	1	10	
	D		L		D		W		L		D		W			W
	5		7		5		21		3		5		19			23

Derbyshire C.C.C.
Batting, *cont.*

	v. Essex (Chelmsford) 1–4 August		v. Leicestershire (Derby) 8–11 August		v. Sussex (Eastbourne) 12–14 August		v. Glamorgan (Swansea) 15–18 August		v. Yorkshire (Chesterfield) 22–25 August		v. Lancashire (Blackpool) 26–28 August	
B. Wood	22	21	0	53*	24	12	38	—	38	68*	36	—
J. G. Wright	0	0	0	11	73	0	42	—	150	—		
P. N. Kirsten			25	9	85	68	38	—	79	22	204*	—
D. S. Steele	0	23	4	1	12	59	26	—	19	53	21	—
G. Miller	7	20	11	1	0	22	14	—	2	2*	27	—
K. J. Barnett	4	18	3	1	0	22	64*	—	11	—	61	—
A. Hill	22	36	5	5	5	16	18	—	42	1	27	—
R. W. Taylor			0	0	16	11*	9	—	25*	—	—	—
C. J. Tunnicliffe	0	5	10	23	12	0	4	—	2	—	1	—
M. Hendrick	18	0					12	—	—	—		
S. Oldham	4	9*	2*	1	7	0						
P. G. Newman			1	0	0*	0	16	—	9*	—	—	—
I. S. Anderson	3*	1									0*	—
M. J. Deakin												
B. J. N. Maher	0	2										
D. G. Moir											16	—
Byes					6	11	16		2	2		
Leg byes	11	5	1	2	8	1	18		13	3	12	
Wides	2	1			2	2	2		2			
No balls		2			6	3	3		6		1	
Total	93	143	62	107	256	227	320		400	151	406	
Wickets	10	10	10	10	10	10	10		8	3	7	
Result	L		L		L		W		L		D	
Points	3		4		6		24		5		7	

Catches

45 – R. W. Taylor (ct 33, st 12)

19 – G. Miller

13 – B. Wood

12 – D. S. Steele and P. N. Kirsten

11 – K. J. Barnett

9 – J. G. Wright, C. J. Tunnicliffe and M. J. Deakin

8 – M. Hendrick, I. S. Anderson and B. J. N. Maher (ct 6, st 2)

6 – A. Hill and substitutes

5 – P. G. Newman and S. Oldham

v. Nottinghamshire (Trent Bridge) 29 August–1 September		v. Middlesex (Derby) 12–15 September		Inns	NOs	Runs	HS	Av
34	43	20	—	37	6	1439	153	46.41
		28	—	32	1	1257	150	40.54
36	3	45	—	35	6	1605	228	55.34
10	27			32	3	902	137	31.10
6	3	12	—	31	3	552	81	19.71
18	1	33	—	23	4	443	67*	23.31
79	17	107	—	32	8	940	107	39.16
2	13	0	—	16	4	236	100	19.66
0	17*	18	—	25	1	246	39	10.25
				9	3	81	18	13.50
				14	5	92	33	10.22
5	3	2*	—	15	4	93	27	8.45
0	6	5	—	15	4	96	44	8.72
				6	—	45	15	7.50
				3	1	6	4*	3.00
6*	4	0	—	4	1	26	16	8.66

4	4	8
3	2	4
1	1	2
4	2	2

208	146	286
10	10	10
L		D
5		2

Derbyshire C.C.C. First-Class Matches – Bowling, 1981	M. Hendrick	S. Oldham	G. Miller	C. J. Tunnicliffe	B. Wood	D. S. Steele
v. Leicestershire (Leicester) 6–8 May	24–4–86–4	18–2–74–1	9–2–39–0	17–5–44–1	7–3–15–0	4–2–15–0
v. Surrey (The Oval) 13–15 May	27.5–13–43–4	21–4–62–2	11–4–23–1	23–6–66–3	14–2–41–0	2–0–13–0
	22–11–25–1	6–3–14–0	16–9–19–2	23–8–64–1	6–2–8–1	
v. Northamptonshire (Northampton) 27–29 May	27–10–51–2	13–6–23–0	12–5–33–1	23–13–34–5		9–3–15–0
v. Warwickshire (Derby) 6–9 June		16.3–2–54–2	14–3–40–1	25–1–49–2	5–0–19–1	21–10–31–0
		3–1–16–0		8–1–12–0		21.4–6–77–6
v. Australians (Derby) 10–12 June			10–2–23–0	13–3–27–0	18–3–41–1	9–6–4–0
v. Essex (Derby) 13–16 June	20–6–46–3			11–0–38–0	6–0–12–2	
	23–6–52–2		14–5–48–0	13–2–27–1	2–1–11–0	17–9–28–1
v. Yorkshire (Sheffield) 17–19 June		25–2–82–1	2–2–0–0	31–4–100–0	17–1–64–2	11–10–3–1
v. Northamptonshire (Derby) 20–28 June		6–1–23–0	21–8–43–2	11–0–59–3	4–2–11–0	9–2–34–1
		8–0–36–0	13–2–65–1	5–0–43–0	5.5–0–40–0	13–1–52–0
v. Lancashire (Chesterfield) 1–3 July		23–5–67–2	30–13–74–0	22–7–76–1	11–3–49–0	
		11–2–43–0	14–6–48–0			20–4–60–1
v. Worcestershire (Chesterfield) 4–7 July	22.2–3–70–0	14–2–57–3	27–8–51–1		3–0–16–0	6–1–16–0
	16.5–3–41–5	9–0–55–1	8–0–52–2		4–0–31–1	2–0–22–0
v. Hampshire (Portsmouth) 15–17 July	26–6–63–2	28–8–80–2		24–6–74–1	20–3–67–2	6–2–9–0
v. Somerset (Taunton) 18–21 July	9.2–1–14–2	24–3–86–2		17.4–4–72–0	20–6–60–1	24–11–36–2
		4–0–17–0		4–0–24–0	4–1–12–1	17–5–70–1
v. Kent (Derby) 25–28 July	25–3–77–0	26.4–5–78–1	5–1–7–0	34–6–127–2	17–6–47–0	1–0–3–0
	11–6–15–0	6–3–5–0	21.2–8–51–2	3–1–8–0		24–11–53–7
v. Gloucestershire (Derby) 29–31 July		9–3–20–1		11.1–2–40–5	4–1–12–0	
		13–1–47–2	7–2–6–1	10–3–29–1		13.5–9–14–3
v. Essex (Chelmsford) 1–4 August	8–2–30–0	11.3–1–35–3	33–5–86–2	19–5–48–3	0.1–0–0–0	13.5–3–25–0
v. Leicestershire (Derby) 8–11 August		4–0–13–0	37–13–71–3	2–0–6–0		44.5–15–85–7
v. Sussex (Eastbourne) 12–14 August		14.4–1–38–0	7–3–20–0	21–6–47–0	7.3–2–19–0	13–3–32–2
			8–0–44–3	11–0–66–0		5–0–47–0
v. Glamorgan (Swansea) 15–18 August	16–3–52–2		11–6–27–4			14.4–7–28–4
	14–4–41–2		10–2–45–2			20.1–5–62–5
v. Yorkshire (Chesterfield) 22–25 August	21–8–24–1		5–2–13–0	24–5–63–3	16–4–38–0	8–1–27–0
	13–2–62–0		5–0–31–0	7–0–46–0	10–1–50–2	4–1–42–0
v. Lancashire (Blackpool) 26–28 August			32–12–62–4	5–1–10–0		8–3–13–0
			31–5–88–1	20–6–54–1	13–3–46–1	16–5–33–1
v. Nottinghamshire (Trent Bridge) 29 August–1 September			9–1–25–0	21.3–2–75–5	8–2–15–0	18–5–37–4
			3–0–20–0	1–0–10–0		7–1–33–0
v. Middlesex (Derby) 12–15 September			29–5–107–0	26–7–78–1	32–12–91–2	
			10–3–20–0	13–1–47–3		
	326.2–91– 792–30 av. 26.40	314.2–55– 102.5–23 av. 44.56	464.2–137– 1281–33 av. 38.81	499.2–105– 1563–42 av. 37.21	254.3–58– 815–17 av. 47.94	403–141– 1019–46 av. 22.15

a A. Hill 0.1–0–4–0
†N. Gifford absent ill
*A. J. Brassington absent hurt
b A. Hill 1–0–1–0

K. J. Barnett	P. N. Kirsten	P. G. Newman	I. S. Anderson	D. G. Moir	J. G. Wright	Byes	Leg byes	Wides	No balls	Total	Wickets
3–0–13–0						6			8	300	6
							5		5	258	10
8–1–32–0	5–2–7–1					2	2		8	181	6
1–0–3–0						6	5			170	8
		20–9–36–3					4		14	247	10
24–5–86–2	5–0–33–0	8–4–24–1				5			17	270	10
	6–1–16–1	14.2–4–28–1	18–7–35–4			4	5		7	190	8
		17–2–51–5				1	4		4	156	10
3–1–6–0		16–4–59–1				4	3		12	250	5
		30–5–100–4				1	12		12	374	9
		13.1–2–39–3				1	7	2	15	234	9
		6–2–27–0				2	7		7	279	1
		21–4–86–2	2–1–8–0				6	3	11	380	5
		11–2–26–1	5–0–36–0				3	1	11	232	2 a
		17–2–71–2				9	9		8	307	7
		7–0–66–0				6	1		1	275	9†
			3–0–17–1			6	9		20	345	8
9–1–22–0			6–0–27–1			3	2		13	335	8
25–6–104–0	8–1–25–0		22–4–73–1		1–1–0–0	5	1	1	5	337	3
						2		7		348	3
			2–0–6–0				1			139	10
		7–4–11–4					3	3		91	10
		8–0–39–2				2	8		5	150	9*
15–1–58–2			1–0–4–0			3	5	1	1	296	10
7–3–11–0			3–1–3–0				1	1	5	196	10
		20–2–73–4					2		19	250	7
		14.1–2–66–2					3	1	8	235	5
		4–0–16–0					8			131	10
		4–0–19–1				2	8		5	182	10
4–0–22–0		14–0–48–0				5	7	1	4	252	4
1.3–0–15–0		9–0–49–2					1		4	300	4
	3–1–4–0	10.1–0–34–4	9–3–37–0	5–1–25–1		2	1		2	190	10
9–1–43–0	5–1–13–0	24–5–60–2		19–3–57–0			6	1	7	408	6
		23–5–59–1		11–3–34–0		11			9	265	10
		1–0–5–0		6.2–1–20–1			1		1	90	1
3–0–8–0		7–2–21–0		11–2–47–0			6		14	372	3
5–2–12–0		13–2–27–3	5–1–14–0	10–4–20–0	1–0–4–0		1		6	152	7 b
117.3–21–435–4	32–6–98–2	341.5–63–1143–47	73–16–257–7	62.2–14–203–2	2–1–4–0						
av. 108.75	av. 49.00	av. 24.31	av. 36.71	av. 101.50	–						

Essex C.C.C.
First-Class Matches – Batting, 1981

	v. Cambridge University (Cambridge) 22–24 April		v. Middlesex (Lord's) 6–8 May		v. Surrey (Chelmsford) 27–29 May		v. Yorkshire (Leeds) 3–5 June		v. Worcestershire (Worcester) 6–9 June		v. Derbyshire (Derby) 13–16 June	
M. S. A. McEvoy	53	—	4	—	56	10	42	—	11	7	9	16
B. R. Hardie	13	—	36	—	0	—	25	—	76	5	3	55*
K. S. McEwan	16	—	33	—	106	25	33	—	51	11	12	1
K. W. R. Fletcher	46	—	20	—	37	10	48	—	127	—		
K. R. Pont	37	—	56	—			89	—	25*	26	8	7
S. Turner	0	—	19	—	15	3	31	—	—	46*	0	58*
R. E. East	27	—	20*	—	11	26*	0	—	—	—	15	—
N. Smith	1	—	7*	—	5	15*	36*	—	—	—	41	—
J. K. Lever	11	—	—	—	0	—	—	—	—	—	2	—
D. L. Acfield	5	—			0*	—	—	—	—	—	8*	—
N. A. Foster	8*	—										
G. A. Gooch			15	—	0	50					29	78
N. Phillip			28	—	12	10	34	—	—	80*	20	16
A. W. Lilley												
D. R. Pringle												
D. E. East												
C. Gladwin												
R. J. Leiper												
Byes	3		4		2	11	4			2	1	4
Leg byes	3		2		2	3	2		3	3	4	3
Wides							1			3		
No balls	17		6		1		9		15	4	4	12
Total	240		250		247	163	354		308	187	156	250
Wickets	10		8		10	6	8		4	4	10	5
Result	D		D		D		D		L		D	
Points	—		7		4		8		8		5	

The match v. Gloucestershire (Chelmsford) 23–26 May was abandoned without a ball being bowled.
† K. W. R. Fletcher retired hurt.

v. Middlesex (Ilford) 17–19 June		v. Sussex (Ilford) 20–23 June		v. Leicestershire (Leicester) 27–30 June		v. Nottinghamshire (Chelmsford) 1–3 July		v. Warwickshire (Edgbaston) 4–7 July		v. Northamptonshire (Southend) 15–17 July		v. Lancashire (Southend) 18–21 July		v. Kent (Canterbury) 29–31 July	
21	14	18	7			9	50	0	36	2	2				
21	70	1	8	15	1	0	9	22	111*	10	45	129	—	71	11
		28	48	54	109*	7	0	40	—	71	14	4	—	102	19
8*	—			2	3	61	55	123*	52	1	0			7	4
87	7	25	0	72*	27	9	6	56	—	8	1			19	34
25	36	47	45	—	3*	41	2	26*	—	3	15	73*	—	51	8*
15	12	29	6	—	—	47	0			0	4	4	—	2	—
1	27	9	9	—	—	39	1*								
2*	1	0	7	—	—	8	—	—	—	19	12	7	—	6	4*
0	7*	2*	0*	—	—	3*	—	—	—	4*	2*	1	—	0	—
				164	87										
13	17	0	45	60*	30	25	5*	0	66*	25	0	0	—	9	1
90	0	3	61									0	—	32	34
								5	—			15	—		
								6	—	28	6	4	—	1*	—
												53	—		
	13				3	19	15	2	5				7	5	3
18	13	3	4	6	10	1	8	14	9	10	3		9	4	3
1	1	2	1			2		1	1					1	
1		2	2	8	3	1	1	8	3	15	4		2		1
303	218	169	246	387	273	272	152	303	283	196	108	308		310	122
9†	9	10	10	4	5	10	7	7	2	10	10	10		10	6
W		L		D		D		W		W		D		W	
24		2		4		4		23		21		8		23	

Essex C.C.C.
Batting, *cont.*

	v. Derbyshire (Chelmsford) 1–4 August		v. Australians (Chelmsford) 8–10 August		v. Kent (Chelmsford) 12–14 August		v. Hampshire (Southampton) 15–18 August		v. Northamptonshire (Northampton) 22–25 August		v. Leicestershire (Colchester) 26–28 August	
M. S. A. McEvoy												
B. R. Hardie	95	—	6	0	28	—	27	12	26	0	5	38
K. S. McEwan	64	—	39	50	59	—	103	5	20	13	141	16
K. W. R. Fletcher	48	—			165*	—	3	14	30	78	23	3
K. R. Pont					10	—	24	18*	23	9		
S. Turner	25	—		14	62*	—					16*	7*
R. E. East	31	—		9*	—	—	26	0	0*	18		
N. Smith												
J. K. Lever	0	—			—	—	21	8	—	—	—	—
D. L. Acfield	2*	—	—	—	—	—	6*	0	—	—	—	—
N. A. Foster												
G. A. Gooch			86	7					146	32	75	105
N. Phillip	5		31	45	35	—	0	6	0	6	0	23
A. W. Lilley	9		21	64	67	—	28	2			33	38
D. R. Pringle	7	—	28	6*			4	16	18	16*	24*	—
D. E. East	0	—	0*	11	—	—	20	19	6*	6	—	10
C. Gladwin												
R. J. Leiper			1	49								
Byes	3		2	5	9			2	8	4	2	2
Leg byes	5			8	5		8		17	4	12	12
Wides	1			2	2						5	
No balls	1		2		11		9	3	6	3	4	2
Total	296		216	270	453		279	105	300	189	340	256
Wickets	10		7	8	5		10	10	7	8	6	7
Result	W		D		W		L		D		W	
Points	23		—		24		6		5		24	

Catches

27 – N. Smith (ct 23, st 4)
25 – D. E. East (ct 20, st 5)
18 – K. W. R. Fletcher
17 – B. R. Hardie and K. S. McEwan
13 – S. Turner
10 – M. S. A. McEvoy and N. Phillip
9 – R. E. East and G. A. Gooch
8 – A. W. Lilley
6 – J. K. Lever
5 – D. L. Acfield and K. R. Pont
2 – D. R. Pringle

v. Glamorgan (Colchester) 29 August–1 September		v. Somerset (Taunton) 9–11 September		v. Surrey (The Oval) 12–15 September		Inns	NOs	Runs	HS	Av
						19	—	367	56	19.31
37	114*	98	16	15	85*	39	4	1339	129	38.25
0	2	0	20	102	2	37	1	1420	141	39.44
6	6			72	128*	29	4	1180	165*	47.20
		0	9			27	3	692	89	28.83
36	31	14	30*			30	10	782	73*	39.10
19	4			8	—	25	4	333	47	15.85
						12	4	191	41	23.87
14*	9	11*	—	5	—	20	4	147	21	9.18
0	—	0	—	0*	—	18	11	40	8*	5.71
						1	1	8	8*	—
16	113	17	122	30	12	19	—	1184	164	62.31
21	4	11	15	22	—	37	4	720	80*	21.81
14	88	30	0	0	2	21	—	616	90	29.33
		0	11*	0	—	13	4	150	28	16.66
5	4	15	—	3	—	17	3	144	28	10.28
						1	—	53	53	53.00
						2	—	50	49	25.00
4	16	1	7	4	12					
6	15	5	6	5	4					
6	4									
3	1	9	4	10	7					
187	411	211	240	276	252					
10	9	10	6	10	3					
	W		D		L					
	21		6		5					

Essex C.C.C. First-Class Matches – Bowling, 1981

	J. K. Lever	N. A. Foster	S. Turner	D. L. Acfield	K. R. Pont	R. E. East
v. Cambridge University	9–3–20–2	13–4–53–0	11–5–20–4	12–8–7–2	11–1–32–1	1.1–1–0–1
(Cambridge) 22–24 April	12–2–40–0	12–1–37–1	17–7–28–2	30–12–43–3		26–11–39–0
v. Middlesex	14.1–1–42–2		21–6–45–2			7–1–13–0
(Lord's) 5–8 May	10–1–27–0		8–4–7–1		14–6–14–0	12–6–13–1
v. Surrey	22.5–4–77–1		19–2–67–1	15–6–24–0		
(Chelmsford) 27–29 May	14–3–33–2		9–2–28–1	9.3–2–35–1		11–2–32–2
v. Yorkshire	21.1–9–49–8		20–9–16–2	2–0–11–0	3–0–19–0	
(Leeds) 3–5 June	31–7–85–2		28–13–53–2	25–12–38–0	9–2–34–0	27–9–37–0
v. Worcestershire	18–7–31–2		10–1–38–0	20–6–34–4		22.1–7–34–2
(Worcester) 6–9 June	17.5–4–91–1		8–0–36–0	4–1–17–0		15–1–62–2
v. Derbyshire	29–10–62–4		17–3–29–0	5–1–7–1	4–0–21–0	8–2–21–0
(Derby) 13–16 June	15–4–36–4		23–5–55–2	6–0–19–0		7–1–18–3
v. Middlesex	22.4–4–75–4		22–8–44–4	15–2–45–1		33–9–65–0
(Ilford) 17–19 June	6–0–16–0		4–0–12–1	20–3–58–5		21.4–2–56–4
v. Sussex	20–2–62–1		19.1–2–66–1	27–6–103–1		31–7–95–0
(Ilford) 20–23 June						
v. Leicestershire	23–8–49–0		14–4–32–0	12–4–35–0	4–0–17–0	20–2–76–0
(Leicester) 27–30 June	12–0–70–1			26–9–57–2		21–10–29–1
v. Nottinghamshire	26–1–81–4		26–0–75–0	14–1–38–0		24–4–75–1
(Chelmsford) 1–3 July	13–0–26–0		22–7–61–2	23–6–43–3		
v. Warwickshire	25–7–64–2		17–3–51–1	20–7–24–2		
(Edgbaston) 4–7 July	17–4–67–1		13–2–39–0	22–11–24–2		
v. Northamptonshire	21–7–47–6		7.5–3–9–2	3–3–0–0		
(Southend) 15–17 July	14–2–43–1		26–12–30–3	23.2–5–32–5		7–2–22–0
v. Lancashire	14–6–23–3		18–7–27–2	16–10–19–1		
(Southend) 18–21 July	18–5–47–2		13–3–36–0	22–7–37–2		20–9–23–0
v. Kent	7–1–22–0		1–0–3–0	32.4–9–55–8		32–9–68–2
(Canterbury) 29–31 July	1–0–9–0			35–17–58–3		35.3–13–49–7
v. Derbyshire	10–5–17–1			14.4–4–21–4		14–5–17–2
(Chelmsford) 1–4 August	5–2–19–0			39–15–56–4		35.5–13–56–4
v. Australians			12–3–54–1	20–4–61–0		18–3–53–2
(Chelmsford) 8–10 August			13–2–41–2	20.5–2–87–2		9–0–47–1
v. Kent	8.4–4–12–3		1–0–1–0	39–10–91–1		39–10–68–5
(Chelmsford) 12–14 August	6–2–20–0			32–10–65–3		33–9–55–7
v. Hampshire	31–6–86–0			19–9–22–1		29–7–64–4
(Southampton) 15–18 August	4–0–15–0			24–5–52–4		20–8–49–0
v. Northamptonshire	13–1–69–3			9–0–42–0		15–5–49–0
(Northampton) 22–25 August	4–2–12–0			15–2–58–1		13–4–27–0
v. Leicestershire	21–7–72–3		5–1–25–0	6–3–3–1		
(Colchester) 26–28 August	30.1–6–103–2		24–5–55–5	9–3–38–0		
v. Glamorgan	19–3–59–2		9–1–30–1	24.5–8–64–6		28–7–56–1
(Colchester) 29 August–1 September	17–2–62–5		8–0–34–1	33–7–84–3		30–8–97–1
v. Somerset	30.2–3–97–6		17–3–56–1	9–1–49–0		
(Taunton) 9–11 September						
v. Surrey	26–3–94–2			5–1–13–0		12–2–34–0
(The Oval) 12–15 September	2–0–18–0			11–0–50–0		3–0–14–0
	680.5–148–	25–5–	485–132–	769.5–232–	45–9–	680.2–190–
	2049–80	90–1	1203–44	1719–76	137–1	1513–53
	av. 25.61	av. 90.00	av. 27.34	av. 22.61	av. 137.00	av. 28.54

* J. A. Ormrod retired hurt

N. Phillip	G. A. Gooch	M. S. A. McEvoy	K. S. McEwan	D. R. Pringle	Byes	Leg byes	Wides	No balls	Total	Wickets
					1	3		10	146	10
					2	6	4	5	204	6
25–9–40–6					1	10		2	153	10
6–1–7–0	10–3–20–0	12–6–20–3	1–1–0–0		1	5		2	116	5
16–3–59–1	22–10–47–3				6	18		2	300	6
9–0–44–0	8–1–29–1				1	16	1	2	221	7
8–2–25–0						8		1	129	10
30–9–61–0		6–1–22–0			4	18		5	357	4
20–5–74–1					1	5	1	3	221	9*
12–0–53–1						13	1	3	276	4
22–2–85–3	12–3–35–1				7	14		8	289	10
6–1–22–0	6–2–29–0				1	5		3	188	9
14–4–28–1						5		1	263	10
3–0–9–0					3	9			163	10
17–3–86–0					7	9	5	3	436	4
24.5–2–89–1					4	12	1	4	319	1
16–3–55–3	1–0–4–0				5	10	4	1	235	7
19–0–63–0					2	9		5	348	5
4–3–7–0						9	1		147	5
22–3–97–2				16–5–31–0	1	12	1	8	289	8
		9–0–57–0	8.5–0–66–0	8–1–36–0	1	4		2	296	3
15–5–25–2						1		4	86	10
6–0–22–1					4	6		6	163	10
11.4–2–33–4					3			6	111	10
15–1–56–1				15–5–20–2	4	14	1	7	245	7
7–4–6–0					2	10			166	10
1–1–0–0					7	3			126	10
11–1–25–3						11	2		93	10
2–1–4–2					5	1		2	143	10
4–0–11–0				15–2–49–2		3	1	8	240	5
6–1–31–2	2–0–10–1			5–0–16–0	1			4	237	8
7–0–31–0					4	9			216	10
5–1–18–0					6	4		2	170	10
21–2–75–1				18–2–83–0	1	5		4	340	7
10.5–3–25–1				7–1–25–1	4	8		2	190	7
10–1–31–0				10–1–46–1	1	7		6	251	4
4–1–4–1	1–0–3–0			7–1–23–0	2	7		3	139	2
15.1–1–46–4				12–3–39–2	4	6		3	198	10
23–8–52–2					1	6	1	3	259	10
15–1–51–0					2	10	1	1	274	10
3–0–12–0					12	8		2	311	10
23–2–126–2				18–5–51–0	4	13	9	3	408	10
16–1–73–4	3–1–14–0			13–4–45–0	3	7	1	4	288	6
12.4–0–64–2				20–1–90–2		7		1	244	5
518.1–87–	65–20–	27–7–	9.5–1–	164–31–						
1725–51	191–6	99–3	66–0	554–10						
av. 33.82	av. 31.83	av. 33.00	—	av. 55.40						

Glamorgan C.C.C.
First-Class Matches –
Batting,
1981

	v. Oxford University (Oxford) 25–28 April		v. Sussex (Hove) 13–15 May		v. Kent (Cardiff) 26 May		v. Australians (Swansea) 27–29 May		v. Worcestershire (Hereford) 3–5 June		v. Surrey (Swansea) 6–9 June	
A. Jones	9	—	109	27	—	—	33	—	63	48	2	44
J. A. Hopkins	16	—	0	0	—	—	11	—	0	28	12	53
D. A. Francis	8	—	28	1								
M. J. Llewellyn	0	—			—	—	0*	—	5	14	7	0
R. C. Ontong	3	—	35	0	—	—	11*	—	26	22	15	2
G. C. Holmes	24*	—										
E. A. Moseley	7	—	0	7	—	—	—	—	23*	17	8	35
E. W. Jones	3	—	0	2	—	—	—	—	1	5*	16	0
M. A. Nash	30*	—	4	0	—	—	—	—	2	4	2	0
R. N. S. Hobbs	—	—	6	4	—	—	—	—	0	—	20*	0*
S. R. Barwick	—	—	3*	11*	—	—	—	—				
Javed Miandad			19	32	—	—	23	—	52	35	14	4
N. G. Featherstone			16	31	—	—	2	—	28	1	19	19
B. J. Lloyd					—	—	—	—	15	2*	12	8
A. A. Jones												
A. L. Jones												
T. Davies												
P. J. Lawlor												
J. G. Thomas												
S. A. B. Daniels												
N. J. Perry												
H. Morris												
Byes	2		2						1		1	18
Leg byes	3		5	2			1		17	4	4	7
Wides	1								1			
No balls	2		3	2			3					2
Total	108		230	119			84		234	180	132	192
Wickets	7		10	10			4		10	8	10	10
Result	D		L		Ab.		D		D		L	
Points	—		6		0		—		6		4	

The match v. Gloucestershire (Cardiff) 6–8 May was abandoned without a ball being bowled.

v. Hampshire (Bournemouth) 10-12 June		v. Leicestershire (Leicester) 13-16 June		v. Warwickshire (Cardiff) 17-19 June		v. Somerset (Swansea) 27-30 June		v. Hampshire (Swansea) 1-3 July		v. Northamptonshire (Northampton) 4-7 July		v. Yorkshire (Cardiff) 15-17 July		v. Gloucestershire (Bristol) 18-21 July	
6	1	33	5	9	—	36	14	2	42	0	42	49	24*	50	64
33	0	111	16	93	—	13	45	0	135	20	0	116	18*	31	27
15	—														
36	6*	26	15	26	—			151*	50	2	43	40	—	116*	18*
		6	8*	10	—	28*	50*	37	—	31	1	70*	—	5*	—
27	—	4	—	50	—	—	7*	14	—	13	4	6	—		
11	—	1	—	9	—			8	—	4	4	20*	—		
27*	1	21	—	14	—			7	7	1	14				
		1*	—					49*	—	2*	6*				
3	—	9	42*	105	—	137*	106	15	34*	0	33	23	—	152	—
113*	9*	58	4	5	—	63	6	17	2*	3	33	0	—		
		10	—	31	—			1	—	21	11				
				0*	—										
						10	12								

v. Hampshire (Bournemouth)		v. Leicestershire		v. Warwickshire		v. Somerset		v. Hampshire (Swansea)		v. Northamptonshire		v. Yorkshire		v. Gloucestershire	
		4	10	12		1	3	4		1	12	3	5	15	
9		12	3	18		7	2	8	12	2	4	11	1	5	4
1		1		26		6	2	3	1	5	5	5	1	1	
		12						1						4	
281	17	309	103	408		301	247	317	283	105	212	343	49	379	113
7	3	10	4	10		4	5	9	4	10	10	6	0	5	1
L		D		W		D		D		L		W		D	
3		5		24		8		8		4		24		8	

Glamorgan C.C.C.
Batting, cont.

	v. Somerset (Taunton) 29–31 July		v. Sri Lankans (Cardiff) 1–3 August		v. Lancashire (Cardiff) 8–11 August		v. Warwickshire (Edgbaston) 12–14 August		v. Derbyshire (Swansea) 15–18 August		v. Middlesex (Lord's) 22–25 August	
A. Jones	33	0			30	48	84	6	22	4	9	16
J. A. Hopkins	0	0	4	16	1	4	37	40	30	10	15	10
D. A. Francis			13	17								
M. J. Llewellyn			0	2								
R. C. Ontong	24	6	28	19	9	0	24	2	10	18	15	45
G. C. Holmes	0	18			1	39*	19	24*	8	1	1	6
E. A. Moseley	25	0			2*	57						
E. W. Jones	0	1			33	0	12	—	0	21	12	15
M. A. Nash	0	36*			0	0	—	—	2	10	1	14
R. N. S. Hobbs	3*	4					—	—	0*	0*		
S. R. Barwick			1*	5								
Javed Miandad	200*	4*			7	72	153*	96	36	79	2	40
N. G. Featherstone	18	68*	83	55	62	13	54	109*	1	11	24	23
B. J. Lloyd	7	14	11	11	0	0	2*	—	4	13	8	21
A. A. Jones			9	5*								
A. L. Jones			0	81								
T. Davies			11	4								
P. J. Lawlor			0	8								
J. G. Thomas					12	6	—	—	10	0	0*	11*
S. A. B. Daniels											0	10
N. J. Perry												
H. Morris												
Byes	10	3	6	5	4	9	1	5		2	3	7
Leg byes	9	1	1	12		3	12	1	8	8	1	3
Wides			1				11				2	1
No balls	7	2			1	1		6		5	3	7
Total	336	157	168	240	162	252	409	289	131	182	96	229
Wickets	9	9†	10	10	10	10	6	4	10	10	10	10
Result	D		D		L		W		L		L	
Points	8		—		5		20		4		3	

Catches   †M. A. Nash retired hurt

56 – E. W. Jones (ct 46, st 10)
27 – N. G. Featherstone
20 – B. J. Lloyd
14 – J. A. Hopkins
12 – M. A. Nash
10 – Javed Miandad
 8 – M. J. Llewellyn
 7 – R. C. Ontong and G. C. Holmes
 6 – R. N. S. Hobbs and T. Davies (ct 5, st 1)
 5 – A. Jones and E. A. Moseley
 4 – S. A. B. Daniels
 3 – A. L. Jones and J. G. Thomas
 2 – D. A. Francis
 1 – S. R. Barwick, A. A. Jones, P. J. Lawlor, N. J. Perry and Substitute

v. Worcestershire (Swansea) 26–28 August		v. Essex (Colchester) 29 August–1 September		v. Leicestershire (Cardiff) 9–11 September		v. Nottinghamshire (Trent Bridge) 12–15 September		Inns	NOs	Runs	HS	Av
42	27	31	0	82	21	5	20	41	2	1192	109	30.56
134	61	46	16			4	11	41	1	1217	135	30.42
								5	—	67	28	13.40
								9	1	43	15	5.37
34	11	5	4	54	6	11	0	40	5	968	151*	27.65
						3	4	23	8	324	70*	26.26
								19	3	306	57	19.12
1	3	1	24	15	8	2	0	31	2	232	33	8.00
11*	22	10	1	22*	0	2	10	31	5	275	36*	10.57
		6*	0					15	10	101	49*	20.20
								4	3	20	11*	20.00
59	0	81	200*	29	105*	7	75	37	7	2083	200*	69.43
1	11	59	0	68	11	0	5	39	5	1105	113*	32.50
12	5	4	0	4	0	14	8	28	2	249	31	9.57
								3	2	14	9	14.00
12*	12	15	36	13	4	9	0	12	1	204	31	18.54
								2	—	15	11	7.50
								2	—	8	8	4.00
				1	13*			8	3	53	13*	10.60
—	0*	2	8	10*	—	0*	0*	8	4	30	10*	7.50
—	0							1	—	0	0	0.00
				5	16			2	—	21	16	10.50
12	8	2	12	4	6		8					
17	10	10	8	5	4		5					
5		1		2								
11		1	2	9	2	3	3					
351	160	274	311	323	196	60	149					
7	10	10	10	9	8	10	10					
L		L		D		L						
8		7		8		4						

Glamorgan C.C.C. First-Class Matches – Bowling, 1981	E. A. Moseley	S. R. Barwick	M. A. Nash	R. N. S. Hobbs	R. C. Ontong	N. G. Featherstone
v. Oxford University (Oxford) 25–28 April	18.1–7–39–2	14–10–10–2	16–7–27–2	22–13–50–4	12–4–27–0	
v. Sussex (Hove) 13–15 May	17.2–3–44–4 7–1–23–0	16–8–33–2 6–1–19–1	15–4–36–0 4–0–17–0	4–0–11–2 14–2–45–0	20–5–52–1 4'–0–12–0	6–1–26–1
v. Kent (Cardiff) 26 May	4–2–3–0	4–1–7–0	8–4–18–2		8–4–8–3	
v. Australians (Swansea) 27–29 May	22–10–23–6	13–7–23–0	18.3–10–20–2		12–3–30–1	
v. Worcestershire (Hereford) 3–5 June	25–7–41–3 10–1–47–2		9–1–31–0 12–3–41–1	30.4–13–67–5 14–3–28–3	18–4–35–1	
v. Surrey (Swansea) 6–9 June	13–2–31–1 17–2–79–3		22–7–62–7 10.4–1–69–1	12–2–47–0	15–5–28–2 14–4–57–2	
v. Hampshire (Bournemouth) 10–12 June	19–3–67–0		13–3–53–0	30.2–4–84–4	7–1–27–0	
v. Leicestershire (Leicester) 13–16 June	15–7–19–1 7–3–12–0		17–7–43–2 15–7–25–1	40.1–11–75–3 22–3–94–1	2–1–3–0 4–1–14–0	
v. Warwickshire (Cardiff) 17–19 June	21.3–2–56–4 11–3–33–2		20–4–65–1 13.2–6–20–4		6–1–27–0	
v. Somerset (Swansea) 27–30 June	13–4–55–3 4–1–4–0		20–3–75–3 10–3–30–1	19.3–4–69–0		2–2–0–0
v. Hampshire (Swansea) 1–3 July	25–6–62–3 6–1–21–0		19.5–5–67–4 10–6–9–1	17–3–65–1 12–7–22–0	12–5–25–1	7–3–12–0
v. Northamptonshire (Northampton) 4–7 July	18–4–41–3 10–1–41–0		22–4–82–3 6–1–23–1	7–2–18–1 12–2–56–1	20.1–3–60–3 19–5–42–0	
v. Yorkshire (Cardiff) 15–17 July	20–4–53–2 21–6–63–6		18–4–37–3 15–2–44–1	8–2–15–0	18.4–3–51–3 23–7–39–0	
v. Gloucestershire (Bristol) 18–21 July			26–2–114–4 17–4–37–2	20–4–88–3 21–5–63–0	9–1–44–0	
v. Somerset (Taunton) 29–31 July	14.4–4–37–6 9–2–29–1		10–1–26–1	3–3–0–1 4–1–12–0	2–0–6–0 6–0–21–0	
v. Sri Lankans (Cardiff) 1–3 August		10–3–26–1 8–3–15–1			21.2–3–62–6 18–3–45–4	1–1–0–0
v. Lancashire (Cardiff) 8–11 August	5–1–12–0 3–1–7–0		28–12–69–3 3–1–7–0		20–4–51–2 22–6–63–1	
v. Warwickshire (Edgbaston) 12–14 August			9.4–1–49–0 20–0–98–2	22–5–58–0 13–1–47–0	19–1–68–2 5–1–37–0	
v. Derbyshire (Swansea) 15–18 August			10–2–32–1	21–6–52–1	23–1–61–4	
v. Middlesex (Lord's) 22–25 August			30–8–80–4		18–6–56–0	
v. Worcestershire (Swansea) 26–28 August			19–9–49–1 8–2–18–0		20–6–67–3 10–2–38–0	
v. Essex (Colchester) 29 August–1 September			19–4–76–3 6–0–33–0	21.5–3–85–5	13.4–2–37–4 21–3–102–3	
v. Leicestershire (Cardiff) 9–11 September			29.2–9–81–5 0.5–0–2–1		5–1–27–0	
v. Nottinghamshire (Trent Bridge) 12–15 September			15.1–2–48–4 3.3–0–15–0		10–0–47–3	
	355.4–88–942–52 av. 18.11	71–33–133–7 av. 19.00	568.5–149–1728–71 av. 24.33	390.3–99–1151–35 av. 32.88	457.5–96–1369–49 av. 27.93	16–7–38–1 av. 38.00

a A. Jones 1–1–0–0
b P. J. Lawlor 5–1–14–0; 8–1–36–1
c N. J. Perry 6–0–31–1; 13–1–57–1
d A. Jones 1–0–4–0

Javed Miandad	B. J. Lloyd	G. C. Holmes	A. A. Jones	J. G. Thomas	S. A. B. Daniels	Byes	Leg byes	Wides	No balls	Total	Wickets
						4	9		5	171	10
						1	2	2	14	195	10
4–2–6–1						1		1	5	155	3
									8	44	5
	14–6–32–1					1	10	3	5	147	10
	15–3–30–0					5	11	1	8	229	10
	12–2–56–2					3	8			183	9
						2	2		6	131	10
	15–4–42–2					12	5		6	317	8
	21–4–50–0					6	9	5		301	
	46–11–99–3					4	8			251	9
	6–3–19–1	17–1–83–2				18	7		4	276	5
6–2–12–2	12–3–28–2		12–1–44–1			3	3	1	8	247	10
			10–4–23–3			7	1	8	8	100	9†
	19–5–56–2	2–0–10–0				6	22	3	7	303	10
	3–2–2–0	6–2–8–1					2			46	2
3–0–19–0	20–4–73–1					9	2		18	340	10
	13–5–33–1					8	3	1	2	111	2 a
	15–7–25–0						10	1	6	243	10
6–1–21–0	13–1–74–0	11–2–50–1				14	3	2	5	331	3
	9–4–22–2					13	6	1	2	185	10
	15–5–31–2					2	7	1	3	205	10
	29.1–7–87–1		15–3–68–1			7	4	6	3	421	9
	39–8–110–4	1–0–4–0	8–2–20–0				6		5	245	6
	19–3–59–2					18	10	5	11	172	10
	11–2–43–1						6	1	9	121	2
	5–1–17–0		16–2–59–3			1	3	2	6	190	10 b
	18–2–48–1		8–2–23–0			4	9	2	3	185	7
	7–2–7–0	3–0–16–1		19.4–4–65–4		11	9	4	5	249	10
6–1–9–0	34.5–10–70–8			7–1–36–1		13	19	4	3	231	10
8–1–21–0	15–3–56–0			7–1–36–0		6	4		17	315	2
	20–2–59–2			16.5–1–92–4			10	1	4	348	10
	44.3–12–98–4			7–1–38–0		16	18	2	3	320	10
	20–2–62–1			17–2–59–1	21–6–79–1	1	11	3	10	361	7
	23–8–33–4				10–2–28–1	13	7	1	8	237	10 c
4–0–20–0	25–3–97–3				3–0–16–0	10	6	2	7	275	5 d
	6–0–22–0				11–3–33–3	4	6	6	3	187	10
	31–4–110–1				7–1–45–0	16	15	4	1	411	9
	26–6–78–3			6–0–29–0	20–5–56–1	5	6			282	10
						1				3	1
	7–2–11–1				14–1–58–2	1	8	1	6	180	10
					3–0–12–0		1		2	30	0
37–7–	619.3–142–	49–9–	69–14–	80.3–10–	89–18–						
108–3	1717–53	193–7	237–8	355–10	327–8						
av. 36.00	av. 32.39	av. 27.57	av. 29.62	av. 35.50	av. 40.87						

* Innings forfeited
† K. D. Smith retired hurt

Gloucestershire C.C.
First-Class Matches – Batting, 1981

	v. Oxford University (Oxford) 13-15 May		v. Australians (Bristol) 31 May-2 June		v. Nottinghamshire (Trent Bridge) 3-5 June		v. Yorkshire (Bristol) 6-9 June		v. Northamptonshire (Bristol) 10-12 June		v. Somerset (Bath) 13-16 June	
B. C. Broad	40	28*	0	—	4	1	50	71	94	0	11	37
B. Dudleston	99	—										
A. W. Stovold	41	61*	1*	—	26	29	6	10	57	0	40	21
A. J. Hignell	102*	—	—	—	38	22	0	13	6	38	55	40*
P. Bainbridge	2	—	—	—	10	3	7	4	84*	5	3*	12
S. J. Windaybank	30	—										
D. A. Graveney	4*	—			48	1	1	13	13	105*	—	—
A. H. Wilkins	—	—	—	—	0	1	2	10	7	0	—	—
A. J. Brassington	—	—	—	—	9	1*						
J. H. Childs	—	—	—	—	3*	0	0*	11*	—	20		
J. Dixon	—	—										
Sadiq Mohammad			15	—	0	7	1	22	38	25	23	33
Zaheer Abbas			60*	—	6	72	71	74	34	50	215*	150*
M. J. Procter			—	—	44	7	19	20	8	46		
B. M. Brain			—	—			7	0	2*	42	—	—
R. Russell												
D. Surridge												
M. R. Whitney												
M. W. Stovold												
D. Lawrence												
R. J. Doughty												
Byes	4				1			5		13	1	4
Leg byes	6	2			4	4	6	4	9	15	5	2
Wides	8	6	1		1			1	2	1	4	
No balls	4		3		6	4	2	10	2	3	4	4
Total	340	97	80		200	152	172	268	356	363	361	303
Wickets	5	0	2		10	10	10	10	8	10	4	4
Result	W		D		L		W		D		D	
Points	—				6		21		8		8	

The match v. Glamorgan (Cardiff) 6–8 May was abandoned without a ball being bowled;
and v. Essex (Chelmsford) 23–26 May; and v. Sussex (Bristol) 27–29 May
†A. J. Brassington absent hurt.

v. Sri Lanka (Bristol) 17–19 June		v. Hampshire (Southampton) 20–23 June		v. Warwickshire (Gloucester) 27–30 June		v. Northamptonshire (Northampton) 1–3 July		v. Sussex (Hove) 4–7 July		v. Worcestershire (Bristol) 15–17 July		v. Glamorgan (Bristol) 18–21 July		v. Derbyshire (Derby) 29–31 July	
70	—	17	49	16	10	9	13	27	17	21	25*	4	45	16	12
		6	35	37	1	26	0	3	57	67	20	104	65*	50	19
—	—	3	22	39	14	72	9	11	8	22	—	7	14	9	45
100*	—	0*	53*	3	43*	14*	53*	21	18	11	—	72	5	0	7
—	2*	—	43*					16	9	16	7	4	0		
		—	—	28*	37*	—	—	1	1*	22*	—	41	—	0	23
—	—			1	—	0	—	10	2	1	—	0	31	2	2
														0	—
—	—	—	—	19*	—	—	—	2*	0*	1*	—	3*	—	2	3
203	—	100	34	3	25	25	6	22	5					4	7
16*	—	101*	16	100	51	135*	128	145	31	71	22*	159	41	0	17
		36	3	31	1	10	—	8	—	—	—				
—	1*														
—	—			—	—									0*	0*
—	—									0	—				
												7	33*	—	—
14		7	4	5	8		3	12			1	7			2
6		4	9	7	1	3	7	6	8	16	6	4	6	3	8
1		2	2	2	3					1	4	6		3	
6		1		10	4	7	5	1	3	2	2	3	5	2	5
416	3	277	270	301	198	301	224	285	159	251	87	421	245	91	150
2	0	5	6	8	6	6	5	10	8	8	2	9	6	10	9†
D		D		D		D		D		D		D		L	
—		4		6		8		6		5		4		4	

Gloucestershire C.C.C. Batting, cont.

	v. Middlesex (Lord's) 1–4 August		v. Surrey (Cheltenham) 8–11 August		v. Hampshire (Cheltenham) 12–14 August		v. Kent (Cheltenham) 15–18 August		v. Worcestershire (Worcester) 22–25 August		v. Somerset (Bristol) 29 August–1 September	
B. C. Broad	0	51	12	76*	16	—	25	5	17	41	6	0
B. Dudleston												
A. W. Stovold	—	39*	35	—	0	—	—	0	4	—	0	7
A. J. Hignell		22	12	—	97	—	12*	25	41	54*	1	38
P. Bainbridge	105*	0*	2	75	61	—	81	57*	24	9	29	13
S. J. Windaybank					46*	—			—	—		
D. A. Graveney	—	5	28	—					21	—	2	11*
A. H. Wilkins	—	2*	0	—	21*	—			1	—	5	10
A. J. Brassington												
J. H. Childs	—	—	0	—					18*	—	4*	6
J. Dixon												
Sadiq Mohammad	78*	3	11	0	43	—	48	6	6	61	6	8
Zaheer Abbas	—	26	17	6*	68	—	136*	2	76	103*	7	72
M. J. Procter												
B. M. Brain			0*	—								
R. Russell												
D. Surridge	—								—	—		
M. R. Whitney												
M. W. Stovold	—	7	39	—	13	—	—	16*	23*	—	0	3
D. Lawrence												
R. J. Doughty											7	10
Byes	7	10	4	3	4		10		3		4	5
Leg byes	3	6	6	4	6		4	4	15	8	3	4
Wides	2			1	2		6			1	2	1
No balls	6	5			4		14	6	1	2		5
Total	201	176	166	165	361		336	121	250	279	76	193
Wickets	1	6	10	2	7		3	5	8	3	10	10
Result	D		W		W		D		W		L	
Points	3		21		24		6		23		4	

A. Second innings forfeited.

Catches
43 – A. W. Stovold (ct 25, st 18)
19 – A. J. Hignell
15 – Sadiq Mohammad
14 – B. C. Broad
12 – J. H. Childs
10 – D. A. Graveney
 9 – Zaheer Abbas
 8 – A. H. Wilkins and R. Russell (ct 7, st 1)
 7 – P. Bainbridge
 6 – M. J. Procter
 4 – A. J. Brassington (ct 3, st 1), M. W. Stovold and Substitutes
 3 – B. M. Brain
 2 – B. Dudleston
 1 – S. J. Windaybank, M. R. Whitney and D. Surridge

v. Lancashire (Old Trafford) 9–11 September		v. Leicestershire (Bristol) 12–15 September		Inns	NOs	Runs	HS	Av
25	41*	115	—	40	4	1117	115	31.02
				1	—	99	99	99.00
43	12*	5	—	35	5	927	104	30.90
80*	—	8	—	33	5	979	102*	34.96
9	—	24	—	36	11	1019	105*	40.76
6	—	24	—	12	3	203	46*	22.55
14	—	8	—	22	7	427	105*	28.46
1	—	8*	—	23	3	117	31	5.85
				3	1	10	9	5.00
17	—	11	—	18	10	120	20	15.00
				—				—
		49	—	32	1	917	203	29.58
17	—	11	—	36	10	2306	215*	88.69
				11	—	225	46	20.45
				6	2	59	47	14.75
				1	1	1	1*	—
		2*	—	2	2	0	0*	—
0	—			2	—	0	0	0.00
1	—			10	3	142	39	20.28
				—				—
				2	—	17	10	8.50

v. Lancashire		v. Leicestershire	
4	4	7	
1	5	6	
	1		
1		3	

219	63	291	A
10	0	9	
D		D	
6		3	

Gloucestershire C.C.C. First-Class Matches – Bowling, 1981

	A. H. Wilkins	J. Dixon	J. H. Childs	P. Bainbridge	D. A. Graveney	B. C. Broad
v. Oxford University	17–7–40–0	5–1–27–0	33–14–48–3	12–7–14–2	10.1–5–9–4	
(Oxford) 13–15 May	20–6–59–2	19–4–52–1	29–11–64–3	7–2–18–1	19–8–38–2	8–3–18–0
v. Australians	29–8–65–3		23.2–3–67–1	15–6–22–0		
(Bristol) 31 May–2 June						
v. Nottinghamshire	23–2–76–0		26–7–73–5	19–4–48–1	1–1–0–0	
(Trent Bridge) 3–5 June	9–2–18–1		6–2–19–0		2–0–9–0	
v. Yorkshire	19–3–40–4		9–4–12–1			
(Bristol) 6–9 June	15–2–43–2		29–8–61–5		2.2–0–9–1	
v. Northamptonshire	13–5–20–1		20–3–89–2	2–0–10–0	28–6–87–0	
(Bristol) 10–12 June						
v. Somerset	24–9–50–3		19–3–83–0	18–3–58–3	6–1–26–1	5–1–18–0
(Bath) 13–16 June	21–3–139–3		11–6–15–1	20–7–68–5	3–1–5–0	3–0–15–0
v. Sri Lankans	7–1–21–0		22–8–61–6	9–1–30–0		
(Bristol) 17–19 June	16–4–64–2		28–8–82–0	6–1–17–0		4–0–32–1
v. Hampshire			24–9–50–0	10–2–26–0	23–5–69–2	10–5–21–1
(Southampton) 20–23 June			10–2–24–0	7–0–37–1	10–4–14–1	4–1–31–0
v. Warwickshire	16–3–60–2		31–5–84–1	11–2–27–1	11–0–37–0	
(Gloucester) 27–30 June	18–6–44–2		23–8–57–0	8–2–17–1	15–5–27–0	
v. Northamptonshire	15–4–67–2		16–4–42–0	12–2–56–0	12.2–5–44–5	
(Northampton) 1–3 July	17–3–58–0		21–7–72–3	17–2–47–2	21–5–56–0	5–0–32–0
v. Sussex	29.5–10–74–3		24–11–43–1	33–6–84–2		
(Hove) 4–7 July	18–1–61–1		8–2–27–0	5.1–0–31–0	10–3–30–1	
v. Worcestershire	17–2–62–0		14–3–52–0	19–5–62–1	9–3–15–1	
(Bristol) 15–17 July	16–1–55–0		1–0–4–0	16–1–60–3		
v. Glamorgan	26.5–3–105–1		35–8–107–2	7–1–24–0	22–4–56–0	
(Bristol) 18–21 July			9–1–35–1	5–0–16–0	6–1–12–0	5–2–18–0
v. Derbyshire	23–3–79–1		22–9–43–5	16–5–42–1	12–4–15–1	
(Derby) 29–31 July						
v. Middlesex	14–3–37–0		8–0–29–0	25–5–71–2	9–1–24–0	11–2–35–1
(Lord's) 1–4 August	15–4–33–0				12–2–38–1	7–1–42–1
v. Surrey	6–1–28–0		19–5–69–6	6–3–15–0	11.3–5–18–4	
(Cheltenham) 8–11 August	2–1–4–0		19–4–54–2		21.1–7–54–6	
v. Hampshire	12–2–42–1		33.5–13–67–5	2–1–1–0	43–19–53–4	
(Cheltenham) 12–14 August	10–5–20–1		17–6–40–2		17–12–18–4	2–0–8–0
v. Kent	24–2–63–1		29–9–58–1		24–6–63–1	20–5–70–2
(Cheltenham) 15–18 August	13–7–32–1		21–10–33–2		18–4–49–0	15–2–60–0
v. Worcestershire	8–1–42–0		42–12–81–4		35.2–11–57–5	1–0–4–0
(Worcester) 22–25 August	10–0–37–0		12–0–54–0		22–2–71–2	
v. Somerset (Bristol)	18.3–5–62–4			18–2–38–4		
29 August–1 September	11–3–32–0		32.3–13–56–9		30–15–50–1	
v. Lancashire	26.5–10–57–8		4–0–17–1	7–4–20–0		9–4–20–0
(Old Trafford)	31–10–62–1		15–5–25–1	16–8–29–2	3–1–5–0	11–5–19–0
9–11 September						
v. Leicestershire						
(Bristol) 12–15 September	19–4–41–2		25–6–65–2	7–3–21–1	11.4–2–20–1	
	630–146–	24–5–	770.4–229–	355.1–85–	480.3–148–	120–31–
	1892–52	79–1	1962–75	1009–33	1078–48	443–6
	av. 36.38	*av. 79–00*	*av. 26–16*	*av. 30.57*	*av. 22.45*	*av. 73.83*

†P. M. Roebuck absent hurt
a B. Duddleston 7–0–30–0
b Zaheer Abbas 5–0–32–3
c D. Lawrence 14–3–62–0; 5–1–24–0
d Zaheer Abbas 2–1–4–0

e M. W. Stovold 1–0–3–0
f M. W. Stovold 1–0–3–0; Zaheer Abbas 5–1–6–0
g R. J. Doughty 19–9–28–2; 8–1–27–0
A. Innings forfeited

D. Surridge	M. J. Procter	Sadiq Mohamad	A. J. Hignell	B. M. Brain	M. R. Whitney	Byes	Leg byes	Wides	No balls	Total	Wickets
							6			144	10
						3	4	4	1	291	10
	19–3–68–3			17–3–40–0		2	11		3	278	7
	24–7–45–4					10	10			262	10
	10–4–21–0	4–1–8–0	0.5–0–10–0			6	1		1	93	1
	15–7–34–2			18–5–34–3		5	5			130	10
	11–5–26–0			20–5–48–2		1	5			193	10
	21.5–3–80–5			14–5–45–1		5	12			348	10
				14–2–60–2		6	9	2	4	316	9 †
						2	1			245	9
19.2–6–47–2					18–5–60–1	7	11	4	5	246	10
12–5–27–1		9–3–45–0	3.2–0–13–2		19–4–86–4	9	17	3	3	398	10
	18–2–79–0			17–3–75–0		11	8	1	9	349	3
	17–3–59–1	14–1–67–0		4–2–10–0		5	1		1	249	3
16–2–65–1	11–2–40–1					3	6	1	2	325	6
10–4–21–0	16–6–30–2	4–1–11–0				9	9			257	8
	9–3–18–1			18–2–74–2		2	6		3	312	10
	1–0–13–0			14–2–53–2		2	10		1	344	7
				24–5–78–3		9	12		4	304	10
				10–3–24–1		11	10	1	2	197	3
				14–3–36–0	20–7–54–3	11	14	8	2	316	5
					17–1–63–1	1	3			186	4
						15	5	1	4	379	3 c
							4			113	1
18–2–62–1						8	7	7	4	267	10
22.3–1–86–0						9	9	1	1	302	3
11–0–49–1		10–2–30–1				4	2		1	202	4 e
				18–8–25–0			4		1	160	10
		9–1–33–2		3–1–7–0		11	7			170	10
						1	8	2		174	10
		12.4–2–34–3					1			121	10
		9–1–43–1				4	6		3	310	6
		20–2–80–3				5	6	2		276	6
14–2–49–1							16	1	1	251	10
11–1–45–1		11–1–61–1				1	7		4	277	6
						5	9	4	1	147	10 g
						7	3	5		180	10
					21–8–62–1	1	1	2	2	182	10
					26–5–74–3	1	11	3	1	230	8
											A.
6–0–25–1							2		3	177	7
139.5–23–476–9 av. 52.85	172.5–45–513–19 av. 27.00	102.4–15–412–11 av. 37.45	4.1–0–23–2 av. 11.50	205–49–609–16 av. 38.06	121–30–399–13 av. 30.69						

Hampshire C.C.C. First-Class Matches – Batting, 1981

	v. Cambridge University (Cambridge) 25–27 April		v. Somerset (Southampton) 6–8 May		v. Australians (Southampton) 20–22 May		v. Leicestershire (Leicester) 27–29 May		v. Middlesex (Basingstoke) 3–5 June		v. Glamorgan (Bournemouth) 10–12 June	
T. M. Tremlett	62	—	46	—	7	—			0	30	—	83
J. M. Rice	35	—					—	14				
M. C. J. Nicholas	19	—	5	0*	58	—	—	4	16	22	—	6
T. E. Jesty	33*	—	4	—	23*	—	—	0	0	57	—	7
D. R. Turner	13*	—	106	—	25*	—	—	17	4	3	—	31*
N. E. J. Pocock	—	—	23	—	—	—	—	15	10	0	—	33
N. G. Cowley	—	—	52	—	—	—	—	12	31	26	—	6*
R. J. Parks	—	—	12*	7*	—	—	—	0	15	33*	—	—
J. W. Southern	—	—	7*	—	—	—	—	35*	20*	3	—	—
K. Stevenson	—	—	—	—	—	—	—	7*	7	11*	—	—
S. J. Malone	—	—			—	—						
C. G. Greenidge			9	—	39	—	—	4	96	57	—	115
M. D. Marshall			10	—			—	33	0	0	—	—
M. J. Bailey												
C. L. Smith												
V. P. Terry												
R. E. Hayward												
C. C. Curzon												
Byes			3				10		1	1	6	
Leg byes	5		16		11		6		4	15	9	
Wides	1		1		1				2	1	5	
No balls	8		5		12		3		5	2		
Total	176		299	7	176		A. 160		211	261	A. 301	
Wickets	3		8	0	3		9		10	9	5	
Result	D		D		D		D		D		W	
Points	—		6		—		4		4		19	

The match v. Surrey (The Oval) 23–26 May was abandoned without a ball being bowled.

A. Innings forfeited.

† N. E. J. Pocock, absent injured.

v. Worcestershire (Worcester) 13–16 June		v. Gloucestershire (Southampton) 20–23 June		v. Lancashire (Old Trafford) 27–30 June		v. Glamorgan (Swansea) 1–3 July		v. Nottinghamshire (Bournemouth) 4–7 July		v. Derbyshire (Portsmouth) 15–17 July		v. Surrey (Portsmouth) 18–21 July		v. Sri Lankans (Bournemouth) 29–31 July	
41	—	8	27	88	3	1	41*	23	8	0	—	1	0		
														31	14
10	—	36	101*	94	34	21	27	1	22*	30	—	0	1		
44	—	81*	35*	3*	31	30	10*	15	—	25	—	9	28		
73	—	55*	—	—	33*	1	—	42	—	48	—	13	38*		
28	—	—	—	—	14	61	—	25	—			8*	—		
4	—			—	6	24	—	4	—	19	—	1	5	67	9
7	—			—	4	25	—	15	—	21	—	19	0		
21*	—	—	6	—	4*									—	33*
17	—			—	—	21	—	1*	—			31	0	—	3*
						5	—							—	—
21	—	140	73	57	58	109	19			109	—	43	3	80	24
40	—	—	—	—	15			8	—	40*	—	7	0	—	5
						13*	—	6	—	4*	—	14	0	4	14
								34	18*	14	—			5	5
														101*	53
														31*	22
2		11	5	3	2	9	8	3		6		3	5		
5		8	1	13	9	2	3	8	4	9		3	7	6	4
5		1		1			1	1				2	2	1	1
19		9	1	1		18	2	4	1	20		10	2	4	2
337		349	249	260	213	340	111	190	53	345		164	91	330	189
10		3	3	3	8	10	2	10	1	8		10	9†	5	8
W		D		W		D		W		W		L		D	
24		6		21		8		21		24		5		—	

Hampshire C.C.C.
Batting, cont.

	v. Kent (Canterbury) 1–4 August		v. Yorkshire (Middlesbrough) 8–11 August		v. Gloucestershire (Cheltenham) 12–14 August		v. Essex (Southampton) 15–18 August		v. Somerset (Taunton) 22–25 August		v. Sussex (Bournemouth) 26–28 August	
T. M. Tremlett											32	17
J. M. Rice	3	24	56*	3	11	2	63	23	0	4		
M. C. J. Nicholas	88*	0	31*	18	0	17	5	43	6	4	2	0
T. E. Jesty	32	1	—	15	84	1	7	5	0	67	34	35
D. R. Turner	0	2	—	6	0	3	53	—	14	13	6	64
N. E. J. Pocock												
N. G. Cowley	3	3	—	20	6	5	30	21	25	0	14	2
R. J. Parks	9	20	—	21	13*	6	34*	7*	0	3	4	7
J. W. Southern	11	6										
K. Stevenson	15	0*	—	—	0	3	—	—	11*	3	28*	3*
S. J. Malone												
C. G. Greenidge	39	25	53*	—							14	36
M. D. Marshall	0	20	—	28*	9	29	75*	10	41	2	1	38
M. J. Bailey			—	4*	7	2	—	—	11	0	0	1
C. L. Smith					28	11	32	39	58	1		
V. P. Terry												
R. E. Hayward	0	14	—	2	5	41*	31	18	0	16*	0	4
C. C. Curzon												
Byes	6			5	1		1	4	1		5	2
Leg byes	8	6	6	5	8	1	5	8	7	3	3	11
Wides					2				1			1
No balls	3	1	4	3			4	2	9	4	5	2
Total	217	122	150	130	174	121	340	180	184	120	148	223
Wickets	10	10	0	7	10	10	7	7	10	10	10	10
Result	L		D		L		W		L		L	
Points	5		3		4		23		5		4	

Catches

52 – R. J. Parks (ct 49, st 3)
25 – C. G. Greenidge
13 – T. E. Jesty
10 – N. E. J. Pocock
 9 – M. C. J. Nicholas
 7 – J. M. Rice and K. Stevenson
 6 – M. D. Marshall
 5 – T. M. Tremlett, C. L. Smith and M. J. Bailey
 4 – J. W. Southern, D. R. Turner and N. G. Cowley
 3 – S. J. Malone, R. E. Hayward and Substitutes
 2 – V. P. Terry
 1 – C. C. Curzon

v. Kent (Bournemouth) 29 August–1 September		v. Sussex (Hove) 2–4 September		v. Warwickshire (Edgbaston) 9–11 September		v. Northamptonshire (Southampton) 12–15 September		Inns.	NOs	Runs	HS	Av
6	54	0	44			14	—	25	1	636	88	26.50
	101*		23	161*	40	31	—	19	3	639	161*	39.93
								32	5	721	101*	26.70
5	14	4	45	—	99	8	—	35	6	891	99	30.72
2	6	31	2			0	—	30	6	704	106	29.33
35	63	34	9	—	35			15	1	393	63	28.07
		1	19	—	3	33	—	29	1	451	67	16.10
5	37*	0	4	—	0*	2	—	29	8	330	34*	15.71
34	4			—	46			13	6	230	46	32.85
26	0	16	8*	—	1	20	—	23	9	232	28*	16.57
2*	23	5	9	—	—	0	—	6	1	44	23	8.80
2	69	17	16	49	64	2	—	30	1	1442	140	49.72
		18	1					23	3	425	75*	21.25
								13	3	67	14	6.70
8	0			81*	32	68	—	15	2	428	81*	32.92
20	0			—	1*	94*	—	7	2	139	94*	27.80
								13	3	285	101*	28.50
								2	1	53	31*	53.00
3	4	4	2			1						
	2	6	9	2	6	14						
						3						
5	2	4	5	7	6	16						
153	278	241	196	300	334	305						
10	10	10	10	1	8	10						
L		L		D		D						
3		5		8		4						

Hampshire C.C.C. First-Class Matches – Bowling, 1981	K. Stevenson	S. J. Malone	J. W. Southern	J. M. Rice	T. E. Jesty	N. G. Cowley
v. Cambridge University (Cambridge) 25–27 April	14–3–26–0	10–5–14–0	22–13–17–0	11–3–26–1	8–6–5–1	11–10–2–2
v. Somerset (Southampton) 6–8 May	28–10–52–1		26–5–60–3		13–6–17–1	24–10–36–1
v. Australians (Southampton) 20–22 May	11–3–36–1	21–5–45–2	32–11–62–2		3–0–9–0	25–4–74–1
v. Leicestershire (Leicester) 27–29 May	12–0–31–0 1.4–0–9–0		7–0–41–0	9–2–25–2 1–0–9–0	28–6–63–1	
v. Middlesex (Basingstoke) 3–5 June	31–4–102–2		13–2–35–1		19–7–44–2	4–0–22–0
v. Glamorgan (Bournemouth) 10–12 June	29–8–94–5		16–8–38–0		7–2–22–0	10–3–21–1
v. Worcestershire (Worcester) 13–16 June	6–2–15–1 21.2–3–63–4		3–1–4–0		21–11–28–4 24–7–56–5	
v. Gloucestershire (Southampton) 20–23 June	23–11–42–2 17–1–72–0		20–3–75–0 28–3–74–1		10–1–31–0	25–7–72–3 25–7–70–2
v. Lancashire (Old Trafford) 27–30 June	24–6–76–1 20–3–56–4		5–0–36–0		19–8–40–0 17–8–29–3	11–1–47–0 6.5–3–5–6–1
v. Glamorgan (Swansea) 1–3 July	25–4–101–2 20–4–61–1	18–4–72–2 9–1–48–0			29–10–65–3 12–3–21–0	11–4–21–0 19–2–78–2
v. Nottinghamshire (Bournemouth) 4–7 July	19–3–86–4 16–7–32–5				10–2–22–2	
v. Derbyshire (Portsmouth) 15–17 July	23.1–8–49–5 20.4–3–54–3				4–2–5–0 24–10–43–3	3–2–1–0
v. Surrey (Portsmouth) 18–21 July	25–4–72–2 10–2–33–2				13–2–38–4 13–3–32–2	
v. Sri Lankans (Bournemouth) 29–31 July	13–2–68–0	15–2–71–2	31–11–97–3	6–2–29–1		14–2–60–1
v. Kent (Canterbury) 1–4 August	19–3–86–2 2–0–6–0		24–5–58–0 28–3–117–2		24.4–7–53–5	15–2–41–0 15–3–37–1
v. Yorkshire (Middlesbrough) 8–11 August	17–5–72–2 8–0–29–0			6–0–25–0	11–6–11–2 4–2–6–0	7–1–32–1 20–3–81–0
v. Gloucestershire (Cheltenham) 12–14 August	10–2–33–2			1–1–0–0	8–1–30–0	30–8–93–1
v. Essex (Southampton) 15–18 August	14–3–54–0 5–1–11–0				10–4–32–2 13–5–25–6	10–0–43–2
v. Somerset (Taunton) 22–25 August	18–4–54–0			10.5–1–55–1	22–3–73–3	
v. Sussex (Bournemouth) 26–28 August	14–3–49–3 9–1–32–0				5–1–24–0 5–0–18–0	9–2–32–1 14–9–17–0
v. Kent (Bournemouth) 29 August–1 September	26–4–103–1 9–1–34–1	25–2–88–3 3–0–12–0	15–8–21–0 12–2–40–00		23–6–62–1	
v. Sussex (Hove) 2–4 September	18–1–91–0	20–4–91–3		3–0–27–0	11–1–60–0	14–1–43–2
v. Warwickshire (Edgbaston) 9–11 September	9–0–55–0 7–0–25–1	17–1–55–1 7–2–17–0	29–10–69–3 41.1–13–108–5	13–3–43–0 4–1–19–0	19–4–52–2 8–2–17–0	15–2–57–1 28–5–134–4
v. Northamptonshire (Southampton) 12–15 September	1–0–2–0	2–1–5–1				3–1–14–0
	595.5–119– 1966–57 av. 34.49	147–27– 578–14 av. 37.00	352.1–98– 952–20 av. 47.60	64.5–13– 258–5 av. 51.60	437.4–136 1033–52 av. 19.86	368.5–92– 1134–27 av. 42.00

† F. C. Hayes absent hurt
a C. L. Smith 4–0–20–0
b R. J. Parks 0.3–0–0–0; R. E. Hayward 2–0–5–0

c C. G. Greenidge 0.4–0–1–0
d C. L. Smith 7–2–21–1; V. P. Terry 0.5–0–4–0
e V. P. Terry 13–4–35–0; C. L. Smith 30–5–108–1

T. M. Tremlett	M. D. Marshall	M. C. J. Nicholas	D. R. Turner	N. E. J. Pocock	M. J. Bailey	Byes	Leg byes	Wides	No balls	Total	Wickets
8–4–10–1						9	2		6	117	5
1–1–0–0	29–9–62–3	1.5–0–4–1				3	13	3	5	255	10
						2	6	3		237	7
	29–10–57–6						4		3	224	10
						4	1			23	0
11–3–14–0	31–9–87–0					8	7	3		322	6
20–6–32–0	26–8–64–1						9	1		281	7
			5–3–7–2	5–3–10–1						17	3
8–2–18–1	19.3–6–46–4					5	2		1	115	10
3–0–10–0	25–11–53–1					6		2		194	10
3–0–14–0	6–0–19–0			0.3–0–10–0		7	4	2	1	277	5
	21.3–10–39–2					4	9	2		270	6
17–4–58–1	27–9–82–4						10			349	6
4–3–2–0	14–5–24–0					1	3	2		123	9†
10–5–27–1					6–0–15–0	4	8	3	1	317	9
					22–3–62–1		12	1		283	4
	20–9–32–4						3			143	10
	16.2–2–64–5						3			99	10
13–8–11–4	21–10–27–1				1–1–0–0	1	4	7		104	10
8–3–17–0	30–14–59–3				7–0–21–1	1	11	1	1	209	10
11–8–5–1	22.4–4–68–3					1	18	2		204	10
18–8–34–1	15.5–4–60–5					8	9	4	1	181	10
					9–1–34–0	8	3			370	7
	23–5–60–2					5	11	1		315	10
	15–4–34–3					8	2		1	205	7
	19–4–49–1						11	5		205	6
	7–4–5–1				23–3–83–0	3	1			208	3
	17–4–51–0				29–4–138–4	4	6	2	4	381	7a
	24–4–67–4				23–5–66–1		8		9	279	10
	11–3–39–4				8–4–25–0	2			3	105	10
	25–8–68–5					13	16	2	6	287	10
			2–1–12–1			4				21	1b
10–1–32–0	15.4–1–62–6				3–0–21–0		9		8	237	10
8–1–18–1	6–3–13–0				9–3–24–1		9	1	2	135	2c
20–4–33–1							14		2	323	6
			1–1–0–0				1			112	2d
23–7–48–2	16–6–30–0					6	13	3	4	416	7
			1.1–0–8–1	2–0–16–0						24	1
						1	12	1		345	9
						11	2	1	1	335	10
			14–2–61–0			1	1		1	228	2e
196–68–	531.3–166–	1.5–0–	23.1–7–	7.3–3–	140–24–						
383–14	1321–68	4–1	88–4	36–1	489–8						
av. 27.35	av. 19.42	av. 4.00	av. 22.00	av. 36.00	av. 61.12						

Kent C.C.C. First-Class Matches – Batting, 1981	v. Nottinghamshire (Canterbury) 6–8 May		v. Warwickshire (Nuneaton) 13–15 May		v. Glamorgan (Cardiff) 26 May		v. Yorkshire (Dartford) 27–29 May		v. Northamptonshire (Northampton) 6–9 June		v. Leicestershire (Tunbridge Wells) 10–12 June	
R. A. Woolmer	15	19	22	119*	3	—	28	24	10	63	—	37
C. J. C. Rowe	9	16	19	0			21	54				
C. J. Tavare	66	1	24	96	6*	—	13	3*	41	135*	—	26
M. R. Benson	7	81	114	—	6	—	3	—	82	51*	—	14
Asif Iqbal	26	39	108	—	5	—	64*	5	5	—	—	26
A. P. E. Knott	47	14	9	—	0	—	6	44	2*	—	—	27
G. W. Johnson	26	5	2*	—	7*	—	2	43	107	0	—	10
J. N. Shepherd	32*	4	0*	—	—	—	59*	8	—	—	—	56*
G. R. Dilley	0	4	—	—	—	—	—	6*	—	—	—	17*
D. L. Underwood	9*	1*	—	—	—	—	—	0*	—	—	—	—
K. B. S. Jarvis	—	1*	—	—	—	—	—	—	—	—	—	—
C. S. Cowdrey					9	—			31*	—		
N. Taylor											—	3
L. Potter												
S. N. V. Waterton												
E. Baptiste												
A. G. E. Ealham												
N. J. Kemp												
R. M. Ellison												
L. J. Wood												
D. G. Aslett												
Byes	4						2		4	4		1
Leg byes	6	7	10	1			2	4	8	3		4
Wides	1		1							1		1
No balls	2		14	2	8				3	1		11
Total	250	192	323	218	44		200	191	293	258	A.	233
Wickets	8	9	6	2	5		6	6	5	2		7
Result	D		L		Ab.		D		D		D	
Points	5		7		0		4		6		1	

A. Innings forfeited

v. Sussex (Tunbridge Wells) 13–16 June		v. Oxford University (Oxford) 17–19 June		v. Australians (Canterbury) 27–29 June		v. Middlesex (Maidstone) 1–3 July		v. Lancashire (Maidstone) 4–7 July		v. Middlesex (Lord's) 15–17 July		v. Leicestershire (Leicester) 18–21 July		v. Derbyshire (Derby) 25–28 July	
20	36			40	—					39	18	6	87	19	0
										4	0	3	16		
33	88	14	63*	12	—	25	28	11	0	11	26*	62	69	156	57
19	15	6	—			7	8	5	0*	33	21*	33	10	108	15
76	14*					7	17	112	—	55	—			—	2
52	0			3	—	45	51*	6	—	24	—	20	44	—	50
13	4*	41	—	27*	—	1	27	30	12*	28	—	13	2	—	3
5	—	12	—			3	16	6	17	13*	—	8	16	—	10*
0*	—					—	—							—	0
1*	—	—	—	—	—	7*	0	10*	—	12	—	9*	6	—	0
—	—	—	—			0	2	—	—	0	—	12	0*	—	0
		70*	—	0	—					60	—	21	35	56*	1
29	99	11	—	5	—	2	6	32	1*						
		6	42*												
		28	—												
		36	—	—	—	1	4	10*	37*			31	22		
				44	—	13	14	22	48						
				5*	—										
		1							4				1		
1	7	4	2	3		1	6	1	2	2	1	5	7	2	1
1				1		1		3		1				7	
1	6	4		7		7	3	2	2	2	1	1	4		
250	270	233	107	147		120	182	250	123	284	67	224	319	348	139
8	5	8	0	6		10	10	8	3	10	1	10	10	3	10
W		W		D		L		D		D		W		L	
20		—		—		4		7		7		22		8	

Kent C.C.C.
Batting, cont.

	v. Essex (Canterbury) 29–31 July		v. Hampshire (Canterbury) 1–4 August		v. Sussex (Eastbourne) 8–11 August		v. Essex (Chelmsford) 12–14 August		v. Gloucestershire (Cheltenham) 15–18 August		v. Surrey (Folkestone) 22–25 August	
R. A. Woolmer					9	9	73	41	1	16	20	0
C. J. C. Rowe												
C. J. Tavare	7	6	4	30	9	72					123*	82
M. R. Benson	57	32	1	21	13	0	36	25	87	36	52	5
Asif Iqbal	11	24	73	40	2	21	58	52	93	40	29	81*
A. P. E. Knott	1	5	0	49*	4	13					21	13*
G. W. Johnson	10	11	16	22	0	12	6	2	30*	48*	7	—
J. N. Shepherd	16	0					21	8				
G. R. Dilley					5	7*						
D. L. Underwood	4*	0	50	—	0	3			—	—	—	39
K. B. S. Jarvis	0	1	1	—	1	0	0*	0	—	—	—	—
C. S. Cowdrey	12	0	53	16	19*	97	0	8	15	3	48	27
N. Taylor	17	19					0	6	60	51		
L. Potter			17	1								
S. N. V. Waterton							8	0*	—			
E. Baptiste	19	18*	28	4	27	7	1	11	0	10	—	—
A. G. E. Ealham												
N. J. Kemp												
R. M. Ellison			55*	11*					11*	59*	2	0
L. J. Wood							0	5				
D. G. Aslett												
Byes	2	7	5	8	6		4	6	4	5	2	8
Leg byes	10	3	11	2	7	11	9	4	6	6	10	4
Wides			1		2	2				2	1	
No balls				1				2	3		1	
Total	166	126	315	205	104	254	216	170	310	276	316	259
Wickets	10	10	10	7	10	10	10	10	6	6	7	6
Result	L		W		L		L		D		D	
Points	4		24		4		3		4		7	

Catches

A. Innings forfeited

47 – A. P. E. Knott (ct 39, st 8)
16 – C. J. Tavare
15 – G. W. Johnson and C. S. Cowdrey
13 – N. Taylor, S. N. V. Waterton (ct 10, st 3) and R. A. Woolmer
10 – D. L. Underwood
9 – M. R. Benson
8 – E. Baptiste
7 – K. B. S. Jarvis and Substitutes
5 – Asif Iqbal
4 – G. R. Dilley and J. N. Shepherd
3 – L. Potter and R. M. Ellison
2 – C. J. C. Rowe and A. G. E. Ealham
1 – D. G. Aslett

	v. Somerset (Folkestone) 26–28 August†		v. Hampshire (Bournemouth) 29 August–1 September		v. Surrey (The Oval) 2–4 September		v. Worcestershire (Canterbury) 13–15 September		Inns	NOs	Runs	HS	Av
	11	0	0	52	26	24	17	—	34	1	904	119*	27.39
									10	—	142	52	14.20
					4	53	135*	—	36	7	1591	156	54.86
	11	0					49	—	36	3	1063	114	32.21
	2	45			88	32			31	3	1252	112	44.71
					65	2	—	—	28	4	617	65	25.70
	27	3	70	—	2	12	17*	—	38	8	698	107	23.26
									20	6	310	59*	22.14
									8	4	39	17*	9.75
	7	1	—	—	0*	3*	—	—	21	10	162	39	14.72
	1	1*	—	—	6	—	—	—	17	4	26	12	2.00
	7	25	33	—	20	19	72	—	27	4	757	97	32.91
	3	0	17	24*					19	2	385	99	22.64
			18	15					6	1	99	42*	19.80
	10	4	—	—					5	1	50	28	12.50
	33	15	22*	—	16	7	—	—	22	4	359	37*	19.94
									5	—	141	48	28.20
									1	1	5	5*	—
	61*	9	1	—	10	18*	—	—	11	6	237	61*	47.40
									2	—	5	5	2.50
			146*	20*	11	11			4	2	188	146*	94.00
	2	6			5	5							
	3	4	14	1	1	10	3						
					1		1						
	8	8	2		3	7	7						
	186	121	323	112	257	204	301	A.					
	10	10	6	2	10	8	3						
	L		W		W		D						
	2		23		23		4						

Kent C.C.C. First-Class Matches – Bowling, 1981	G. R. Dilley	K. B. S. Jarvis	D. L. Underwood	J. N. Shepherd	R. A. Woolmer	G. W. Johnson
v. Nottinghamshire	18–4–73–1	17–3–51–2	17–6–15–1	20–5–52–1	4–1–12–0	34–13–69–2
(Canterbury) 6–8 May	12–6–38–1	6–0–27–0	25–7–51–2	6–2–12–0		25–9–52–3
v. Warwickshire	17–3–53–0	15–5–36–2	18–7–37–1	13–3–35–0	8–4–11–2	21–6–30–2
(Nuneaton) 13–15 May	15–3–45–0	11–2–57–0	23–2–88–1	3–0–13–0	2–0–11–0	24.2–4–75–3
v. Yorkshire	10–2–30–1	9–1–18–2	13–4–49–0	8–4–10–0	2–0–4–0	12–2–43–2
(Dartford) 27–29 May	4–0–15–0	7–0–29–1	17–6–31–1	6–1–19–1		10–7–4–2
v. Northamptonshire	20.5–3–69–3	20–4–84–3	23–7–54–2	8–1–29–0		21–7–46–0
(Northampton) 6–9 June	9–1–43–0	10–2–30–1	12.3–0–53–3	4–0–25–1		14–2–56–2
v. Leicestershire	5–0–14–0	24–9–66–2	31–15–40–2	46–10–132–3		14–4–43–0
(Tunbridge Wells) 10–12 June						
v. Sussex	18–3–57–3	16.5–0–67–1	23–10–48–1	25–7–70–0	4–1–15–0	11–0–28–0
(Tunbridge Wells) 13–16 June	10–0–63–2	11–0–82–5	2–2–0–2			1–0–11–0
v. Oxford University		6–3–14–0	23–11–43–2	15–8–29–1		21–9–30–5
(Oxford) 17–19 June		6–4–3–2	27.5–17–51–4	24–2–64–1		15–4–27–1
v. Australians	5–1–15–0		29–12–61–2		8–2–21–2	8–1–33–0
(Canterbury) 27–29 June						
v. Middlesex		28.4–14–45–3	6–3–6–1	32–10–84–1		12–4–17–3
(Maidstone) 1–3 July		7–2–20–1	14–3–29–6	13.3–3–25–2		7–2–9–0
v. Lancashire		25–10–57–2	4–4–0–1	25–5–72–2		4–1–22–0
(Maidstone) 4–7 July		21–7–62–2	31–12–44–2	27–9–58–2		21–6–49–1
v. Middlesex		23.2–7–53–3	10–4–18–2	31–12–61–5		
(Lord's) 15–17 July		9–2–26–0	20–4–54–0	14–4–31–0		17–2–56–0
v. Leicestershire		19.5–7–78–7	12–5–39–0	21–7–56–1		2–1–5–0
(Leicester) 18–21 July		17–0–69–4	4–2–7–1	16–4–42–4		
v. Derbyshire	16–4–44–2	22–6–41–1	29–11–62–2	21–7–58–1		16.1–5–42–3
(Derby) 25–28 July	3–0–12–0	4–0–22–0	15–3–44–0	10–0–42–1		9–1–38–0
v. Essex		13–2–39–0	42.2–14–93–7	17–1–65–1		24–9–52–2
(Canterbury) 29–31 July		8–2–15–0	17.5–7–61–5	3–2–5–0		13–2–34–1
v. Hampshire		12.4–2–54–2	34–12–72–5			23–7–45–2
(Canterbury) 1–4 August		5–1–19–0	27.5–12–58–4			25–11–33–6
v. Sussex	13–1–55–0	27.4–7–66–6	17–7–25–0		8–2–24–0	
(Eastbourne) 8–11 August		4–1–18–0	3–0–17–0			2–0–6–0
v. Essex		21–2–73–1		14–4–47–0		46–7–113–0
(Chelmsford) 12–14 August						
v. Gloucestershire		16–4–55–1	16–5–64–0		11–1–43–0	20–1–88–1
(Cheltenham) 15–18 August		7–0–36–2	15–6–30–1			8–3–20–0
v. Surrey		21–6–72–3	32–13–65–1			18–7–53–2
(Folkestone) 22–25 August		8–1–36–0	17–0–92–1			19–5–91–4
v. Somerset		13–2–41–0	54.4–22–118–7			54–19–107–3
(Folkestone) 26–28 August						
v. Hampshire		19–3–79–4	8.2–5–12–2			
(Bournemouth) 29 August–1 September		9–2–34–3	31–12–72–3			31–10–85–3
v. Surrey		22–6–65–7				
(The Oval) 2–4 September		29.3–3–82–5	8–2–27–0			5–0–11–0
v. Worcestershire	3–1–6–1	3–1–9–1	5–2–10–0			5–1–7–0
(Canterbury) 12–15 September	5–1–29–0	12–1–55–2	16.1–6–48–3			15–5–42–4
	183.5–33–661–14	586.3–137–1885–81	774.3–282–1788–78	422.3–111–1136–28	47–11–141–4	627.3–177–1572–57
	av. 47.21	*av.* 23.27	*av.* 22.92	*av.* 40.57	*av.* 35.25	*av.* 27.57

a A. P. E. Knott 2–2–0–0; N. J. Kemp 7–1–32–0   b N. Taylor 4–0–23–0   c M. R. Benson 4–0–28–0

C. J. C. Rowe	Asif Iqbal	E. Baptiste	C. S. Cowdrey	R. M. Ellison	C. J. Tavare	Byes	Leg byes	Wides	No balls	Total	Wickets
							7	3	11	293	7
1–0–4–0						7	5		2	198	6
						1	11		3	217	7
5–0–25–0							7		4	325	6
						4	5		1	164	5
1–1–0–0						9	5			112	5
						4	12	1	7	306	8
						1	13		3	224	7
							5		8	308	8
							5		11	301	5
	1–0–17–1					1	4		4	182	10
		8.5–2–32–1					4	1	2	155	10
		6–1–16–1	5–2–8–1			1	6	1	6	183	10
		25–10–63–1	17–6–27–1		2–1–5–0		15		11	283	6 a
		18–6–38–2					6	2	11	209	10
							9	1	4	97	9
		20.4–7–37–5					7	2	6	203	10
	4–0–32–0	10–1–39–0					6		5	318	7 b
	4–2–12–0		5–1–21–0			1			1	167	10
			2–0–9–0		9–1–91–0	1	8	3		367	0 c
14–2–60–0		16–3–55–1	3–0–16–1			1	8	1	7	266	10
		12–4–42–1				2	2		2	166	10
			4–1–18–1			4	17	3	8	297	10
			5.1–0–29–0			2	2			191	1
		5–1–17–0	8–0–34–0			5	4	1		310	10
						3	3		1	122	6
		8–2–16–0		5–1–13–1		6	8		3	217	10
		2–0–5–0					6		1	122	10
		24–6–91–1	6–0–29–0			1	10	1	8	310	9
		4–1–8–2					1		1	51	2
		6.1–0–28–0	5–0–41–0			9	5	2	11	453	5 d
	0.4–0–0–0	9–1–24–0		15.2–3–28–1		10	4	6	14	336	3
		8–0–25–2					4		6	121	5
		17–4–52–1	4–1–8–0	8–3–28–0		3	11	1	2	295	8
		5–0–39–2					14		2	274	7
		6–1–12–0		1–0–4–0		3	9		15	309	10
		15–3–37–4	1–0–5–0	6–1–12–0		3			5	153	10
		9.4–0–53–1	5–3–12–0	6–3–14–0		4	2		2	278	10
		17–5–25–2		12–7–11–1		4	3	4	3	115	10
		28–5–90–2	5–0–14–2	17–0–34–1		5	13		1	286	10
								2	4	38	2
						3	1		8	186	9
21–3–89–0	9.4–2–61–1	280.2–63–844–29	75.1–14–271–6	70.2–18–144–4	11–2–96–0						
—	av. 61.00	av. 29.10	av. 45.16	av. 36.00	—						

d L. J. Wood 43–11–124–4

Lancashire C.C.C.
First-Class Matches –
Batting,
1981

	v. Cambridge University (Cambridge) 2–5 May		v. Northamptonshire (Northampton) 6–8 May		v. Somerset (Old Trafford) 13–15 May		v. Yorkshire (Old Trafford) 23–26 May		v. Worcestershire (Worcester) 29 May		v. Surrey (Old Trafford) 3–5 June	
A. Kennedy	65	—	0	6	16	31	5	—	0	—	64	4
G. Fowler	143	—	41	18*	7	5	14	—	105*	—	47	75
F. C. Hayes	11	—	0	4*	2*	0*	126	—				
D. Lloyd	39	—	21	—	66	5	47	—	26	—	63	0
S. J. O'Shaughnessy	5	—	19	—			0	—	6	—		
J. Abrahams	9*	—			5	5						
J. Simmons	18*	—	22	—			3	—	—	—	0	—
D. P. Hughes	—	—	7	—	87	8	37	—	33*	—	32	5*
C. J. Scott	—	—					—	—	—	—	—	—
P. J. W. Allott	—	—	10*	—	27	5	0*	—			6*	0
P. G. Lee	—	—	2	—	9	4					—	—
C. H. Lloyd			38	—	17	22					74	49*
M. A. Holding			15	—	0	13			—	—	0*	—
B. W. Reidy					0	21	38	—	—	—	18	55
N. V. Radford							26*	—	—	—		
I. Cockbain												
K. A. Hayes												
G. Speak												
T. J. Taylor												
Byes			1						1		7	
Leg byes	3		4		4	2	9		7		10	9
Wides	1				1		1		2		1	
No balls	20		4		3		4		5		10	2
Total	314		184	28	244	121	310		185		332	199
Wickets	5		10	1	10	10	8		3		7	5
Result	D		D		L		D		W		D	
Points	—		5		3		6		12		8	

† F. C. Hayes absent hurt.

v. Sussex (Hove) 6–9 June		v. Warwickshire (Old Trafford) 10–12 June		v. Surrey (The Oval) 17–19 June		v. Nottinghamshire (Liverpool) 20–23 June		v. Hampshire (Old Trafford) 27–30 June		v. Derbyshire (Chesterfield) 1–3 July		v. Kent (Maidstone) 4–7 July		v. Sri Lankans (Old Trafford) 15–17 July	
14	35	0	31	3	2	13	47	21	13	180	39	18	8	48	—
9	14	72	65*	36	18	8	33	43	13	54	58	14	41	33	—
0	7	8	23	9	1	23	98	—	—						
5	0	4	—	36	19	26	128*	37	22	17	86*	12	32	4	—
				24	1	2*	—	25*	0	—	—	35	—	38	—
		34	—	23	24	25	—			19*	—	10	59*	14	—
5	15							30*	8*			5	65*		
21	0	126	5*	32	17	18	5*	85	33	19	—	29	54	18	—
														0	—
10	14	4	—	0*	4	0	—	—	0	—	—	5*	6		
5*	4	12*	—												
1	31	33	—	84	13	1	—	80	23	56	34*	30	38		
				0	0*										
50	3	33	—	9	23	55	—	18	0						
0	75*	5*	—			0	—	—	5			15	—	8	—
										15*	—	15	4		
														11	—
														0*	—
														2	—
2	1	1		2	21	4	1		1						
7	2	9		8	1	3	6	10	3	6	3	7	6	3	
		1					1		2	3	1	2			
2	3	10				1	1			11	11	6	5	4	
131	204	352	124	266	144	179	320	349	123†	380	232	203	318	183	
10	10	9	2	10	10	10	3	6	9	5	2	10	7	10	
L		D		L		D		L		D		D		D	
2		5		6		2		5		5		5		—	

Lancashire C.C.C.
Batting, *cont.*

	v. Essex (Southend) 18–21 July		v. Nottinghamshire (Trent Bridge) 25–28 July		v. Middlesex (Southport) 29–31 July		v. Worcestershire (Old Trafford) 1–4 August		v. Glamorgan (Cardiff) 8–11 August		v. Warwickshire (Edgbaston) 15–18 Augt	
A. Kennedy	18	32	0	12	35	7	45	—	22	10	53	16
G. Fowler	4	30	24	0	32	51	66	—	7	26	55	141
F. C. Hayes											5	61
D. Lloyd	5	6							0	27	108	19
S. J. O'Shaughnessy	5	31	2	9	20	0					1	—
J. Abrahams	33	18	5	74	3	17	7	—	1	14	28	11*
J. Simmons	1	36*	12	18	7	4	6	—	15	9		
D. P. Hughes	26	1	11	30	4	0	1	—	2	4	5	30*
C. J. Scott			3*	27*	0*	10*	12	—	4	10	5	6
P. J. W. Allott	0	—	22	0	6	13	17*	—				
P. G. Lee							—	—	0	0*	7	—
C. H. Lloyd	0	65	59	13	91	69	97	—	65	16		
M. A. Holding												
B. W. Reidy			0	0	1	39	70*		96	28	26*	—
N. V. Radford	10	0*	7	6	23	13			8*	48	3	—
I. Cockbain												
K. A. Hayes							0	—				
G. Speak	0*	—										
T. J. Taylor												
Byes	3	4		4			10		11	13		4
Leg byes		14	4	7	5	8	12		9	19	19	7
Wides		1	1	8			4		4	4	5	1
No Balls	6	7		1	17	10	11		5	3	6	3
Total	111	245	150	209	244	241	358		249	231	326	299
Wickets	10	7	10	10	10	10	8		10	10	10	5
Result	D		L		L		W		W		D	
Points	4		5		4		23		22		6	

Catches

29 – C. J. Scott (ct 25, st 4)
26 – G. Fowler (ct 23, st 3)
17 – D. P. Hughes
16 – B. W. Reidy
14 – J. Simmons
13 – C. H. Lloyd and D. Lloyd
11 – N. V. Radford
 8 – J. Abrahams
 6 – P. J. W. Allott
 5 – A. Kennedy
 4 – I. Cockbain
 3 – F. C. Hayes and Substitutes
 2 – S. J. O'Shaughnessy and M. A. Holding

v. Leicestershire (Old Trafford) 22–25 August		v. Derbyshire (Blackpool) 26–28 August		v. Yorkshire (Leeds) 29 August–1 September		v. Gloucestershire (Old Trafford) 9–11 September		Inns	NOs	Runs	HS	Av
34	4	30	3	14	—	44	2	42	—	1044	180	24.85
3	33	52	18	39	—	11	2	42	3	1560	143	40.00
14	24	8	46					20	3	470	126	27.64
17	3	20	146*	13	—	23	40	35	3	1122	146*	35.06
								18	2	223	38	13.93
								22	4	438	74	24.33
				31*	—	4	26	22	6	340	65*	21.25
17	22	3	86	54	—	8	27	39	5	1002	126	29.47
7*	0	0	—	0	—	11	4	16	5	99	27*	9.00
5	7			2	—	0	14*	26	7	177	27	9.31
5	0	4	—	10	—	2*	—	14	4	64	12*	6.40
		21	6	145	—	39	14	31	2	1324	145	45.65
				6	—	32	—	8	2	66	32	11.00
15	26							23	2	624	96	29.71
		2*	76*					19	7	330	76*	27.50
20	50	45	13	13	—	2	85	10	1	262	85	29.11
								2	—	11	11	5.50
								2	2	0	0*	—
0	0*	0	—					4	1	2	2	0.66
		2				1	1					
10	2	1	6	10		1	11					
6	1		1	2		2	3					
10	3	2	7	7		2	1					
163	175	190	408	346		182	230					
10	10	10	6	10		10	8					
L		D		W		D						
5		2		24		5						

Lancashire C.C.C. First-Class Matches – Bowling, 1981	P. J. W. Allott	P. G. Lee	J. Abrahams	D. P. Hughes	J. Simmons	S. J. O'Shaughnessy
v. Cambridge University (Cambridge) 2–5 May	21–8–48–1	17–7–38–1	10–4–13–0	19–10–34–1	20–9–35–1	7–2–12–0
v. Northamptonshire (Northampton) 6–8 May	25.3–12–48–8 13–6–34–1	17–5–42–0 9–2–45–0		1–1–0–0 13–4–38–0	1–1–0–0 17–7–39–0	2–0–17–0
v. Somerset (Old Trafford) 13–15 May	24–6–78–1 12–5–23–4	12–6–27–0 6–2–16–1	24–5–75–0 3–1–4–0	6–1–25–0		
v. Yorkshire (Old Trafford) 23–26 May	33.2–6–105–6				12–2–44–1	15–3–38–0	5–0–21–0
v Worcestershire (Worcester) 29 May	15–2–61–3				4–0–38–0	
v. Surrey (Old Trafford) 3–5 June	21–5–82–3 8–3–26–0	13–2–34–0 2–0–12–0		4–1–11–0	14–6–41–2 13–6–20–2	
v. Sussex (Hove) 6–9 June	28–7–75–3	23–8–65–0		12–3–27–0	6–1–34–1	
v. Warwickshire (Old Trafford) 10–12 June	15–1–42–1 19–4–48–3	7–1–20–0 4–1–14–0	4–1–19–2 24–7–54–0	5–2–12–0		
v. Surrey (The Oval) 17–19 June	33.3–8–94–5 13–1–48–2		7–2–32–0			8–1–17–3
v. Nottinghamshire (Liverpool) 20–23 June	21–5–63–1		14–0–49–0	13–1–45–1		8–0–25–0
v. Hampshire (Old Trafford) 27–30 June	16–0–49–0 22.3–7–80–4			16.5–2–52–1 12–3–49–1	10–3–29–0 7–0–33–0	11–1–23–1 11–3–24–1
v. Derbyshire (Chesterfield) 1–3 July	22–6–68–0 12–3–46–2		8–0–29–1 5–3–7–1	13–5–34–0 4–2–3–0	22.5–7–43–3 21–7–39–5	5–0–25–0 2–2–0–0
v. Kent (Maidstone) 4–7 July	25–5–62–3 8–2–30–0		7–1–16–0	14–2–34–3	15–1–36–0	5–0–26–0 3.2–0–12–2
v. Sri Lankans (Old Trafford) 15–17 July			15–3–46–1	9–3–22–1		
v. Essex (Southend) 18–21 July	23–8–58–1		6–1–23–1	2–0–11–0	17–4–36–1	13–3–49–2
v. Nottinghamshire (Trent Bridge) 25–28 July	22–8–43–3 12–0–41–0			8–2–25–1	12–2–25–0	
v. Middlesex (Southport) 29–31 July	31–9–74–3 5–0–29–0		15–1–41–2 3.1–0–30–1	21–3–67–1	15–6–34–0 7–1–28–1	1–0–3–0
v. Worcestershire (Old Trafford) 1–4 August	14–4–39–2 8–1–19–1	6–1–25–0 2–0–12–0	19–8–27–3 20.4–9–39–2	17–6–26–1 23–10–40–4	20–11–21–4 23–8–40–2	
v. Glamorgan (Cardiff) 8–11 August		17.1–2–49–4 20–8–44–6	4–1–29–0	7–2–20–1 11–3–51–1	12–5–22–3 38–10–81–3	
v. Warwickshire (Edgbaston) 15–18 August		17–6–35–0 14–4–42–3	14–2–34–0	8–6–3–0		16–6–64–1 6–2–27–1
v. Leicestershire (Old Trafford) 22–25 August	23.4–8–59–4 16–7–29–1	23–8–50–6 13–3–44–0				
v. Derbyshire (Blackpool) 26–28 August		26–6–87–0		26–6–80–3		
v. Yorkshire (Leeds) 29 August–1 September	23–13–63–4 20–3–78–4	10–3–38–2 3–1–8–0			10–7–6–0 3–1–11–0	
v. Gloucestershire (Old Trafford) 9–11 August	15–2–47–1 1–0–2–0	24–5–69–2		9–1–19–0 6–2–8–0	4–3–4–1 6–2–7–0	
	621.3–165– 1701–75 av. 22.68	285.1–81– 816–25 av. 32.64	202.5–49– 567–14 av. 40.50	291.5–83– 780–21 av. 37.14	331.5–111 740–21 av. 25.51	103.2–20– 345–11 av. 31.36

a T. J. Taylor 14–6–25–0
b T. J. Taylor 23–5–63–2

c T. J. Taylor 31–6–75–2
d I. Cockbain 6–1–14–0; G. Fowler 1–0–12–0

A. Kennedy	D. Lloyd	M. A. Holding	B. W. Reidy	N. V. Radford	G. Speak	Byes	Leg byes	Wides	No balls	Total	Wickets
4–0–24–0	6–3–10–1					5	8	3	4	234	5
		20–7–43–2				5	3			141	10
	2–0–7–0	14–2–62–3				3	4	1	3	253	4
	7–0–24–1	23–4–63–1	1–0–9–0			1	7			309	3
		20.3–7–37–5					8	1		89	10
			16–2–52–0	28–6–74–2		1	9		4	348	9
		16–2–44–2		4–0–27–0		4	5	4		183	5
	2.2–0–18–2	27–12–65–2					3			254	10
	9–1–35–1	22–5–60–5					2		1	156	8
	28–2–74–1			17–2–100–2		12	10			397	7
			3–0–20–0	5–1–33–0			1			135	3
	20–5–27–1			12–3–49–0		5	7		2	218	4
	9–4–35–0	31–9–86–2	1–0–4–0			15	7			290	10
		13.2–2–65–2				2	9			124	6
	16–4–29–0		12–3–33–0	18–3–73–1		6	6			329	3
	7–4–13–0		4–1–23–0	20–9–53–1		3	13	1	1	260	3
				5–1–16–0		2	9			213	8
	12–3–32–0			17–3–65–0			5	1	1	303	4
	15–8–31–1			8–4–19–0			3			149	9
10–2–26–1				13–3–60–1			1	3	2	250	8
	8–1–23–0			4–0–34–1		4	2		2	123	3
				12–1–47–1	10–1–32–0	4	4		4	184	3 a
	9–1–20–0			24.2–3–71–4	5–0–22–0	7	9		2	308	10
			11.3–6–11–2	28–8–107–5		1	5			167	10
2–0–10–0			10.3–0–44–0	11–2–45–0			2		1	193	2
			26–7–67–3	18–1–75–0		2	2		4	366	9
			4–0–26–0				2		2	120	2
										138	10
			8–1–19–1			5	1			175	10
	3–0–16–1			13–3–50–1		4			1	162	10
	4–2–12–0			3–0–22–0		9	3		1	252	10
6–1–20–1			22–2–98–2	12–5–24–1		1	12	6	7	301	5
	6–3–7–0		4–2–8–0	13–4–28–1			2	1	7	125	5
							2			111	10
	20–2–106–2		6–1–22–0				6			270	5 b
9–3–20–0	17–4–60–1			18–2–68–0			12		1	406	7 c
		24–7–39–4					3			149	10
		27–9–76–6					7	1		181	10
		30.1–7–74–6				4	1		1	219	10
2–1–2–0	5–2–7–0	3–2–1–0				4	5	1		63	0 d
33–7–	205.2–49–	271–75–	129–25–	303.2–64–	15–1–						
102–2	586–12	715–40	436–8	1140–21	54						
av. 51.00	av. 48.83	av. 17.87	av. 54.50	av. 54.28	—						

Leicestershire C.C.C.
First-Class Matches – Batting, 1981

	v. Derbyshire (Leicester) 6–8 May		v. Nottinghamshire (Trent Bridge) 13–15 May		v. Hampshire (Leicester) 27–29 May		v. Oxford University (Oxford) 3–5 June		v. Kent (Tunbridge Wells) 10–12 June		v. Glamorgan (Leicester) 13–16 June	
N. E. Briers	101*	—	23	41	0	—	10	51	50	—	49	30*
J. F. Steele	3	—	8	16	9	11*	56	—	40	—	20	65
D. I. Gower	42	—	18	35	109	—			115	—	7	11
B. F. Davison	45	—	57	3	60	—	75*	—	23	—	0	86
J. C. Balderstone	4	—	27	0	22	7*	16	7	46	—	91	16
R. W. Tolchard	2	—	0	12	0	—	16*	55	0	—	8*	—
P. B. Clift	73	—	0	13								
A. M. E. Roberts	16*	—	20	43	5	—						
N. G. B. Cook	—	—	8	4	2	—	—	2*	0*	—	6	—
G. J. Parsons	—	—	1	21	1*	—	—	22	21*	—	6	27
L. B. Taylor	—	—	1*	1*	2	—			—	—	9	—
J. P. Agnew					7	—	—	1	0	—	11*	—
T. J. Boon							49	0	0	—	32	12*
D. A. Wenlock							—	0				
P. Booth							—	35*				
R. A. Cobb												
M. A. Garnham												
I. P. Butcher												
Byes							4				4	18
Leg byes	6		2	4	4	1	4	2	5		8	7
Wides				1			7					
No balls	8		5	1	3		7	3	8			4
Total	300		170	195	224	23	240	178	308		251	276
Wickets	6		10	10	10	0	4	7	8	A.	9†	5
Result	D		L		D		W		D		D	
Points	8		5		2		—		3		3	

The match v. Northamptonshire (Northampton) 23–26 May was abandoned without a ball being bowled.

A. Innings forfeited.

† R. W. Tolchard, retired hurt.

v. Cambridge University (Leicester) 17–19 June		v. Essex (Leicester) 27–30 June		v. Yorkshire (Bradford) 1–3 July		v. Somerset (Leicester) 4–7 July		v. Sri Lankans (Leicester) 11–13 July		v. Warwickshire (Coventry) 15–17 July		v. Kent (Leicester) 18–21 July		v. Nottinghamshire (Hinckley) 29–31 July	
12	—	—	65	14	38	23	23			33	—	89	5	12	11
83	—	15	16	4	4	0	19			64	—	0	3	116	5*
		156*	67												
		—	4	31	4	8	29	60	31	39	—	82	12	123*	30
44	—	127*	12	44	73	10	71			15	—	0	18	100	7
								104*	9*	1	—	6	17	27	42
				52	0					23	—			9	5
—	—			13*	2	6*	0*	—	0	13	—	4	0	—	—
17*	—	—	14*	4	0	0	0	—	7	20	—	50	4	1	—
—	—	—	—					—	—	4*	—	2*	1*	—	—
9	—	—	7*	23	2*	9	7	25*	5*			2	26		
1	—			24	18	18	44	31	10	83	—	14	0	21	1*
								29	62						
10	—	—	13	0	7	30	21								
11	—					4	37	15	20						
49	—	—	17	29	16	1	13	13	30	36*	—	0	74	0	17
								14	42						
7		4	5		4	1	11	4	7	2		1	2		
2		12	10	3	9		6	6	8	13		8	2	16	5
		1	4	1	3		1	2	1			1		6	1
4		4	1	7	14	6	8			11		7	2	6	1
249		319	235	249	194	116	290	303	232	357		266	166	431	124
8		1	7	10	10	10	10	6	8	9		10	10	8	6
D		D		L		L		D		W		L		W	
—		5		4		4		—		23		7		23	

Leicestershire C.C.C. Batting, cont.	v. Sussex (Leicester) 1–4 August		v. Derbyshire (Derby) 8–11 August		v. Surrey (The Oval) 12–14 August		v. Worcestershire (Leicester) 15–18 August		v. Lancashire (Old Trafford) 22–25 August		v. Essex (Colchester) 26–28 August	
N. E. Briers	116	—	3	—	21	18	103	41*	3	61	6	42
J. F. Steele	97	51	23	—	0	17	33	5	0	6	0	30
D. I. Gower			28	—					63	67*	0	22
B. F. Davison	25	30*	14	—	1	72	23*	74	7	—		
J. C. Balderstone	17	6	26	—	82	19	150*	50	4	46	28	1
R. W. Tolchard	41	19*	33	—	0	21*	—	—				
P. B. Clift			10	—	12	6*	—	18*	18	20	42	6
A. M. E. Roberts					29	21					40	57
N. G. B. Cook	—	—	8*	—	8	—	—	—	3	62	2	22
G. J. Parsons	5	—	3	—			—	—	9*	—		
L. B. Taylor	—	—	22	—	11*	—	—	—	0	—	1	5*
J. P. Agnew	8*	—							1	—		
T. J. Boon	13	44			56	12	—	49			0	10
D. A. Wenlock												
P. Booth												
R. A. Cobb											24	17
M. A. Garnham	16	—	19	—	0	—	—	—	1	2*	42*	36
I. P. Butcher												
Byes	1				5	8	6	8			4	1
Leg byes	4	2	1		7	1	5		2	6	6	6
Wides	5		1				1					1
No balls	10	3	5		3		1	3			3	3
Total	358	155	196		235	195	322	248	111	270	198	259
Wickets	8	3	10		10	6	2	4	10	5	10	10
Result	W		W		D		D		W		L	
Points	22		21		5		8		20		3	

Catches

52 – M. A. Garnham (ct 45, st 7)

20 – B. F. Davison

18 – N. G. B. Cook

16 – D. I. Gower, J. C. Balderstone and R. W. Tolchard (ct 15, st 1)

11 – J. F. Steele

10 – J. P. Agnew

8 – P. B. Clift

7 – N. E. Briers, L. B. Taylor and T. J. Boon

5 – R. A. Cobb and Substitutes

4 – G. J. Parsons

2 – A. M. E. Roberts

1 – P. Booth and D. A. Wenlock

A. Innings forfeited

v. Northamptonshire (Leicester) 29 August–1 September		v. Middlesex (Leicester) 2–4 September		v. Glamorgan (Cardiff) 9–11 September		v. Gloucestershire (Bristol) 12–15 September		Inns	NOs	Runs	HS	Av
22	5	0	48	17	—	—	9	36	3	1195	116	36.21
								32	2	819	116	27.30
53	117*	11	15	62	0	—	11	21	3	1009	156*	56.05
55	2	0	8	47	2*	—	36	35	5	1188	123*	39.60
11	10	46	5	4	—	—	4	39	3	1266	150*	35.16
		3	42*	26	—	—	51*	24	8	535	104*	33.43
17	73	29	27	45	—	—	21	17	2	430	73	28.66
		17	10	0	—	—	0*	17	2	347	57	23.13
5	—	0	4	9*	—	—	—	24	7	183	62	10.76
15*	4*							23	7	252	50	15.75
5*	—	9*	1	0	—	—	—	16	9	74	22	10.57
								16	6	143	26	14.30
0	ɔ							26	2	542	83	22.58
								4	—	91	62	22.75
								7	1	116	35*	19.33
54	—	45	0	43	—	—	5	12	—	275	54	22.91
0	41	0	7	18	0*	—	35	27	4	512	74	22.26
								2	—	56	42	28.00
6	3	8	3	5	1							
7	6	1	3	6			2					
1	2	3					3					
251	263	172	173	282	3		177					
9	6	10	10	10	1	A.	7					
W		L		D		D						
20		2		7		3						

Leicestershire C.C.C. First-Class Matches – Bowling, 1981	A. M. E. Roberts	G. J. Parsons	L. B. Taylor	N. G. B. Cook	P. B. Clift	J. F. Steele
v. Derbyshire	12–7–14–1	14–5–40–2	16.1–9–28–7	4–2–7–0	10–2–22–0	
(Leicester) 6–8 May	16–3–50–3	23–3–81–1	22–6–58–0	34–14–72–0	13–6–18–0	23–13–13–0
v. Nottinghamshire	14–2–46–3	19–0–75–2	21–4–68–3	10–5–26–0	15.2–4–51–2	
(Trent Bridge) 13–15 May	6–3–4–0	10–4–26–2	9.4–3–30–0	10–5–20–0	1–0–3–0	
v. Hampshire						
(Leicester) 27–29 May	16–4–34–2	10–1–28–3	13–2–39–2	14–2–30–2		7–3–10–0
v. Oxford University		19–8–47–3		19.3–8–44–3		7–4–4–0
(Oxford) 3–5 June		11–1–41–2		16–11–19–1		12–5–27–1
v. Kent						
(Tunbridge Wells)		13–3–30–1	8–3–17–0	44–19–84–4		27–6–63–2
10–12 June						
v. Glamorgan		25–6–77–2	24–6–45–4	38–15–68–3		16–2–40–1
(Leicester) 13–16 June		5–1–13–0	9–3–17–1	16–8–26–2		4–2–8–0
v. Cambridge University		11–3–23–0	14–2–30–4	10–4–18–1		11.4–4–31–4
(Leicester) 17–19 June		6–0–8–0		3–0–8–0		12–5–21–0
v. Essex		21–4–64–0	11–3–49–2	23–5–98–1		16–4–34–1
(Leicester) 27–30 June		5–0–27–1		27–8–106–3		22–2–76–1
v. Yorkshire	23–3–71–2	25–3–76–0		12–3–37–0		10–2–25–0
(Bradford) 1–3 July	7.5–0–49–1	8–0–29–0				
v. Somerset		24.3–2–115–4		15–1–58–1		14–0–37–1
(Leicester) 4–7 July		2–1–6–0		4–4–0–0		
v. Sri Lankans		14.5–3–84–3	15–1–77–1	16–6–29–2		
(Leicester) 11–13 July		6–3–19–0	5–0–15–0	11–0–46–1		
v. Warwickshire	16.4–7–41–2	17–4–44–4	16–6–26–4	15–8–17–0		
(Coventry) 15–17 July	17–4–58–1	5–1–9–0	17–3–36–3	22–12–25–2		7.5–4–11–3
v. Kent		20–3–75–3	17–4–64–4	8–3–11–0		2–0–6–0
(Leicester) 18–21 July		16–5–42–0	16.3–2–72–3	34–12–74–0		14–1–44–1
v. Nottinghamshire	16.4–5–55–4	11–3–24–2	13–3–52–1	13–1–35–0		15–3–26–3
(Hinckley) 29–31 July	18–6–58–0	16–6–37–3	21–5–54–1	31–10–92–5		10–1–39–0
v. Sussex		10–0–32–0	13–2–39–3	19–8–48–1		7–0–23–1
(Leicester) 1–4 August		2–0–11–0	4–0–28–1	24–5–81–7		21–3–87–1
v. Derbyshire		6–2–14–0	15–7–19–6	6–2–10–1		15–8–18–3
(Derby) 8–11 August		6–2–18–1	5–4–4–0	32–18–25–4	21.1–9–26–3	14–7–17–2
v. Surrey	21–4–65–2		27–7–90–3	28.4–6–59–2	18–4–58–3	8–2–19–0
(The Oval) 12–14 August	13–2–44–2		6–3–7–0	19–6–37–3	15–3–37–1	4–0–23–0
v. Worcestershire		20–5–72–2	22–7–60–1	19.4–8–31–2	19–3–54–3	7–0–27–1
(Leicester) 15–18 August		12–2–29–1	14–1–55–1	17–7–22–2	5–1–17–0	5–3–11–0
v. Lancashire		21–6–46–2	14–4–28–2	1–0–2–0	23–10–32–5	1–0–4–0
(Old Trafford)		5–0–21–0	6.1–1–16–2	11–1–66–2	15–4–47–6	
22–25 August						
v. Essex	19–6–60–1		24.4–3–93–4	20–4–62–0	19–4–52–0	11–2–43–1
(Colchester) 26–28 August	12–3–54–1		12–0–75–2	14.4–3–31–3	14–1–80–1	
v. Northamptonshire		18.1–2–66–1	20–2–61–1	13–2–55–0	15–7–29–1	
(Leicester)		5–2–3–0	4–0–16–0	25.3–9–71–1	24–3–62–1	
29 August–1 September						
v. Middlesex	23–3–65–1		27–7–72–3	27–4–102–0	27–7–70–0	
(Leicester) 2–4 September						
v. Glamorgan	28–10–71–5		31–10–75–2	21–2–83–0	16–4–60–1	
(Cardiff) 9–11 September	17–5–49–5		19–4–54–1	14–2–44–1	9.5–1–34–0	
v. Gloucestershire	14–2–35–1		15–4–59–3	33–9–95–3	28–9–47–2	
(Bristol) 12–15 September						
	310.1–79–	462.3–94–	547.1–131–	795–262–	308.2–82–	322.3–86–
	923–37	1452–45	1628–75	1974–63	799–29	787–27
	av. 24.94	av. 32.26	av. 21.70	av. 31.33	av. 27.55	av. 29.14

*Hampshire forfeited first innings   a R. W. Tolchard 2–0–14–0
†Innings forfeited   b T. J. Boon 3–0–7–0

N. E. Briers	J. C. Balderstone	J. P. Agnew	P. Booth	D. A. Wenlock	Byes	Leg byes	Wides	No balls	Total	Wickets
						7		1	119	10
5–3–2–0	2–2–0–0				5	9	5	2	315	4
2–0–4–0					2	4	1	2	279	10
						5	2		90	2
					10	6		3	160	9
		6–3–21–2	6–1–25–1	8–3–10–1	4	3	1	6	165	10
	12–4–17–4	10–4–25–1	5–3–3–0		4	2		4	142	10
	7–3–16–0	2–1–6–0			1	4	1	11	233	7†
	3–1–3–0	17–4–47–0			4	12	1	12	309	10
	10–2–26–1				10	3			103	4
		14–2–49–0	10–5–16–1		3	8	4	1	183	10
13–4–32–2	1–0–1–0	4–2–2–0	7–3–17–0			7		2	98	2
	4–0–17–0	17–0–84–0	6–1–21–0		6	6		8	387	4
	1–0–15–0	7–1–21–0	6–0–15–0			10		3	273	5
2–1–5–0		17–1–72–5	19–3–52–3		5	8		7	358	10
					2	9			89	3
		25–5–76–3	17–3–58–1		7	1	1	3	356	10
4.2–0–27–0		3–1–15–0			4		1		53	0
		19–1–83–4		3–0–15–0	1	8	4	3	304	10
		6–0–21–0		4–0–22–0	1	3	2		143	1 a
					5	1		2	136	10
					9	10	2		160	10
		15–4–62–3				5		1	224	10
	8–3–11–2	26–8–64–4			1	7		4	319	10
					1	5	2		200	10
	25–10–52–1					12	1	9	354	10
6–1–24–1	5–1–16–0	13–4–54–1			5	3		6	250	7
	2–0–13–0	3–0–29–0			2	9			260	10
						1			62	10
	6–2–15–0					2			107	10
6–1–9–0	2–0–7–0				6	9	12		334	10
	6.3–0–30–4				2	4		1	185	10
	5–2–17–1				2	4		1	268	10
2–1–1–0	8–5–14–0				7	3	4	5	175	4 b
		14–7–25–1				10	6	10	163	10
		3–0–19–0				2	1	3	175	10
4–0–7–0					2	12	5	4	340	6
					2	12		2	256	7
12–4–22–1	11–3–42–0				4	11		10	300	4
	18–2–58–0					1			211	3
8–0–38–1	5–0–28–0				14	5		13	407	5
	5–1–14–1				4	5	2	9	323	9
	2–1–3–0				6	4		2	196	8
	11–1–29–0				7	6		3	281	9
										†
64.2–15–	159.3–43–	221–48–	76–19–	15–3–						
171–5	444–14	775–24	207–6	47–1						
av. 34.20	av. 31.71	av. 32.29	av. 34.50	av. 47.00						

Middlesex C.C.C.
First-Class Matches – Batting, 1981

	v. M.C.C. (Lord's) 29 April–1 May		v. Essex (Lord's) 6–8 May		v. Yorkshire (Leeds) 13–15 May		v. Nottinghamshire (Uxbridge) 27–29 May		v. Hampshire (Basingstoke) 3–5 June		v. Somerset (Lord's) 6–9 June	
J. M. Brearley	41	43	16	23	47	3	—	53	135	—	2	—
P. R. Downton	13	10	4	41	—	0	—	14*	0*	—	—	—
C. T. Radley	32	23	13	16	1	5	—	18	19	—	87	
M. W. Gatting	101*	—	0	21*	158	44	—	7				
R. O. Butcher	15	25*	9	4			—	0	48		106*	—
G. D. Barlow	5	40*	19	3	73*	28	—	32			32	
P. H. Edmonds	35	—	10	0*			—	16	25*	—	11*	—
J. E. Emburey	3*	—	1	—	—	38	—	31*				
V. A. P. van der Bijl	—	—										
M. W. W. Selvey	—	—	33	—	—	0	—	—	23		—	—
W. G. Merry	—	—			—	—					—	—
J. R. Thomson			35	—	—	13	—	—				
W. W. Daniel			0*	—	—	2*	—	—				
W. N. Slack					19	3			22	—	17	—
K. P. Tomlins									32	—		
J. D. Monteith									—	—		
N. G. Cowans												
C. R. V. Taylor												
S. P. Hughes												
C. R. Cook												
K. D. James												
C. Metson												
Byes		1	1	1	5			1	1	8		
Leg byes	4	4	10	5	12	2		6		7		7
Wides					1					3		
No balls	20	3	2	2	13	4		2				3
Total	269	149	153	116	329	142	A.	180	322		265	
Wickets	6	3	10	5	4	9		6	6		4	
Result	D		D		W		D		D		D	
Points	—		4		24		1		8		6	

The match v. Sussex (Lord's) 23–26 May was abandoned without a ball being bowled.
A. Innings forfeited.

v. Oxford University (Oxford) 10-12 June		v. Australians (Lord's) 13-16 June		v. Essex (Ilford) 17-19 June		v. Nottinghamshire (Trent Bridge) 27-30 June		v. Kent (Maidstone) 1-3 July		v. Kent (Lord's) 15-17 July		v. Worcestershire (Lord's) 18-21 July		v. Lancashire (Southport) 29-31 July	
		4	132*	113	45	2	131	4	1						
		19	1			5	20	0	0	44	—	9	7	35	—
44	19*	28	33	8	54	0	10	5	40	0	—	12	0	14	26*
36	—	32	75			8	22								
8	—	26	5	48	8	58	53	6	4	2	—	54	66		
3	14*	18	—			2	1	101	23	7	174*	7	0	177	33
31	—	0	0*	15	6	7	93	0	0	26	—	0	33	9	—
36	—	0	—			0	23					16	6		
		0	3	57	2	55	1	17	3	11	—			8	—
14*	—							1*	2*	7*	—	0	—		
5	—	6	—	3	1*					0	—				
		3*	—	7*	4*	1	11	9	10*			2*	10*	5	—
65	4			1	14					56	181*	4	248*	0	41
				3	4			29	0	7	—	1	57	0	—
				1	8					5	—			16*	—
10	—														
19	—			1	5										
						4*	4*	18	0			0	—	15*	—
														79	16*
3		1			3	1	1			1	1	1	7	2	
4		3	9	5	9	4	16	6	9		8		6	2	2
9	2	1		1		2	8	11	4		3	2	4	4	2
287	39	150	261	263	163	151	396	209	97	167	367	108	444	366	120
10	1	10	5	10	10	10	10	10	9	10	0	10	7	9	2
D		D		L		W		W		D		D		W	
—		—		7†		21		22		5		4		23	

† Points lost for playing unregistered player.

Middlesex C.C.C.
Batting, *cont.*

	v. Gloucestershire (Lord's) 1–4 August		v. Warwickshire (Lord's) 8–11 August		v. Northamptonshire (Northampton) 12–14 August		v. Surrey (The Oval) 15–18 August		v. Glamorgan (Lord's) 22–25 August		v. Yorkshire (Lord's) 26–28 August	
J. M. Brearley			58	100					72	—		
P. R. Downton	—	—	6	—	0	23*	40*	17	28*	—	3	—
C. T. Radley	69*	49			20	29	28	51	40	—	56	29*
M. W. Gatting			13	7*					99	—		
R. O. Butcher			2	2*	10	1	7	27	2	—	72	2
G. D. Barlow	58	11	30	—	54	33	9	5	41	—	10	12
P. H. Edmonds	—	—	4	—	19	0	0	0	16*	—	9	—
J. E. Emburey			11	—					24	—		
V. A. P. van der Bijl												
M. W. W. Selvey	—	—	5	—	8	0	1	15*				
W. G. Merry												
J. R. Thomson												
W. W. Daniel	—	—	10*	—	34	17*	0	2	—	—	53*	—
W. N. Slack	74	81	130	65	64	67	17	7	14	—	4	7
K. P. Tomlins	77*	15									79*	2*
J. D. Monteith					10	8	0	0			3	—
N. G. Cowans												
C. R. V. Taylor												
S. P. Hughes	—	—	1		6*	0	0	7	—	—	2	—
C. R. Cook	4	34*			0	11	32	1			36	1
K. D. James	—	5*										
C. Metson												
Byes	9	4	5	6	12	8		5	1		6	
Leg byes	9	2	9	1	3	4	5	7	11		13	2
Wides	1				3				3		5	3
No balls	1	1		3	9	2			10		15	8
Total	302	202	284	184	252	203	139	144	361		366	66
Wickets	3	4	10	2	10	9	10	10	7		9	4
Result	D		W		D		L		W		W	
Points	4		23		4		4		24		23	

Catches

49 – P. R. Downton (ct 41, st 8)

32 – R. O. Butcher

23 – P. H. Edmonds

19 – C. T. Radley

17 – J. E. Emburey

15 – M. W. Gatting

10 – J. M. Brearley

 9 – G. D. Barlow

 8 – J. D. Monteith

 7 – M. W. W. Selvey and K. P. Tomlins

 6 – W. N. Slack and C. R. V. Taylor

 5 – C. R. Cook

 4 – J. R. Thomson and S. P. Hughes

 2 – W. W. Daniel and N. G. Cowans

 1 – W. G. Merry, K. D. James, C. P. Metson and Substitute

v. Sussex (Hove) 29 August–1 September		v. Leicestershire (Leicester) 2–4 September		v. Surrey (Uxbridge) 9–11 September		v. Derbyshire (Derby) 12–15 September		Inns	NOs	Runs	HS	Av
		72	—	21	31	145	10	25	1	1304	145	54.33
7	11	—	—	14*	—			27	6	371	44	17.66
41	51	101*	—	44	56*	3*	3	40	7	1177	101*	35.66
		0	—	169	38	186*	10	19	4	1026	186*	68.40
6	1			10	7	—	1	33	3	695	106*	23.16
36	3	152	—	35	17*	7	8	38	5	1313	177	39.78
7	6	0*	—	11	—	—	2	31	6	391	93	15.64
		—	—	2	—	—	5	14	2	196	38	16.33
								—				
		—	—					18	1	242	57	14.23
								5	4	24	14*	24.00
								6	1	63	35	12.60
0	15			0*	—	—	—	22	11	195	53*	17.72
14	0	4	—	60	10	11	68*	32	3	1372	248*	47.31
23	28	46	—					16	3	403	79*	31.00
0	10*	—	—			—	—	11	2	61	16*	6.77
								1	—	10	10	10.00
								3	—	25	19	8.33
0*	0			—	—			14	5	57	18	6.33
16	19							12	2	249	79	24.90
								1	1	5	5*	—
						—	38*	1	1	38	38*	—
	4	14		10	4							
2	6	5		11	2	6	1					
	1											
2	2	13		5		14	6					
154	157	407		392	165	372	152					
10	10	5		8	4	3	7					
L		W		W		D						
5		24		23		5						

Middlesex C.C.C. First-Class Matches – Bowling, 1981

	M. W. W. Selvey	W. G. Merry	P. H. Edmonds	J. E. Emburey	M. W. Gatting	W. W. Daniel
v. M.C.C. (Lord's) 29 April–1 May	23–9–55–3 3–0–8–0	21–8–56–2 7–1–17–2	11–2–17–0 11–4–28–0	17–4–32–0 7–3–25–0	3–1–5–0 3–1–6–0	
v. Essex (Lord's) 6–8 May	16–5–35–0		10–1–45–1	20–5–39–1	2–2–0–0	20.5–4–53–2
v. Yorkshire (Leeds) 13–15 May	31–10–91–5 11–3–30–0	6–2–19–0 8–2–28–2		8–1–14–1 17–7–33–2	1–0–2–0	14.3–4–29–1 14.4–1–64–6
v. Nottinghamshire (Uxbridge) 27–29 May	13–5–26–0		30–11–60–1	27.5–5–94–1	3–1–9–0	12–7–22–1
v. Hampshire (Basingstoke) 3–5 June	32–12–79–5 21–5–67–1		5–3–7–0 29–14–45–2			18.2–5–47–3 24–3–60–2
v. Somerset (Lord's) 6–9 June	33.3–11–78–3 5–1–18–0	15–1–58–2 12–0–43–1	18–4–54–0 5–1–12–0			23–4–58–1 9–3–26–1
v. Oxford University (Oxford) 10–12 June		9–3–30–0 2–1–4–0	27.1–14–35–3 38–10–65–2	28–8–70–1 46.5–15–88–7	13–3–40–3 4–2–3–0	
v. Australians (Lord's) 13–15 June	18–5–42–2 6–2–7–1		13–7–14–1 11–3–30–0	11.4–5–12–2 11–3–28–1	3–1–7–0 3–1–12–0	16–5–23–2 7–1–19–1
v. Essex (Ilford) 17–19 June	12–4–36–0 8–2–24–1		20–2–70–2 29.3–5–56–3			19–1–71–3 4–0–17–0
v. Nottinghamshire (Trent Bridge) 27–30 June	10–2–31–0		4–1–19–0 19–6–47–1	23–6–57–0 26–14–30–5		21.5–5–89–4 9.1–3–16–1
v. Kent (Maidstone) 1–3 July	16–8–34–3 11–2–34–1	6–2–13–1 7–3–12–1	2–2–0–0 11–1–31–1			19–7–38–3 15.1–0–48–4
v. Kent (Lord's) 15–17 July	29–10–90–3 4–1–7–2	19–3–54–0	14–2–37–1 6–1–16–0			22–0–74–4 6–0–31–0
v. Worcestershire (Lord's) 18–21 July		13–1–44–2	15–5–32–1 11–3–26–1	28–8–77–0 9–1–29–0		26–5–91–4 6–2–17–2
v. Lancashire (Southport) 29–31 July	12–3–37–1 12–1–36–2		18–8–24–1 10–5–16–0			18.3–4–56–1 24–7–82–5
v. Gloucestershire (Lord's) 1–4 August	12.1–1–63–0 9–2–18–0		17–3–50–0 36–4–43–4			7–4–9–0 12–4–37–1
v. Warwickshire (Lord's) 8–11 August	1–0–2–0 12–4–23–0		42–20–57–4 42.3–19–53–5	37.3–11–52–5 38–11–80–5		7–1–16–0 8–2–23–0
v. Northamptonshire (Northampton) 12–14 August	6.2–0–27–1		38–9–79–3 29.5–10–57–5			10–0–36–1 3–1–2–0
v. Surrey (The Oval) 15–18 August	5–1–16–0		32–7–104–2 3–1–6–0			6.3–1–18–3 3–0–16–0
v. Glamorgan (Lord's) 22–25 August			16–7–20–3 32–13–57–4	11–6–19–1 29–7–74–3		14–3–27–2 12–2–35–2
v. Yorkshire 26–28 August			35–9–60–3 24–9–36–2			20–5–52–3 14.5–2–34–1
v. Sussex (Hove) 29 August–1 September			21.5–6–44–3 4–2–10–0			9–0–23–0
v. Leicestershire (Leicester) 2–4 September	10.2–4–26–1 6–1–14–0		34–12–60–3 27–9–46–0	36–12–59–5 28.5–8–49–5		
v. Surrey (Uxbridge) 9–11 September			37–5–121–4 18–4–32–1	41–8–134–5 16.1–6–37–5		16–0–78–0 13–3–40–3
v. Derbyshire (Derby) 12–15 September			52.1–16–93–6	49–10–124–4	1–0–4–0	9–4–17–0
	388.2–114– 1054–35 av. 30.11	125–27– 378–13 av. 29.07	909–280– 1814–73 av. 24.84	566.5–164– 1256–59 av. 21.28	36–12– 88–3 av. 29.33	514.2–103– 1494–67 av. 22.29

a V. A. P. van der Bijl 26–11–32–1; 3–1–6–0
b W. N. Slack 2–0–5–0
c W. N. Slack 8–1–28–0
d K. D. James 10–3–21–0; 4–0–13–0
e G. D. Barlow 0.3–0–7–0

J. R. Thomson	S. P. Hughes	K. P. Tomlins	J. D. Monteith	C. T. Radley	N. G. Cowans	Byes	Leg byes	Wides	No balls	Total	Wickets
							8		5	210	7 a
						3	7	1		101	2
16–2–66–4						4	2		6	250	8
14–6–39–3							9	1	3	207	10
8–0–25–0							1	1	1	183	10
8–0–33–0						1	12		1	258	3
12–0–44–1			3–0–17–0			1	4	2	5	211	10 b
14–1–42–3			7–1–24–1	1–0–4–0		1	15	1	2	261	9
18–2–59–3						3	6		8	324	9
9–1–31–2							3		5	166	4 c
11–5–34–2					12–1–26–1	8	14	1	4	262	10
6–2–11–0					9–1–24–1	1	12			208	10
15–4–35–2							10	2	1	146	9†
11–2–33–1				1–0–4–0		6	5			144	4
14.3–4–36–2			23–6–70–2			13	13	1		303	9‡
6–1–34–0			20–4–60–5				18	1	1	218	9
	30–7–102–6					3	7		1	309	10
	12–3–20–3					6	6		1	126	10
	13–5–26–3						1	1	7	120	10
	14–4–48–2						6		3	182	10
			12–3–24–1			2	1	2		284	10
			7–2–10–0	1–0–1–0		1			1	67	2
	17.2–2–94–2					2	3		2	345	10
	6–0–30–1						1			103	4
	29–7–75–6		11–3–30–1				5		17	244	10
	22.5–5–74–3		5–2–15–0				8		10	241	10
	11–4–25–1	2–0–15–0				7	3	2	6	201	1 d
	12–0–44–1					10	6		5	176	6
	4–1–10–0					10	4	1	2	154	10
	3–0–7–0					2	5		3	196	10
	22–2–74–1		35–8–105–1			6	14		3	344	7
	8–0–20–0		26–6–68–5			12	4		3	166	10
	5–2–8–0		28–9–85–4			14	10		4	259	10
			0·3–0–3–0							25	0
	12–5–21–2					3	1	2	3	96	10
	14–1–42–1			1–0–3–0		7	3	1	7	229	10
	27–5–85–2	6–2–7–0	21–6–43–0				6	1	10	264	9
	14–1–49–2	1–0–4–0	15–5–22–4			7	8		7	167	10
	34–11–94–2	20–5–54–2	9–3–20–0				10		7	252	10
	5–0–28–0	1–0–4–0		1–0–9–0			1	1		60	0 e
					10–3–15–1	8	1		3	172	10
					13–0–58–5	3	3			173	10
	17–2–52–1					9	6	5	6	411	10
	4–0–28–0					4	3		1	145	10
					10–1–32–0	8	4	2	2	286	10
162.3–30– 522–23 av. 22.69	336.1–67– 1056–42 av. 25.14	30–7– 84–2 av. 42.00	222.3–58– 596–24 av. 24.83	5–0– 21–0 —	54–6– 155–8 av. 19.37						

†G. M. Wood retired hurt
‡K. W. R. Fletcher retired hurt

Northamptonshire C.C.C.
First-Class Matches – Batting, 1981

	v. Cambridge University (Cambridge) 29 April–1 May		v. Lancashire (Northampton) 6–8 May		v. Derbyshire (Northampton) 27–29 May		v. Warwickshire (Edgbaston) 3–5 June		v. Kent (Northampton) 6–9 June		v. Gloucestershire (Bristol) 10–12 June	
G. Cook	131	—	16	5	51	—	42	—	17	10	29	—
W. Larkins	117	—	39	8	2	—	157	—	77	74	30	—
R. G. Williams	26	—	22	18	3	—	30	—	2	19	8	—
A. J. Lamb	18	—	1	133*	51	—	7	—	65	31	78	—
P. Willey	14	—	0	37	8	—					79	—
T. J. Yardley	4	—	20	41*	3	—	0	—	36	55*	96*	—
G. Sharp	9	—	14	—	25*	—	30	—	14	6	0	—
R. M. Carter	15*	—	6	—	4	—	10	—	42*	4	1	—
N. A. Mallender	7*	—	5*	—	12	—						
T. M. Lamb	—	—	10	—	0*	—					1	—
B. J. Griffiths	—	—	0	—								
R. M. Tindall							29*	—	28	7	9	—
D. J. Wild									1	1*		
C. D. Booden											0	—
Kapil Dev												
R. J. Boyd-Moss												
Sarfraz Nawaz												
J. P. C. Mills												
D. Capel												
N. Priestley												
I. G. Peck												
Byes	1		5	3	6		1		4	1	5	
Leg byes	5		3	4	5		9		12	13	12	
Wides	1			1			3		1			
No balls	14			3			7		7	3		
Total	362		141	253	170		325		306	224	348	
Wickets	7		10	4	8		7		8	7	10	
Result	W		D		D		D		D		D	
Points	—		4		3		7		5		7	

The match v. Leicestershire, 23–26 May, (Northampton) was abandoned without a ball being bowled.

v. Sussex (Northampton) 17–19 June		v. Derbyshire (Derby) 20–23 June		v. Surrey (The Oval) 27–30 June		v. Gloucestershire (Northampton) 1–3 July		v. Glamorgan (Northampton) 4–7 July		v. Australians (Northampton) 11–13 July		v. Essex (Southend) 15–17 July		v. Sri Lankans (Northampton) 18–20 July	
146*	0	32	120*	14	11	10	84	42	59	46	25	16	0	60	78
4	39	0	126	20	55*			57	18	29	21	0	55		
133	0	22	—	16	77	29	80	13	142*			10	60	41	37
5*	102*	91	17*	14	24	162	79	6	76	5	8	3	6	0	56*
				45	38					47	12				
—	49	27	—	14	3	18	1	41	—	19	38*	11	0		
—	—	24	—	36	14*	14	23*			36	0	9	4		
—	—	0	—	4	1	17	0	18	—	0	2*	1	15		
—	—	2	—	16	—	0	—	4*	—	4	—	1*	6	—	—
—	—	—	—	6*	—	8	—	0	—	4	—	0	0*	—	—
—	16	7	—			21	9					30	2	0	8
				22	—	4*	12*	26	—						
		4*	—												
—	31					18	43								
								19	12*	2	19			90	—
								0	—	34*	32	0	1	68	6
														37	0*
														20*	—
4	4	1	2	7	1	2	2		14	1			4	5	12
3	3	7	7	8	6	6	10	10	3	7	8	1	4	2	5
	4	2		1				1	2						
5	4	15	7	1		3	1	6	5	18	2	4	6	5	3
300	252	234	279	224	230	312	344	243	331	252	167	86	163	328	205
2	6	9	1	10	6	10	7	10	3	10	7	10	10	7	4
D		W		D		D		W		D		L		D	
7		18		6		6		22		—		4		—	

Northamptonshire C.C.C. Batting, cont.	v. Worcestershire (Stourbridge) 29-31 July		v. Warwickshire (Northampton) 1-4 August		v. Somerset (Weston-super-Mare) 8-11 August		v. Middlesex (Northampton) 12-14 August		v. Yorkshire (Wellingborough) 15-18 August		v. Essex (Northampton) 22-25 August	
G. Cook	52	16	19	15	10	75	51	51	23	66	30	8
W. Larkins	43	58	3	130	20	40	3	8	16	20	17	0
R. G. Williams	—	4	4	64	16	4	14	0	4	4	—	72*
A. J. Lamb	86	12	79	88	58	5	159	40	30	73	117	47*
P. Willey					9*	0						
T. J. Yardley	8	65*	34	15*	53	6	11	19*	21	0	0	—
G. Sharp	44*	0	28	0	0	28	46	1			69*	—
R. M. Carter									2	9	4*	—
N. A. Mallender	10*	7	13	—	1	11*	—	0	5	1	—	—
T. M. Lamb	—	0*	14*	—	4	3*	—	13	1	1	—	—
B. J. Griffiths	—	—	2	—	0*	—	—	0	0	0*	—	—
R. M. Tindall												
D. J. Wild												
C. D. Booden												
Kapil Dev	79	4										
R. J. Boyd-Moss	25	10	8	5			6	4	15	12		
Sarfraz Nawaz			6	13*	19	14	31*	11			—	—
J. P. C. Mills												
D. Capel												
N. Priestley												
I. G. Peck									13*	2		
Byes		6		2	1	2	6	12	4	5	1	2
Leg byes	9	9	10	6	10	7	14	4	12	14	7	7
Wides		1	2			10			2			
No balls	3	7	1	4			3	3	8		6	3
Total	359	199	223	342	201	205	344	166	156	207	251	139
Wickets	6	8	10	6	9†	8	7	10	10	10	4	2
Result	D		L		W		D		L		D	
Points	6		6		22		8		5		6	

Catches
47 – G. Sharp (ct 45, st 2)
23 – T. J. Yardley and G. Cook
20 – A. J. Lamb
15 – R. G. Williams
 9 – R. M. Carter and N. A. Mallender
 8 – T. M. Lamb and Sarfraz Nawaz
 6 – Substitutes
 4 – B. J. Griffiths and R. J. Boyd-Moss
 3 – R. M. Tindall and N. Priestley (ct 1, st 2)
 2 – W. Larkins, P. Willey and I. G. Peck (ct 1, st 1)
 1 – C. D. Booden, D. Capel, D. J. Wild and Kapil Dev

v. Nottinghamshire (Cleethorpes) 26–28 August		v. Leicestershire (Leicester) 29 August–1 September		v. Yorkshire (Scarborough) 9–11 September		v. Hampshire (Southampton) 12–15 September		Inns	NOs	Runs	HS	Av
1	2	117	71	0	2	106*	—	43	3	1759	146*	43.97
				61	16	6	—	35	1	1369	157	40.26
2	0	63	22	30	3	103	—	38	2	1203	142*	33.41
15	73	36*	78*	0	5	10*	—	43	9	2049	162	60.26
				0	27	—	—	13	1	316	79	26.33
6	18	25*	—	46	0	—	—	35	8	803	96*	29.74
2	6	—	—	50	12	—	—	29	5	544	69*	22.66
11	2	—	—			—	—	17	3	132	42*	9.42
3	7			0	5*	—	—	20	6	123	18	8.78
11*	0*	—	—	31	4	—	—	21	8	128	31	9.84
4	2	—	—	1*	3	—	—	16	5	30	8	2.72
								8	1	126	29*	18.00
								10	3	106	30	15.14
								2	1	4	4*	4.00
								5	—	175	79	35.00
		5	23*					14	2	165	25	13.75
22	45	—	—	0	48			16	3	366	90	28.15
1	15	29	16					6	—	135	68	22.50
								2	1	37	37	37.00
								1	1	20	20*	—
								2	1	15	13*	15.00
4		4		5	2	1						
2	6	11	1	2	5	1						
				1	3							
1	5	10		5		1						
85	181	300	211	232	135	228						
10	10	4	3	10	10	2						
L		L		L		D						
4		8		6		6						

† P. Willey retired hurt.

Northamptonshire C.C.C. First-Class Matches – Bowling, 1981	B. J. Griffiths	N. A. Mallender	T. M. Lamb	P. Willey	R. G. Williams	R. M. Carter
v. Cambridge University	12.3–6–15–2	8–2–15–0	13–2–26–2	32–11–46–5	15–7–24–1	
(Cambridge) 29 April–1 May	12.4–9–8–1	6–2–16–0	4–1–11–1	40–16–72–5	31–12–43–3	7–2–19–0
v. Lancashire	19–7–36–1	19–6–46–3	19–14–47–3	20–7–26–1		5–1–20–2
(Northampton) 5–8 May	7–3–17–0	5–0–5–1	4–2–3–0			2–0–3–0
v. Derbyshire	21–6–67–1	18–5–51–1	20–6–44–2	17–2–41–0	6–0–27–0	6–2–22–1
(Northampton) 27–29 May						
v. Warwickshire	24–7–53–1	20–3–67–2	23–8–35–1		20–9–32–4	16–3–35–2
(Edgbaston) 3–5 June	25–8–68–1	10–5–16–1	21–10–42–3		38–17–69–1	7–3–20–0
v. Kent	6–1–14–0		25–10–57–1		34–13–74–0	16–3–60–2
(Northampton) 6–9 June			18–6–39–1		19–4–50–1	14–4–40–0
v. Gloucestershire			24–6–79–0	34–14–72–3	5–0–18–0	22–2–88–3
(Bristol) 10–12 June			27–8–49–3	39–16–71–3		16–1–65–1
v. Sussex	20–6–51–0		16.3–2–47–2		19–5–58–3	7–1–29–1
(Northampton) 17–19 June	10–3–40–1		6.5–2–35–0		2–0–8–0	
v. Derbyshire	24–5–70–1		23–6–54–0		19.4–4–60–0	12–2–36–1
(Derby) 20–23 June	12–4–20–1		14–1–35–0		22–2–57–2	10–1–51–0
v. Surrey	22–3–69–2		29–6–77–4	26–10–54–2	4–2–28–0	3–0–17–0
(The Oval) 27–30 June	15–5–53–1		16–2–45–1		11–2–25–2	3–0–23–0
v. Gloucestershire	16.3–4–63–1		19–1–68–2		11–3–43–1	
(Northampton) 1–3 July	17–6–41–2		13–3–37–2		11–2–43–0	2–0–15–0
v. Glamorgan	15.1–3–50–8	4–0–17–0	4–1–8–0		10–3–13–2	
(Northampton) 4–7 July	17–4–41–1	4–2–7–0	14–4–49–3		15.5–7–28–2	
v. Australians	24–7–48–2	23–4–74–1	22–10–40–0	24–4–67–1		
(Northampton) 11–13 July						
v. Essex	24–10–45–2	15.3–2–45–4	10–3–27–0			
(Southend) 15–17 July	13–5–27–4	8–1–42–4	5.1–0–9–2			
v. Sri Lankans	14–3–42–0	12–4–22–2	14–3–19–0		31.3–10–70–3	
(Northampton) 18–20 July	8–1–23–1	4–1–16–0	2–0–2–0		13–1–45–0	
v. Worcestershire	20–4–76–2	14–3–48–0	19–4–61–1		20–1–75–1	
(Stourbridge) 29–31 July	11–0–55–1	12–0–56–1	11–0–36–1		14–1–80–2	
v. Warwickshire	29.1–12–64–4	15–6–34–2	10–3–23–0		3–3–0–0	
(Northampton) 1–4 August	14–2–74–1	16–2–71–1	7–0–36–0		21–4–76–1	
v. Somerset	12.5–3–27–3	10–1–30–2	20–8–50–4			
(Weston-super-Mare)	19–3–59–2	16–5–52–2	11–5–31–4		10–0–32–1	
v. Middlesex	24–8–61–2	14–6–22–2	13–2–26–1		37.3–14–64–4	
(Northampton) 12–14 August	5–0–24–0	9–5–22–2	6–2–17–1		25–5–88–5	
v. Yorkshire	24–13–38–2	23–11–37–6	11–1–30–0		30–7–88–2	
(Wellingborough) 15–18 August	9–3–20–0	5–2–10–0	13–8–15–3		11–1–39–0	4.4–0–11–0
v. Essex	21–5–42–0	19–2–50–2	19–4–61–1		1–0–8–0	5–0–37–0
(Northampton) 22–25 August	7–0–31–0	9–2–24–1	9–3–10–1		14.2–2–38–0	12–1–52–4
v. Nottinghamshire	20–5–48–3	19–3–50–1	22–5–51–2		23–5–69–1	2–0–6–0
(Cleethorpes) 26–28 August						
v. Leicestershire	13–5–43–1		18–0–30–0		34–11–101–5	9–4–16–1
(Leicester) 29 August–1 September	9–0–35–3		8–0–55–0		26.2–5–100–1	1–0–6–0
v. Yorkshire	16–2–71–2	12–0–60–1	21.4–6–68–4	22–9–30–2		
(Scarborough) 9–11 September	21–6–43–4	23.2–5–73–3	25–9–50–3	13–2–37–0	4–1–13–0	
v. Hampshire	29–9–73–6	24–1–92–4	23–7–64–0	14–4–38–0		3–2–5–0
(Southampton) 12–15 September						
	682.5–196–	396.5–91–	673.1–184–	281–95–	612.1–163–	184.4–32–
	1845–70	1170–49	1698–59	557–22	1686–48	676–18
	av. 26.35	av. 23.87	av. 28.77	av. 25.18	av. 35.12	av. 37.55

a G. Cook 3–3–0–0
b C. D. Booden 19–4–61–1; 14–3–30–2
c G. Cook 5–1–28–0; A. J. Lamb 5–1–22–0
d C. D. Booden 3–0–19–0; 15–4–37–0

W. Larkins	R. M. Tindall	Sarfraz Nawaz	D. J. Wild	R. J. Boyd-Moss	Kapil Dev	Byes	Leg byes	Wides	No balls	Total	Wickets
						2	4		1	133	10
						5	9		4	187	10
						1	4		4	184	10
										28	1
							4	1	4	261	6
						3	7	2	3	237	10
5–2–12–0	4–3–1–2						5			233	8 a
	4–0–21–0		22–7–52–2			4	8		3	293	5
4–0–20–0	12–0–57–0		12–2–43–0			4	3	1	1	258	2
4.1–2–17–1	1–0–8–0						9	2	2	356	8 b
1.1–0–7–1	17–6–59–0					13	15	1	3	363	10 c
					19–5–51–1	5	8		1	250	7
					9–2–24–2	2	2			111	3
							5	3	5	252	2 d
6–1–22–2	6–1–23–0						1		11	257	5
			17–4–61–1			2	10	1	1	320	9
			11–1–36–0			9	8		1	200	4
			5–0–36–0	21–9–81–2			3		7	301	6
			5–0–27–0	13–6–39–0		3	7		5	224	5 e
		5–2–9–0				1	2		5	105	10
		13–2–42–2		12–4–24–2		12	4		5	212	10
1–0–13–0		24–8–50–3		14–2–66–1		11	2		5	415	8 f
		19–4–54–4					10		15	196	10
		11–4–23–0					3		4	108	10
		13–3–41–1	8–1–51–0			7	13		14	292	6 g
		5–1–12–0				9	8			134	1 h
				4–0–4–0	19–1–84–1		7	1	10	376	5
				4–1–28–1	15–1–37–0	5	7	4	9	317	6
		22–4–62–3				2	6		10	201	10
		20–2–84–6		1–0–10–0		1		1	12	365	9
		10–1–56–1					3		3	169	10
		11–1–42–1				4	3		13	236	10
		14–2–51–1		2–1–1–0		12	3	3	9	252	10
		8–0–33–1		2–0–5–0		8	4		2	203	9
				3–1–8–0		10	17		10	238	10
							6		3	126	4 i
		19–3–71–4				8	17		6	300	7
		5–0–23–1				4	4		3	189	8
		17.5–3–58–2				13	7	6	11	319	10
		17–4–47–1				6	7		1	251	9
		6–2–18–1				3	6	2		263	6 j
		12–0–39–1				4	14		1	287	10
						3	16		1	236	10
							14	3	16	305	10
21.2–5– 91–4 av. 22.75	44–10– 169–2 av. 84.50	251.5–46– 815–33 av. 24.69	80–15 306–3 av. 102.00	42–9– 156–4 av. 39.00	96–24– 316–6 av. 52.66						

e G. Cook 1.4–0–7–1

f G. Cook 7–1–36–0; T. J. Yardley 1–0–3–0

g G. Cook 4–1–13–0

h D. J. Chapel 3–0–6–0; A. J. Lamb 3–1–13–0

i G. Cook 4–0–22–1

j G. Cook 12–4–38–0

Nottinghamshire C.C.C
First-Class Matches – Batting, 1981

	v. Kent (Canterbury) 6–8 May		v. Leicestershire (Trent Bridge) 13–15 May		v. Middlesex (Uxbridge) 27–29 May		v. Gloucestershire (Trent Bridge) 3–5 June		v. Cambridge University (Cambridge) 6–9 June		v. Yorkshire (Bradford) 13–16 June	
P. A. Todd	4	1	81	40	61	—	96	48*			1	—
R. T. Robinson	33	19	1	17	10	—	60	5	77	30*	28	—
D. W. Randall	81	37	37	18*	12	—					5	—
C. E. B. Rice	1	84	66	—	117*	—	3	—			67	—
B. Hassan	97*	3	0	8*					91*	—		
M. J. Harris	23	25*	4	—	44*	—	9	—			4	—
R. J. Hadlee	2	14*	66	—			9	—			142*	—
B. N. French	31	1	0	—			3	—	6	—	25	—
E. E. Hemmings	—	—	4	—			7	—	14	—	28	—
P. J. Hacker	—	—	3*	—					—	—		
K. E. Cooper	—	—	8				6	—			1*	—
J. D. Birch					—	—	29	—	35	—	3	—
M. K. Bore					—	—			—	—		
R. E. Dexter							10	32*	57	21*		
K. Saxelby							10*	—	6	—		
R. Illingworth									—	—		
C. Scott												
N. I. Weightman												
Byes	7	7	2		1		10	6	1		2	
Leg byes	3	5	4	5	12		10	1	9	2	12	
Wides			1	2								
No balls	11	2	2	2	1			1	2		4	
Total	293	198	279	90	258		262	93	298	53	322	
Wickets	7	6	10	3	3		10	1	6	0	8	
Result	D		W		D		W		W		D	
Points	5		23		3		23		—		8	

The match v. Derbyshire (Derby) 23–26 May was abandoned without a ball being bowled.

v. Somerset (Bath) 17–19 June		v. Lancashire (Liverpool) 20–23 June		v. Middlesex (Trent Bridge) 27–30 June		v. Essex (Chelmsford) 1–3 July		v. Hampshire (Bournemouth) 4–7 July		v. Worcestershire (Trent Bridge) 11–14 July		v. Yorkshire (Trent Bridge) 18–21 July		v. Lancashire (Trent Bridge) 25–28 July	
32	1	16	—	29	3	27	18	1	6	2	9*	22	41	19	112
10	4	8	—	20	13	1*	49*	10	4*	8	3*	3	—		
43	1	162*	—	0	0					65	—	87	4	1	52*
8	4	102	—	44	20	166*	17	105*	9	152	—	172	7*	80	—
				24	15	1	12	8	12						
15	36*					2*	0								
10	20	—	—	82	5	14	—	2	40	39	—	42*	—	23	—
12	9	—	—	30	14					23	—	0	—	0	—
9	1	—	—	25*	10*	—	—	0	2	10	—	2	—	2	—
										1*	—	6	—	0*	—
		—	—	7	27			0	1	13	—	0	—	4	—
63	11	29*	—	30	6	111	40*	4	6	0	—	0	50*	9	—
0	5	—	—	7	0	—	—	0	4						
						10	1	4	4	40	—	4	—	19	0*
5*	2	—	—												
								6	8						
														4	26
1	1	6		3	6	2				12	1		6	1	
7	2	6		7	6	9	9	3	3	17		7	3	5	2
1							1			1			1		
6				1	1	5				19		9	3		1
222	97	329		309	126	348	147	143	99	402	13	354	115	167	193
10	10	3		10	10	5	5	10	10	10	0	10	2	10	2
L		D		L		D		L		W		W		W	
3		8		8		8		4		24		24		21	

Nottinghamshire C.C.C. Batting, cont.	v. Leicestershire (Hinckley) 29–31 July		v. Surrey (Trent Bridge) 1–4 August		v. Worcestershire (Worcester) 8–11 August		v. Sussex (Trent Bridge) 15–18 August		v. Warwickshire (Edgbaston) 22–25 August		v. Northamptonshire (Cleethorpes) 26–28 August	
P. A. Todd	14	35	6	—	19	13	7	5	13	52*	18	—
R. T. Robinson					3	19	0	24	32	12	91	—
D. W. Randall	76	101	0	—	8	55	4	0	117	1*	19	—
C. E. B. Rice	21	22	21	—	33	7	4	58	50	—	3	—
B. Hassan			61		3	51*	58*	79	24	—	47	—
M. J. Harris												
R. J. Hadlee	8	34	98	—	28	—	1	11	32	17	0	—
B. N. French	11	0	25	—	12	—	4	1	1	—	3	—
E. E. Hemmings	44	19	7	—	20*	—	11	10*	2	—	15	—
P. J. Hacker			8*	—								
K. E. Cooper	1	2	0	—	11	—	4	0	0*	—	16	—
J. D. Birch	3	13	43	—	13	65*	4	18	20	—	63*	—
M. K. Bore	6*	1*			11*		1	4*	—	—	7	—
R. E. Dexter	7	0										
K. Saxelby												
N. Illingworth												
C. Scott												
N. I. Weightman	1	105	3	—								
Byes	1		4			1					13	
Leg byes	5	12	14		9	2	2	10	3	1	7	
Wides	2	1	3								6	
No balls		9				1	2	3	9	2	11	
Total	200	354	293		170	214	102	223	303	79	319	
Wickets	10	10	10		9	10	10	9	9	2	10	
Result	L		W		W		D		W		W	
Points	2		23		21		4		24		24	

Catches
53 – B. N. French (ct 51, st 2)
25 – C. E. B. Rice
21 – D. W. Randall
18 – J. D. Birch
15 – B. Hassan
14 – R. J. Hadlee
12 – R. T. Robinson and R. E. Dexter
8 – M. J. Harris, P. A. Todd and K. E. Cooper
6 – E. E. Hemmings
4 – M. K. Bore
3 – K. Saxelby, C. Scott (ct 1, st 2), and N. I. Weightman
2 – P. J. Hacker
1 – N. Illingworth and Substitute

v. Derbyshire (Trent Bridge)	29 August–1 September	v. Glamorgan (Trent Bridge)	12–15 September		Inns	NOs	Runs	HS	Av
1	11	17	18*		37	4	899	112	27.24
38	30*	16	9		33	7	687	91	26.42
42	47*	18	—		29	5	1093	162*	45.54
8	—	11	—		30	4	1462	172	56.23
29	—	18	—		20	5	641	97*	42.73
					10	4	162	44*	27.00
12	—	0	—		26	3	745	142*	32.39
24	—	26	—		23	—	231	31	11.34
4	—	11	—		23	4	257	44	13.52
					5	4	18	8*	18.00
20	—	11	—		20	2	132	27	7.33
62*	—	27	—		27	6	757	111	36.04
5	—	9*	—		14	5	60	11*	6.66
					14	3	209	57	19.00
					4	2	23	10*	11.50
					—				—
					2	—	14	8	7.00
					5	—	139	105	27.80

v. Derbyshire (Trent Bridge)	29 August–1 September	v. Glamorgan (Trent Bridge)	12–15 September
11		1	
	1	8	1
		1	
9	1	6	2

v. Derbyshire (Trent Bridge)	29 August–1 September	v. Glamorgan (Trent Bridge)	12–15 September
265	90	180	30
10	1	10	0
W		W	
23		21	

Nottinghamshire C.C.C. First-Class Matches – Bowling, 1981	C. E. B. Rice	R. J. Hadlee	E. E. Hemmings	P. J. Hacker	K. E. Cooper	M. J. Harris
v. Kent	13.3–6–28–0	21–6–47–2	18–3–54–2	18–6–51–1	18–4–57–3	
(Canterbury) 6–8 May	5–1–11–0	16–6–26–2	29–10–80–6		6–0–37–0	7–1–31–0
v. Leicestershire	13–2–50–1	17–8–24–3	2–2–0–0	7–0–37–2	19.1–3–52–4	
(Trent Bridge) 13–15 May	18–6–45–2	19–6–43–2	4.2–2–4–2	14–3–39–1	14–3–58–2	
v. Middlesex						
(Uxbridge) 27–29 May	6–1–21–0	8–2–9–0	16–5–53–3		7–0–36–0	
v. Gloucestershire	18–9–32–3	20–9–46–2	11–6–13–0		12–3–33–1	
(Trent Bridge) 3–5 June	13–2–49–1	12–6–18–0	12–5–21–6		7–5–11–1	
v. Cambridge University			19.2–10–32–3	17–8–34–4		
(Cambridge) 6–9 June			37.1–15–85–3	14–5–38–2		1–0–8–0
v. Yorkshire	17–9–8–2	19–12–16–4	18.1–7–31–4		5–0–18–0	
(Bradford) 13–16 June	28–11–52–3	31–9–78–0	60–25–95–2		27–10–41–0	
v. Somerset	4–1–11–0	30–8–77–3	31–9–82–1			
(Bath) 17–19 June						
v. Lancashire		17.1–8–25–7	20–5–40–0		25–8–53–2	
(Liverpool) 20–23 June		12–7–35–0	40–12–93–0		19–4–49–0	
v. Middlesex	12–3–41–2	15–3–57–4	6.3–0–16–2		10–4–28–2	
(Trent Bridge) 27–30 June	22–3–50–1	22–8–45–2	35–5–94–3		17–4–59–0	
v. Essex	25–5–86–3	25.3–9–60–6	14–1–48–0			
(Chelmsford) 1–3 July	7–3–14–2	9–2–34–0	20–8–34–1			
v. Hampshire	19–6–50–4	28.3–9–59–4	6–0–12–0		18–7–42–2	
(Bournemouth) 4–7 July	5–1–9–0	3–0–11–0	6.3–5–8–1			
v. Worcestershire	9–2–14–1	14–4–43–3	3–0–13–1	10–0–43–1	12.2–6–13–4	
(Trent Bridge) 11–14 July	17–4–48–2	21–5–43–2	16–2–70–0	14–4–33–3	20–6–69–2	
v. Yorkshire	8–4–10–2	11.5–3–26–4	12–5–18–2	8–2–17–1	11–5–21–1	
(Trent Bridge) 18–21 July	23–7–62–0	36–12–90–4	48–15–92–3	22.3–5–51–2	18–7–35–1	
v. Lancashire	10–3–30–1	18–4–47–5		14.3–6–35–2	15–4–33–2	
(Trent Bridge) 25–28 July	20–7–40–2	28–5–57–3	25–15–33–1	21.4–9–37–2	11–3–22–1	
v. Leicestershire	19–2–53–3	17.5–3–54–2	35–3–102–1		28–9–75–0	
(Hinckley) 29–31 July	1–0–19–0	7–0–54–2	5.5–0–45–3			
v. Surrey	17–5–50–3	23–7–63–3		10–3–25–2	16–9–23–2	
(Trent Bridge) 1–4 August	17–4–44–6	15–7–15–3	4–1–26–1	5–1–6–0	4–2–2–0	
v. Worcestershire		12.5–2–34–3	26–7–66–6			
(Worcester) 8–11 August		9–3–17–3	28.2–13–64–4			
v. Sussex	11–2–22–2	15.2–4–26–1	36–10–94–5		15–1–39–1	
(Trent Bridge)	1.1–1–0–1	8–4–15–2	26–8–57–4			
v. Warwickshire	29–5–104–3	28–9–59–4	14–2–53–0		20–3–70–2	
(Edgbaston) 22–25 August	6–2–8–1	9–6–8–3	8–4–5–2		7–3–17–2	
v. Northamptonshire	10–3–25–4	16.4–6–34–5			6–0–19–1	
(Cleethorpes)	14–1–55–3	16–4–35–3	16–6–44–1		6–3–7–2	
v. Derbyshire	14–3–33–1	31–11–57–1	34.4–16–59–7		10–2–21–0	
(Trent Bridge)	14–3–33–1	31–11–57–1	34.4–16–59–7		10–2–21–0	
29 August–1 September	20–11–22–3	10–2–21–0	36–10–70–6		6–2–10–1	
v. Glamorgan	8.1–1–14–2	12–4–18–4			10–3–25–4	
(Trent Bridge)	15–6–38–1	17–8–38–4	29–11–51–4		4–2–6–0	
12–15 September						
	494.5–142–	708.4–231–	808.5–263–	175.4–52–	423.3–125–	8–1–
	1248–65	1564–105	1857–90	446–23	1081–43	39–0
	av. 19.20	av. 14.89	av. 20.63	av. 19.39	av. 25.13	—

A. First innings forfeited.

† E. J. O. Hemsley absent injured.

M. K. Bore	K. Saxelby	N. Illingworth	R. T. Robinson	Byes	Leg byes	Wides	No balls	Total	Wickets
				4	6	1	2	250	8
					7			192	9
					2		5	170	10
					4	1	1	195	10
									A.
22–7–52–3				1	6		2	180	6
	19.2–5–64–4			1	4	1	6	200	10
	12.2–0–45–2				4		4	152	10
21–8–29–2	14–7–15–1	6–3–12–0			4		4	126	10
31–15–46–2	12–5–28–2	1–0–4–1		5	9		1	224	10
					1		4	78	10
39–13–79–2				1	4	1	4	355	7
32–9–94–2	23–4–97–2			3	3	6	7	380	9
18–5–43–1	9–2–10–0			4	3		1	179	10
45–11–95–2	10–1–34–1		1–0–5–0	1	6	1	1	320	3
				1	4	2	2	151	10
37.5–7–121–4				1	16	2	8	396	10
30–7–55–1				19	1	2	1	272	10
20.4–5–46–4				15	8		1	152	7
6–2–11–0				3	8	1	4	190	10
4–0–20–0					4		1	53	1
					4		2	132	10
				4	9	2	4	282	9†
					6		6	104	10
					21	4	9	364	10
					4	1		150	10
				4	7	8	1	209	10
42–11–125–2					16		6	431	8
					5		1	124	6
				2	9		3	175	10
				8	1	1		103	10
14–5–37–1				4	5			146	10
20–10–36–3				8	4		3	132	10
19–12–18–0					7		2	208	10
32–13–71–3					1			144	10
8–3–20–0				9	12		4	331	9
3.2–1–8–2					2	1		49	10
				4	2		1	85	10
8–2–29–1					6		5	181	10
14–6–26–1				4	3	1	4	208	10
9–5–14–0				4	2	1	2	146	10
							3	60	10
1–1–0–0				8	5		3	146	10
476.5–158– 1075–36 av. 29.86	99.4–24– 293–12 av. 24.41	7–3– 16–1 av. 16.00	1–0– 5–0 —						

Somerset C.C.C.
First-Class Matches –
Batting, 1981

	v. Oxford University (Oxford) 29 April–1 May		v. Hampshire (Southampton) 6–8 May		v. Lancashire (Old Trafford) 13–15 May		v. Australians (Taunton) 23–25 May		v. Sussex (Hove) 3–5 June		v. Middlesex (Lord's) 6–9 June	
B. C. Rose	18	—	0	—	21	4	11*	—	15	39	23	6*
J. W. Lloyds	19	—	14	—	127	17	11*	—	22	2	12	8
P. W. Denning	28	—	29	—	31*	0	—	—	72	1	63	75*
P. M. Roebuck	16	—	75	—	40*	10	—	—	31	25	68	33
P. A. Slocombe	62*	—										
D. Breakwell	—	—	53	—	—	14*	—	—	5	—	12	7
D. J. S. Taylor	16*	—	2	—	—	20	—	—	48*	31*	6	—
N. F. M. Popplewell	35	—										
C. H. Dredge	—	—	4*	—	—	3	—	—	0	—	—	—
K. F. Jennings	—	—										
H. R. Moseley	—	—	12	—					4*	—	2*	—
I. T. Botham			5	—	—	0	—	—				
V. J. Marks			15	—	—	0	—	—	3	25*	0	26*
J. Garner			22	—	—	0	—	—	52	—	29	—
I. V. A. Richards					82	12	—	—	13	22	92	3
M. Olive												
N. Russom												
R. L. Ollis												
Byes	9		3		1					1	3	
Leg byes	5		13		7	8			6	4	6	3
Wides			3			1	1		1	2	8	5
No balls	1		5					2	1	2	8	5
Total	209		255		309	89	25		272	152	324	166
Wickets	5		10		3	10	0		9	5	9	4
Result	W		D		W		D		D		D	
Points	—		4		24		—		4		4	

† P. M. Roebuck absent hurt.
A. Innings forfeited.

v. Gloucestershire (Bath) 13-16 June		v. Nottinghamshire (Bath) 17-19 June		v. Worcestershire (Worcester) 20-23 June		v. Glamorgan (Swansea) 27-30 June		v. Surrey (Taunton) 1-3 July		v. Leicestershire (Leicester) 4-7 July		v. Sussex (Taunton) 11-14 July		v. Derbyshire (Taunton) 18-21 July	
21	85*	1	—	18	107	40	18	35	3			6	82	1	52
6	2	0	—							73	43*	3	68	0	98
8	12	39	—	11	14*	4	—	65	50*	9	—	31	61	71	5*
—	13*					51	6*	31	27	0	—	91	40*		
		50	—	13	37					6	5*				
58	53			2	—	10	—					0	21*	46	—
18	4	10	—	32*	—	5	—	4	—	13	—	0	1	17*	—
		47	—	14	39*			2	5	17	—	8	4	27	—
		2*	—					4*	—	0*	—	0	0	—	—
2*	10	36*	—	9	—	9*	—	14	—	10	—	0*	1		
41	1					123*	—					15	72		
49	9	70	—	33	—	0	—	1	16*	2	—			48	—
90	16	0	—	20	—	18	—	3	—	18	—			0*	—
2	37	106	—	63	118	2	15*	4	68	196	—	8	26	16	130
				18	8	3	5	19	19						
6		3		1	2	6		5	5	7	4		10	3	5
9	2	3		11	1	22		2	5	1			7	2	1
2	1	6			4	3	2			1	1	1	10		1
4		7		1	2	3		1	4	13	5				
316	245	380		246	331	303	46	190	200	356	53	104	367	335	337
9†	9	9		10	4	9	2	10	5	10	0	10	10	8	3
D		W		D		D		D		W		L		D	
5		24		3		5		5		24		4		4	

Somerset C.C.C.
Batting, *cont.*

	v. Glamorgan (Taunton) 29–31 July		v. Yorkshire (Sheffield) 1–4 August		v. Northamptonshire (Weston-super-Mare) 8–11 August		v. Worcestershire (Weston-super-Mare) 12–14 August		v. Hampshire (Taunton) 22–25 August		v. Kent (Folkestone) 26–28 August	
B. C. Rose	3	37	1	6	20	34	25	4	23	4*	39	—
J. W. Lloyds	2	20	9	22	36	0	13	1	50	4	25	—
P. W. Denning	0	—	16	15	25	32	0	25	11	—	98	—
P. M. Roebuck	39*	1*	50	16	24	8	4	1*	7	—	51	—
P. A. Slocombe												
D. Breakwell	3	—										
D. J. S. Taylor	11	—	20	18*	0	1	3	—	27	—	4	—
N. F. M. Popplewell	5	—	36	51*	9	26	46	5	21	—	21	—
C. H. Dredge	14	—	6	—	2*	1*	5*	—			4*	—
K. F. Jennings			4	—								
H. R. Moseley			9*	—	1	19	2	—	15	—	3	—
I. T. Botham					42	49			34	—		
V. J. Marks	30	—	9	58	3	23	7	12*	13	—	0	—
J. Garner	4	—							19*	—	0	—
I. V. A. Richards	17	47*	8	153	1	23	150	41	30	9*	37	—
M. Olive												
N. Russom							12	12*				
R. L. Ollis												
Byes	18					4	1		13	4	3	
Leg byes	10	6	6	7	3	3	2	3	16		9	
Wides	5	1		1					2			
No balls	11	9	9	2	3	13	10	3	6		15	
Total	172	121	183	349	169	236	280	107	287	21	309	
Wickets	10	2	10	6	10	10	10	5	10	1	10	
Result	D		W		L		W		W		W	
Points	5		21		5		23		23		22	

Catches

62 – D. J. S. Taylor (ct 56, st 6)
22 – B. C. Rose
18 – I. V. A. Richards
14 – P. W. Denning
13 – P. M. Roebuck
10 – J. W. Lloyds and J. Garner
9 – C. H. Dredge and H. R. Moseley
8 – V. J. Marks
7 – I. T. Botham
3 – N. F. M. Popplewell
2 – K. F. Jennings and D. Breakwell
1 – P. A. Slocombe, M. Olive, N. Russom, R. L. Ollis and Substitute

v. Gloucestershire (Bristol) 29 August–1 September		v. Warwickshire (Edgbaston) 2-4 September		v. Essex (Taunton) 9-11 September		v. Warwickshire (Taunton) 12-15 September		Inns	NOs	Runs	HS	Av
13	6	70	37	2	—	—	75	39	4	1005	107	28.71
6	75	0	42	1	—	—	6	35	2	837	127	25.36
9	23	14	102*	10	—	—	28	36	6	1087	102*	36.23
18	2	72	17	70	—	—	89*	34	8	1057	91	40.65
								6	2	173	62*	43.25
								13	2	284	58	25.81
19	1	19*	—	20	—	—	—	28	7	370	48*	17.61
21	8	0	5	26	—	—	35	25	2	513	51*	22.30
0*	6*	—	—			—	—	16	10	51	14	8.50
								1	—	4	4	4.00
2	1	—	—	1*	—	—	—	21	8	162	36*	12.46
				88	—	—	56	12	1	525	123*	47.81
0	18	81*	2*	27	—	—	9*	30	7	589	81*	25.60
20	7	—	—	6	—			18	2	326	90	20.25
				128	—	—	59	33	3	1718	196	57.26
								6	—	72	19	12.00
								2	1	24	12*	24.00
20	18	22	0					4	—	60	22	15.00
5	7		4	4			11					
9	3	9	8	13			2					
4	5			9			2					
1		13	3	3			8					
147	180	300	220	408		A.	378					
10	10	6	5	10			6					
	W		W		D		W					
	20		24		8		18					

Somerset C.C.C. First-Class Matches – Bowling, 1981	H. R. Moseley	C. H. Dredge	J. W. Lloyds	D. Breakwell	K. F. Jennings	J. Garner
v. Oxford University	9–4–16–4	13.1–4–18–1	5–1–12–3	9–3–13–1	2–1–1–1	
(Oxford) 29 April–1 May	2–2–0–0	7–6–3–1	22.2–9–44–3	23–7–38–6		
v. Hampshire	16–5–36–1	14–3–41–0	8–1–30–1	4–0–18–0		26–9–38–3
(Southampton) 6–8 May						
v. Lancashire		23–9–49–2		4–0–16–1		25–8–59–5
(Old Trafford) 13–15 May						17.2–3–57–5
v. Australians		17–6–34–0	5–1–14–0	17–3–37–2		22–9–37–1
(Taunton) 23–25 May						
v. Sussex	23–6–71–3	24–4–93–1		18–3–52–0		22–9–37–0
(Hove) 3–5 June	4–1–17–0	4–1–6–0		16–0–69–3		7–1–13–1
v. Middlesex	20–3–55–2	15–1–50–0	4–0–25–0	9–0–35–0		18–1–52–1
(Lord's) 6–9 June						
v. Gloucestershire	15–3–56–1		3–0–16–0	14–4–29–0		26–4–81–0
(Bath) 13–16 June	10–2–21–1		14–3–64–1			10–3–20–0
v. Nottinghamshire	14–4–38–2	18–5–34–3				20.5–7–52–2
(Bath) 17–19 June	15–3–39–2		3–3–0–0			21.4–9–29–6
v. Worcestershire	16–3–73–1			28–7–82–0		22–6–66–2
(Worcester) 20–23 June						
v. Glamorgan	18–2–60–0			6–0–19–0		23.3–5–64–3
(Swansea) 27–30 June	9–1–22–1			17–2–66–1		14–5–22–2
v. Surrey	18–2–69–2	22–6–60–3				23–4–73–3
(Taunton) 1–3 July	15–3–47–2	13–0–45–1				15–2–40–1
v. Leicestershire	12–5–28–2	10–1–40–1				17–6–41–7
(Leicester) 4–7 July	24–11–49–1	20–8–38–1	4–2–8–0			28–7–65–5
v. Sussex	13–6–32–1	14–3–37–1	1–0–4–0	2–0–4–0		
(Taunton) 11–14 July		14–2–28–1	3–0–17–0	27–8–64–2		
v. Derbyshire		22.3–3–70–3	1–0–6–0	36–7–126–3		32–8–45–0
(Taunton) 18–21 July						
v. Glamorgan		23–2–103–2		7–0–32–0		33–12–68–3
(Taunton) 29–31 July		21.3–6–41–4		4–0–19–0		16–7–20–2
v. Yorkshire	16–4–44–4	20–7–40–1			22–3–52–3	
(Sheffield) 1–4 August	13–2–70–1	16.5–6–43–6			5–0–21–0	
v. Northamptonshire	8–2–23–0	16–6–43–1				
(Weston-super-Mare)	12–3–33–2	12.4–5–16–0	1–0–4–0			
8–11 August						
v. Worcestershire	8–0–33–2	23.4–5–75–4				
(Weston-super-Mare)	21–1–75–3	18.2–5–53–4				
12–14 August						
v. Hampshire	15–4–36–0					21–6–39–3
(Taunton) 22–25 August	10–4–22–1					14–6–25–7
v. Kent	13–4–28–2	15–6–33–2	1–0–4–0			19.2–4–53–3
(Folkestone)		6–3–20–1	8–4–11–0			19–8–37–4
26–28 August						
v. Gloucestershire	6–3–6–0	10.4–3–37–6				17–5–24–4
(Bristol)	8–3–11–0	25–6–63–3	1–0–2–0			26.4–7–56–6
29 August–1 September						
v. Warwickshire	12–2–33–2	19–4–44–1	12–0–36–1			15.2–5–30–2
(Edgbaston) 2–4 September	5–0–16–1	5–0–9–0	21–0–77–0			12–3–25–4
v. Essex	14–2–53–2					18–11–29–3
(Taunton) 9–11 September	16–0–60–3					14–2–52–0
v. Warwickshire	6–1–19–0	10–3–20–0	27–5–108–1			
(Taunton)						
12–15 September						
	436–101–	493.2–129–	144.2–29–	241–44–	29–4–	615.4–182–
	1291–49	1286–54	482–10	719–19	74–4	1349–88
	av. 26.34	av. 23.81	av. 48.20	av. 37.84	av.18.50	av. 15.32

†M. A. Nash retired hurt   a M. Johnson absent hurt   b P. Willey retired hurt

I. T. Botham	V. J. Marks	P. W. Denning	B. C. Rose	I. V. A. Richards	N. F. M. Popplewell	Byes	Leg byes	Wides	No balls	Total	Wickets
						1	2			63	10
						6	9			100	10
26–6–71–1	17–3–40–2					3	16	1	5	299	8
		2–0–2–0	2–0–5–0							7	0
24–7–77–2	8–2–35–0						4	1	3	244	10
17–3–62–4							2			121	10
22–9–36–2	30.4–6–59–2			2–0–7–0		1	4	3		232	8
	25–5–82–2			1–0–10–0		2	7		6	360	6
	17.5–3–53–2						5		1	164	8
	18–5–38–1						7		3	265	4
25–7–99–2	13–2–40–0			7–2–26–0		1	5	4	4	361	4
9–1–45–0	28–4–74–1	1–0–16–0		13–1–53–0		4	2		4	303	4
	9–6–10–0			15–6–31–2	15–3–42–0	1	7	1	6	222	10
	7–2–26–1					1	2			97	10
	34–7–91–2			13–2–61–1	10–3–34–0	6	8		10	431	6
16–0–81–0	24–6–63–0					1	7		6	301	4
15–3–61–0	22–5–51–0			9.4–2–18–1		3	2		2	247	6
	3.4–2–20–2				11–4–32–0		7	1	13	275	10
	14–5–38–1				9–1–32–1	5	8		4	219	7
	1–1–0–0					1			6	116	10
	27–15–26–1			29–7–44–0	21–8–34–1	11	6	1	8	290	10
34.5–10–90–6				5–1–15–0	13–5–31–2	2	6	1	11	233	10
17–5–39–0			0.5–0–4–0	9–0–50–0	6–0–25–1	8	6		1	242	4
	37–4–111–1			14–1–66–0	13–1–53–0	4	9		5	495	7
	8–4–23–0			22.1–6–55–4	10–3–29–0	10	9		7	336	9
	19–4–56–1			7–4–15–2		3	1		2	157	9 †
	14–7–16–1				4–0–16–0	5	7			180	10
	13–3–40–2						11			185	9 b
22–8–81–3	5–2–10–0				12.3–2–33–5	1	10			201	96
12–0–50–3	17–7–29–2			6–1–23–0	10–2–31–1	2	7	10		205	8
	10–6–26–1				9–1–33–1		2		1	188	10 c
	8–3–14–1				13–3–36–2	3	5		1	198	10
12.2–2–34–3				9–3–21–3	11–3–36–1	1	7	1	9	184	10
6–1–46–1	6.1–4–8–1			3–0–12–0			3		4	120	10
	25–12–48–3			4–1–7–0		2	3		8	186	10
	29.3–14–34–5			1–0–1–0		6	4		8	121	10
						4	3	2		76	10
	18–7–46–1					5	4	1	5	193	10
	38–11–71–3					6	4		1	225	10
	32–8–116–5				3–0–7–0		3			253	10
16–6–53–3	4–0–21–0				11.5–1–40–2	1	5		9	211	10
16–5–46–2	10–2–17–1			5–0–16–0	7–1–32–0	7	6		4	240	6
11.4–2–41–1	35–10–96–3			11–1–54–0	5–1–22–1	1	7	2	5	375	6
											A.
613.5–75– 1012–33 av. 30.66	627.5–187– 1528–48 av. 31.83	3–0– 18–0 —	2.5–0– 9–0 —	185.5–38– 585–13 av. 45.00	194.2–42– 598–18 av. 33.22						

c N. Russom 7–3–18–2; 3–0–11–0   A. Innings forfeited

Surrey C.C.C.
First-Class Matches –
Batting,
1981

	v. Cambridge University (Cambridge) 6–8 May		v. Derbyshire (The Oval) 13–15 May		v. Essex (Chelmsford) 27–29 May		v. Lancashire (Old Trafford) 3–5 June		v. Glamorgan (Swansea) 6–9 June		v. Worcestershire (The Oval) 10–12 June	
A. R. Butcher	1	133*	2	33	73	25	13*	0*			3	7
G. S. Clinton	123	9	123	2	40	16	13	79*	18	10	1	69
G. P. Howarth	27	75	1	1	0	4			5	77		
R. D. V. Knight	10	13*	3	21	96	84	42	36	12	21	3	62
G. R. J. Roope	14	—	7	55*	9	26	0	2	1	7	38	—
D. M. Smith	29	—	21	15	14	13	16	0	43	8	23	42*
R. D. Jackman	18*	—			—	3*					2*	—
C. J. Richards	12	—	62	34	37*	10	7	0	19	53		
S. T. Clarke	5	—	4	—	—	—	79	15	0	100*	6	24
R. G. L. Cheatle	5*	—										
P. I. Pocock	—	—	3	—	—	—	7	—	11*	—	46	—
D. J. Thomas			20	8*	5*	20*	3	0	8	3	5	29*
P. H. L. Wilson			2*	—								
M. A. Lynch							46	21	1	15	33	16
Intikhab Alam							25	0			1	0
G. Monkhouse									3	0*		
I. R. Payne												
A. Needham												
A. J. Stewart												
D. B. Pauline												
K. Mackintosh												
Byes	2	1		2	6	1			2	12		
Leg byes	7	4	5	2	18	16	3	2	2	5	1	13
Wides		1				1					1	3
No balls	4	1	5	8	2	2		1	6	6	7	9
Total	257	237	258	181	300	221	254	156	131	317	170	274
Wickets	8	2	10	6	6	7	10	8	10	8	10	6
Result	D		D		D		D		W		W	
Points	—		5		8		4		20		21	

The match v. Hampshire (The Oval) was abandoned without a ball being bowled.

v. Lancashire (The Oval) 17–19 June		v. Northamptonshire (The Oval) 27–30 June		v. Somerset (Taunton) 1–3 July		v. Yorkshire (Harrogate) 4–7 July		v. Warwickshire (The Oval) 11–14 July		v. Sussex (Hove) 15–17 July		v. Hampshire (Portsmouth) 18–21 July		v. Sussex (Guildford) 29–31 July	
25	2			22	3			93	10	7	39*	26	15	12	13
35	20	5	26	66	4	15	22	37	0	5	0	21	10	60	17
								90	110*	6	25				
5	32	77	48	18	57	21	13			61	18	48	6	47	11
2	2*	2	96*	46	18	63	11	5	10			19	25	12	7
76	29*	18	2	0	34	13	84*					3	0	24	13*
8	—	28*	—	0	—	18	51	—	9*	4	—	20*	6	9	—
		3	—	5*	18*	19	5	—	30	11	—	25	36	20	—
0	—	24	—									3	26		
0*	—	11*	—	21	—	0*	3			7*	—	0	2*	0*	—
0	8	29	—	26	2	4	29	—	14	47	—			30	—
38	20	38	6*	19	66*	2	8	45*	10	12	3*	17	19	75	20
79	0	71	4	31	0	1	1	—	42	5	—			0	27*
						18	0	—	0	0	—	1	14		
								6*	1						
15	2	2	9		5			1	6	1	1	1	8	11	
7	9	10	8	7	8	10	14	13	15	4		18	9	5	6
1		1		1		2		3	3	1		2	4	2	1
1	1	1	1	13	4	6	5	7	4	4	4		1	4	4
290	124	320	200	275	219	192	246	300	264	175	90	204	181	311	119
10	6	9	4	10	7	10	10	4	9	10	3	10	10	10	5
W		D		D		L		D		D		W		W	
22		8		7		5		6		4		22		23	

Surrey C.C.C.
Batting, *cont.*

	v. Nottinghamshire (Trent Bridge) 1–4 August		v. Gloucestershire (Cheltenham) 8–11 August		v. Leicestershire (The Oval) 12–14 August		v. Middlesex (The Oval) 15–18 August		v. Kent (Folkestone) 22–25 August		v. Kent (The Oval) 2–4 September	
A. R. Butcher	12	0	45	90	37	24	33	19*	116	89	2	139
G. S. Clinton	4	7	21	0	15	79	6	6*	3	54	2	4
G. P. Howarth			7	18	24	10						
R. D. V. Knight	0	6	8	5	0	0	35	—	0	1	26	13
G. R. J. Roope	94*	21	27	11	2	18	20	—	81	44	5	10
D. M. Smith	9	0					71	—	31	13	6	29
R. D. Jackman	1	0	41	16	17*	5	6*	—	19*	5*	11	15
C. J. Richards	11	6			63	3	0	—	11	4	21	22
S. T. Clarke	22	34										
R. G. L. Cheatle												
P. I. Pocock			0	0*	1	9	15	—	4*	—		
D. J. Thomas	7	7*			18	1						
P. H. L. Wilson			0*	1			0	—	—			
M. A. Lynch	0	4	4	1	118	20*	41	—	0	4	19	10
Intikhab Alam	1	8	0	2	12	9	4	—	13	44*	1	6
G. Monkhouse											6*	0*
I. R. Payne											2	10
A. Needham												
A. J. Stewart			2	8								
D. B. Pauline												
K. Mackintosh												
Byes	2	8		11	6	2	14		3		4	5
Leg byes	9	1	4	7	9	4	10		11	14	3	13
Wides		1							1		4	1
No balls	3			1	12	1	4		2	2	3	9
Total	175	103	160	170	334	185	259	25	295	274	115	286
Wickets	10	10	10	10	10	10	10	0	8	7	10	10
Result	L		L		D		W		D		L	
Points	5		5		8		23		6		4	

Catches

45 – G. R. J. Roope (ct 44, st 1)

37 – C. J. Richards (ct 30, st 7)

16 – R. D. V. Knight and D. M. Smith

14 – A. R. Butcher

8 – P. I. Pocock, S. T. Clarke and M. A. Lynch

7 – G. S. Clinton and D. J. Thomas

6 – R. D. Jackman

5 – I. R. Payne

3 – G. P. Howarth and A. J. Stewart

2 – Intikhab Alam, G. Monkhouse, P. H. L. Wilson and Substitutes

1 – R. G. L. Cheatle

v. Middlesex (Uxbridge) 9–11 September		v. Essex (The Oval) 12–15 September		Inns	NOs	Runs	HS	Av
75	20	32	154*	38	6	1444	154*	45.12
114	2	1	27	44	2	1191	123	28.35
				16	1	480	110*	32.00
31	34	5	12	41	1	1041	96	26.02
		9	10	37	4	829	96*	25.12
5	0			32	4	684	84*	24.42
0	19	—	—	26	10	331	51	20.68
40	33	60*	—	31	4	680	63	25.18
				14	1	342	100*	26.30
				1	1	5	5*	—
8	6*			21	10	154	46	14.00
				24	5	323	47	17.00
				4	2	3	2*	1.50
58	23	120*	6	37	6	958	120*	30.90
21	0	46	15*	31	3	469	79	16.75
28*	0	—	—	6	4	37	28*	18.50
				8	—	45	18	5.62
				2	1	7	6*	7.00
				2	—	10	8	5.00
5	0	0	12	4	—	17	12	4.25
		—	—					
9	4	3						
6	3	7	7					
5		1						
6	1	4	1					
411	145	288	244					
10	10	6	5					
	L	W						
	7	23						

Surrey C.C.C. First-Class Matches – Bowling, 1981	S. T. Clarke	R. D. Jackman	P. I. Pocock	R. D. V. Knight	G. Monkhouse	D. M. Smith
v. Cambridge University	20–7–47–4	21–10–46–2	33–12–62–0	16–4–40–2		
(Cambridge) 6–8 May	6–3–8–1	7–2–23–2	17–8–23–2	5–1–7–0		7–4–10–0
v. Derbyshire	24–8–42–3		9–4–12–0	19–8–35–0		6–3–5–0
(The Oval) 13–15 May	5–3–5–0					
v. Essex	20.2–6–36–5	16–4–39–1	28–6–93–1	19–6–40–2		
(Chelmsford) 27–29 May	14–5–26–2	15–2–47–0	16.3–3–41–3	10–2–35–1		
v. Lancashire	23–5–63–1		21–7–65–1	18–7–48–1		
(Old Trafford) 3–5 June	12–4–22–3		16–3–51–1	5–0–23–0		
v. Glamorgan	26.3–9–66–6		11–4–28–2	14–8–18–2	4–0–10–0	
(Swansea) 6–9 June	17–4–42–0		37.1–17–54–4	8–5–14–0	5–2–9–0	
v. Worcestershire	21–3–44–2	19.2–4–74–2		11–4–28–0		
(The Oval) 10–12 June	11–4–15–0	4–0–17–0	8–2–24–0	7–1–21–0		
v. Lancashire	33–10–80–5	31–11–62–1	17–7–33–1			
(The Oval) 17–19 June	17.3–2–41–4	12–2–25–4	14–3–27–0			
v. Northamptonshire	25–7–41–1	24–6–48–3	10–5–21–0	11–2–23–2		
(The Oval) 27–30 June	5–0–9–0	11–4–21–0	21–10–40–3	7–2–28–0		
v. Somerset		27–6–70–6	6–2–13–0	5–0–22–0		
(Taunton) 1–3 July		12–3–37–1	12–1–29–0	5–1–8–1		
v. Yorkshire		27.3–8–47–5	2–1–1–0			
(Harrogate) 4–7 July		14–1–50–0	10–0–46–0			
v. Warwickshire		22–1–73–2				
(The Oval) 11–14 July		9.4–2–33–0				
v. Sussex		31–11–76–0	28–8–61–2			
(Hove) 15–17 July						
v. Hampshire	21.2–10–41–5	19–4–52–2	7–0–19–0	6–3–6–0		
(Portsmouth) 18–21 July	10–1–25–2	16–6–30–5	6–5–1–2	6–4–2–0		
v. Sussex		20–3–66–2	25–8–48–3	14–2–40–0		
(Guildford) 29–31 July		19–8–40–3	12.4–3–32–2			
v. Nottinghamshire	28–7–81–5	19–5–60–1		17–5–46–1		
(Trent Bridge) 1–4 August						
v. Gloucestershire		11–2–22–3	29–12–59–3			
(Cheltenham) 8–11 August		8–3–27–0	18–3–58–1			
v. Leicestershire		14–2–27–0	34–8–99–4	6–2–12–0		
(The Oval) 12–14 August		7–1–12–0	22–5–68–1			
v. Middlesex		8–1–19–1	23–7–46–2	9–3–13–1		
(The Oval) 15–18 August		4–1–4–1	26–10–41–2			
v. Kent		21.5–6–67–2	21–5–64–1	20–5–66–2		
(Folkestone) 22–25 August		10–4–20–3	20–3–73–1			
v. Kent		26–4–90–4		11–0–38–1	23–7–53–3	
(The Oval) 2–4 September		20–2–46–2		10–2–35–0	16–2–45–3	5–1–23–1
v. Middlesex		12–4–48–0	28.1–15–117–2		8–1–21–0	
(Uxbridge)		3–0–6–0	14.4–3–62–2		2–0–7–0	
9–11 September						
v. Essex		21.5–5–83–5		10–2–37–0	20–4–60–1	
(The Oval)		4–0–12–1			5–1–19–0	
12–15 September						
	339.4–98–	577.1–138–	603.1–190–	269–79–	73–17–	18–8–
	734–49	1519–64	1511–46	685–16	224–7	38–1
	av. 14.97	av. 23.73	av. 32.84	av. 42.81	av. 32.00	av. 38.00

a R. G. L. Cheatle 12–3–33–1; 6–1–19–0
b G. P. Howarth 3–0–12–0
c G. P. Howarth 4–2–12–10
d M. A. Lynch 6–3–6–3
e M. A. Lynch 2–0–6–0
f M. A. Lynch 3–1–9–0
g A. Needham 5–1–30–0; 11–4–27–1

† N. E. J. Pocock absent injured
h M. A. Lynch 1–0–2–0; 1–0–3–0
i M. A. Lynch 1.4–0–9–0
j D. B. Pauline 2–0–14–0
k K. Mackintosh 10–2–46–0; 9–3–19–2
l M. A. Lynch 14–3–62–0

G. R. J. Roope	A. R. Butcher	D. J. Thomas	P. H. L. Wilson	I. R. Payne	Intikhab Alam	Byes	Leg byes	Wides	No balls	Total	Wickets
6-2-15-0						6	6			240	10 a
						3	6			126	5 b
12-3-22-1		23-6-52-2	9-1-31-0			10	13	4	7	233	6
	4-3-10-1	4-4-0-0				1			3	31	1 c
		11-2-34-0				2	2		1	247	10
						11	3			163	6
11-4-30-2		22-7-57-2			11-1-41-0	7	10	1	10	332	7
		17-6-63-1			7-1-29-0		9		2	199	5
		3-1-5-0				1	4			132	10
		14-2-40-3				18	7		2	192	10 d
		17-5-51-1			19-3-66-5	2	4	1	3	273	10
		7-0-35-0			14-1-49-1		5		2	168	2
		13-1-48-1			14.1-4-33-2	2	8			266	10
		6-1-18-1			9-6-11-1	21	1			144	10
		7-0-24-0			20.3-8-50-4	7	8	1	1	224	10
		3-0-14-1			26.3-3-105-1	1	6			230	6 e
3-0-18-0		16.4-5-38-2			14-6-21-2	5	2		1	190	10
		12-0-50-0			20-4-55-3	5	5		2	200	5 f
		10-2-26-0		5-2-9-0	34-15-65-5	6	3			157	10
		12-3-29-3		23-4-64-2	17.4-2-84-0	4	4		2	283	5
		20.1-6-54-0		22-7-65-2	17-3-65-1	1	10	2		300	5 g
		14-3-26-3			14-10-5-2		10	2	1	104	6
		25-4-77-2		9-3-17-1	21.4-9-44-5	4	6	2	2	289	10
				11-4-28-2		3	3	2	10	164	10
				6-2-17-0		5	7	2	2	91	9 †
		15-1-64-3			28.5-8-63-2	4	11	1	5	302	10
		16-7-31-5			4-0-8-0	6	5	1	4	127	10
		17-3-71-1			9.3-3-14-2	4	14	3		293	10
			3-1-4-0		27-7-69-4	4	6			166	10 h
	4.3-2-13-1		3-0-4-0		15-1-52-0	3	4	1		165	2
		12-5-22-2			25.1-5-60-3	5	7		3	235	10
	8-1-28-2		7-3-4-1		27.3-5-74-2	8	1			195	6
	7-3-15-2		5-0-15-0		10.3-5-26-4		5			139	10
	8-4-16-2		2-0-8-0		31.5-10-63-4	5	7			144	10
			19-3-61-2		15-4-44-0	2	10	1	1	316	7
	12-0-59-2		7-4-18-0		17-4-68-0	8	4			259	6 i
5-0-17-1				10-3-50-1		5	1		3	257	10
					9-1-32-2	5	10	1	7	204	8
	8-1-33-0				28-4-133-4	10	11		5	392	8 j
	3-0-16-0				12-2-68-2	4	2			165	4
2-0-3-0					19-12-28-4	4	5		10	276	10 k
	10-1-57-0				22-6-60-0	12	4		7	252	3 l
39-9–	64.3-15–	323.5-77–	48-9–	86-25–	560.5-153–						
105-4	247-10	933-34	141-2	250-8	1585-65						
av. 26.25	av. 24.70	av. 27.44	av. 70.50	av. 31.25	av. 24.38						

Sussex C.C.C.
First-Class Matches – Batting, 1981

	v. Worcestershire (Worcester) 6–8 May		v. Glamorgan (Hove) 13–15 May		v. Somerset (Hove) 3–5 June		v. Lancashire (Hove) 6–9 June		v. Cambridge University (Cambridge) 10–12 June		v. Kent (Tunbridge Wells) 13–16 June	
G. D. Mendis	31	79*	5	44	14	22	46	—			55	80
J. R. T. Barclay	0	55	47	17	19	5	24	—	7	—	65	4
T. D. Booth-Jones	5	11	17	42	95	7	8	—	0	—	60	3
P. W. G. Parker	15	7*	4	39*	108	36	136	—	36	—	60*	3
Imran Khan	9	—	13	6*	74	24	23	—			45	11
C. M. Wells	10	—	5	—					79	—		
I. A. Greig	46	—	39	—	1	19	71	—	50	—	0	19
I. J. Gould	16	—	18	—	19*	23	1	—	0	—	—	28
G. S. Le Roux	49*	—	7	—	—	17*	10*	—			—	5
G. G. Arnold	46*	—	9	—	—	—	—	—			—	4*
C. E. Waller	—	—	12*	—	—	—	—	—	51*	—	—	0
C. P. Phillipson					15*	5	56*	—	22	—	0*	16
A. M. Green									21	—		
A. P. Wells									63	—		
A. N. Jones									1*	—		
J. R. Heath												
T. J. Head												
A. C. S. Pigott												
D. J. Smith												
Byes	2		1	1	2		12		9			1
Leg byes	11	6	2		7	5	10		2		5	4
Wides		3	2	1								
No balls	12	2	14	5	6	1			7		11	4
Total	252	163	195	155	360	164	397		348		301	182
Wickets	8	2	10	3	6	8	7		9		5	10
Result	D		W		D		W		W		L	
Points	3		21		6		24		—		7	

The match v. Middlesex (Lord's) 23–26 May was abandoned without a ball being bowled; and v. Gloucestershire (Bristol) 27–29 May.

v. Northamptonshire (Northampton) 17–19 June		v. Essex (Ilford) 20–23 June		v. Sri Lankans (Hastings) 27–30 June		v. Gloucestershire (Hove) 4–7 July		v. Somerset (Taunton) 11–14 July		v. Surrey (Hove) 15–17 July		v. Warwickshire (Hove) 18–21 July		v. Surrey (Guildford) 29–31 July	
30	33	119	—			78	95	25	12	5	—	12	32	14	2
107*	0	24	—	0	0*	41	6	13	4	15	—	26	23	14	3
—	6	2	—	25	7	41	19	0	75	16	—	17	9	43	0
37	53*	132	—	14	15	30	50*	19	105*	58	—	45	50	21	17
18	15*	98*	—	14	47	38	—	1	12*	19	—	5	25*	92	3
10	—	37*	—	1	—	11	3*	0	19	78*	—	34	7	32	0
4	—	—	—			0	—	25	—	52	—	18	—	8	13
9	—	—	—					65*	—	11	—	20	—	15	10
13*	—	—	—			18*	—	13	—	2	—	0	—	25	11
—	—	—	—	21	—	7	—	22	—	14	—	0*	—	0*	13
8	—	0*	—	17	2	11	—	30	—	5	—	19	2*	17	39*
				36	38										
				4*	—	4	—								
				5	101*										
				14	7										
5	2	7		5		9	11	2	8	4			4	4	6
8	2	9		4	8	12	10	6	6	6		3	9	11	5
		5			2		1	1		2			1	1	1
1		3		1	1	4	2	11	1	2		9	7	5	4
250	111	436		161	228	304	197	233	242	289		208	169	302	127
7	3	4		10	6	10	3	10	4	10		10	5	10	10
D		W		W		D		W		D		W		L	
3		24		—		7		22		6		22		8	

Sussex C.C.C.
Batting, cont.

	v. Leicestershire (Leicester) 1–4 August		v. Kent (Eastbourne) 8–11 August		v. Derbyshire (Eastbourne) 12–14 August		v. Nottinghamshire (Trent Bridge) 15–18 August		v. Australians (Hove) 22–24 August		v. Hampshire (Bournemouth) 26–28 August	
G. D. Mendis	34	137	61	—	17	1	65	0	18	19	12	51
J. R. T. Barclay	101	5	79	—	37*	—	5	4			0	38
T. D. Booth-Jones	19	4	6	4								
P. W. G. Parker	29	16	0	9*	82*	41	37	6	2	14		
Imran Khan	0	13	12	—	2	107*	14	11			100	—
C. M. Wells					11	1	1	4	2	0	32	20*
I. A. Greig	34	11	86	0	0	5	20	43	43	28	16	—
I. J. Gould	4	25	26	36*	38	29	5	42			35*	—
G. S. Le Roux	7*	9	2	—	40	—	18*	23			1	—
G. G. Arnold	—	9	4*	—	2*	—	20	0			0	—
C. E. Waller	—	1*	—	—	—	—	1	4*			2	—
C. P. Phillipson	8*	19	14	—	0	39*	13	6	36*	29	13	—
A. M. Green									12	0		
A. P. Wells												
A. N. Jones									8	0		
J. R. Heath									2	56	9	14*
T. J. Head									0	52*		
A. C. S. Pigott									7	39		
D. J. Smith									2	1		
Byes	5	2	1						1	8		
Leg byes	3	9	10	1	2	3	7	1		5	9	9
Wides			1			1				1		1
No balls	6		8	1	19	8	2		17	9	8	2
Total	250	260	310	51	250	235	208	144	150	261	237	135
Wickets	7	10	9	2	7	5	10	10	10	10	10	2
Result	L		W		W		D		L		W	
Points	4		24		23		6		—		22	

Catches

63 – I. J. Gould (ct 59, st 4)
28 – J. R. T. Barclay
27 – C. P. Phillipson
20 – P. W. G. Parker
13 – I. A. Greig
11 – C. E. Waller
8 – G. G. Arnold
7 – Imran Khan
6 – T. D. Booth-Jones, T. J. Head, G. S. Le Roux and G. D. Mendis
4 – C. M. Wells
2 – J. R. Heath and Substitutes
1 – A. M. Green, A. P. Wells, A. N. Jones and A. C. S. Pigott

v. Middlesex (Hove) 29 August–1 September		v. Hampshire (Hove) 2–4 September		v. Yorkshire (Hove) 12–15 September			Inns	NOs	Runs	HS	Av
31	34*	58	15*	45	26		38	3	1457	137	41.62
17	24*	9	1	—	33		37	4	872	107*	26.42
		0	—	10	12*		27	—	541	95	20.03
37	—	33	—	48*	—		37	9	1348	136	48.14
7	—	111	8*	80	30*		27	6	857	107*	40.80
24	—	118*	—	6	—		21	4	513	111	30.17
51	—	43	—	35	—		34	4	911	118*	30.36
9	—	13*	—	—	—		26	3	594	52	25.82
4*	—						20	7	340	65*	26.15
0	—	—	—	—	—		17	7	180	46*	18.00
27	—	5	—	12*	—		15	6	148	51*	16.44
							30	10	485	56*	24.25
							5	—	107	38	21.40
							1	—	63	63	63.00
				—	—		5	2	17	8	5.66
28	—						7	2	215	101*	43.00
							4	1	63	52*	21.00
		—	—				2	—	46	39	23.00
							2	—	3	2	1.50

v. Middlesex		v. Hampshire		v. Yorkshire	
		6		1	
10	1	13		9	1
	1	3			
7		4		4	
252	60	416	24	250	102
10	0	7	1	5	2
W		W		W	
23		24		23	

Sussex C.C.C. First-Class Matches – Bowling, 1980	G. G. Arnold	Imran Khan	G. S. Le Roux	I. A. Greig	J. R. T. Barclay	C. E. Waller
v. Worcestershire	21–4–59–0	14–2–27–0	7–3–13–0	6–1–16–0		
(Worcester) 6–8 May	4–0–17–0	14–4–33–1	12–3–28–2	2–0–12–0	13–5–28–0	12–4–24–1
v. Glamorgan	20–4–42–2	23.5–7–41–3	21–4–59–3	16–5–45–1	11–2–24–1	3–1–9–0
(Hove) 13–15 May	12.1–2–39–6	16–3–38–0	17–5–38–4			
v. Somerset	19.4–3–60–3	21–3–60–3	17–2–61–2	3–0–13–0	22–8–70–1	1–0–1–0
(Hove) 3–5 June	11–1–44–1	13–2–36–2	8–2–35–0		4–0–9–0	7–0–21–1
v. Lancashire	24–12–35–3	16.3–3–50–4	15–6–35–3			
(Hove) 6–9 June	9–3–17–1	17–1–75–1	16–3–54–2	17.3–7–21–6		5–0–31–0
v. Cambridge University				21–7–45–5	6.5–1–17–1	20–9–37–1
(Cambridge) 10–12 June				22.4–6–43–7	9–5–5–1	24–11–36–0
v. Kent	17–8–20–0	27–9–58–2	14.2–1–55–1	20–2–54–0	6–1–20–0	16–5–41–3
(Tunbridge Wells)	10–3–18–0	3–1–6–0	9–3–24–0		40–8–87–2	44–10–119–3
13–16 June						
v. Northamptonshire	19–3–61–1	14–4–39–0	14–0–89–0	9–2–34–0	5.4–0–22–0	13–3–43–1
(Northampton) 17–19 June	10–2–37–0	14–2–41–2	16–0–66–2	6.5–0–33–1	2–0–27–0	8–3–33–0
v. Essex	17–3–35–2		14–3–29–2		16.4–2–47–4	20–6–51–1
(Ilford) 20–23 June	12–5–21–0		6–1–26–1	5–1–13–1	30.4–6–90–4	31–10–86–4
v. Sri Lankans						11.5–4–11–2
(Hastings) 27–30 June					20.2–5–75–4	22–10–43–4
v. Gloucestershire	9–2–16–0			10–1–51–2	40–10–82–3	34.4–10–94–5
(Hove) 4–7 July	12–4–24–0			8–1–23–2	17–4–45–3	21–6–56–2
v. Somerset	11.5–3–30–4		6–0–39–2	7–1–33–4		
(Taunton) 11–14 July	34–8–104–0		33.2–10–107–8	22–3–85–1	5–2–12–0	11–2–28–0
v. Surrey	10–3–17–0	15–5–33–1	22–7–57–3	14–4–41–4	3.4–1–4–1	4–0–13–0
(Hove) 15–17 July	5–1–12–0	10–0–36–0	9–3–16–2	1–0–8–0	10.1–4–11–0	6–4–2–1
v. Warwickshire	19.5–5–52–3	11–3–26–2	22–4–71–1	18–3–55–1	16–8–15–2	11–5–14–0
(Hove) 18–21 July		14–1–55–2	16–3–36–6	8–2–29–1		
v. Surrey	9–5–17–0	16–2–57–0	17.2–4–48–4	18–2–55–4	20–5–70–0	20–4–42–2
(Guildford) 29–31 July	11–3–34–2	14–2–46–1	5–1–10–0			7.3–2–18–2
v. Leicestershire	27–8–76–2	25–10–66–0	31–8–83–5	15–1–58–1	2–0–8–0	18–6–47–0
(Leicester) 1–4 August	5–2–9–0	10–5–15–1	7–3–16–0	4–1–12–0	11–1–37–1	17–3–61–1
v. Kent	17–5–26–4	15.5–5–33–2	15–6–15–1	7–3–15–3		
(Eastbourne) 8–11 August	19–3–60–0	22–6–51–4	20.5–4–68–3	15–6–46–2		7–4–16–0
v. Derbyshire	21.2–6–44–3	19–4–55–1	18–3–47–1	22–3–75–4		6–1–13–0
(Eastbourne) 12–14 August	12–4–16–0	17.1–5–52–5	9–2–21–1	5–1–20–0		26–8–46–1
v. Nottinghamshire	2–1–2–0	7–1–11–1	3–1–8–1		18–4–41–3	19–5–36–5
(Trent Bridge) 15–18 August		27–9–53–3	13–5–18–3		23–3–56–3	29–5–83–0
v. Australians				22.3–2–76–4		
(Hove) 22–24 August				10–3–41–0		
v. Hampshire	9–2–28–1	17–4–50–4	8.2–3–22–2	16–4–34–3		1–0–1–0
(Bournemouth)	16–4–35–2	18.5–5–47–2	15–1–55–2	15–5–53–4	4–2–6–0	5–1–11–0
26–28 August						
v. Middlesex	2.2–0–14–0	15.4–2–41–4	16–5–32–3	14.4–2–45–3	1–1–0–0	8–3–18–0
(Hove)		22–6–52–6	20–6–30–3	18–4–31–0		11–4–31–1
29 August–1 September						
v. Hampshire		21–1–57–1	15–1–46–1	26.3–6–75–6	8–3–11–0	4–0–12–0
(Hove) 2–4 September		16–2–58–2	16–6–46–3	18.2–5–57–4		1–0–5–0
v. Yorkshire		20.2–11–11–4	24–9–39–2	17–3–46–0	2–1–1–0	2–2–0–0
(Hove) 12–15 September		15–3–55–1	11–2–40–2	16–3–58–2		5.2–0–31–3
	458.1–122–1121–40 av. 28.02	565.1–133–1464–66 av. 22.18	559.1–133–1582–81 av. 19.53	477–100–1469–76 av. 19.32	374–93–936–34 av. 27.52	512.2–151–1264–44 av. 28.72

a G. D. Mendis 0.3–0–2–0
† M. D. Moxon and R. G. Lumb absent hurt

A. N. Jones	C. M. Wells	I. J. Gould	P. W. G. Parker	C. P. Phillipson	A. C. S. Pigott	Byes	Leg byes	Wides	No balls	Total	Wickets
						1	5	1	2	158	0
							3			145	4
						2	5		3	230	10
							2		2	119	10
							6		1	272	9
						1	4		2	152	5
						2	7		2	131	10
						1	2		3	204	10
11–2–31–2	9–1–18–1						5		12	165	10
6–1–11–1	10–3–36–1					7			5	143	10
							1		1	250	8
		3–1–2–0	3–3–0–0				7	1	6	270	5
						4	3		5	300	2
						4	3	4	4	252	6
							3	2	2	169	10
						3	4	1	2	246	10
17–2–71–3	17–5–48–4			2–0–15–0		2	5		6	158	10
5–1–9–2	6–1–15–0					1	3	1	2	149	10
5–0–23–0						12	6		1	285	10
							8		3	159	8
								1	1	104	10
						10	7	10	4	367	10
						1	4	1	4	175	10
						1			4	90	3
						2	4	2	8	249	10
						1	2	1	2	126	10
						11	5	2	4	311	10
							6	1	4	119	5
						1	4	5	10	358	8
							2		3	155	3
						6	7	2		104	10
							11	2		254	10
						6	8	2	6	256	10
	17–3–55–2					11	1	2	3	227	10
							2		2	102	10
							10		3	223	9
15–2–68–4	7–2–35–0				16–1–49–2	3	1	1	3	236	10
10–0–30–1	8–2–30–1		2–0–19–0		11–1–47–0	1	3		3	176	3 a
						5	3		5	148	10
						2	11	1	2	223	10
							2		2	154	10
						4	6	1	2	157	10
	2–1–1–0				7–1–25–1	4	6		4	241	10
					7–1–14–1	2	9		5	196	10
12–2–33–4						4	12	2	5	153	10
2–1–7–0						2		1	4	198	8 †
83–11– 283–17 av. 16.64	76–18– 238–9 av. 26.44	3–1– 2–0 —	5–3– 19–0 —	2–0– 15–0 —	41–4– 135–4 av. 33.75						

Warwickshire C.C.C.
First-Class Matches – Batting, 1981

	v. Yorkshire (Edgbaston) 6–8 May		v. Kent (Nuneaton) 13–15 May		v. Worcestershire (Edgbaston) 26 May		v. Northamptonshire (Edgbaston) 3–5 June		v. Derbyshire (Derby) 6–9 June		v. Lancashire (Old Trafford) 10–12 June	
D. L. Amiss	53	—	43	32	11	—	38	17	109	127	28	40
K. D. Smith	34	—	17	—	16	—	14	2	16	4	56	56
T. A. Lloyd	3	—	24	48	37	—	30	42	0	42	31	2
G. W. Humpage	11	—	58	36	42	—					19*	81*
A. I. Kallicharran	30	—	35	135	9	—	13	59	30	12	0*	2
Asif Din	14	—	22	43	8	—	9	26	15	43	—	23*
D. C. Hopkins	17	—										
C. Lethbridge	69	—										
R. G. D. Willis	12	—	—	6*	16*	—						
W. Hogg	0	—	—	—	9	—	5	0	16	7	—	—
D. R. Doshi	1*	—			4*	—	3	—	0*	1*	—	—
A. M. Ferreira			0	9								
G. C. Small			3*	5*	9	—	17	15	19	0		
S. P. Perryman			—	—			1*	12*	1	2	—	—
C. Maynard							70	0	22	0		
S. J. Rouse							22	55*	1	10	—	—
G. P. Thomas												
S. H. Wootton												
R. I. H. B. Dyer												
P. R. Oliver												
S. P. Sutcliffe												
D. M. Smith												
Byes			1		2		3					5
Leg byes	7		11	7	8		7	5	4	5	1	7
Wides					4		2					
No balls	9		3	4	3		3		14	17		2
Total	260		217	325	185		237	233	247	270	135	218
Wickets	10		7	6	9		10	8	10	10	3	4
Result	D		W		L		D		D		D	
Points	5		20		0		5		4		3	

The match v. Oxford University (Oxford) 27–29 May was abandoned.

† K. D. Smith retired hurt.

A. Innings forfeited.

v. Glamorgan (Cardiff) 17–19 June		v. Sri Lanka (Edgbaston) 20–23 June		v. Gloucestershire (Gloucester) 27–30 June		v. Essex (Edgbaston) 4–7 July		v. Surrey (The Oval) 11–14 July		v. Leicestershire (Coventry) 15–17 July		v. Sussex (Hove) 18–21 July		v. Yorkshire (Scarborough) 29–31 July	
103	0			22	18	47	38	110	29	27	31	1	58	32	0
9	1*														
11	14	15	39	78	0	94	18	16	0	11	7	89	7	7	24
32	20	73	—	146	110	17	119*	126	16	19	13	8	9	27	49
0	0	121*	29*												
17	0	5	70*	5	43	30	73*	17	5	24	7	57	9	28	16
34	10	0	—												
				—	6										
11	11	—	—	—	11*	3	—	—	—	26	0	1*	0*	3	3
4	4	—	—	—	—	—	—	—	—	3*	0	5	4	2*	0*
				3*	19	45*	—	0*	27	0	21	36	21	35	39
0	0	19	—	—	0	1	—	—	0*	2	15	12	0	13	5
11*	16*	2*	—			4*	—	—	6*	4	1*	11	5	0	12
		9	40	43	6	11	41	14	8*					3	52
		13	77	16	26*	15	—	4*	0	3	44	6	0		
										9	0	7	7		
														122	67
3	7		10	3	9	1	1	1		5	9	2	1		1
3	1	11	2	6	9	12	4	10	10	1	10	4	2	6	8
1	8	5		1		1		2	2		2	2	1	1	1
8	8	1	1	2		8	2		1†	2		8	2	9	19
247	100	274	268	325	257	289	296	300	104	136	160	249	126	288	296
10	9†	7	3	6	8	8	3	5	6	10	10	10	10	10	10
	L		D		D		L		D		L		L		D
	4		—		7		6		5		2		6		4

Warwickshire C.C.C.
Batting, *cont.*

	v. Northamptonshire (Northampton) 1–4 August		v. Middlesex (Lord's) 8–11 August		v. Glamorgan (Edgbaston) 12–14 August		v. Lancashire (Edgbaston) 15–18 August		v. Nottinghamshire (Edgbaston) 22–25 August		v. Worcestershire (Worcester) 29 August–1 September	
D. L. Amiss	14	4	20	53	132	4	4	32	83	1	145	24
K. D. Smith			58*	33	30	93	39	3	4	3	0	20
T. A. Lloyd	24	38	5	10	100*	4	74	0	32	1	29	120
G. W. Humpage	0	28	7	5	26*	102	31	15	65	6	8	111
A. I. Kallicharran							91*	21			82*	16*
Asif Din	25	37	0	13	—	54	31	17*	0	1		
D. C. Hopkins												
C. Lethbridge											0	—
R. G. D. Willis			11	11					33*	11		
W. Hogg	5	20	0	4	—	2	—	—	2	4	—	—
D. R. Doshi	1*	3*	35	0*	—	15			12*	1*		
A. M. Ferreira	67	24	0	32	—	1	—	—	40	1	9*	—
G. C. Small	15	4			—	15	—	—	1	3	—	—
S. P. Perryman	8	1	0	0	—	1*	—	—				
C. Maynard												
S. J. Rouse												
G. P. Thomas	15	21										
S. H. Wootton												
R. I. H. B. Dyer												
P. R. Oliver	9	171*	1	25	—	42	5*	27*	34	14	11	—
S. P. Sutcliffe											—	—
D. M. Smith												
Byes	2	1	10	2	6		1		9		9	4
Leg byes	6		4	5	4	10	12	2	12	2	6	2
Wides		1	1			1	6	1		1	1	
No balls	10	12	2	3	17	4	7	7	4			
Total	201	365	154	196	315	348	301	125	331	49	300	297
Wickets	10	9	10	10	2	10	5	5	9	10	6	4
Result	W		L		L		D		L		L	
Points	22		5		6		7		8		4	

Catches

46 – G. W. Humpage (ct 36, st 10)

13 – D. L. Amiss

11 – Asif Din

10 – T. A. Lloyd

8 – G. C. Small

7 – A. I. Kallicharran

6 – G. P. Thomas (ct 5, st 1) and C. Maynard (ct 5, st 1)

5 – S. P. Perryman

4 – K. D. Smith, A. M. Ferreira, D. R. Doshi and S. H. Wootton

3 – C. Lethbridge

2 – R. I. H. B. Dyer, W. Hogg, P. R. Oliver and Substitutes

1 – D. M. Smith, R. G. D. Willis, D. C. Hopkins and S. J. Rouse

v. Somerset (Edgbaston) 2–4 September		v. Hampshire (Edgbaston) 9–11 September		v. Somerset (Taunton) 12–15 September		Inns	NOs	Runs	HS	Av
42	17	46	56	31	—	41	—	1722	145	42.00
4	51	0	22	29	—	26	2	614	93	25.58
51	138	45	39	46	—	43	1	1445	138	34.40
59	12	36	50	65	—	38	4	1657	146	48.73
19	1	45	54	119	—	23	6	923	135	54.29
		45	9	37	—	37	4	878	73*	26.60
						1	—	17	17	17.00
1	7*	0	18	—	—	10	1	146	69	16.22
						8	3	106	33*	21.20
5	2	31	12			27	3	193	31	8.04
0	0					22	12	98	35	9.80
		67*	54	35*	—	24	6	585	67*	32.50
21*	4			—	—	26	4	198	21*	9.00
						20	9	98	16*	8.16
						4	—	92	70	23.00
						4	1	88	55*	29.33
						12	1	263	52	23.90
						11	2	204	77	22.66
						4	—	23	9	5.75
8	18					14	3	554	171*	50.36
4	0	0	1*	—	—	4	1	5	4	1.25
		16*	5			2	1	21	16*	21.00
6		1	11	1						
4	3	12	2	7						
		1	1	2						
1			1	5						
225	253	345	335	376	A.					
10	10	9	10	6						
	L		D		L					
	4		4		4					

Warwickshire C.C.C. First-Class Matches – Bowling, 1981	R. G. D. Willis	W. Hogg	S. P. Sutcliffe	C. Lethbridge	D. R. Doshi	Asif Din
v. Yorkshire (Edgbaston) 6–8 May	28–8–60–5	25–4–102–2 5–2–5–0		17–3–77–1	31.4–11–72–1 10–3–29–0	2–0–11–1 13–3–40–0
v. Kent (Nuneaton) 13–15 May	13–3–36–0	13–4–42–0 14–3–55–0				2–0–21–0
v. Worcestershire (Edgbaston) 26 May	9–1–35–1	10–0–22–2		3–0–14–0	9.2–1–54–1	1–0–4–0
v. Northamptonshire (Edgbaston) 3–5 June		20–7–44–0			27–12–72–0	
v. Derbyshire (Derby) 6–9 June		19–4–46–0 6–2–12–0			26–7–53–1 4–0–22–1	
v. Lancashire (Old Trafford) 10–12 June	27–4–58–3	22–7–57–0			23–5–85–3 17–0–61–1	
v. Glamorgan (Cardiff) 17–19 June		23–7–47–3		19–1–78–1	35.1–9–78–3	
v. Sri Lanka (Edgbaston) 20–23 June		14–2–60–0 5–0–40–0		8–1–41–0	28–8–64–2 6–2–20–1	1–1–0–0
v. Gloucestershire (Gloucester) 27–30 June	13.2–2–40–1 14–3–32–2	14–4–50–2 8–1–22–0			25–5–74–1 17–8–34–0	4–1–9–0
v. Essex (Edgbaston) 4–7 July		20–5–71–3 10–1–62–1			17–5–34–0 18–2–82–1	
v. Surrey (The Oval) 11–14 July		15.5–3–47–0 18–2–69–1			26–5–62–0 25–9–67–1	1–0–5–0
v. Leicestershire (Coventry) 15–17 July		16–3–59–2			47.1–19–90–4	1–0–1–0
v. Sussex (Hove) 18–21 July		16–3–54–4 15–4–49–1			6.2–3–7–3 12.5–6–40–1	1–0–4–0
v. Yorkshire (Scarborough) 29–31 July		22–4–85–1			37–15–73–5	
v. Northamptonshire (Northampton) 1–4 August		18.4–5–46–4 17–1–65–4			7–0–31–0 21–2–83–1	9–0–52–1
v. Middlesex (Lord's) 8–11 August	15–7–26–1 8–0–25–0	12.5–3–50–4			40–5–97–4 25–3–83–1	2–0–11–0 1–0–7–0
v. Glamorgan (Edgbaston) 12–14 August		15–3–57–3 7–0–21–0			18–2–86–1 29–0–132–2	7–1–45–0 1–0–28–0
v. Lancashire (Edgbaston) 15–18 August		27–8–56–4 19–1–92–4				8–1–45–1
v. Nottinghamshire (Edgbaston) 22–25 August	7–1–26–0 4.1–0–32–0	9–1–34–1 1–0–17–0			26.3–6–94–4 1–0–17–0	
v. Worcestershire (Worcester) 29 August–1 September		10–0–58–0 12–0–66–1	22.4–1–67–1 11–0–78–0	7–0–34–0 10–0–53–1		
v. Somerset (Edgbaston) 2–4 September		14–3–40–2 11–2–35–1	32–7–72–2 21.3–4–68–2	11–2–26–2 1–0–4–0	27.3–6–68–0 26–4–86–2	
v. Hampshire (Edgbaston) 9–11 September		16–3–57–0	16.3–5–51–0 13–0–75–1	12–2–70–1 10–2–50–1		2–0–9–0 12–1–68–1
v. Somerset (Taunton) 12–15 September			7.4–0–74–0	15–1–54–0		2–1–11–1
	138.3–29– 370–13– av. 28.46	520.2–102– 1794–50– av. 35.88	124.2–17– 485–6– av. 80.83	113–12– 501–7– av. 71·57	669.3–163– 1950–45– av. 43.33	70–9– 371–5– av. 74.20

a D. C. Hopkins 10–1–33–0; 3–1–2–0   b S. H. Wootton 1–0–7–0   c D. M. Smith 12–3–43–0; 11–0–55–1

A. I. Kallicharran	T. A. Lloyd	A. M. Ferreira	G. C. Small	S. P. Perryman	S. J. Rouse	Byes	Leg byes	Wides	No balls	Total	Wickets
						1	8	2	30	396	10 a
8–2–14–1	3–0–14–0						5		3	112	1
1–0–1–0		22–6–81–3	19–3–57–2	21–5–60–1			10	1	14	323	6
4–0–18–0		14–2–70–0	12–2–39–1	7.4–0–33–1			1		2	218	2
2–1–13–0			7–2–31–0			1	10	1	2	187	4
			19–4–68–3	19–6–75–2	14.3–4–46–2	1	9	3	7	325	7
	1–0–1–0		13.2–2–51–0	24–8–60–4	14–1–59–0	2	10	1	17	300	5
			4.4–0–26–0	5–0–28–0	1–0–11–0		6	2	2	109	1
				21–5–78–2	12–2–53–0	1	9	1	10	352	9
16–0–63–1					1–1–0–0					124	2
	1–0–14–0		27–3–86–1	22–4–49–1		12	18		26	408	10
			17–1–98–3	14–4–52–5		8	6	1	5	335	10
			5–1–16–0	5–0–13–1					2	91	2
		8–0–43–0	20–4–70–4			5	7	2	10	301	8
		10–1–31–2	9–0–47–2			8	1	3	4	198	6 b
		23.4–7–68–2	18–2–54–1	17–6–51–1		2	14		1	8	303	7
	1–0–1–0	8–1–42–0	7–1–44–0	7–0–34–0		5	9	1	3	283	2
		20–5–59–2	15–4–57–1	14–3–46–1		1	13	3	7	300	4
		10–3–24–1	24–4–76–6			6	15	3	4	264	9
		31–6–65–1	21–2–77–1	12–2–39–1		2	13		11	357	9
		18–4–39–0	13–0–57–2	12–1–35–1			3		9	208	10
		7–2–26–1	8–1–33–2			4	9	1	7	169	5
		38–13–92–3	12–2–54–1	19–4–57–0			19	1	3	384	10
		16–3–58–2	13–4–42–3	8–0–33–1			10	2	1	223	10
		8–0–46–0	5–0–44–0	6–0–40–0		2	6		4	342	6
	10–2–27–0	8–1–31–0		9–1–28–0		5	9			284	10
	3–0–11–0	2–1–1–1		16–7–47–0		6	1		3	184	2
		21–2–65–1	17–0–78–0	14–2–54–1		1	12	11		409	6
		14.5–3–52–1	6–2–21–0	5–0–23–1		5	1		6	289	4
4–1–17–0		29–5–86–2	20.5–3–76–4	22.5–5–61–0			19	5	6	326	10
	5–0–38–0	13–2–74–0	6–1–18–0	3–1–17–0		4	7	1	3	299	5
		28–4–121–3	4–1–16–0				3		9	303	9
			2–0–10–1			1			2	79	2
		10–1–35–1	11–1–46–0			5	3		3	251	2
0.5–0–7–0		14–2–86–1	7–0–42–1			3	5	2	5	347	4
			14–2–72–0				9		13	300	6
			4–0–12–0			4	8		3	220	5
		24–8–61–0					2		7	300	1 c
		18–0–73–4				1	6		6	334	8
											*
		21–1–113–1	15–0–72–3	3–0–33–0			11	2	8	378	6
35.5–4–	24–2–	436.3–83–	395.5–52–	305.4–64–	42.3–8–						
133–2–	106–0–	1542–32–	1590–42–	1046–24–	169–2–						
av. 66.50	—	av. 48.18	av. 37.85	av. 43.58	av. 84.50						

*Innings forfeited.

Worcestershire C.C.C.
First-Class Matches – Batting, 1981

	v. Sussex (Worcester) 6–8 May		v. Cambridge University (Cambridge) 13–15 May		v. Warwickshire (Edgbaston) 26 May		v. Lancashire (Worcester) 29 May		v. Glamorgan (Hereford) 3–5 June		v. Essex (Worcester) 6–9 June	
J. A. Ormrod	45*	19	100*	—					6	25	84*	—
G. M. Turner	104*	38	—	—	2	—	0	—	18	7	26	101
P. A. Neale	—	31*	24	—	9	—	13	—	16	0	9	19
E. J. O. Hemsley	—	3	9	—	37	—	1	—	18	21	9	27*
Younis Ahmed	—	44	18	—	106*	—	83*	—	80	74	18	65
S. P. Henderson	—	7*					6	—				
J. Birkenshaw	—	—	0	—	—	—	4	—	18	2		
N. Gifford	—	—			—	—	—	—	16*	6	21	—
P. B. Fisher	—	—					—	—			0	—
J. D. Inchmore	—	—	—	—	—	—	63*	—			12	40*
A. P. Pridgeon	—	—			—	—	—	—	7	6*	13*	—
D. J. Humphries			64*	—	17*	—			19	2		
J. Cumbes			—	—					0	0*		
D. N. Patel					2	—			6	29	19	7
H. L. Alleyne					—	—	—	—			0	—
M. S. Scott												
M. J. Weston												
T. S. Curtis												
W. R. K. Thomas												
A. J. Webster												
Byes	1		2		1		4		5	3	1	
Leg byes	5	3	6		10		5		11	8	5	13
Wides	1		1		1		4		1		1	1
No balls	2		1		2				8		3	3
Total	158	145	225		187		183		229	183	221	276
Wickets	0	4	4		4		5		10	9	9†	4
Result	D		D		W		L		D		W	
Points	4		—		12		0		5		19	

† J. A. Ormrod retired hurt.
‡ N. Gifford absent ill.
A. E. J. O. Hemsley absent injured.

v. Surrey (The Oval) 10–12 June		v. Hampshire (Worcester) 13–16 June		v. Somerset (Worcester) 20–23 June		v. Yorkshire (Worcester) 27–30 June		v. Sri Lankans (Worcester) 1–3 July		v. Derbyshire (Chesterfield) 4–7 July		v. Nottinghamshire (Trent Bridge) 11–14 July		v. Gloucestershire (Bristol) 15–17 July	
21	73	9	28	47	—	168	11	45	13	40	67	51	0	43	57
0	12*	14	43	101	—	102	65			7	52	15	10	38	29
5	—	7	0	4*	—	4*	19			22	0	6	—		
116	24*	0	33	87	—	9*	5			32	107	32	80	83*	46*
								37	3					1	—
						—	12	34	—	1	8				
17	—	1	18			—	8*			37*	—	2	29*		
28*	—	0	6					19*	7*			5	41		
		22	0					1	—			0*	4		
3	—	0	1*							—	2*	5	61		
				42	—	—	27			15	7			3*	17*
4	—			—	—			10	—			4	34		
13	—	34	6	105*	—	—	26*	47	72	100*	3	2	4	4	9
10	—	0*	1	0	—	—	—			—	0				
46	52	20	50	21	—	12	68	41	73	27	21	4	0	109	24
								9	22						
								8	5						
								44	13*						
2		5	6	6			18	4	3	9	6		4	11	1
4	5	2		8		8	9	1	14	9	1	4	9	14	3
1		1		2				1					2	8	
3	2	1		10			3			8	1	2	4	2	
273	168	115	194	431		303	271	301	225	307	275	132	282	316	186
10	2	10	10	6		3	7	10	6	7	9‡	10	9A.	5	4
L		L		D		W		D		L		L		D	
7		4		8		22		—		6		2		7	

Worcestershire C.C.C.
Batting, cont.

	v. Middlesex (Lord's) 18–21 July		v. Australians (Worcester) 25–27 July		v. Northamptonshire (Stourbridge) 29–31 July		v. Lancashire (Old Trafford) 1–4 August		v. Nottinghamshire (Worcester) 8–11 August		v. Somerset (Weston-super-Mare) 12–14 August	
J. A. Ormrod	61	19*			161	101	16	33	10	0	1	20
G. M. Turner	28	37*	28	145*	125	38	43	15	16	1	7	2
E. J. O. Hemsley					2	22*	26	45			46	20
Younis Ahmed	35	0	36	14			23	17	17	47	9	60
S. P. Henderson	9	16	4	0								
J. Birkenshaw			32	54	—	—						
N. Gifford	22	—	11*	5*	—	—	3*	1	6	0	8	31
P. B. Fisher			3	11								
J. D. Inchmore	29	—			—	14	5	10	41	0	18	26
A. P. Pridgeon	0*	—	9	1	—	—	0	20*	12	7	2*	1*
D. J. Humphries	58	—			0*	20	9	0	15	41	53	1
J. Cumbes			2	5*								
D. N. Patel	36	15	28	39	21	87	8	15	15	8	30	10
H. L. Alleyne	1	—							5*	1*	3	16
M. S. Scott	59	15	3	29	43	10	1	2	0	8	8	2
M. J. Weston			2	11								
T. S. Curtis					6*	—	4	11	0	4		
W. R. K. Thomas												
A. J. Webster												
Byes			10	5		5			5		4	8		3
Leg byes	2		4	10	7	7		1	5	4	2	5
Wides	3				1	4						
No balls	2	1	17	15	10	9				3	1	1
Total	345	103	189	344	376	317	138	175	146	132	188	198
Wickets	10	4	10	8	5	6	10	10	10	10	10	10
Result	D		L		D		L		L		L	
Points	8		—		6		2		4		5	

Catches
43 – D. J. Humphries (ct 29, st 14)
21 – G. M. Turner
12 – Younis Ahmed
11 – E. J. O. Hemsley
10 – J. Birkenshaw and D. N. Patel
9 – P. A. Neale
8 – M. S. Scott and A. P. Pridgeon
5 – N. Gifford and P. B. Fisher
3 – M. J. Weston and J. D. Inchmore
2 – J. Cumbes and H. L. Alleyne
1 – J. A. Ormrod and Substitutes

†A late official correction from Worcestershire has amended A. P. Pridgeon's total to 34 and J. Cumbes' to 15 not out.

v. Leicestershire (Leicester) 15–18 August		v. Gloucestershire (Worcester) 22–25 August		v. Glamorgan (Swansea) 26–28 August		v. Warwickshire (Worcester) 29 August–1 September		v. Kent (Canterbury) 12–15 September		Inns	NOs	Runs	HS	Av
										6	3	279	100*	93.00
56	11	47	111	23	130*	147*	139	—	46	42	4	2101	168	55.28
13	2	2	66*	20	2	48	0		16	41	5	1247	145*	34.63
73	0	7	—	45	8	—	38*	—	16	30	5	540	73	21.60
4	83*	42	15	0	46			16*	31	39	8	1637	116	52.80
										9	1	83	37	10.37
										10	—	165	54	16.50
22	—	3	—	14	—	—	—	—	3*	23	8	284	37*	18.93
										8	3	74	28*	14.80
19	—	37	19	1	—			—	25	21	2	428	63*	22.52
0	—	4*	—	†34	—	—	—	—	0*	22	11	122	20*	11.09
46	—	14	4	5	8*	—	5*	—	17	28	7	575	64*	27.30
0*	—	14	—	†15*	—	—	—			9	4	54	19*	10.80
10	43	9	28	22	43	24*	138	3	3	40	4	1155	138	32.08
										13	3	43	16	4.30
18	17*	54	25	29	13	21	12	6	25	37	1	968	109	26.88
						—	—	7*	2	6	1	53	22	10.60
						—	—			7	1	38	11	6.33
										2	1	57	44	57.00
								—	6	1	—	6	6	6.00
2	7		1	13	10	5	3		3					
4	3	16	7	7	6	3	5		3					
	4	1		1	2		2	2	1					
1	5	1	1	8	7	3	5	4	8					
268	175	251	277	237	275	251	347	38	186					
10	4	10	6	10	5	2	4	2	9					
D		L		W		W		D						
3		6		20		21		1						

Worcestershire C.C.C. First-class Matches – Bowling, 1981	J. D. Inchmore	A. P. Pridgeon	Younis Ahmed	N. Gifford	J. Birkenshaw	P. A. Neale
v. Sussex	25–8–65–4	26–5–64–1	8–2–21–0	26–9–41–2	15–4–36–1	
(Worcester) 6–8 May	7–1–29–0	6–0–15–0	4–0–31–0	9–4–20–1	9–0–42–0	4–0–15–0
v. Cambridge University	14–4–37–0	11–4–17–0		29–6–65–1	24–4–54–1	
(Cambridge) 13–15 May	4–2–5–0	8–1–17–0	7–3–12–1	24–9–51–0	15–5–29–1	11.1–0–53–0
v. Warwickshire	10–1–39–2	10–1–38–3	10–0–36–1	10–1–28–1		
(Edgbaston) 26 May						
v. Lancashire	6–1–26–0	10–1–42–1		4–0–13–0	4.5–0–40–0	
(Worcester) 29 May						
v. Glamorgan		18.4–3–46–3		32–12–70–3	17–6–32–0	
(Hereford) 3–5 June		15–5–38–1		29–8–63–3	14–7–15–0	
v. Essex	17–3–60–0	22–7–72–2		19–5–46–1		
(Worcester) 6–9 June	8–1–26–1	13.4–2–42–0		9.2–0–26–1		
v. Surrey		22.3–6–49–4		6–1–21–2		
(The Oval) 10–12 June		12–0–61–0		16.4–1–83–3		
v. Hampshire	19–2–83–3	23–1–75–1		22.3–6–60–2		
(Worcester) 13–16 June						
v. Somerset		22–5–69–3		31–17–37–2		
(Worcester) 20–23 June		12–1–44–0	4–0–12–0	46–12–93–2		
v. Yorkshire		23–5–56–1	4–1–5–0	32–4–98–2	8–2–24–1	
(Worcester) 27–30 June		12–3–27–3		37–10–82–4	11–2–41–1	
v. Sri Lankans	20–4–57–1				26–4–67–1	
(Worcester) 1–3 July						
v. Derbyshire		25.5–4–63–5	18–2–42–1	37–8–61–2		
(Chesterfield) 4–7 July		19–5–41–1		1–1–0–0	26–2–131–3	4–0–34–0
v. Nottinghamshire	24–3–81–1	37–5–82–4		25.4–3–74–2		
(Trent Bridge) 11–14 July				5.3–2–9–0		
v. Gloucestershire	17–2–60–3	20–5–48–2		31–7–84–2		
(Bristol) 15–17 July	6–2–13–2	7–2–20–0				
v. Middlesex	11–0–32–2	10–3–30–0				
(Lord's) 18–21 July	28–4–101–1	25.3–0–120–0		31–5–112–1		
v. Australians		17–5–30–2		23–5–59–0	17–2–52–1	
(Worcester) 25–27 July		4–0–25–0		13–0–86–2	3–0–28–0	
v. Northamptonshire	13–0–66–0	16–2–55–0		41–9–129–3	6–0–40–1	
(Stourbridge) 29–31 July	5–1–15–0	9–3–26–2		35–15–75–2	7–2–13–0	
v. Lancashire	15–2–46–1	21–5–46–2	5–1–15–0	40–12–96–0		
(Old Trafford) 1–4 August						
v. Nottinghamshire	6–1–17–1	11–4–15–2		27–6–64–4		
(Worcester) 8–11 August		7–0–20–0		27–8–54–1		
v. Somerset	20–2–85–5	31–4–91–3		15.4–6–31–1		
(Weston-super-Mare) 12–14 August	7–1–14–1	11–0–44–1				
v. Leicestershire	18–4–55–0	24–2–98–1		22–4–46–0		
(Leicester) 15–18 August	4–1–10–0	11–0–40–0	2–0–9–0	17–2–98–1		
v. Gloucestershire	21–7–52–0	19–5–54–3		31–15–56–2		
(Worcester) 22–25 August	6–1–25–0	7–0–45–0		20.5–1–95–1		
v. Glamorgan	19–4–42–2	26–4–74–2		24–6–72–1		
(Swansea) 26–28 August		4–2–11–0		35–13–67–6		
v. Warwickshire		28–6–93–2		11–2–26–0		
(Worcester) 29 August–1 September		7–1–13–0		29.5–11–78–1		
v. Kent	5–1–25–0	9–2–22–1		37.4–7–107–1		
(Canterbury) 12–15 September						
	355–63–	673.1–119–	62–9–	963.4–253–	202.5–40–	19.1–0–
	1166–30	1978–56	183–3	2476–63	644–11	102–0
	av. 38.86	*av.* 35.32	*av.* 61.00	*av.* 39.30	*av.* 58.54	—

a W. R. K. Thomas 17–4–54–0   b T. S. Curtis 4–2–13–1   c A. J. Webster 6–0–18–0   d Innings forfeited

J. Cumbes	E. J. O. Hemsley	H. L. Alleyne	D. N. Patel	M. S. Scott	M. J. Weston	Byes	Leg byes	Wides	No balls	Total	Wickets
						2	11		12	252	8
							6	3	2	163	2
22–5–69–5	5–0–24–0					6	5	1	3	281	7
15–6–18–1	7–0–32–0						3			220	4
		10–2–27–1				2	8	4	3	185	9
		12–1–49–1				1	7	2	5	185	3
29–14–39–1			18–8–28–3			1	17	1		234	10
15–5–34–1			13–5–26–3				4			180	8
		16–1–72–0	7.4–0–40–1				3		15	308	4
		11–3–35–2	12–1–46–0			2	3	3	4	187	4
9–0–40–1		17–5–46–2	1–0–5–0			1	1	7		170	10
4–1–10–0		18–4–64–3	6–0–31–0				13	3	9	274	6
		29–5–79–4	3–1–9–0			2	5	5	19	337	10
17.4–3–44–2		25–5–75–3	3–2–8–0			1	11		1	246	10
7–1–33–0		14–4–50–1	38–12–84–4	4–1–7–0		2	1	4	1	331	4
		22–7–57–2	17–0–69–1				9		1	319	7
		11–4–33–2	18–3–56–0			2	9	1		251	10
19–4–53–1		28.5–6–76–5			5–1–14–0	1	13	3	12	350	10 a
		13–3–31–0	19–3–40–0			2	5	1	3	248	10
		14–1–41–0	20–4–78–0			2	9		1	337	4
		27–5–84–2	9–1–32–1			12	17	1	19	402	10
			5–3–3–0			1				13	0
		17–4–40–1					16	1	2	251	8
		8–0–31–0	4–2–10–0			1	6	4	2	87	2
		14–1–43–8				1			2	108	10
		3.3–1–19–2	26–5–75–3			7	6		4	444	7
20.5–7–62–4			28–6–81–3			3	6			293	10
3–0–26–0			10–0–66–1		0.4–0–4–0		6			241	3
			18–4–57–2				9		3	359	6
			24–12–34–3			6	9	1	7	199	8 b
			49–11–118–5			10	12	4	11	358	8
		7–3–15–0	26–10–50–2				9			170	9
		5–0–25–1	26–1–111–1			1	2		1	214	4
		17–2–60–1				1	2		10	280	10
		14–2–43–3					3		3	107	5
29–3–91–1			3–0–19–0			6	5	1	1	322	2
17–6–38–3	2–0–21–0		6–2–21–0			8			3	248	4
22–8–55–3			6–2–14–0			3	15		1	250	8
			21–0–103–2				8	1	2	279	3
28–4–84–2			10–1–34–0			12	17	5	11	351	7
7–1–26–0			29–11–48–4			8				160	10
34–7–96–3			20–7–48–1		6–2–21–0	9	6	1		300	6
8–1–30–0			38–11–111–1	6–0–30–0	4–0–29–0	4	2			297	4
			33–3–118–0				3	1	7	301	3 c
											d
306.3–76–	14–0–	324.63–	595.3–137–	10–1–	15.4–3–						
848–28	77–0	1019–39	1749–43	47–0	68–0						
av. 30.28	—	av. 26.12	av. 40.67	—	—						

Yorkshire C.C.C.
First-Class Matches – Batting, 1981

	v. Oxford University (Oxford) 2–5 May		v. Warwickshire (Edgbaston) 6–8 May		v. Middlesex (Leeds) 13–15 May		v. Lancashire (Old Trafford) 23–26 May		v. Kent (Dartford) 27–29 May		v. Essex (Leeds) 3–5 June	
G. Boycott	51	—	24	51*	22	29	35	—	5	33		
R. G. Lumb	63	—					14	—	20	11*	0	53
C. W. J. Athey	1	—	25	39	72	11	3	—	14	0	0	57
J. H. Hampshire	10	—	64	—	21	46			29	17	39*	18
J. D. Love	0	—	161	—	0	6	154	—	53*	26		
P. Carrick	1	—	11	—	4	28	1	—	—	—	5	—
D. L. Bairstow	79*	—	17	—	16	2	49	—	16*	—	0	53*
A. Sidebottom	52*	—	0	—	34	10	15*	—			45	—
C. M. Old	—	—	23*	—	6	30*	28	—	—	—	16	—
J. P. Whiteley	—	—	10	—	0*	11			—	—	7	—
G. B. Stevenson	—	—	20	—	1	0	3	—	17	11	2	—
S. N. Hartley			0	14*	18	7	32	—			1	33*
M. Johnson							0*	—	—	0*		
M. D. Moxon											5	116
P. G. Ingham												
A. Ramage												
S. J. Dennis												
P. R. Hart												
K. Sharp												
S. J. Rhodes												
S. Stuchbury												
P. Jarvis												
Byes	5		1				1		4	9		4
Leg byes	4		8		9	1	9		5	5	8	18
Wides	2		2	5	1	1			1		1	5
No balls	10		30	3	3	1	4		1		1	5
Total	278		396	112	207	183	348		164	112	129	357
Wickets	6		10	1	10	10	9		5	5	10	4
Result	D		D		L		D		D		D	
Points	—		8		3		7		3		3	

† M. Johnson absent hurt.
‡ R. G. Lumb and M. D. Moxon absent hurt.

v. Gloucestershire (Bristol) 6–9 June		v. Nottinghamshire (Bradford) 13–16 June		v. Derbyshire (Sheffield) 17–19 June		v. Worcestershire (Worcester) 27–30 June		v. Leicestershire (Bradford) 1–3 July		v. Surrey (Harrogate) 4–7 July		v. Glamorgan (Cardiff) 15–17 July		v. Nottinghamshire (Trent Bridge) 18–21 July	
		18	124			8	3								
29	21	3	0	145	—	17	45	35	—						
0	6	6	19			64	4	20	6	6	2	12	43	22	34
21	12	16	42	24	—	94	15	112	1*	1	127	35	75*	0	82
		2	97	16	—	44	34	9	18	10	0	30	0	9	12
0	8	21	5	3	—	22*	2								
27*	16	0	6	19	—	12	73*	84	13*	32	33*	1	6	35	16
9	42	1	37*	8*	—			9	—						
1	1	3	15*	0	—	15*	55	13	—	11	38*				
7	10*	0	—	12*	—	—	7	0	—	18	—			1*	19*
						33	1	32	—			29	3	4	12
				7	—					10	63	18	0	2	106
9	8	·		111	—			22	40	22	10	22	4	6	23
15	11														
2	52	3*	—	4	—					32*	—	9	8	2	4
						—	0	2*	—	5	—	0*	1	4	4
										1	—	3	11	4	4
										4	41	7	18		
5	1			1	1		2	5	2	6	4	13	2		
5	5	1	4	12		9	9	8	9	3	4	6	7	6	21
				1								1	1		4
		4	4	12		1		7			2	2	3	6	9
130	193	78	355	374		319	251	358	89	157	283	185	205	104	364
10	10	10	7	9		7	10	10	3	10	5	10	10	10	10
L		D		D		L		W		W		L		L	
4		3		6		4		24		21		3		4	

Yorkshire C.C.C.
Batting, cont.

	v. Sri Lankans (Sheffield) 22-24 July		v. Warwickshire (Scarborough) 29-31 July		v. Somerset (Sheffield) 1-4 August		v. Hampshire (Middlesbrough) 8-11 August		v. Northamptonshire (Wellingborough) 15-18 August		v. Derbyshire (Chesterfield) 22-25 August	
G. Boycott	43	—					10	39			122*	—
R. G. Lumb									32	24	11	24
C. W. J. Athey	46	—	44	—	17	0	64*	8	123*	0	14	34
J. H. Hampshire							13	118*	2	2	84	8
J. D. Love	29	—	34	—	37	51	2	31*	3	6*	0	84*
P. Carrick	1*	—	27	—	0	7	20*	—	20	—		
D. L. Bairstow			62	—	19	70	71	—	2	—	4*	88*
A. Sidebottom									13	—		
C. M. Old	—	—					—	—			—	—
J. P. Whiteley	—	—	9*	—	7*	5			1	—		
G. B. Stevenson	—	—	44	—	14	17			0	—		57
S. N. Hartley	27	—	59	—	18	2	4	—	2	6*		
M. Johnson			0	—	2	—						
M. D. Moxon			29	—	25	2						
P. G. Ingham												
A. Ramage	—	—										
S. J. Dennis					1	5*	—	—				
P. R. Hart												
K. Sharp	116	—	51	—	28	15	5	8	3	79		
S. J. Rhodes	—	—										
S. Stuchbury			2	—								
P. Jarvis												
Byes					5			3	10		5	
Leg byes	7		19		7	11	11	1	17	6	7	1
Wides	2		1				5				1	
No balls	4		3						10	3	4	4
Total	275		384		180	185	205	208	238	126	252	300
Wickets	5		10		10	9†	6	3	10	4	4	4
Result	D		D		L		D		W		W	
Points	—		7		5		2		22		22	

Catches

49 – D. L. Bairstow (ct 43, st 6)

22 – C. W. J. Athey

17 – J. H. Hampshire and J. D. Love

9 – S. N. Hartley

8 – G. B. Stevenson, J. P. Whiteley and M. D. Moxon

6 – K. Sharp

4 – P. Carrick, G. Boycott and A. Sidebottom

2 – C. M. Old and Substitute

1 – R. G. Lumb, P. R. Hart and M. Johnson

v. Middlesex (Lord's) 26–28 August		v. Lancashire (Leeds) 29 August–1 September		v. Northamptonshire (Scarborough) 9–11 September		v. Sussex (Hove) 12–15 September		Inns	NOs	Runs	HS	Av
								16	2	617	124	44.07
27	56	2	14	12	9	39	—	25	1	706	145	29.41
30	15	4	26					38	2	891	123*	24.75
36	10	5	40	19	120	14	53	37	4	1425	127	43.18
66	8	1	7	57	0	21	43	38	4	1161	161	34.14
0	22	0	4	6	15	0	6	27	3	239	28	9.95
52*	0	15	0	62	7	12*	14	38	11	1083	88*	40.11
0	2	23	47	21	1	0	7	21	4	376	52*	22.11
				5	12			17	5	272	55	22.66
1*	8*	9	5	1*	16*			23	11	164	19*	13.66
0	6	33	0	10	0	2	4	27	—	355	57	13.44
33	0	53	26	44	4	19	46	29	3	654	106	25.15
								4	2	2	2	1.00
				31	32	1	—	19	—	518	116	27.26
						17	18	4	—	61	18	15.25
								9	2	116	52	16.57
								7	3	14	5*	3.50
								5	—	23	11	4.60
2	18							14	—	395	116	28.21
								—				—
		1*	4*					3	2	7	4*	7.00
						5	0*	2	1	5	5	2.50
	7			4	3	4	2					
6	8	3	7	14	16	12						
1			1			2	1					
10	7			1	1	5	4					
264	167	149	181	287	236	153	198					
9	10	10	10	10	10	10	8‡					
L		L		W		L						
6		4		23		3						

Yorkshire C.C.C. First-Class Matches – Bowling, 1981	C. M. Old	G. B. Stevenson	P. Carrick	J. P. Whiteley	A. Sidebottom	S. N. Hartley
v. Oxford University (Oxford) 2–5 May	4–3–4–1 7–0–24–0	5–1–11–2 11–6–16–2	15–6–20–2 12–4–25–0	19–4–50–4 18–3–28–3	4–1–14–0 7–3–18–1	
v. Warwickshire (Edgbaston) 6–8 May	21–8–68–2	21–5–68–2	6.1–3–7–1	9–7–24–1	17–5–35–2	9–1–31–1
v. Middlesex (Leeds) 13–15 May	24.2–8–48–1 24–8–52–5	20–4–67–0 17–1–70–3	12–2–48–0	9–1–32–0	18–2–70–2 4.2–1–13–1	11–3–27–1
v. Lancashire (Old Trafford) 23–26 May	20–6–52–3	22–8–78–4	29–11–64–1		6–1–25–0	9–3–26–0
v. Kent (Dartford) 27–29 May	23–11–33–2	19–3–57–2 5–0–12–0	10–1–60–1 21–2–76–4	20.4–5–76–2		
v. Essex (Leeds) 3–5 June	27–8–73–1	20–2–105–2	12–2–29–0	10–0–52–0	17.3–4–44–4	13–4–35–1
v. Gloucestershire (Bristol) 6–9 June	18.1–9–41–4 11–3–36–0		10–4–30–1 35–10–73–3	26–10–51–2	15–4–50–3 21–5–68–5	
v. Nottinghamshire (Bradford) 13–16 June	26–7–89–2		21–7–105–2	7–3–14–0	23–12–40–1	
v. Derbyshire (Sheffield) 17–19 June	19–10–26–1		49–13–88–1	33–6–95–3	14–7–29–2	13–1–62–1
v. Worcestershire (Worcester) 27–30 June	15–8–21–1 13–2–44–2	24–6–93–1 9.5–0–46–2	18.4–4–53–0 21–3–68–0	24–2–74–1 22–2–72–3		
v. Leicestershire (Bradford) 1–3 July	21–5–65–4 26–11–40–2	18–5–73–1 20.3–8–51–3		2–0–10–0 20–10–40–1	13–1–42–1	
v. Surrey (Harrogate) 4–7 July	12–3–34–3 33–7–92–3			1–0–2–0 6–3–9–0		
v. Glamorgan (Cardiff) 15–17 July		26–4–77–2 4–1–20–0				12–1–36–0
v. Nottinghamshire (Trent Bridge) 18–21 July		24–5–58–5 2–0–19–0		14–2–52–0		13–3–55–1 4–0–33–0
v. Warwickshire (Scarborough) 29–31 July		17–3–66–0 32–8–103–4	24–11–48–1 30–15–45–3	16–5–46–1 14–4–43–1		5–0–15–1
v. Somerset (Sheffield) 1–4 August		16–2–61–3 25–3–105–2	4–1–6–0 20–9–70–0	15–5–28–2 4.2–0–32–0		
v. Hampshire (Middlesbrough) 8–11 August	3–1–5–0	11–1–47–0 19–7–41–5	13–3–38–0 16–10–36–1			4–1–11–0 1–0–2–0
v. Northamptonshire (Wellingborough) 15–18 August		18–8–28–3 17–6–45–0	27–12–37–3 25.2–13–57–3	5–0–27–0 13–2–24–1	14–7–25–2 20–8–62–6	3–1–13–1
v. Derbyshire (Chesterfield) 22–25 August	19–2–63–0 5–0–12–0	23.2–5–96–1 9–4–23–1	17–2–79–3 14.5–2–58–1		26–4–110–2 4–1–8–1	4–0–29–0 4–1–25–0
v. Middlesex (Lord's) 26–28 August		22–5–76–2	22–6–56–1 10.2–4–9–1	34–4–90–2 12–6–20–2	24–6–66–4	7–2–20–1
v. Lancashire (Leeds) 29 August–1 September		23.4–6–56–1	10–4–28–0	13–2–64–4	23–6–70–2	7–1–27–0
v. Northamptonshire (Scarborough) 9–11 September	12–1–53–4 5–0–15–2	10–2–58–0 12.2–2–46–7	9–3–37–0 6–3–8–1	12–4–36–1 13–3–33–0	14–6–35–5 9–2–23–0	
v. Sussex (Hove) 12–15 September		12–0–84–1 2–1–1–0	11.5–1–54–1		12–2–52–3	5.1–0–32–1
	388.3–121– 990–43 *av. 23.02*	537.4–122– 1857–61 *av. 30.44*	532.1–171– 1412–35 *av. 40.34*	392–93– 1124–34 *av. 33.05*	305.5–88– 899–47 *av. 19.12*	124.1–22– 479–9 *av. 53.22*

† A. Hill retired hurt.
J. D. Love 12–4–31–0
J. H. Hampshire 5–0–22–1

M. D. Moxon 6–0–23–0
a D. L. Bairstow 3–1–7–0
b D. L. Bairstow 3–0–7–0

c S. Stuchbury 12–0–49–2; 15–3–45–1
d J. H. Hampshire 2–2–0–0
f S. Stuchbury 15–4–82–3

G. Boycott	M. Johnson	A. Ramage	C. W. J. Athey	S. J. Dennis	P. R. Hart	Byes	Leg byes	Wides	No balls	Total	Wickets
						3	12	1	5	120	10
						2	6		4	123	6
5–2–11–0							7		9	260	10
4–2–6–0						5	12	1	13	329	4
2–1–1–0							2		4	142	9
	13–3–51–0						9	1	4	310	8
	15–2–46–1					2	2			200	6
	4–0–23–0						4			191	6
						4	2	1	9	354	8
		10–2–43–2					6		2	172	10
		8–3–17–0	1–0–3–0			5	4	1	10	268	10
		17–4–56–3				2	12		4	322	8
		13–0–77–0				5	9		13	480	9 †
				15–3–54–0			8			303	3
				1–0–11–0		18	9		3	271	7
				13–4–48–3			3	1	7	249	10
			6–2–14–1	19–11–19–3		4	9	3	14	194	10
		14–1–63–3		14.4–1–53–3	18–10–22–1		10	2	6	192	10
		22–5–65–5		18.3–5–50–1	4–0–11–0		14		5	246	10
		20–3–62–1	9–1–23–0	25–5–75–2	19–4–51–1	3	11		5	343	6
		3–0–7–0	2.1–0–8–0			5	1		1	49	0 a
		31.5–4–117–4			17–3–56–0		7		9	354	10
		9.1–0–43–0				6	3	1	3	115	2 b
	17.1–4–48–4						6	1	9	288	10 c
	12–4–31–0		4–0–0–1			1	8	1	19	296	10
	15–4–38–0			17–3–35–5			6		9	183	10
	9.4–0–64–2			19–1–68–2			7	1	2	349	6
				11–2–39–0			6		4	150	0
				9–1–38–1		5	5		3	130	7 d
						4	12	2	8	156	10
						5	14			207	10
			10–1–20–0			2	13	2	6	400	8
			6.4–1–39–0			2	3			151	3
			4–2–4–0			6	13	5	15	366	9
							2	3	8	66	4
							10	2	7	346	10 f
						5	2	1	5	232	10
						2	5	3		135	10
						1	9		4	250	5 g
							1			102	2 h
11–5– 18–0 —	85.5–17– 301–7 av. 43.00	148–22– 550–18 av. 30.55	39.3–7– 111–2 av. 55.50	162.1–36– 490–20 av. 24.50	58–17– 140–2 av. 70.00						

g P. Jarvis 13–0–68–0; 5–2–6–0
h J. D. Love 8–0–40–0

K-Close of Play

Cricket was alive and well in 1981 and thousands responded to the excitement and entertainment which was provided. The Test series between England and Australia caught the public imagination, but the interest did not end there. The NatWest Trophy, the successor to the Gillette Cup, maintained the fine tradition of the sixty-over knock-out competition in producing matches of quality and excitement. The Schweppes County Championship, the supreme test of consistent ability for the first-class cricketer, was contested to the pen-ultimate day of the season and there was some wonderful cricket throughout the country. There was no really weak county. Warwickshire's bowling was inadequate and was their main reason for finishing bottom of the Schweppes table, but their batting was attractive enough, with Lloyd, Oliver, Humpage and the under-praised Amiss playing some memorable innings, and they ran close to winning the John Player League. Worcestershire and Northants, too, were not strong in bowling and though both have some fine batsmen, one would be surprised if they carried off a major honour in the next few years. The same must be said of Leicestershire although they appear to have achieved stability in team selection even if the batting remains fragile. Balderstone, however, deserves the highest praise for his consistent application. He has been ill-served by selectors. Cook still promises much as does Garnham, and Clift's value to the side was apparent when he missed several weeks through injury. Lancashire often looked a jaded side. They were unimpressive in the field and desperately need a spin attack. They were better at saving games than winning them, but in Fowler they have a fine player and one hopes that he will not be burdened with a wicket-keeping job in which he is painfully inefficient. For Allott one anticipates an excellent future. Yorkshire have six players in the side who have played international cricket in the past eighteen months and still they struggle. A special medal should be struck for David Bairstow whose enthusiasm never flagged in any adversity.

Gloucestershire, deprived of Procter, but with Zaheer in marvellous form, saw their young players begin to advance. Glamorgan are recovering slowly from the traumas of 1979. Malcolm Nash is a leader of the traditional school and, in Javed Miandad, he has a batsman of world class. There is a need for more youth, but there were signs that some good young talent is emerging. The cricket scene will be sadder without Robin Hobbs. As Intikhab, too, has retired, leg-spin appears to be dead. Intikhab has been an exciting cricketer and a charming man. Surrey really defy their lack of talent to achieve much through dedication and hard work and with the advance of Lynch and the growing confidence of Clinton, the talent itself is now blossoming. One only wishes that Howarth were used to better advantage. Kent remain an enigma. There is much talent in the county. Benson was the most exciting new batsman of the season and Jarvis had a fine year. Knott recaptured his old zest and Underwood bowled well, and yet all is not right. Derbyshire applied themselves well and deserved success. Kim Barnett is beginning to look very good and will be better when he brings his off-side play up to the standard of his leg-side. Essex did not always select their side wisely and it was selection that cost them at least one of the three honours for which at one time they were contending. This is harsh criticism, however, for they are an attractive side and well led. Hardie was a tower of strength amid the more exotic talents of Gooch, McEwan and Fletcher, all of whom played well. Lever and Acfield had fine seasons and once more Turner was the heart of the side. It will be hard to replace him for Pringle at present is struggling to attain the high standard of the side, particularly in the field. David East was the find of the season and may well play for England within the next four years. Hampshire deserve every praise, especially Nick Pocock who has raised them from the depths. They are weak in spin, but they are enjoying their cricket again. At full strength Middlesex were a fine side, but their batsmen took too long to find form. Brearley is still vital to their success.

Somerset can be an exciting side, but too much depends on Richards and Garner, and their spin attack has not developed. Botham in the Tests is a memory that most of us will cherish for ever. Nottinghamshire may not have been one of the great sides, but their team work and enthusiasm was warming to those who watched. Rice was a leader by example and he was served by players who put team first. Birch, Hassan, Todd and the rest all scored valuable runs, and Randall was as good as ever he had been when selected for England. He is a spark to kindle any side. Hadlee was magnificent and so, too, was Eddie Hemmings. Here is a player's player, the backbone of the game and a very fine bowler. It is good that he was one who gained a championship medal after years of endeavour. For my part, I thought that Sussex were the best side in the country although they had the crisis of belief that used to attack Essex some years ago before they finally won honours. Parker was a glory to behold and it is shameful that he was not selected for India. Mendis, Barclay and the rest all performed nobly. They were a joy in the field. Ian Greig was a revelation and none who saw him at university could have predicted that he would blossom so. Le Roux and Imran were superb in hostility and stamina, and surely they will bring Sussex honours in the next couple of years. It would be only right that Geoff Arnold should be there to share them.

All books which have been received by the editor are reviewed in the following pages. We are indebted to E. K. BROWN, *the distinguished cricket bookseller, for his appended list of publications received during the year.*

ARCHIE: A BIOGRAPHY OF A. C. MACLAREN, Michael Down; George Allen & Unwin; 193 pp., £8–95
The publishers are to be congratulated in their efforts in giving us this book. Michael Down explores the great A.C.'s life with objectivity and humour and a picture emerges of a man who was more talented at cricket than in negotiating the business affairs of day-to-day life. It reads well and gives a glint of the golden age.

W. G. GRACE: HIS LIFE AND TIMES, Eric Midwinter; George Allen & Unwin; 175 pp., £9–95
There may have been protestations when another book on W.G. was announced, but surely none can argue with the quality of this volume. What

is so important about this truly excellent book is that Eric Midwinter relates the man to his time. He no longer moves as a giant abstraction out of time, but he is set clearly in the social conditions, a time of history that was as colossal as the man himself.

MIKE PROCTER AND CRICKET, Mike Procter; Pelham Books, 196 pp., £5–95
It is sad that this book arrived just as Mike Procter was ending his association with county cricket. It is a solid account of his cricketing life and he offers some opinions which deserve serious consideration.

PLAYFAIR CRICKET ANNUAL, edited by Gordon Ross; Queen Anne Press, 240 pp. £1–00
Is there any regular at cricket matches who does not have this book in his pocket? It remains a splendid little volume, and this year there was the addition of the University sides. You should not be without this book. It is not out of place here, I hope, to recommend Gordon Ross's other work, *The Cricketer International Quarterly Facts and Figures.* Neat and accurate, it is good value every three months at 90p.

CRICKET UMPIRING, David Constant (with Pat Murphy); Pelham Books, 120 pp. £5–95
This is the last in the Sporting Skills series on Cricket and gives excellent hints to club and village umpires as well as helping us to understand how umpires work at top level.

TIME TO DECLARE, Basil D'Oliveira; Dent, 180 pp., £5–95
Basil D'Oliveira passed through his stormy career with dignity and honour and this autobiography, the second he has offered us, reveals both those qualities of this likeable man. He is forthright and honest without ever being cheap and the book is interesting both from the point of view of cricket, and humanity.

A SONG FOR CRICKET, David Rayvern Allen; Pelham Books, 219 pp. £10–95
I am not sure whether this book comes under the province of cricket, music or music-hall, but as I am a lover of all three, I found it highly acceptable. It is a beautifully produced book, but it is more than a delight to hold and look at, for it is eminently readable. David Rayvern Allen is a man of wit and culture and the two qualities combine well here. This scholarly work, never stuffy, will give pleasure to many and promises to be a book that one wishes to return to at frequent intervals.

WISDEN CRICKETERS ALMANACK, edited by John Woodcock; Queen Anne Press: 1231 pp., Hardback £7–95; Softback £6–95
This is John Woodcock's first year with Wisden and the achievement is remarkable. With subtle additions and changes, he has given this marvellous annual a revitalised freshness. None who love the game can be without it.

YORKSHIRE AND BACK, Ray Illingworth; Macdonald Futura, 221 pp., Paperback
£1–50
This is the paperback edition of Ray Illingworth's book written in association
with Don Mosey which was reviewed in last year's *Pelham*. At £1–50 this is
excellent value though recent happenings have made it somewhat dated.

TEST MATCH SPECIAL, edited by Peter Baxter; Queen Anne Press, 159 pp. £6–95
The joy that the B.B.C. commentators give to their millions of listeners is
reflected in this publication. Although the jokes and comments are better heard
than read, the book is a valuable one in that it will give much pleasure to
many who, for various reasons, may never see a Test match, but who still feel
part of the 'family'.

THE WISDEN BOOK OF COUNTY CRICKET, Christopher Martin-Jenkins, with
statistics edited by Frank Warwick; Queen Anne Press, 447 pp., £11–95
This is a splendid book. It contains career records of every first-class county
player, a magnificent achievement, and it has a good-humoured history of
county cricket as a starter. Christopher Martin-Jenkins manages to capture
the essential flavour of each county so that the book is not only an indispensable
work of reference, but it is very good reading. Highly recommended.

CRICKET CHOICE, Alec Bedser; Pelham Books, 204 pp., £6–95
Initially one had expected that this would be a book taking us behind the scenes
of the Test selectors, but although the book does not do this, we are not
disappointed. With years of rich experience, Alec Bedser comments upon the
great players of the past thirty to forty years. There is astute observation here
and the book never dissolves into mere flattery. It goes much of the way in
taking us into the mind of a Test selector of long-standing.

THE WISDEN BOOK OF CRICKET RECORDS, compiled and edited by Bill Frindall;
Queen Anne Press, 618 pp., £14
The books that have been published under the name of Wisden in the past
three years have, with one exception, been an exciting addition to cricket
literature and statistics. Bill Frindall's book is another triumph in the series
and must quickly become an indispensable companion to the cricket buff. I
am very glad that Mr Frindall pays tribute to the work of the Association
of Cricket Statisticians. Their work is splendidly meticulous and a credit to
the game they love. *The Wisden Book of Cricket Records* is an up-dating of
Mr Frindall's earlier *Kaye Book of Cricket Records*, but the present volume
is at once more comprehensive and more appealing. Mr Frindall and his helpers
have filled a void and we are in their debt. No one who is fascinated by the
game can afford to ignore this book. It may not be a book that one would
read from cover to cover, but oh the hours of happy delving.

ANOTHER DAY, ANOTHER MATCH, Brian Brain; George Allen & Unwin, 115 pp.,
£5–95
This is the second diary of a cricket season to have been offered and, like the
first, by Bob Willis, it is ultimately disappointing. Willis's book was disappoint-

ing because it had little to say and was too preoccupied with Test cricket; the disappointment with Brain's book is the style in which it is written; the 'ghost' has missed the maturity of the man and reduced him to a common denominator of semi-literacy. This is a pity because the book has so much that is of interest. The county game is still the back-bone of cricket and it breeds a comradeship which is open only to those who play it. The book captures some of this spirit, but often sacrifices it in search of controversy where none exists, for example in the passing waspish comments on Malcolm Nash, comments which are far from justified. There is, however, much that is interesting from behind the scenes at Gloucestershire, particularly in the honest assessments of the players. There is, too, Brian Brain's own enthusiasm and love of the game. It is touching to read of his excitement when he first captained Gloucestershire in 1980 and to realise that we who follow the game took his appointment to the captaincy in Procter's absence as axiomatic and thereby missed the moment. He is a good man and cricket will be poorer when he leaves the scene.

MIDDLESEX COUNTY CRICKET CLUB REVIEW 1980–81, edited by Alvan Seth-Smith; 136 pp., £1–50
It was right that there should be a publication to celebrate the Middlesex triumphs of 1980 and it is equally right that the man to undertake the compilation of this fine statistical record should be Alvan Seth-Smith, a cultured enthusiast of the Middlesex cause. This is a delightful handbook wherein the complete record of the events of 1980 is enhanced by some most readable contributions from Mike Brearly, Vincent van der Bijl, Robert Brooke, Alan Lee and Alec Waugh. It is excellent value, splendidly illustrated and a credit to its compiler.

P. G. H. FENDER, Richard Streeton; Faber & Faber, 194 pp., £5–95
Dick Streeton's long-awaited study of Percy Fender has proved to be no anti-climax. Meticulously researched, the book provides not only a fine appraisal of the controversial Surrey captain, but gives a clear picture of cricket in the decade after the First World War. It is written with clarity and perception and will remain a most important contribution to cricket literature.

ENGLAND v. WEST INDIES 1981, THE ENGLAND TEAM TOUR BOOK, edited by Peter Smith; Pelham Books, 192 pp., £6–95
This is a novel venture in that it provides an official view of the tour with comments by the players, Boycott excepted. An interesting volume.

Appleyard, F. S. *Water Orton. A Hundred Years of Cricket* £3–00
Association of Cricket Statisticians *A Guide to Important Matches Played in the British Isles, 1709–1863* £2–00; *Irish Cricket, 1839–1980* £2–00; *Scottish Cricket, 1855–1980* £2–00
Boycott, Geoffrey *Opening Up* (Barker) £5–95; *In the Fast Lane* (Barker) £6–95
Brown, L. H. *Victor Trumper & the 1902 Australians* (Secker & Warburg) £9–95
Compton, D. *Compton on Cricketers Past and Present* (Cassell) £6–95